GLOBAL STUDIES

THE MIDDLE EAST

Fourth Edition

STAFF

Ian A. Nielsen	Publisher
Brenda S. Filley	Production Manager
Lisa M. Clyde	Developmental Editor
Charles Vitelli	Designer
Cheryl Greenleaf	Permissions Coordinator
Shawn Callahan	Graphics
Libra Ann Cusack	Typesetting Supervisor
Juliana Arbo	Typesetting
Diane Barker	Editorial Assistant

GLOBAL STUDIES

THE MIDDLE EAST

Fourth Edition

William Spencer

The Dushkin Publishing Group, Inc., Sluice Dock, Guilford, Connecticut 06437

The Middle East

OTHER BOOKS IN THE GLOBAL STUDIES SERIES

- Africa
- China
- Commonwealth of Independent States and Central/Eastern Europe
- Japan and the Pacific Rim
- Latin America
- Western Europe
  India and South Asia

- Available Now

©1992 by The Dushkin Publishing Group, Inc., Guilford,
Connecticut 06437. All rights reserved. No part of this book
may be reproduced, stored, or transmitted by any means—
mechanical, electronic, or otherwise—without written
permission from the publisher.

Fourth Edition

Manufactured by The Banta Company, Harrisonburg,
Virginia 22801

Library of Congress Catalog Number: 90-081363

ISBN: 1-56134-074-X

ISSN: 1056-6848

The Middle East

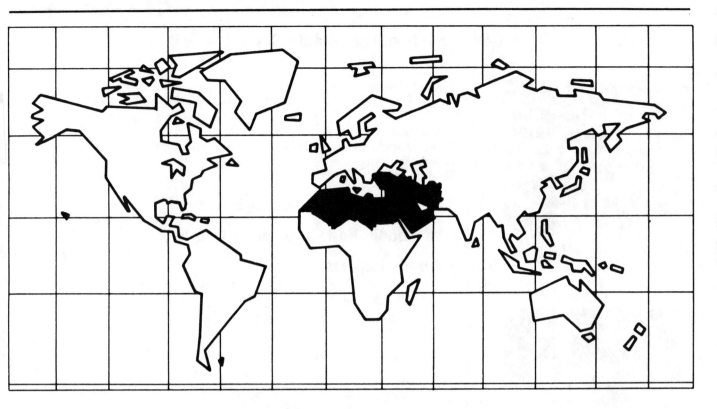

AUTHOR AND EDITOR

Dr. William Spencer

The author and editor for *Global Studies: The Middle East* was formerly Professor of Middle East/North African History at Florida State University and in recent years has been Visiting Professor at Rollins College, Jacksonville University, and the University of Florida. During a 35-year career specializing in Middle Eastern affairs, he has published and lectured extensively and has held various U.S. government and international organization and foundation assignments. His special area of interest is Islamic North Africa. As a curriculum consultant for school systems, colleges, and universities, Dr. Spencer has developed workshops and short courses designed to help U.S. educators develop a better understanding of this region.

CONSULTANT

Elizabeth Bouvier Spencer

Elizabeth Spencer is an artist and teacher who has traveled with her husband to the Middle East on many research trips. She is responsible for much of the material in this book on home and family life, architecture, and housing, aside from her contributions as grammarian and amanuensis extraordinary.

SERIES CONSULTANT

H. Thomas Collins
Washington, D.C.

Contents

Global Studies: The Middle East

Page 11

Page 26

Page 69

150 Articles from the World Press

Introduction

THE GLOBAL AGE

As we approach the end of the twentieth century, it is clear that our future will be considerably more international in nature than we ever believed was possible. Each day print and broadcast journalists make us aware that our world is becoming increasingly smaller and substantially more interdependent.

The energy crisis, world food shortages, and regional conflicts in the Middle East and other areas that threaten to involve us all make it clear that the distinctions between domestic and foreign problems are all too often artificial—that many seemingly domestic problems no longer stop at national boundaries. As Rene Dubos, the 1969 Pulitzer Prize recipient stated: ". . . [I]t becomes obvious that each [of us] has two countries, [our] own and planet Earth." As global interdependence has become a reality, it has become vital for the citizens of this world to develop literacy in global matters.

THE GLOBAL STUDIES SERIES

It is the aim of this Global Studies series to help readers acquire a basic knowledge and understanding of the regions and countries in the world. Each volume provides a foundation of information—geographic, cultural, economic, political, historical, artistic, and religious—which will allow readers to understand better the current and future problems within these countries and regions and to comprehend how events there might affect their own well-being. In short, these volumes attempt to provide the background information necessary to respond to the realities of our Global Age.

Author and Editor

Each of the volumes in the Global Studies series has been crafted under the careful direction of an author/editor—an expert in the area under study. The author/editors teach and conduct research and have traveled extensively through the countries about which they are writing.

In this Middle East volume, the author/editor has written the regional essays and the country reports. In addition, he has been instrumental in the selection of the world press articles which relate to each of the regional sections.

Contents and Features

The Global Studies volumes are organized to provide concise information and current world press articles on the regions and countries within those areas under study.

Regional Essays

For *Global Studies: The Middle East, Fourth Edition*, the author/editor has written two narrative essays focusing on the religious, cultural, sociopolitical, and economic differences and similarities of the countries and peoples in the region. The purpose of the regional essays is to provide readers with an effective sense of the diversity of the area as

(United Nations photo/Yutaka Nagata)

The Global Age is making all countries and all people more interdependent.

well as an understanding of its common cultural and historical backgrounds. Accompanying the regional essays is a two-page map showing the political boundaries of each of the countries within the region.

Country Reports

Concise reports are written for each of the countries within the region under study. These reports are the heart of each Global Studies volume. *Global Studies: The Middle East, Fourth Edition*, contains 20 country reports.

The country reports are comprised of five standard elements. Each report contains a small, semidetailed map visually positioning the country amongst its neighboring states; a detailed summary of statistical information; a current essay providing important historical, geographical, political, cultural, and economic information; a historical timeline offering a convenient visual survey of a few key historical events; and four graphic indicators, with summary statements about the country in terms of development, freedom, health/welfare, and achievements.

A Note on the Statistical Summaries

The statistical information provided for each country has been drawn from a wide range of sources. The nine most frequently referenced are listed on page 234. Every effort has been made to provide the most current and accurate information available. However, occasionally the information cited by these sources differs to some extent; and, all too often, the most current information available for some countries is dated. Aside from these difficulties, the statistical summary of each country is generally quite complete and reasonably current. Care should be taken, however, in using these statistics (or, for that matter, any published statistics) in making hard comparisons among countries. We have also included comparable statistics on the United States, which follow on the next two pages.

World Press Articles

Within each Global Studies volume are reprinted a number of articles carefully selected by our editorial staff and the author/editor from a broad range of international periodicals and newspapers. The articles have been chosen for currency, interest, and their differing perspectives on the subject countries and regions. There are a total of twenty-one articles in *Global Studies: The Middle East, Fourth Edition*.

The articles section is preceded by a *Topic Guide* as well as an *Annotated Table of Contents*. The Annotated Table of Contents offers a brief summary of each article, while the Topic Guide indicates the main theme(s) of each article. Thus, readers desiring to focus on articles dealing with a particular theme—say, religion—may refer to the Topic Guide to find those articles.

Spelling

In many instances articles from foreign sources may use forms of spelling that are different from our own. Many Fourth World publications reflect the European usage. In order to retain the flavor of the articles and to make the point that our system is not the only one, spellings have not been altered to conform with our system.

Glossary, Bibliography, Index

At the back of each Global Studies volume, readers will find a *Glossary of Terms and Abbreviations*, which provides a quick reference to the specialized vocabulary of the area under study and to the standard abbreviations (OPEC, PLO, etc.) used throughout the volume.

Following the glossary is a *Bibliography*, which is organized into general works, national histories, literature in translation, current-events publications, and periodicals that provide regular coverage on the Middle East.

The *Index* at the end of the volume is an accurate reference to the contents of the volume. Readers seeking specific information and citations should consult this standard index.

Currency and Usefulness

This fourth edition of *Global Studies: The Middle East*, like other Global Studies volumes, is intended to provide the most current and useful information available necessary to understand the events that are shaping the cultures of the region today.

We plan to issue this volume on a regular basis. The statistics will be updated, regional essays rewritten, country reports revised, and articles completely replaced as new and current information becomes available. In order to accomplish this task we will turn to our author/editor, our advisory boards, and—hopefully—to you, the users of this volume. Your comments are more than welcome. If you have an idea that you think will make the volume more useful, an article or bit of information that will make it more current, or a general comment on its organization, content, or features that you would like to share with us, please send it in for serious consideration for the next edition.

(United Nations photo/John Isaac)

Understanding the problems and life-styles of other countries will help make us literate in global matters.

United States of America

Comparing statistics on the various countries in this volume should not be done without recognizing that the figures are within the timeframe of our publishing date and may not accurately reflect today's conditions. Nevertheless, comparisons can and will be made, so to enable you to put the statistics of different countries into perspective, we include here comparable statistics on the United States. These statistics are drawn from the same sources that were consulted for developing the statistical information for each country report.

The United States is unique. It has some of the most fertile land in the world, which, coupled with a high level of technology, allows the production of an abundance of food products—an abundance that makes possible the export of enormous quantities of basic foodstuffs to many other parts of the world. The use of this technology also permits the production of goods and services that exceeds what is possible in a majority of the rest of the world. In the United States are some of the most important urban centers in the world focusing on trade, investment, and commerce as well as art, music, and theater.

GEOGRAPHY

Area in Square Kilometers (Miles):
9,578,626 (3,618,770)
Capital (Population): Washington, D.C.
(639,000)
Climate: temperate

PEOPLE

Population

Total: 253,978,000 (adjusted 1990
census)
Annual Growth Rate: 0.8%
Rural/Urban Population Ratio: 21/79
Ethnic Makeup of Population: 80%
white; 11.5% black; 6.2% Spanish
origin; 1.6% Asian and Pacific
Islander; 0.7% American Indian,
Eskimo, and Aleut

Health

Life Expectancy at Birth: 72 years
(male); 79 years (female)
Infant Mortality Rate (Ratio):
9.1/1,000
Average Caloric Intake: 138% of FAO
minimum
Physicians Available (Ratio): 1/410

Religion(s)

55% Protestant; 36% Roman
Catholic; 4% Jewish; 5% Muslim and
others

Education

Adult Literacy Rate: 99.5% (official)
(estimates vary significantly)

COMMUNICATION

Telephones: 182,558,000 (79.1/100
Newspapers: 1,679 dailies;
approximately 63,000,000 circulation

TRANSPORTATION

Highways—Kilometers (Miles):
6,229,633 (3,871,143)
Railroads—Kilometers (Miles):
270,312 (167,974)
Usable Airfields: 16,685

GOVERNMENT

Type: federal republic
Independence Date: July 4, 1776
Head of State: President George Bush
Political Parties: Democratic Party;
Republican Party; others of minor
political significance
Suffrage: universal at 18

MILITARY

Number of Armed Forces: 2,127,940
*Military Expenditures (% of Central
Government Expenditures):* 27.1%
Current Hostilities: none

ECONOMY

Per Capita Income/GNP:
$18,400/$5,200 billion
Inflation Rate: 4%
Natural Resources: metallic and
nonmetallic minerals; petroleum;
arable land
Agriculture: food grains; feed crops;
oilbearing crops; cattle; dairy
products
Industry: diversified in both capital-
and consumer-goods industries

FOREIGN TRADE

Exports: $363 billion
Imports: $492 billion

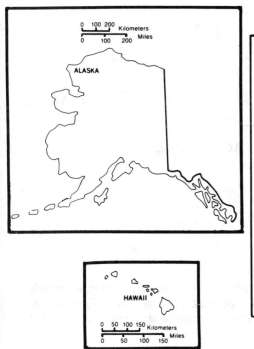

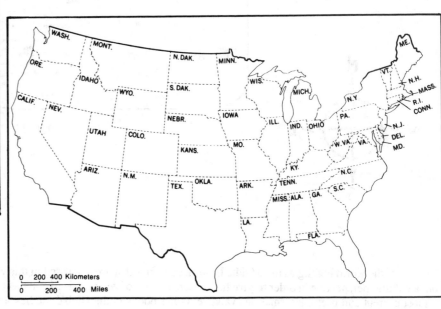

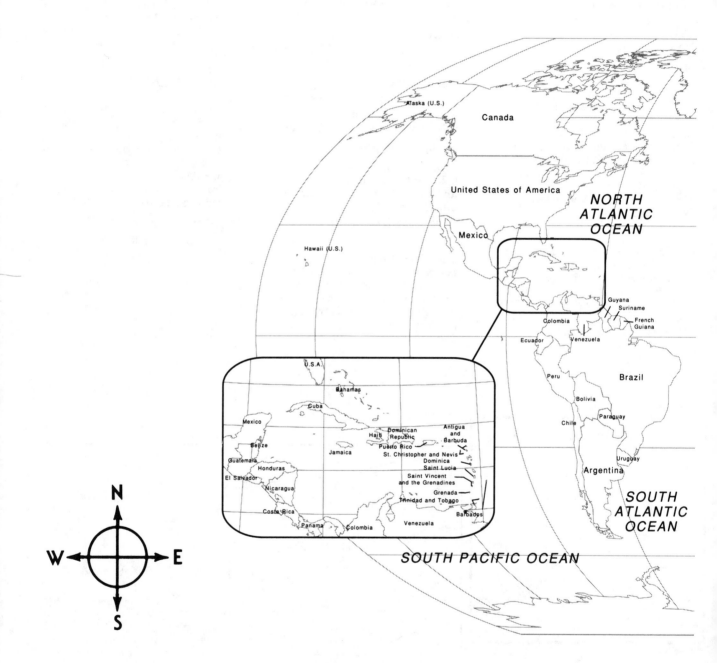
This map of the world highlights the Middle Eastern countries that are discussed in this volume. All of the following essays are written from a cultural perspective in order to give the readers a sense of what life is like in these countries. The essays are designed to present the most current and useful information available. Other books in the Global Studies series cover different global areas and examine the current state of affairs of the countries within those regions.

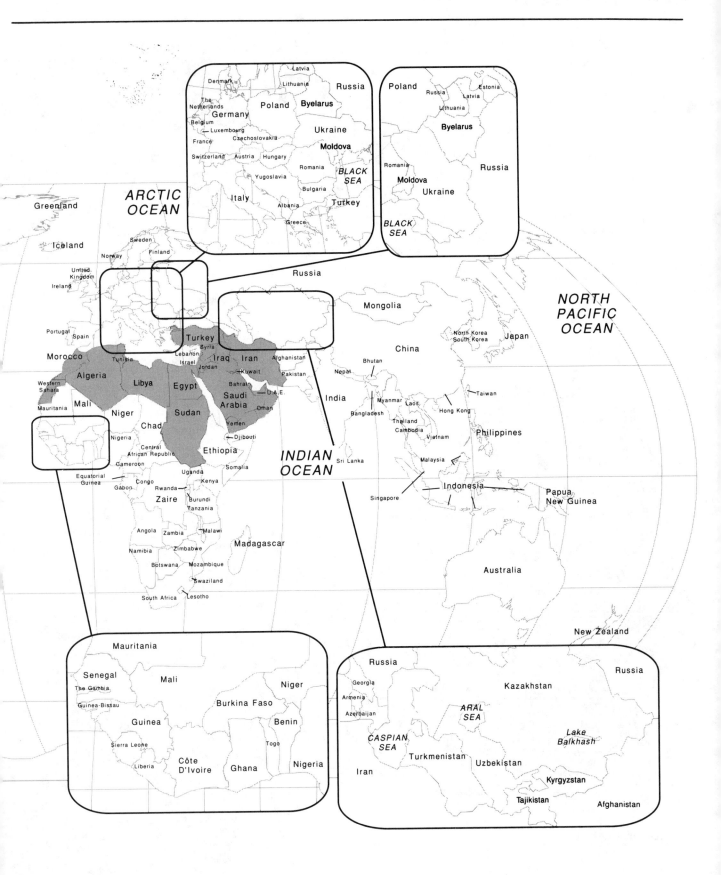

The Middle East

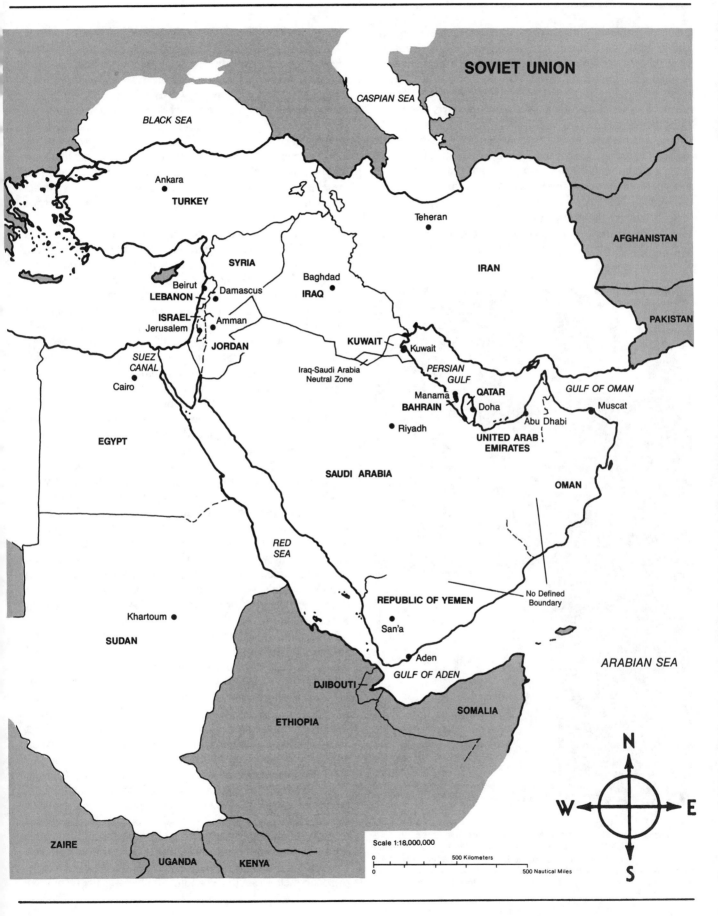

SOVIET UNION

CASPIAN SEA

BLACK SEA

Ankara

TURKEY

Teheran

AFGHANISTAN

SYRIA

IRAN

Beirut
LEBANON
Damascus

Baghdad

PAKISTAN

ISRAEL
Jerusalem

Amman

IRAQ

JORDAN

KUWAIT

Kuwait

SUEZ
CANAL

Iraq-Saudi Arabia
Neutral Zone

PERSIAN
GULF

GULF OF OMAN

Cairo

Manama

QATAR

BAHRAIN

Doha

Muscat

Abu Dhabi

EGYPT

Riyadh

UNITED ARAB
EMIRATES

SAUDI ARABIA

OMAN

RED
SEA

No Defined
Boundary

Khartoum

REPUBLIC OF YEMEN

SUDAN

San'a

ARABIAN SEA

Aden

GULF OF ADEN

DJIBOUTI

SOMALIA

ETHIOPIA

N

ZAIRE

W   E

UGANDA   KENYA

Scale 1:18,000,000

0   500 Kilometers

0   500 Nautical Miles

S

The Middle East: Islam in Ferment

Until quite recently the world of Islam, centered in the Middle East, was a remote grey area to most Americans. To those who passed through the area en route to the invasions of occupied Europe in World War II, it was a hot, dusty place, peopled by men dressed in what appeared to be bed sheets, who sat in fly-blown cafes at the outskirts of military bases drinking endless glasses of hot sweet tea and speaking an incomprehensible language. This stereotype changed little in the intervening years except for the addition of the little state of Israel, whose Jewish peoples made the desert bloom and more than stood their ground militarily against the children of those men in bed sheets.

Seen against the strong image of Israel, that country's Middle Eastern neighbors seemed unimportant. Americans knew little of their history or of their struggle to attain

(UN photo)

The Middle East did not make a real impact on the American consciousness until 1979, when the followers of the Ayatollah Khomeini seized the U.S. Embassy in Teheran and held its occupants hostage for more than a year. The extent to which the fundamentalist Shia Muslims would follow Khomeini was little recognized before this event.

dignity and stability in the new world of independent states. Many Americans shared only a vague awareness of a religious group called Muslims (mistakenly called Mohammedans), who inhabited the Middle East in large numbers and practiced a religion known as Islam. But in political terms, the Muslims seemed powerless, disorganized, always on the brink of conflict. With the exception of Israel, often seen as an extension of the United States, the predictability that Americans had come to expect of governments like their own was not to be found among the quarrelsome leaders of these new Middle Eastern states. Thus the thunderous impact of Islam on the United States came with little advance warning or preparation.

The American public abruptly came face to face with militant Islam in 1979, when the U.S. Embassy in Teheran, Iran was seized by supporters of Ayatollah Khomeini and its occupants were held hostage. Their enforced detention for more than a year made yellow ribbons a symbol of America's captivity to Islam and led to the political downfall of President Jimmy Carter but produced relatively little development in Americans' understanding of Islamic peoples. Later, misreading of their motivations by the Reagan administration led to the disastrous assignment of American marines to Lebanon as part of a multinational peacekeeping force after the 1982 Israeli invasion of that country. In 1983 a truck carrying what was later described as the largest non-nuclear bomb ever exploded blew up the U.S. Marine barracks in Beirut, killing 241 marines.

In the mid-1980s the Islamic Jihad, a Shia Lebanese secret organization linked to Iran through Hizbullah (Party of God), Lebanon's most powerful Shia group, initiated a campaign of kidnappings of Americans and other foreigners in Beirut. Other shadowy organizations such as Revolutionary Justice and Islamic Holy War for the Liberation of Palestine followed suit. American involvement in Lebanon after the Israeli invasion, and revelations of the Reagan administration's secret arms deals with Iran, shifted the kidnappers' focus to one of revenge for American and Israeli actions against the "sacred Islamic soil" of Lebanon, whereas the original reason for the hostage-taking had been to obtain the release of "Islamic brothers" held in Israeli and European jails for terrorist activities.

Altogether some 14 Americans plus Briton Terry Waite, personal representative of the Archbishop of Canterbury, and a number of British, French, German, and Italian citizens were held hostage for periods up to 7 years. The longest-held was AP Middle East Bureau Chief Terry Anderson. Between 1986 and 1990 there were no hostage releases, but in 1990–1991 protracted negotiations by UN Secretary-General Javier Perez de Cuellar and his mediators, through intermediaries in Iran (the protecting umbrella for Lebanese Shia organizations and essentially the only outside force capable of influencing the kidnappers), led to the resolution of the "hostage problem." One contributing factor in the complex negotiations was the release by Israel of Shia Lebanese prisoners held in south Lebanon. Another was the resolution of the Lebanese Civil War and establishment of de facto Syrian control over most of that country. However, Islamic Jihad's release of Anderson in December 1991 was accompanied by a statement reemphasizing both the political and the Islamic aspects of the long-running hostage issue. It stated, in part: "The confrontation created by the kidnappings made the world listen to the voice of oppressed people and unmasked the ugly American and Israeli faces . . . but after finishing several stages we decided to free our last captive, thus folding this page in the hostage file before glorious Christmas."

This sequence of shocks since 1979 has brought the United States face to face with what appears to be a new phenomenon of confrontation in the Middle East between Muslims and Westerners. To give the phenomenon a name, we call it *Islam in ferment.*

What has caused this ferment? What does it consist of, and why is it directed so violently against the United States? Is it a new phenomenon, or is it a natural progression for Islam, arising out of the circumstances in which Muslims find themselves in the late twentieth century? What are the elements in the Islamic ferment? We address these questions in this report.

THE CONCEPT OF JIHAD

Jihad is one of the most important elements in the Islamic ferment. It may be defined as "sacred struggle," "striving" (*i.e.,* of the individual to carry out God's will), or, when exercised against the enemies of Islam, "holy war." The Afghan *mujahideen* (resistance fighters) who fought during the 1980s to expel Soviet forces from their homeland characterized their struggle as a jihad, as did Iranian Revolutionary Guards challenging U.S. forces in the Persian Gulf, to give just two of many examples.

But jihad can also be directed against apostates or weak believers *within* the House of Islam. In 1979 Muslims who seized the Great Mosque in Mecca, Saudi Arabia, argued that the Saudi government should be replaced, on these grounds: Islam does not allow secular kings or dynasties, and the Saudi government had deviated from "true" Islamic law and principles. And during the trial of those arrested for the 1981 assassination of Egyptian President Anwar al-Sadat, their leader argued that there were three reasons for the justness of their act: 1) the incompatibility of Egypt's laws with Islamic law; 2) Sadat's peace with Israel; and 3) the sufferings of "good" Muslims under the regime.[1]

A third form of jihad-inspired violence within Islamic society has developed out of the religious divisions of Islam into Sunni and Shia groups. The Muslim Brotherhood, to give an example, is a Sunni organization spread throughout the Islamic world that seeks the replacement of all existing regimes by a universal Islamic state faithful to the ideals and practices of the original community of believers founded by Muhammad. As a result, it has at times been banned, proscribed, and ruthlessly repressed by those regimes. In Syria, the Brotherhood represents the principal opposition to

(Aramco Photo)

One of the Five Pillars of Islam, or five basic duties of Muslims, is to go on a pilgrimage to Mecca in Saudi Arabia once in their lifetime. Once there they circle seven times around the Black Box (the Ka'ba, pictured above), kiss the Black Stone, drink from the well of Zam Zam, and perform other sacred rites.

the Alawi Shia minority government of President Hafez al-Assad. The Brotherhood's main power base was the city of Hama, home of a conservative Sunni population. From Hama, Brotherhood members carried out a series of assassinations of Alawi officials and made two attempts on the life of the Syrian president. They called him "an enemy of Allah" and a Maronite (Lebanese Christian). In 1982, after the discovery of an Air Force plot to overthrow him which was linked to the Brotherhood, Assad ordered his troops into the city and all but obliterated it in the process of crushing his opposition.[2]

These militant events have not occurred in isolation. They are part of the struggle of Muslim peoples to come to terms with the modern world, and to define an appropriate role for Islam in that world.

THE KORAN: THE HOLY BOOK OF ISLAM

Muslims believe that the Koran is the literal Word of God, and that Muhammad was chosen to receive God's Word through the Angel Gabriel as a *rasul* (messenger). But the Koran does not cancel out the Bible and Torah, which preceded it. The Koran is viewed, rather, as providing a corrective set of revelations for these previous revelations from God, which Muslims believe have been distorted or not followed correctly. To carry out God's Word, as set down in the Koran, requires a constant effort to create the ideal Islamic society, one "that is imbued with Islamic ideals and reflects as perfectly as possible the presence of God in His creation."*

The Koran was revealed to Muhammad over the 22-year period of his ministry (A.D. 610–632). The revelations were of varying lengths and were originally meant to be committed to memory and recited on various occasions, in particular the daily prayers. Even today, correct Koranic practice requires memorization and recitation; during the fasting month of Ramadan, one section per day should be recited aloud.

In its original form, the Koran was either committed to memory by Muhammad's listeners or written down by one or more literate scribes, depending upon who was present at the revelation. The scribes used whatever materials were at hand: "paper, leather, parchment, stones, wooden tablets, the shoulder-blades of oxen or the breasts of men."** The first authoritative version was compiled in the time of the third caliph, Uthman, presumably on parchment. Since then the Holy Book has been translated into many other languages as Islam spread to include non-Arab peoples.

All translations stem from Uthman's text. It was organized into 114 *suras* (chapters), with the longest at the beginning and the shortest at the end. (The actual order of the revelations was probably the reverse, since the longer ones came mostly during Muhammad's period in Medina, when he was trying to establish guidelines for the community.)***

Many of the revelations provide specific guides to conduct or social relationships:

When ye have performed the act of worship, remember Allah sitting, standing and reclining . . . Worship at fixed times hath been enjoined on the believers. . . .

(IV, 103)

Establish worship at the going down of the sun until the dark of night, and at dawn. Lo! The recital of the Koran at dawn is ever witnessed.

(XVII, 78–79)

Make contracts with your slaves and spend of your own wealth that God has given you upon them. . . .

(XXIV, 33)

If you fear that you will be dishonest in regard to these orphan girls, then you may marry from among them one, two, three or four. But if you fear you will not be able to do justice among them, marry only one.

(IV, 3)

Much of the content of the Koran is related to the ethical and moral. It is an Arab Koran, given to Arabs "in clear Arabic tongue" (*Sura* XLI, 44) and characterized by a quality of style and language that is essentially untranslatable. Muslim children, regardless of where they live, learn it in Arabic, and only then may read it in their own language (but always accompanied by the original Arabic). Recitals of selections from the Koran are a feature of births, marriages, funerals, festivals, and other special events, and are extraordinarily effective, whether or not the listener understands Arabic.****

*Peter Awn, "Faith and Practice," in Marjorie Kelly, ed., *Islam: The Religious and Political Life of a World Community* (New York: Praeger, 1984), pp. 2–7.

**The Qur'an, The First American Version, Translation and Commentary by T. B. Irving (Brattleboro, VT: Amana Books, 1985), Introduction, XXVII.

***On this topic see Fazlur Rahman, *Major Themes of the Qur'an* (Chicago: Bibliotheca Islamica, 1980), *passim*.

****"The old preacher sat with his waxen hands in his lap and uttered the first Surah, full of the soft warm coloring of a familiar understanding . . . His listeners followed the notation of the verses with care and rapture, gradually seeking their way together . . . like a school of fish following a leader, out into the deep sea." Lawrence Durrell, *Mountolive* (London: Faber and Faber, 1958), p. 265.

The difficulty for fundamentalist Muslims in defining such a role stems from the fact that their religion operates under very specific divine rules of conduct. These rules were laid down 14 centuries ago by Muhammad the Messenger, who received them as revelations from God. The sum total of these revelations is the Koran, the Holy Book of Islam. Because Muslims believe that the Koran is the literal word of God, they also believe that it is not subject to change but only to interpretation within a narrow range.

The conflict over interpretation of jihad has had a great deal to do with the ferment visible in Islam today. For example, members of Islamic Jihad believe that their interpretation of a *holy war* against the enemies of Islam is the correct one. The holy-war definition of jihad is the one most familiar to non-Muslims. Muslims have always believed that God intended them to struggle to establish Islam as a universal religion, although conversion of other monotheists (Jews and Christians) would not be required as long as these communities recognized the superiority of Islam. The military interpretation of jihad has led to the division of the world into the Dar al-Islam ("House of Islam") and the Dar al-Harb ("House of Dissidence"), the area yet to be brought into the House of Islam.[3]

Members of al-Dawa, on the other hand, interpret jihad as

a *struggle* to overthrow the Islamic government of Iraq, because they deem it unjust and believe that it does not follow correct Islamic principles or apply strict Islamic law to the state.

A third definition of jihad, the *striving* of the individual for justice, is perhaps the most controversial. Islam teaches that if rulers, appointed or elected over some Islamic territory, become unjust, their subjects should bear the injustices with fortitude; God will, in due course, reward their patience. Some Muslims interpret this injunction to mean that they should strive to help the leaders to see the error of their ways—by whatever action is necessary. Centuries ago a secret society, the Hashishin ("Assassins," so called because they reportedly were users of hashish) carried out many assassinations of prominent officials and rulers, claiming that God had inspired them to rid Islamic society of tyrants. Since Islam emphasizes the direct relationship of people to God, and therefore people's responsibility to do right in the eyes of God and to struggle to help other believers follow the same right path, it becomes most dangerous when individuals feel that they do not need to subject themselves to the collective will but, rather, to impose their own concept of justice on others.

In our own day, jihad is associated with the struggle of Shia Muslims for social, political, and economic rights within Islamic states. Inspired by the example of Iran, they seek to establish a true Islamic government in the House of Islam. But Iranian Muslims are not only militant, they are also strongly nationalistic. In this respect, they differ sharply in their approach to Islamic reform from the approaches of other militant Islamic groups, notably the Muslim Brotherhood. Its founder, Hassan al-Banna, stressed the gradualist approach, rejecting narrow or exclusivist philosophies and declaring that the Brotherhood stood ready to assist Muslim governments in the improvement of society through "basic Islamification of beliefs, moral codes and ruling institutions."[4]

No such strictures affect Iranians' view of jihad. An important element in their belief system derives from their special relationship with their religious leaders, particularly the late Ayatollah Khomeini. In his writings and sermons, Khomeini stressed the need for violent resistance to unjust authorities.

The best example of "internal" Islamic jihad in recent years developed during the annual *Hajj* ("Great Pilgrimage") to Mecca in August 1987. Iranian pilgrims, taking literally Khomeini's injunction that the Hajj is the ideal forum for demonstration of "the proper use of Islam in politics," staged a political rally after midday prayer services. Demonstrators carrying posters of Khomeini shouted, "Death to America! Death to the Soviet Union! Death to Israel!" Saudi police attempting to control them were attacked, and the demonstration swiftly grew into a riot. When it was over, more than 400 had been killed, including 85 policemen, and 650 injured. "To take revenge for the sacred bloodshed is to free the holy shrines from the wicked

Wahhabi," an Iranian government official told a crowd in Teheran.[5]

ISLAMIC ORIGINS

Despite the fact that Islam has coexisted with Christianity for 14 centuries, the long history of conflict between these two religions makes mutual understanding difficult. F. E. Peters notes that "holy war against the Franks did not spring immediately to the mind of every Muslim . . . until the Franks made it clear by their behavior and propaganda (in the Crusades) that they were engaged in a holy war over Jerusalem."[6] The most negative view of Islam by Westerners is largely the result of the Crusades, highly colored by generations of Sunday-school textbooks. However, Islam developed among a particular people, the Arabs; was built on earlier foundations of Christianity and Judaism; and was primarily concerned with the transmission of the spiritual message of God to humankind as a corrective measure. It is an article of faith among Arab nationalists and Muslim Arab scholars that the Arabs were chosen as a people to receive God's revelations because they were cousins of the Jews through Abraham and therefore were included in the Judeo-Christian tradition. But they did not have scriptures of their own.

Islam was founded in the seventh century A.D. by Muhammad, a merchant in the small town of Mecca in southwestern Arabia. Muslims believe Muhammad's religious teachings came from revelations that he received orally from God via the Angel Gabriel. After Muhammad's death, these revelations were put into book form in the *Koran* ("Recitation"), the Holy Book of Islam.

During Muhammad's lifetime, the various revelations he received were used to guide his followers along the "Way" of conduct (*Sharia,* in Arabic) acceptable to God. The Arabs followed traditional religions in Muhammad's time, worshiping many gods. Muhammad taught belief in one God—Allah—and in the Word of God sent down to him as messenger. For this reason, Muhammad is considered the Prophet of Islam.

Muhammad's received revelations plus his own teachings issued to instruct his followers make up the formal religious system known as Islam. The word *Islam* is Arabic and has been translated variously as "submission," "surrender" (*i.e.*, to God's will), and the fatalistic "acceptance." A better translation might be "receptiveness." Those who receive and accept the Word of God as transmitted to Muhammad and set down in the Koran are called *Muslims*.

Islam is essentially a simple faith. Five basic duties are required of the believer; they are often called the *Five Pillars* because they are the foundations of the House of Islam. They are:

1. The confession of faith: "I testify that there is no God but God, and Muhammad is the Messenger of God."

2. Prayer, required five times daily, facing in the direction of Mecca, the holy city.

THE ISLAMIC CALENDAR

The Islamic calendar is a lunar calendar. It has 354 days in all, divided into 7 months of 30 days, 4 months of 29 days, and 1 month of 28 days. The first year of the calendar, A.H. 1 (*Anno Hegira,* the year of Muhammad's "emigration" to Medina to escape persecution in Mecca), corresponds to A.D. 622.

In the Islamic calendar, the months rotate with the moon, coming at different times in the year from year to year. It takes an Islamic month 33 years to make the complete circuit of the seasons. The fasting month of Ramadan moves with the season and is most difficult for Muslims when it takes place in high summer.

3. Fasting during the daylight hours in the month of Ramadan, the month of Muhammad's first revelations.

4. Alms giving, a tax or gift of not less than two-and-one-half percent, to the community for the help of the poor.

5. Pilgrimage, required at least once in one's lifetime, to the House of God in Mecca.

It is apparent from the above description that Islam has many points in common with Judaism and Christianity. All three are monotheistic religions, having a fundamental belief in one God. Muslims believe that Muhammad was the "seal of the Prophets," the last messenger and recipient of revelations. But they believe that God revealed Himself to other prophets before Muhammad, starting with Abraham, Moses, and the Old Testament prophets, down through history to Jesus. Muslims part company with Christians over the divinity of Jesus, the Resurrection, and the Trinity. They stay close to Judaism on matters of dietary restrictions and the interpretation of divine law by a body of religious scholars.

In addition to the revelations in the Koran, Muhammad based his leadership on his own wisdom and understanding of human behavior. Muhammad's own life is considered by Muslims as a model to follow. His decisions, called *hadith* ("sayings" or "traditions"), supplement the Koran as a guide to the correct conduct or code of behavior of Muslims. This code is called the *Sunna,* translated literally as "Beaten Path."

ISLAMIC DIVISIONS: SUNNI AND SHIA

The great majority (90 percent) of Muslims are called *Sunni Muslims.* They follow the Sunna, practice the rituals of the religion, and accept the progression of Islamic history from Muhammad through a line of successors called *caliphs* (in Arabic, *Khalifa*—"agent," "successor," or "deputy") acting on his behalf down to the current division into sovereign Islamic states. But a significant minority (10 percent), while accepting the bases of Islam, reject its historical and political development. They are called *Shia Muslims* (commonly, but incorrectly, Shiites). The split between these two groups dates back to the aftermath of Muhammad's death in A.D. 632.

Muhammad left no instructions as to a successor (caliph). Since he had said that there would be no more revelations after him, a majority of his followers favored the election of a caliph who would hold the community together and carry on his work. But a minority felt that Muhammad had intended to name his closest male blood relative, Ali, as his successor. Supporters of Ali declared that the succession to Muhammad was a divine right inherited by his direct descendants. Hence they are known as Shia ("Partisans") of Ali.

The first three caliphs—Abu Bakr, 'Umar, and 'Uthman—were chosen by majority vote by the Mecca community. Under their leadership, Arab armies expanded Islam's territory far outside Arabia, changing what had been essentially a religious community into a political power through the conversion of non-Arab peoples to Islam and the imposition of rule by Islamic caliphs. These conquests compounded Sunni-Shia differences.

Ali was eventually elected as the fourth caliph, but by this time the divisions were so deep that his election was disputed. An extremist group, the Kharijites, who felt that Muhammad's original purpose in founding the Islamic community had been distorted, decided to assassinate him and his major rival, on the grounds that Ali had accepted arbitration in his dispute with this rival over the election. The Kharijites argued that the office of caliph could not be bartered away; it was a sacred trust transmitted from God to Muhammad. One of them murdered Ali outside a mosque in A.D. 661.

Ali's younger son and designated successor, Husayn, was ambushed and killed in A.D. 680 by the army of Yazid, the son of the fourth caliph's major rival, near the town of Karbala (in modern Iraq). This event led to the founding of a hereditary dynasty, the Umayyads. The Umayyad caliphs moved the Islamic capital from Mecca to Damascus. But the intrigues and rivalries of Muslim leaders continued to hamper political stability. A century and a half later a rival group overthrew the Umayyads and established a third caliphate, the Abbasids. The caliphal capital was moved eastward, to Baghdad, where it endured for 500 years and developed the distinctive features of *Islamic* civilization, the successor in many respects of Greek and Roman civilization and precursor of European civilization.

The Abbasid caliphs were Sunnis, and Shia resistance to them as presumed usurpers of the rightful heritage of Ali and his descendants resulted in much persecution. Shia rebellions were put down with bloody massacres by the ruling Sunnis. Forced to go underground, the Shia Muslims began to practice *taqiya* ("dissimulation"). Outwardly they bowed to the authority of Sunni rulers, but secretly they continued to believe in the divine right of Ali's descendants to rule the Islamic world.

Most Shia Muslims recognize a line of 12 direct descendants of Muhammad, through Ali and Husayn, as their *Imams,* or spiritual leaders. When the twelfth Imam died, a number of Shia religious leaders declared that he was not dead but hidden (alive, present in this world, but invisible) and would return at the end of time to pronounce the Day of Judgment. Until the hidden Imam returned, the religious leaders would provide leadership and interpretation of God's will and make decisions on behalf of the Shia community. This doctrine gave the Shia religious leaders more authority over Shia Muslims than Sunni religious leaders have over Sunni Muslims. This helps to explain the tremendous power and prestige that Ayatollah Khomeini, leader of the revolution that established an Islamic republic in Iran, held among his people.

With one exception, Shia Muslims remained a minority in Islamic lands and did not acquire political power. The exception was Iran. In the early 1500s Shaykh Safi, the leader of a religious brotherhood in northern Iran, preached a jihad against the Ottoman Turks, accusing them of unjust practices and discrimination against the non-Turkish subjects of their empire. His successor, as head of the brotherhood, claimed to be descended from Ali, which entitled him to act on behalf of the Hidden Imam. In order to obtain further sanction for his wars with the Ottomans, the successor reached an agreement with Shia religious leaders, whereby they would recognize him as ruler of Iran in return for a commitment to establish Shia Islam as the majority there.

Since that time Shia Islam has been the strongest bond unifying the Iranian people, regardless of ethnic, linguistic, or social differences. The relationship between the shahs of Iran and the clergy underwent many vicissitudes, from coexistence, to persecution, to a grudging acceptance. But it was not until Shah Mohammed Reza Pahlavi began to tamper with the bonds linking the Iranian people with their religious leaders, through his programs of social modernization, particularly in the areas of emancipation and literacy, that the relationship became totally an adversary one.

SHIA MUSLIMS AND MARTYRDOM

The murder of Husayn, far more than that of his father, provided the Shia community with a martyr figure. This is due to the circumstances surrounding his death—the lingering image of Muhammad's grandson, with a small band of followers, surrounded in the waterless desert to be cut down by the vastly superior forces of Yazid, has exerted a powerful influence on Shia. Shia Muslims identify themselves with Husayn in terms of a heroic martyr struggling against superior odds. The sense of martyrdom among Shia Muslims is reinforced by their low socioeconomic status in most Islamic countries outside Iran. This sense and belief in their leaders make Shia Muslims more willing than their Sunni brethren to give their lives for their cause of social justice and defense of Islam.

ISLAM AND EUROPE: CHANGING ROLES

In November 1979 the Islamic world marked the start of 14 centuries since the founding of the religion. The early centuries were marked by many brilliant achievements. An extensive network of trade routes linked the cities of the Islamic world. It was a high-fashion world in which the rich wore silks from Damascus ("damask"), slept on fine sheets from Mosul ("muslin"), sat on couches of morocco leather, and carried swords and daggers of Toledo steel. Islamic merchants developed many institutions and practices used in modern economic systems, such as banks, letters of credit, checks and receipts, accounting, and bookkeeping. Islamic agriculture, based on sophisticated irrigation systems developed for the arid Middle East, introduced to the Western world the cultivation of citrus fruits, vegetables such as eggplant and radishes, coffee, cotton, and sugar.

Islamic medical technology reached a level of excellence in diagnosis and treatment unequalled in Europe until the nineteenth century. Muslim mathematics gave us our Arabic numerals and the concept of zero. Muslim navigators made possible Columbus's voyages through their knowledge of seamanship and inventions such as the sextant and the compass. Their libraries were the most extensive in existence at that time.

The level of achievements of Islamic civilization during these centuries (roughly A.D. 750–1200) was far superior to that of Europe. The first Europeans to come in direct contact with Islamic society were Crusader knights who invaded the Middle East in order to recapture Jerusalem from its Muslim rulers. The Crusaders marveled at what they saw, even though they were the sworn enemies of Islam. Those who returned to Europe brought with them new ideas and products from the Islamic world, as well as many English words derived from Arabic, including sofa, algebra, crimson, and admiral.

One of the great contributions of Islam to world culture is the art—or, more precisely, the scientific art—of calligraphy.

'ASHURA

A special Shia festival not observed by Sunnis commemorates the 10 days of 'Ashura, the anniversary of the death of Husayn. Shia Muslims mark the occasion with a series of ritual dramas that may be compared to the Christian Passion Play, except that they may be performed at other times during the year. Particularly in Iran, the ritual, called Ta'ziyeh, is presented by strolling troupes of actors who travel from village to village to dramatize the story with songs, poetry, and sword dances. Ta'ziyeh also takes place in street parades in cities, featuring penitents who lash themselves with whips or slash their bodies with swords. Freya Stark, the great English travel writer, describes one such procession in her book, *Baghdad Sketches:*

> All is represented, every incident on the fateful day of Karbala, and the procession stops at intervals to act one episode or another. One can hear it coming from far away by the thud of beaters beating their naked chests, a mighty sound like the beating of carpets, or see the blood pour down the backs of those who acquire merit with flails made of knotted chains with which they lacerate their shoulders; and finally the slain body comes, headless, carried under a bloodstained sheet through wailing crowds.

Writing has been highly prized in the Islamic world ever since the first scribes took down God's Word as transmitted to Muhammad and transcribed it as the Koran. Echoing the Messenger of God, one master has described it as the algebra of the soul traced by the most spiritualized organ of the body, the right hand. Calligraphy reaches its apogee in the arabesque, the intricate retracing in Arabic script of noble thoughts and praises of Allah, the One God. No mosque, no Islamic public building, can be considered completed until it is adorned with arabesques.

Islamic calligraphy is infinitely detailed, requiring a high degree of professional training and artistic skill. The ink is specially made; the other essential calligraphic tool, the pen, receives equal care. Although both preparation and writing of calligraphic work are exacting processes, one of the by-products of the contemporary revival of Islamic studies has been a renaissance of traditional Islamic arts, with renewed attention to calligraphy as one which bridges the gap between the Muslim and Allah, recalling the time when religion suffused ordinary life with its rich textures.

The hostility between Muslims and Christians, generated by the Crusades, was intensified by the rise of the Ottoman Turks, one of the many newly converted Islamic peoples, to power in the Islamic world. By the 1400s they had established a powerful Islamic military state. In 1453 the Ottomans captured Constantinople, capital of the East Roman (Byzantine) Empire, and soon controlled most of Eastern Europe.

During the centuries of Ottoman rule many people from the Christian European provinces became converts to Islam. Islamic peoples from other parts of the empire also migrated there, drawn by opportunities for land or other inducements, and often Ottoman soldiers were given land grants in return for service to the state. Muslims in Eastern Europe remained there after countries such as Yugoslavia, Romania, Bulgaria, and Albania gained their independence from the sultan. Until recently their governments did not interfere substantially with the personal lives of their Muslim subjects. However, the wave of nationalism that swept over Eastern Europe in the wake of Soviet efforts under Mikhail Gorbachev to revitalize the Communist system led at least one government—that of Bulgaria—to begin a forcible assimilation of its Muslim minority.

The Ottoman state not only ruled Eastern Europe for nearly 4 centuries but also dominated such emerging European nations as Russia, Austria, France, and England. These nations were struggling to limit the powers of absolute monarchs, develop effective military technology, and build systems of representative government. The Ottomans and the various Islamic peoples they governed did not think that any of these things were necessary. The Ottoman sultan was also the caliph of Islam. He was convinced that God had given him the right to rule and to know what was best for the people. Ottoman military success against Europe seemed to prove that God had given the Islamic world a stronger army, superior military technology, and a more effective way of life. The Ottomans were so sure of the superiority of Islam over anything that could be devised in the Christian West that they allowed Christian and Jewish communities under their control to practice their beliefs and rituals freely under their own leaders, in return for payment of a special tax and admission of their inferior military and political status in exchange for Ottoman protection.

Gradually these roles were reversed. The first reversal came with the defeats of Ottoman armies by various European powers. The Ottoman sultans were forced to sign treaties with rulers they deemed inferior. Worse yet, they lost territories with each defeat. In the early nineteenth century European powers seized control of Egypt, while in Eastern Europe the Greeks, Romanians, Serbs, and other subject peoples won their independence with European support. The defeat in Egypt was particularly shocking to Ottoman leaders, because Egypt had been part of the Islamic heartland for a thousand years.

An even greater shock came with the discovery by Muslims that the despised Europeans had developed a relatively advanced technology. Upper-class Muslim visitors to European lands in the late nineteenth century were astonished by this technology. Electric lights, railroads, broad boulevards sweeping through cities, telegraph lines, factories, and a long list of labor-saving inventions were all new to the Muslims. Most Islamic peoples were still living much as their ancestors had lived for centuries. When this apparent superiority in technology was added to European military dominance, it seemed to thoughtful Muslims that something had gone wrong.

The question was, What had gone wrong? How had it happened that the Islamic world had fallen behind Europe? Some Muslims believed that all one could do was to await the inevitable; God Himself had decided that it was time to bring the world to an end, and, therefore, the decline of Islam was a logical consequence. Other Muslims believed that the problem had developed because they had not been true to their religion or observed correctly the obligations of the faith. A third group of Muslims were convinced that Islam itself had to be "changed, modified, adapted or reformed to suit modern conditions . . . so as to overcome Western domination."[7]

The contrast between the second and third approaches to Islamic reform has been important in forming the Middle Eastern states of today. Two states, Saudi Arabia and, more recently, Iran, developed out of a movement to reestablish the Islamic community of Muhammad in its original form, basing their campaign on calls for strict adherence to the Koran and the Sunna. The other Middle Eastern states developed on an ad hoc basis through Western tutelage and gradual acceptance of Western methods and technology.

ISLAMIC FUNDAMENTALISM

The fundamentalism that appears to pervade the Islamic world today has its roots in earlier, nineteenth-century movements that sought to revitalize Islam through internal reform, thus enabling Islamic societies to resist foreign control. Some of these movements sought peaceful change; others were more militant. The most prominent of the militant groups was the Wahhabi movement, which laid the basis for the Saudi Arabian state, a pure Islamic state in form, law, and practice. Another was the Sanusiyah, founded by a prominent scholar who sought to unite the nomadic and seminomadic peoples of Libya into a brotherhood. This movement was also based on strict interpretation and application of the Koran. A third movement, Mahdism, developed in the Sudan; its purpose was not only to purify Sudanese Islam but also to drive out the British who had invaded the Sudan from Egypt. The aims of these three movements were essentially parochial and territorial, either to expel foreigners from Islamic soil or to impose a "purification" on their tribal neighbors.

Twentieth-century reform movements such as the Muslim Brotherhood have concentrated their efforts on removal of secular Islamic governments, which in their view do not conform to the principles of the true faith and therefore are illegitimate. Islamic reform on the scale of the Christian Protestant Reformation has yet to be attempted, and the establishment of fixed national boundaries by Islamic governments bent on preserving their legitimacy makes it unlikely that a global Islamic state will emerge in the foreseeable future.

Fundamentalism is a somewhat incomplete term to apply to the twentieth-century Islamic movements, because it suggests to Westerners a religious view that is antimodernist, literal in interpretation, and with a strong emphasis on traditional ethics. Some fundamentalists would reestablish Islamic society peacefully through internal change, but others would revolutionize Islam in the manner of Marxist or other European revolutionary movements. Shia Muslim factions in Lebanon, such as the Hizbullah, view the revolutionary struggle as one aimed at expelling foreign influences first and achieving social justice second. This revolutionary movement, once centered around Khomeini in Iran, is committed to the rule of the religious leaders; while Libya's Muammar al-Qadhafi would eliminate the influence of the religious leaders entirely, substituting rule by "people's committees." The only common ground for these movements and groups is their fundamental opposition to the onslaught of materialistic Western culture. Their desire is to reassert a distinct Islamic identity for the societies they claim to represent.

The great danger to Islam is that, rather than being a true revival of the religion, these movements have disfigured its nature. Some of them would modernize Islam by grafting onto the religion negative and spiritually devastating ideas borrowed from the West. In the name of religious fervor, they close the door to the kind of open dialogue that could produce general agreement or understanding of what form Islam should take. A common concern among Muslims is how to achieve *Islamic modernization,* meaning a future wherein political and social development and economic

(UN photo/John Isaac)

The mosque at Khan El Khalili, Egypt.

progress appropriate for the realities of the twentieth century are firmly rooted in Islamic history and values.

Islamic modernizers and fundamentalists alike view Islam as a divinely ordained alternative to capitalism and communism. Where they differ is that many leaders and professional persons throughout the Islamic world are Western-educated; they seek to superimpose Western principles and values on Islamic society. The struggle of fundamentalists to reestablish *Islamic* law as the law of the land, prohibit banks from charging interest, emphasize propriety of dress and decorum for women, and reform the curriculum in universities for greater Islamic emphasis sets the two groups at odds, although their long-term goals are essentially the same.

In recent years Islamic fundamentalists have undertaken political action through either legitimate parties or violence outside the political process. The Muslim Brotherhood has been the most successful of these parties, representing the

MUSLIM HOUSING: FORM FOLLOWS FUNCTION

Muslim families in the Middle East live in many different kinds of houses. A common feature is the suitability of the traditional Islamic residence to the surrounding environment. Nomads in the desert live in woven goat-hair tents, easily dismantled when ready to break camp. In Syria and Turkey one finds the cone-shaped beehive house, built of mud brick, which can be put up easily by unskilled labor and costs little in the way of materials. The high dome of the beehive collects the hot, dry air and releases it through narrow openings, while the dome shape sheds rainfall before the mud brick can absorb moisture and crumble. The construction provides natural air conditioning; interior temperatures remain in the 75°F–85°F range, while the outside temperatures may reach 140°F. The beehive house illustrates Frank Lloyd Wright's dictum that "form follows function."

Further illustrations of ingenious designs to suit the harsh climate are the cave houses in southern Tunisia. Caves have been hollowed out from a central shaft below the desert floor. (The movie *Star Wars* was filmed here.) Most residences on the Persian/Arab Gulf, where strong winds blow, have open-sided towers above the rooftops to catch any wind and funnel it into the rooms below. Many city residences are built with tiny windows, and are joined together and covered by deep overhangs to provide shade for passersby.

In San'a in the Yemen Arab Republic, houses are several stories high, gaily decorated and painted with slatted overhangs for women to look out of without being seen. Some farmers in northern Tunisia utilize hay to construct their houses. These hay houses are sometimes elaborate and contain windows and wooden doors.

Mud brick, cut and sun dried, has been the Middle East's common building material for 8,000 years. Today, with the increased use of reinforced concrete, steel, and other prefabricated building materials, and air condition-

(UN photo/W. Graham)

This cave house in the Matmata Mountains suits the harsh climate of southern Tunisia.

ing, Middle Eastern cities have begun to take on the look of cities everywhere. Not only have most Middle Eastern cities lost their distinctive look, but widespread use of cement instead of the traditional and easily available building materials has had more dire consequences. To raise the cash to buy cement for housing in rural areas, someone must leave the village, thus disrupting family life.

---

main opposition to government in Jordan and Egypt, although it is proscribed in Syria. The National Salvation Front (FIS) in Algeria was instrumental in breaking the stranglehold of that country's single party on political and social life in 1989–1991. The Islamic Republic of Iran continues to adhere at least pro forma to the principles of its founder, Khomeini, who insisted that no Islamic state could be either just or representative unless governed by religious leaders and obedient to Islamic laws and customs. Qadhafi, Libya's revolutionary leader, in the past challenged all Islamic regimes on the grounds that Western institutions of government, however modified, were basically hostile to Islam.

Yet the majority of Islamic fundamentalists in Middle Eastern countries are Western-educated and -oriented, with ideas of democracy and social justice derived from familiar democratic models. As Bernard Lewis points out, "Even the

Islamic Republic of Iran has a written constitution and an elected assembly, as well as a kind of episcopate, for none of which is there any prescription in Islamic teaching nor any precedent in the Islamic past."[8] Fundamentalism may be state-sponsored, as in Saudi Arabia and Iran, or oppositionist, as in Algeria, Egypt, and Jordan. (The controversy over Salman Rushdie's novel *The Satanic Verses,* because of the author's "unflattering" portrait of Muhammad and the resulting charges of blasphemy, making him a heretic in the eyes of true believers, underscores the difficulty for both fundamentalists and modern secular Muslims of bringing their faith into harmony with the values of the contemporary world.) But because Islam does not distinguish between sacred and secular authority, in the long run it is likely that the religion will remain largely what it is, a guide to conduct and a shaping force in social matters, rather than a political instrument.

(UN photo/John Isaac)

A common concern among Muslims is how to achieve Islamic modernization, wherein social development considers the realities of the twentieth century. This dichotomy is illustrated by these Egyptian women in traditional dress waiting for a bus, a modern convenience.

ISLAMIC SOCIETY IN TRANSITION

I have come, I know not where,
  but I have come.
And I have seen a road before me,
  and have taken it.[9]

Most Muslims inhabit a world still dominated by Islamic law, custom, spirituality, and belief, despite the waves of violence, puritanical reaction, revolution, ideological conflict, and power struggles among leaders that have threatened it. Islam is not only the bond that unites diverse peoples over a vast territory; it also brings equilibrium to counterbalance the visible disruptions that increasingly affect Islamic life.

Islam is a complete system providing spiritual, social, moral, and, to a considerable extent, political rules and guidelines for its followers. To become a Muslim is to enter into that system. But there are vast cultural differences among the world's estimated 850 million Muslims. Other than religion, an Indonesian Muslim has little in common with an American Muslim.[10] The only time these differences disappear is during the annual Great Pilgrimage to Mecca. At that time all Muslims, rich and poor, famous and unknown, become merely pilgrims, indistinguishable from one another in their seamless white *ihrams* as they circle seven times around the Ka'ba, kiss the Black Stone, drink from the well of Zam Zam, and perform the other rites associated with the return to the sacred center of their faith.[11]

In the Islamic lands of the Middle East, however, Islam provides a cultural uniformity that transcends ethnic, linguistic, and other differences between social groups. This Middle Eastern Islamic cultural order has many components, both real and intangible. The former include architecture, dress, arts and crafts, food, and living accommodations. In addition to these physical aspects of the culture, a wide range of social activities has evolved, built on religious foundations. The traditional social rituals of childbirth, marriage, adulthood, and death, the festival celebrations, are duplicated with minor variations across the region. The intangible components of the system are harder to define, and they are perhaps more Middle Eastern than purely Islamic. Yet there is a common pattern of behavior. Most Middle Easterners practice bargaining in both business and personal relationships, emphasize the family as the responsible social unit above political parties and even nations, and follow a formal code of etiquette governing all aspects of behavior.

ARCHITECTURE: AN EXPRESSION OF RELIGIOUS FAITH

Islamic architecture is centered on the *mosque,* the house of worship. The first mosque was a simple structure of palm branches laid over a frame of tree trunks to provide shade from the desert sun for worshippers. As time passed, Muslim architects built more magnificent structures, dedicating their work to the glory of God, much as medieval Christian artisans did with the great cathedrals of Europe. The mosque today remains the dominant architectural feature of every Islamic village and town. The presence of at least one mosque in every city neighborhood or district provides Islamic cities with a distinctive skyline of domes and minarets.

Until recently all Islamic cities were also marked by a distinct spatial order, and many still are. The order began with an encircling series of massive walls and gates, closed at night to frustrate invasion or criminal actions. There was a separate, often fortified quarter marking the presence of the central government, the market (*suq*) with its tiny artisans' shops and sacks of spices, residential quarters, and religious institutions. Residential suburbs and subdivisions similar to those of many American cities have developed only in recent years. Traditionally, one was either in the city or out of it, one was either a city dweller or a rural peasant.

HOUSING AND FAMILY LIFE

Within the residential quarters of Islamic cities there existed, and in large measure still exists, a kinship arrangement very different from that of the typical American subdivision. The households of each quarter claim either a kinship relation or close personal ties to one another. Everyone knows everyone else, and most households are related. In one residential

(UN photo/J. Isaac)

Privacy is emphasized in the communities of the Middle East. The nondescript walls behind this Moroccan child may very well hold beautiful courtyards with fruit trees, flowers, and fountains.

quarter of the town of Boujad, Morocco, the great majority of households claim descent from a common ancestor, the founder of the group from which they descended patrilineally. Other households regard themselves as being under the protection of that group.

The resulting close cooperation establishes what anthropologists call the notion of closeness (*qaraba*), which defines the social organization of the quarter. Closeness is essential to the proper functioning of society. Christine Eickelman describes the *hayyan* (family cluster) in inner Oman as an essential support network for village women. The hayyan consists of those women (some of them relatives, others not related) whom each woman regards as her confidantes, and to whom she will confide matters that she may not reveal even to her own husband or immediate family. Visits among hayyan members

are made on a daily basis, aside from the support provided in stressful situations such as birth, marriage, or death. Hayyan members also provide mutual protection and even share housework and child care.[12]

Within the Islamic family, the father has the final say on all matters, which gives him, in theory, absolute authority. However, the role of women in family life is crucial to its continuation. Women in Muslim families not only ensure successive generations, but they are also responsible for the discipline and informal education of the young. Mothers hold the family together through the transmission of cultural and religious traditions and values learned from *their* mothers. A tragic result of the turmoil in Lebanon and the Palestinian resistance movement in the occupied West Bank and Gaza Strip has been the breakup of the family, the loss of parental authority, and the substitution of war and violence for traditional family values among Lebanese and Palestinian youth.

Communities in the Middle East emphasize the private over the public life of residents. It is not possible for someone walking along a town or city residential street to know much about the economic or social circumstances of those who live there. Homes have blank, windowless walls facing the street; entry is usually through a massive studded door set in the wall, a brass hand serving as a knocker. Inside one may find, in a wealthier home, low-ceilinged rooms furnished with rich carpets, banquettes, and ottomans in lieu of chairs and sofas (though this is disappearing), and in the center an open courtyard with flowers, fruit trees, and a plashing fountain.

FAMILY CELEBRATIONS

Throughout the Middle East, the family is still the most important social unit, so much so that when rulers like King Hussein of Jordan and King Hassan II of Morocco describe their relationship with their subjects they do so in terms of "my family" or "my children." Economic dislocations, the gap between illiterate parents and educated children, and new social legislation have all affected the family. But the extended family is still where the individual places his or her trust, loyalty, and obedience.

Most celebrations and holidays in the Middle East are related to religion; the national "holiday" or independence day (usually from colonial rule) is the only exception, although secular Turkey observes a number of holidays associated with the birth of the republic. Both Jewish and Islamic festivals spring from the very roots of their respective faiths. Thus in September 1990 Israelis and Diaspora Jews alike observed the High Holy Days, or "Days of Awe," that begin annually with Rosh Hashana, the Jewish New Year (the 5,751st in the Jewish calendar) and end with Yom Kippur, the Day of Atonement. The observant Jew fasts, prays, stays home, and refrains from all work or physical activity on Yom Kippur. (In a bitterly ironic reminder of Jews' vulnerability in a secular age, Egyptian and Syrian armies attacked Israel in October 1973, the day of Yom Kippur in that year.)

Muslim households observe a similar pattern. The entire month of Ramadan, for example, is set aside as a period of fasting to commemorate God's first revelations to Muhammad. Fasting Muslims go without any nourishment—not even a drop of water may pass their lips—during the daylight hours, until a white thread cannot be distinguished from a black one after sunset. Then a cannon booms to mark the end of the fast, and families gather for the evening meal, followed by sweets for the children and visits to friends and neighbors. Shops and cafes remain open all night, mosques are crowded with worshippers, and a *hafiz* ("reciter") reads from the Koran on street corners until by the 27th of the month the entire Koran has been read. When the month ends and the cannon booms for the last time, Muslims celebrate *Id*

al-Fitr, the "Breaking of the Fast." This festival may last for several days.

A CUISINE SUITED TO THE ENVIRONMENT

Middle Eastern cooking largely transcends political, linguistic, religious, and other differences. It is a highly varied cuisine that makes much use of natural, unrefined foods. The pungent smells of lamb roasting over charcoal, stuffed eggplant and roasted sweet peppers, tiny cups of thick coffee and hot, sweet tea are common across national boundaries. The basics of Middle Eastern cooking originated in ancient Persia (modern Iran) and have been continually refined, with subtle differences developing from country to country.

Beef is relatively scarce in the region due to the aridity and lack of pasture, although this is changing with the introduction of Texas cattle and other breeds suited to the arid climate. There is abundant lamb and chicken, and people eat a great variety of seafood. Because of the lack of cattle, more olive oil is used in cooking than butter, and goat and sheep cheeses are more common than cheese made from cows' milk. Yogurt is a staple dessert but it is also used in soups and sauces. Potatoes are seldom used, but rice pilaf made with chicken broth, onions, and currants is popular. There is an almost limitless variety of herbs and spices.

Little milk is drunk, due to the lack of dairy cows and pasteurization. Fresh orange juice and guava juice are common, along with other fruit juices. Desserts are usually fruit, and sometimes cheese. Middle Easterners are also fond of rich, sweet pastries such as baklava and cakes, which are reserved for holidays and special occasions.

Coffee was discovered growing wild in the mountains of Yemen hundreds of years ago, and was brought to Europe by Ottoman Turkish soldiers during the siege of Vienna, Austria. Coffee is usually drunk strong and heavily sugared in tiny cups. Mint tea is also very popular in the Middle East, particularly in Morocco, where it is heavily laced with sugar and is drunk from small glasses. The elaborate tea-making ceremony is an important part of a formal meal.

Each region of the Middle East has its distinctive cuisine or special dishes that serve as symbolic centers of social life. Thus cous-cous, a traditional North African specialty, has a special place in the family meal ritual in that region. Its base is semolina wheat, to which is added vegetables, lamb or chicken, and varied spices.

The best cous-cous, as any Moroccan, Algerian, or Tunisian will tell you, is served at home, where it becomes the centerpiece of the meal on Friday, the Islamic Sabbath. Custom calls for each diner to spoon a mound from the main platter into his or her bowl and add a ladleful of the sauce, premixed with the hot paste so that the meat and vegetables blend into a delicious potpourri of tastes. A glass of hot, sweet mint tea completes the ritual.

Over the years minor variations of the basic cous-cous recipe have evolved, but whatever the recipe, the subtle, tantalizing blend of tastes and textures calls to mind the world of North African Islam.

Middle Easterners are very conscious of their need to make use of every part of the things they grow. The date palm is a good illustration of this ecologically sound practice. The leaves of the date palm provide rope, baskets, mats and rugs, cleaning pads, and shelter for people and animals. People eat the dates; camels feed on the pits. The trunk of the palm is used for roof beams, rafters, and window frames.

As is true elsewhere in the world, in the Middle East the traditional distinctive culinary arts and specialties are giving way to a homogenized "international" cuisine, just as shoes and plastic sandals now adorn Middle Easterners' feet. Labor-saving devices such as microwave ovens and refrigerators simplify the task of meal preparation in Middle Eastern homes, and McDonald's and Kentucky Fried Chicken houses have introduced a fast-food wedge into Middle Eastern life. But a strong undercurrent of traditionalism pervades Islamic society in the region. This undercurrent has been strengthened by the relative success of Khomeini's revolution in Iran and the appeal of this revolution to Muslims as a force independent of both the United States and the former Soviet Union. Traditions die hard anyway, and the more isolated Muslims become by their own choice from Western thought, behavior, and practice, the more likely it is that all elements in their social system that reflect preferences and values, including food, will remain appropriate to the system.

CHALLENGES TO THE MUSLIM FAMILY

The Muslim family in the Middle East today is subject to many of the same strains and stresses as those that affect families everywhere, but they have somewhat greater impact on Muslim families because of their suddenness. The Middle East did not have the lengthy period of conditioning and preparation that Europe and the United States had due to the Industrial Revolution. The story is told that when some Turkish villagers saw their first automobile, early in the 1940s, they could not believe that it ran on its own power. Where is the donkey that will pull it? they wondered. Similarly, King Ibn Saud, former ruler of Saudi Arabia, was faced with angry opposition by the religious leaders of the kingdom when he wished to install a radio network to link the far-flung cities and towns of his realm. He satisfied the religious leaders by having the Koran read over a radio hookup between Mecca and Riyadh, his capital, pointing out to them that if the machine could carry the Word of God, then God must have approved its use.

One of the challenges to family solidarity in the contemporary Middle East is "Western" secular education, which separates parents from their children who have been educated to acquire university degrees and enter the world of modern technology. Until recently this education had to be obtained abroad. As a result, a generation of young Muslim men (and, increasingly, women) trained and educated in Western countries have returned to take up leadership positions in their own countries. Particularly in the 1970s and early 1980s, oil-producing Arab countries channeled oil revenues into education, setting up universities, medical centers, and technical institutes of high quality, staffed initially by expatriates but in the 1990s largely by indigenous personnel.

A more difficult challenge to the Muslim family, and to the economy and society in general, has been posed by labor emigration. In the 1970s and early 1980s several million Turks, Yemenis, Moroccans, Tunisians, Egyptians, and others emigrated either to Europe or to Arab oil-prospecting states on work contracts. Although their work was seldom of a skilled nature, the pay differential was enormous. Remittances from expatriate labor were important to the home economies, particularly of oil-less Islamic states. However, the recession of the 1980s and the drop in oil prices resulted in the departure of the majority of these expatriate workers, not only weakening their economies but also giving a further jolt to family life with the return of a long-absent and fully Westernized father to his traditional Muslim family.

Women's rights in the Islamic Middle East remain a thorny issue. Early Islam preserved the Arabian tradition of a patriarchal society; *Sura 4:34* of the Koran is often cited as divine intent to place men in charge of women, since God has endowed them with the necessary qualifications and has made them breadwinners. The establishment of Islamic states with a commitment to secular nation-building has led to increased participation by women in the labor force in these states, their participation being justified (in Islamic terms) as a necessary contribution to economic development. Secular national leaders such as Mustafa Kemal Ataturk in Turkey and Habib Bourguiba in Tunisia introduced laws to provide legal safeguards for women's rights and enhance their personal status. Western educational institutions such as the American University of Beirut and the American University at Cairo have contributed to the relaxation of Islamic strictures on male-female relationships that have marked modern Islamic societies in Egypt, Lebanon, and Jordan (where two-thirds of the student body in the national university are female).

The 1979 Iranian Revolution inaugurated a period of reversal in the struggle for women's rights. Religious leaders seeking to reverse the secularizing policies of the shah set rigid Islamic standards of decorum, modesty and dress, and behavior for women; they also decreed the removal of women from the labor force. Rejection of Western attitudes and views of the position of women of Western society spread throughout the Islamic Middle East, where it is now a component of fundamentalism. In 1986 the Egyptian Parliament passed a law abrogating divorce rights for women; it was subsequently annulled, under pressure not only from women's groups but also from male intellectuals and large landowners, who feared repercussions.

To a considerable extent, the Iranian-inspired rejection of women's hard-won personal status is a form of backlash.

Thus in 1990 a group of upper-class women in Saudi Arabia who drove their cars in downtown Riyadh in defiance of an unwritten edict were not only forcibly escorted back to their homes but became the first victims of legal sex discrimination in an Islamic state, when the Saudi government hastily passed a law banning not only driving but all forms of protest and demonstration by women.

NOTES

1. R. Hrair Dekmejian, *Islam in Revolution* (Syracuse: Syracuse University Press, 1985), p. 99.

2. Emmanuel Sivan, *Radical Islam: Medieval Theology and Modern Politics* (New Haven: Yale University Press, 1985), p. 41. Reports the comment of an imprisoned Brotherhood member that underscores this violence: "These regimes are animated by vicious hatred of Islam; no dialogue with them is possible, for their sole answer is repression" (p. 41). Thomas L. Friedman, in *From Beirut to Jerusalem* (New York: Farrar Straus Giroux, 1989) devotes a chapter to "Hama Rules" to describe the uses of power by secular rulers in Islamic nation-states.

3. Peter Awn, "Faith and Practice," in Marjorie Kelly, ed., *Islam: The Religious and Political Life of a World Community* (New York: Praeger, 1984), p. 26.

4. Tareq Y. Ismael and Jacqueline S. Ismael, *Government and Politics in Islam* (New York: St. Martin's Press, 1985), pp. 64–67.

5. *Time* (August 17, 1987). The Koran, *Sura II,* verse 197, enjoins: "Anyone who undertakes the Pilgrimage should not engage in . . . any immorality or wrangling."

6. F. E. Peters, "The Early Muslim Empires," in Kelly, *op. cit.*, p. 86.

7. Seyyed Hossein Nasr, "Islam in the West Today, an Overview," in C. K. Pullapilly, ed., *Islam in the Contemporary World* (Notre Dame: Cross Roads Books, 1980), p. 7.

8. Bernard Lewis, "The Roots of Muslim Rage," in *The Atlantic Monthly* (September 1990), p. 60.

9. Eliya Abu Madi, quoted in Michael Asher, *In Search of the Forty Days' Road* (London: Longman, 1984), p. 132.

10. There are between 1.5 million and 3 million Muslims in the United States and Canada. Most are immigrants, but the number of converts from the black and white communities, particularly in the U.S., is growing rapidly. See Yvonne Y. Haddad, "Muslims in the United States," in Kelly, *op. cit.*, pp. 258–272.

11. The American Muslim leader Malcolm X has a moving description of the pilgrimage in which he participated, in his autobiography, *The Autobiography of Malcolm X* with Alex Haley (New York: Ballantine Books, 1973).

12. Christine Eickelman, *Women and Community in Oman* (New York: New York University Press, 1984), pp. 80–111.

The Middle East: Theater of Conflict

The Middle East, a region approximately equal in size to the continental United States and slightly larger in population, extends from the Atlantic coast of Morocco, in North Africa, to the mountains of Afghanistan, where the Indian subcontinent begins. The Middle East is thus intercontinental rather than continental, with the diversity of topography, climate, and physical and social environments characteristic of the two continents, Africa and Asia, that define its territory. Geography and location have dictated a significant role in world affairs for the Middle East throughout recorded history; humankind's earliest cities, governments, organized societies, and state conflicts were probably located there. In the twentieth century this traditional role has been confirmed by the exploitation of mineral resources vital to the global economy and by the rivalries of nations that regard the Middle East as strategically important to their national interests.

The contemporary Middle East is very different, however, from its predecessors of 100 or 200 years ago. One important difference is political. When the United States became independent of England there were three more or less "sovereign" Middle Eastern nation-states and empires: the Sherifian Sultanate of Morocco; the Ottoman Turkish Empire; and Iran, reunited by force under the new Qajar dynasty, which would remain in power until it was succeeded by the Pahlavi dynasty in the 1920s. These three states were still in place late in the nineteenth century, but European influence and control over their rulers had effectively robbed them of most of their independence. Since then—a process accelerated since World War II—the Middle East map has been redrawn many times. The result of the redrawing process is the contemporary Middle East, 20 independent states with diverse political systems overlaying a pastiche of ethnic groups, languages, customs, and traditions.

The diversity of these states is compensated for, in part, by the cohesion provided by various unifying factors. One of these factors is geography. The predominance of deserts, with areas suitable for agriculture compressed into small spaces where water was available in dependable flow, produced the *oasis-village* type of social organization and agricultural life. Beyond the oases evolved a second type of social organization suited to desert life, called *nomadism*. Another type of village settlement evolved in plateau and mountain regions, wherever the topography afforded physical protection for the defense of the community. In Egypt, and to a lesser extent in the Tigris-Euphrates river valleys, *villages* were established to take advantage of a dependable water supply for crop irrigation. Peoples living in the region

(UN photo)

Humankind's earliest governments, cities, and organized societies were probably located in what today is known as the Middle East. This ancient Roman town of Timgad, Algeria, testifies to people's continued attempts to live in the arid expanses of this part of the world.

mirrored these lifestyles, with the Middle Eastern city developing as an urban refinement of the same traditions.

The broad set of values, traditions, historical experiences, kinship structures, and so on, usually defined as "culture," is a second cohesive factor for the Middle East's peoples. Islam, for example, is either the official state religion or the leading religion in all but one (Israel) of the 20 states. The Arabic language, due to its identification with Islam, is a bond even for those peoples who use another spoken and/or written language (such as Turkish, Hebrew, or Farsi); and in any case, the social order of Islam is another unifying force.

A third unifying factor, while it is intangible and difficult to define, is a common historical experience. Without exception, the 20 states of the Middle East are the products of twentieth-century international politics and the clash of interests of outside powers. Clashing national interests and external involvement in regional affairs have set the tone for the internal and regional conflicts of Middle Eastern states. Thus, the intercommunal violence in modern Lebanon has its roots in foreign (French and British) support for various communal groups in the 1860s, setting the groups against one another under the guise of protecting them from the Ottoman government and its misrule. But Lebanon is only one example of a broad historical process. Throughout Middle Eastern history, invaders and counterinvaders have rolled across the region, advancing, conquering, and being conquered, while below the surface of conflict other peoples have crisscrossed the land in peace, building homes, establishing cities, forming the bedrock of settlement and social development.

THE LAND ISLAND

Until recently the Middle East was compartmentalized. Its peoples had little awareness of one another and even less of the outside world. Months of arduous travel were needed for a directive from the caliph in Baghdad, the chief personage of the theocratic Islamic state, to reach his viceroy in far-off Morocco. Communications within the region were relatively poor, so that often residents of one village would know nothing of what was going on in other nearby villages—that is, if they were at peace and not feuding. Travel for caravans between cities was uncertain and often dangerous; the Tuareg of the Western Sahara Desert, a nomadic society, made a good living by charging tolls and providing mounted escorts for merchants crossing the desert.

Consequently, the combination of vast distances, poor communications, and geographical isolation brought about the early development of subregions within the larger Middle East. As early as the tenth century A.D., three such subregions had been defined: North Africa, the Arab lands traditionally known to Europeans as the Near East, and the highland plateaux of Turkey and Iran. In the twentieth century these three areas were further separated from one another by foreign political control—the French in North Africa, the French and British jointly in the Arab lands, with Turkey and Iran nominally independent but subject to pressures from various outside powers. Alan Taylor's phrase "the Arab balance of power," referring to the "patterns of equilibrium, dislocation and readjustment that unfolded among the Arab states . . ." applies equally well to the interaction of peoples and nations within the subregions.[1]

Many years ago naval historian Alfred Thayer Mahan defined the Middle East as a central part of the "land island" or heartland whose possession would enable some powerful nation to dominate the world. Mahan's definition stemmed from his view of naval power as an element in geopolitics; he saw the United States, as a growing naval power, and Russia, expanding across Asia, as the competitors for world domination in the twentieth century.

Mahan was not original in his geopolitical assessment. In the nineteenth century the United Kingdom and Russia, the two superpowers of the period, were engaged in a "Great Game" of imperial expansion in Asia—the British *from* India, and the Russians moving southward from Moscow across the steppes *toward* India.[2] Each power worked assiduously to expand its territory or sphere of interest at the expense of the other. Their perceived national interests were thousands of miles from London and Moscow, in the mountains of Tibet, the Caucasus, or along the Amu Darya (Oxus) River that today separates Iran from Central Asia.

The Great Game was still being played in different locations, but under similar rules, by the United States and the Soviet Union during the 1980s; the Reagan administration's commitment to a strongly anti-Communist policy revived the Great Game in new locations. Thus former President Ronald Reagan insisted in 1983–1984 that American Marines were in Lebanon to defend vital U.S. interests. In 1987 the United States accepted a request from Kuwait to "reflag" Kuwaiti tankers in the Persian Gulf and provide them with naval protection, ostensibly to thwart Iran but also to forestall a Soviet move into the region. Reagan had warned Iran and Iraq earlier that any attempt to close the Strait of Hormuz to oil-tanker traffic would be regarded as a threat to the free world's access to Middle East oil and therefore to American national interests. Before its disintegration, the Soviet Union from time to time made equally strong pronouncements.[3]

SUBREGIONAL CONFLICTS

The periodic outbreak of local or subregional conflicts characteristic of Middle Eastern societies, which stem from their tribal or ethnic origins, has brought the region to the forefront of world affairs in recent years. Such conflicts as the Lebanese Civil War, the Iran-Iraq War, the Gulf War, the ongoing Arab-Israeli conflict, and the conflict in the Western Sahara between Morocco and the Saharan nationalist movement Polisario (Popular Front for the Liberation of Saguia al-Hamra and Rio de Oro), which is fighting to establish an independent state, have not only drawn in outside powers but also have often developed an internal rhythm that is difficult to control.

Although thus far these Middle Eastern conflicts have been confined to their areas of origin or mediated by outside powers to reduce tension levels, some U.S. policy-makers continue to fear that they might spread and involve other nations in a wider war, possibly proving or at least demonstrating the effectiveness of the "domino theory" often invoked as a guide to modern international relations.

The domino theory holds that tensions or unresolved disputes between two nations will widen as neighboring nations are drawn inevitably into the dispute, even without taking sides. The uninvolved nations will then become involved, as the particular dispute becomes buried in the rivalries of competing national interests. At some point a specific incident ignites a general war, as nation after nation falls like a domino into the widening conflict. The classic example of the theory is World War I.

While the applicability of the domino theory to the Middle East has yet to be proven, thus far regional conflict there has not affected long-term global commerce or national survival, and international terrorist acts identified with Middle Eastern governments remain sporadic and uncoordinated. But there are very real limits to involvement or effective management, even by the superpowers. Former U.S. President Reagan recognized these limits implicitly by withdrawing American Marines from Lebanon; and when Egypt's then-President Anwar al-Sadat ordered the withdrawal of all Soviet military advisers from his country some years ago, home they went.

A final point about these conflicts is that they are all direct results of European intervention in the Middle East. For much of its history the Middle East was a region without defined borders, other than the intangible limits fixed for Muslims by their religion. Even the Ottoman Empire, the major power in the region for more than 5 centuries, did not mark off its territories into provinces with precise boundaries until well into the 1800s. But the European powers brought a different set of rules into the area. They laid down fixed borders sanctified by treaties, played ruler against ruler, divided and conquered. It is this European ascendancy, building on old animosities while creating new ones, that laid the groundwork for today's conflicts.

THE IRAN-IRAQ WAR:
BATTLE OF ISLAMIC BROTHERS

The Iran-Iraq War broke out in September 1980, when Iraqi forces invaded Iran and occupied large portions of Khuzestan Province. This measure was in retaliation for Iranian artillery attacks across the border and efforts by Iranian agents to subvert the Iraqi Shia Muslim population, along with propaganda broadcasts urging Iraqis to overthrow the regime of Saddam Hussein. But as is the case with most Middle Eastern conflicts, the causes of the war are complex.

One factor is the ancient animosity between Iranians and Arabs, which dates back to the seventh century A.D., when invading Arab armies overran the once powerful Sassanid Empire of Iran, defeating the Iranian army at the famous

ARABS AND IRANIANS

Arabs and Iranians (or Persians) are nearly all Muslims. But they have very different ethnic origins and linguistic and geographical backgrounds as well as different histories. The Arabs originated in the Arabian Peninsula and began to migrate to other parts of the Middle East after the rise of Islam. The Iranians were a loosely organized nomadic people from Central Asia who migrated into the Iranian plateau 3,000 years ago and became sedentary farmers and herders. They displayed early a talent for political organization and military prowess.

Around 600 B.C. an Iranian prince, Cyrus, founded what is usually considered to be the world's first true empire. His successors, the Achaemenian dynasty, expanded Iranian territory east to the Indus River and westward to the edge of Asia on the Mediterranean Sea. Despite a checkered history since then, Iranians have retained a lofty sense of their contributions to civilization beginning with this period.

The Arabs, in contrast, gained their sense of unity and leadership through Islam. Today the Arabs form the majority of the population in North Africa, the Near Eastern Arab states, and Sudan and are an important minority in Iran. Except for Iraq and the Persian Gulf states, where there are significant Iranian communities, Iranians have largely remained in their country of origin.

battle of Qadisiya in 637. The Iranians were converted to Islam with relative ease, yet they looked down on the Arabs as uncivilized nomads who needed to be taught the arts of government and refined social behavior. The Arabs, in turn, despised the Iranians for what they considered their effeminateness—their love of gardens and flowers, their appreciation of wine and fine banquets. These attitudes never entirely disappeared.[4] After the 1980 invasion the controlled Iraqi press praised it as Saddam Hussein's Qadisiya, reminding readers of the earlier Arab success.

In recent years the two countries have been at swords' points over a number of issues. One is occupation of three small islands at the mouth of the Persian Gulf. The British had included them in their protectorate over eastern Arabia and transferred them to the United Arab Emirates after that country became independent. But Iran's Shah Mohammed Reza Pahlavi contested the transfer on the grounds that historically they had belonged to Iran. In 1971 an Iranian commando force seized the islands. Although the islands had never belonged to Iraq, the Iraqis denounced the occupation as a violation of *Arab* sovereignty and mounted a campaign among the predominantly Arab population of Iran's Khuzestan Province, adjacent to the border, to encourage them to revolt against the central government.

Another issue was the shah's support for Kurdish guerrillas who had been fighting the Iraqi government for years to obtain autonomy for their mountain region. The shah also resented Iraq's grant of asylum to the Ayatollah Khomeini in

1963, because of Khomeini's continued anti-shah activities and propaganda broadcasts into Iran.

These disagreements intensified after the overthrow of the shah in 1979. Iraq accused the Khomeini regime of mistreatment of Khuzestan Arabs and of sending agents to incite its own Shia Muslim population to rebel. Iraqi governments have been dominated by the Sunni Muslim population since independence, although more than half percent of the population are Shia. The regime of Saddam Hussain, like its predecessors, is paranoid about opposition in general but about Shia opposition in particular.[5]

The personal hatred between Saddam and Khomeini contributed to the war. They had been bitter enemies since 1978, when Saddam ordered Khomeini expelled from Iraq and accused him of working with Iraqi Shia Muslim leaders to undermine the regime. But differences in their views on the nature of authority and of social development set the two leaders in opposition. For Saddam Hussain, the development of Islamic society to the fullest is best achieved by a secular Socialist party (e.g., the Ba'th); Islam is tangential. Khomeini, in the republic he fashioned for Iran based on his Islamic political philosophy, argued for authority to be vested in religious leaders like himself since they are qualified by wisdom, moral uprightness, and insight to know what is best for the Islamic community.

One issue often overlooked as a cause of the war is a territorial dispute, dating back many centuries, that has been aggravated by European intervention in the Middle East. The dispute concerns the Shatt al-Arab, the 127-mile waterway from the junction of the Tigris and Euphrates Rivers south to the Persian Gulf. The waterway was a bone of contention between the Ottoman and Iranian Empires for centuries, due to its importance as a trade outlet to the Gulf. It came entirely under Ottoman control in the nineteenth century. But with the collapse of the Ottoman Empire in World War I, the new kingdom of Iraq set up by the United Kingdom came in conflict with a revitalized Iran over navigation and ownership rights. Iran demanded ownership of half of the Shatt al-Arab under international law, which would mean to mid-channel at the deepest point. Iraq claimed the entire waterway across to the Iranian side. Conflict intensified as both countries built up their oil exports in the 1960s and 1970s. In 1969 Iranian Shah Reza Pahlavi threatened to occupy Iran's side of the waterway with gunboats, and began a program of military support to Kurdish (Sunni Muslims) rebels fighting the Iraqi government.

Iran was much wealthier and militarily stronger than Iraq at that time, and Iraq could do little about Iranian support for the Kurds. But the Iraqis did have the Shatt al-Arab as a bargaining chip, in that their rights were embodied in several treaties. In 1975, after lengthy negotiations, Houari Boumedienne, then the president of Algeria, interrupted an oil ministers' conference in Algiers to announce that "our fraternal countries Iran and Iraq have reached agreement on their differences."[6] Iraq agreed to recognize Iranian ownership of the Shatt from bank to mid-channel, and Iran agreed to stop supporting Kurdish rebels in Iraq.

The advantage to Iraq of bringing an end to the Kurdish rebellion was offset by the humiliation felt by Iraqi leaders because they had bartered away a part of the sacred Arab territory. Hussain considered the agreement a personal humiliation because he had been the chief negotiator. When he became president, he said that he had negotiated it under duress and that Iraq would one day be strong enough to revoke it.[7]

The fall of Shah Reza Pahlavi, followed by the internal upheaval in Iran let loose by the 1979 Revolution, seemed to Saddam Hussain to be an excellent opportunity to reverse Iraq's humiliation. In September 1980 he announced that the 1975 treaty was null and void, and he demanded Iran's recognition of Iraqi sovereignty over the entire Shatt al-Arab. He also called for the return of the three islands seized by the shah's forces in 1971 and the transfer of predominantly Arab areas of Khuzestan to Iraqi control. Although the two countries were roughly equal in military strength at the time, purges in Iranian Army leadership, low morale, and lack of spare parts for weapons due to the U.S. economic boycott convinced Saddam that a limited attack on Iran would almost certainly succeed.[8]

However, the quick and easy victory anticipated by the Iraqis did not materialize. Political expectations proved equally erroneous. Iraq had expected the Arabs of Khuzestan to support the invasion, but they remained loyal to the Khomeini regime. The Iraqi forces failed to capitalize on their early successes and were stopped by determined Iranian resistance. The war quickly turned into a stalemate.

In 1981–1982 the momentum shifted strongly in Iran's favor. The war became a patriotic undertaking as thousands of volunteers, some barely teenagers, headed for the front. An Iranian operation, appropriately code-named Undeniable Victory, routed three Iraqi divisions. Iran's blockade of Iraqi oil exports put a severe strain on the Iraqi economy. After the defeat Saddam withdrew all Iraqi forces from Iranian territory and asked for a ceasefire. But Iran refused; Khomeini set the ouster of "the traitor Saddam" as a precondition for peace.

Iraqi forces fared better on their own soil and threw back a number of large-scale Iranian assaults, with huge casualties. Subsequent U.S.S.R. deliveries of missiles and new aircraft gave Iraq total air superiority. In early 1985 the Iraqis launched a campaign of "total war, total peace," combining air raids on Iranian ports and cities with an all-out effort to bring international pressure on Iran to reach a settlement.

In March 1985 Iranian forces launched another major offensive toward Basra from their forward bases in the Majnoon Islands, deep in the marshes, which they had captured by surprise in 1984. Although they were driven back with heavy losses, a year later the Iranian forces captured the Fao (Faw) Peninsula southeast of Basra in another surprise attack and moved to within artillery range of Iraq's second city.

(Gamma-Liaison/François Lochon)

These young Iranians, taken prisoner by Iraq, were typical of those fighting in the Iran-Iraq War. The Iranians' patriotic fervor produced thousands of volunteers, some as young as 12.

With the war on the ground stalemated, conflict shifted in 1986 and 1987 to the sky and sea lanes. Iraq's vast air superiority enabled the country to carry the war deep into Iranian territory, with almost daily bombing raids on Iranian cities, industrial plants, and oil installations.

But the most dangerous aspect of the conflict stemmed from Iraqi efforts to interdict Iranian oil supplies in order to throttle its enemy's economy. The war had a high-risk potential for broader regional conflict from the start, and in 1984 Iraqi missile attacks on tanker traffic in the Persian Gulf came close to involving other states in the region in active participation.

The internationalization of the war predicted by many analysts became a reality in its seventh year, like a plague of locusts. The secret dealings with the United States (revealed in the 1987 Iran-Contra hearings) had immeasurably strengthened Iran's air power and defenses; Iraq lost one-fifth of its aircraft in a series of battles in the marshes. Iranian arms dealers were successful in purchasing weaponry from many sources. One of their major suppliers was China, from which they purchased a number of Silkworm missiles that were installed at secret launching sites along the coast facing the Strait of Hormuz and the Fao Peninsula. At the same time Iranian Revolutionary Guards established bases in various small harbors from whence they could mount missile and grenade attacks in fast patrol boats against ships passing in the Gulf. The government warned that tankers bound for Kuwait and other Gulf ports would be attacked if Iraq continued its air raids.

However, the direct cause of the internationalization of the war was an Iraqi air raid on the U.S. naval frigate *Stark* on May 17, 1987. Thirty-seven American sailors were killed in the raid. (Although about 230 ships have been attacked by Iraq or Iran since 1984, the *Stark* was the first warship and suffered the heaviest casualties.) Saddam called the attack a "tragic mistake" and apologized. The United States drastically increased its naval forces in the Gulf and in the following month accepted a request from Kuwait for tanker protection under the American flag, along with naval escorts. In June 1987 the first convoy of "reflagged" Kuwaiti tankers traversed the Gulf without incident, escorted by U.S. warships and overflying jets from the aircraft carrier *Constellation.*

Predictably, Iran's threat to make the Gulf "safe for every one or no one," following the U.S. buildup in the region, affected nearby countries as well as international shipping. Saboteurs blew up oil installations and factories in the United Arab Emirates, Bahrain, and Saudi Arabia. Revolutionary Guardsmen carried out their earlier threats with hit-and-run strafing and grenade attacks on passing tankers. But the most serious danger came from floating mines strewn at random in shipping lanes. After a number of tankers had been damaged, the United States and several European countries previously uninvolved in the conflict, notably Italy, began sending minesweepers to the area.

With the Gulf in a state of high tension, the United Nations Security Council mounted a major effort to end the war. In July 1987 the council unanimously approved Resolution 598. It called for an immediate ceasefire, withdrawal of all forces to within recognized international boundaries, repatriation of all prisoners, and negotiations under UN auspices for a permanent peace settlement. Iraq accepted the resolution, but Iran temporized. Its president, Ali Khamenei, told the UN General Assembly: "The Security Council's stance in relation to the war imposed on us has not changed up to this moment."[9]

A year later Iran accepted Resolution 598, in an abrupt about-face. A number of factors combined to bring about this change, but the principal one was probably Iraqi success on the battlefield. Iraqi forces recaptured the Fao Peninsula in early 1988; this success was followed by several other offensives that recovered all the territory in Iraq taken by Iranian forces. Iranian morale sagged after a series of unexpected Iraqi missile attacks on both military and civilian targets deep inside Iran. And the Iranian economy continued to weaken as the destruction of oil installations and factories by Iraqi aircraft took its toll.

Khomeini's death in June 1989 removed a major obstacle to peace negotiations. The Ayatollah had been persuaded with great difficulty to approve the ceasefire, and his uncompromising hatred of Saddam Hussein was not shared by many associates.

A real peace settlement would enable both regimes to turn their full attention to the enormous problems of reconstruction. Unfortunately, their diametrically opposed positions on war gains worked against dialogue. Iran insisted on the withdrawal of Iraqi troops from its territory as a first step, while Iraq demanded that prisoner exchanges and clearing of the Shatt al-Arab should precede withdrawal.

For the next 2 years UN mediators shuttled between Baghdad and Teheran without effect. But Iraq's invasion of Kuwait in August 1990 brought about a drastic change in the relationship. Saddam Hussain, desperately searching for allies, abruptly agreed to the peace terms set by the UN and accepted by Iran in March. The terms specified a withdrawal of Iraqi troops from 1,560 square miles of occupied Iranian territory, prisoner exchanges, freedom of navigation in the Strait of Hormuz and the Gulf, and clearance of the Shatt al-Arab. The last Iraqi troops left Iran on August 21, and an exchange of 54,000 Iranian POWs for 50,000 Iraqis was completed in September. (In a strange turnabout, Iraqi pilots later flew the bulk of the Iraqi Air Force to sanctuary in Iran during the buildup of UN coalition forces in Saudi Arabia to drive Iraq from Kuwait.) But in terms of the results of the bitter war between Islamic brothers, Iraq lost more than it gained.

THE GULF WAR

On August 2, 1990, the Iraqi Army, which had been mobilized along the border, invaded and occupied Kuwait, overcoming light resistance as the ruling emir and his family escaped into exile. The invasion climaxed a long dispute between the two Arab neighbors over oil production quotas, division of output from the oil fields of the jointly controlled Neutral Zone along the border, and repayment of Iraqi debts to Kuwait from the war with Iran. Saddam Hussain had criticized Kuwait for producing more than its quota as allotted by OPEC, thus driving down the price per barrel and costing Iraq some $7 billion to $8 billion in lost revenues. The Iraqi leader also charged Kuwait with taking more than its share of the output of the Neutral Zone. The Iraqi charges found considerable support from other Arab states, most of which consider the Kuwaitis to be stingy and arrogant. However, an Arab League summit meeting of oil ministers failed to resolve the dispute. Kuwait agreed only to a 1-month adherence to its OPEC quota and continued to press for repayment of Iraqi war debts.

What had been initially been an inter-Arab conflict was globalized by the invasion. Although Iraq called its occupation a recovery of part of the Arab homeland, which had been "stolen" from the Arabs by the British and given its independence under false premises, the action was viewed as aggression by nearly all the countries in the world. The UN Security Council on August 6 approved Resolution 660, calling for an immediate withdrawal of Iraqi forces from Kuwait and restoration of the country's legitimate government. Pending withdrawal, a worldwide embargo would be imposed on Iraq, covering exports as well as imports and including medical and food supplies as well as military equipment. A similar resolution approved by the League of Arab States denounced Iraq's aggression against the "broth-

(A/P Wide World Photos)

During Operation Desert Storm, the U.S.-UN–led coalition mobilized a large number of air strikes that routed Iraqi forces. These F/A-18 fighters met with little resistance as they flew sorties over Iraqi defensive positions.

erly Arab state of Kuwait" and demanded immediate Iraqi withdrawal and restoration of Kuwaiti independence.

The invasion divided the Arab states, as several, notably Yemen and Sudan, agreed with Iraq's contention that Kuwait was historically part of Iraq and that Kuwaiti arrogance was partly responsible for the conflict. Others took the opposite view. Egyptian President Hosni Mubarak accused Saddam Hussain of breaking a solemn pledge not to invade Kuwait. Saudi Arabia, fearing that it might be Iraq's next victim, requested U.S. help under the bilateral defense treaty to protect its territory. U.S. President George Bush and then-Soviet President Mikhail Gorbachev issued a joint pledge for action to expel Iraqi forces from Kuwait. A massive military buildup followed, largely of U.S. forces but with contingents from a number of other countries, including several Arab states. Although led by U.S. military commanders, the collective force operated under the terms of UN Resolution 660 and was responsible ultimately to the Security Council as a military coalition.

The UN embargo continued in effect for 6 months but failed to generate an Iraqi withdrawal from Kuwait, despite its severe impact on the civilian population. The only concession made by Saddam Hussain during that period was the release of foreign technicians (many of them Americans) who had been working in Kuwait at the time of the invasion. As a result, the coalition forces launched the so-called Operation Desert Storm on January 16, 1991. With total air superiority and superior military technology they made short work of Iraq's army as thousands fled or surrendered. On the express orders of President Bush, the campaign was halted on February 7, after Iraqi forces had been expelled from Kuwait. Yet Saddam Hussein remained in power, and uprisings of the Kurdish and Shia populations in Iraq were crushed by the reorganized Iraqi Army, which remained loyal to its leader. Although many felt that Saddam should be punished as well as driven from power, it was the consensus of U.S. policy-makers that no alternative to the Iraqi leader existed and that a breakup of Iraq into competing factions would enable Iran to dominate the region and perhaps resume its anti-Western destabilizing activities.

In any case, Iraq's defeat shifted the balance of power in the Middle East. The embargo on exports and imports continued, although the UN agreed in principle to allow the country to sell enough of its oil to pay for desperately needed medical and food supplies. A 1,440-strong UN observer force from 27 nations was set up to monitor the Iraq-Kuwait border and report possible violations of the ceasefire, while a Rapid Strike Force based in eastern Turkey was given the responsibility to cross the border into Iraq in the event of Iraqi attacks on the Kurdish population.

The UN also established compliance procedures for Iraq's alleged nuclear and chemical warfare programs and sent teams of inspectors to oversee the dismantling of those facilities that seemed to show evidence of the country's nuclear capability. Continued Iraqi noncooperation and Saddam's rejection of a UN plan to monitor its arms industry in return for approval of a $1.6 billion oil sale to pay for food and medicine imports led the Security Council in early 1992 to extend economic sanctions indefinitely.

THE ARAB-ISRAELI CONFLICT

The basis of the Arab-Israeli conflict (or, more narrowly, the Palestinian-Israeli conflict) rests on ownership of land. It is not ownership in the proprietary sense, documented by title deeds and mortgages, but in the sense of a *homeland,* a place claimed by a particular people on emotional, symbolic, and physical grounds. The land in question, generally referred to as Palestine (*Falastina,* in Arabic) since Roman times, is the claimed homeland of two peoples, Israelis and Palestinians.

The Israelis are the returned Jews, immigrants to Palestine from many lands plus the small community of Jews who have always lived there. The Palestinians are the dispersed descendants of settlers whose attachment to Palestine dates back to antiquity. The Jews, as Israelis, have been in possession of their homeland since 1948; yet most of them regard possession as the fulfillment of God's original covenant with Abraham, patriarch of the Hebrew people. The sense of Palestine as a homeland among Palestinians was not based on strong religious feelings; it was more of an

automatic attachment based on long residence, something not to be questioned. Nor was it particularly *Arab,* since the Arabs were spread over many lands and did not have the overriding sense of a particular place given to them by some divine ordinance. But the exile of the majority of Palestinians after the establishment of the State of Israel in 1948 generated among them an emotional commitment to their Palestinian homeland every bit as strong as that of the Israelis.

In the twentieth century the question of a Palestine homeland was given form and impetus by two national movements, Zionism and Arab nationalism. Zionism, the first to develop political activism in implementation of a national ideal, organized large-scale immigration of Jews into Palestine. These immigrants, few of them skilled in agriculture or the vocations needed to build a new nation in a strange land, nevertheless succeeded in changing the face of Palestine. In a relatively short time a region of undeveloped sand dunes near the coast evolved into the city of Tel Aviv and unproductive marshland was transformed into profitable farms and kibbutz settlements.

Arab nationalism, slower to develop, grew out of the contacts of Arab subject peoples in the Ottoman Empire with Europeans, particularly missionary-educators sent by their various churches to work with the Christian Arab communities. It developed political overtones during World War I, when British agents such as T. E. Lawrence encouraged the Arabs to revolt against the Turks, their "Islamic brothers." In return, the Arabs were given to understand that the United Kingdom would support the establishment of an independent Arab state in the Arab lands of the empire. An Anglo-Arab army entered Jerusalem in triumph in 1917 and Damascus in 1918, where an independent Arab kingdom was proclaimed, headed by the Emir Faisal, leader of the revolt.

The Arab population of Palestine took relatively little part in these events. But European rivalries and conflicting commitments for disposition of the provinces of the defeated Ottoman Empire soon involved them directly in conflict over Palestine. The most important document affecting the conflict was the Balfour "Declaration," a statement of British support for a Jewish homeland in Palestine in the form of a letter from Foreign Secretary Arthur Balfour to Lord Rothschild, a prominent Jewish banker and leader of the Zionist Organization.

Although the Zionists interpreted the statement as permission to proceed with their plans for a Jewish National Home in Palestine, neither they nor the Arabs were fully satisfied with the World War I peace settlement, in terms of the disposition of territories. The results soon justified their pessimism. The Arab kingdom of Syria was dismantled by the French, who then established a mandate over Syria under the League of Nations. The British set up a mandate over Palestine, attempting to balance support for Jewish aspirations with a commitment to develop self-government for the Arab population, in accordance with the terms of the mandate as approved by the League of Nations. It was an impossible task, and in 1948 the British gave up, handing the

ZIONISM

Zionism may be defined as the collective expression of the will of a dispersed people, the Jews, to recover their ancestral homeland. This idealized longing was given concrete form by European Jews in the nineteenth century. In 1882 a Jewish law student, Leon Pinsker, published *Auto-Emancipation,* a book that called on Jews, who were being pressed at the time between the twin dangers of anti-Semitism and assimilation into European society, to resist these dangers by establishing a Jewish homeland *somewhere.* Subsequently a Viennese journalist, Theodor Herzl, published *The Jewish State,* in which he advocated a homeland established by immigrant Jews from all parts of the world as a secular commonwealth that could become a model for all nations through its revival of the ancient Jewish nation formed by a covenant with God. The Zionist Organization, formed as a result of Herzl's efforts, held its first conference at Basle, Switzerland, in 1896. Although the conferees considered other locations for the Jewish homeland, such as Argentina and Uganda, they eventually fixed upon Palestine as the logical site for the homeland.

The Zionist program, which led ultimately to the establishment of the State of Israel, generated sharp disagreement within global Jewry. Although some Orthodox Jews supported the program—Mizrachi, one of its earliest movements, was Orthodox—the majority held that only God could ordain a Jewish *state* and that therefore Zionism would have to build a Jewish homeland in strict accordance with the rules and practices of Judaism. The small "religious" parties representing Orthodox views play a role disproportionate to their size in Israeli political life and are often the key to survival of coalition governments in the rough and tumble of national politics.

"Palestine problem" back to the United Nations as successor to the League of Nations. The UN had approved a partition plan for Palestine in November 1947, and after the termination of the mandate the Zionists proclaimed the establishment of the State of Israel.

Israel was established against the formal opposition of the neighboring Arab states, and since 1948 Israeli resolve has been tested in five wars with them. None of these wars led directly to a peace settlement, and except for Egypt, Israel remains in a state of armistice and nonrecognition with these states.

Most state-to-state disputes are susceptible to arbitration and often outside mediation, particularly when they involve borders or territory. But Palestine is a special case. Its location astride communication links between the eastern and western sections of the Arab world made it essential to the building of a unified Arab nation, the goal of Arab leaders since World War I. Its importance to Muslims as the site of one of their holiest shrines, the Dome of the Rock in Jerusalem, is underscored by Jewish control—a control made possible by the "imperialist enemies of Islam," in the Arab Muslim view, and reinforced by the relatively lenient treatment given by an Israeli court to Jewish terrorists arrested for trying to blow up the shrines on the Dome and build a new temple on the site. Also, since they lack an outside patron, both the dispersed Palestinians and those remaining in Israel look to the Arab states as the natural champions of their cause.

Yet the Arab states have never been able to develop a coherent, unified policy toward Israel in support of the Palestine cause. There are several reasons for this failure. One is the natural rivalry of Arab leaders, a competitiveness that has evolved from ancient origins, strong individualism, and family pride. Other reasons include the overall immaturity of the Arab political system and the difficulty of distinguishing between rhetoric and fact. The majority of Arab states today are still struggling to develop separate, viable political systems and create legitimacy for their governments. But because rhetoric urges them to subscribe to the ideal of a single Arab nation, they are torn between the ideal of this nation and the reality of separate nations. With the exception of Egypt, they lack the collective maturity that would enable them to negotiate on a firm basis with Israel. This lack of maturity has been amply demonstrated in the past, as opportunities to make some sort of durable peace, even on somewhat unfavorable terms, were squandered regularly. The Arab states are thus probably more of a liability than an asset to the Palestinian cause.

Another reason for Arab disunity stems from the relationship of the Arab states with the Palestinians. During the British mandate, the Arab Higher Committee, the nexus of what became the Palestine national movement, aroused the anger of Arab leaders in neighboring countries by refusing to accept their authority over the committee's policies in return for financial support. After the 1948 Arab-Israeli War the dispersal of Palestinians into Arab lands caused further friction; the Palestinians, often better educated than their reluctant hosts and possessed of greater political skills, seemed to threaten the authority of some Arab leaders and to dominate some Arab economies. Finally, the performance of the Arab states in the wars with Israel was a bitter disillusionment to the Palestinians. Constantine Zurayk of the American University of Beirut expressed their shame in his book, *The Meaning of Disaster*:

> Seven Arab states declare war on Zionism, stop impotent before it and turn on their heels. . . . Declarations fall like bombs from the mouths of officials at meetings of the Arab League, but when action becomes necessary, the fire is still and quiet. . . .[10]

Without the interference of Arab state rhetoric and inept Arab military intervention, it is possible that the Palestinians might have come to terms with their Jewish neighbors long ago. As early as the 1930s, some Jews sought accommodation with Palestinian leaders. Chaim Weizmann, later the first president of Israel, wrote to an American friend: "Palestine is to be shared by two nations . . . Palestine must be built without violating (by) one iota the legitimate rights of the Arabs."[11] Martin Buber, distinguished Jewish philosopher and theologian, argued tirelessly for Jewish-Arab har-

(Israeli Government Tourism Administration)

The Dome of the Rock in Jerusalem is the site of one of the holiest Muslim shrines. The Israeli control of Jerusalem is one of the reasons the Palestinian Muslims turn to the Arab states for assistance in regaining control of the area.

mony. In 1947, on the eve of the UN partition resolution, he warned: "What is really needed by each of the two peoples . . . in Palestine is self-determination, autonomy . . . but this most certainly does not mean that each is in need of a state in which it will be the sovereign."[12]

More recently, Uri Avnery, a prominent Zionist and Knesset member, writing in the afterglow of Israel's triumph over the Arab states in the Six-Day War, said, "The government (should) offer the Palestine Arabs assistance in setting up a national republic of their own . . . (which) will become the natural bridge between Israel and the Arab world."[13]

THE BALFOUR DECLARATION

The text of the Balfour Declaration is as follows:

"I have much pleasure in conveying to you on behalf of His Majesty's Government the following declaration of sympathy with Jewish Zionist aspirations which has been submitted to and approved by the Cabinet:

"His Majesty's Government view with favor the establishment in Palestine of a National Home for the Jewish people and will use their best endeavors to facilitate the achievement of this project, it being clearly understood that nothing shall be done which may prejudice the civil and religious rights of existing non-Jewish communities in Palestine or the rights and political status enjoyed by Jews in any other country. . . ."

Mark Heller, of Tel Aviv University, goes further: "Rather than avoiding a comprehensive peace with the Palestinians, Israel should therefore pursue the Palestine-state settlement as the primary goal of its foreign and national security policy."[14] Peace Now, an organization of Israeli military reservists, students, intellectuals, and young kibbutzim established in 1977, takes dead aim both at the occupation of the West Bank and the building of Jewish settlements there. "We cannot feel free while we rule another people. . . . Peace Now stands . . . for the Zionism that bases itself on the ethical right of every people to national self-expression . . . (it) believes that the peace process . . . is necessary for the maintenance of the democratic character of Israeli society."[15]

Professor Yehoshafat Harkabi, a former chief of military intelligence and an Israeli hawk turned dove, argues that the "Bar Kokhba syndrome," which sees in that foredoomed rebellion of a second-century Jewish leader against the Romans a "rationalization for a policy of vainglory, characterized by contempt for obstacles, underestimation of the adversary, blind faith in the power of will," imposes on the nation a set of goals beyond its reach.[16]

Unfortunately, strong countervailing pressures are working against a Palestinian-Israeli settlement. The increasing number of voices being raised for restitution of Palestinian rights, including withdrawal from the West Bank and Gaza Strip to "trade land for peace," are matched by an equal number demanding full annexation of the territories and possibly expulsion of the entire Arab population. Other than a total commitment to a united Jerusalem as their traditional capital, Israelis are divided down the middle on almost every other issue.

Another sore point involves the policy of land acquisition on the West Bank for new Jewish settlements. This policy, which was strictly controlled by successive Labor governments, accelerated after Menachem Begin and his Likud bloc came to power in 1977. By 1985 Israel had acquired 51.6 percent of the West Bank through various methods, including condemnation. The expanding Jewish settlements on the West Bank are a major obstacle to Palestinian-Israeli agreement, especially since Jewish settlers work with the military against the Arab population in both subtle and violent ways.

The difficulty of establishing a consensus in Israel on Palestinian "rights" has been compounded by U.S. policy toward the conflict. Since President Harry Truman recognized the State of Israel minutes after Jewish leaders proclaimed its independence, in the wake of the first Arab-Israeli War, eight American presidents have attempted to deal with the issue. It can be argued that only two of them, Dwight D. Eisenhower and Jimmy Carter, were at all successful—Eisenhower for forcing Israel to withdraw from occupied Arab territory (the Sinai) in 1956, and Carter for bringing about the first recognition of Israel by an Arab state, through the Camp David peace treaty. But no American president as yet has been able to close the gap between Palestinian land aspirations and Israeli control of Palestine as the "land of the Covenant." The most positive step yet taken by any U.S. administration toward meeting Palestinian desires was the statement made by Carter in 1977, when he defined for them a homeland as precise as that defined for the Jewish National Home by the Balfour Declaration.

Domestic political pressures, the broad sympathy of Americans for Israel, and pragmatic support for the country as a dependable key ally in the volatile Middle East all work against commitments by any U.S. administration to put sufficient pressure on Israel to bring about a solution to the problem that is acceptable to the Palestinians.

Such a solution is made more difficult by the position held by the Palestine Liberation Organization, the international exponent organization of the Palestinian cause. The PLO at its founding in 1964 issued a charter calling for the destruction of Israel and the establishment of a sovereign Palestinian Arab state. The PLO until recently was also ambivalent about its acceptance of UN Resolutions 242 and 338, which call for Israeli withdrawal from the occupied West Bank and Gaza Strip as a prelude to peace negotiations.

During the 20-year Israeli occupation of the territories, the Palestinians there undertook few initiatives on their own to challenge the occupation. An entire generation grew up under Israeli control, living in squalid refugee camps or towns little changed since Ottoman times and deprived of even the elemental human rights supposedly guaranteed to an occupied population under international law. But in December 1987 a series of minor clashes between Palestinian youths and Israeli security forces escalated into a full-scale revolt

(UN photo/Kata Bader)

Life in the Sahara Desert is often percieved as nomadic, with the people living in tents and riding camels. To some extent this is still true, but there are many towns that offer a more settled way of life, such as this town in the Algerian Sahara.

against the occupying power. This single event, called (in Arabic) the *intifada* (literally, "resurgence"), has changed the context of the Israeli-Palestinian conflict more decisively than any other in recent history.

The intifada caught not only the Israelis but also the PLO by surprise. Having lost their Beirut base due to the Israeli invasion of 1982, PLO leaders found themselves in an unusual situation, identified internationally with a conflict from which they were physically separated and could not control directly or even influence to any great degree. As more and more Palestinians in the territories were caught up in the rhythm of struggle, the routine of stone-throwings, waving of forbidden Palestinian flags, demonstrations, and cat-and-mouse games with Israeli troops, the PLO seemed increasingly irrelevant to the Palestinian cause.

Yet this organization, particularly its leader, Yassir Arafat, has a talent for theater, for dramatic moves that not only keep

(UN photo/Y. Nagata)

The Western Sahara region is flat and very hot. It currently appears that this land eventually will be integrated with Morocco.

the cause in the international spotlight but also provide hope for several million Palestinians that an apparently unwinnable conflict may someday be won. This talent was amply demonstrated in December 1988, the first anniversary of the intifada. Arafat concluded a meeting of the PLO National Council, the organization's executive body, in Tunis, Tunisia, with the historic statement that in addition to formal acceptance of Resolutions 242 and 338 as the basis for peace negotiations, the PLO would recognize Israel's right to exist.

Arafat amplified the statement at a special UN General Assembly session in Geneva, Switzerland, formally accepting Israeli sovereignty over its own territory and renouncing the use of terrorism by the PLO.

The evidence of five wars and innumerable small conflicts suggests that the Arab-Israeli conflict will remain localized. Israel's invasion of Lebanon, like its predecessors, remained localized once the United States had intervened, and proved only a temporary setback for the PLO, a displacement. Israel and the Arab states continue to be haunted by the Palesti-

nians, an exiled, dispersed people who refuse to be assimilated into other populations or give up their hard-won identity. Mohammed Shadid observes that "Palestine is the conscience of the Arab world and a pulsating vein of the Islamic world . . . perhaps the only issue where Arab nationalism and Islamic revivalism are joined."[17]

The Palestinians are equally present on the Israeli conscience. General Ariel Sharon's Lebanon War, ironically code-named "Operation Peace in Galilee," was intended to solve the Palestine problem by rough surgery—decapitation of the PLO head on the assumption that the trunk and arms (the West Bank Palestinians) would have no further reason for resisting incorporation into the Israeli state. The Lebanon War caused the downfall of one Israeli government and the eclipse of Sharon himself, proving for the fifth time in Arab-Israeli history that military solutions do not work for essentially political problems. Sharon's continued presence in the Israeli government and his popularity among right-wing "hawks" do not augur well for a future Israeli-

Palestinian relationship based on mutal acceptance and toleration. As the minister of Housing, the former general in 1990–1991 presided over a large-scale expropriation and establishment of new Jewish settlements in the West Bank, a program regarded by the leaders of nearly all outside powers as a major obstacle to Arab-Israeli peace.

The Arab nations that surround Israel, although politically new, are heirs to a proud and ancient tradition, reaching back to the period when Islamic-Arab civilization was far superior to that of the Western world. Unfortunately, this tradition and the self-proclaimed commitment to Arab brotherhood have yet to bring them together in a united front toward Israel. One of the few common Arab policies toward Israel has been the Arab boycott, but it was observed spottily over the years and formally abandoned in 1990.

A major obstacle to Arab unity is the variety of political systems that exist in the individual Arab states. These range from patriarchal absolute rule in Saudi Arabia by a ruling family to the multiparty system of Lebanon. Ranged in between are constitutional monarchies, single-party authoritarian regimes, governments dependent upon a single individual, and so on. The only true Arab unification yet achieved is the merger of the two Yemens, the Marxist People's Democratic Republic and the tribal Yemen Arab Republic, into a single Yemeni republic. Arab states have been able to combine in certain inter-Arab groupings such as the Arab Maghrib Union and the Gulf Cooperation Council, but without giving up any of their fractious sovereignty.

The Gulf War, although abortive in the sense that it failed in its secondary objective of overthrowing an aggressive Arab leader, generated a significant shift in the alignment of the Arab states. This new alignment, plus an element of self-interest on the part of those Arab states that had opposed Iraq and the reduction of Soviet influence in the region, prompted the United States to press both the Arabs and Israelis for mutual recognition and the resolution of outstanding differences. As a result, the first direct peace talks between Arab and Israeli representatives since the 1949 armistice got under way in 1991. Although little more than an agenda for future meetings was achieved and even the makeup of the Palestinian delegation was challenged by Israel, the very fact that three subsequent rounds of talks took place early in 1992 suggested that the gulf separating these ancient adversaries might some day be bridged.

THE WESTERN SAHARA: WHOSE DESERT?

It is a fearsome place, swept by sand-laden winds that sting through layers of clothing, scorched by 120°F temperatures, its flat, monotonous landscape broken occasionally by dried-up *wadis* (river beds). The Spanish called it Rio de Oro, "River of Gold," in a bitter jest, for it has neither. Rainfall averages 2 to 8 inches a year in a territory the size of Colorado. The population is largely nomadic. Before the twentieth century this region, which we know today as the Western Sahara, was outside the control of any central authority. Other than a brief period of importance as the

headquarters of the Almoravids, a dynasty that ruled most of North Africa for about a century, the Western Sahara was a backwater.

As a political entity, the Western Sahara resulted from European colonization in Africa in the late nineteenth century. The United Kingdom and France had a head start in establishing colonies. Spain was a latecomer. By the time the Spanish joined the race for colonies, little was left for them in Africa. Since they already controlled the Canary Islands off the West African coast, it was natural for them to claim Rio de Oro, the nearest area on the coast.

In 1884 Spain announced a protectorate over Rio de Oro. The other European powers accepted the Spanish claim under the principle that "occupation of a territory's coast entitled a colonial power to control over the interior."[18] But Spanish rights to the Saharan interior clashed with French claims to Mauritania and the French effort to control the independent Sultanate of Morocco to the north. After the establishment of a joint Franco-Spanish protectorate over Morocco in 1912, the boundaries of the Spanish colony were fixed, with Mauritania on the south and east and Morocco to the north. The nomads of the Western Sahara now found themselves living within fixed boundaries defined by outsiders.[19]

The Spanish moved very slowly into the interior. The entire Western Sahara was not "pacified" until 1934. Spain invested heavily in development of the important Western Sahara phosphate deposits but did little else to develop the colony.

The Spanish population was essentially a garrison community, living apart from the Sahrawis, the indigenous Saharan population, in towns or military posts. A few Sahrawis went to Spain or other European countries, where they received a modern education, and upon their return began to organize a Saharan nationalist movement. Other Sahrawis traveled to Egypt and returned with ideas of organizing a Saharan Arab independent state. But a real sense of either a Spanish Saharan or an independent Sahrawi identity was slow to emerge.[20]

Serious conflict over the Spanish Sahara developed in the 1960s. By that time both Morocco and Mauritania had become independent. Algeria, the third African territory involved in the conflict, won its independence after a bloody civil war. All three new states were highly nationalistic and were opposed to the continuation of colonial rule over any African people, but particularly Muslim peoples. They encouraged the Sahrawis to fight for liberation from Spain, giving arms and money to guerrilla groups and keeping their borders open.

However, the three states had different motives. Morocco claimed the Western Sahara on the basis of historical ties dating back to the Almoravids, plus the oath of allegiance sworn to Moroccan sultans by Saharan chiefs in the nineteenth and twentieth centuries. Kinship was also a factor; several important Saharan families have branches in Morocco, and both the mother and the first wife of the founder of Morocco's current ruling dynasty, Mulay Ismail, were from Sahrawi families.

The Mauritanian claim to the Spanish Sahara was based not on historical sovereignty but on kinship. Sahrawis have close ethnic ties with the Moors, the majority of the population of Mauritania. Also, Mauritania feared Moroccan expansion, since its territory had once been included in the Almoravid state. A Saharan buffer state between Mauritania and Morocco would serve as protection for the Mauritanians.

Algeria's interest in Spanish Sahara was largely a matter of support for a national liberation movement against a colonial power. The Algerians made no territorial claim to the colony. But Algerian foreign policy has rested on two pillars since independence: the right to self-determination of subject peoples, and the principle of self-determination through referendum. Algeria consistently maintains that the Saharan people should have these rights.

In the 1960s Spain came under pressure from the United Nations to give up its colonies. After much hesitation, in August 1974 the Spanish announced that a referendum would be held under UN supervision to decide the colony's future.

The Spanish action brought the conflict to a head. King Hassan II declared that 1975 would be the year of testing for Morocco's recovery of the Sahara. A new Sahrawi nationalist organization, Polisario, organized in Mauritania, emerged as the dominant force in the colony. Attacks on Spanish garrisons increased the pressure on Spain to withdraw. Then, in October 1975, Hassan announced that he would lead a massive, peaceful march of civilians, armed only with Korans, into the Spanish Sahara to recover sacred Moroccan territory. The "Green March" of half a million unarmed Moroccan volunteers into Spanish territory seemed an unusual, even risky, method of validating a territorial claim, but it worked. In 1976 Spain reached agreement with Morocco and Mauritania to partition the territory into two zones, one-third going to Mauritania and two-thirds to Morocco. The Moroccan Zone included the important phosphate deposits.

The Polisario rejected the partition agreement and announced formation of the Sahrawi Arab Democratic Republic (S.A.D.R.), "a free, independent, sovereign state ruled by an Arab democratic system of progressive unionist orientation and of Islamic religion."[21] The action gave the Polisario a government-in-exile and international maneuvering room. Algeria recognized the S.A.D.R. in March 1976.

Polisario tactics of swift-striking attacks from hidden bases in the vast desert were highly effective in the early stages. Mauritania withdrew from the war in 1978, when a military coup overthrew its government. The new Mauritanian rulers signed a peace treaty in Algiers with Polisario representatives. Morocco, not to be outdone, promptly annexed the Mauritanian share of the territory and beefed up its military forces. A fortified "Sand Wall," which was built in stages from the former border with Rio de Oro down to the Moroccan-Mauritanian border and in 1987 extended about

350 miles to the Atlantic Ocean, provided the Moroccan Army with a strong defensive base from which to launch punitive raids against its elusive foe. The new segment also cut off the Polisario's access to the sea; Polisario raiders had begun to intercept and board fishing vessels in attempts to disrupt development of that important Moroccan resource and to bring pressure on foreign countries (such as Spain) that use the fishing grounds to push Morocco toward a settlement.

Although a large number of member states of the Organization of African Unity subsequently recognized the Sahrawi republic, Morocco blocked its admission to the OAU on the grounds that it was part of Moroccan territory. However, the drain on Moroccan resources of indefinitely maintaining a 100,000-man army in the desert led King Hassan II to soften his obduracy, particularly in relation to Algeria. With both countries affected by severe economic problems and some political instability, a rapprochement became possible in the late 1980s. Diplomatic relations were restored in 1988, and in 1989 Morocco joined Algeria, Libya, Tunisia, and Mauritania in the Arab Maghrib Union. The AMU charter binds member states not to support resistance movements in one anothers' territory, and as a result Algeria withdrew its backing for the S.A.D.R. and closed Polisario offices in Algiers.

In August 1988 Hassan also reluctantly accepted a UN plan for a referendum on the Western Sahara. However, face-to-face talks between the king and Polisario leaders in 1989 resulted in nothing more than a reaffirmation of the referendum principle. The most probable reason for Hassan's delay was summed up by foreign diplomats: "The King won't allow it to happen unless he knows he can win."

By June 1991 Hassan seemed to feel that he would win. He accepted the UN plan, which was then approved by the Security Council. A ceasefire went into effect as a result and, during the summer, a UN observer force of 2,000 people was mobilized for deployment in the region to supervise the referendum. This was originally set for September 6, but the process was halted by technical problems—notably the determination of voter eligibility—and renewed conflict in which each side accused the other of breaking the ceasefire. By March 1992 the ceasefire was again established and the UN had a peacekeeping mission in place. This UN observer force will again attempt to supervise the referendum.

If or when a Saharan referendum takes place, the results are likely to favor integration with Morocco. An amnesty announced by King Hassan in 1990 for all Saharan exiles and Polisario leaders was accepted by a number of them. A more significant change was the influx of thousands of Moroccan settlers drawn by free housing and other inducements to develop Morocco's "new frontier," centered around its huge phosphate deposits. UN voting registrars faced an almost-impossible task in separating them from the pre-1974 population for ballot purposes, and it seemed highly unlikely that they would vote to separate themselves from their own country.

NOTES

1. Alan R. Taylor, *The Arab Balance of Power* (Syracuse: Syracuse University Press, 1982), Preface, XIII.

2. "Turkistan, Afghanistan, Transcaspia . . . they are the pieces on a chessboard upon which is played out a game for the domination of the World." Lord Curzon, Viceroy of India, quoted in Shabbir Hussain *et al.*, *Afghanistan Under Soviet Occupation* (Islamabad, Pakistan: World Affairs Publications, 1980), p. 54.

3. "The Soviet Action in Afghanistan was made necessary by the real threat of seeing the country transformed into an imperialist military platform on the Southern frontier of the U.S.S.R." Former Soviet leader Leonid Brezhnev, quoted in Hussain, *op. cit.*, p. 7.

4. Terence O'Donnell, *Garden of the Brave in War* (New York: Ticknor and Fields, 1980), p. 19, states that in visits to remote Iranian villages he was told by informants that the Arabs never washed, went around naked, and ate lizards.

5. Daniel Pipes, "A Border Adrift: Origins of the Conflict," in Shirin Tahir-Kheli and Shaheen Ayubi, eds., *The Iran-Iraq War: New Weapons, Old Conflicts* (New York: Praeger, 1983), pp. 10–13.

6. *Ibid.*, quoted on p. 20.

7. Stephen R. Grummon, *The Iran-Iraq War: Islam Embattled*, The Washington Papers/92, Vol. X (New York: Praeger, 1982), p. 10.

8. William O. Staudenmaier, "A Strategic Analysis," in Tahir-Kheli and Ayubi, *op. cit.*, pp. 29–33.

9. *The Christian Science Monitor* (September 23, 1987).

10. Quoted in Barry Rubin, *The Arab States and the Palestine Conflict* (Syracuse: Syracuse University Press, 1981), p. 7.

11. Letter to James Marshall, January 17, 1930, in Camilo Dresner, ed., *The Letters and Papers of Chaim Weizmann*, Vol. 14 (New Brunswick: Rutgers University Press, 1979), pp. 208–211.

12. Martin Buber, *Land of Two Peoples*, ed. Paul Mendes-Flohr (New York: Oxford University Press, 1983), p. 199.

13. Uri Avnery, *Israel Without Zionists* (New York: Macmillan, 1968), pp. 187, 189.

14. Mark A. Heller, *A Palestinian State: The Implications for Israel* (Cambridge: Harvard University Press, 1983), p. 154.

15. R. D. McLaurin, Don Peretz, and Lewis Snider, eds., *Middle East Foreign Policy: Issues and Processes* (New York: Praeger, 1982), p. 154.

16. Quoted in Milton Viorst, *Sands of Sorrow: Israel's Journey From Independence* (New York: Harper & Row, 1987), pp. 272–273.

17. Mohammed Shadid, *The United States and the Palestinians* (New York: St. Martin's Press, 1981), p. 195.

18. John Damis, *Conflict in Northwest Africa: The Western Sahara Dispute* (Stanford: Hoover Institution Press, 1983), p. 110.

19. "The borders zigzagged from Zag in the north to Zug in the south." David Lynne Price, *The Western Sahara*, The Washington Papers/63, Vol. VII (Beverly Hills: Sage Publications, 1979), p. 11.

20. Damis, *op. cit.*, p. 13, notes that a tribal assembly (Jama'a) was formed in 1967 for the Sahrawis but that its 43 members were all tribal chiefs or their representatives; it had only advisory powers.

21. Quoted from *Le Monde*, in Damis, *op. cit.*, p. 75.

Algeria (Democratic and Popular Republic of Algeria)

GEOGRAPHY

Area in Square Kilometers (Miles):
2,381,740 (919,352) (about 3 times
the size of Texas)
Capital (Population): Algiers
(1,483,000)
Climate: mild winters and hot
summers on coastal plain; less rain
and cold winters on high plateau;
considerable temperature variation in
desert, February-May

PEOPLE

Population
Total: 25,714,000
Annual Growth Rate: 3.1%
Rural/Urban Population Ratio: 51/49
Ethnic Makeup of Population: 99%
Arab-Berber; less than 1% European

Health
Life Expectancy at Birth: 64 years
(male); 66 years (female)
Infant Mortality Rate (Ratio):
82/1,000
Average Caloric Intake: 96% of FAO
minimum
Physicians Available (Ratio): 1/1,302

Religion(s)
99% Sunni Muslim (state religion);
1% Christian and Hebrew

Education
Adult Literacy Rate: 52%

COMMUNICATION
Telephones: 769,000
Newspapers: 6 dailies

THE CASBAH

The romantic image of the Casbah of Algiers purveyed by Hollywood
films is rudely shattered by a walk through the narrow, twisted streets of
the old corsair fortress. The tall houses lean inward, producing a
claustrophobic gloom. Algiers' Casbah does not have the colorful
outdoor markets and artisans of other North African capitals. Today it is
an urban slum. Riots broke out there in 1985 protesting its crowded and
substandard living conditions. The government responded with force,
but agreed to begin demolition of tenements, thus ending 200 years of
colorful existence.

TRANSPORTATION
Highways—Kilometers (Miles): 78,410
(48,446)
Railroads—Kilometers (Miles): 3,836
(2,378)
Usable Airfields: 145

GOVERNMENT
Type: republic
Independence Date: July 5, 1962
Head of State: ruling council, led by
Mohammed Boudiaf
Political Parties: multiparty system
Suffrage: universal at 18

MILITARY
Number of Armed Forces: 125,500
*Military Expenditures (% of Central
Government Expenditures):* 5.4%
Current Hostilities: none

ECONOMY
Currency ($ U.S. Equivalent): 16.3
Algerian dinars = $1
Per Capita Income/GNP:
$2,450/$63.5 billion
Inflation Rate: 17%
Total Foreign Debt: $26.06 billion
Natural Resources: crude oil; natural
gas; iron ore; phosphates; uranium;
lead; zinc; mercury
Agriculture: wheat; barley; oats;
olives; grapes; dates; citrus fruits;
sheep; cattle
Industry: petroleum; light industries;
natural gas; petrochemicals;
electrical; automotive plants; food
processing

FOREIGN TRADE
Exports: $8.6 billion
Imports: $8.9 billion

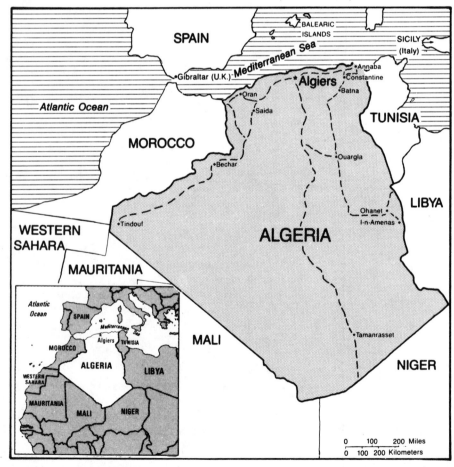

* Capital   — Rivers   -- Roads

ALGERIA

The modern state of Algeria occupies the central part of North Africa, a geographically distinctive and separate region of Africa that also includes Morocco and Tunisia. The name of the state comes from the Arabic word *al-Jaza'ir*, "the islands," because of the rocky islets along this part of the Mediterranean coast, which were a hazard to ships in the days of sail. The name of the capital, Algiers, is derived from the same origin.

The official name of the state is the Democratic and Popular Republic of Algeria. It is the second-largest country in Africa (after Sudan). The overall population density is low considering its size, but Algeria has one of the highest birth rates in the world, although the rate dropped significantly in 1988–1989, due in part to a government-sponsored promotional program encouraging spacing of children in families. Also, the housing shortage and high unemployment in recent years have forced many Algerians to delay marriage, with a consequent natural reduction in the number of births.

GEOGRAPHY

Algeria's geography is another obstacle to broad economic and social development. About 80 percent of the land is uncultivatable desert, and only 12 percent is arable without irrigation. Most of the population live in a narrow coastal plain and in a fertile, hilly inland region called the Tell (Arabic for "hillock"). The four Saharan provinces comprise more than half the land area but have only 3 percent of the population. Yet the mineral resources that have made possible Algeria's transformation in 2 decades from a land devastated by civil war to one of the Third World's success stories are all located in the Sahara.

Economic growth, however, has been uneven, affecting the rural and lower-class urban populations largely unfavorably. The large-scale exodus of rural families into the cities, with consequent neglect of agriculture, has resulted in a vast increase in urban slums. Economic disparities were a major cause of riots in 1988, which led to political reforms and the dismantling of the socialist system responsible for Algerian development since independence.

Algeria is unique among newly independent Middle Eastern countries in that it gained its independence through a civil war. For more than 130 years (1830–1962) it was occupied by France and became a French department (similar to a U.S. state). With free movement from mainland France to Algeria, and vice versa, the country was settled by large numbers of Europeans who became the politically dominant group in the population, although they were a minority. The modern Algerian nation is the product of the interaction of native Muslim Algerians with the European settlers, who also considered Algeria home.

Algeria's geography is a key to the country's past disunity. In addition to its vast Saharan territory, Algeria is broken up into discontinuous regions by a number of rugged mountain ranges. The Mediterranean coastline is narrow and is backed throughout its length by mountains, notably the imposing Kabyle range. The Algerian Atlas range, a continuation of the Moroccan Atlas, is a complex system of deep valleys, high plateaus, and peaks ranging up to 6,000 feet. In southeastern Algeria is the most impressive range in the country, the Aurès, a great mountain block. These diverse mountain regions were an obstacle to the development of any form of Algerian social and national unity until recent times.

The original inhabitants of the entire North African region were Berbers, a people of unknown origin grouped into various tribes and speaking different dialects of a now-lost Berber language. (The Tuareg, a nomadic people still living in the Algerian Sahara and neighboring countries, use a written language called Tifinagh. Theirs is the only surviving Berber script. The main Berber-speaking populations are found in Kabylia, the Aurès [Chaouia], and the Mzab region of the northern Sahara. Tuareg also inhabit the central Algerian Sahara and spill over into neighboring Mali and Niger.) Altogether, Berbers form about 20 percent of the population.

The Arabs, who brought Islam to North Africa in the seventh century A.D., converted the Algerian Berbers after a fierce resistance. The Arabs brought their language as a unifying feature, and religion linked the Algerians with the larger Islamic world. Most follow the Sunni rite of Islam, but a significant compact minority, about 100,000, are Shia. They refer to themselves as Ibadis, from their observance of an ancient Shia rite, and live in five "holy cities" clustered in a remote Saharan valley where centuries ago they took refuge from Sunni rulers of northern Algeria. Their valley, the Mzab, has always maintained religious autonomy from Algerian central governments. The much larger Berber population of Kabylia has also resisted central authority, whether Islamic or French, throughout Algerian history. One of many pressures on the government today is that of an organized Kabyle movement which seeks greater autonomy for the region and an emphasis on Berber language in schools, along with the revitalization of Kabyle culture.

HISTORY: THE CORSAIR REGENCY

The foundations of the modern Algerian state were laid in the sixteenth century with the establishment of the Regency of Algiers, an outlying province of the Ottoman Empire. Algiers in particular, due to its natural harbor, was developed for use by the Ottomans as a naval base for wars against European fleets in the Mediterranean. The Algerian coast was the farthest extent westward of Ottoman power. Consequently, Algiers and Oran, the two major ports, were exposed to constant threats of attack by Spanish and other European fleets. They could not easily be supported, or governed directly, by the Ottomans. The regency, from its beginnings, was a state geared for war.

The regency was established by two Greek-born Muslim sea captains, Aruj and Khayr al-Din (called Barbarossa by his European opponents because of his flaming red beard). The brothers obtained commissions from the Ottoman sultan for expeditions against the Spanish. They made their principal base at Algiers, then a small port that Khayr al-Din expanded into a powerful fortress and naval base. His government consisted of a garrison of Ottoman soldiers sent by the sultan to keep order, along with a naval force called the corsairs.

Corsairing or piracy (the choice of term depended upon one's viewpoint) was a common practice in the Mediterranean, but the rise to power of the Algerine corsairs converted it into a more or less respectable profession.[1] The cities of Tunis, Tetuanq, and Salé in Morocco and Tripoli, Libya also had corsair fleets, but the Algerine corsairs were so effective against European shipping that for 300 years (1500–1800) European rulers called them "the scourge of the Mediterranean." One factor in their success was their ability to attract outstanding sea captains from various European countries. Renegades from Italy, Greece, Holland, France, and England joined the Algerine fleet, converted to Islam, and took Muslim names as a symbol of their new status. Some rose to high rank.

Government in Algiers passed through several stages and eventually became a system of deys. The deys were elected by the Divan, a council of the captains of the Ottoman garrison. Deys were elected for life, but most of them never fulfilled their tenure, due to constant intrigue, military

(UN photo/Ruth Massey)

Eighty percent of Algeria is uncultivatable, and only 12 percent is arable without irrigation. This crop is being harvested in the fertile inland region that makes up Algeria's small agricultural area.

coups, or assassinations. Yet the system provided considerable stability, security for the population, and wealth and prestige for the regency. These factors probably account for its durability; the line of deys governed uninterruptedly from the late 1600s to 1830.

Outside of Algiers and its hinterland, authority was delegated to local chiefs and religious leaders who were responsible for tax collection and remittances to the dey's treasury. The chiefs were kept in line by generous subsidies. It was a system well adapted to the fragmented society of Algeria and one that enabled a small military group to rule a large territory at relatively little cost.[2]

The French Conquest

In 1827 the dey of Algiers, enraged at the French government's refusal to pay an old debt incurred during Napoleon's wars, struck the French consul on the shoulder with a fly-whisk in the course of an interview. The king of France, Charles X, demanded an apology for the "insult" to his representative. None was forthcoming, so the French blockaded the port of Algiers in retaliation. But the dey continued to keep silent. In 1830 a French army landed on the coast west of the city, marched overland, and entered it with almost no resistance. The dey surrendered and went into exile.[3]

The French, who had been looking for an excuse to expand their interests in North Africa, now were not sure what to do with Algiers. The overthrow of the despotic Charles X in favor of a constitutional monarchy in France confused the situation even further. But the Algerians considered the French worse than the Turks, who were at least fellow Muslims. In the 1830s they rallied behind their first national leader, the Emir Abd al-Qadir.

Abd al-Qadir was the son of a prominent religious leader and, more important, was a descendant of the Prophet Muhammad. Abd al-Qadir had unusual qualities of leadership, military skill, and physical courage. From 1830 to 1847 he carried on guerrilla warfare against a French army of more than 100,000 men with such success that at one point the French signed a formal treaty recognizing him as head of an Algerian nation in the interior. Abd al-Qadir described his strategy in a prophetic letter to the king of France:

France will march forward, and we shall retire. But France will find it necessary to retire, and we shall return. We shall weary and harry you, and our climate will do the rest.[4]

In order to defeat Abd al-Qadir, the

French commander used "total war" tactics, burning villages, destroying crops, killing livestock, and levying fines on peoples who continued to support the emir. These measures, called "pacification" by France, finally succeeded. In 1847 Abd al-Qadir surrendered to French authorities. He was imprisoned for several years, in violation of a solemn commitment, and was then released by Emperor Napoleon III. He spent the rest of his life in exile.

Although he did not succeed in his quest, Abd al-Qadir is venerated as the first Algerian nationalist, able by his leadership and Islamic prestige to unite warring groups in a struggle for independence from foreign control. Abd al-Qadir's green and white flag was raised again by the Algerian nationalists during the second war of independence (1954–1962), and it is the flag of the republic today.

Algérie Française

After the defeat of Abd al-Qadir, the French gradually brought all of present-day Algerian territory under their control. The Kabyles, Berbers living in the rugged mountain region east of Algiers, were the last to submit. The Kabyles had submitted in 1857, but they rebelled in 1871 after a series of decrees by the French government had made all Algerian Muslims subjects but not citizens, giving them a status inferior to French and other European settlers.

The Kabyle rebellion had terrible results, not only for the Kabyles but for all Algerian Muslims. More than a million acres of Muslim lands were confiscated by French authorities and sold to European settlers. A special code of laws was enacted to treat Algerian Muslims differently from Europeans, with severe fines and sentences for such "infractions" as insulting a European or wearing shoes in public. (It was assumed that a Muslim caught wearing shoes had stolen them.)

After 1871 Algeria legally became a French department. But in terms of exploitation of natives by settlers, it may as well have remained a colony. One author notes that "the desire to make a settlement colony out of an already populated area led to a policy of driving the indigenous people out of the best arable lands."[5] Land confiscation was only part of the exploitation of Algeria by the *colons* (French settlers). They developed a modern Algerian agriculture integrated into the French economy, providing France with much of its wine, citrus, olives, and vegetables. Colons owned 30 percent of the arable land and 90 percent of the best farmland. Special taxes were imposed on the Algerian Muslims; the colons were exempted from paying most taxes.

The political structure of Algeria was even more favorable to the European minority. The colons were well represented in the French National Assembly, and their representatives made sure that any reforms or new laws intended to improve the living conditions or political rights of the Algerian Muslim population would be blocked.

In fairness to the colons, it must be pointed out that many of them had come to Algeria as poor immigrants and worked hard to improve their lot and to develop the country. By 1930, the centenary of the French conquest, many colon families had lived in Algiers for two generations or more. Colons had drained malarial swamps south of Algiers and developed the Mitidja, the country's most fertile region. A fine road and rail system linked all parts of the country, and French public schools served all cities and towns. Algiers even had its own university, a branch of the Sorbonne. It is not surprising that to the colons, Algeria was their country, "Algérie Française." Throughout Algeria they rebaptized Algerian cities with names like Orléansville and Philippeville, with paved French streets, cafes, bakeries, and little squares with flower gardens and benches where old men in berets dozed in the hot sun.

Jules Cambon, governor-general of Algeria in the 1890s, once described the country as having "only a dust of people left her." What he meant was that the ruthless treatment of the Algerians by the French during the pacification had deprived them of their natural leaders. A group of leaders developed slowly in Algeria, but it was made up largely of *evolués*, persons who had received French educations, spoke French better than Arabic, and had accepted French citizenship as the price of status.[6]

Other Algerians, several hundred thousand of them, served in the French Army in the two world wars. Many of them became aware of the political rights that they were supposed to have but did not. Still others, religious leaders and teachers, were influenced by the Arab nationalist movement for independence from foreign control in Egypt and other parts of the Middle East.

Until the 1940s the majority of the evolués and other Algerian leaders did not want independence. They wanted full assimilation with France and Muslim equality with the colons. Ferhat Abbas, a French-trained pharmacist who was the spokesperson for the evoluées, said in 1936 that he did not believe that there was such a thing as an Algerian nation separate from France.

Abbas and his associates changed their minds after World War II. In 1943 they had presented to the French government a manifesto demanding full political and legal equality for Muslims with the colons. It was blocked by colon leaders, who feared they would be drowned in a Muslim sea. On May 8, 1945, the date of the Allied victory over Germany in World War II, a parade of Muslims celebrating the event but also demanding equality led to violence in the city of Sétif. Several colons were killed, and in retaliation army troops and groups of colon vigilantes swept through Muslim neighborhoods, burning houses and slaughtering thousands of Muslims. From then on Muslim leaders concluded that independence through armed struggle was the only choice left to them.

The War for Independence

November 1 is an important holiday in France. It is called *Toussaint* (All Saints' Day). On that day French people remember and honor all the many saints in the pantheon of French Catholicism. It is a day devoted to reflection and staying at home.

In the years after the Sétif massacre there had been scattered outbreaks of violence in Algeria, some of them by the so-called Secret Organization (OS) that had developed an extensive network of cells in preparation for armed insurrection. In 1952 French police accidentally uncovered the network and jailed most of its leaders. One of them, a former French Army sergeant named Ahmed Ben Bella, subsequently escaped and went to Cairo, Egypt.

As the date of Toussaint 1954 neared, Algeria seemed calm. But appearances were deceptive. Earlier in the year nine former members of the OS had laid plans in secret for armed revolution. They divided Algeria into six *wilayas* (departments), each with a military commander. They also planned a series of coordinated attacks for the early-morning hours of November 1, when the French population would be asleep and the police preparing for a holiday. Bombs exploded at French Army barracks, police stations, storage warehouses, telephone offices, and government buildings. The revolutionaries circulated leaflets in the name of the National Liberation Front (FLN), warning the French that they had acted to liberate Algeria from the colonialist yoke and calling on Algerian Muslims to join in the struggle to rebuild Algeria as a free Islamic state.

There were very few casualties as a result of the Toussaint attacks; for some time the French did not realize that they had a revolution on their hands. But as violence continued, regular army troops were sent to Algeria to help the hard-pressed police and the colons. Eventually, there were 400,000 French troops in Algeria, as opposed to about 6,000 guerrillas. But the French consistently refused to consider the situation in Algeria as a war. They called it a "police action." Others called it "the war without a name."[7] Despite their great numerical superiority, they were unable to defeat the FLN.

Elsewhere the French tried various tactics. They divided the country into small sectors, with permanent garrisons for each sector. They organized mobile units to track down the guerrillas in caves and hideouts. About 2 million villagers were moved into barbed-wire "regroupment camps," with a complete dislocation of their way of life, in order to deny the guerrillas the support of the population.

The war was settled not by military action but by political negotiations. The French people and government, already worn down by the effects of World War II and Indochina (Vietnam), grew sick of the slaughter, the plastic bombs exploding in public places (in France as well as Algeria), and the brutality of the army in dealing with guerrilla prisoners. A French newspaper editor expressed the general feeling: "Algeria is ruining the spring. This land of sun and earth has never been so near us. It invades our hearts and torments our minds."[8]

The colons and a number of senior French army officers were the last to give up their dream of an Algeria that would be forever French. Together, the colons and the army forced a change in the French government. General Charles de Gaulle, the French wartime resistance hero, returned to power after a dozen years in retirement. But de Gaulle, a realist, had no intention of keeping Algeria forever French. He began secret negotiations with FLN leaders for Algerian independence.

The colons and the army officers made one last effort. In 1961 four generals led an insurrection in Algiers against de Gaulle and demanded his removal from office. However, the majority of the army remained loyal. A ceasefire came into effect on March 19, 1962. However, the Secret Army Organization (OAS), a group of army dissenters and colon vigilantes, then launched a new campaign of violence, terror, and indiscriminate murders of Muslims. Bombs exploded in Muslim hospitals and schools; victims were shot at random as they walked the streets. The OAS hoped that the FLN would break the ceasefire to protect its fellow Muslims and thus bring back the French Army. But the FLN held firm.

A REUNITED NATION

Algeria became independent on July 5, 1962. Few nations have started their existence under worse circumstances. Estimates of casualties vary, but by the end of the war hundreds of thousands of men, women, and children, Muslims, colons, and soldiers had been killed or wounded or had simply disappeared. A painful loss to the new nation was the departure of almost the entire European community. The colons panicked and crowded aboard ships to cross the Mediterranean and resettle in various European countries, but especially in France, a land they knew only as visitors. Nearly all of Algeria's managers, landowners, professional class, civil servants, and skilled workers left.

The new Algerian government was also affected by factional rivalries among its leaders. The French writer Alexis de Tocqueville once wrote, "In rebellion, as in a novel, the most difficult part to invent is the end." The FLN revolutionaries had to invent a new system, one that would bring dignity and hope to people dehumanized by 130 years of French occupation and 8 years of savage war.

The first leader to emerge from intra-party struggle to lead the nation was Ahmed Ben Bella, who had spent the war in exile in Egypt but had great prestige as the political brains behind the FLN. Ben Bella laid the groundwork for an Algerian political system centered on the FLN as a single legal political party, and in September 1963 he was elected president. Ben Bella introduced a system of autogestion (workers' self-management), by which tenant farmers took over the management of farms abandoned by their colon owners and restored them to production as cooperatives. Autogestion became the basis for Algerian socialism, the basis of development for decades.

Ben Bella did little else for Algeria, and he alienated most of his former associates by his ambitions for personal power. In June 1965 he was overthrown in a military coup headed by the defense minister, Colonel Houari Boumedienne. Ben Bella was sentenced to house arrest for 15 years, pardoned and exiled in 1980. While in exile, he founded the Movement for a Democratic Algeria in opposition to the regime. In 1990 he returned to Algeria and announced plans to lead a broad-based opposition party in the framework of the multiparty system.

Boumedienne declared that the coup was a "corrective revolution, intended to reestablish authentic socialism and put an end to internal divisions and personal rule."[9] The government was reorganized under a Council of the Revolution, all military men, headed by Boumedienne, who subsequently became president of the republic. After a long period of preparation and gradual assumption of power by the reclusive and taciturn Boumedienne, a National Charter (constitution) was approved by voters in 1976. The charter defines Algeria as a Socialist state with Islam as the state religion, basic citizens' rights guaranteed, and leadership by the FLN as the only legal political party. A National Popular Assembly (the first elected in 1977) is responsible for legislation.

In theory, the Algerian president has no more constitutional powers than the American president. However, in practice, Boumedienne was the ruler of the state, being president, prime minister, and commander of the armed forces rolled into one. In November 1978 he became ill from a rare blood disease; he died in December. For a time it appeared that factional rivalries would again split the FLN, especially as Boumedienne had named neither a vice president nor a prime minister, nor had he suggested a successor.

The Algeria of 1978 was a very different nation from that of 1962. The scars of war had mostly healed. The FLN closed ranks and named Colonel Chadli Bendjedid to succeed Boumedienne as president for a 5-year term. In 1984 he was reelected. But the process of ordered socialist development was abruptly and forcibly interrupted in October 1988. A new generation of Algerians, who had come of age long after the war for independence, took to the streets, protesting high prices, lack of jobs, inept leadership, a bloated bureaucracy, and other grievances.

The riots accelerated the process of Algeria's "second revolution" toward political pluralism and dismantling of the single-party socialist system. President Bendjedid initially declared a state of emergency, and for the first time since independence the army was called in to restore order. Some 500 persons were killed in the rioting, most of them jobless youth. But the president moved swiftly to mobilize the nation in the wake of the violence. Voters approved in national referendum changes in the governing system to allow political parties to form outside the FLN. Another constitutional change, also effective in 1989, made the Cabinet and prime minister responsible to the National Assembly.

The president retained his popularity during the upheaval and was reelected for a third term, winning 81 percent of the votes. A number of new parties were formed in 1989 to contest future Assembly elections. They represented a variety of political and social positions. Thus, the Peoples' Movement for Algerian Renewal advocates a "democratic Algeria, representative of moderate Islam," while the National Algerian Party, more fundamentalist in its views, has a platform of full enforcement of Islamic law and the creation of 2 million new jobs. The Front for Socialist Forces (FFS), founded many years ago by exiled FLN leader Hocine Ait Ahmed, resurfaced with a manifesto urging Algerians to support "the irreversible process of democracy."

For its part, the government sought to revitalize the FLN as a genuine mass party on the order of the Tunisian Destour, while insisting that it would not duplicate its neighbor country's *democratie de facade* but embark on real political reforms. Recruitment of new members was extended to rural areas in a vigorous recruitment campaign. Although press freedom was confirmed in the constitutional changes approved by the voters, control of the major newspapers and media was shifted from the government to the FLN, to provide greater exposure.

FOREIGN POLICY

During the first decade of independence Algeria's foreign policy was strongly nationalistic and anti-Western. Having won their independence from one colonial power, the Algerians were vocally hostile to the United States and its allies, calling them enemies of popular liberation. Algeria supported revolutionary movements all over the world, providing funds, arms, and training. The Palestine Liberation Organization, rebels against Portuguese colonial rule in Mozambique, Muslim guerrillas fighting the Christian Ethiopian government in Eritrea—all benefited from active Algerian support.

Since the mid-1970s Algeria has moderated its anti-Western stance in favor of nonalignment and good relations with both East and West. The government broke diplomatic relations with the United States in 1967, due to American support for Israel, and did not restore them for a decade. Relations improved thereafter to such a point that Algerian mediators were instrumental in resolving the 1979–1980 American-Iranian hostage crisis, since Iran regarded Algeria as a suitable mediator, Islamic yet nonaligned.

The only foreign-policy issue on which Algeria remains adamant is the Western Sahara. The Algerians believe strongly in the right of Western Saharan peoples to determine their own future. This commitment has embroiled them in conflict with Morocco, since the Moroccans claim ownership of the Western Sahara as an integral part of their territory. The two countries fought a brief border war in 1963 over ownership of iron mines near the border town of Tindouf. The Algerian policy of allowing sanctuary and bases to the Polisario, the military force of the Sahrawi Arab Democratic Republic, led to a number of clashes between Moroccan and Algerian troops. Algeria formally recognized the Sahrawi Republic in 1980 and has led the fight within the Organization of African Unity to have it seated as an OAU member.

In recent years the government has made serious efforts to develop dialogue with Morocco toward resolving the dispute under the terms of a UN-sponsored referendum. President Bendjedid and Morocco's King Hassan II developed a good working relationship in the course of several summit meetings in 1987 and 1988. Diplomatic relations between the two countries were restored, and prisoners held since border clashes in the early 1970s were released. Algeria also in 1988 supported the "agreement in principle" between the Moroccan government and the Polisario worked out by UN negotiators for a referendum on the future of the Western Sahara. As a result, aid to the Polisario has been sharply reduced while the government concentrates on internal economic and political reform.

Elsewhere, Algeria has been successful in improving relations with other North African states. In 1987 it mediated successfully with Libyan leader Muammar Qadhafi to obtain compensation for Tunisian workers expelled from Libya. In February 1989 Algeria joined with Morocco, Tunisia, Libya, and Mauritania in the establishment of the Arab Maghrib Union. Algerian negotiators had pushed hard for the union, not only as a means of ending centuries of border disputes and political rivalries but also to create a strong regional market. One of its first successes, also a particular success for Algerian diplomacy, was the signing of a peace treaty between Chad and Libya.

THE ECONOMY

Algeria's Saharan oil and natural-gas resources were developed by the French, and commercial production began in 1958. The French government ruled the Algerian Sahara under a separate military administration. The Sahara was not affected by the war for independence and exports of crude oil continued, mostly to metropolitan France, throughout the war. The oil fields were turned over to Algeria after independence, but the French concessionaires continued to manage them until 1970, when the oil industry was nationalized.

Algeria's petroleum reserves are estimated to be 8 billion barrels. The country is a member of the Organization of Petroleum Exporting Countries and follows agreed-upon OPEC guidelines and quotas governing production and pricing. Fortunately for Algeria's ambitious development plans, its low-sulfur crude is in great demand in the industrialized nations. The Gulf War led to a significant improvement in the economy. Higher oil prices brought a $1.4 billion increase in revenues, resulting in 1990 in the first budget surplus since 1987.

THE FUTURE

Considering the devastation of an 8-year war, the departure of nearly all skilled professionals and educated leaders in all fields, and vicious infighting among leaders in the period immediately after independence, Algeria has accomplished a great deal in a short time. President Boumedienne brought stability of leadership, initiated agrarian reform, and defined the direction of development in the 1976 National Charter as a uniquely Algerian form of socialism, Islamic yet suited to the country's special circumstances.

His successor had a more difficult road to follow. The persistent economic crisis caused by lowered oil prices and global oversupply led the government to borrow heavily to finance industrial expansion. Gross domestic product growth was negative in 1987 (−1.4 percent) and in 1988 (−2.7 percent). But in 1990 the downturn was reversed; GDP grew by 3 percent.

Long-term problems revolve around Algeria's agricultural limitations. About 42 percent of the labor force are employed in agriculture, yet the amount of arable land equals less than 2.2 acres per rural resident. The country still must import 70 percent of its food, but lower food costs in 1990–1991 due to the decline in the dollar's value (hard currency must be used for food imports) eased the impact on the long-suffering Algerian consumer.

Rapid population growth and urban migration have also created a serious urban-housing shortage. The worst locust plague in 30 years combined with severe drought in 1987–1988 to slow agricultural development, one of the keys to a successful move away from state socialism toward balanced growth and greater involvement of the private sector. Structural improve-

| Establishment of the Regency of Algiers 1518-1520 | The French conquest, triggered by the "fly-whisk incident" 1827-1830 | The defeat of Abd Al-Qadir by French forces 1847 | Algeria becomes an overseas department of France 1871 | The Blum-Viollette Plan, for Muslim rights, is annulled by colon opposition 1936 |

ments took top priority. In 1988, 3,500 state farms were converted to collective farms, but with individual farmers holding title to lands. Low-income urban migrants were encouraged to return to farming, with financial incentives provided, and the autogestion system, introduced as a stopgap measure after independence and enshrined later in FLN economic practice when it seemed to work, was totally abandoned.

In July 1987 Algeria marked the 25th anniversary of its independence. Of its three presidents, one, Boumedienne, established the institutions of government on a sound, permanent basis, while a second, Bendjedid, succeeded in broadening the leadership. Neither made any concessions to interest groups that might undermine the single-party system. Thus, internal stability was achieved at the expense of popular participation in the nation-building process. Also, Boumedienne's emphasis on development of a huge industrial structure under state management on the Soviet model, and based upon expanding oil and gas exports, not only created external debt problems but also discouraged private initiative. In a speech to FLN leaders in 1985, President Bendjedid warned: "We are on the threshold of the year 2000, when the era when we could count on oil and gas will be finished. Algerians should roll up their sleeves and stop considering the state as a milking cow."[10] In 1991 the government formally scrapped socialism in favor of a free-market economy. Under new rules, state-controlled enterprises are to be turned over to private management. The first 11 such enterprises were turned over early in the year; they included Peugeot-Algérie, henceforth serviced by a network of private dealerships, and the government-owned pharmaceuticals plant. Disadvantages of the conversion, notably loss of jobs and higher prices, should be more than offset by greater efficiency and improved production.

THE FUNDAMENTALIST CHALLENGE

Despite the growing appeal of Islamic fundamentalism in numerous Arab countries in recent years, Algeria until very recently seemed an unlikely site for the rise of a strong fundamentalist movement.

(UN photo/Kata Bader)

The rapid growth in the population of Algeria, coupled with urban migration, has created a serious urban-housing shortage, as this apartment building in Algiers testifies.

The country's long association with France, its lack of historic Islamic identity as a nation, and 3 decades of single-party socialism militated against such a development. But the failure of successive Algerian governments to resolve severe economic problems, plus the lack of representative political institutions nurtured within the ruling FLN, brought about the rise of fundamentalism as a political force during the 1990s. Fundamentalists took an active part in the 1988 riots, and with the establishment of a multiparty system they organized a political party, the Islamic Salvation Front (FIS). It soon claimed 3 million adherents among the 25 million Algerians.

FIS candidates won 55 percent of urban mayoral and council seats in the 1989 local and municipal elections. The FLN

Ferhat Abbas issues the Manifesto of the Algerian People 1943	Civil war, ending with Algerian independence 1954–1962	Ben Bella is overthrown by Boumedienne 1965	The National Charter commits Algeria to revolutionary socialist development 1976	President Boumedienne dies 1978

1980s–1990s

Land reform is resumed with the breakup of 200 large farms into smaller units

The last street and shop signs in French Algiers are replaced by Arabic ones, in an Arabization campaign

The trial of Islamic fundamentalists ends with the release of the majority and short prison terms for the leaders

President Bendjedid steps down; the Islamic Salvation Front becomes a force

conversely managed to hold on to power largely in the rural areas. Fears that FIS success might draw army intervention and spark another round of revolutionary violence led the government to postpone for 6 months the scheduled June 1991 elections for an enlarged 430-member National People's Assembly. An interim government, under technocrat Prime Minister Sid Ahmed Ghozal, was formed to oversee the transition process.

In accordance with President Bendjedid's commitment to multiparty democracy, the first stage of Assembly elections took place on December 26, 1991, with FIS candidates winning 188 out of 231 contested seats. But before the second stage could take place, the army stepped in. FIS leaders were arrested and the elections were postponed indefinitely. President Bendjedid resigned on January 17, 1992, well ahead of the expiration (in 1993) of his third 5-year term. He said he had done so as a sacrifice in the interest of restoring stability to the nation and preserving democracy. Mohammed Boudiaf, a hero of the War for Independence but for many years an exile in Morocco, returned to become head of a ruling council dominated by military leaders.

The great fear among the military and of most educated and articulate Algerians was that the FIS would put into practice its commitment to an Algerian state ruled by Islamic law, with consequent loss of rights and status for women and other restrictions unsuited to a modern secular state. In February, after a cycle of violence had developed, Boudiaf declared a state of emergency. FIS headquarters was closed and its remaining leaders arrested, while the military government readied a constitutional amendment that would prohibit political parties based on religion. But these moves carried built-in risks: either an escalation of violence, led by young toughs called Afghans (because as unemployed youth they had fought with the Afghan mujahiddin against Soviet forces); or a total loss of confidence in the democratic process by the Algerian population.

NOTES

1. On the corsairs see William Spencer, *Algiers in the Age of the Corsairs* (Norman: University of Oklahoma Press, 1976), Centers of Civilization Series. "The corsair, if brought to justice in maritime courts, identified himself as *corsale* or *Korsan,* never as fugitive or criminal; his occupation was as clearly identifiable as that of tanner, goldsmith, potter or tailor." P. 47.

2. Raphael Danziger, *Abd al-Qadir and the Algerians* (New York: Holmes and Meier, 1977), notes that Turkish intrigue kept the tribes in a state of near constant tribal warfare, thereby preventing them from forming dangerous coalitions. P. 24.

3. The usual explanation for the quick collapse of the regency after 300 years is that its forces were prepared for naval warfare but not for attack by land. *Ibid.,* pp. 36–38.

4. Quoted in Harold D. Nelson, *Algeria, A Country Study* (Washington: American University, Foreign Area Studies, 1979), p. 31.

5. Marnia Lazreg, *The Emergence of Classes in Algeria* (Boulder: Westview Press, 1976), p. 53.

6. For Algerian Muslims to become French citizens meant giving up their religion, for all practical purposes, since Islam recognizes only Islamic law and to be a French citizen means accepting French laws. Fewer than 3,000 Algerians became French citizens during the period of French rule. Nelson, *op. cit.,* pp. 34–35.

7. John E. Talbott, *The War Without a Name: France in Algeria, 1954–1962* (New York: Alfred A. Knopf, 1980).

8. Georges Suffert, in *Esprit,* 25 (1957), p. 819.

9. Nelson, *op. cit.,* p. 68.

10. *Africa Research Bulletin,* Political Series (February 1985).

DEVELOPMENT

Expansion of natural-gas production and exports and discovery of several new oil fields indicate that hydrocarbons will continue to provide the bulk of revenue (97% in 1988) for some time to come. Efforts to reduce oil dependence resulted in a major zinc discovery, with 20 million tons of reserves, in the Bejaia area in 1991.

FREEDOM

The new Algerian Constitution allows multiparty participation in local and national elections. In addition to the FIS, 28 new parties registered for the abortive National Assembly elections in 1991.

HEALTH/WELFARE

The 1984 Family Law improved the status of women in marital and work matters. But a 1990 Arabization Law discriminates against the Berber minority and French-educated middle classes by making Arabic the official language and requiring its exclusive use in schools and all business transactions. It was pushed through the Assembly by Islamic fundamentalists.

ACHIEVEMENTS

With one of the world's highest population growth rates, housing is a priority. From 1980 to 1984, 430,000 new units were built. The 1985–1989 5-year plan called for a 15% increase in new housing, with 250,000 units needed annually.

Bahrain (State of Bahrain)

GEOGRAPHY

Area in Square Kilometers (Miles):
678 (260) (about 4 times the size of
Washington, D.C.)
Capital (Population): Manama
(146,000)
Climate: hot and humid,
April–October; temperate,
November–March

PEOPLE

Population
Total: 490,000
Annual Growth Rate: 3.1%
Rural/Urban Population Ratio: 18/82
Ethnic Makeup of Population: 63%
Bahraini; 13% Asian; 10% other
Arab; 8% Iranian; 6% others

Health
Life Expectancy at Birth: 70 years
(male); 75 years (female)
Infant Mortality Rate (Ratio):
22/1,000
Average Caloric Intake: n/a
Physicians Available (Ratio): 1/991

Religion(s)
66% Shia Muslim; 30% Sunni
Muslim; 4% Christian

Education
Adult Literacy Rate: 40%

COMMUNICATION
Telephones: 120,000
Newspapers: 7 Arabic; 2 English
language (one weekly, one daily)

PEARLING: AN ANCIENT INDUSTRY

Pearl diving dates back 5,000 years; the ancient Epic of Gilgamesh
describes a diver tying stones to his feet to descend to the bed of the sea
and pluck the magic flowers. Before the discovery of oil, pearl fishing
was the main occupation and source of income of Bahrain. As recently
as the 1930s there were 900 dhows, with 20,000 divers and crew. The
pearling industry slumped with the introduction of cheaper Japanese
cultured pearls, and oil development finished it. But Bahraini pearls are
still highly valued, and a few dhows continue to bring them in, using
methods unchanged for centuries.

TRANSPORTATION
Highways—Kilometers (Miles): 255
(158)
Railroads—Kilometers (Miles): none
Usable Airfields: 2

GOVERNMENT
Type: traditional emirate (cabinet-
executive system)
Independence Date: August 15, 1971
Head of State: Emir Isa bin Salman
al-Khalifa
Political Parties: prohibited; several
small, clandestine leftist and
fundamentalist groups active
Suffrage: none

MILITARY
Number of Armed Forces: Bahrain
Defense Force (army, navy, and air
force), 5,800
*Military Expenditures (% of Central
Government Expenditures):* 9.2%
Current Hostilities: territorial dispute
with Qatar

ECONOMY
Currency ($ U.S. Equivalent): 0.37
Bahrain dinar = $1
Per Capita Income/GNP: $9,994/$4.6
billion
Inflation Rate: −2.3%
Total Foreign Debt: n/a
Natural Resources: oil; associated and
nonassociated natural gas; fish
Agriculture: eggs; vegetables; dates;
dairy and poultry farming
Industry: petroleum processing and
refining; aluminum; ship repair;
natural gas; shrimping and fishing

FOREIGN TRADE
Exports: $2.3 billion
Imports: $2.6 billion

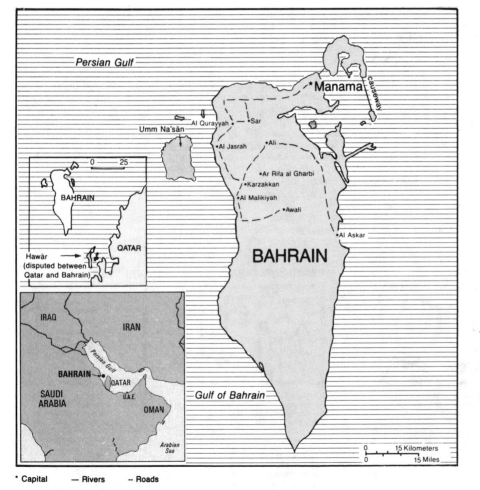

BAHRAIN

Bahrain is the smallest Arab state. It is also the only Arab island state, consisting of an archipelago of 33 islands, 5 of them inhabited. The largest island, also named Bahrain (from the Arabic *bahr-ayn,* or "two seas"), has an area of 216 square miles. This island contains the capital, Manama, and two-thirds of the population. Bahrain's population density is thus one of the highest in the Middle East.

Although separated from the Arabian mainland, Bahrain is not far; it is 15 miles from Qatar and the same distance from Saudi Arabia. A causeway linking Bahrain with mainland Saudi Arabia opened in 1986, technically ending its insular status. The causeway has given strong stimulus to Bahraini business, much of it brought by Saudi visitors who drive across it to take advantage of the facilities of the freer Bahraini society, such as movie theaters and bar lounges.

Bahrain is unusual among the Persian Gulf states in that it started to develop its economy early. Oil was discovered there in 1932. Its head start in exportation of oil enabled the government to build up an industrial base over a long period and to build a large, indigenous, skilled labor force. Unlike other Gulf states, Bahrain has a native majority of the population; 63 percent are native-born Bahrainis.

HISTORY

Archaeologists believe that in ancient times Bahrain was the legendary Dilmun, the land of immortality of the Sumerians of Mesopotamia. Dilmun was an important trade center between Mesopotamian cities and the cities of the Indus Valley in western India.

During the centuries of Islamic rule in the Middle East, Bahrain (it was renamed by Arab geographers) became wealthy from the pearl-fishing industry. By the fourteenth century it had 300 villages. Bahraini merchants grew rich from profits on their large, lustrous, high-quality pearls. Bahraini sea captains and pearl merchants built lofty palaces and other stately buildings on the islands.

The Portuguese were the first Europeans to land on Bahrain, which they seized in the early sixteenth century as one of a string of fortresses along the coast to protect their monopoly over the spice trade. They ruled by the sword in Bahrain for nearly a century before they were ousted by Iranian invaders. The Iranians, in turn, were defeated by the al-Kalifas, a clan of the powerful Anaizas. In 1782 the clan leader, Shaykh Ahmad al-Khalifa,

established control over Bahrain and founded the dynasty that rules the state today. (The al-Khalifas belong to the same clan as the al-Sabahs, rulers of Kuwait, and are distantly related to the Saudi Arabian royal family.)

A British Protectorate

In the 1800s Bahrain came under British protection in the same way as other Gulf states. The ruler Shaykh Isa, whose reign was one of the world's longest (1869–1932), signed an agreement making the United Kingdom responsible for Bahrain's defense and foreign policy. He also agreed not to give any concessions for oil exploration without British approval. The agreement was important because the British were already developing oil fields in Iran. Control of oil in another area would give them an added source of fuel for the new weaponry of tanks and oil-powered warships of World War I. The early development of Bahrain's oil fields and the guidance of British political advisers helped prepare the country for independence.

INDEPENDENCE

Bahrain became fully independent in 1971. The British encouraged Bahrain to join with Qatar and seven small British-protected Gulf states, the Trucial States, in a federation. But Bahrain and Qatar felt they were more advanced economically, politically, and socially than were the Trucial States and therefore did not need to federate.

A mild threat to Bahrain's independence came from Iran. In 1970 Shah Mohammed Reza Pahlavi claimed Bahrain, on the basis of Iran's sixteenth-century occupation plus the fact that a large number of Bahrainis were descended from Iranian emigrants. The United Nations discussed the issue and recommended that Bahrain be given its independence on the grounds that "the people of Bahrain wish to gain recognition of their identity in a fully independent and sovereign state."[1] The shah accepted the resolution, and Iran made no further claims on Bahrain during his lifetime.

The gradual development of democracy in Bahrain reached a peak after independence. Shaykh Khalifa (now called *emir*) approved a new Constitution and a law establishing an elected National Assembly of 30 members. The Assembly met for the first time in 1973; but only 2 years later it was dissolved by the emir.

What Had Happened?

Bahrain is an example of a problem common in the Middle East: the conflict be-

tween traditional authority and popular democracy. Fuad Khuri describes the problem as one of a "tribally controlled government that rules by historical right, opposed to a community-based urban population seeking to participate in government through elections. The first believes and acts as if government is an earned right, the other seeks to modify government and subject it to a public vote."[2]

Governmental authority in Bahrain is defined as hereditary in the al-Khalifa family, according to the 1973 Constitution. The succession passes from the ruling emir to his eldest son. The Council of Ministers (many members of which also belong to the ruling family) serves as an advisory body to the emir. Since Bahrain has no tradition of representative government or political parties, the National Assembly was set up to broaden the political process without going through the lengthy period of conditioning necessary to establish a multiparty system. Members were expected to debate laws prepared by the Council of Ministers and to assist with budget preparation. But as things turned out, Assembly members spent their time arguing with one another or criticizing the ruler instead of dealing with issues. When the emir dissolved the Assembly, he said that it was preventing the government from doing what it was supposed to do.

Although the ruling emir's authority remains absolute, in practical terms the country's small size, close-knit ruling family, and web of social relationships encourage political participation at a local and informal level and make the exercise of power more patriarchal than authoritarian. By primordial custom, the ruling emir holds a traditional *majlis* (public assembly) each week for all citizens, who may complain about laws or present petitions or grievances for redress.

FOREIGN RELATIONS

Bahrain has been important to the United States in its Middle East policy for many years, due to its strategic location in the Persian Gulf and its excellent naval-base facilities, built by the British during the protectorate. The base was an essential staging-point for U.S. warships protecting convoys during the Iran-Iraq War. As a result, the state received more military aid than its size and tiny armed forces (at that time, approximately 2,850) would normally warrant. A 1988 agreement provided for delivery of F-16 jets and Stinger missiles as well as for help with construction of a military air base next to the naval base. The army was also beefed up, with delivery of 60 M-60 tanks.

THREATS TO NATIONAL SECURITY

The 1979 Revolution in Iran caused much concern in Bahrain. The new Iranian government revived the old territorial claim, and a Teheran-based Islamic Front for the Liberation of Bahrain called on Shia Muslims in Bahrain to overthrow the Sunni regime of the emir. In 1981 the government arrested a group of Shia Bahrainis and others and charged them with a plot against the state, backed by Iran. The plotters had expected support from the Shia population, but this did not materialize. After seeing the results of the Iranian Revolution, few Bahraini Shia Muslims wanted the Iranian form of fundamentalist Islamic government. In 1982, 73 defendants were given sentences ranging from 7 years' to life imprisonment. Bahrain's prime minister told a local newspaper that the plot didn't represent a real danger, "but we are not used to this sort of thing so we had to take strong action."[3]

The Shia community has remained quiet and politically uninvolved since the 1982 trial, and the end of the Iran-Iraq War plus the Ayatollah Khomeini's death removed the main causes for potential internal unrest. But as is usually the case in countries with a narrow economic base, a youthful population (34 percent under age 14), and few outlets for political expression, the possibility of an Iran-backed Shia uprising against the Sunni majority still exists.

A STABLE AND DIVERSIFIED ECONOMY

Bahrain was among the first Persian Gulf states to enter the oil business. Today the Bahrain Petroleum Company (Bapco) manages the production, refining, and export of crude oil. However, the refinery has mostly old equipment, and refining methods are inefficient. What is more, at current production rates, it is expected that reserves will be depleted by the year 2000.

The country's economic management is characterized by a lack of dynamism and conservative policies, in keeping with its patriarchal political system. Yet in order to compensate for lowered oil production and dwindling reserves, the government is aggressively seeking to expand production of other mineral resources in order to diversify the economic base. Expansion of a liquefied-natural-gas plant increased production to 170 million cubic feet per day by the end of 1989; reserves are estimated at 9 billion cubic feet. Another ambitious project is making Bahrain a major exporter of aluminum. Ironically, a positive side benefit of the costly Iran-Iraq

(UN photo/Ian Steele)

Bahrain may be the first of the Gulf states to get out of the oil business, due to its dwindling reserves. Other income-generating industries are being explored, and recently Bahrain has replaced Lebanon as the Middle East's principal international banking and trade center. The need for an effective educational system to supply an informed labor force is paramount, as these children at a nursery school near Manama attest.

War accrued to the Bahraini ship-repair business. The Arab Shipbuilding and Repair Yard (ASRY), set up in 1968 by the Organization of Arab Oil Exporting Countries, recorded its first profits in 1987 and 1988, with use of its 450,000-ton drydock averaging close to 90 percent as damaged ships limped in for repairs.

A CENTER FOR INTERNATIONAL FINANCE

In recent years Bahrain has replaced Beirut, Lebanon as the Middle East's princi-

pal international banking and trade center. The Bahraini government established so called Offshore Banking Units (OBUs). Foreign banks may open OBUs, which cannot provide local banking services but can accept deposits from governments or large financial organizations such as the World Bank and can make loans for development projects. OBUs are offshore in the sense that a Bahraini cannot open a checking account or borrow money. However, OBUs bring funds into Bahrain without interfering with local growth or undercutting local banks.

Periodic
occupation of
Bahrain by Iran
after the
Portuguese
ouster
1602–1782

The al-Khalifa
family seizes
power over
other families
and groups
1783

Bahrain
becomes a
British
protectorate
1880

Independence
1971

The new Consti-
tution establishes
a Constituent As-
sembly, but the
ruler dissolves it
shortly thereafter
1973–1975

1980s–1990s

An Iran-backed
plot against the
government is
thwarted

A clash with
Qatar over
ownership of the
Fasht al-Dibal
reef is mediated
by the Gulf
Cooperation
Council in
Bahrain's favor

The causeway
linking mainland
Saudi Arabia to
Bahrain is
completed

Both inshore and offshore banking sectors were badly affected by the world oil glut and slump in prices of the early 1980s. By 1987 several British and other foreign banks had ceased operations in Bahrain, and expenditures to cover bad debts had reduced OBU assets by 70 percent. The Iran-Iraq ceasefire gave offshore banking a temporary boost, but long-term prospects, especially after the Iraqi invasion of Kuwait in 1990, seemed dubious at best. The Bank of America closed its OBU office in August, and expatriate managers of most other OBUs took "extended vacations abroad." By mid-1991 the entire OBU system in Bahrain was down 50 percent in deposits.

THE FUTURE

One key to Bahrain's future may be found in a Koranic verse (Sura XIII, II):

Lo! Allah changeth not the condition of a people until they first change what is in their hearts.

For a brief time after independence, the state experimented with representative government. But the hurly-burly of politics, with its factional rivalries, trade-offs, and compromises found in many Western democratic systems, did not suit the Bahraini temperament or experience. Democracy takes time to mature, and Emile Nakhleh reminds us that "any serious attempt to democratize the regime will ultimately set tribal legitimacy and popular sovereignty on a collision course."[4]

Also, Bahrain's neighbors are ruled by similar patriarchal governments. It is doubtful that it could move rapidly toward a democratic system unless, or until, these neighbors undertake the same process. To date, the ruling family has succeeded in drawing potential opposition groups into the governing process without giving away too much power. Barring a major upsurge in antigovernment Islamic fundamentalism among the Shia majority, this process should continue in an orderly fashion.

A second action that should help to assure an orderly future for Bahrain was the establishment of the Gulf Cooperation Council in 1981, which linked the country in a framework of regional cooperation with Saudi Arabia, Kuwait, Qatar, Oman, and the United Arab Emirates. The GCC was envisaged initially as a mutual defense arrangement, but over the long term its political accomplishments should outweigh the development of a coordinated military system. The members' common goals of gradual democratization, sustained national development, and the building of successful integrated societies are probably most likely to be attained by a tandem movement forward on the part of their patriarchal governments. The power structure in Bahrain, based on the traditional rule of the al-Khalifa family, may appear undemocratic in principle, but in practice it does provide the stable framework within which national life and a new consensus will develop as a matter of course.[5]

NOTES

1. United Nations Security Council Resolution 287, 1970. Quoted from Emile Nakhleh, *Bahrain* (Lexington: Lexington Books, 1976), p. 9.

2. Fuad I. Khuri, *Tribe and State in Bahrain* (Chicago: University of Chicago Press, 1981), p. 219.

3. *Gulf Daily News* (May 15, 1982).

4. Nakhleh, *op. cit.*, p. 11.

5. See Michael Jenner, *Bahrain: Gulf Heritage in Transition* (London: Longman, 1984), p. 115.

DEVELOPMENT

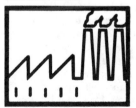

Oil production in 1990 was 90.2 million barrels, down from the levels of previous years. Plans for diversification were halted by the Gulf War; to reduce its oil dependence, the government plans to expand aluminum and natural-gas production.

FREEDOM

The first labor union was approved in 1983, although it is a worker-management committee rather than a trade union. In 1984 the government decreed equal pay for equal work for men and women. A UN-funded project, begun in 1987, trains 300 Bahraini women each year to become self-supporting in handcrafts, tailoring, and other vocations.

HEALTH/WELFARE

The Arab University of the Gulf, based in Manama but financed by all the Gulf states, opened in 1988 with an enrollment of 5,000 students.

ACHIEVEMENTS

Although Bahrain is a modern state, some aspects of its traditional past survive. One is the art of dhow building. Next door to the huge Arab Shipbuilding and Repair, which handles supertankers, young ship builders learn how to build the broad-beamed, seaworthy dhow without plans, measuring tapes, or welding equipment.

Egypt (Arab Republic of Egypt)

GEOGRAPHY

Area in Square Kilometers (Miles):
1,001,258 (386,650) (about the size of
Oregon and Texas combined)
Capital (Population): Cairo (more
than 11 million in greater Cairo area)
Climate: dry, hot summers; moderate
winters

PEOPLE

Population

Total: 54,139,000
Annual Growth Rate: 2.6%
Rural/Urban Population Ratio: 56/44
Ethnic Makeup of Population: 90%
Eastern Hamitic (Egyptian, Bedouin,
Arab, Nubian); 10% Greek, Italian,
Syro-Lebanese

Health

Life Expectancy at Birth: 59 years
(male); 61 years (female)
Infant Mortality Rate (Ratio):
68/1,000
Average Caloric Intake: 116% of FAO
minimum
Physicians Available (Ratio): 1/616

Religion(s)

94% Muslim (mostly Sunni); 6%
Coptic Christian and others

Education

Adult Literacy Rate: 44%

THE ASWAN DAM

The High Dam at Aswan began as a political decision of the Egyptian
government under Gamal Abdel Nasser, whose goal was to increase
available cultivable land and generate electricity for industrialization in
order to lift Egypt out of poverty. When Western institutions refused to
finance the dam, he turned to the Soviet Union. Construction began in
1960 and the dam went into operation in 1971. By 1974 revenues had
exceeded construction costs. The dam has made possible electrification
of all Egyptian villages; and in Lake Nasser, its reservoir, a fishing
industry has been established to replace the sardine industry lost in the
Mediterranean due to reduction in Nile flow. Yet the dam is a mixed
blessing for Egypt. Land reclamation through irrigation is proving far
more costly than expected, and Nile water control has led to increased
salinity.

COMMUNICATION

Telephones: 600,000
Newspapers: 11 dailies in Cairo, 6 in
Alexandria

TRANSPORTATION

Highways—Kilometers (Miles):
47,025 (29,343)

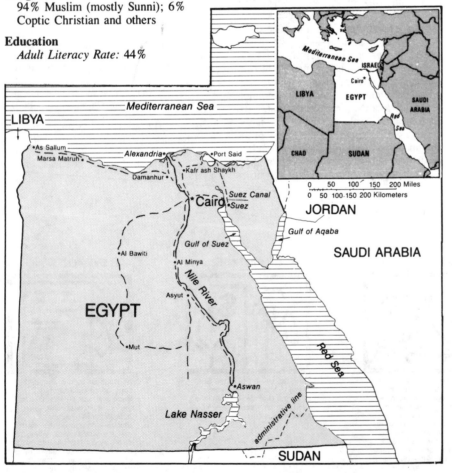

* Capital — Rivers - - Roads

Railroads—Kilometers (Miles): 4,548
(2,819)
Usable Airfields: 86

GOVERNMENT

Type: republic
Independence Date: July 23, 1952
Head of State: President Mohammed
Hosni Mubarak
Political Parties: National
Democratic Party (dominant);
Socialist Liberal Party; Socialist
Labor Party; National Progressive
Unionist Grouping; others; all must
be government approved
Suffrage: universal over 18

MILITARY

Number of Armed Forces: 370,000
*Military Expenditures (% of Central
Government Expenditures):* 14%
Current Hostilities: none

ECONOMY

Currency ($ U.S. Equivalent): 3.23
Egyptian pounds = $1
Per Capita Income/GNP: $640/$25.6
billion
Inflation Rate: 11%
Total Foreign Debt: $48.8 billion
Natural Resources: petroleum and
natural gas; iron ore; phosphates;
manganese; limestone; gypsum; talc;
asbestos; lead; zinc
Agriculture: cotton; rice; onions;
beans; citrus fruits; wheat; corn;
barley; sugarcane
Industry: textiles; food processing;
chemicals; petroleum; construction;
cement; light manufacturing

FOREIGN TRADE

Exports: $2.5 billion
Imports: $7.4 billion

EGYPT

The Arab Republic of Egypt is located at the extreme northeastern corner of Africa, with part of its territory, the Sinai Peninsula, serving as a land bridge to Southwest Asia. The country's total land area is 386,650 square miles. However, 96 percent of this area is uninhabitable desert. Except for a few scattered oases, the only settled and cultivable area is a narrow strip along the Nile River. The vast majority of Egypt's population is concentrated in this strip; thus, real population density is very high. Urban density is also very high. The combination of rapid population growth and limited arable land presents serious obstacles to national development.

Modern Egypt identifies itself as an Arab nation and has taken an active part in the development of other Arab states. Not one of the wealthier Arab countries in natural resources, it has a higher level of education and more skilled professionals than do most other Arab countries. Egyptian teachers, doctors, nurses, engineers, and agricultural specialists have contributed significantly to the development of Arab countries that are wealthier but do not have many skilled workers, such as Libya, Kuwait, and Saudi Arabia.

HISTORY

Although Egypt is a twentieth-century nation in terms of independence from foreign control, it has a distinct national identity and a rich culture that date back thousands of years. The modern Egyptians take great pride in their brilliant past; this sense of the past gives them patience and a certain fatalism which enable them to withstand misfortunes that would crush most peoples. The Egyptian peasants, the *fellahin,* are as stoic and enduring as the water buffaloes they use to do their plowing. Since the time of the pharaohs, Egypt has been invaded many times, and it was under foreign control for most of its history. When Gamal Abdel Nasser, the first president of the new Egyptian republic, came to power in 1954, he said he was the first native Egyptian to rule the country in nearly 3,000 years.

It is often said that Egypt is "the gift of the Nile." The mighty river, flowing north to the Mediterranean with an enormous annual spate that deposited rich silt along its banks, attracted nomadic peoples to settle there as early as 6000 B.C. They developed a productive agriculture based on the river's seasonable floods. They

(UN photo/John Isaac)

These pyramids at Giza are among the most famous mementos of Egypt's brilliant past.

lived in plastered mud huts, in small but compact villages. Their villages are not too different from those one sees today in parts of the Nile Delta.

Each village had its "headman," the head of some family more prosperous or industrious (or both) than the others. Gradually the arrival of other nomadic desert peoples brought about the evolution of an organized system of government. Since the Egyptian villagers did not have nearby mountains or wild forests to retreat into, they were easily governable.

The institution of kingship was well established in Egypt by 2000 B.C., and in the time of Ramses II (1300–1233 B.C.) Egyptian monarchs extended their power over a large part of the Middle East. All Egyptian rulers were called *pharaohs,* although there was no hereditary system of descent and many different dynasties ruled during the country's first 2,000 years of existence. The pharaohs had their capital at Thebes, but they built other important cities on the banks of the Nile. Pharaonic architecture, based on simple yet accurate instruments and a great deal of human labor, produced extraordinary structures, such as the Pyramids, the Sphinx, the Temples at Philae, and royal tombs and palaces. These structures, even in ruin, give evidence of the high level of civilization of Pharaonic Egypt.

In the first century B.C. Egypt became part of the Roman Empire. The city of Alexandria, founded by Alexander the Great, became a center of Greek and Roman learning and culture. Later it became a center of Christianity. The Egyptian Coptic Church was one of the earliest organized churches. The Copts, direct descendants of the early Egyptians, are the principal minority group in Egypt today. When Arab invaders brought Islam to Egypt, they were welcomed by the Copts. In return, Arab Islamic rulers protected the Copts, respecting their Christian faith and not requiring conversion to Islam, although some Copts did convert. The Copts have been useful to Islamic governments in Egypt ever since, because of their high level of education and management skills.

Egypt also had, until very recently, a small but long-established Jewish community that held a similar position under various Muslim rulers. Most of them emigrated to Israel after 1948. Eleven thousand were deported in 1956 after the Israeli invasion of the Suez Canal Zone.

THE INFLUENCE OF ISLAM

Islam was the major formative influence in the development of modern Egyptian society. Islamic armies from Arabia invaded Egypt in the seventh century A.D. Large numbers of nomadic Arabs followed, settling the Nile Valley until over time they became the majority in the population. Egypt was under the rule of the caliphs ("successors" of the Prophet Muhammad) until the tenth century, when a Shia group broke away and formed a separate government. The leaders of this group also called themselves caliphs. To show their independence, they founded a new capital in the desert south of Alexandria. The name they chose for their new capital was prophetic: al-Qahira, "City of War," the modern city of Cairo.

In the sixteenth century Egypt became a province of the Ottoman Empire. It was then under the rule of the Mamluks, originally slaves or prisoners of war who were converted to Islam. Many Mamluk leaders had been freed and then acquired their own slaves. They formed a military aristocracy, constantly fighting with one another for land and power. The Ottomans found it simpler to leave Egypt under Mamluk control, merely requiring periodic tribute and taxes.

EGYPT ENTERS THE MODERN WORLD

At the end of the eighteenth century rivalry between Britain and France for control of trade in the Mediterranean and the sea routes to India involved Egypt. The French General Napoleon Bonaparte led an expedition to Egypt in 1798. However, the British, in cooperation with Ottoman forces, drove the French from Egypt. A confused struggle for power followed. The victor was Muhammad Ali, an Albanian officer in the Ottoman garrison at Cairo. In 1805 the Ottoman sultan appointed him governor of Egypt.

Although he was not an Egyptian, Muhammad Ali had a vision of Egypt under his rule as a rich and powerful country. He began by forming a new army consisting of native Egyptians instead of mercenaries or slave-soldiers. This army was trained by European advisers and gave a good account of itself in campaigns, performing better than the regular Ottoman armies.[1]

Muhammad Ali set up an organized, efficient tax-collection system. He suppressed the Mamluks and confiscated all the lands they had seized from Egyptian peasants over the years, lifting a heavy tax burden from peasant backs. He took personal charge of all Egypt's exports. Cotton, a new crop, became the major Egyptian export and became known the world over for its high quality. Dams and irrigation canals were dug to improve cultivation and expand arable land. Although Muhammad Ali grew rich in the process of carrying out these policies, he was concerned for the welfare of the peasantry. He once said, "One must guide this people as one guides children; to leave them to their own devices would be to render them subject to all the disorders from which I have saved them."[2]

Muhammad Ali's successors were called *khedives* ("viceroys"), in that they ruled Egypt in theory on behalf of their superior, the sultan. In practice, they acted as independent rulers. Under the khedives, Egypt was again drawn into European power politics, with unfortunate results. The Suez Canal was opened in 1869, during the reign of Khedive Ismail. Ismail was the most ambitious of Muhammad Ali's descendants. The Suez Canal was only one of his grandiose public-works projects, by which he intended to make Egypt the equal of any European power. But he used up Egypt's revenues and finally had to sell the Egyptian government's share in the company that had built the canal to the British government in order to pay his debts.

Ismail's successors were forced to accept British control over Egyptian finances. In 1882 a revolt of army officers threatened to overthrow the khedive. The British intervened and established a de facto protectorate, keeping the khedive in office in order to avoid conflict with the Ottomans.

EGYPTIAN NATIONALISM EMERGES

The British protectorate lasted from 1882 to 1956. An Egyptian nationalist movement gradually developed in the early 1900s, inspired by the teachings of religious leaders and Western-educated officials in the khedives' government. They advocated a revival of Islam and its strengthening to enable Egypt and other Islamic lands to resist European control.

During World War I Egypt was a major base for British campaigns against the Ottoman Empire. The British formally declared their protectorate over Egypt in order to "defend" the country, since legally it was still an Ottoman province. The British worked with Arab nationalist leaders against the Turks and promised to help them form an independent Arab nation after the war. Egyptian nationalists were active in the Arab cause, and although at that time they did not particularly care about being a part of a new Arab nation, they wanted independence from the United Kingdom.

At the end of World War I Egyptian nationalist leaders organized the *Wafd* (Arabic for "delegation"). The delegation in 1918 presented demands to the British for the complete independence of Egypt. The British rejected the demands, saying that Egypt was not ready for self-government. The Wafd then turned to violence, organizing boycotts, strikes, and terrorist attacks on British soldiers and on Egyptians accused of cooperating with the British.

Under pressure, the British finally abolished the protectorate in 1922. But they retained control over Egyptian foreign policy, defense, and communications as well as the protection of minorities and foreign residents and of Sudan, which had been part of Egypt since the 1880s. Thus, Egypt's "independence" was a hollow shell.

Egypt did regain control over internal affairs. The government was set up as a constitutional monarchy under a new king, Fuad. Political parties were allowed, and in elections for a Parliament in 1923 the Wafd emerged as the dominant party. But neither Fuad nor the son who succeeded him, Farouk, trusted Wafd leaders. They feared that the Wafd was working to establish a republic. For their part, the Wafd leaders did not believe that the rulers were seriously interested in the good of the country. So Egypt waddled along for 2 decades with little progress.

THE EGYPTIAN REVOLUTION

During the years of the monarchy the Egyptian Army gradually developed a corps of professional officers, most of them from lower- or middle-class Egyptian backgrounds. They were strongly patriotic and resented what they perceived to be British cultural snobbery as well as the United Kingdom's continual influence over Egyptian affairs.

The training school for these young officers was the Egyptian Military Academy, founded in 1936. Among them was Gamal Abdel Nasser, the eldest son of a village postal clerk. Nasser and his fellow officers were already active in anti-British demonstrations by the time they entered the academy. During World War II the British, fearing a German takeover of Egypt, reinstated the protectorate. Egypt became the main British military base in the Middle East. This action galvanized the officers into forming a revolutionary movement. Nasser said at the time that it roused in him the seeds of revolt. "It made [us] realize that there is a dignity to be retrieved and defended."[3]

When Jewish leaders in Palestine organized Israel in May 1948, Egypt, along with other nearby Arab countries, sent troops to destroy the new state. Nasser and several of his fellow officers were sent

(UN photo)

In 1952 the Free Officers organization persuaded Egypt's King Farouk to abdicate. The monarchy was formally abolished in 1954 when Gamal Abdel Nasser became Egypt's president, prime minister, and head of the Revolutionary Command Council.

to the front. The Egyptian Army was defeated; Nasser himself was trapped with his unit, was wounded, and was rescued only by an armistice. Even more shocking to the young officers was the evident corruption and weakness of their own government. The weapons they received were inferior and often defective, battle orders were inaccurate, and their superiors proved to be incompetent in strategy and tactics.

Nasser and his fellow officers attributed their defeat not to their own weaknesses but to their government's failures. When they returned to Egypt, they were determined to overthrow the monarchy. They formed a secret organization, the Free Officers. It was not the only organization dedicated to the overthrow of the monarchy, but it was the best disciplined and had the general support of the army.

On July 23, 1952, the Free Officers launched their revolution. It came six

months after "Black Saturday," the burning of Cairo by mobs protesting the continued presence of British troops in Egypt. The Free Officers persuaded King Farouk to abdicate, and they declared Egypt a republic. A nine-member Revolutionary Command Council (RCC) was established to govern the country.

EGYPT UNDER NASSER

In his self-analytical book, *The Philosophy of the Revolution,* Nasser wrote, " . . . I always imagine that in this region in which we live there is a role wandering aimlessly about in search of an actor to play it."[4] Nasser saw himself as playing that role. Previously he had operated behind the scenes, but always as the leader to whom the other Free Officers looked up. By 1954 Nasser had emerged as Egypt's leader. When the monarchy was formally abolished in 1954, he became president, prime minister, and head of the RCC. Cynics said that Nasser came along when Egypt was ready for another king; the Egyptians could not function without one!

Nasser came to power determined to restore dignity and status to Egypt, to eliminate foreign control, and to make his country the leader of a united Arab world. It was an ambitious set of goals, and Nasser was only partly successful in attaining them. But in his struggles to achieve these goals, he brought considerable status to Egypt. The country became a leader of the "Third World" of Africa and Asia, nations newly freed from foreign control.

Nasser was successful in removing the last vestiges of British rule over Egypt. British troops were withdrawn from the Suez Canal Zone, and Nasser nationalized the canal in 1956, taking over the management from the private foreign company that had operated it since 1869. That action made the British furious, since the British government had a majority interest in the company. The British worked out a secret plan with the French and the Israelis, neither of whom liked Nasser, to invade Egypt and overthrow him. British and French paratroopers seized the canal in October 1956, but the United States and the Soviet Union, in an unusual display of cooperation, forced them to withdraw. It was the first of several occasions when Nasser turned military defeat into political victory. It was also one of the few times when Nasser and the United States were on the same side of an issue.

Between 1956 and 1967 Nasser developed a close alliance with the Soviet Union—at least, it seemed that way to the United States. Nasser's pet economic project was the building of a high dam at Aswan, on the upper Nile, to regulate the annual flow of river water and thus enable Egypt to reclaim new land and develop its agriculture. He applied for aid from the United States through the World Bank to finance the project, but he was turned down, largely due to his publicly expressed hostility to Israel. Again Nasser turned defeat into a victory of sorts. The Soviet Union agreed to finance the dam, which was completed in 1971, and subsequently to equip and train the Egyptian Army. Thousands of Soviet advisers poured into Egypt, and it seemed to American and Israeli leaders that Egypt had become a dependency of the Soviet Union.

The lowest point in Nasser's career came in June 1967. Israel invaded Egypt and defeated his Soviet-trained army, along with those of Jordan and Syria, and occupied the Sinai Peninsula in a lightning 6-day war. The Israelis were restrained from marching on Cairo only by a United Nations ceasefire. Nasser took personal responsibility for the defeat, calling it al-Nakba ("The Catastrophe"). He announced his resignation, but the Egyptian people refused to accept it. The public outcry was so great that he agreed to continue in office. One observer wrote, "The irony was that Nasser had led the country to defeat, but Egypt without Nasser was unthinkable."[5]

Nasser had little success in his efforts to unify the Arab world. One attempt was a union of Egypt and Syria, which lasted barely 3 years (1958–1961). Egyptian forces were sent to support a new republican government in Yemen after the overthrow of that country's autocratic ruler. But they became bogged down in a civil war there and had to be withdrawn. Other efforts to unify the Arab world also failed. Arab leaders respected Nasser but were unwilling to play second fiddle to him in an organized Arab state. In 1967, after the Arab defeat, Nasser lashed out bitterly at the other Arab leaders. He said, "You issue statements, but we have to fight. If you want to liberate [Palestine] then get in line in front of us."[6]

Inside Egypt, the results of Nasser's 18-year rule were also mixed. Although he talked about developing representative government, Nasser distrusted political parties and remembered the destructive rivalries under the monarchy that had kept Egypt divided and weak. The Wafd and all other political parties were declared illegal. Nasser set up his own political organization to replace them, called the Arab Socialist Union (ASU). It was a mass party, but it had no real power. Nasser and a few close associates ran the government and controlled the ASU. The associates took their orders directly from Nasser; they called him *El-Rais*—"The Boss."

As he grew older, Nasser, plagued by health problems, became more dictatorial, secretive, and suspicious. The Boss tolerated no opposition and ensured tight control over Egypt with a large police force and a secret service that monitored activities in every village and town.

Nasser died in 1970. Ironically, his death came on the heels of a major policy success, the arranging of a truce between the Palestine Liberation Organization and the government of Jordan. Despite his health problems, Nasser had seemed indestructible, and his death came as a shock. Millions of Egyptians followed his funeral cortege through the streets of Cairo, weeping and wailing over the loss of their beloved Rais.

ANWAR AL-SADAT

Nasser was succeeded by Vice President Anwar al-Sadat, in accordance with constitutional procedure. Sadat had been one of the original Free Officers and had worked with Nasser since their early days at the Military Academy. In the Nasser years, Sadat came to be regarded as a lightweight, always ready to do whatever The Boss wanted.

Many Egyptians did not even know what Sadat looked like. A popular story was told of an Egyptian peasant in from the country to visit his cousin, a taxi driver. As they drove around Cairo, they passed a large poster of Nasser and Sadat shaking hands. "I know our beloved leader, but who is the man with him?" asked the peasant. "I think he owns that cafe across the street," replied his cousin.

When Sadat became president, however, it did not take long for the Egyptian people to learn what he looked like. Sadat introduced a "revolution of rectification," which he said was needed to correct the errors of his predecessor.[7] These included too much dependence on the Soviet Union, too much government interference in the economy, and failure to develop an effective Arab policy against Israel. He was a master of timing, taking bold action at unexpected times to advance Egypt's international and regional prestige. Thus, in 1972 he abruptly ordered the 15,000 Soviet advisers in Egypt to leave the country, despite the fact that they were training his army and supplying all his military equipment. His purpose was to reduce Egypt's dependence on one foreign power, and as he had calculated, the United States now came to his aid.

A year later, in October 1973, Egyptian forces crossed the Suez Canal in a surprise attack and broke through Israeli defense lines in occupied Sinai. The attack was coordinated with Syrian forces invading Israel from the east, through the Golan Heights. The Israelis were driven back with heavy casualties on both fronts, and although they eventually regrouped and won back most of the lost ground, Sadat felt he had won a moral and psychological victory. After the war Egyptians believed that they had held their own with the Israelis and had demonstrated Arab ability to handle the sophisticated weaponry of modern warfare.

Anwar al-Sadat's most spectacular action took place in 1977. It seemed to him that the Arab/Israeli conflict was at a stalemate. Neither side would budge from its position, and the Egyptian people were angry at having so little to show for the 1973 success. In November he addressed a hushed meeting of the People's Assembly and said, "Israel will be astonished when it hears me saying . . . that I am ready to go to their own house, to the Knesset itself, to talk to them."[8] And he did so, becoming for a second time the "Hero of the Crossing,"[9] but this time to the very citadel of Egypt's enemy.

Sadat's successes in foreign policy, culminating in the 1979 peace treaty with Israel, gave him great prestige internationally. Receipt of the Nobel Peace Prize, jointly with Israeli Prime Minister Menachem Begin, confirmed his status as a peacemaker. His pipe-smoking affability and sartorial elegance endeared him to U.S. policy-makers.

The view that more and more Egyptians held of their world-famous leader was less flattering. Religious leaders and conservative Muslims objected to Sadat's luxurious style of living. The poor resented having to pay more for basic necessities. The educated classes were angry about Sadat's claim that the political system had become more open and democratic when, in fact, it had not. The Arab Socialist Union was abolished and several new political parties were allowed to organize. But the ASU's top leaders merely formed their own party, the National Democratic Party, headed by Sadat. For all practical purposes, Egypt under Sadat was even more of a single-party state under an authoritarian leader than it had been in Nasser's time.

Sadat's economic policies also worked to his disadvantage. In 1974 he announced a new program for postwar recovery, *Infitah* ("Opening"). It would be an open-door policy, bringing an end to Nasser's state-run socialist system. Foreign investors would be encouraged to invest in Egypt, and foreign experts would bring their technological knowledge to help develop industries. Infitah, properly applied, would bring an economic miracle to Egypt.

Rather than spur economic growth, however, Infitah made fortunes for a few, leaving the great majority of Egyptians no better off than before. Chief among those who profited were the Sadat family. Corruption among the small ruling class, many of its members newly rich contractors, aroused anger on the part of the Egyptian people. In 1977 the economy was in such bad shape that the government increased bread prices. Riots broke out and Sadat was forced to cancel the increase.

On October 6, 1981, President Sadat and government leaders were reviewing an armed-forces parade in Cairo to mark the eighth anniversary of the Crossing. Suddenly, a volley of shots rang out from one of the trucks in the parade. Sadat fell, mortally wounded. The assassins, most of them young military men, were immediately arrested. They belonged to Al Takfir Wal Hijra ("Repentance and Flight from Sin"), a secret group that advocates the reestablishment of a pure Islamic society in Egypt—by violence, if necessary. Their leader declared that the killing of Sadat was an essential first step in this process.

Islamic fundamentalism developed rapidly in the Middle East after the Iranian Revolution. The success of that revolution was a spur to Egyptian fundamentalists. They accused Sadat of favoring Western capitalism through his Infitah policy, of making peace with the enemy of Islam (Israel), and of not being a good Muslim. At their trial, Sadat's assassins said that they had acted to rid Egypt of an unjust ruler, a proper action under the laws of Islam.

Sadat may have contributed to his early death (he was 63) by a series of actions taken earlier in the year. About 1,600 people were arrested in September 1981 in a massive crackdown on religious unrest. They included not only religious leaders but also journalists, lawyers, intellectuals, provincial governors, and leaders of the country's small but growing opposition parties. Many of them were not connected with any fundamentalist Islamic organization. It seemed to most Egyptians that Sadat had overreacted, and at that point he lost the support of the nation. In contrast to Nasser's funeral, few tears were shed at Sadat's. His funeral was attended mostly by foreign dignitaries. One of them said that Sadat had been buried without the people and without the army.

(UN photo/M. Tzoraras)

Nasser died in 1970 and was succeeded by Vice President Anwar al-Sadat. Sadat, virtually unknown by the Egyptian people, took many bold steps in cementing his role as leader of Egypt.

MUBARAK IN POWER

Vice President Hosni Mubarak, former Air Force commander and designer of Egypt's 1973 success against Israel, succeeded Sadat without incident. Mubarak dealt firmly with Islamic fundamentalism at the beginning of his regime. He was given emergency powers and approved death sentences for five of Sadat's assassins in 1982. But he moved cautiously in other areas of national life, in an effort to disassociate himself from some of Sadat's more unpopular policies. The economic policy of Infitah, which had led to widespread graft and corruption, was abandoned; stiff sentences were handed out to a number of entrepreneurs and capitalists, including Sadat's brother-in-law and several associates of the late president.

Mubarak also began rebuilding bridges with other Arab states that had been damaged after the peace treaty with Israel. Egypt was readmitted to membership in the Islamic Conference, the Islamic Development Bank, the Arab League, and other Arab regional organizations. In 1990 the Arab League headquarters was moved from Tunis back to Cairo, its original location. Egypt backed Iraq with arms

and advisers in its war with Iran, but Mubarak broke with Saddam Hussain after the invasion of Kuwait, accusing the Iraqi leader of perfidy. Some 35,000 Egyptian troops served with the Un-U.S. coalition during the Gulf War; and, as a result of these efforts, the country resumed its accustomed role as the focal point of Arab politics.

Despite the peace treaty, relations with Israel continued to be difficult. One bone of contention was removed in 1989 with the return of the Israeli-held enclave of Taba, in the Sinai Peninsula, to Egyptian control. It had been operated as an Israeli beach resort.

The return of Taba strengthened the government's claim that the 10-year-old peace treaty had been valuable overall in advancing Egypt's interests. Also, the Palestine Liberation Organization's historic announcement in December 1988 that it would accept the existence of Israel and a two-state solution for Palestine encouraged Egyptian opposition parties to expand their contacts with members of the "peace camp" in Israel. However, brutal Israeli treatment of Palestinians in the occupied territories since the Intifada (uprising) of 1987 continued to hamper rela-

Period of the pharaohs 2500–671 B.C.	The Persian conquest, followed by Macedonians and rule by Ptolemies 671–30 B.C.	Egypt becomes a Roman province 300 B.C.	Invading Arabs bring Islam A.D. 641	The founding of Cairo 969	Egypt becomes an Ottoman province 1517–1800	Napoleon's invasion, followed by the rise to power of Muhammad Ali 1798–1831

tions between the two former enemies.

Internal Politics

Although Mubarak's unostentatious life-style and firm leadership encouraged confidence among the Egyptian regime, the system he inherited from his predecessors remained largely impervious to change. The first free multiparty national elections held since the 1952 Revolution took place in 1984, although they were not entirely free, because a law requiring political parties to win at least 8 percent of the popular vote limited party participation. Mubarak was reelected easily for a full 6-year term (he was the only candidate), and his ruling National Democratic Party won 73 percent of seats in the Assembly. The New Wafd Party was the only party able to meet the 8-percent requirement.

New elections for the Assembly in 1987 indicated how far Egypt's embryonic democracy has progressed under Mubarak. This time, four opposition parties aside from his own party presented candidates. Although the National Democratic Party's plurality was still a hefty 69.6 percent, 17 percent of the electorate voted for candidates from a coalition of the Socialist Labor and Liberal Socialist Parties plus members of the newly respectable Muslim Brotherhood, who were running as independents. The New Wafd's percentage of the vote rose to 10.9 percent. A huge banner in downtown Cairo on election day proclaimed: "Citizens: The Phony Parliament Is Over. The Future Is Up To You." Although charges of voting irregularities—a long-standing Egyptian tradition—were made by the opposition, the ruling party's success and the fact that the National Unionist Progressive Party (Tagammu), the major leftist group, failed to win a seat, indicated a broad national preference for Mubarak's brand of secular representation.

The growing success of Islamic fundamentalism in other states, notably Iran, Lebanon, and Tunisia, encouraged Egyptian fundamentalists to make a strong bid toward restoring Islamic law and practice in Egypt. The country's hopelessly muddled economy, its strategic importance, and the deep religious convictions of its people made it a likely target.

Under pressure from fundamentalist groups, the Constitutional Court in 1985 annulled a 1979 law giving women rights in divorce cases comparable to those held by women in countries such as the United States. Fundamentalist groups then called demonstrations demanding replacement of all Egyptian laws by Islamic Sharia law, and Islamic preachers thundered denunciations of the regime from their pulpits, calling it un-Islamic. The government responded by arresting a number of the most militant preachers. They were jailed briefly and forbidden to conduct services, with substitute clerics appointed from the civil service to replace them. Counterpressure from women's groups, supported by the Egyptian lawyers' union and other professional organizations, caused the Constitutional Court to rescind the annulment of the divorce law in 1986.

Although the possibility remains of another presidential assassination or a coup by one or more of Egypt's underground organizations, the regime's strategy of encouraging fundamentalist participation in the political process began to bear fruit in 1987. The Muslim Brotherhood took an active part in the parliamentary election, and 35 members won seats. The Brotherhood also voted in favor of Mubarak's nomination for a second presidential term—again, he was the only candidate. The ruling party also won 143 of 144 seats in the Shura, the upper house of the People's Assembly, in the 1989 elections to that body, to continue the trend of centralized party domination that has governed Egypt since the start of the republic. However, the Higher Constitutional Court ruled in 1990 that the 1987 People's Assembly election was invalid because a 1986 amendment to the election law discriminated against independent candidates. The Assembly was allowed to remain in session pending new elections, but all laws passed would not be legally binding.

Although the majority of both the Egyptian people and fundamentalist groups support government policy, some of the smaller, more militant groups continue to work outside the system. By 1989 some 1,500 Islamic militants were under detention. In 1990 and 1991 fundamentalists shifted strategy, seeking to undermine communal harmony by attacks on Coptic Christians.

Despite these obstacles, Mubarak continued to move the country slowly toward a less centralized political system. Three new political parties were approved in 1990—the Egyptian Greens, Misr al-Fatat, and the Democratic Unionists—making a total of nine opposition parties.

A STRUGGLING ECONOMY

Egypt's economy rests upon a narrow and unstable base, due to rapid demographic growth and limited arable land and because political factors have adversely influenced national development. The country has a relatively high level of education and as a result is a net exporter of skilled labor to other Arab countries. But the overproduction of university graduates has produced a bloated and inefficient bureaucracy, because the government is required to provide a position for every graduate who cannot find other employment.

Agriculture is the most important sector of the economy, accounting for 30 percent of national income. The major crops are long-staple cotton and sugarcane. Egyptian agriculture since time immemorial has been based on irrigation from the Nile River. In recent years greater control of irrigation water through the Aswan High Dam, expansion of land devoted to cotton production, and improved planting methods have begun to show positive results.

The new Aswan High Dam, completed in 1971 upstream from the old one (built in 1906), was expected to increase production and solve population pressure on the land by bringing vast desert areas under cultivation. However, increased costs of reclamation have offset the value of the dam in providing a regulated flow of Nile water for irrigation. The prolonged drought in the Sahel and Sahara Desert has begun to threaten seriously Egyptian water management and use of its sole water resource. In 1987 water levels in Lake Nasser were at their lowest since the lake was filled. The level was actually below the amount needed to run the Aswan power station, which supplies 20 percent of Egypt's requirements.

Egypt was self-sufficient in foodstuffs as recently as the 1970s but now must import 60 percent of its food require-

The Suez Canal opens to traffic 1869	The United Kingdom establishes a protectorate 1881	The Free Officers overthrow the monarchy and establish Egypt as a republic 1952	An Anglo-French-Israeli invasion of the Canal Zone after nationalization of Suez operations 1954, 1956	Union with Syria into the United Arab Republic 1958–1961	The Six-Day War with Israel ends in occupation of the Gaza Strip and the Sinai Peninsula by Israelis 1967	Nasser dies; Sadat succeeds as head of Egypt 1970	A peace treaty is signed at Camp David between Egypt and Israel 1979

1980s–1990s

Sadat is assassinated; he is succeeded by Mubarak	U.S. jets intercept an Egyptian airliner carrying Palestinian hijackers of an Italian cruise ship	The first free multiparty elections since the 1952 Revolution; the Brotherhood Charter is signed with Sudan to allow equal partnership in Nile Valley development
A crackdown on Islamic fundamentalists, with arrests of several religious leaders		

ments. Such factors as rapid population growth, rural-to-urban migration with consequent loss of agricultural manpower, and Sadat's open-door policy for imports have combined to produce this negative food balance. Subsidies for basic commodities, which cost the government nearly $2 billion a year, are an important cause of inflation, since they keep the budget continuously in deficit. Fearing a recurrence of the 1977 Bread Riots, the government kept prices in check. But in May 1990 they were raised drastically to secure IMF development financing. As a result, inflation jumped to 30 percent.

Egypt has significant oil and natural-gas reserves and in recent years has become a major oil-producing country. Proven oil reserves are 4.5 billion barrels. Discoveries in the Western Desert and the Gulf of Suez have increased output to 870,000 barrels per day, half of which is committed to meet increased domestic demand. Recent natural-gas discoveries will make Egypt a major world producer; production by 1992 is expected to meet domestic energy requirements.

Egypt also derives revenues from Suez Canal tolls and user fees, from tourism, and from remittances from Egyptian workers abroad, mostly working in Saudi Arabia and other oil-producing Gulf states. However, the flow of remittances from the approximately 4 million expatriate workers was reduced and then all but cut off with the Iraqi invasion of Kuwait. Egyptians fled from both countries in panic, arriving home as penniless refugees. With unemployment already 20 per-

cent and housing in short supply, the government faced an enormous assimilation problem apart from its loss of revenue. The United States helped by agreeing to write off $4.5 billion in Egyptian military debts.

One encouraging sign of brighter days is the expansion of local manufacturing industries, in line with government efforts to reduce dependence upon imported goods. A 10-year tax exemption plus remission of customs duties on imported machinery have encouraged a number of new business ventures, notably in the clothing industry.

In 1987 Mubarak gained some foreign help for Egypt's cash-strapped economy when agreement was reached with the International Monetary Fund for a standby credit of $325 million over 18 months to allow the country to meet its balance-of-payments deficit. The Club of Paris, a group of public and private banks from various industrialized countries, then rescheduled $12 billion in Egyptian external debts over a 10-year period.

But Egypt's chronically debt-ridden economy and inability to deal effectively with population growth, unemployment, and shortages of hard currency do not augur well for sustained long-term growth. IMF aid was suspended in 1988, when the country failed to meet such performance targets as a 10-percent reduction in the budget deficit.

In 1991 the Club of Paris agreed to reduce Egypt's official foreign debt to $20 billion and to provide $8 billion for development in compensation for revenues lost

during the Gulf War. With IMF standby credits of $372 million in hand after the agreed-on price increases, Egypt could float on, like the Nile, for a while longer.

NOTES

1. An English observer said, "In arms and firing they are nearly as perfect as European troops." Afaf L. Marsot, *Egypt in the Reign of Muhammad Ali* (Cambridge: Cambridge University Press, 1984), p. 132.
2. *Ibid.*, p. 161.
3. Quoted in P. J. Vatikiotis, *Nasser and His Generation* (New York: St. Martin's Press, 1978), p. 35.
4. Gamal Abdel Nasser, *The Philosophy of the Revolution* (Cairo: Ministry of National Guidance, 1954), p. 52.
5. Derek Hopwood, *Egypt: Politics and Society 1945–1981* (London: George Allen and Unwin, 1982), p. 77.
6. Quoted in Vatikiotis, *op. cit.*, p. 245.
7. Hopwood, *op. cit.*, p. 106.
8. David Hirst and Irene Beeson, *Sadat* (London: Faber and Faber, 1981), p. 255.
9. "Banners slung across the broad thoroughfares of central Cairo acclaimed The Hero of the Crossing (of the October 1973 War)." *Ibid.*, pp. 17–18.

DEVELOPMENT

Rapid population growth and limited arable land prompted the government in 1990 to begin developing 1.1 million acres on both sides of the Suez Canal for farming, using Nile water pumped under the canal and diverted for irrigation.

FREEDOM

Egypt's political system is modeled on that of France under de Gaulle. All decision-making powers are held by the president. The People's Assembly is merely an arena for debate. However, Mubarak has opened up the political process by allowing opposition political parties. There are an active press and publishing industry and considerable freedom for journalists.

HEALTH/WELFARE

A 10-year program to end illiteracy for 8 million out-of-school adults began in 1991. It also will create 20,000 jobs for university graduates as tutors.

ACHIEVEMENTS

Revenues from Suez Canal tolls were $1.3 billion in 1988. Expansion and deepening of the canal were undertaken in 1989 to allow passage of supertankers. U.S. aid over the period 1979–1989 resulted in several large infrastructure projects, such as modernization of the Cairo telephone and sewer systems.

Iran (Islamic Republic of Iran)

GEOGRAPHY
Area in Square Kilometers (Miles):
1,648,000 (636,294) (about the size of
Alaska and Pennsylvania combined)
Capital (Population): Teheran
(6,200,000)
Climate: semiarid; subtropical along
Caspian coast

PEOPLE

Population
Total: 55,000,000
Annual Growth Rate: 3.2%
Rural/Urban Population Ratio: 45/55
Ethnic Makeup of Population: 63%
Persian; 18% Turkic and Baluchi;
13% other Iranian; 3% Kurdish; 3%
Arab and other Semitic

Health
Life Expectancy at Birth: 63 years
(male); 63 years (female)
Infant Mortality Rate (Ratio):
113/1,000
Average Caloric Intake: 114% of FAO
minimum
Physicians Available (Ratio): 1/2,992

A RICH AND INVENTIVE HERITAGE

Well before the great age of Islamic civilization, Iranian artists, writers,
skilled craftspeople and agriculturalists, along with generals, priests,
and administrators, had woven a rich cultural fabric, like an intricate
Persian carpet, into Iranian life. The stimulus of Islamic scientific and
technological inquiry brought an added dimension. One still sees houses
built centuries ago, with wind towers rising from the rooftops. They are
multisided, with tall hollow grooves to catch the wind from whatever
direction it blows and channel it down directly or across pools of water
to the rooms beneath. These towers, developed long ago by Iranian
Islamic scientists, provide residents with natural air conditioning.

Religion(s)
93% Shia Muslim; 5% Sunni
Muslim; 2% Zoroastrian, Jewish,
Christian, and Baha'i

Education
Adult Literacy Rate: 68%

COMMUNICATION
Telephones: 2,143,000
Newspapers: 17 dailies (circulation of
two largest: 570,000)

TRANSPORTATION
Highways—Kilometers (Miles):
139,368 (86,408)
Railroads—Kilometers (Miles): 4,601
(2,859)
Usable Airfields: 146

GOVERNMENT
Type: theocratic republic
Independence Date: February 1, 1979
Head of State: Supreme Legal Guide
Ali Khamenei; President Ali Akbar
Hashemi Rafsanjani
Political Parties: none dominant;
several legal since 1990
Suffrage: universal over 15

MILITARY
Number of Armed Forces: 640,000
*Military Expenditures (% of Central
Government Expenditures):* 11.7%
Current Hostilities: none

ECONOMY
Currency ($ U.S. Equivalent): 65
rials = $1
Per Capita Income/GNP: $1,200/$93
billion
Inflation Rate: 40%
Total Foreign Debt: virtually none
Natural Resources: petroleum; natural
gas; some mineral products
Agriculture: rice; barley; wheat;
sugar beets; cotton; dates; raisins;
tea; tobacco; sheep; goats
Industry: crude-oil production and
refining; textiles; cement; food
processing; metal fabricating

FOREIGN TRADE
Exports: $13.5 billion
Imports: $9.5 billion

* Capital   — Rivers   -- Roads

IRAN

The Islamic Republic of Iran is the second-largest country in the Middle East. Iran is in many respects a subcontinent, ranging in elevation from Mount Demavend (18,386 feet) to the Caspian Sea, which is below sea level. Most of Iran consists of a high plateau ringed by mountains. Much of the plateau is covered with uninhabitable salt flats and deserts, the Dasht-i-Kavir and Dasht-i-Lut, the latter being one of the most desolate and inhospitable regions in the world. The climate is equally forbidding. The so-called Wind of 120 Days blows throughout the summer in eastern Iran, bringing dust and extremely high temperatures.

Most of the country receives little or no rainfall. Settlement and population density are directly related to the availability of water. The most densely populated region is along the Caspian Sea coast, which has an annual rainfall of 80 inches. The province of Azerbaijan, in the northwest, the province of Khuzestan, along the Iraqi border, and the urban areas around Iran's capital, Teheran, are also heavily populated.

Water is so important to the Iranian economy that all water resources were nationalized in 1967.[1] Lack of rainfall caused the development of a sophisticated system of underground conduits, called qanats, to carry water across the plateau from a water source, usually at the base of a mountain. Many qanats were built thousands of years ago and are still in operation. They make existence possible for much of Iran's rural population.

Until the twentieth century the population was overwhelmingly rural; but due to rural-urban migration, the urban population has increased steadily. Nearly all of this migration has been to Teheran.[2] Yet the rural population has increased overall. This fact has had important political consequences for Iran under the monarchy as well as under the republic. Attachment to the land, family solidarity, and high birth rates have preserved the strong rural element in Iranian society as a force for conservatism and loyalty to religious leaders, who then are able to influence whatever regime is in power. Indeed, the rural population strongly supported the Khomeini regime and contributed much of the volunteer manpower recruited to defend the country after the invasion by Iraqi forces in 1980.

ETHNIC AND RELIGIOUS DIVERSITY

Due to Iran's geographic diversity, the population is divided into a large number of separate and often conflicting ethnic groups. Ethnic Iranians constitute the majority. The Iranians (or Persians, from Parsa, the province where they first settled) are an Indo-European people whose original home was probably in Central Asia. They moved into Iran around 1100 B.C. and gradually dominated the entire region, establishing the world's first empire (in the sense of rule over various unrelated peoples in a large territory). Although the Persian Empire eventually broke up, the Persian language, system of government, and cultural/historical traditions have given Iran an unbroken national identity to the present day.

The largest ethnic minority group is the Azeri (Azerbaijani) Turks. The Azeris live in northwestern Iran. Their ethnic origin dates back to the ancient Persian Empire, when Azerbaijan was known as Atropene. The migration of Turkish peoples into this region in the eleventh and twelfth centuries A.D. encouraged the spread of the Turkish language and of Islam. These were reinforced by centuries of Ottoman rule, although Persian remained the written and literary language of the people.

Turkish dynasties originating in Azerbaijan controlled Iran for several centuries and were responsible for much of premodern Islamic Iran's political power and cultural achievements. In the late nineteenth and early twentieth centuries Azeris were in the forefront of the constitutional movement to limit the absolute power of Iranian monarchs. They formed the core of the first Iranian Parliament. The Azeris have consistently fought for regional autonomy from the central Iranian government in the modern period and refer to their province as "Azadistan, Land of Freedom."[3]

The Kurds are the second-largest ethnic minority. Iran's Kurdish population is concentrated in the Zagros mountains along the Turkish and Iraqi border. The Kurds are Sunni Muslims, as distinct from the Shia majority. The Iranian Kurds share a common language, culture, social organization, and ethnic identity with the Kurds in Iraq, Turkey, and Syria. All Kurds are strongly independent mountain people who lack a politically recognized homeland and who have been unable to unite to form one. The Kurds of Iran formed their own Kurdish Republic, with Soviet backing, after World War II. But the withdrawal of Soviet troops, under international pressure, caused its collapse. Since then Iranian Kurdish leaders have devoted their efforts toward greater regional autonomy. Kurdish opposition to the central Iranian government was muted during the rule of the Pahlavi dynasty (1925–1979), but it broke into the open after the establishment of the republic. The Kurds feared that they would be oppressed under the Shia Muslim government headed by Ayatollah Khomeini, and boycotted the national referendum approving the republic.[4] Kurdish leaders maintained a de facto autonomy during the early years of the Khomeini regime, but the army restored central government control in 1985.

The Arabs are another important minority group (Iran and Turkey are the two Middle Eastern Islamic countries with a non-Arab majority). The Arabs live in Khuzestan Province along the Iraqi border. The Baluchi, also Sunni Muslims, are located in southeast Iran and are related to Baluchi tribes in Afghanistan and Pakistan. They are seminomadic and have traditionally opposed any form of central government control. The Baluchi were the first minority to oppose openly the fundamentalist Shia policies of the Khomeini government.

Lesser non-Muslim minorities include the Armenians, Jews, Assyrians (an ancient Christian sect), and Zoroastrians, followers of the major religion of the Persian and Sassanid Empires, who worshipped Ahura Mazda, the god of light, and regarded fire as sacred because it was a purifier of life. The Bahais, a splinter movement from Islam founded by an Iranian mystic named the *Bab* ("Door," i.e., to wisdom) and organized by a teacher named Baha'Ullah in the nineteenth century, are the largest non-Muslim minority group. Although Baha'Ullah taught the principles of universal love, peace, harmony, and brotherhood, his proclamations of equality of the sexes, ethnic unity, the oneness of all religions, and of a universal rather than a Muslim God aroused the hostility of Shia religious leaders. The Bahais were tolerated and prospered under the Pahlavis, but the republican government, due to its strong insistence on Shia authoritarianism, undertook a campaign of violent persecution that some observers called the "genocide of a noncombatant people."[5] By 1987 this campaign had resulted in the execution of more than 200 Bahais. Nearly 800 more were in prison, most of them charged with espionage. Amnesty International reported a case in 1985 in which a court ruled that an Iranian Muslim who had killed a Bahai with a "premeditated blow" should not be prosecuted and the victim's family could not claim compensation, because they were Bahais. Out of a total pre-1979 Bahai population of 350,000, some 30,000 had fled the country by 1987. Pressure from human-rights organi-

Iranian society today has a considerable level of cultural conformity. Shia Islam is the dominant religion of Iran, and observance of this form of Islam permeates society, as this prayer-meeting at Teheran University attests.

zations and a critical 1990 UN report have resulted in improved treatment for the Bahais, although their religion remains proscribed.

CULTURAL CONFORMITY

Despite the separatist tendencies in Iranian society caused by the existence of these various ethnic groups and religious divisions, there is considerable cultural conformity. Most Iranians, regardless of background, display distinctly Iranian values, customs, and traditions. Unifying features include the Persian language, Islam as the overall religion, the appeal (since the sixteenth century) of Shia Islam as an Iranian nationalistic force, and a sense of nationhood derived from Iran's long history and cultural continuity.

Iranians at all levels have a strongly developed sense of class structure. It is a three-tier structure, consisting of upper, middle, and lower classes, although some scholars distinguish two lower classes: the urban wage earner and the landed or landless peasants. The basic socioeconomic unit in this class structure is the patriarchal family, which functions in Iranian society as a tree trunk does in relation to

its branches. The patriarch of each family is not only disciplinarian and decision maker, but also guardian of the family honor and inheritance.

The patriarchal structure, in terms of the larger society, has defined certain behavioral norms. These include the seclusion of women, ceremonial politeness *(ta'aruf)*, hierarchical authoritarianism with domination by superiors over subordinates, and the importance of face *(aberu)*, maintaining "an appropriate bearing and appearance commensurate with one's social status."[6] Under the republic, these norms have been increasingly Islamized as religious leaders have asserted the primacy of Shia Islam in all aspects of Iranian life.

HISTORY

Modern Iran occupies a much smaller territory than that of its pre-Islamic or some of its Islamic predecessors. The Persian Empire included nearly all of the current Middle East. The Sassanid kings, contemporaries of Roman emperors (A.D. 226–651) and heirs to much of the territory of Cyrus and Darius, made Zoroastrianism the official state religion under

a powerful priestly caste. The Sassanid system of administration was taken over by the Arabs when they brought Islam to Iran, because they lacked experience in political organization or government beyond the tribal level.

The establishment of Islam brought significant changes into Iranian life. Arab armies defeated the Sassanid forces at the Battle of Qadisiya (A.D. 637) and the later Battle of Nihavand (A.D. 641), which resulted in the death of the last Sassanid king and the fall of his empire. The Arabs gradually established control over all of the former Sassanid territories, converting the inhabitants to Islam as they went. But the well-established Iranian cultural and social system provided refinements for Islam that were lacking in its early existence as a purely Arab religion. The Iranian converts to Islam converted the religion from a particularistic Arab faith to a universal faith. Islamic culture, in the broad sense, embracing literature, art, architecture, music, certain sciences and medicine, owes a great deal to the contributions of Iranian Muslims such as the poets Hafiz and Sa'di, the poet and astronomer Omar Khayyam, and many others.

Shia Muslims, currently the vast majority of the Iranian population and represented in nearly all ethnic groups, were in the minority in Iran during the formative centuries of Islam. Only one of the Twelve Shia Imams—the eighth, Reza—actually lived in Iran. (His tomb at Meshed is now the holiest shrine in Iran.) *Taqiya,* or concealment, the Shia practice of hiding one's beliefs to escape Sunni persecution, added to the difficulties of the Shia in forming an organized community.

In the sixteenth century the Safavids, who claimed to be descendants of the Prophet Muhammad, established control over Iran with the help of Turkish tribes. The first Safavid ruler, Shah Ismail, proclaimed Shiism as the official religion of his state and invited all Shias to move to Iran, where they would be protected. Shia domination of the country dates from this period. Shia Muslims converged on Iran from other parts of the Islamic world and became a majority in the population.

The Safavid rulers were bitter rivals of the Sunni Ottoman sultans and fought a number of wars with them. The conflict was religious as well as territorial. The Ottoman sultan assumed the title of caliph of Islam in the sixteenth century after the conquest of Egypt, where the descendants of the last Abbasid caliph of Baghdad had taken refuge. As caliph, the sultan claimed the right to speak for, and rule, all Muslims. The Safavids rejected this claim and called on Shia Muslims to struggle against him. In recent years the Khomeini government issued a similar call to Iranians to carry on war against the Sunni rulers of Iraq, indicating that Shia willingness to struggle and incur martyrdom if necessary was still very much alive in Iran.

King of Kings

The Qajars, a new dynasty of Turkish tribal origin, came to power after a bloody struggle at the end of the eighteenth century. They made Teheran their capital. Most of Iran's current borders were defined in the nineteenth century by treaties with foreign powers—Britain (on behalf of India), Russia, and the Ottoman Empire. Due to Iran's military weaknesses, the agreements favored the outside powers and the country lost much of its original territory.

Despite Iran's weakness in relation to foreign powers, the Qajar rulers sought to revive the ancient glories of the monarchy at home. They assumed the old Persian title *Shahinshah,* "King of Kings." At his coronation, each ruler sat on the Peacock Throne, the gilded, jewel-encrusted treasure brought to Iran by Nadir Shah, conqueror of northern India and founder of the short-lived Iranian Afshar dynasty. They assumed other grandiose titles, such as "Shadow of God on Earth" and "Asylum of the Universe." A shah once told an English visitor, "Your King, then, appears to be no more than a first magistrate. I, on the other hand, can elevate or degrade all the high nobles and officers you see around me!"[7]

Qajar pomp and power, however, masked serious internal weaknesses. The shahs ruled by manipulating ethnic and communal rivalries to their own advantage. When they were faced with dangerous opposition, they retreated, and they made concessions only to retract them once the danger was past. Marriages helped to establish a network of power radiating outward from the royal family to leading upper-class families; one shah married 192 times and married off 170 sons and daughters to cement alliances.[8]

Nasr al-Din Shah, Iran's ruler for most of the nineteenth century, was responsible for a large number of concessions to European bankers, promoters, and private companies. His purpose was to demonstrate to European powers that Iran was becoming a modern state and to find new revenues without having to levy new taxes, which would have aroused more dangerous opposition. The various concessions helped to modernize Iran, but they bankrupted the treasury in the process. The shah also wanted to prove to the European powers that Iran had a modern army. A contract was signed with Russia for officers from the Cossacks, a powerful Russian group, to train an elite Iranian military unit, the Cossack Brigade.

In the mid-nineteenth century the shah was encouraged by European envoys to turn his attention to education as a means of creating a modern society. In 1851 he opened the Polytechnic College, with European instructors, to teach military science and technical subjects. The graduates of this college, along with other Iranians who had been sent to Europe for their education and a few members of aristocratic families, became the nucleus of a small but influential intellectual elite. Along with their training in military subjects they acquired European ideas of nationalism and progress. They were "government men" in the sense that they worked for and belonged to the shah's government.

But they also came to believe that the Iranian people needed to unite into a nation, with representative government and a European-style educational system, in order to become a part of the modern world. The views of these intellectuals put them at odds with the shah, who cared nothing for representative government or civil rights, only for tax collection. The intellectuals found themselves also at odds with the religious leaders (mullahs), who controlled the educational system and feared any interference with their superstitious, illiterate subjects.

The intellectuals and mullahs both felt that the shah was giving away Iran's assets and resources to foreigners. For a long time the intellectuals were the only group to complain; the illiterate Iranian masses could not be expected to protest against actions they knew nothing about. But in 1890 the shah gave a 50-year concession to a Briton named Talbot for a monopoly over the export and distribution of tobacco. Faced with higher prices for the tobacco they grew themselves, Iranians staged a general strike and boycott, and the shah was forced to cancel the concession. The pattern of local protest leading to mass rebellion, with all population groups uniting against an arbitrary ruler, was to be duplicated in the Constitutional Revolt of 1905 and again in the 1979 Revolution.

By the end of the nineteenth century the people were roused to action, the mullahs had turned against the ruler, and the intellectuals were demanding a Constitution that would limit his powers. One of the intellectuals wrote, "It is self-evident that in the future no nation—Islamic or non-Islamic—will continue to exist without constitutional law . . . The various ethnic groups that live in Iran will not become one people until the law upholds their right to freedom of expression and the opportunity for [modern] education."[9] Nearly a century and two revolutions later Iran is still struggling to put this formula into operation.

According to Roy Mottahedeh, "the bazaar and the mosque are the two lungs of public life in Iran."[10] The bazaar, like the Greek agora and the Roman forum, is the place where things are bought, deals are consummated, and political issues are aired for public consideration or protest. The mosque is the bastion of religious opinion; its preachers can, and do, mobilize the faithful to action through thundering denunciations of rulers and government officials. Mosque and bazaar came together in 1905 to bring about the first Iranian Revolution, a forerunner at least in pattern of the 1979 revolt. Two sugar merchants were bastinadoed (a punishment, still used in Iran, of beating the soles of the feet with a cane) because they refused to lower their prices; they complained that high import prices set by the government gave them no choice. The bazaar then closed down in protest. With commercial activity at a standstill, the shah agreed to establish a "house of justice" and to promulgate a constitution. But 6 months later he had done nothing. Then a mullah was arrested, shot, and killed for criticizing the ruler in a Friday sermon. Further protests were met with mass arrests and then gunfire; "a river of blood now divided the court from the country."[11]

In 1906 nearly all of the religious leaders left Teheran for the sanctuary of Qum, Iran's principal theological-studies center. The bazaar closed down again, a general strike paralyzed the country, and thousands of Iranians took refuge in the British Embassy in Teheran. With the city paralyzed, the shah gave in. He granted a Constitution that provided for an elected Majlis (Parliament), the first limitation on royal power in Iran in its history. Although four more shahs would occupy the throne, two of them as absolute rulers, the 1906 Constitution and the elected legislature survived as brakes on absolutism until the 1979 Revolution. In this sense, the Islamic Republic is the legitimate heir to the constitutional movement.

The Pahlavi Dynasty

Iran was in chaos at the end of World War I. British and Russian troops partitioned the country, and after the collapse of Russian power due to the Communist Revolution, the British dictated a treaty with the shah that would have made Iran a British protectorate. Azeris and Kurds talked openly of independence, and a Communist group, the Jangalis, organized a "Soviet Republic" of Gilan along the Caspian coast.

The only organized force in Iran at this time was the Cossack Brigade. Its commander was Reza Khan, a villager from an obscure family who had risen through the ranks on sheer ability. In 1921 he seized power in a bloodless coup, but he did not overthrow the shah. The shah appointed him prime minister and then left the country for a comfortable exile in Europe, never to return.

Iran's neighbor, Turkey, had just become a republic, and many Iranians felt that Iran should follow the same line. But the religious leaders wanted to keep the monarchy, fearing that a republican system would weaken their authority over the illiterate masses. The religious leaders convinced Prime Minister Reza that Iran was not ready for a republic. In 1925 Reza was crowned as shah, with an amendment to the Constitution that defined the monarchy as belonging to Reza Shah and his male descendants in succession. Since he had no family background to draw upon, Reza chose a new name for his dynasty:

Pahlavi. It was a symbolic name, derived from an ancient province and language of the Persian Empire.

Reza Shah was one of the most powerful and effective monarchs in Iran's long history. He brought all ethnic groups under the control of the central government and established a well-equipped standing army to enforce his decrees. He did not tamper with the Constitution; instead, he approved all candidates for the Majlis and outlawed political parties, so that the political system was entirely responsible to him.

Reza Shah's New Order

Reza Shah wanted to build a "new order" for Iranian society, and he wanted to build it in a hurry. He was a great admirer of Mustafa Kemal Ataturk, founder of the Turkish republic. Like Ataturk, he believed that the religious leaders were an obstacle to modernization, due to their control over the masses. He set out to break their power through a series of reforms. Lands held in religious trust were leased to the state, depriving the religious leaders of income. A new secular code of laws took away their control, since the secular code would replace Islamic law. Other decrees prohibited the wearing of veils by women and the fez, the traditional brimless Muslim hat, by men. When religious leaders objected, Reza Shah had them jailed; on one occasion he went into a mosque, dragged the local mullah out in the street, and horsewhipped him for criticizing the ruler in a Friday sermon.

In 1935 a huge crowd went to the shrine of Imam Reza, the eighth Shia Imam, in Meshad, to hear a parade of mullahs criticize the shah's ruthless reform policies. Reza Shah ringed the shrine with troops, and when the crowd refused to disperse they opened fire, killing a hundred people. It was the first and last demonstration organized by the mullahs during his reign. Only one religious leader, a young scholar named Ruhollah al-Musavi al-Khomeini, consistently dared to criticize the shah, and he was dismissed as being an impractical teacher.

Iran declared its neutrality during the early years of World War II. But Reza Shah was sympathetic to Germany; he had many memories of British interference in Iran. He allowed German technicians and advisers to remain in the country, and he refused to allow war supplies to be shipped across Iran to the Soviet Union. In 1941 British and Soviet armies simultaneously occupied Iran. Reza Shah abdicated in favor of his son, Crown Prince Mohammed, and was taken into exile on a

British warship. He never saw his country again.

Mohammed Reza Pahlavi

When the new shah came to the throne few suspected that he would rule longer than his father and hold even more absolute power. Mohammed Reza Pahlavi was young (22) and inexperienced, and found himself ruling a land occupied by British and Soviet troops and threatened by Soviet-sponsored separatist movements in Azerbaijan and Kurdistan. Although these movements were put down with U.S. help, a major challenge to the shah developed in 1951–1953.

A dispute over oil royalties between the government and the Anglo-Iranian Oil Company (AIOC) aroused intense national feeling in Iran. Mohammed Mossadegh, a long-time Majlis member and ardent nationalist, was asked by the shah in 1951 to serve as prime minister and to implement the oil-nationalization laws passed by the Majlis. The AIOC responded by closing down the industry, and all foreign technicians left the country. The Iranian economy was not affected at first, and Mossadegh's success in standing up to the company, which most Iranians considered an agent of foreign imperialism, won him enormous popularity.[12]

Mossadegh served as prime minister from 1951 to 1953, a difficult time for Iran due to loss of oil revenues and internal political wrangling. Although his policies embroiled him in controversy, Mossadegh's theatrical style—public weeping when moved, fainting fits, a preference for conducting public business in pajamas from his bed, a propensity during speeches to emphasize a point by ripping the arm from a chair—enhanced his appeal to the Iranian people. His radio "fireside chats" soon won him a mass following; he became more popular than the shy, diffident young shah, and for all practical purposes he ruled in Iran.

However, by 1953 economic difficulties and Mossadegh's repressive measures had cost him most of his popularity. A contest of wills between the shah and his prime minister followed, ending as the shah left the country. However, the United States, through the CIA (which feared that a communist plot to take over Iran was behind Mossadegh), helped to mobilize mass demonstrations against Mossadegh. Fortunately for the shah, the prime minister's support base was shallow, coming mostly from leftist intellectuals and members of the Tudeh (Masses), a pro-Soviet political party. The army officer corps, the middle class and the *bazaris*, the powerful community of merchants and small business owners in city bazaars, stood firm behind their ruler, while CIA agents with discreet use of minimal funds mobilized the masses in huge street parades. In August 1953 the shah returned to his country in triumph. He then gradually gathered all authority in his hands and developed the vast internal security network that eliminated parliamentary opposition.[13]

By the 1960s the shah felt that he was ready to lead Iran to greatness. In 1962 he announced the Shah-People Revolution, also known as the White Revolution. It had six basic points: land reform, public ownership of industries, nationalization of forests, voting rights for women, workers' profit sharing, and a literacy corps to implement compulsory education in rural areas. The plan drew immediate opposition from landowners and religious leaders. But only one spoke out forcefully against the shah: Ayatollah Ruhollah Khomeini, now the most distinguished of Iran's religious scholars. "I have repeatedly pointed out that the government has evil intentions and is opposed to the ordinances of Islam," he said in a public sermon.[14] His message was short and definite: the shah is selling out the country; the shah must go.

Khomeini continued to criticize the shah, and in June 1963 he was arrested. Demonstrations broke out in various cities. The shah sent the army into the streets, and again a river of blood divided ruler from country. Khomeini was released, rearrested, and finally exiled to Iraq. For the next 15 years he continued attacking the shah in sermons, pamphlets, and broadsides smuggled into Iran through the "bazaar network" of merchants and village religious leaders. Some had more effect than others. In 1971, when the shah planned an elaborate coronation at the ancient Persian capital of Persepolis to celebrate 2,500 years of monarchy, Khomeini declared, "Islam is fundamentally opposed to the whole notion of monarchy. The title of King of Kings . . . is the most hated of all titles in the sight of God. . . . Are the people of Iran to have a festival for those whose behavior has been a scandal throughout history and who are a cause of crime and oppression . . . in the present age?"[15]

Yet, until 1978, the possibility of revolution in Iran seemed to be remote. The shah controlled all the instruments of power. His secret service, SAVAK, had informers everywhere. The mere usage of a word such as "oppressive" to describe the weather was enough to get a person arrested. Whole families disappeared into the shah's jails and were never heard from again.

The public face of the regime, however, seemed to indicate that Iran was on its way to wealth, prosperity, and international importance. The shah announced a 400-percent increase in the price of Iranian oil in 1973 and declared that the country would soon become a "Great Civilization." Money poured into Iran, billions more each year. The army was modernized with the most sophisticated U.S. equipment available. A new class of people, the "petro-bourgeoisie," became rich at the expense of other classes. Instead of the concessions given to foreign business firms by penniless Qajar shahs, the twentieth-century shah became the dispenser of opportunities to businesspeople and bankers to develop Iran's great civilization with Iranian money—an army of specialists imported from abroad.

In 1976 the shah seemed at the pinnacle of his power. His major adversary, Khomeini, had been expelled from Iraq and was now far away in Paris. U.S. President Jimmy Carter visited Iran in 1977 and declared, "Under your leadership (the country) is an island of stability in one of the more troubled areas of the world."[16] Yet a month later 30,000 demonstrators marched on the city of Qum, protesting an unsigned newspaper article (reputed to have been written by the shah) that had attacked Khomeini as being anti-Iranian. The police fired on the demonstration and a massacre followed.

Gradually, a cycle of violence developed. It reflected the distinctive rhythm of Shia Islam, wherein a death in a family is followed by 40 days of mourning and every death is a martyr for the faith. Massacre followed massacre in city after city. In spite of the shah's efforts to bring modernization to his country, it seemed to more and more Iranians that he was trying to undermine the basic values of their society by striking at the religious leaders. Increasingly, marchers in the streets were heard shouting, "Death to the shah!"

Even though the shah held absolute power, he seemed less and less able or willing to use his power to crush the opposition. It was as if he were paralyzed. He wrote in his last book, "A sovereign may not save his throne by shedding his countrymen's blood. . . . A sovereign is not a dictator. He cannot break the alliance that exists between him and his people."[17] The shah vacillated as the opposition intensified. His regime was simply not capable of self-reform or of accepting the logical consequences of liberalization, of free elections, a return to constitutional monarchy, and the emergence of legitimate dissent.[18]

THE ISLAMIC REPUBLIC

The shah and his family left Iran for good in January 1979. Ayatollah Ruhollah Khomeini returned from exile practically on his heels, welcomed by millions who had fought and bled for his return. The shah's Great Civilization lay in ruins. Like a

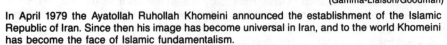

(Gamma-Liaison/Goodman)

In April 1979 the Ayatollah Ruhollah Khomeini announced the establishment of the Islamic Republic of Iran. Since then his image has become universal in Iran, and to the world Khomeini has become the face of Islamic fundamentalism.

transplant, it had been an attempt to impose a foreign model of life on the Iranian community, a surgical attachment that had been rejected.

In April 1979 Khomeini announced the establishment of the Islamic Republic of Iran. He called it the first true republic in Islam, since the original community of believers was formed by Muhammad. Khomeini said that religious leaders would assume active leadership, serve in the Majlis, even fight Iran's battles as "warrior mullahs." A Council of Guardians was set up to interpret laws and ensure that they were in conformity with the sacred law of Islam. Although the republic is governed under a Constitution with an elected president and legislature, final authority is reserved to a Velayat-e-Faqih ("Supreme Legal Guide"), who is responsible only to God.

Khomeini, as the first Supreme Guide, embodied the values and objectives of the republic. Because he saw himself in that role, he consistently sought to remain above factional politics yet to be accessible to all groups and render impartial decisions. But the demands of the war with Iraq, the country's international isolation, conflicts between radical Islamic fundamentalists and advocates of secularization and other divisions forced the aging Ayatollah into a day-to-day policy-making role. It is a role that he was not well prepared for, given his limited experience beyond the confines of Islamic scholarship. Quite possibly the war with Iraq, for example, could have been settled earlier if it were not for Khomeini's vision of a pure Shia Iran fighting a just war against the atheistic secular regime of Saddam Hussein.

A major responsibility of the Council of Guardians was to designate—with his approval—a successor to Khomeini as Supreme Legal Guide. In 1985 the council chose Ayatollah Hossein Ali Montazeri, a former student and close associate of the bearded patriarch, to succeed him. Montazeri, although politically inexperienced and lacking Khomeini's charisma, had directed the exportation of Iranian Islamic fundamentalist doctrine to other Islamic states after the Revolution, with some success. This responsibility had identified him abroad as the architect of Iranian-sponsored terrorist acts such as the taking of hostages in Lebanon. But during his brief tenure as Khomeini's designated successor he helped make changes in prison administration, revamped court procedures to humanize the legal system and reduce prisoner mistreatment, and urged a greater role for opposition groups in political life. However, Montazeri resigned in March 1989 after publishing an open letter, which aroused Khomeini's ire, criticizing the mistakes made by Iranian leaders during the Revolution's first decade.

The Islamic Republic staggered from crisis to crisis in its initial years. Abol Hassan Bani-Sadr, a French-educated intellectual who had been Khomeini's right-hand man in Paris, was elected president in 1980 by 75 percent of the popular vote. But it was one of the few postrevolutionary actions that united a majority of Iranians. Although the United States, as the shah's supporter and rescuer in his hour of exile, became Iran's "Great Satan" and thus helped to maintain revolutionary fervor, the prolonged crisis over the holding of American hostages by guards who would take orders from no one but Khomeini embarrassed Iran and damaged its credibility more than any gains made from tweaking the nose of a superpower.

Revolutions historically often seem to end by devouring those who carry them out. A great variety of Iranian social groups had united to overthrow the shah. They had different views of the future; an "Islamic republic" meant different things to different groups. The Revolution first devoured all those associated with the shah, in a reign of terror intended to compensate for 15 years of repression. Islamic tribunals executed thousands of people—political leaders, intellectuals, and military commanders.

The major opposition to Khomeini and his fellow religious leaders came from the radical group Mujahideen-i-Khalq. The Mujahideen favored an Islamic socialist republic and were opposed to too much government influence by religious leaders. However, the Majlis was dominated by the religious leaders, many of whom had no experience in government and knew little of politics beyond the village level. As the conflict between these groups sharpened, bombings and assassinations occurred almost daily.

The instability and apparently endless violence during 1980–1981 suggested to the outside world that the Khomeini government was on the point of collapse. Iraqi President Saddam Hussein thought so, and in September 1980 he ordered his army to invade Iran, an action that proved to be a costly mistake. President Bani-Sadr was dismissed by Khomeini after an open split developed between him and religious leaders over the conduct of the war, and he subsequently escaped to France. A series of bombings carried out by the Mujahideen in mid-1981 killed a number of Khomeini's close associates, including the newly elected president of the republic.

The Khomeini regime showed considerable resilience in dealing with its adversaries. The Mujahideen were ruthlessly repressed in 1983. This organization had been in the vanguard of the struggle against the shah, but once the republic had been established, the religious leaders came to view its Marxist, and therefore atheist, members as their major internal enemy. The Mujahideen's principal leader, Massoud Rajavi, escaped to France, but many of his associates were hunted down and killed. In 1986 the French expelled him, along with about a thousand of his supporters, as part of an effort to cultivate better relations with Iran. The Iraqi government granted him asylum.

Toward the end of the Iran-Iraq War the Mujahideen took advantage of Iraqi successes to seize several towns inside Iran, freeing political prisoners and executing minor officials, such as prison wardens, without trial. But the organization has little internal support in the country. Its Marxist views are not shared by the majority of people, and Mujahideen claims of 90,000 executions and more than 150,000 political prisoners held by the regime are believed to be wildly exaggerated.

However, the Rafsanjani government is as ruthless as the shah's was in hunting down its opponents. In 1990 Rajavi's brother was killed by unknown gunmen in Geneva, Switzerland. In August 1991 Shahpour Bakhtiar, the last prime minister under the monarchy, was murdered under similar circumstances in Paris, where he had been living in exile. Although the elderly Bakhtiar had been opposed to the shah as well as to Khomeini, fellow exile and former Iranian President Bani-Sadr charged that the regime had a hit list of opponents, including himself and the former prime minister, slated for execution.

The other main focus of opposition was the Tudeh (Masses) Party. Although considered a Communist party, its origins were in the constitutional movement of 1905–1907, and it has always been more nationalistic than Soviet oriented. The shah banned the Tudeh after an assassination attempt on him in 1949, but it revived during the Mossadegh period of 1951–1953. After the shah returned from exile in 1953, the Tudeh was again banned and went underground. Many of its leaders fled to the Soviet Union. After the 1979 Revolution the Tudeh again came out into the open and collaborated with the Khomeini regime. It was tolerated by the religious leaders for its nationalism, which made its Marxism acceptable. Being militarily weak at that time, the regime also wished to remain on good terms with its Soviet neighbor. However, the rapprochement was brief. In 1984 top Tudeh leaders were arrested in a series of surprise raids and given long prison terms.

PROSPECTS

The Revolution that overturned one of the most ruthless authoritarian regimes in history has been in effect long enough to provide some clues to its future direction. One clue is the continuity of internal politics. Despite wreaking savage vengeance on persons associated with the shah's regime, Khomeini and his fellow mullahs preserved most of the Pahlavi institutions of government. The Majlis, civil service, secret police, and armed forces were continued as before, with minor modifications to conform to strict Islamic practice. The main addition was a parallel structure of revolutionary courts, paramilitary Revolutionary Guards (Pasdaran), workers' and peasants' councils, plus the Council of Guardians as the watchdog over legislation.

In the first years of the Revolution the mullah, in his somber robe and turban, inspired more respect among Iranians than the "Mr. Engineer" type in his Western business suit, the symbol of modernization in the shah's time. But later, political institutions, and particularly the Majlis, began to show a growing secular configuration. The 1984 Majlis, for example, included more professionals and technicians than its predecessor and fewer religious leaders.

The 1985 presidential election in Iran continued this secular trend. The ruling Islamic Republican Party (since dissolved) nominated President Ali Khamenei for a second term, against token opposition. However, Mehdi Bazargan, the republic's first prime minister, who subsequently went into opposition and founded the Freedom Movement, announced that he would be a candidate. The Council of Guardians vetoed his candidacy on the grounds that his opposition to the war with Iraq, although well publicized, would be damaging to national solidarity if he ran for president. Although Khamenei won reelection handily, nearly 2 million votes were cast for one of the two opposition candidates, a religious leader. The relatively high number of votes for this candidate reflected increasing dissatisfaction with the Khomeini regime's no-quarter policy toward Iraq, rather than opposition to the regime itself.

The formal end of the war with Iraq—resulting in the recovery of all Iranian territory, repatriation of prisoners, opening of the Shatt al-Arab, and freedom of navigation in the Strait of Hormuz and the

Persian Gulf— was regarded by the population as a victory for Iranian persistence and patience. But in its foreign relations, the regime remains unpredictable. It played an active behind-the-scenes role in the release of Western hostages in Lebanon in 1990 and 1991, possibly reflecting a desire for improved relations with Western countries, both for economic reasons and to enable Iran to resume its important role in regional affairs. Balancing these efforts is a determined campaign to eliminate opponents even at the risk of alienating other nations, as shown by the murder of ex-Prime Minister Bakhtiar and the refusal by the regime to suspend the death sentence of Salman Rushdie, author of *The Satanic Verses*. This campaign underscores the division in the government between the "pragmatists," who seek accommodation with the West, and the "hardliners," who want no accommodation at all.

The division has continued to hamper internal political and social development. The ruling Islamic Republican Party set up by Khomeini was dissolved several years ago when the Imam decreed that it was superfluous. In 1990 three political parties were approved by the Majlis in preparation for scheduled 1992 elections. But, in principle, political action in Iran remained more a product of fractious individualism than of organized political parties.

A similar fractiousness and individualism affects social issues in Iran. Thus the imposition after the Revolution of the strict Islamic dress code for women, including the full veil (*hejab*), was relaxed slightly in 1984, whereupon fundamentalists led violent demonstrations to compel the government to reinstate it. Middle-class women, many of them emancipated in the shah's time, became second-class citizens under the republic, segregated or discriminated against the work place and threatened with the death penalty for violations of the dress code.

IRAN AFTER KHOMEINI

In June 1989 Ayatollah Ruhollah Khomeini died of a heart attack in a Teheran hospital. He was 86 years old and had struggled all his life against the authoritarianism of two shahs, but his vision of a unified, purified Islamic republic in Iran had lasted barely a decade.

Behind him the Imam left a society reshaped by his uncompromising Islamic ideals and principles. Every aspect of social life in republican Iran is governed by these principles, from prohibition of the production and use of alcohol and drugs to a strict dress code for women outside the home, compulsory school prayers, em-

phasis on theological studies in education, and required fasting during Ramadan. One positive result of this Islamization program has been a renewed awareness among Iranians of their cultural identity and pride in their heritage.

Khomeini also bequeathed many problems to his country. The most immediate problem concerned the succession to him as Supreme Legal Guide. Earlier he had appointed an Expediency Council to resolve differences between the Majlis and the Council of Constitutional Guardians, a 12-member group that determines whether or not laws passed by the Majlis are compatible with Islam.

The succession question was resolved quickly. The Assembly of Theological Experts, a body comprising the country's senior theologians and religious jurists, elected President Ali Khamenei as the new Guide. Khamenei, a *Hojatulislam* (lower-ranking religious leader) had been scheduled to step down as president in October 1989, since he was limited by law to two 4-year terms. Khomeini's mantle of religious infallibility was passed on to Grand Ayatollah Ali Araki, his 95-year-old former teacher, and Iranians in the Imam's inner circle of followers were urged to go to the senior cleric for guidance in personal and spiritual matters.

The 1989 Presidential Election

Amendments to the 1979 interim Constitution were approved by the voters in a July 1989 referendum to make it into a more permanent document. The most important amendment abolished the office of prime minister. Henceforth Cabinet ministers will be responsible directly to the president. Another important change provides that any theologian may be elected as Supreme Legal Guide, regardless of rank.

The presidential election was advanced from the scheduled October date to July in order to expedite the post-Khomeini transfer of leadership. There were only two candidates: Speaker of the Majlis Ali Akbar Hashemi Rafsanjani and former Agriculture Minister Sheibani. The credentials of 78 other candidates were dismissed by the Council of Constitutional Guardians for various reasons. As had been expected, Rafsanjani won handily, garnering 95 percent of the 14.1 million votes cast. His first Cabinet, which was approved by the Majlis after considerable debate but by comfortable majorities in each case, consisted almost exclusively of pragmatists and technocrats; missing were a number of hardliners who had consistently opposed the president's policies of improved relations with the non-Islamic

The Persian Empire under Cyrus the Great and his successors includes most of ancient Near East and Egypt 551–331 B.C.	The Sassanid Empire establishes Zoroastrianism as the state religion A.D. 226–641	Islamic conquest at the battles of Qadisiya and Nihavard 637, 641	The Safavid shahs develop national unity based on Shia Islam as the state religion 1520–1730

world and foreign investment to aid post-war reconstruction.

Rafsanjani's election and the establishment of a "moderate" leadership pragmatically committed to improved Iranian relations with the outside world and economic progress at home produced some changes, especially in the former arena. Iran remained neutral during the Gulf War, signing a formal peace treaty with Iraq to end their former hostilities and allowing Iraqi pilots sanctuary in the early stages of the conflict. (However, their aircraft have yet to be returned to Iraq.) Iran also used its influence over the Lebanese Shia Hizbullah militia in 1991 to help UN negotiators secure the release of the last American hostages in Lebanon.

THE ECONOMY

Iran's bright economic prospects during the 1970s were largely dampened by the 1979 Revolution. Petroleum output was sharply reduced, and the war with Iraq crippled industry as well as oil exports. Khomeini warned Iranians to prepare for a decade of grim austerity before economic recovery would be sufficient to meet domestic needs. After the ceasefire with Iraq, Khomeini enlarged upon his warning, saying that the world would be watching to see if the Revolution would be destroyed by postwar economic difficulties.

The end of the war with Iraq and Iran's strong external fiscal position—nearly all foreign debts were paid by 1990 and reserves were $7 billion—suggest that the Imam's fears had been exaggerated. Serious problems remain, including 25 percent unemployment, 40 percent inflation, and an inefficient and cumbersome bureaucracy. The middle class has been hard hit; per capita income for its members plummeted, from $1,600 in 1988 to $1,200 in 1991. Such peculiarly Iranian customs as *khodyari* ("voluntary sacrifice"), by which parents are required to pay the costs of free public education for their children, have had a negative effect on personal economies. However, the 1990–1991 budget of $80 billion, $28 billion of it for development, was to be financed entirely from internal sources. Deficit spending, the bugbear of many oil-producing countries, has become a relic of the past in post-Khomeini Iran.

Until 1970 Iran was self-sufficient in food. The White Revolution redistributed a considerable amount of land, most of it from estates that Reza Shah had confiscated from their previous owners. But the new owners, most of them former tenant farmers, lacked the capital, equipment, and technical knowledge needed for a productive agriculture. The revolutionary period caused another upheaval in agriculture, as farmers abandoned their lands to take part in the struggle and fighting between government forces and ethnic groups disrupted production. Production dropped 3.5 percent in 1979–1980, the first full year of the Islamic Republic of Iran, and continued to drop at the same rate through 1982. A rural development agency, the Crusade for Construction, was formed in 1979 to encourage urban migrants to return to the land; funds were made available to help them reestablish themselves in rural areas and aid small farmers with projects such as roads, schools, electricity, and small-scale dams to provide a dependable water supply. But opposition from well-to-do landowners, who were expected to pay most of the costs of the projects, along with budget cutbacks during the war and time-consuming disputes over land titles hampered the agency's effectiveness.

Another rural development program, Jihad-i-Sazandegi, begun in 1989, has been more effective because of its emphasis on an integrated system of meeting social needs on the basis of allocation of various components of rural infrastructure to different villages within a particular district, enabling these districts to become self-sufficient.

Petroleum is Iran's major resource and the key to economic development. Oil was discovered there in 1908, making the Iranian oil industry the oldest in the Middle East. Until 1951 the Anglo-Iranian Oil

(UN photo)

Iran is a land of paradox, with political upheaval contrasted with the serene majesty of some of the world's most beautiful monuments. Picture above are the dome and minarets of the Madraseh-yi-Madar-i-Shah, a religious college.

The constitutional movement limits the power of the shah by the Constitution and legislature 1905–1907	The accession of Reza Shah, establishing the Pahlavi dynasty 1925	The abdication of Reza Shah under Anglo-Soviet pressure; he is succeeded by Crown Prince Mohammed Reza 1941	The oil industry is nationalized under the leadership of Prime Minister Mossadegh 1951–1953	The shah introduces the White Revolution 1963	Revolution overthrows the shah; Iran becomes an Islamic republic headed by Ayatollah Khomeini 1979–1980

1980s–1990s

The Khomeini regime rejects UN Security Council resolution for ceasefire and peace talks with Iraq	The war with Iraq comes to an end; Khomeini dies	Iran's economy recovers; foreign relations improve

Company produced, refined, and distributed all Iranian oil. After the 1951–1953 nationalization period, when the industry was closed down, a consortium of foreign oil companies—British, French, and American—replaced the AIOC. In 1973 the industry was again nationalized and operated by the state-run National Iranian Oil Company.

After the Revolution political difficulties affected oil production, as the United States and its allies boycotted Iran due to the hostage crisis, and other customers balked at the high prices ($37.50 per barrel in 1980 as compared to $17.00 per barrel a year earlier). The war with Iraq was a further blow to the industry. Japan, Iran's biggest customer, stopped purchases entirely in 1981–1982. War damage to the important Kharg Island terminal reduced Iran's export capacity by one-third, and the Abadan refinery was severely crippled. Periodic Iraqi raids on other Iranian oil terminals in more distant places such as Lavan and Qeshm, reachable by longer-range aircraft, seriously decreased Iran's export output. Yet the economy displayed an extraordinary ability to rebound from economic crises. The end of the war set off a major reconstruction effort. The Abadan refinery, the country's oldest and largest, resumed production in 1989 after a 9-year hiatus. Industrial plants, the Ahwaz and Isfahan steel complexes, petrochemical facilities, and ports were restored to service. A major natural-gas strike near the Caspian Sea, completion of the new Nur-Kangan refinery on the Persian Gulf coast, and

planned resumption of gas exports to Russia are hoped to generate greatly increased revenues from hydrocarbons.

Another favorable economic prospect, with political implications for the 1990s, is the conclusion of the work of an international tribunal in The Hague, Netherlands, to resolve claims by U.S. companies against Iran for services and equipment provided during the shah's regime and counterclaims by Iran for nondelivery of equipment. By 1990 U.S. claims had been reduced to $2 billion, with settlement of an Amoco claim for $600 million. The United States in turn paid Iran $200 million in compensation for undelivered military equipment.

NOTES

1. Richard F. Nyrop, ed., *Iran, A Country Study* (Washington: American University, Foreign Area Studies, 1978), p. 12.

2. Teheran is a relatively new city for Iran. It was founded in the early nineteenth century and was chosen as the capital due to its central location. In 1900 its population was 200,000. *Ibid.*, p. 77.

3. Byron J. Good, "Azeri," in R. V. Weekes, ed., *Muslim Peoples: A World Ethnographic Survey,* 2nd edition (Westport: Greenwood Press, 1984), p. 69.

4. Daniel G. Bates, "Kurds," in *Ibid.*, p. 425.

5. *cf. The New Yorker* (February 4, 1985), p. 31. The writer notes that "merely being a member of that Bahai community is now, in effect, a crime."

6. Golamreza Fazel, "Persians," in Weekes, *op. cit.*, p. 610. "Face-saving is in fact one of the components of *Ta'aruf,* along with assertive masculinity *(gheyrat).*"

7. John Malcolm, *History of Persia,* 2 vols. (London: John Murray, 1829), Vol. II, p. 303.

8. Ervand Abrahamian, *Iran Between Two Revolutions* (Princeton: Princeton University Press, 1982), p. 48.

9. Roy Mottahedeh, *The Mantle of the Prophet* (New York: Simon & Schuster, 1985), p. 52.

10. *Ibid.*, p. 34.

11. Abrahamian, *op. cit.*, p. 83.

12. "Oil is our blood!" the crowds in Teheran chant enthusiastically. Ryszard Kapuscinski, "Reflections—Iran, Part I," *The New Yorker* (March 4, 1985), p. 82.

13. Robert Graham, *Iran: The Illusion of Power* (New York: St. Martin's Press, 1978), pp. 61–62.

14. Imam Khomeini, *Islam and Revolution,* transl. by Hamid Algar (Berkeley: Mizan Press, 1981), p. 175.

15. *Ibid.*, p. 202.

16. Mohammed Reza Pahlavi, Shah of Iran, *Answer to History* (New York: Stein and Day, 1980), pp. 152–153.

17. *Ibid.*, p. 167.

18. Sepehr Zabih, *Iran's Revolutionary Upheaval: An Interpretive Essay* (San Francisco: Alchemy Books, 1979), pp. 46–49.

DEVELOPMENT

Revenues from oil and gas exports rose to $15 billion in 1990, the highest since the Revolution. The 1990–1994 5-year-plan sets investment at $394 billion, only $27 billion from foreign sources.

FREEDOM

Amendments to the 1979 Constitution make Iran more of a "presidential republic" than in the past, with extensive powers reserved to the president, who acts as his own prime minister. However, the tradition of vigorous dissent, with the Majlis serving as a forum for public debate (among other functions), continues.

HEALTH/WELFARE

A large-scale program to combat illiteracy, currently 32%, sets up 400 literacy centers throughout the country. The 14 million adult illiterates in Iran will be required to attend these centers.

ACHIEVEMENTS

Jihad-i-Sazandegi, a rural community organization, has had great success in providing paved access roads, electricity, and potable water to 11,000 villages. Recently the organization set up 40,000 Islamic village councils in 650 districts to integrate farms, small industries, schools, health clinics, and tractor stations on a district-by-district basis.

Iraq (Republic of Iraq)*

GEOGRAPHY

Area in Square Kilometers (Miles):
434,924 (167,924) (larger than
California)
Capital (Population): Baghdad
(3,400,000)
Climate: mostly hot and dry

PEOPLE

Population

Total: 18,782,000
Annual Growth Rate: 3.5%
Rural/Urban Population Ratio: 29/71
Ethnic Makeup of Population: Arab;
Kurdish; Turkish, Assyrian, and
others

Health

Life Expectancy at Birth: 65 years
(male); 68 years (female)
Infant Mortality Rate (Ratio):
67/1,000
Average Caloric Intake: 127% of FAO
minimum
Physicians Available (Ratio): 1/3,324

Religion(s)

55% Shia Muslim; 40% Sunni
Muslim; 5% Christian and others

Education

Adult Literacy Rate: 90%

COMMUNICATION

Telephones: 624,685
Newspapers: 4 main dailies in
Baghdad (one in English with
200,000 circulation)

TRANSPORTATION

Highways—Kilometers (Miles):
25,500 (15,810)

Railroads—Kilometers (Miles): 2,032
(1,259)
Usable Airfields: 96

GOVERNMENT

Type: officially a republic; in reality a
single-party secular state with an
absolute ruler
Independence Date: October 3, 1932,
as kingdom; July 14, 1958, as
republic
Head of State: President-for-Life
Saddam Hussain, who also heads the
Revolutionary Command Council
Political Parties: Ba'th (Iraqi branch
of Arab Socialist Resurrection Party),
only legal party
Suffrage: universal for adults

MILITARY

Number of Armed Forces: n/a
*Military Expenditures (% of Central
Government Expenditures):* n/a
Current Hostilities: none

ECONOMY

Currency ($ U.S. Equivalent): 0.03
Iraqi dinar = $1
Per Capita Income/GNP: n/a
Inflation Rate: 1,400%
Total Foreign Debt: n/a
Natural Resources: oil; natural gas;
phosphates; sulfur; lead; gypsum
Agriculture: wheat; barley; rice;
cotton; dates; poultry
Industry: petroleum; petrochemicals;
textiles; cement

FOREIGN TRADE

Exports: $11.4 billion
Imports: $11.0 billion

*Note: The effects of Iraq's war with the
coalition forces led by the United States
(January 16–February 28, 1991) cannot be
accurately reflected in these statistics.
Those noted are the most current available.

EVEN BEFORE BABYLON

Four thousand years ago Babylon was a world-class city, capital of a
great empire centered in the Tigris-Euphrates plain. Biblical tradition
holds that the Tower of Babel, where men first "spake in tongues," was
located there. The Garden of Eden was nearby according to tradition.
The Hanging Gardens, laid out on artificial hills by a king to please his
queen, who was homesick for her northern mountains, were one of the
Seven Wonders of the ancient world. Saddam Hussain, who fancies
himself a modern Nebuchadnezzar, a decade ago ordered the rebuilding
of Babylon as a historic monument, using 15'million bricks baked by the
method used in the original construction of the city. Every 100th brick
bears his name in Arabic. However, work stopped during the Gulf War
and has not resumed, due to lack of funds and qualified staff.

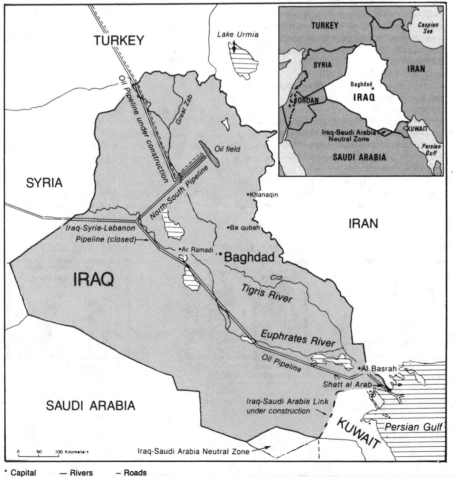

IRAQ

The Republic of Iraq is a young state in a very old land. In ancient times its central portion was called Mesopotamia, meaning "land between the rivers." The rivers are the Tigris and the Euphrates, rivers that originate in the highlands of Turkey and flow southward for more than a thousand miles to join in an estuary called the Shatt al-Arab, which carries their joint flow into the Persian (or, to Iraqis, the Arab) Gulf.

The fertility of the land between the rivers encouraged human settlement and agriculture from an early date. The oldest farming community yet discovered anywhere was unearthed near Nineveh, capital of the Assyrian Empire, in 1989; it dates back to 9000 B.C. Other settlements grew in time into small but important cities, with local governments, their economies based on trade and crafts production in addition to agriculture. And the process of using a written alphabet with characters rather than symbols probably originated here.

Modern Iraq (an Arabic word meaning "cliff" or, less glamorously, "mudbank") occupies a much larger territory than the original Mesopotamia. The current total land area is 167,924 square miles, about the size of California. Iraqi territory also includes a Neutral Zone of 3,522 square miles on the border with Saudi Arabia. Iraq's other borders are with Turkey, Syria, Jordan, Kuwait, and Iran. These borders were established by the British on behalf of the newly formed Iraqi government, which they controlled after World War I. The only one in dispute is the boundary with Iran down the Shatt al-Arab. This dispute has a long history of bitter conflict behind it, and it was one of the major causes of the war between Iraq and Iran that broke out in 1980.

HISTORY

During its long and rich history, the land between the rivers has seen many empires rise and fall. Assyrians, Babylonians, Chaldeans, Persians, and others contributed layer upon layer to Mesopotamian civilization. Archaeologists digging at the site of Nimrud, a major Assyrian city, uncovered in 1989 the 2,700-year-old tomb of a royal princess within the grounds of the palace of King Ashurnasirpal II, containing a vast store of her jewelry—55 pounds in all.

Despite the many varied influences, the most important influence in Iraqi social and cultural life today comes from the conquest of the region by Islamic Arabs. In A.D. 637 an Arab army defeated the Persians, who were then rulers of Iraq, near the village of Qadisiya, not far from modern Baghdad, a victory of great symbolic importance for Iraqis today. Arab peoples settled the region and intermarried with the local population, producing the contemporary Iraqi-Arab population.

During the early years of Islam, Iraq played an important role in Islamic politics. It was a center of Shia opposition to the Sunni Muslim caliphs. The tombs of Ali, Muhammad's son-in-law and the fourth and last leader of a united caliphate, and his son Husayn, martyred in a power struggle with his Damascus-based rival Yazid, are both in Iraq, at Najaf and Karbala respectively.

In the period of the Abbasid caliphs (A.D. 750–1258) Iraq was the center of a vast Islamic empire stretching from Morocco on the west to the plains of India. Caliph al-Mansur laid out a new capital for the world of Islam, some 60 miles from the ruins of Babylon. He named his new capital Baghdad, possibly derived from a Persian word for "garden," and, according to legend, laid bricks for its foundations with his own hand. Baghdad was a round city, built in concentric circles, each one walled, with the caliph's green-domed palace and mosque at the center. It was the world's first planned city, in the sense of having been laid out on a definite urban configuration and design. Under the caliphs, Baghdad became a center of science, medicine, philosophy, law, and the arts, at a time when London and Paris were mud-and-wattle villages. The city became wealthy from the goods brought by ships from Africa, Asia, and the Far East, since it was easily reachable by shallow-draught boats from the Gulf and the Indian Ocean moving up the Tigris to its harbor.

Baghdad was destroyed by an invasion of Central Asian Mongols in A.D. 1258. The Mongols overran most of the Middle East. In addition to ravaging cities, they ruined the complex irrigation system that made agriculture possible and productive in the land between the rivers. Modern Iraq has yet to reach the level of agricultural productivity of Abbasid times, even with the use of sophisticated technology.

After the fall of Baghdad, Iraq came under the rule of various local princes and dynasties. In the sixteenth century it was included in the expanding territory of the Safavid Empire of Iran. The Safavid shah championed the cause of Shia Islam, and as a result, the Ottoman sultan, who was Sunni, sent forces to recover the area from his hated Shia foe. Possession of Iraq went back and forth between the two powers, but eventually the Ottomans established control.

Iraq was administered as three separate provinces under appointed Ottoman governors. The governors paid for their appointments and were interested only in recovering their losses. The result was heavy taxation and indifference to social and economic needs. The one exception was the province of Baghdad. It was governed by a man whom today we would call an enlightened administrator. This governor, Midhat Pasha, set up a provincial newspaper, hospitals, schools, munitions factories, and a fleet of barges to carry produce downriver to ports on the Gulf. His administration also ensured public security and an equitable taxation system. Midhat Pasha later became the grand vizier (prime minister) of the Ottoman Empire and was the architect of the 1876 Constitution, which limited the powers of the sultan.

The British Mandate

World War I found England and France at war with Germany and the Ottoman Empire. British forces occupied Iraq, which they rechristened Mesopotamia, early in the war. British leaders had worked with Arab leaders in the Ottoman Empire to launch a revolt against the sultan and in return promised that they would help the Arabs form an independent Arab state once the Ottomans had been defeated. A number of prominent Iraqi officers who were serving in the Ottoman Army then joined the British and helped them in the Iraqi campaign.

The British promise, however, was not kept. The British had made other commitments, notably to their French allies, to divide the Arab provinces of the Ottoman Empire into British and French "zones of influence." An independent Arab state in those provinces was not in the cards.

The most the British (and the French) would do was to organize protectorates, called *mandates,* over the Arab provinces, promising to help the population become self-governing within a specified period of time. The arrangement was approved by the new League of Nations in 1920. Iraq became a British mandate, with a government under British advisers, but was headed by its own monarch, King Faisal I.

The British kept their promise with the mandate. They worked out a Constitution for Iraq in 1925 that established a constitutional monarchy with an elected Legislature and a system of checks and balances. Political parties were allowed, although most of them were groupings around prominent personalities and had no platform other than independence from the United Kingdom.[1] In 1932 the mandate formally ended, and Iraq became an independent kingdom under Faisal. The British kept the use of certain air bases, and their large capital investment in the oil industry was protected through a 25-year treaty of alliance. Otherwise the new Iraqi nation was on its own.

The Iraqi Monarchy, 1932–1958

The new kingdom cast adrift on perilous international waters was far from being a unified nation. It was more of a patchwork of warring and competing groups. The Muslim population was divided into Sunni and Shia, as it is today, with the Sunnis forming a minority but controlling the government and business and dominating urban life. The Shia, although a majority, were mostly rural peasants and farmers, many of them migrants to the cities, where they formed a large underclass. The Kurds, the largest non-Arab Muslim group, had been incorporated arbitrarily into the kingdom by the action of the League of Nations, when it confirmed the British mandate. They bitterly resented both Arab and British administration.

The country also had large Christian and Jewish communities, the latter tracing its origins back several thousand years to the exile of Jews from Palestine to Babylonia after the conquest of Jerusalem by Nebuchadnezzar. The Christians made up several denominational groups, such as Chaldeans (Assyrians), pre-Islamic residents of Mesopotamia, Yazidis ("devil-worshippers"), and Sabeans, lineal descendants of the ancient Babylonians. The Christians were protected and favored by the British, especially in the police and civil services; the British found them more cooperative than the Sunni Arabs.

These social and ethnic divisions, plus the economic and educational gaps between rural peasants and urban merchants and landowners, made the new state all but impossible to govern, let alone develop politically.[2]

King Faisal I was the single stabilizing influence in Iraqi politics, and his untimely death in 1933 was critical. His son and successor, Ghazi, was more interested in racing cars than anything else and was killed at the wheel of one in 1939. Ghazi's infant son succeeded him as King Faisal II, while Ghazi's first cousin became regent until the new ruler came of age.

Lacking strong direction from the top, leadership in the kingdom shifted among a small group of politicians, landlords, wealthy merchants, and local leaders. They controlled the legislature and the Cabinet. One author notes that in the period 1932–1936, there were 22 different governments, headed by various prime ministers.[3] No effort was made to broaden the base of participation in the government or to develop responsible political parties. Nuri al-Said, who served many times as prime minister, compared the Iraqi political system to a small pack of cards. You must shuffle them often, he said, because the same faces keep turning up.

THE REVOLUTION OF 1958

By the late 1950s the regime had become out of step with the rest of the Arab world and out of touch with its people. It was aligned with the West through the 1955 Baghdad Pact, a treaty linking Iraq, Iran, Pakistan, and Turkey with the United Kingdom and sponsored by the United States. Iraq's membership alienated most Iraqi young people, who were Arab nationalists, from their own government. Increasing oil revenues seemed to enrich only the already-prosperous landlords, merchants, and politicians.

Resentment crystallized in the Iraqi Army. On July 14, 1958, a group of young officers overthrew the monarchy in a swift, predawn coup. The king, regent, and royal family were killed. Iraq's new leaders proclaimed a republic that would be reformed, free, and democratic, united with the rest of the Arab world and opposed to all foreign ideologies, "Communist, American, British or Fascist."[4]

Iraq has been a republic since the 1958 Revolution, and July 14 remains a national holiday. But the republic has passed through many different stages, with periodic coups, changes in leadership, and political shifts, most of them violent. Continuing sectarian and ethnic hatreds, maneuvering of political factions, ideological differences, and lack of opportunities for legitimate opposition to express itself without violence have created a constant sense of insecurity among Iraqi leaders. A similar paranoia affects Iraq's relations with its neighbors. The competition for influence in the Arab world and the Persian/Arab Gulf and other factors combine to keep the Iraqi leadership constantly on edge.

This pattern of political instability showed itself in the coups and attempted coups of the 1960s. The republic's first two leaders were overthrown after a few years. Several more violent shifts in the Iraqi government took place before the Ba'th Party seized control in 1968. Since that time the party has dealt ruthlessly with internal opposition. A 1978 decree outlawed all political activity outside the Ba'th for members of the armed forces. Many Shia clergy were executed in 1978–1979 for leading antigovernment demonstrations after the Iranian Revolution, and following Saddam Hussein's election to the presidency he purged a number of members of the Revolutionary Command Council (RCC) on charges of a plot to overthrow the regime.

THE BA'TH PARTY IN POWER

The Ba'th Party in Iraq began as a branch of the Syrian Ba'th founded in the 1940s by two Syrian intellectuals, Michel Aflaq, a Christian teacher, and Salah al-Din Bitar, a Sunni Muslim. Like its Syrian parent, the Iraqi Ba'th was dedicated to the goals of Arab unity, freedom, and socialism. However, infighting among Syrian Ba'th leaders in the 1960s led to the expulsion of Aflaq and Bitar. Aflaq went to Iraq, where he was accepted as the party's true leader. Eventually he moved on to Paris, where he died in 1989. His body was brought back to Iraq for burial, giving the Iraqi Ba'th a strong claim to legitimacy in its struggle with the Syrian Ba'th for hegemony in the movement for Arab unity.

The basis of government under the Ba'th is the 1970 provisional Constitution, issued unilaterally by the Revolutionary Command Council, the party's chief decision-making body. It defined Iraq as a sovereign peoples' democratic republic. The Constitution also provided for an elected National Assembly, although its powers were limited to ratification of laws and decisions made by the RCC. In 1980 and again in 1984 elections were held for such an Assembly, the first since the 1958 Revolution which overthrew the monarchy.

An abortive coup in 1973, which pitted a civilian faction of the Ba'th against the military leadership headed by President Bakr, stirred party leaders to attempt to broaden their base of popular support. They reached agreement with the Iraqi Communist Party to set up a Progressive National Patriotic Front. Other organizations and groups joined the front later. Although the Iraqi Communist Party had cooperated with the Ba'th on several occasions, the agreement marked its first legal recognition as a party. However, mutual distrust between the two organizations deepened as Ba'th leaders struggled to mobilize the masses. The Communists withdrew from the Front in 1979 and refused to participate in parliamentary elections. Their party was declared illegal in 1980 and has not been reinstated, largely due to its support for Iran during the Iran-Iraq War.

SADDAM HUSSEIN

Politics in Iraq since the 1958 overthrow of the monarchy have been marked by extreme secrecy. The intrigues and maneuvers of factions within the Ba'th take place off-screen, and there is no tradition of public pressure to bring them to account. In assessing the strengths, capabilities, and prospects for survival of Iraq's Ba'th leaders, a good question beyond "Who are they?" is "Will the Iraqi ruling class please stand up?"[5] But in the late 1970s and early '80s one of its leaders, Saddam Hussain, emerged from the pack to become an absolute ruler.

Saddam Hussain's early history did not suggest such an achievement. He was born in 1937 in the small town of Tikrit, on the Tigris halfway between Baghdad and Mosul. Tikrit's chief claim to fame, until the twentieth century, was that it was the birthplace of Saladin, hero of the Islamic world in the Middle Ages against the Crusaders. (The Iraqi leader has at times identified himself with Saladin as another great Takriti, although Saladin was a Kurd and Saddam Hussain's distrust for the Kurds is well known.) His family, who were freeholding tribal cultivators from the village of Shawish near Takrit, belonged to the Begat tribe of the Al Bu Nasser tribe, farming about 12 acres of land there. While still in school he became a founding member of the Iraqi branch of the Ba'th Party and took part in its struggles against rival groups, surviving endless internal conflicts to work his way up to vice chair of the Revolutionary Command Council and finally to chair the body, after his elderly predecessor had retired due to ill health. As chair he became automatically president of Iraq under the 1970 Constitution. As there are no constitutional provisions limiting the terms of office for the position, in 1990 the National Assembly named him president-for-life.

Saddam Hussain is a somewhat unusual head of state, in that he holds supreme elective offices although he has never stood as a candidate in an election and serves as commander of the armed forces although he has never served in the military. He does have considerable leadership assets, such as personal courage, a gambler's instinct in decision-making, personal magnetism, and charisma. But his major asset is his control over the party, the army, and secret services, and the absolute loyalty of his supporters. He has also placed family members in important positions, to such an extent that the government is often referred to as the "Takriti regime."[6]

The Iran-Iraq War provided a severe test for the Ba'th and its leader. A series of Iraqi defeats with heavy casualties in the mid-1980s suggested that the Iranian demand for Hussain's ouster as a precondition for peace might ignite a popular

(Homer Sykes/Katz/Woodfin)

The image of Saddam Hussain has become part of the Iraqi landscape; his portrait appears in public buildings, at the entrances to cities, in homes, even on billboards along highways.

uprising against him. But Iranian advances into Iraqi territory, and in particular the capture of the Fao Peninsula and the Majnoon oil fields, united the Iraqis behind Saddam Hussain. For one of the few times in its history, the nation coalesced around a leader and a cause.

The Iraqi leader used this support to cultivate a more popular public image. In addition to visiting the war front regularly, he traveled to villages for whistle-stop appearances, helped with the harvests, and mingled with the people. Portraits of Saddam Hussain in field marshal's uniform, Bedouin robes, Ba'th Party green fatigues, or Italian designer suits, complete with the peasant *keffiyeh* (headscarf) of his native region, are common everywhere in Iraq—in public buildings, at the entrances to cities, in offices and even homes, or on huge highway billboards.

RECENT DEVELOPMENTS

The end of the war with Iran and Saddam Hussain's popularity as the heroic defender of the Iraqi Arab nation against the Shia Iranian enemy prompted a certain lifting of Ba'thist repression and authoritarian rule. Emergency wartime regulations in force since 1980 were relaxed in 1989, and an amnesty was announced for all political exiles except "agents of Iran."

In July 1990 the RCC and the Arab Ba'th Regional Command, the party's governing body, approved a draft constitution which was expected to replace the 1970 interim one after submission to the voters in the fall for their anticipated approval. In addition to legalizing opposition political parties, the new constitution would establish press freedom, civil liberties, and elections for a Consultative Assembly, which would work in tandem with the existing National Assembly in framing laws. The RCC promised that it would disband after the constitutional referendum and elections for the Consultative Assembly.

The August 1990 invasion of Kuwait and the resulting Gulf War in early 1991 halted these moves toward a broadening of the political process. But inasmuch as Iraq's defeat on the battlefield was not followed by the overthrow of Saddam Hussain, the process has resumed in recent months. Marking the Ba'th Party's 23rd anniversary, the Iraqi leader launched a restructuring of the party to strengthen its power base, to restore public confidence, and, at least on the surface, to continue inching toward a pluralist political system. Elections were held for local and provincial party leaders, the first since 1979, and a number of long-time Ba'thist government officials were defeated.

However, the RCC approved amendments to the new draft constitution that would ban any parties based on religion, race, or ties with foreign governments. All prospective parties would be required to include support for Iraqi territorial integrity in their founding principles.

A change in Ba'th Party rules would also allow members to resign without being subjected to interrogation by security forces. Another move toward revitalization of the moribund governing system was the annulment of wartime labor laws limiting the rights, pay, and freedom to work of civil servants. During the Iran-Iraq War and also during the Gulf War, they had been prohibited from leaving government service to take higher-paying jobs in private industry or from taking second or third jobs to supplement their meager government salaries ($50 to $70 per month). In addition, the 1989 amnesty offer was renewed; it would include Shia and Kurdish rebels and soldiers who deserted their units during the Gulf War.

THE KURDS

The Kurds, the largest non-Arab minority in Iraq today, form a relatively compact society in the northern mountains. Kurdish territory was included in the British mandate after World War I, because British troops were already there and the territory was known to have important oil resources. The Kurds agitated for self-rule periodically during the monarchy, and for a few months after World War II formed their own republic in Kurdish areas straddling the Iraq-Iran and Iraq-Turkey borders.

In the 1960s the Kurds rebelled against the Iraqi government, which had refused to meet their three demands (self-government in Kurdistan, use of Kurdish in schools, and a greater share in oil revenues). The government sent an army to the mountains but was unable to defeat the Kurds, masters of guerrilla warfare. Conflict continued intermittently into the 1970s, with periodic ceasefires. Although the 1970 Constitution named Arabs and Kurds as the two nationalities in the Iraqi nation and established autonomy for Kurdistan, the Iraqi government had no real intention of honoring its pledges to the Kurds.

A major Iraqi offensive in 1974 had considerable success against the Kurdish *Pesh Merga* ("Resistance"), even capturing several mountain strongholds. At that point, the shah of Iran, who had little use for Saddam Hussain, began to supply arms to the Pesh Merga. The shah also kept the Iraq-Iran border open as sanctuary for the guerrillas.

In 1975 a number of factors caused the shah to change his mind. He signed an agreement with Saddam Hussain, redefining the Iran-Iraq border to give Iran control over half the Shatt al-Arab. In return, the shah agreed to halt support for the Kurds. The northern border was closed, and without Iranian support, Kurdish resistance collapsed. For more than a decade the Kurdish region was relatively quiet. But in 1986 Iran, in another twist of policy, resumed support for Kurdish resistance groups. The main group, the Patriotic Union of Kurdistan, agreed to put its fighters under Iranian command, and in turn the Khomeini regime renounced its goal of an Islamic republic in Iraq. Early in 1987 joint Kurdish-Iranian forces captured a number of villages and mountain strongpoints in northern Iraq. But after the ceasefire with Iran, the Iraqi government turned on the Kurds. Disregarding international criticism, the army swept into Kurdish areas, using mustard gas and other chemical weapons to crush the resistance and destroying many Kurdish villages. More than 60,000 Kurds took refuge in Turkey.

A second exodus of Kurdish refugees took place in 1991, after uprisings of Kurdish rebels in northern Iraq were brutally suppressed by the Iraqi Army, which had remained loyal to Saddam Hussain. The United States and its allies sent troops and aircraft to the Iraqi-Turkish border and barred Iraq from using its own air space north of the 36th Parallel, the main area of Kurdish settlement. Several hundred thousand refugees subsequently returned to their homes and villages.

However, de facto Kurdish control of northern Iraq and U.S. protection of the Kurds have yet to produce a formal agreement between them and the Iraqi government. Negotiations between leaders of the two main Kurdish groups—the Kurdish Democratic Party (KDP), headed by Masoud Barzani, and the Patriotic Union of Kurdistan (PUK), led by Jalal Talabani—and the government began in earnest in March 1991. The negotiations are based on a 1970 autonomy agreement, originally made with these same leaders by Saddam Hussain, but never implemented. The agreement would make Kurdish an official language, establish a Kurdish university, provide for internal autonomy for Kurdistan with greater representation for Kurds in the government, and give the Kurds a greater share in oil revenues from northern oil fields.

THE SHIA COMMUNITY

Although Shias form the largest population group in Iraq, they have been ruled by the Sunni minority ever since independence. With a few exceptions (notably the current prime minister, Saadun Hammadi), the Shia have been consistently underrepresented in successive Ba'thist governments. Iraq's Shias remained loyal during the war with Iran, but the only concession by the government to their status or economic deprivation was the rebuilding of sacred Shia shrines such as the tomb of the Imam Hussein, whose dome was gold-leafed at considerable expense.

After the defeat and expulsion of Iraqi forces from Kuwait, Shia rebels staged an uprising and briefly seized control of the holy cities of Najaf and Karbala. Some 300 local Ba'thist officials were executed as the rebels took out their economic and political frustration on them as agents of the regime. But the army remained loyal to Saddam Hussain, and elite units supported by tanks and artillery crushed the outnumbered rebels. About 600 were killed, most of them in an Alamo-type last stand in the shrines, which were badly damaged.

THE ECONOMY

Iraq's economy is based on oil production and exports, but it has a well-developed agriculture (Iraq is the world's leading exporter of dates) due to the fertile soil and water resources of the Tigris and Euphrates Rivers. It also has a large population and a skilled labor force available for industrial development.

Since the Ba'th Party took control in 1968 its economic policies have emphasized state control and guidance of the economy, under the Ba'thist rubric of guided socialism. But starting in 1987 the regime began a major economic restructuring program. More than 600 state organizations were abolished, and young technocrats replaced many senior ministers. In 1988 the government began selling state-run industries to private management, reserving only heavy industry and hydrocarbons for state operation. Light industries such as breweries and dairy plants will henceforth be run by the private sector.

The oil industry was developed by the British during the mandate but was nationalized in the early 1970s. Nationalization and price increases after 1973 helped to accelerate economic growth. The bulk of Iraqi oil shipments are exported via pipelines across Turkey and Syria. During the war with Iran the Turkish pipeline proved essential to Iraq's economic survival, since the one across Syrian territory was closed and Iraq's own refineries and ports were put out of commission by

| Border province of the Ottoman Empire 1520–1920 | British mandate 1920–1932 | Independent kingdom under Faisal I 1932 | The monarchy is overthrown by military officers 1958 | The Ba'th Party seizes power 1963 | The Algiers Agreement between the shah of Iran and Hussain ends Kurdish insurrection 1975 | 1980s–1990s |

| Iraqi forces invade Iran, initiating war; diplomatic relations are restored with United States after a 17-year break | A pipeline is completed from Iraqi oil fields to port Yanbu on the Red Sea, bypassing the Gulf; the war with Iran comes to an end after 8 bitter years | Iraq invades and occupies Kuwait, leading to the intense but brief Gulf War; Saddam Hussain retains power |

Iranian attacks. Turkey closed this pipeline during the 1990–1991 Gulf crisis, a decision that proved a severe strain for the Iraqi economy (not to mention a huge sacrifice for coalition-member Turkey).

Iraq has proven oil reserves of 100 billion barrels, the fifth largest in the world, and new discoveries continue to augment the total. Oil output was cut to 2 million barrels per day in 1986–1987, in accordance with quotas set by the Organization of Petroleum Exporting Countries, but was increased to 4.5 million b/d in 1989 as the country sought to recover economically from war damage.

The country also has natural-gas reserves of 2.69 billion cubic meters and significant deposits of phosphate rock, sulfur, lead, gypsum, and iron ore.

The economic impact of the 8-year Iran-Iraq War was heavy, causing delays in interest payments on foreign loans, defaults to some foreign contractors, and postponement of major development projects except for dams, deemed vital to agricultural production. The war also was a heavy drain on Iraqi finances; arms purchases between 1981 and 1985 cost the government $23.9 billion, and by 1986 the external debt was $12 billion. By 1988 the debt burden had gone up to nearly $60 billion, although half this total had been given by the Arab Gulf states as war aid and was unlikely ever to be repaid.

PROSPECTS

Iraq's economic recovery after the war with Iran, despite heavy external debts, suggested rapid growth in the 1990s. Gross domestic product was expected to rise by 5 percent a year due to increasing oil revenues. Even in 1988, Iraq's GDP of $50 billion was the highest in the Arab world, after Saudi Arabia's. With a well-developed infrastructure and a highly trained work force, Iraq appeared ready to move upward in the ranks of the developed nations.

The Gulf War all but destroyed these optimistic prospects. Bombing raids destroyed much of the country's infrastructure, knocking out electricity grids and sewage and water-purification systems. The UN embargo, which was continued after the war as a device to force Saddam's compliance with UN resolutions regarding Iraqi nuclear and chemical warfare facilities, hit hardest on the population. The wheat harvest for 1991–1992 was 837,000 tons, a 60-percent drop from prewar totals, due to the embargo on farm machinery and pesticide and fertilizer imports. Shortages of medical equipment and supplies, and refusal to allow Iraq to sell oil to pay for food and medicines (although these were subsequently exempted from the embargo), intensified malnutrition and prospects of high levels of child mortality, well above the normal for a country such as Iraq.

Yet its isolation not only increased Iraqi will to resist the embargo but united the population behind Saddam. The first anniversary of the Gulf War generated huge patriotic celebrations throughout the country as Iraqis celebrated their leader's "Steadfastness and Defiance" in resisting U.S. and UN pressures. With anti-Saddam opposition confined to exile groups, it seemed unlikely in 1992 that the leader would be overthrown other than by foreign intervention.

NOTES

1. The parties had names like "Free," "Awakening," "Nationalists," and "National Independence." Richard F. Nyrop, *Iraq: A Country Study* (Washington: American University, Foreign Area Studies, 1979), p. 38.

2. " . . . sectors were divided within themselves, politicians working against their colleagues, shaykhs perpetuating traditional rivalries . . . fellahin resenting the exploitation of urban landlords and tribal shaykhs alike. . . ." Mohammad A. Tarbush, *The Role of the Military in Politics: A Case Study of Iraq to 1941* (London: Kegan Paul, 1982), p. 50.

3. *Ibid.*, p. 50.

4. Nyrop, *op. cit.*, pp. 48–49.

5. Joe Stork, "State Power and Economic Structure . . ." in Tim Niblock, ed., *Iraq: The Contemporary State* (London: Croom Helm, 1982), p. 44.

6. See Milton Viorst, "Letter From Baghdad," *The New Yorker* (June 24, 1991), p. 61.

DEVELOPMENT

Iraq's development program was halted during the Gulf War. The country's resources have since been concentrated on rebuilding the war-damaged infrastructure.

FREEDOM

A draft constitution legalizing opposition parties and providing for press freedom and civil rights was approved by the National Assembly in 1990. Neither the draft constitution nor the agreement for Kurdish autonomy and rights has been approved by the ruling Revolutionary Command Council. Unless they are Iraq will likely remain a one-party state, one of the most repressive in the world.

HEALTH/WELFARE

A "social contract" between the Ba'th and the Iraqi people has exchanged dictatorial government for social and economic progress. The result has been a better life for the population. By 1990 child mortality was reduced 66%, life expectancy was up from 48 years to an average 65 years, and adult literacy has risen from 30% to almost 90%.

ACHIEVEMENTS

Opening of the new lube oil refinery at Basra, once the embargo is lifted, will add significantly to Iraq's exports. The refinery has a capacity of 100,000 tons of lubricants and 150,000 tons of asphalt a year.

Israel (State of Israel)

GEOGRAPHY
Area in Square Kilometers (Miles): 20,325 (7,850) (about the size of Delaware)
Capital (Population): Jerusalem (457,000), not recognized by United States and most other governments that maintain embassies in Tel Aviv (322,000)
Climate: temperate, except in desert areas

PEOPLE

Population
Total: 4,371,000 (excludes East Jerusalem and settlements on West Bank and Gaza Strip)
Annual Growth Rate: 1.7%
Rural/Urban Population Ratio: 11/89
Ethnic Makeup of Population: 83% Jewish; 17% non-Jewish (mostly Arab)

Health
Life Expectancy at Birth: 74 years (male); 78 years (female)
Infant Mortality Rate (Ratio): 10/1,000
Average Caloric Intake: 115% of FAO minimum
Physicians Available (Ratio): 1/345

Religion(s)
83% Jewish; 13% Muslim; 2% Christian; 2% Druze

Education
Adult Literacy Rate: 88% (Jewish); 70% (Arab)

COMMUNICATION
Telephones: 1,940,000
Newspapers: 23 dailies, 20 in Hebrew

COOPERATIVE SETTLEMENTS

A unique feature of Israeli society is the cooperative settlements called *moshavim* and *kibbutzim*, originally developed to meet the needs of an untrained Jewish immigrant population having to adjust to difficult conditions in a new land. The moshavim are cooperative small land-holders' associations. All members work their own land, but their economic and social security are assured by the cooperative in the village where they live. The kibbutzim are collective ownership communities with communal living arrangements. Members pool their labor, income, and expenses. All kibbutzniks have equal rights; action is voluntary and liability is shared. Kibbutz members have contributed significantly to the building of a Jewish state in Palestine; David Ben-Gurion, Israel's principal leader for 3 decades, lived in and retired to Kibbutz Sde Boker, in the Negev.

TRANSPORTATION
Highways—Kilometers (Miles): 12,980 (8,047)
Railroads—Kilometers (Miles): 790 (498)
Usable Airfields: 53

GOVERNMENT
Type: parliamentary democracy with numerous parties reflecting religious, minority, and other group interests

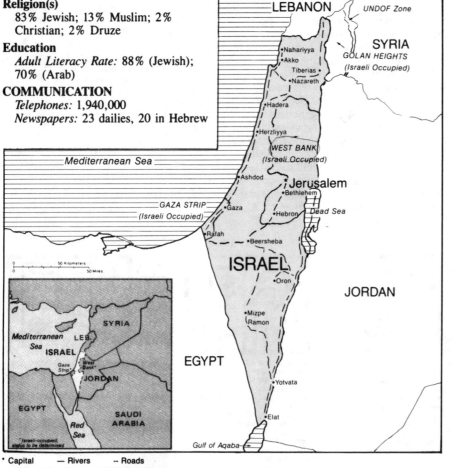

and membership
Independence Date: May 14, 1948
Head of State: President Chaim Herzog; *Head of Government:* Prime Minister Yitzhak Shamir
Political Parties: Likud Bloc, currently ruling alone but formerly in coalition with Labor and then with minor religious parties; Labor Alignment, main opposition; various minor parties
Suffrage: universal over 18

MILITARY
Number of Armed Forces: 141,000
Military Expenditures (% of Central Government Expenditures): 26%
Current Hostilities: periodic conflict with the Palestinian population in the West Bank and Gaza Strip

ECONOMY
Currency ($ U.S. Equivalent): 1.32 shekels = $1
Per Capita Income/GNP: $9,790/$36 billion
Inflation Rate: 48%
Total Foreign Debt: n/a
Natural Resources: copper; phosphates; bromide; potash; clay; sand; sulfur, bitumen; manganese
Agriculture: citrus and other fruits; vegetables; beef, dairy, and poultry products
Industry: food processing; diamond cutting and polishing; textiles and clothing; chemicals; metal products; transport and electrical equipment; potash mining; high-technology electronics

FOREIGN TRADE
Exports: $10.7 billion
Imports: $13.1 billion

ISRAEL

Israel, the Holy Land of Judeo-Christian tradition, is a very small state about the size of Delaware. Its population is also smaller than that of most of its neighbors, with low birth and immigration rates. Both its size and population growth would be manageable if it were not for the fact that its territory, boundaries, and very existence are in dispute.

The country occupies a larger land area than it held at the time of its independence in 1948, due to expansion wars with its neighbors. Its borders with Lebanon, Syria, and Jordan were established by armistice agreements and remain provisional pending a final peace settlement. The border with Egypt, which extends southward from the Mediterranean Sea to the Gulf of Aqaba, along the eastern side of the Sinai Peninsula, was defined by the 1979 Egyptian-Israeli peace treaty and confirmed by the withdrawal of Israeli troops from the Sinai in 1982. Egypt is thus far the only one of its neighbors to

have any formal relations with Israel. (A provisional agreement between Israel and Lebanon for the withdrawal of Israeli troops was subsequently cancelled by the Lebanese government.)

Although it is small, Israel has a complex geography, with a number of distinct regions. The northern region, Galilee, is a continuation of the Lebanese mountains, but at a lower altitude. The Galilee uplands drop steeply on three sides: to the Jordan Valley on the east, a narrow coastal plain on the west, and southward to the Valley of Esdraelon, a broad inland valley from the Mediterranean to the Jordan River. This lowland area is fertile and well watered and has become important to Israeli agriculture.

Another upland plateau extends south from Esdraelon for about 90 miles. It contains the ancient Jewish heartland—Judea and Samaria, often referred to as the West Bank—with Nablus, Hebron, and Jerusalem as the main cities. This plateau gradually levels off into semidesert, the

barren wilderness of Judea. The wilderness merges imperceptibly into the Negev, a desert region that comprises 60 percent of the land area but has only 12 percent of the population. Despite the importance to Israel of the Negev's mineral resources, the nuclear reactor and facility at Dimona, and the port of Eilat, the region has received little in the way of development funds in recent years and remains the least developed and most impoverished in the country, with a 25-percent unemployment rate and low productivity.

CURRENT TERRITORY

Israeli territory currently includes four areas occupied during the 1967 and 1973 wars: the Gaza Strip on the Mediterranean, the Golan Heights along the Syrian border, the West Bank of the Jordan River, and East Jerusalem. The Gaza Strip was part of Egypt; the West Bank and East Jerusalem were Jordanian territories. The Golan Heights, which Israel considers strategically important to its defenses, was annexed unilaterally in 1981, although it is legally within Syria, in the United Nations demilitarized zone.

Israeli occupation of the West Bank and East Jerusalem have generated a great deal of controversy within Israel as well as internationally. Many Israelis consider the West Bank as an integral part of the Jewish homeland granted by God to Abraham and his descendants; they refer to the territory as Judea and Samaria exclusively. A small but growing number of Israelis openly advocate the expulsion of the entire Arab population from the West Bank, and some urge that expulsion be extended to Arabs living in Israel proper. Other Israelis feel that the West Bank should either be returned to Jordan or become a self-governing Palestinian state; they call it "trading land for peace."

In the case of East Jerusalem, there is no disagreement among Israelis. They regard Jerusalem as a single city and as their spiritual and political capital. However, almost all other nations consider Tel Aviv, near the coast, as the Jewish capital and maintain their embassies there. A resolution in the U.S. Congress to recognize Jerusalem as the capital has only symbolic significance.

THE POPULATION

The great majority of the Israeli population is Jewish. Judaism is the state religion, and Hebrew, the ancient liturgical language revived and modernized in the twentieth century, is the official language, although English is widely used. Language and religion, along with shared historical traditions, a rich ancient culture, and a commitment to the survival of

(Israeli Government Tourism Administration)

Israelis regard Jerusalem as the political and spiritual capital of Israel. East Jerusalem was annexed from Jordan after the 1967 Six-Day War, and returning this part of the city to Jordan has never been considered seriously.

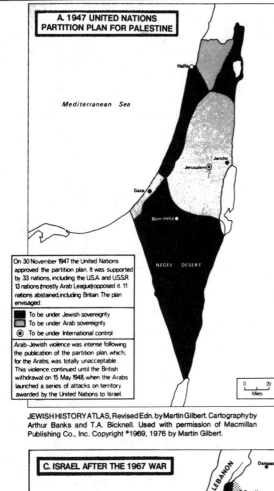

A. 1947 UNITED NATIONS PARTITION PLAN FOR PALESTINE

Mediterranean Sea

Haifa

Jericho

Jerusalem

Gaza

Beer-sheba

NEGEV DESERT

On 30 November 1947 the United Nations approved the partition plan. It was supported by 33 nations, including the U.S.A. and U.S.S.R. 13 nations (mostly Arab League) opposed it. 11 nations abstained, including Britain. The plan envisaged:

- To be under Jewish sovereignty
- To be under Arab sovereignty
- To be under International control

Arab-Jewish violence was intense following the publication of the partition plan, which, for the Arabs, was totally unacceptable. This violence continued until the British withdrawal on 15 May 1948, when the Arabs launched a series of attacks on territory awarded by the United Nations to Israel.

0   20
Miles

JEWISH HISTORY ATLAS, Revised Edn. by Martin Gilbert. Cartography by Arthur Banks and T.A. Bicknell. Used with permission of Macmillan Publishing Co., Inc. Copyright ®1969, 1976 by Martin Gilbert.

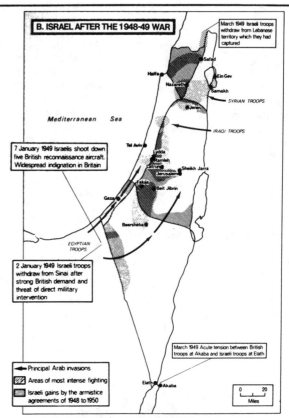

B. ISRAEL AFTER THE 1948-49 WAR

March 1949 Israeli troops withdraw from Lebanese territory which they had captured

Safad

Ein Gev

Haifa

Nazareth

Samakh

SYRIAN TROOPS

Jenin

IRAQI TROOPS

Mediterranean Sea

Tel Aviv

7 January 1949 Israelis shoot down five British reconnaissance aircraft. Widespread indignation in Britain

Lydda
Ramleh
Latrun
Jerusalem

Sheikh Jarra

Fahma

Beit Jibrin

Gaza

EGYPTIAN TROOPS

Beersheba

2 January 1949 Israeli troops withdraw from Sinai after strong British demand and threat of direct military intervention

March 1949 Acute tension between British troops at Akaba and Israeli troops at Elath

Elath   Akaba

- Principal Arab invasions
- Areas of most intense fighting
- Israeli gains by the armistice agreements of 1948 to 1950

0   20
Miles

JEWISH HISTORY ATLAS, Revised Edn. by Martin Gilbert. Cartography by Arthur Banks and T.A. Bicknell. Used with permission of Macmillan Publishing Co., Inc. Copyright ®1969, 1976 by Martin Gilbert.

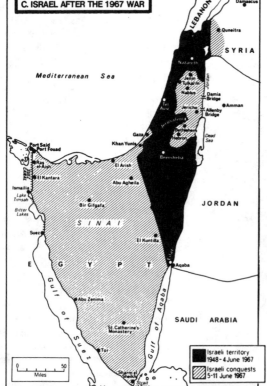

C. ISRAEL AFTER THE 1967 WAR

LEBANON

Damascus

Quneitra

SYRIA

Nazareth

Mediterranean Sea

Jenin
Tulkarm
Nablus

Damia Bridge

Tel Aviv

Jericho

Allenby Bridge

Amman

Jerusalem

Gaza

Bethlehem

Hebron

Dead Sea

Khan Yunis

Port Said
Port Fouad

Ras el Aish

El Arish

El Kantara

Abu Agheila

Ismailia

Lake Timsah

Bir Gifgafa

Bitter Lakes

SINAI

JORDAN

Beersheba

Suez

El Kuntilla

E G Y P T

Aqaba

Gulf of Suez

Abu Zenima

Gulf of Aqaba

SAUDI ARABIA

St. Catherine's Monastery

Tor

Sharm el Sheikh

Strait of Tiran

0   50
Miles

- Israeli territory 1948-4 June 1967
- Israeli conquests 5-11 June 1967

JEWISH HISTORY ATLAS, Revised Edn. by Martin Gilbert. Cartography by Arthur Banks and T.A. Bicknell. Used with permission of Macmillan Publishing Co., Inc. Copyright ®1969, 1976 by Martin Gilbert.

0 Miles   100

LEBANON

Beirut

SYRIA

Damascus

MEDITERRANEAN SEA

Golan Heights

Haifa

ISRAEL

Tel-Aviv

West Bank

R Jordan

Amman

Jerusalem

Gaza

Dead Sea

Port Said

JORDAN

Suez Canal

SINAI

EGYPT

Suez

Eilat

Aqaba

Gulf of Suez

Gulf of Aqaba

SAUDI ARABIA

RED SEA

- Israeli-controlled areas

Borders of Israel and Israeli controlled areas as depicted in THE ECONOMIST of July 20, 1985.

the Jewish state, have fostered a strong sense of national unity among the Israeli people. They are extremely nationalistic, and these feelings are increased because of hostile neighbors. Most Israelis believe that their neighbors are determined to destroy their state, and this belief has helped to develop a "siege mentality" among them.

Although Israeli Jews are a unified people, in a state sense, they have come out of widely varying backgrounds and places of origin. Because Jews were dispersed throughout the world for nearly 2,000 years, they barely survived as a people. The two main population groups in terms of origin are the Ashkenazic (European) and Sephardic (Oriental) Jews. The Ashkenazi, the founders of the Jewish state, came from various European countries.[1] The Sephardim, Jews from "Oriental" lands—Turkey, various Arab countries, and North Africa—were later immigrants, except for those indigenous to Palestine. The two groups had little in common except their religion. They had become so isolated from each other over centuries of dispersal that they spoke different languages and could not communicate. Hebrew, until the twentieth century, was one of the few communication links among widely scattered Jewish communities, being used as a literary and liturgical language.

The diversity among incoming Jews, and particularly the Sephardic communities, was so great during the early years of independence that the government developed a special orientation program of Hebrew language and culture, called Ulpan (which is still in use), to help with their assimilation. Some Sephardic groups have prospered and gained economic and political equality with Ashkenazis; Foreign Minister David Levy, for example, originally emigrated from Morocco. However, the majority of Sephardim have yet to attain full equality, and this is an added cause of tension.

Another difference among Israelis has to do with religious practice. The Chasidim or Orthodox Jews strictly observe the rules and social practices of Judaism and live in their own separate neighborhoods within cities. Reform Jews, by far the majority, are Jewish in their traditions, history, and faith, but modify their religious practices to conform to the demands of modern life and thought. Both the Orthodox and Reform Jews have chief rabbis who sit on the Supreme Rabbinical Council, the principal interpretive body for Judaism. There are also two small Jewish communities of ancient origin, the Karaites and the Samaritans, who reject rab-

(UN photo/John Isaac)

The Wailing Wall, a focal point of Jewish worship, is all that remains of the ancient temple destroyed by the Roman legions led by Titus in A.D. 70. The Wailing Wall stands as a place of pilgrimage for devout Jews throughout the world.

binical authority and keep themselves separate from the main body of Jews.

Other than occasional incidents of friction, Reform and Orthodox communities coexisted until the rise to power of Begin's Likud bloc. Begin's own party, Herut, always emphasized the biblical heritage of Israel. But during his period in office several small religious parties, representing orthodox or fundamentalist views, acquired political power, because they were essential to the coalition system that makes government possible in Israel. Friction between the 200,000-member Orthodox community and the secular majority has increased markedly in recent years as the religious parties exert their political power, by attempting to impose Judaic law over the entire nation, by the continued exemption of seminary students from military service, and by taking an increasing share of the national budget for synagogue construction and upkeep.

Differences in historical experiences have also divided the Ashkenazi. Most lived in Eastern Europe, almost completely isolated from other Jews as well as from their Christian neighbors. "They were closed off in a gigantic ghetto called the Pale of Settlement, destitute, deprived of all political rights, living in the twilight of a slowly disintegrating medieval world."[2] However, by the nineteenth century Jews in Western Europe had become politically tolerated, relatively well off, and, due to the "Enlightenment," found most occupations and professions open to them.[3] These "emancipated" Jews played a crucial role in the Zionist movement,

but the actual return to Palestine and settlement was largely the work of Ashkenazis from Eastern Europe.

The Soviet Union, ironically, with a Jewish population of 3.5 million, did not have diplomatic relations with Israel, although consular relations were established in 1990. Soviet Jews were allowed to emigrate after 1987 under the then-new *glasnost* ("openness") policy of Party Secretary Mikhail Gorbachev. A U.S. limit on entry of Soviet Jews accelerated emigration to Israel, and some 270,000 had emigrated by mid-1991. Most of them were highly qualified and well educated yet were often unable to find suitable jobs or housing. The Israeli government's pledge to accept up to 1 million Soviet Jews began to find fewer and fewer takers, in view of Israel's own economic difficulties. Average arrivals per month had dropped from 9,000 in 1991 to barely 3,000 by early 1992.

The Aliyah policy, described by Prime Minister Yitzhak as "one of the foundations of our existence and faith," was responsible for the ingathering of two other isolated Jewish exile communities in 1991. Some 14,000 Ethiopian Jews were airlifted to Israel just prior to the fall of the Marxist government there. The government had approved the airlift in return for payment of $35 million. A second airlift of 300 Jews from the isolated Eastern European country of Albania followed the establishment of diplomatic relations between the two countries.

Modern Israel has two important non-Jewish minorities. The larger (750,000) is the Palestine Arabs, descendants of the original Arab population who stayed on after the establishment of the state. Israel's Arab population was ruled under military administration from 1948 until 1966, when restrictions were lifted and the Arabs ostensibly became full citizens. However, they are not allowed to serve in the armed forces and are discriminated against in myriad ways, including job opportunities, pay scales, and access to higher education. It is only recently, with the coming of age of a new generation of Arabs better educated and politically more articulate than their elders, that the Arabs have begun to press for full equality with Jews in Israeli life. In 1948 they were primarily village farmers, but by 1985, 60 percent were employed in industry, construction, and public services, and a small but substantial Arab industrial sector was emerging. In 1986 a survey of 10 Arab towns found that the population included 1,130 university graduates, a 13-percent increase over 1983.

A second non-Jewish minority, the Druze, live not only in Israel but also in mountain enclaves in Lebanon and Syria. They form a majority of the population in the Golan Heights, occupied by Israeli forces in the 1967 Six-Day War and annexed in 1981. They are a secret sect, practicing a form of Islam that split off from the main body of this religion in the tenth century. Other Druze villages are located near Haifa in northern Israel. Most Druze have remained loyal to the Israeli state. In return, they have been given full citizenship, may serve in the armed forces, and are guaranteed freedom to practice their faith under their religious leaders. The exception to this pattern is the Druze population of the Golan Heights, about 15,000 people grouped in 3 large villages. This community has refused Israeli citizenship and continues to agitate for the return of the area to Syrian control. The Israeli annexation separated many Druze families, who can communicate with family members on the Syrian side of the border only through a "shouting fence" of megaphones in the UN-patrolled "no-man's land" that separates the two countries.

Another small minority, the Circassians, are descended from tribal warriors originally from the Caucasus who were brought to the area in Crusader times. They are Sunni Muslims, but they also serve in the armed forces and are integrated into Israeli society. A Circassian serving as an army lieutenant became the center of a significant court case in 1987 when he was freed from prison by the Supreme Court after he had been falsely accused by the intelligence service, Shin Beth, of collaboration with the enemy in Lebanon.

HISTORY

For most Jews, the establishment of the modern State of Israel is the fulfillment of God's promise of the Land of Canaan to Abraham and his descendants as their home. The original promise still stands to religious Jews, but the people of Israel did not keep their covenant with God, according to one interpretation, and at various times in their history were carried off into captivity or dispersed into exile by invaders. Each period of exile is called *Diaspora* ("Dispersion"). The most important one, in terms of modern Israel, took place in the first century A.D. At that time Palestine was part of the Roman Empire. The Jews rebelled against Rome. The Roman general Titus (who later became emperor) besieged Jerusalem and captured the city in A.D. 70. He destroyed most of it, including the Temple, the focal point of Jewish worship. The majority of Jews either fled into exile or were forcibly deported. (A portion of the Western Wall of the Temple was not destroyed and stands as a place of pilgrimage for devout Jews who come from all over the world to pray beside it. It is called the Wailing Wall.) For 2,000 years Jews were dispersed all over the world.

Diaspora Jews were often persecuted in the lands where they lived, and they were almost always distrusted, feared, and restricted to certain occupations. They were better off in some places than in others. In Spain, Egypt, and other Islamic lands, Jews served as judges, prime ministers, and financial advisers to local rulers. The Jews in these countries were known as "People of the Book," respected for their knowledge and their sacred books. But no matter how Jews were treated in the lands of the Diaspora, they always felt that they were strangers. Their dream was to return to their homeland.

Zionism

Until the late nineteenth century there was no organized movement among Jews to return to Palestine. A few pious Jews, usually elderly, made the long and dangerous journey to Palestine to live out their days in prayer and perhaps to be buried in the cemetery on the Mount of Olives.[4]

The organized movement for a Jewish return to Palestine to fulfill the biblical promise is called *Zionism*. It became, however, more of a political movement formed for a particular purpose: to establish by Jewish settlement a homeland where dispersed Jews may gather, escape persecution, and knit together the strands

of traditional Jewish faith and culture. As a political movement, it differs sharply from spiritual Zionism, the age-old dream of the return. Most Orthodox Jews and traditionalists opposed *any* movement to reclaim Palestine; they believed that it is blasphemy to do so, for only God can perform the miracle of restoring the Promised Land. The establishment of the Israeli state and its development by a secular political system, and policies evolved from modern Jewish nationalism rather than Judaism, have created a dilemma in the Jewish community which has yet to be resolved.[5]

Zionism as a political movement began in the late nineteenth century. Its founder was Theodore Herzl, a Jewish journalist from Vienna, Austria. Herzl had grown up in the Enlightenment period. Like other Western European Jews, he came to believe that a new age of full acceptance of the Jewish community into European life had begun. He was bitterly disillusioned by the wave of Jewish persecution that swept over Eastern Europe after the murder of the liberal Russian czar, Alexander II, in 1881. He was even more disillusioned by the trial of a French Army officer, Alfred Dreyfus, for treason. Dreyfus, who was Jewish, was convicted after angry protests that he was a member of a vast Jewish conspiracy to overthrow the French government.

Herzl concluded from these events that the only hope for the long-suffering Jews, especially those from Eastern Europe, was to live together separate from non-Jews. In his book *The Jewish State* he wrote: "We have sincerely tried everywhere to merge with the national communities in which we live, seeking only to preserve the faith of our fathers. It is not permitted to us."[6]

In 1897 Herzl organized a conference of Jewish leaders in Basle, Switzerland. This first World Zionist Conference ended with a declaration that "the aim of Zionism is to create for the Jewish people a home in Palestine secured by public law."[7] To reach this goal, the Zionists would promote settlement of Palestine by Jewish farmers, artisans, and tradespeople.

Palestine at that time was part of the Ottoman Empire. The Zionists hoped to be allowed to buy land in Palestine for Jewish settlements. But the Ottoman government would not allow them to do so. Small groups of Eastern European Jews escaping persecution made their way to Palestine and established communal agricultural settlements called *kibbutzim*. Those immigrants believed that hard work was essential to the Jewish return to the homeland. Work was sacred, and the only

(Consultate General of Israel, Information Office)

David Ben-Gurion, pictured here at the head of the table, at an early Israeli Cabinet meeting. Also shown (in front, on the right) is Golda Meir, a later prime minister of Israel.

thing that gave the Jews the right to the soil of Palestine was the "betrothal of toil." This belief became a founding principle of the Jewish state.

The Balfour Declaration

Although the Zionist movement attracted many Jewish supporters, it had no influence with European governments, nor with the Ottoman government. The Zionists had difficulty raising money to finance land purchases in Palestine and to pay for travel of emigrants.

It appeared in the early 1900s that the Zionists would never reach their goal. But World War I gave them a new opportunity. The Ottoman Empire was defeated, and British troops occupied Palestine. During the war a British Zionist named Chaim Weizmann, a chemist, had developed a new type of explosive that was valuable to the British war effort against Germany. Weizmann and his associates pressed the British government for a commitment to support a home for Jews in Palestine after the war. In 1917 Arthur Balfour, the British foreign secretary, wrote a letter to Lord Rothschild, a wealthy banker and Zionist leader, outlining the British agree-

ment to help the Zionists establish a Jewish national home in Palestine. Although the letter was general in its terms, the Zionists accepted it as a British commitment to their cause. Since then the letter has been referred to as the Balfour Declaration.[8]

The British Mandate

The peace settlement arranged after World War I by the new League of Nations gave Palestine to the United Kingdom as a mandate. The Zionists understood this to mean that they could now begin to build a Jewish national home in Palestine, through large-scale immigration. They established a Jewish agency under Weizmann's leadership to organize the immigration.

However, most of the Zionist leaders had never been to Palestine. They imagined it as an empty land waiting to be developed by industrious Jews; they did not realize that it was already inhabited by a large Arab population. The Palestinian Arabs had been there for centuries; many families still lived in the villages settled by their ancestors. They regarded Palestine as their national home. The basic conflict between the Arabs and Israel arises from

the claim of two different peoples to the same land.

Palestinian Arabs were opposed to the mandate, the Balfour Declaration, and to Jewish immigration. They turned to violence on several occasions, against the British and the growing Jewish population. In 1936 Arab leaders called a general strike to protest Jewish immigration, which led to a full-scale Arab rebellion. The British tried to steer a middle ground between the two communities. But they were unwilling (or unable) either to accept Arab demands for restrictions on Jewish immigration and land purchases or Zionist demands for a Jewish majority in Palestine. British policy reports and White Papers during the mandate wavered back and forth. Thus, in 1937 a report recommended partition, while a 1939 White Paper recommended a self-governing Arab state with an end to Jewish immigration.

One important difference between the Palestinian Arab and Jewish communities was in their organization. The Jews were organized under the Jewish Agency, which operated as a "state within a state" in Palestine. Jews in Europe and the United States also contributed substantially to the agency's finances and made arrangements for immigration. The Palestinian Arabs, in contrast, were led by heads of urban families who often quarreled with one another. The Palestinian Arab cause also did not have outside Arab support; leaders of neighboring Arab states were weak and were still under British or French control.

Adolf Hitler's policy of genocide (total extermination) of Jews in Europe, developed during World War II, gave a special urgency to Jewish settlement in Palestine. American Zionist leaders condemned the 1939 British White Paper and called for unrestricted Jewish immigration into Palestine and the establishment of an independent, democratic Jewish state. After World War II the British, still committed to the White Paper, blocked Palestine harbors and turned back the crowded, leaking ships carrying desperate Jewish refugees from Europe. World opinion turned against the British. In Palestine itself, Jews formed their own defense organization, Haganah, and underground Jewish terrorist groups such as the Irgun Zvai Leumi and the Stern Gang developed a campaign of murder and sabotage to force the British to end the mandate and establish Palestine as an independent Jewish state.

PARTITION AND INDEPENDENCE

In 1947 the British decided that the Palestine mandate was unworkable and asked the United Nations to come up with a solution to the problem of "one land, two peoples." A UN Special Commission on Palestine recommended partition of Palestine into two states, one Arab, one Jewish, with an economic union between them. A minority of UNSCOP members recommended a federated Arab/Jewish state, with an elected legislature and minority rights for Jews. The majority report was approved by the UN General Assembly on November 29, 1947 by a 33–13 vote, after intensive lobbying by the Zionists. The partition plan established a Jewish state consisting of 56 percent of Palestine, and an Arab state with 43 percent of the area. The population at that time was 60 percent Arab and 40 percent Jewish. Due to its special associations for Jews, Muslims, and Christians, Jerusalem would become an international city administered by the UN.

The Jews accepted the partition plan and made plans to take over their state after the withdrawal of British forces. The Arabs, now backed by the newly independent Arab states, rejected the plan. Conflict between two communities turned to civil war as the deadline approached for the end of the mandate. On May 14, 1948,

the last British soldier left Palestine. Zionist leaders declared the independence of the State of Israel, which was immediately recognized by the United States and the Soviet Union, even as the armies of five Arab states were converging on the new nation to destroy it.

INDEPENDENT ISRAEL

Long before the establishment of Israel, the nation's first prime minister, David Ben-Gurion, had come to Palestine as a youth. After a clash between Arab nomads and Jews from the kibbutz where he lived had injured several people, Ben-Gurion wrote prophetically, "It was then I realized . . . that sooner or later Jews and Arabs would fight over this land, a tragedy since intelligence and good will could have avoided all bloodshed."[9] In the 4 decades of independence, Ben-Gurion's prophecy has been borne out in five Arab/Israeli wars. In between those wars, conflict between Israel and the Palestinians has gone on more or less constantly like a running sore.

Some 700,000 to 800,000 Palestinians fled Israel during the War for Independence. After the 1967 Six-Day War, an additional 380,000 Palestinians became refugees in Jordan. Israeli occupation of the West Bank brought a million Palestinians under military control.

The unifying factor among all Palestinians is the same as that which had united the dispersed Jews for 20 centuries: the recovery of the sacred homeland. Abu Iyad, a top Palestine Liberation Organization leader, once said, " . . . our dream . . . [is] the reunification of Palestine in a secular and democratic state shared by Jews, Christians and Muslims rooted in this common land. . . . There is no doubting the irrepressible will of the Palestinian people to pursue their struggle . . . and one day, we will have a country."[10]

The land vacated by the Palestinians has been transformed in the 4 decades of Israeli development. Those Israelis actually born in Palestine—now in their third generation—call themselves Sabras, after the prickly-pear cactus of the Negev. The work of Sabras and of a generation of immigrants has created a highly urbanized society, sophisticated industries, and a productive agriculture. Much of the success of Israel's development has resulted from large contributions from Jews abroad, from U.S. aid, from reparations from West Germany for Nazi war crimes against Jews, and from bond issues. Yet the efforts of Israelis themselves cannot be underestimated. David Ben-Gurion once wrote, "Pioneering is the lifeblood of our

people. . . . We had to create a new life consonant with our oldest traditions as a people. This was our struggle."[11]

ISRAELI POLITICS: DEMOCRACY BY COALITION

Israel is unique among Middle Eastern states in having been a multiparty democracy from its beginnings. The country has no written constitution, although one has been proposed by potential jurists. In place of a constitution there are organic laws that define the organization and powers of government and the obligations and rights of citizens. The most important of these is the Law of Return, enacted in 1950, which states that any Jew in the world may emigrate to Israel and receive full citizenship.

The Knesset is the hub of the Israeli political system. Its 120 members are elected for 4-year terms under a system of proportional representation from party lists. The party with the most votes in each election chooses a prime minister and Cabinet to run the government. However, the Israeli Cabinet is responsible to the Knesset for all policies. As is the case with the British political system, the prime minister can be called to account at any time by the Knesset and forced to resign by a nonconfidence vote.

The Labor Party of David Ben-Gurion controlled the government for the first 3 decades of independence. However, the party seldom had a clear majority in the Knesset. As a result, it was forced to join in coalitions with various small parties. Israeli political parties are numerous. Many of them have merged with other parties over the years or have broken away to form separate parties. The Labor Party itself is a merger of three socialist labor organizations. The two oldest parties are Agudath Israel World Organization (founded in 1912), which is concerned with issues facing Jews outside of Israel as well as within, and the Israeli Communist Party (Rakah, founded in 1919).

The Labor Party's control of Israeli politics began seriously to weaken after the October 1973 War. Public confidence was shaken by the initial Israeli defeat, heavy casualties, and evidence of Israel's unpreparedness. Austerity measures imposed to deal with inflation increased Labor's unpopularity. In the 1977 elections the opposition, the Likud bloc, won more seats than Labor but fell short of a majority in the Knesset. The new prime minister, Menachem Begin, was forced to make concessions to smaller parties in order to form a governing coalition.

Begin and his party won reelection in 1981, aided by the national euphoria over the peace treaty with Egypt. But the coalition began to unravel swiftly thereafter. The Israeli invasion of Lebanon put the finishing touches on the unraveling process. It seemed to many Israelis that for the first time in its existence, the state had violated its own precept that wars should be defensive and waged only to protect Israeli land. The ethical and moral implications of Israel's occupation, and in particular the massacre by Lebanese Christian militiamen of Palestinians in refugee camps in Beirut who were supposedly under Israeli military protection, led to the formation in 1982 of Peace Now, an organization of Israelis committed to total Arab/Israeli peace. Peace Now activists held daily vigils in Jerusalem, during the war, publicly listing Israeli casualties. This campaign and the killing of an activist during a protest demonstration were important contributing factors to Begin's as yet unexplained resignation in 1983. Afterward the former prime minister remained in seclusion in a state of deep depression, and on March 8, 1992, Menachem Begin died, at the age of 78.

THE 1984 ELECTIONS

Elections were held in July 1984, a year ahead of schedule due to the economic crisis and disagreement over the Lebanese invasion. The Labor Party returned to power but again failed to win a majority. After lengthy negotiations, Labor and Likud reached agreement on the first "government of national unity" in Israel's history. The unusual arrangement provides for alternating 2-year terms as prime minister for each party leader. Prime Minister Shimon Peres took office in September 1984 and was succeeded by Yitzhak Shamir, the Likud leader, in October 1986.

The broad political differences between Labor and Likud that had been papered over to establish coalition government in 1984 broke open again in the 1988 elections. In addition to their deep disagreement over methods of handling the Palestinian uprising in the occupied territories, the two parties differed over long-term peace-settlement policies, Jewish settlements on the West Bank, and other matters. Thus, the Labor proposal of "trading land for peace" with a treaty guaranteeing Israel's right to exist clashed with Likud's insistence on never yielding any part of the sacred Jewish homeland.

The election results underscored equally deep divisions in the population. Neither party won a clear majority of seats in the Knesset; Likud took 40 seats, Labor 39. Four minority ultrareligious parties gained

(UN photo/Saw Lwin)

The outcome of the 1984 Israeli elections presented a difficult problem. The Labor Party was returned to power but failed to win a majority due to the showing of the Likud Party. A compromise was reached: Prime Minister Shimon Peres, the head of the Labor party, took power in September 1984 and Yitzhak Shamir (above), the head of the Likud Party, became prime minister in 1986.

the balance of power, with 15 percent of the popular vote and 18 seats.

With majority government ruled out, it appeared that for Israel to have any government at all, major concessions to these religious parties would be required to make a ruling coalition feasible. One such concession would be an amendment to the Law of Return to allow only Orthodox rabbis to determine who is a Jew for citizenship purposes. The demand aroused a storm of protest, not only in Israel but also among Jews abroad, most of whom are either Conservative or Reform and would be excluded under the law. The proposal was eventually defeated by the Knesset, and after protracted negotiations the two parties reached agreement on another coalition government, in December 1988, with Shamir as prime minister and Peres as finance minister. However, in 1990 Labor withdrew from the coalition in disagreement with Likud over the issue of negotiations for Palestinian autonomy. Since then Shamir has presided over a government with a bare majority of 66 seats in the Knesset, continuing in office through the support of religious parties and despite the deep division in Israeli society over the Palestinian issue.

The divisiveness of the issue was underlined by the exposure of a Jewish underground terrorist organization responsible for violent attacks on West Bank Palestinians as well as an attempt to blow up the Islamic shrines on the Dome of the Rock in Jerusalem. The government was bitterly criticized after a number of underground members were given life sentences by a military court in 1985. Several of the sentences were later commuted by President Chaim Herzog.

Religious extremism reached its apex in 1984 when Brooklyn, NY-born Rabbi Meir Kahane founded Kach, a political party that advocates expulsion of all Arabs from the country. After his election to the Knesset—which gave him parliamentary immunity—Kahane began visiting Arab villages, organizing anti-Arab demonstrations, and warning the villagers by loudspeaker to leave Israel or else risk physical harm. The Knesset subsequently passed a law prohibiting any political party that advocates racism in any form from participation in national elections. On that basis, the Israeli Supreme Court barred Kach and its founder from participating in the 1988 elections. Kahane's subsequent murder (while on a speaking tour in the United States) removed one element of extremism from the Israeli body politic. But violence by other groups—armed Jewish settlers on the West Bank, countering violence by the Palestinian population, and clashes and counterclashes involving Israeli troops and Shia guerrillas in south Lebanon—continued to underline the ever-present xenophobia engrained in Israeli minds and making accommodation with the country's adversaries difficult.

POLARIZATION

Israel's obsession with security has at times affected its relations with Diaspora Jewry and especially with American Jews. The Pollard affair, in which an American Jew, Jonathan Jay Pollard, was convicted of spying for Israel against the United States, aroused much resentment among American Jews. Although the Israeli government maintained that the affair was a "rogue operation" undertaken by one secret intelligence unit without the knowledge or approval of its superiors or Cabinet officials, the fact that Pollard's principal spymasters were rewarded with higher positions angered many. Jews abroad as well as some Israelis questioned the value of an operation directed at Israel's main ally. "Is Israel becoming an ugly little Spartan state instead of 'the light of the world' we want it to try to be?" asked one prominent American Jewish leader.[12] Although Pollard was not the first person to spy on the United States on behalf of Israel, his reports to his Israeli handlers on National Security Agency intelligence-collection systems and military satellite photography were more damaging to American security than those of any previous Israeli agent.[13]

A divisive internal issue involved Shin Beth, Israel's counterpart to the U.S. Federal Bureau of Investigation. Shin Beth agents had been charged with the fatal beatings of two Palestinian bus hijackers in 1984, immediately after their capture, but the case had been covered up by the government and the agents granted immunity on grounds of national security. The organization's methods of torture and interrogation in the West Bank and Gaza Strip had long been condoned for the same reason. But the exoneration of an army lieutenant after exposure of brutal methods used by Shin Beth agents to obtain a false confession, added to reports of increased brutality on the West Bank, led to a public outcry. As was the case after the invasion of Lebanon, a commission of inquiry was formed to investigate the organization's methods, and several officials resigned.

During his 25 months as prime minister, Shimon Peres chalked up a number of impressive accomplishments. The withdrawal of Israeli forces from Lebanon in 1985 was a significant achievement; an opinion poll in December indicated that

68 percent of the population supported his policies. Inflation was brought under control, and the economy revived. In foreign affairs, the prime minister took the bold step of "going to the enemy" when he traveled to Morocco for face-to-face talks with King Hassan II. However, his efforts to advance the peace process and resolve the Palestinian problem through Israeli/Jordanian cooperation failed when King Hussein severed Jordan's relationship with the West Bank.

THE INTIFADA

The Palestinian *intifada* (literally, a "resurgence") in the West Bank and Gaza Strip, which began in December 1987, came as a rude shock to Israel. Coming as it did barely $2^1/_2$ years after the trauma of the Lebanon War, the uprising found the Israeli public as well as its citizen army unprepared. The recall of middle-aged reservists and dispatch of new draftees to face stone-throwing Palestinian children created severe moral and psychological problems for many soldiers. Dr. John Freymann, an eye-witness to the first Palestinian-Israeli conflict, wrote sadly: "Forty years later the grandsons of the refugees I saw huddled in these camps clash daily with the grandsons of the Israelis with whom I endured the siege of Jerusalem."[14]

Military authorities devised a number of methods to deal with the uprising, and although many of them were strongly criticized in Israel as well as abroad as being inhumane if not illegal under international law, Defense Minister Rabin justified them as necessary to restore public security. One of the hardest blows to the Palestinian population was the closing of all West Bank schools in January 1989; Rabin claimed that they had become staging grounds for violence and were teaching nationalism rather than educating Palestinian children. The schools were reopened in July after the government had come under intense international pressure, but the West Bank's four universities and community colleges remained closed, and Israeli authorities even interfered with home education provided in lieu of formal education, arresting teachers for giving classes in their homes.

Other army methods included deportation of prominent activists, demolition of houses, beatings of children, use of plastic dum-dum bullets on demonstrators, wholesale arrests, and detention for indefinite periods under "security" regulations left over from the British mandate. By mid-September 1989 the human cost of the intifada had reached 400 dead, several

thousand injured, and 6,000 Palestinians under indefinite detention.

The government also tried to break the Palestinian resistance through arbitrary higher taxes, arguing that this was necessary to compensate for revenues lost due to refusal of Palestinians to pay taxes, a slowdown in business, and lowered exports to the territories. A Value Added Tax (VAT) imposed on olive presses just prior to the processing of the West Bank's major crop was a particular hardship. Along with the brutality of its troops, the tax-collection methods drove Palestinians and Israelis further apart, making the prospect of any future amicable relationship questionable.

For its part, the intifada offered an opportunity for Palestinians to settle old scores or extend clan vendettas by accusing rivals of collaboration with Israel. In 1989 alone, some 50 "collaborators" were murdered by their fellow Palestinians.

The stepped-up immigration of Soviet Jews to Israel revitalized the intifada after a period of relative inactivity. Government expropriation of land in the West Bank for housing for immigrant families and the expansion of existing Jewish settlements triggered a new outburst of violence. Palestinian resentment was also fueled by the belief, supported by evidence, that because the newcomers could not find professional employment they were taking menial jobs normally held by West Bank and Gaza residents.

In October 1990 the most serious incident since the start of the intifada occurred in Jerusalem. Palestinians stoned a Jewish group, the Temple Mount Faithful, who had come to lay a symbolic cornerstone for a new Jewish Temple near the Dome of the Rock. Israeli security forces then opened fire, killing some 20 palestinians and injuring more than 100. The UN Security Council approved a resolution condemning Israel for excessive response—one of hundreds that the Israeli state has ignored over the years. Israel appointed an official commission to investigate the killings, but the commission exonerated the security forces, saying that they had acted in self-defense.

Shamir's Election Plan

In May 1989, responding to threats by Labor to withdraw from the coalition and precipitate new elections, the government approved a plan drafted by Defense Minister Rabin for elections in the West Bank and Gaza as a prelude to "self-government." Under the plan, the Palestinians would elect 1 representative from each of 10 electoral districts to an Interim Council. The Council would then negotiate with Israeli representatives for autonomy for the West Bank and Gaza as defined in the 1979 Camp David treaty. Negotiations on the final status of the territories would begin within 3 years of the signing of the autonomy agreement.

The success of UN-U.S. coalition forces in expelling the Iraqi Army from Kuwait created an additional problem for intifada leaders. They had strongly supported Saddam Hussain's "linkage" of Iraqi withdrawal from Kuwait with Israeli withdrawal from the occupied territories; they had even applauded the Scud missile attacks on Israeli cities. However, the United States launched an all-out effort after the Gulf War to convene a Middle East peace conference that would once and for all settle the Palestinian question.

The U.S.-sponsored peace conference, which began in October 1991 in Madrid, Spain, further divided the Israeli public, since it represented a commitment to peace and possible withdrawal from occupied territories that some Israeli groups would not accept. The religious parties walked out from the ruling coalition; and, although the Shamir government was able to survive several no-confidence motions, its days were clearly numbered. Elections originally scheduled for the Knesset for November 1991 were rescheduled, upon demand from the opposition, for June. In addition, the political field was crowded even further by a new party, the National Movement for Democracy and Aliya (DA), representing Soviet immigrant Jews.

Perhaps the one hope for a knitting together of the Israeli people to resolve the country's political isolation and come to terms with the Palestinians lay in the Labor Alignment's ability to win a clear-cut election. In February 1992 the party held its annual Congress and elected former Defense Minister Yitzhak Rabin to succeed Shimon Peres as party leader. Rabin enjoyed widespread popularity as the official who had managed to contain the intifada and was committed, along with his party, to eventual Palestinian self-rule and withdrawal from the occupied territories. These characteristics stood in sharp contrast to Shamir's inflexible opposition (and that of hardline elements in the population to any settlement). Under such conditions, the voters would at least be given a clear choice.

A revolution on another front has involved the Arab population living in Israel itself. Israeli Arabs generally backed the uprising, but their major efforts have been to achieve parity with their Israeli neighbors in matters of jobs, education, housing, representation in the Knesset, and improved social services. The first all-

Arab party in the country's history was formed in 1988; its platform emphasized these issues, and it won one seat in the Knesset in the elections. In 1989 Arab Muslim fundamentalists defeated the incumbents in municipal elections in seven Arab municipalities, including Nazareth, the largest Arab city, and Umm al-Fahm, the major Arab village. However, the feared onset of pro-Khomeini violence against Israelis did not occur, as the new local administrators and mayors focused their efforts on such services as libraries, community centers, health clinics, and expanded jobs for their constituents.

THE ECONOMY

In terms of national income and economic and industrial development, Israel is ahead of a number of Middle Eastern states that have greater natural resources. Agriculture is highly developed; Israeli engineers and hydrologists have been very successful in developing new irrigation and planting methods that not only "make the desert bloom" but also are exported to other developing nations under the country's technical-aid program. Agriculture contributes 7.5 percent of gross domestic product annually. Israel is mostly self-sufficient in food, although a number of basic commodities, such as dairy products, are heavily subsidized.

Small industries provide the bulk of the national income. The most important industrial export is diamonds, accounting for 25 percent of exports. The aircraft industry is the largest single industrial enterprise. However, the industry has fallen on hard times. The national airline, El Al, suffered through a major strike in 1982 and was placed in receivership, although it continued to operate. The major industry project, the largely U.S.-financed Lavi jet fighter, was scrapped in 1987 by the Cabinet by a one-vote margin. Opponents of the project pointed out that its cost overruns would more than make up for savings created by the austerity program, which had brought inflation down to manageable limits.

Israel has 34 producing oil wells and produces a very small amount of natural gas, which meets only a fraction of domestic needs. After the 1967 War and the occupation of the Sinai Peninsula, Israel was able to exploit Sinai petroleum resources as well as the Alma oilfields in the Gulf of Suez. Twenty-five percent of domestic oil needs came from the Alma fields. In accordance with the Egyptian-Israeli peace treaty, all of these fields were returned to Egypt, with the stipulation that Israel be able to purchase Sinai oil at less than prices set by the Organization of

Petroleum Exporting Countries for Egyptian oil on the world market. Israel has also bought oil from Iran from time to time and from certain African oil-producing countries. Still, fuel imports are a huge drain on the economy. There are, however, considerable deposits of bromine, magnesium, and phosphates in the Negev and Dead Sea.

The internal strengths of the Israeli economy are more than offset by the weaknesses caused by its international political position. The burden of the more or less permanent state of siege has imposed an artificially high level of military expenditures, usually a quarter of the national budget. Inflation, fed by regular cost-of-living increases under government-labor contracts, topped 100 percent annually between 1980 and 1984. It reached a plateau of 800 percent in 1985 and has since dropped to about 48 percent. The shekel, which replaced the pound in 1980 as a medium of exchange, was kept artificially high in order to curb inflation, resulting in a drop in export values.

Israel has survived and prospered economically as a state due to the availability of foreign support. Awareness of this outside resource has kept the nation in an illusion of economic plenty. But just as Israel must one day come to political terms with its Arab neighbors, it must at some point stand on its own feet economically as a Middle Eastern state rather than a dependency of states outside the region. Efforts in this direction would be a healthy sign of a maturing nation.

However, maturity has been slow to develop. Prior to 1977, when the Likud came to power, the economy was managed by the state or by Histadrut, the many-tentacled labor confederation that functions as a union but also as employer and controlling voice in many industries and bargains with the government on equal terms for labor contracts. Likud Prime Minister Begin went all out, abolishing foreign-exchange controls, the travel tax, and import licenses, and allowing the currency to float and Israelis to open foreign bank accounts. The result was rampant inflation, balance-of-payments deficits, and a huge increase in imports of luxury goods paid for in foreign currencies, a major factor in the decline in reserves. But there was no offsetting reduction in the welfare-state structure originally created to absorb immigrants, or in the huge Socialist bureaucracy which had two out of three Israelis working for the government. Government policy of linking wage increases to price rises generated an inflationary spiral. U.S. aid, because it was disbursed freely with-

| The Zionist movement is organized by Theodor Herzel **1896** | The Balfour Declaration **1917** | British mandate over Palestine **1922–1948** | A UN partition plan is accepted by the Jewish community; following British withdrawal, the State of Israel is proclaimed **1947–1948** | Armistices are signed with certain Arab states, through U.S. mediation **1949** | The Six-Day War; Israeli occupation of East Jerusalem, the Gaza Strip, and the Sinai Peninsula **1967** | Yom Kippur War **1973** | Opposition leader Menachem Begin's Likud bloc wins the election **1977** | Peace treaty with Egypt **1979** |

1980s–1990

The Israeli invasion of Lebanon	Withdrawal of Israeli forces from Lebanon	Home-grown Palestinian resistance to Israeli occupation in the West Bank and Gaza Strip intensifies; Shamir head caretaker government as Peres attempts the setup of a new government at the turn of the decade
Knesset elections result in deadlock between Labor and Likud; resolved by coalition government and 2-year alternation of prime ministers	Conviction of Jonathan Pollard for espionage drives wedge between Israelis and the U.S. Jewish community	

out demands that the Israeli government introduce needed structural economic reforms, encouraged Israelis to believe that no matter how profligate they were, Uncle Sam would always bail them out.

The Peres government took office amid warnings from U.S. advisers as well as its own economists that the economy would soon collapse if reforms were not introduced immediately. Warned that even the U.S. Congress might be less willing to consider aid increases without a clear commitment to austerity, the Israeli government introduced a draconian package of reforms in 1984. It included wage and price freezes and an almost total ban on imports of nonessential goods. Another set of measures, in 1985, reduced subsidies, raised taxes, devalued the Israeli shekel, eliminated cost-of-living increases in labor contracts, and abolished some 10,000 civil-service jobs.

But even these steps failed to revive the sluggish economy. In 1988–1989 a drop in exports, reduced tourism due to the intifada, and the costs of the occupation led to budget deficits of 6 to 7 percent. Inflation was held in line only through currency devaluations of 18 percent, while unemployment rose to 9.7 percent, with a fourth of the working population jobless in such areas as the Negev.

In July 1989 a new austerity program, prepared by Finance Minister Peres, was approved by the government. It would cut workers' pay and fringe benefits, in an effort to draw skilled retired workers back into the labor force and thus increase productivity. The currency was devalued

by an additional 13 percent, and prices on subsidized food products and gasoline increased. However, the influx of Soviet Jews in the early 1990s threatened to undercut economic stability, putting a severe strain on housing and other services as well as affecting employment.

NOTES

1. Ashkenazi derived from Ashkenaz (Genesis 10:3) is the name given to Jews who lived in Europe, particularly Germany, and followed particular traditions of Judaism handed down from biblical days. Sephardim (from Sepharah, Obadiah 1:20) refers to Jews originally from Spain who were expelled and emigrated to the Middle East—North Africa. R. J. Zwi Werblowsky and Geoffrey Wigoder, eds., *The Encyclopedia of the Jewish Religion* (New York: Holt, Rinehart & Winston, 1965).

2. Dan V. Segre, *A Crisis of Identity: Israel and Zionism* (Oxford: Oxford University Press, 1980), p. 25.

3. The "Enlightenment" resulted from the French Revolution and its declaration of Liberty, Equality, and Fraternity (Brotherhood), meaning that all people are created equal. "Under the new spirit of equality, ghetto walls crumbled." Abraham Shulman, *Coming Home to Zion* (Garden City: Doubleday, 1979), p. 11.

4. Jews believe that those buried there will be the first to be resurrected when the Messiah comes through the "Gate of Compassion" on a white donkey and proclaims The Day of Judgment. Chaim Bernant, *The Walled Garden* (New York: MacMillan, 1974), p. 249.

5. Segre, *op. cit.*, points out that Israel contains "the first community of Jews officially dissociated from the idea that Jews are a people distinguished from all others by their special relationship with God."

6. Quoted in Shulman, *op cit.*, p. 14.

7. *The Middle East and North Africa 1984–1985*, 31st edition (London: Europa Publications, 1984), "Documents on Palestine," p. 58.

8. The letter qualifies this commitment by adding that "nothing shall be done which may prejudice the civil and religious rights of existing non-Jewish communities in Palestine . . ." John Kimche, *Palestine or Israel* (London: Secker and Warburg, 1973), Appendix I, p. 343.

9. David Ben-Gurion, *Memoirs* (Cleveland: World Publishing Company, 1970), p. 58.

10. Abu Iyad with Eric Rouleau, *My Home, My Land: A Narrative of the Palestinian Struggle*, transl. by Linda Butler Koseoglu (New York: New York Times Books, 1981), pp. 225–226.

11. Ben-Gurion, *op. cit.*, p. 57.

12. Robert Schreiber, in *New Outlook*, 30, 5/6 (May/June 1987), p. 42.

13. *cf.* Stephen Green, in *The Christian Science Monitor* (May 22, 1989), pp. 19–22, from an unpublished book on the subject.

14. John Freymann, in *Foreign Service Journal* (May 1988), p. 30.

DEVELOPMENT

With outside aid, Israel has been able to develop a strong industrial sector that emphasizes high-technology industries. However, inflation, falling industrial production, and high unemployment continue to affect economic development. The U.S. in 1991 provided $650 million to aid reconstruction of cities damaged by Iraqi Scud missiles in the Gulf War.

FREEDOM

Israeli citizens enjoy extensive civil rights. But security constraints frequently place limitations on these rights, such as censorship of publications. Rights of women are also limited at times by the intervention of religious authorities. Thus women have been barred from praying aloud at the Wailing Wall.

HEALTH/WELFARE

Immigration of Soviet Jews has created problems in the job market, particularly in the professional sector. While Israeli medical schools graduate 280 doctors annually, in 1 week alone, some 300 Jewish doctors arrived from the (former) Soviet Union. Other professional Soviet Jews must take menial jobs to survive, crowding out Palestinians who held those jobs in the past.

ACHIEVEMENTS

Israel is the world's largest exporter of bromine. Sophisticated agricultural techniques, such as use of solar power and drip irrigation, which were pioneered in the country, have not only increased crop yields but also export of food crops. Although not a European Community member, Israel has preferential trade access to EC members.

Jordan (The Hashimite Kingdom of Jordan)

GEOGRAPHY

Area in Square Kilometers (Miles):
93,740 (37,727) (slightly larger than Indiana)
Capital (Population): Amman (900,000)
Climate: predominantly dry

PEOPLE

Population
Total: 3,065,000
Annual Growth Rate: 3.8%
Rural/Urban Population Ratio: 33/67
Ethnic Makeup of Population: 98% Arab; 1% Circassian; 1% Armenian

Health
Life Expectancy at Birth: 65 years (male); 69 years (female)
Infant Mortality Rate (Ratio): 53/1,000
Average Caloric Intake: 102% of FAO minimum
Physicians Available (Ratio): 1/881

Religion(s)
95% Sunni Muslim; 5% Christian

Education
Adult Literacy Rate: 75%

"ROSE-RED CITY HALF AS OLD AS TIME"

A sunset view of the rose-red glow of the ancient Jordanian city of Petra, capital of the Nabataeans 20 centuries ago, is a never-to-be-forgotten sight. Built at the crossroads of major caravan routes between Egypt, Arabia, and Mesopotamia, Petra was carved from the red sandstone cliffsides of a narrow valley into a city housing 30,000 people. The best-preserved building is Pharaoh's Treasury, which was probably a second-century A.D. tomb of a Nabataean king. Petra was the Nabataean capital for 4 centuries and continued to flourish for another 3 centuries after conquest by Rome in A.D. 106, until its abandonment due to lack of water.

COMMUNICATION
Telephones: 189,500
Newspapers: 4 dailies (one in English); 3 weeklies

TRANSPORTATION
Highways—Kilometers (Miles): 4,095 (2,539)
Railroads—Kilometers (Miles): 619 (386)
Usable Airfields: 19

GOVERNMENT
Type: constitutional monarchy
Independence Date: May 25, 1946
Head of State: King Hussein I; parliamentary system of prime minister (Taher al-Masri) and Cabinet; bicameral Legislature
Political Parties: Jordanian Arab National Democratic Alliance (JANDA); Muslim Brotherhood; minor parties
Suffrage: universal over 20

MILITARY
Number of Armed Forces: 84,250
Military Expenditures (% of Central Government Expenditures): 26%
Current Hostilities: none

ECONOMY
Currency ($ U.S. Equivalent): 0.65 Jordanian dinar = $1
Per Capita Income/GNP: $1,640/$4.3 billion
Inflation Rate: −1%
Total Foreign Debt: $7.4 billion
Natural Resources: phosphate; potash
Agriculture: vegetables; fruits; olive oil; wheat
Industry: phosphate mining; petroleum refining; cement production; light manufacturing

FOREIGN TRADE
Exports: $926 million
Imports: $2.1 billion

* Capital   — Rivers   – – Roads   – - Department Boundaries

JORDAN

The Hashimite Kingdom of Jordan (formerly called Transjordan; usually abbreviated to Jordan) is one of the smaller Middle Eastern nations. The country formerly consisted of two regions: the East Bank (lying east of the Jordan River) and the West Bank of the Jordan. Israel occupied the West Bank in 1967, although the region continued to be legally and administratively attached to Jordan and salaries of civil servants and others were paid by the Jordanian government. In 1988 King Hussein formally severed the relationship, leaving the West Bank under Israeli occupation de facto as well as de jure. Between 1948 and 1967 Jordanian-occupied territory also included the old city of Jerusalem (East Jerusalem), which was annexed during the 1948 Arab-Israeli War.

Modern Jordan is an artificial nation, the result of historical forces and events that shaped the Middle East in the twentieth century. It had no prior history as a nation and was known simply as the land east of the Jordan River, a region of diverse peoples, some nomadic, others sedentary farmers and herders. Jordan's current neighbors are Iraq, Syria, Saudi Arabia, and Israel. Their joint borders were all established by the British after World War I, when the United Kingdom and France divided the territories of the defeated Ottoman Empire between them.

Jordan's borders with Iraq, Syria, and Saudi Arabia do not follow natural geographical features. They were established mainly to keep nomadic peoples from raiding; over time, these borders have been accepted by the countries concerned. However, a serious border question for Jordan concerns the boundary with Israel. The Israeli occupation of the West Bank and East Jerusalem in June 1967 set up an artificial border between the East and West Banks. The Palestinian refugees in Jordan and the country's military weakness vis-à-vis Israel have served as destabilizing elements in the government's efforts to build an integrated Jordanian nation.

HISTORY

The territory of modern Jordan was ruled by outside powers until it became an independent nation in the twentieth century. Under the Ottoman Empire, it was part of the province of Syria. The Ottoman authorities in Syria occasionally sent military patrols across the Jordan River to "show the flag" and collect taxes, but otherwise they left the people of the area to manage their own affairs.[1]

This tranquil existence ended with World War I. The Ottomans were defeated

(Jordan Information Bureau)

This is the crowning monument to Rome's occupation of Petra, the Nabataean stronghold in the south Jordan mountains. The city, which had been rock-cut by its Nabataean founders into the tombs and monuments of a death cult, was resculpted by Rome into a Graeco-Roman architectural marvel.

and their provinces were divided into protectorates, called *mandates*, set up by the League of Nations and assigned to the United Kingdom and/or France to administer and prepare for eventual self-government. The British received a mandate over Palestine and extended its territory to include Transjordan, the land east of the River Jordan. Due to their commitment to help Jews dispersed throughout the world to establish a national home in Palestine, the British decided to govern Transjordan as a separate mandate.

The terms of the mandate system required the protecting power (in this case, the United Kingdom) to appoint a native ruler. During the war the British had worked with Sharif Husayn, a prominent Arab leader in Mecca who held the honorary position of Protector of the Holy Shrines of Islam, to organize an Arab revolt against the Ottomans. Two of the sharif's sons, Faisal and Abdullah, had led the revolt, and the British felt they owed them something. When Iraq was set up as a mandate, the British made Faisal its king. Abdullah was offered the Transjordan territory. Because the population was primarily pastoral, he chose the traditional title of emir, rather than king, as being more appropriate.

EMIR ABDULLAH

Through his father Abdullah traced his lineage back to the Hashim family of Mecca, the clan to which the Prophet Muhammad belonged. This ancestry gave him a great deal of prestige in the Arab world, particularly among the nomads of Transjordan, who had much respect for a person's genealogy. Abdullah used the connection assiduously to build a solid base of support among his kinspeople. When the country became fully independent in 1946 and Abdullah took the title of king, he named his new state the Hashimite Kingdom of Jordan.

Abdullah's new country had little to recommend it to outsiders except some fine Roman ruins and a great deal of empty land. It was a peaceful, quiet place, consisting entirely of what is today the East Bank of the Jordan River, with vaguely defined borders across the desert. The population was about 400,000, mostly rural peasants and nomads; the capital, Amman, was little more than a large village spread over some of those Roman ruins.

During the period of the mandate (1921–1946) Abdullah was advised by resident British officials. The British helped him draft a Constitution in 1928, and Transjordan became independent in everything except financial policy and foreign relations. But Emir Abdullah and his advisers ran the country like a private club. In traditional Arab desert fashion, Abdullah held a public meeting outside his palace every Friday; anyone who wished could come and present a complaint or petition to the emir.

Abdullah did not trust political parties or institutions such as a parliament, although he agreed to issue the 1928 Constitution as a step toward eventual self-government. He also laid the basis for a regular army. A British Army officer, John Bagot Glubb, was appointed in 1930 to train the Transjordanian Frontier Force to curb Bedouin raiding across the country's borders. Under Glubb's command, this frontier force eventually became the Arab Legion; during Emir Abdullah's last years, it played a vital role not only in defending the kingdom against the forces of the new State of Israel but also in enlarging Jordanian territory by the capture of the West Bank and East Jerusalem.[2]

When the United Kingdom gave Jordan its independence in 1946, the country was not vastly different from the tranquil emirate of the 1920s. But events beyond its borders soon overwhelmed it, like the duststorm rolling in from the desert that sweeps everything before it. The conflict between the Arab and Jewish communities in neighboring Palestine had become so intense and unmanageable that the British decided to terminate their mandate. They turned the problem over to the United Nations, and in November 1947 the UN General Assembly voted to partition Palestine into separate Arab and Jewish states, with Jerusalem to be an international city under UN administration.

(Jordan Information Bureau)

Amman, the capital of Jordan, is a city built on seven hills. Against the slope of one hill is this large Roman amphitheater (center), now restored to its original seating capacity of 6,000 spectators.

The partition plan was not accepted by the Palestine Arabs, and as British forces evacuated Palestine in 1947–1948, they prepared to fight the Jews for possession of all Palestine. The State of Israel was proclaimed in 1948. Armies of the neighboring Arab states, including Jordan, immediately invaded Palestine. But they were poorly armed and untrained. Only the Jordanian Arab Legion gave a good account of itself. The legion's forces seized the West Bank, originally part of the territory allotted to a projected Palestinian Arab state by the UN. The legion also occupied the old city of Jerusalem (East Jerusalem). Subsequently, Abdullah annexed both territories, despite howls of protest from other Arab leaders, who accused him of land grabbing from his "Palestine brothers" and ambitions to rule the entire Arab world.

Jordan now became a vastly different state. Its population tripled with the addition of half a million West Bank Arabs and half a million Arab refugees from Israel. Abdullah still did not trust the democratic process. But he realized that he would have to take firm action to strengthen Jordan and help the dispossessed Palestinians who now found themselves reluctantly included in his kingdom. He approved a new Constitution, one that provided for a bicameral legislature (similar to the U.S. Congress), with an appointed Senate and an elected House of Representatives. He appointed prominent Palestinians to his Cabinet. A number of Palestinians were appointed to the Senate; others were elected to the House of Representatives.

On July 20, 1951, King Abdullah was assassinated as he entered the Al Aqsa Mosque in East Jerusalem for Friday prayers. His grandson, Hussein, was at his side and narrowly escaped death. Abdullah's murderer, who was killed immediately by royal guards, was a Palestinian. Many Palestinians felt that Abdullah had betrayed them by annexing the West Bank and because he was thought to have carried on secret peace negotiations with the Israelis (recent evidence suggests that he did so). In his *Memoirs,* King Abdullah wrote, "The paralysis of the Arabs lies in their present moral character. They are obsessed with tradition and concerned only with profit and the display of oratorical patriotism."[3]

Abdullah dealt with the Israelis because he despaired of Arab leadership. Ironically, Abdullah's proposal to the United Kingdom in 1938 for a unified Arab-Jewish Palestine linked with Jordan, if it had been accepted, would have avoided five wars and hundreds of thousands of casualties. Yet this same proposal forms the basis for discussion of the Arab-Israeli settlement today.[4]

KING HUSSEIN

Abdullah's son, Crown Prince Talal, succeeded to the throne. He suffered from mental illness (probably schizophrenia) and had spent most of his life in mental hospitals. When his condition worsened, his senior advisers convinced him to abdicate in favor of his eldest son, Hussein. Hussein became king in 1953.

King Hussein's is one of the longest reigns in the contemporary world, and he remains one of the few surviving examples of monarchy. Thus far he has faced and overcome a number of crises. These crises have stemmed from Jordan's involvement in the larger Arab-Israeli conflict and its pivotal location in that conflict.

Hussein faced a serious threat to his rule shortly after he became king. Elections for the new National Assembly, in 1956, resulted in a majority for parties representing the West Bank.[5] A tug of war between king and Assembly followed. At one point it was rumored that Hussein had been killed. Hussein, who was very much alive, jumped into a jeep and rode out to the main army base at Zerqa, outside Amman, where he showed himself to his troops to prove he was still in command. The army remained loyal to him, and the alleged coup never materialized. The Zerqa incident illustrates two things about Jordanian politics. One is Hussein's sense of timing, his ability to take bold actions designed to throw his opponents off guard. The second is the importance of army support to the monarchy. The great majority of soldiers in the Arab Legion are still drawn from Bedouins. An observer once said that Jordan is an army with a country attached to it. Through years of attempted assassinations, internal crises, and threats from outside, King Hussein's survival has depended on army loyalty and his own survival skills.

The June 1967 Six-Day War produced another crisis in Jordan, this one not entirely of its own making. Israeli forces occupied 10 percent of Jordanian territory, including half of its best agricultural lands. The Jordanian Army suffered 6,000 casualties, most of them in a desperate struggle to hold the Old City of Jerusalem against Israeli attack. Nearly 300,000 more Palestinian refugees from the West Bank fled into Jordan. To complicate things further, guerrillas from the Palestine Liberation Organization, formerly based in the West Bank, made Jordan their new headquarters. The PLO considered Jordan as its base for the continued struggle against Israel. Its leaders talked openly of removing the monarchy and making Jordan an armed Palestinian state.

By 1970 Hussein and the PLO were headed toward open confrontation. The guerrillas had the sympathy of the population, and successes in one or two minor clashes with Israeli troops had made them arrogant. They swaggered through the streets of Amman, directed traffic at intersections, stopped pedestrians to examine their identity papers. Army officers complained to King Hussein that the PLO was really running the country. The king became convinced that unless he moved against the guerrillas his throne would be in danger. He declared martial law and in September 1970 ordered the army to move against them. (King Hussein lifted some aspects of martial law in 1989 and cancelled it in 1991.)

The ensuing Civil War lasted until July 1971, but in the PLO annals it is usually referred to as "Black September," because of its starting date and because it ended in disaster for the guerrillas. Their bases were dismantled and most of the guerrillas were driven from Jordan. The majority went to Lebanon, where they reorganized and in time became as powerful as they had been in Jordan, mainly because the Lebanese government was too weak to control them.

Since 1970 there have been no serious internal threats to Hussein's rule. Jordan shared in the general economic boom in the Arab world that developed as a result of the enormous price increases in oil after the 1973 Arab-Israeli War. Consequently, Hussein was able to turn his attention to the development of a more democratic political system. Like his grandfather, he did not entirely trust political parties or elected legislatures, and he was leery of the Palestinians' intentions toward him. He was also convinced that Jordan rather than the PLO should be the natural representative of the Palestinians. But he realized that in order to represent them effectively and to build the kind of Jordanian state that he could safely hand over to his successors, he would need to develop popular support in addition to that of the army. Accordingly, Hussein set up a National Consultative Council in 1978, as what he called an interim step toward democracy. The Council had a majority of Palestinians (those living on the East Bank) as members.

Hussein's arbitrary separation of Jordan from the West Bank has had important internal implications for internal politics in the kingdom. It enabled the king to proceed with political reforms without the need to involve the Palestinian population there. The timetable was accelerated by nationwide protests in 1989 over price increases for basic commodities. The protests turned swiftly to violence, resulting in the most serious riots in national history. Prime Minister Zaid Rifai was dismissed; he was held personally responsible for the increases and for the country's severe financial problems, although these were due equally to external factors. King Hussein appointed a caretaker government headed by his cousin to oversee the transitional period before national elections for the long-promised lower chamber of the Legislature.

In 1990 the king and leaders of the major opposition organization, the Jordanian National Democratic Alliance (JANDA), signed a historic National Charter which provides for a multiparty political system. Elections were set under the Charter for an 80-member House of Representatives. Nine seats would be reserved for Christians and three for Circassians, an ethnic Muslim minority originally from the Caucasus.

The election results gave the Islamic fundamentalist Muslim Brotherhood 22 seats, plus 10 for other fundamentalist groups. However, JANDA and independent promonarchy candidates won a comfortable majority in the House. In any case, the Charter requires all political parties to swear allegiance to the monarchy, so Hussein's rule was in no danger.

In July 1991 the king cancelled martial law, which had been in effect since the 1967 Arab-Israeli War. All curbs on freedom of speech, public assembly, and the press were also lifted. A new Cabinet, headed by Palestinian-born Taher al-Masri, took office. All political parties and groups in the kingdom were represented except the Muslim Brotherhood, which refused to join "any government that is ready to negotiate with Israel."

The unthinkable came to pass in late 1991 and early 1992, as Jordan joined other Arab states and a Palestinian delegation in a U.S.-sponsored peace conference—held initially in Madrid, Spain, and subsequently in other world capitals—in an effort to resolve the Palestinian conflict and normalize Israeli-Arab state relations. The Jordanian government's decision to join the peace talks led to a political crisis which threatened briefly to unravel the fragile web of democracy. Eighty members of the lower house of Parliament, most of them members of the Muslim Brotherhood, introduced a no-confidence motion against the Cabinet of Prime Minister al-Masri for "treachery to Jordan and the Arab nation." However, the motion failed, and in January 1992 Jordanian

| Establishment of the British mandate of Transjordan 1921 | The first Constitution is approved by the British-sponsored Legislative Council 1928 | Treaty of London; the British give Jordan independence and Abdullah assumes the title of emir 1946 | The Arab Legion occupies the Old City of Jerusalem and the West Bank during the first Arab-Israeli War 1948 | Jordanian forces are defeated by Israel in the Six-Day War; Israelis occupy the West Bank and Old Jerusalem 1967 | "Black September"; Civil War between army and PLO guerrillas ends with expulsion of the PLO from Jordan 1970–1971 | Hussein suspends the National Assembly 1974 |

1980s–1990s

| New electoral law reserves seats for West Bank Palestinian refugees in the lower House of Representatives; a 5-year development program is announced for the West Bank | Women are allowed to vote; Jordan resumes full diplomatic relations with Egypt and Syria | Politically, economically, and socially, Jordan is one of the primary losers in the Gulf crisis; martial law is lifted |

and Israeli representatives began their first-ever formal peace talks, held under U.S. sponsorship in Washington, D.C.

Jordan's support for Iraq during the Gulf War not only deprived the country of its main source of oil but cost $1.79 billion in lost exports and transit fees for oil shipments across its territory. Saudi Arabia discontinued its financial subsidy, as did other Gulf states, while the burden of refugees from Kuwait put an added strain on the economy.

THE ECONOMY

Jordan does not have oil, but it is rich in phosphates. Reserves are estimated at 2 billion tons, and new deposits are constantly being reported. Phosphate rock is one of the country's main exports, along with potash, which is mined on the Jordanian side of the Dead Sea.

Although oil has not yet been discovered in commercial quantities, Jordan does have deposits of 800 million tons of shale oil. Shale oil requires vastly greater expenditures and highly sophisticated techniques to produce, and the return per ton is far less in number of barrels than it is from a ton of crude petroleum. Consequently, Jordan is unlikely to become an oil-producing country for years to come.

The mainstay of the economy is agriculture. The most productive agricultural area is the Jordan Valley. A series of dams and canals from the Jordan and Yarmuk rivers has increased arable land in the valley by 264,000 acres and has made possible production of high-value vegetable crops for export to nearby countries.

However, politics continues to interfere with the development of agriculture.

The Israeli occupation of the West Bank deprived Jordan of 80 percent of its citrus-growing area and 45 percent of its vegetable gardens. Israeli bombardments destroyed much of the irrigation system for the Yarmuk and Jordan rivers in 1967, while Israeli noncooperation has blocked the development of a Tennessee Valley Authority–type project for the Jordan Valley, which would benefit both countries.

The Jordanian economy has always been affected by outside factors, which tend to undercut domestic efforts toward development. Aid from Arab oil-producing countries and remittances from the large expatriate skilled labor force are the main sources of economic support. Although this Arab aid has not been consistently forthcoming, the country did achieve high growth rates until 1987. At that time a combination of high development-investment rates, inflation, and declining agricultural exports led to a severe economic recession. A 1989 agreement with the International Monetary Fund required an austerity program, including reduction of subsidies on basic commodities, currency devaluation, and other measures, as a prerequisite for further aid, the IMF goal for Jordan being a balanced budget by 1993. The first attempt to reduce subsidies led to riots. But the changed political climate in the country due to the National Charter enabled the government to proceed to comply with IMF requirements without opposition. Subsidies were reduced drastically in September 1991; henceforth, basic commodities will be sold to consumers at fixed low prices on a ration basis, with savings to the state of $89 million a year.

NOTES

1. The Ottomans paid subsidies to nomadic tribes to guard the route of pilgrims headed south for Mecca. Peter Gubser, *Jordan: Crossroads of Middle Eastern Events* (Boulder: Westview Press, 1983).

2. Years later Glubb wrote, "In its twenty-eight years of life it had never been contemplated that the Arab Legion would fight an independent war." Quoted in Harold D. Nelson, ed., *Jordan, A Country Study* (Washington: American University, Foreign Area Studies, 1979), p. 201.

3. King Abdullah of Jordan, *My Memoirs Completed*, translated by Harold W. Glidden (London: Longman, 1951, 1978), preface, xxvi.

4. The text of the proposal is in Abdullah's *Memoirs,* pp. 89–90.

5. The party with the largest number of seats, the National Socialists, openly opposed most of Hussein's policies. See Naseer Aruri, *Jordan: A Study in Political Development (1925–1965)* (The Hague: Martinus Nijhoff, 1967), p. 159.

DEVELOPMENT

The austerity program introduced to meet IMF requirements began to show results in 1991, as exports rose 67%, to $1.2 billion. Conversely, imports went up only 19%, enabling the country to post its first current account surplus in 10 years.

FREEDOM

Although King Hussein retains ultimate authority over the state, as confirmed in the Constitution, the 1990 National Charter carries constitutional government a step further in its provision for a bicameral Legislature, consisting of an appointed Senate and an elected House of Representatives responsible for legislation.

HEALTH/WELFARE

With population growth one of the highest in the world, the government must maintain a large expatriate labor force while also expanding local industry. Refugees from the 1990–1991 crisis in the Gulf have sorely strained Jordan's resources.

ACHIEVEMENTS

Jordanians are in great demand as skilled technicians in other Arab states. As of 1987 some 400,000 were employed outside the country, sending back remittances of $880 million.

Kuwait (State of Kuwait)*

GEOGRAPHY

Area in Square Kilometers (Miles):
17,818 (6,880) (slightly smaller than
New Jersey)
Capital (Population): Kuwait
(454,000)
Climate: intensely hot and dry in
summer; short, cool winters

PEOPLE

Population
Total: 2,080,000
Annual Growth Rate: 3.7%
Rural/Urban Population Ratio: 5/95
Ethnic Makeup of Population: 25%
native; 39% other Arab; 20% South
Asian; 4% Iranian; 12% others

Health
Life Expectancy at Birth: 71 years
(male); 76 years (female)
Infant Mortality Rate (Ratio):
15/1,000
Average Caloric Intake: n/a
Physicians Available (Ratio): 1/669

Religion(s)
85% Muslim; 15% Christian, Hindu,
Parsi, and others

Education
Adult Literacy Rate: 71%

COMMUNICATION
Telephones: 419,200
Newspapers: 5 Arabic and 2 English
dailies; 418,000 combined circulation

TRANSPORTATION
Highways—Kilometers (Miles): 3,800
(2,356)

Railroads—Kilometers (Miles): none
Usable Airfields: 4

GOVERNMENT
Type: nominal constitutional
monarchy
Independence Date: June 19, 1961
Head of State: Emir Jabir al-Ahmad
al-Sabah
Political Parties: prohibited
Suffrage: adult males resident before
1920 and their male descendents
(eligible voters 3% of citizenry)

MILITARY
Number of Armed Forces: n/a
*Military Expenditures (% of Central
Government Expenditures):* n/a
Current Hostilities: none

ECONOMY
Currency ($ U.S. Equivalent): 0.29
Kuwaiti dinar = $1
Per Capita Income/GNP: $16,105/
$19.1 billion
Inflation Rate: 1%
Total Foreign Debt: n/a
Natural Resources: petroleum; fish;
shrimp
Agriculture: virtually none
Industry: crude and refined oil;
fertilizer; chemicals; construction
materials

FOREIGN TRADE
Exports: $11.4 billion
Imports: $6.3 billion

*Note: The effects of the 1991 Gulf War
between Iraq and the coalition forces
headed by the United States cannot be
accurately reflected in these statistics.
Those included here are the most current
available.

DRINKING WATER FROM THE SEA

There is almost no fresh water in Kuwait, and less than 1 percent of the
land is arable. Rainfall is rare, less than 4 inches annually. Aridity was
manageable while the population was small, but the demands of growth
have put a severe strain on the water supply. For this reason, the Kuwaiti
government has become a world leader in the desalination of sea water
to provide fresh water. It pioneered in the 1950s with a sea-water
distillation plant producing 80,000 gallons of fresh water daily. (Production reached 20 billion gallons in the late 1970s and continues to rise.)
Other plants followed, and today Kuwait receives all of its fresh water
through the desalination process. A reverse osmosis desalination system
was designed to provide emergency water supplies to hospitals in 1988.

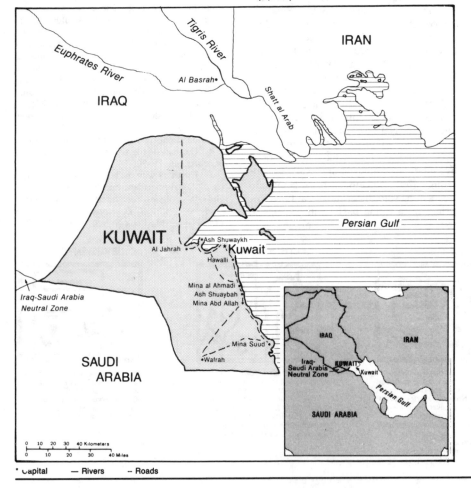

KUWAIT

Kuwait is the second smallest of the Arab states, after Bahrain; it is about the size of New Jersey. The country consists of a wedge-shaped, largely desert territory located near the head of the Persian Gulf and just southwest of the Shatt al-Arab. Kuwaiti territory includes the islands of Bubiyan and Failaka in the Gulf, both of them periodically claimed by Iraq. Kuwait also shares a Neutral Zone, consisting mainly of oil fields, which it administers jointly with Iraq and Saudi Arabia; oil production is supposedly divided equally among them. The Iraqi accusation that Kuwait was taking more than its share was one of the points of contention between the two neighbors that led to Iraq's invasion of Kuwait in 1990.

Kuwait's location has given the country great strategic importance in the twentieth-century rivalries of regional powers and their outside supporters. The country played a major role in the Iran-Iraq War, supporting Iraq financially and serving as a conduit for U.S. naval intervention through the reflagging of Kuwaiti tankers. The Iraqi invasion reversed roles, with Iraq the aggressor and Kuwait both the victim and the target of UN–U.S.-led military action during the brief Gulf War.

HISTORY

Kuwait was inhabited entirely by nomads until the early 1700s. Then a number of clans of the large Anaiza tribal confederation settled along the Gulf in the present area of Kuwait. They built a fort for protection from nomadic raids—*Kuwait* means "little fort" in Arabic—and elected a chief to represent them in dealings with the Ottoman Empire, the major power in the Middle East at that time. The ruling family of modern Kuwait, the al-Sabah, traces its power back to this period.

Kuwait prospered under the al-Sabahs. Its well-protected natural harbor became headquarters for a pearl-fishing fleet of 800 dhows (ships). The town (also called Kuwait) became a port of call for British ships bound for India.

In the late 1700s and early 1800s Kuwait was threatened by the Wahhabis, fundamentalist Muslims from central Arabia. Arab piracy also adversely affected Kuwait's prosperity. Kuwait's ruling shaykhs paid tribute to the Ottoman sultan in return for protection against the Wahhabis. However, the shaykhs began to fear that the Turks would occupy Kuwait, so they turned to the British. In 1899 Shaykh Mubarak, who reigned from 1896 to 1915, signed an agreement with the United Kingdom for protection. In return, he agreed to accept British political advisers and not to have dealings with other foreign governments. In this way, Kuwait became an autonomous (self-governing) state under British protection.

Shaykh Mubarak's period of reign was important for another reason. During the 1890s Kuwait had given refuge to Ibn Saud, a leader from central Arabia whose family had been defeated by its rivals. Ibn Saud left Kuwait in 1902, traveled in secret to Riyadh, the rivals' headquarters, and seized the city in a surprise raid. Kuwait thus indirectly had a hand in the founding of its neighbor state, Saudi Arabia.

INDEPENDENCE

Kuwait continued its peaceful ways under the paternalistic rule of the al-Sabahs until the 1950s. Then oil production increased rapidly. The small pearl-fishing port became a booming modern city. In 1961 the United Kingdom and Kuwait jointly terminated the 1899 agreement and Kuwait became fully independent under the al-Sabahs.

A threat to the country's independence developed almost immediately, as Iraq refused to recognize Kuwait's new status and claimed the territory on the grounds that it had once been part of the Iraqi Ottoman province of Basra. Iraq was also interested in controlling Kuwaiti oil resources. The ruling shaykh, now called *emir*, asked the United Kingdom for help, and British troops rushed back to Kuwait. Eventually, the Arab League agreed that several of its members would send troops to defend Kuwait—and, incidentally, to ensure that the country would not revert to its previous protectorate status. The Arab contingents were withdrawn in 1963. A revolution had overthrown the Iraqi government earlier in the year, and the new government recognized Kuwait's independence.

REPRESENTATIVE GOVERNMENT

Kuwait differs from other patriarchally ruled Arabian Peninsula states in having a Constitution which provides for an elected National Assembly. The Assembly consists of 50 members elected for 4-year terms. Friction developed between the Assembly and the ruling family soon after independence. Assembly members criticized Shaykh Abdullah and his relatives, as well as the Cabinet, for corruption, press censorship, refusal to allow political parties, and insufficient attention to public services. Since all members of the ruling family were on the government payroll, there was some justification for the criticism.

Abdullah died in 1965, but his successor, Shaykh al-Sabah, accepted the criticism as valid. Elections were held in 1971 for a new Assembly, although the voting was hardly representative, since only adult male Kuwaiti citizens have the franchise and only 58,000 Kuwaitis were eligible to vote. Since there are no political parties in the country, candidates were elected by profession.

Unfortunately for democracy in Kuwait, the new Assembly paid more attention to criticism of the government than to lawmaking. In 1976 it was suspended by Shaykh al-Sabah. He died the following year, but his successor, Shaykh Jabir, reaffirmed the ruling family's commitment to the democratic process. A new Assembly was formed in 1981, with a different membership. The majority were traditional patriarchs loyal to the rulers, along with technical experts in various fields, such as industry, agriculture, and engineering. But the new Assembly fared little better than its predecessor in balancing freedom of expression with responsible leadership. The ruler suspended it, along with the Constitution, in 1986.

Pressure for political reform has increased significantly in recent years and was accelerated in the aftermath of the Iraqi invasion and the flight of the ruling family. Prior to the invasion the ruler had convened a National Council of 75 members as a transitional body to "appraise our parliamentary experiment." Sixty-two percent of the country's 62,000 eligible male voters participated in the election of members, although opposition leaders representing various groups (political parties are prohibited) had urged a boycott. The Council was reconvened after the restoration of Kuwaiti independence, and the ruler promised to hold elections in October 1992 for a new National Assembly. Elections and restoration of the 1962 Constitution had been two key demands of opposition leaders as the price for loyalty to the ruling family during the Iraqi occupation.

VULNERABILITY

Kuwait's location and its relatively open society make the country vulnerable to external subversion. In the early 1970s the rulers were the target of criticism and threats from other Arab states because they did not publicly support the Palestinian cause. For years afterward Kuwait provided large-scale financial aid not only to the Palestine Liberation Organization but also to Arab states such as Syria and Jordan, which were directly involved in the struggle with Israel because of their common borders. The Kuwait National Assembly cancelled its aid to Syria in 1985.

(UN photo/B. Cirone)

Before the advent of tremendous oil revenues, most Kuwaitis relied on traditional livelihoods that revolved around a nomadic life. The nomadic population has now dwindled to a small segment of the population. The need to cope with new surroundings is typified by this Bedouin family confronting city life.

A new vulnerability surfaced with the Iranian Revolution of 1979, which overthrew the shah. Kuwait has a large Shia Muslim population, while its rulers are Sunni. Kuwait's support for Iraq and the development of closer links with Saudi Arabia (and indirectly the United States) angered Iran's new fundamentalist rulers. Kuwaiti oil installations were bombed by Iranian jets in 1981, and in 1983 truck bombs severely damaged the American and French embassies in Kuwait City. The underground organization Islamic Jihad claimed responsibility for the attacks and threatened more if Kuwait did not stop its support to Iraq. Kuwaiti police arrested 17 persons; they were later jailed for complicity in the bombings. Since Islamic Jihad claims links to Iran, the Kuwaiti government suspected an Iranian hand behind the violence and deported 600 Iranian workers.

Tension with Iran intensified in the mid-1980s as Iranian jets and missile-powered patrol boats attacked Kuwaiti tankers in the Gulf and pro-Iranian terrorists carried out a series of hijackings. A 1988 hijacking caused international concern when a Kuwaiti Airways 747 jet with several members of the royal family aboard was seized and its passengers held for 16 days while being shuttled from airport to airport. The hijackers demanded the release of the 17 truck bombers as the price for hostage freedom. The Kuwaiti government refused to negotiate, and after the hostages were released through mediation by other Arab states, it passed a law making hijacking punishable by death.

Fear of Iran led Kuwait to take a major role in forming the Gulf Cooperation Council in 1981. The country also began to beef up its armed forces, balancing U.S. with Soviet military aid. But the United States assumed the major protector's role after the spread of the Iran-Iraq War to Gulf sea lanes threatened to involve Kuwait directly. Thirteen Kuwaiti tankers were reflagged as American ships and provided with U.S. naval escort protection. (After the Gulf War in 1991 the United States signed a 10-year defense pact with Kuwait, the first of its kind in the region.)

THE IRAQI OCCUPATION

The 7 months of Iraqi occupation (August 1990–February 1991) had a devastating effect on Kuwait. Some 5,000 Kuwaitis were killed; the entire population was held hostage to Iraqi demands. Oil production stopped entirely. Iraqi forces opened hundreds of oil storage tanks as a defense measure, pouring millions of gallons into the sea, creating a serious environmental hazard. (As they retreated the Iraqis also set 800 oil wells afire, destroying production capabilities and posing enormous technological problems. These conflagrations were not extinguished for nearly a year.) In Kuwait City, basic water, electricity, and other services were cut off, public buildings damaged, shops and homes vandalized, and over 3,000 gold bars, the backing for the Kuwaiti currency, taken to

| Establishment of the al-Sabah family as the rulers of Kuwait **1756** | Agreement with the United Kingdom making Kuwait a protectorate **1899** | Independence, followed by Iraqi claim and British/Arab League intervention **1961–1963** | Elections for a new National Assembly **1971** | The ruler suspends the Assembly on the grounds that it is a handicap to effective government **1976** | |

●■■■■■■■■■■■■■■■■■■■■■■■■■■■■■●■■■■■■■■■■■■■■■■■■■■■■■■■■■■■■■■■■■■●■■■■■■■●■■■■■■■■■■■■■■■■■■●■■■■■■■■■■■■■ **1980s–1990s**

| Bombings of public installations by Islamic Jihad; 17 persons are arrested; massive deportation of Iranians after public buildings and oil installations are sabotaged | The National Assembly is dissolved after friction with the ruler and Council of Ministers affects public policy; the government places the tanker fleet under U.S. protection by reflagging ships and providing naval escorts in the Gulf | Iraqi forces occupy Kuwait: Kuwait is liberated by U.S.–led coalition forces in the Gulf War |

Iraq. Nearly half the population fled the country during the occupation. The National Council estimated that it would cost $8 billion to compensate Kuwaiti families for their suffering.

THE PEOPLE: A MINORITY AMONG MINORITIES

Kuwait has a very high birth rate—about 3.7 percent annually—and until the economic recession in the region, the country had a high rate of immigration. As a result, there are more non-Kuwaitis than Kuwaitis in the population. Just 40 percent of the population hold citizenship, which is only granted to those who can prove that their grandfathers were in Kuwait in 1920. All others live on sufferance on 2-year residency permits.

About one-third of the total population, both citizens and non-citizens, are Shia Muslims. After the 1979 Revolution in Iran they were blamed for much of the unrest in the country, and Shia terrorists were charged directly for the 1983 truck bombings of embassies in Kuwait City. In 1989 two of the jailed terrorists were released and deported. The improvement in Kuwait-Iran relations that followed the end of the Iran-Iraq War lessened this Shia antigovernment activity, and Shias and Sunni Kuwaitis suffered equally under the Iraqi occupation.

The largest homogeneous population group is the Palestinians. Originally refugees from what is now Israel, they are generally better educated and more active politically than the native Kuwaitis, although denied citizenship. They were the focus of opposition to the ruling family, and a number of them collaborated with the Iraqi occupation forces. After the Gulf War more than 600 Palestinians were tried and sentenced to prison terms for collaboration, in some cases for nothing more than wearing a Saddam Hussein T-shirt. As a result of uncertain economic conditions plus the government's resolve to reduce its dependence on foreign workers, thousands of Palestinians lost their jobs. Some 300,000 out of the 400,000 Palestinians in Kuwait emigrated in 1991, most of them going to Jordan as penniless refugees.

THE ECONOMY

Kuwait's only abundant resource is petroleum. Less than 0.1 percent of the land can be cultivated, and there is almost no fresh water. Drinking water comes from seawater converted to fresh by huge desalination plants.

Prior to the Iraqi invasion, oil production in Kuwait had reached 1.6 million barrels per day. With reserves of 100 billion barrels, the third highest in the world, the state could anticipate more than 200 years of oil revenues. These revenues made possible a stable and strong per capita income in the recession of the 1980s. (In point of fact, one factor in the conflict with Iraq was Kuwait's continued production in excess of Organization of Petroleum Exporting Countries (OPEC) quotas and its refusal to share revenues from output in the Neutral Zone with Iraq.)

Recovery from the Iraqi occupation has been difficult for Kuwait. The last oil wells set ablaze by retreating Iraqi troops were capped by February 1992, although a number of them continue to spray oil fumes into the air, posing a danger both to wildlife and to humans. Although oil production has resumed, the 400,000 barrel-per-day rate is well below pre-invasion figures; renewed oil exports did not begin until July 1991. Payments of $22 billion in subsidies plus Kuwait's $16 billion cash contribution to the United States for war costs have been a further drain on the economy. The government has extensive foreign investments including U.S. real estate and U.S. Treasury bonds and CDs, but financial strictures forced it to negotiate its first major loans in 1991 from U.S. and European banks, in order to spur lagging reconstruction efforts.

DEVELOPMENT

The Kuwait Fund for Arab Economic Development (KFAED), formed in 1961, has been the conduit for aid to Arab and some African and Asian less developed countries from Kuwait's vast oil revenues. Most of the funds are provided for transportation, electricity, and agricultural projects.

FREEDOM

The Iraqi occupation and the exile of the ruling family spurred demands for a reconstituted National Assembly and the establishment of full civil rights. But the only concession announced by the ruler since his return is a pledge to hold elections in October 1992. The press is relatively free, and prepublication censorship was lifted in early 1992.

HEALTH/WELFARE

The country's oil wealth has enabled it to provide free health care, education, housing, jobs, and even telephone service to all subjects. Kuwait has a high literacy rate, and a large percentage of high-school graduates continue their schooling in Kuwait or abroad.

ACHIEVEMENTS

The University of Kuwait, with a student body of 17,000, serves the country as well as the larger Arab world with a distinguished faculty and ultramodern facilities, notably in medicine. Kuwait also sends a large number of students abroad for training in technical fields not yet offered at the university.

Lebanon (Republic of Lebanon)

GEOGRAPHY

Area in Square Kilometers (Miles):
10,452 (4,015) (smaller than
Connecticut)
Capital (Population): Beirut
(1,500,000)
Climate: Mediterranean (hot, humid
summers; cool, damp winters)

PEOPLE

Population
Total: 3,340,000
Annual Growth Rate: 0.7%
Rural/Urban Population Ratio: 19/81
Ethnic Makeup of Population: 93%
Arab; 6% Armenian; 1% others

Health
Life Expectancy at Birth: 65 years
(male); 70 years (female)
Infant Mortality Rate (Ratio):
48/1,000
Average Caloric Intake: 99% of FAO
minimum
Physicians Available (Ratio): 1/771

Religion(s)
55% Christian (Maronite, Greek
Orthodox and Catholic, Roman
Catholic, and Protestant); 44%
Muslim (Sunni and Shia) and Druze;
1% others

Education
Adult Literacy Rate: 75%

COMMUNICATION
Telephones: 150,400
Newspapers: 37 dailies; 30 in Arabic

TRANSPORTATION
Highways—Kilometers (Miles): 7,370
(4,580)
Railroads—Kilometers (Miles): 417
(258)

Usable Airfields: 9

GOVERNMENT
Type: parliamentary republic
Independence Date: November 22,
1943
Head of State: President Elias Hrawi
Political Parties: various parties
identified with religious or
denominational groups. A majority of
these parties formed a National Unity
government in 1990, headed by Prime
Minister Omar Karami
Suffrage: compulsory for males over
21; authorized for women over 21
with elementary-school education

MILITARY
Number of Armed Forces: 21,800
*Military Expenditures (% of Central
Government Expenditures):* n/a
Current Hostilities: The Lebanese
Army has disarmed all militias and
controls the country, with the
exception of Israel's self-proclaimed
"security zone" along the southern
border. In 1992 Lebanese troops
began replacing UN peacekeeping
forces in south Lebanon. Periodic
clashes between Israeli forces and
Palestinian and Shia guerrillas in the
security zone continue

ECONOMY
Currency ($ U.S. Equivalent): 880
Lebanese pounds = $1
Per Capita Income/GNP: $690/$1.8
billion
Inflation Rate: 60%
Total Foreign Debt: $520 million
Natural Resources: limestone
Agriculture: citrus fruit; wheat; corn;
barley; potatoes; tobacco; olives;
onions
Industry: food processing; cement; oil
refining; light industry; textiles;
chemicals

FOREIGN TRADE
Exports: $700 million
Imports: $2.3 billion

IQTA': THE SOCIAL BASE OF LEBANESE POLITICS

Unlike most modern nations, Lebanon still operates politically and
socially under an *iqta'*—a feudal social system. Lebanese society is
organized into an intricate network of families and clans, each headed by
a *zaim* (literally, "boss"). Family and clan loyalties are given to the zaim
rather than the state, and the zaim in turn looks after the welfare of his
family and clan in a sort of patron-client relationship. The rivalries of
zaims and their private armies, along with deep-rooted religious hatreds,
have dominated Lebanese life up to the present.

* Capital   — Rivers   -- Roads

LEBANON

The Republic of Lebanon is located at the eastern end of the Mediterranean Sea. The coastal plain, which contains the capital, Beirut, and all other important cities, is narrow, rising just a few miles east of Beirut to a rugged mountain range, Mount Lebanon. Beyond Mount Lebanon is the Biqa', a broad fertile valley that is the country's main wheat-growing region. At the eastern edge of the Biqa', the land rises again abruptly to the snow-capped Anti-Lebanon Range, which separates Lebanon from Syria.

Lebanon's location has always been important strategically as well as commercially. Many invaders passed through it over the centuries on their conquests— Egyptians, Assyrians, Persians, Crusaders, Arabs, and Turks. However, these invaders were seldom able to control Mount Lebanon. For this reason, the mountain served as a refuge for ethnic and religious minorities, and it became in time the nucleus of the modern Lebanese state.

Lebanon's commercial importance stemmed from the fact that its seaports were a natural outlet for goods from Syria, Jordan, and other inland areas. The port of Beirut, in normal times, is one of the busiest in the world.

Lebanon is not yet a unified nation in the same sense as the American, British, or Japanese nations. Each religious sect, each ethnic group, and sometimes even families within a sect or group distrust and at times mortally hate the others. Abdo Baaklini, a Lebanese political scientist, describes the system as one of a feudal hierarchy with fluctuating political influence, as "powerful families asserted themselves to acquire power and prominence."[1]

HISTORY

In ancient times Lebanon was known as Phoenicia. The Phoenicians were great traders who traveled throughout the Mediterranean and probably out into the Atlantic Ocean as far north as Cornwall in England in search of the tin, copper, and iron ore valued for many uses in the ancient world. Phoenician merchants established trading posts, some of which eventually grew into great cities.

In Phoenicia itself, no central government was ever established. Phoenician towns like Byblos, Tyre, Sidon, and Tripoli were independent states, often in conflict or rivalry over trade with one another. This city-state rivalry has always been a feature of Lebanese life and is another reason for the lack of a national Lebanese sense of unity.

(UN photo/J. K. Isaac)

Invasions have played an important role in the history of Lebanon. The Crusades began in 1095, when the Western Christians were finally expelled. The 200 years of their occupation are still in evidence, as shown in the photograph above. This view of Ayta az Zutt, in the southeastern area of Lebanon, shows the remains of a Crusader's castle on the distant hill.

Lebanon began to develop a definite identity much later, in the seventh century A.D., when a Christian group, the Maronites, took refuge in Mount Lebanon after they were threatened with persecution by the government of the East Roman or Byzantine Empire because of theological disagreements over the nature of Christ. The Muslim Arabs brought Islam to coastal Lebanon at about the same time, but they were unable to dislodge or convert the Maronites. Mount Lebanon's sanctuary tradition attracted other minority groups, Muslim as well as Christian. Shia Muslim communities moved there in the ninth and tenth centuries to escape persecution from Sunni Muslims, the Islamic majority. In the eleventh century the Druze, an offshoot of Islam, who followed the teachings of an Egyptian mystic and also faced persecution from Sunni Muslims, established themselves in the southern part of Mount Lebanon. These communities were originally quite separate but in the modern period of Lebanese history have tended to overlap, a fact, as David Gordon says, "that makes both for unity and in troubled times for a dangerous struggle for turf."[2]

Lebanon acquired a distinct political identity in the sixteenth and seventeenth centuries under certain powerful families.

The Ottoman Turks conquered it, along with the rest of the Middle East, but were content to leave local governance in the hands of these families in return for tribute. The most prominent were the Ma'an family, who were Druze. Their greatest leader, Fakhr al-Din (1586–1635), established an independent principality including all of present-day Lebanon, Israel, and part of Syria. It was during al-Din's rule that French religious orders were allowed to establish missions in the country, which facilitated later European intervention in Lebanon.

The Ma'ans were succeeded by the Shihabs, who were Maronites. Their descendants continue to hold important positions in the country, underscoring the durability of the extended-family system which still dominates Lebanese politics. They also allied the Maronite Church with the Catholic Church in Rome, an action that had great consequences in the twentieth century, when the Maronites came to view Lebanon as "a Christian island in a Muslim sea," preserving its unique Lebanese identity only through Western support.

European countries began to intervene directly in Lebanon in the nineteenth century, due to conflict between the Maronite and Druze communities. Mount Lebanon was occupied by Egyptian armies of the Ottoman khedive (viceroy) of Egypt, Muhammad Ali, in the 1830s. Egyptian development of Beirut and other coastal ports for trade purposes, particularly exports of Lebanese silk (still an important cash crop) at the expense of Mount Lebanon, and heavy taxes imposed by the khedive's overseers led to peasant uprisings in 1840 and 1857. By then the Ottomans had reestablished their authority, with European help. However, the European powers refused to allow the sultan to change Mount Lebanon's special status as an autonomous province. Ottoman governors resorted to intrigues with Maronite and Druze leaders, playing one against the other. The result was a Maronite-Druze civil war, which broke out in 1860. The cause was insignificant—"an affray between two boys, the shooting of a partridge or the collision of two pack animals," asserts one author; but whatever the spark, the two communities were ready to go for each other's throats.[3]

Although the Maronite fighters greatly outnumbered the Druze, the latter had better leadership. The Druze massacred 12,000 Christians and drove 100,000 from their homes during a 4-week period. At that point, the European powers intervened to protect their coreligionists. French troops landed in Beirut and moved

on to occupy Damascus. France and England forced the Ottoman sultan to establish Mount Lebanon as a self-governing province headed by a Christian governor. The province did not include Beirut. Although many Lebanese emigrated during this period, because Mount Lebanon was small, rather poor, and provided few job opportunities, those who stayed (particularly the Maronites) prospered. Self-government under their own leader enabled them to develop a system of small, individually owned farms and to break their former dependence on absentee landowners. A popular saying among Lebanese at the time was, "Happy is he who has a shed for one goat in Mount Lebanon."[4]

The French Mandate

After the defeat of Ottoman Turkey in World War I Lebanon became a French mandate. The French had originally intended the country to be included in their mandate over Syria, but in 1920, due to pressure from Maronite leaders, they separated the two mandates. "New" Lebanon was much larger than the old Maronite-Druze territory up on Mount Lebanon. The new "Greater Lebanon" included the coast; in short, the area of the current Lebanese state. The Maronites found themselves linked not only with the Druze but also with both Sunni and Shia Muslims. The Maronites already distrusted the Druze, out of bitter experience. Their distrust was caused by fear of a Muslim majority and fear that Muslims, being mostly Arabs, would work to incorporate Lebanon into Syria after independence.

France gave Lebanon its independence in 1943, but French troops stayed on until 1946, when they were withdrawn due to British and American pressure on France. The French made some contributions to Lebanese development during the mandate, such as the nucleus of a modern army, development of ports, roads, and airports, and an excellent educational system dominated by the Université de St. Joseph, training ground for many Lebanese leaders. The French language and culture served until recently as one of the few things unifying the various sects and providing them with a sense of national identity.

THE LEBANESE REPUBLIC

The major shortcoming of the mandate was the French failure to develop a broad-based political system with representatives from the major religious groups. The French very pointedly favored the Maronites. A Constitution, originally issued in 1926, established a republican system under an elected president and a Legislature. Members would be elected on the

basis of 6 Christians to 5 Muslims. The president would be elected for a 6-year term and could not succeed him- or herself. (The one exception was Bishara Khuri [1943–1952], who served during and after the transition period to independence. The Constitution was amended to allow him to do so.) By private French-Maronite agreement, the custom was established whereby the Lebanese president would always be chosen from the Maronite community.

In the long term, perhaps more important to Lebanese politics than the Constitution is the National Pact, an oral agreement made in 1943 between Bishara al-Khuri, as head of the Maronite community, and Riad al-Sulh, his Sunni counterpart. The two leaders agreed that, first, Lebanese Christians would not enter into alliances with foreign (i.e., Christian) nations and Muslims would not attempt to merge Lebanon with the Muslim Arab world; and second, that the 6-to-5 formula for representation in the Assembly would apply to all public offices. The pact has never been put in writing, but in view of the delicate balance of sects in Lebanon, it has been considered by Lebanese leaders, particularly the Maronites, as the only alternative to anarchy.

Despite periodic political crises and frequent changes of government due to shifting alliances of leaders, Lebanon functioned quite well during its first 2 decades of independence. The large extended family, although an obstacle to broad nation building, served as an essential support base for its members, providing services that would otherwise have to have been drawn from government sources. These services included education, employment, bank loans, investment capital, and old-age security. Powerful families of different religious groups competed for power and influence but also coexisted, having had "the long experience with each other and with the rules and practices that make coexistence possible."[5]

The freewheeling Lebanese economy was another important factor in Lebanon's relative stability. Per capita annual income rose from $235 in 1950 to $1,070 in 1974, putting Lebanon on a level with some of the oil-producing Arab states, although the country does not have oil. The private sector was largely responsible for national prosperity. A real-estate boom developed, and many fortunes were made in land speculation and construction. Tourism was another important source of revenues; in 1974 alone, 1.5 million tourists visited Lebanon. Many banks and foreign business firms established their headquarters in Beirut because of its excellent communications with the outside world, its educated, multilingual labor force, and the absence of government restrictions.

THE 1975–1976 CIVIL WAR

The titles of books on Lebanon in recent years often contain adjectives such as "fractured," "fragmented," and "precarious." These provide a generally accurate description of the country's changed situation as a result of the Civil War of 1975–1976. The main destabilizing element, and the one that precipitated the conflict, was the presence and activities of the Palestinians.

In some ways, Palestinians have contributed significantly to Lebanese national life. The first group, who fled there after the 1948 Arab-Israeli War, consisted mostly of cultured, educated, highly urbanized people who gravitated to Beirut and were absorbed quickly into the population. Many of them became extremely successful in banking, commerce, journalism, or as faculty members at the American University of Beirut. A second Palestinian group arrived as destitute refugees after the 1967 Six-Day War. Ever since, they have been housed in refugee camps run by the United Nations Relief and Works Agency (UNRWA). The Lebanese government provides them with identity cards but no passports, and for all practical purposes they are stateless persons.

Neither group was a threat to Lebanese internal stability until 1970, although Lebanon backed the Palestine Liberation Organization cause and did not interfere with guerrilla raids from its territory into Israel. After the PLO was expelled from Jordan, the organization made its headquarters in Beirut. This new militant Palestinian presence in Lebanon created a double set of problems for the Lebanese. Palestinian raids into Israel brought Israeli retaliation, which caused more Lebanese than Palestinian casualties. Yet the Lebanese government could not control the Palestinians. To many Lebanese, especially the Maronites, their government seemed to be a prisoner in its own land.

In April 1975 a bus carrying Palestinians returning from a political rally was ambushed near Beirut by the Kata'ib, members of the Maronite Phalange Party. The incident triggered the year-long Lebanese Civil War of 1975–1976. The war officially ended with a peace agreement arranged by the Arab League.[6] But the bus incident brought to a head conflicts derived from the opposing goals of various Lebanese power groups. The Palestinian goal was to use Lebanon as a springboard for the liberation of Palestine. The Maronites' goal was to drive the

(UN photo)

After being expelled from Jordan in 1970, the Palestine Liberation Organization moved its headquarters to Beirut. In 1982 it was forced out of Lebanon by the Israeli Army, with American assistance. Yasser Arafat, above, is the head and familiar symbol of the PLO.

Palestinians out of Lebanon and preserve their privileged status. Sunni Muslim leaders sought to reshape the National Pact to allow for equal participation with the Christians in the political system. Shia leaders were determined to get a better break for the Shia community, generally the poorest and least represented in the Lebanese government.[7] The Druze, also interested in greater representation in the system and traditionally hostile to the Maronites, disliked and distrusted all of the other groups.

Like most civil wars, the Lebanese Civil War was fought by its own people. But Lebanon's location, its international importance as a trade, banking, and transit center, and the various factions' need for financial backing ensured outside involvement in the conflict. Syrian troops intervened, at the request of the Arab League, first to enforce the 1976 ceasefire and then to crush the Palestinians. The Israelis helped a Lebanese renegade officer to set up an "independent free Lebanon" adjoining the Israeli border. The complexity of the situation was described in graphic terms by a Christian religious leader:

The battle is between the Palestinians

and the Lebanese. No! It is between the Palestinians and the Christians. No! It is between Christians and Muslims. No! It is between Leftists and Rightists. No! It is between Israel and the Palestinians on Lebanese soil. No! It is between international imperialism and Zionism on the one hand, and Lebanon and neighboring states on the other.[8]

THE ISRAELI INVASION

The immediate result of the Civil War was to divide Lebanon into separate territories, each one controlled by a different faction. The Lebanese government, for all practical purposes, could not control its own territory. Israeli forces, in an effort to protect northern Israeli settlements from constant shelling by the Palestinians, established control over southern Lebanon. The Lebanese-Israeli border, ironically, became a sort of "good fence" open to Lebanese civilians for medical treatment in Israeli hospitals.

In March 1978 PLO guerrillas landed on the Israeli coast near Haifa, hijacked a bus, and drove it toward Tel Aviv. The hijackers were overpowered in a shootout with Israeli troops, but 35 passengers were killed along with the guerrillas. Israeli forces invaded southern Lebanon in retaliation and occupied the region for 2 months, eventually withdrawing after the United Nations, in an effort to separate Palestinians from Israelis, set up a 6,000-member Interim Force in Lebanon (UNIFIL), made up of units from various countries, in the south. But the Interim Force was not able to do much to control the Palestinians; most Lebanese and Israelis referred sarcastically to the force as the "United Nothings."

The Lebanese factions themselves continued to tear the nation apart. Political assassinations of rival leaders were frequent. Many Lebanese settlements became ghost towns; they were fought over so much that their residents abandoned them. Some 300,000 Lebanese from the Israeli-occupied south fled to northern cities as refugees. In addition to the thousands of casualties, a psychological trauma settled over Lebanese youth, the "Kalashnikov generation" that knew little more than violence, crime, and the blind hatred of religious feuds. (The Kalashnikov, a Soviet-made submachine gun, became the standard toy of Lebanese children.)[9]

The Israeli invasion of Lebanon in June 1982 was intended as a final solution to the Palestinian problem. It didn't quite work out that way. The Israeli Army surrounded Beirut and succeeded with American intervention in forcing the evacuation of PLO guerrillas from Lebanon. Some of the Lebanese factions were happy to see them go, particularly the Maronites and the Shia community in the south. But they soon discovered that they had exchanged one foreign domination for another. The burden of war, as always, fell heaviest on the civilian population. A Beirut newspaper estimated almost 50,000 civilian casualties in the first 2 months of the invasion. Also, the Lebanese discovered that they were not entirely free of the Palestinian presence. The largest number of PLO guerrillas either went to Syria and then returned secretly to Lebanon or retreated into the Biqa' Valley to take up new positions under Syrian Army protection.

Israeli control over Beirut enabled the Christians to take savage revenge against the remaining Palestinians. In September 1983 Christian Phalange militiamen entered the refugee camps of Sabra and Shatila in West Beirut and massacred hundreds of people, mostly women and children. The massacre led to an official Israeli inquiry and censure of Israeli government and military leaders for indirect responsibility. But the Christian-dominated Lebanese government's own in-

quiry failed to fix responsibility on the Phalange.

PROSPECTS

The Civil War supposedly ended in 1976, but it was not until 1990 that the central government began to show results in disarming militias and establishing its authority over the fragmented nation. Until then, hostage taking and clan rivalries underlined the absence in Lebanon of a viable national identity.

The 1982 Israeli invasion brought a change in government, with the Phalange leader, Bashir Gemayel, elected to head a "government of national salvation." Unfortunately for Bashir, his ruthless career had enabled him to compile an impressive list of enemies. He was killed by a bomb explosion at Phalange headquarters before he could take office. Gemayel was succeeded by his older brother, Amin. The new president was persuaded by American negotiators to sign a troop-withdrawal agreement with Israel. However, the agreement was not supported by leaders of the other Lebanese communities, and in March 1984 Gemayel unilaterally repudiated it. The Israelis then began working their way out of the "Lebanese quagmire" on their own, and in June 1985 the last Israeli units left Lebanon. (However, the Israelis did reserve a "security zone" along the border for necessary reprisals for attacks by the PLO or Shia guerrillas.)

Behind them the Israelis left a country that had become almost ungovernable. Gemayel's effort to restructure the national army along nonsectarian lines came to nothing, since the army was not strong enough to disband the various militias. The growing power of the Shia Muslims, particularly the Shia organization Amal, presented a new challenge to the Christian leadership, while the return of the Palestinians brought bloody battles between Shia and PLO guerrillas. As the battles raged, ceasefire followed ceasefire and conference followed conference, without noticeable success.

The Israeli withdrawal left the Syrians as the major power brokers in Lebanon. In 1985 Syrian President Hafez al-Assad masterminded a comprehensive peace and reform agreement with Elie Hobeika, commander of the Christian Lebanese Forces, with Shia Muslim and Druze leaders concurring. The agreement would provide for the election of an enlarged Parliament, with equal representation for Christians and Muslims, and would change the Lebanese National Pact to apportion greater power in the government and the army to Muslims. But before the pact could be put into effect, one of

Hobeika's rivals, privately encouraged by President Gemayel, overthrew him. Hobeika fled into exile in Syria. With his departure the Civil War resumed, fueled by seemingly endless factional conflicts.

SYRIA INTERVENES

The collapse of peace efforts led Syria to send 7,000 heavily armed commandos into West Beirut in 1987 to restore law and order. They did restore a semblance of order to that part of the capital and opened checkpoints into East Beirut. But the Syrians were unable (or perhaps unwilling) to challenge the powerful Hizbollah faction (reputed to have held most Western hostages), which controlled the rabbit warren of narrow streets and tenements in the city's southern suburbs.

Aside from Hizbollah, Syria's major problem in knitting together Lebanon under its tutelage was with the Maronite community. With President Gemayel's 6-year term scheduled to end in September 1988, the Syrians lobbied hard for a candidate of their choice. (Under the Lebanese parliamentary system, the president is elected by the Chamber of Deputies.) Unfortunately, due to the Civil War, only 72 of the 99 deputies elected in 1972, when the last elections were held, were still in office. They rejected Syria's candidate, former President Suleiman Franjieh (1970–1976), because of his identification with the conflict and his ties with the Assad regime. When the Chamber failed to agree on an acceptable candidate, the office became vacant. Gemayel's last act before leaving office was to appoint General Michel Aoun, commander of Christian troops in the Lebanese Army, to head an interim government. But the Muslim-dominated civilian government of Prime Minister Salim al-Hoss contested the appointment, declaring that it remained the legitimate government of the country.

BREAKDOWN OF A SOCIETY

The assassination in 1987 of Prime Minister Rachid Karami, when a bomb hidden in the army helicopter in which he was traveling blew up and destroyed the aircraft, underlined graphically the mindless rejection of law and order of the various Lebanese factions. The only show of Lebanese unity in many years occurred at the funeral of former President Camille Chamoun, dead of a heart attack at age 87. Chamoun's last public statement, the day before his death, was particularly fitting to this fractured land. "The nation is headed toward total bankruptcy and famine," he warned. The statement brought to mind the prophetic observations of a historian, written 25 years ago: "Lebanon is too conspicuous and successful an example of political democracy and economic liberalism to be tolerated in a region that has turned its back on both systems."[10]

The death of the Mufti (the chief religious leader) of the Sunni Muslim community in a car-bomb attack in 1989 confirmed Chamoun's gloomy prediction. The Mufti had consistently called for reconciliation and nonviolent coexistence between Christian and Muslim communities. The political situation remained equally chaotic. Rene Moawwad, a respected Christian lawyer, was elected by the Chamber to fill the presidential vacancy. However, he was murdered after barely 17 days in office. The Chamber then elected Elias Hrawi, a Christian politician from the Maronite stronghold of Zahle, as president. General Aoun contested the election, declaring himself the legitimate president of Lebanon, and holed up in the presidential palace in East Beirut, defended strongly by his Maronite militiamen.

But the Maronite community was as fragmented as the larger Lebanese community. Aoun's chief Christian rival, Samir Geagea, rejected his authority, and early in 1990 a renewed outbreak of fighting between their militias left East Beirut in a shambles, with more than 3,000 casualties. After another shaky ceasefire had been reached, Syrian Army units supporting the regular Lebanese Army surrounded the Christian section. Aoun's palace became an embattled enclave, with supplies available only by running the Syrian blockade or humanitarian relief.

Aoun's support base eroded significantly in the spring, when his rival recognized the Hrawi government as legitimate and endorsed the Taif Accord.[11] In October Hrawi formally requested Syrian military aid for the Lebanese Army. After an all-out assault on the presidential palace by joint Syrian-Lebanese forces, the general surrendered, taking refuge in the French Embassy and then going into exile.

Aoun's departure enabled the Hrawi government to begin taking the next step toward rebuilding a united Lebanon. This involved disarming the militias. To facilitate the process, Syrian forces withdrew from Beirut, although continuing to control eastern and northern Lebanon from bases in the Matn region and the Biqa' Valley as a hedge against Israel. The Syrian withdrawal, ironically, would help to strengthen the same Lebanese political institutions that Syria had sought to control in the past. But Syria's President Assad was realistic. "Lebanon and Syria are one nation and one people, but they are two distinct states," he told an inter-

viewer.[12] It was the first clear statement from any Syrian leader that Lebanon had a legitimate existence as a state.

By mid-1991 all the militias had been disarmed as the Lebanese regular Army extended its control to all of Lebanon except for the self-proclaimed Israeli "security zone" along the border and the Jezzine area in the far south, still controlled by the Israeli-backed South Lebanese Army.

The restoration of central government authority was accompanied by steps to establish political unity. The Chamber of Deputies approved in December 1990 a Cabinet of representatives of the various religious communities. However, Geagea and Druze leader Walid Jumblatt refused to join, saying that it was biased toward Syria. The Chamber also approved amendments to the Taif Accord that reduced the powers of the president and ended Christian dominance over ministerial posts and staffs of public institutions.

A new Chamber of Deputies took office in 1991; its 108 seats are equally divided between Christians and Muslims. Rather than delay the formation of the "Second Lebanese Republic" (as its backers hoped it would be), the Hrawi government appointed 40 new members to the Chamber to fill seats left vacant by death or resignation of its predecessor, observing the democratic process by choosing from a slate of 348 candidates.

LEBANON AND THE WORLD

Aside from its vulnerability to international and inter-Arab rivalries because of internal conflicts, Lebanon in the 1980s drew world attention for its involvement in hostage taking. Lebanese militias such as Hizbollah, a Shia group backed by Iran as a means of exporting the Islamic Revolution, and shadowy organizations with names like Islamic Jihad, Revolutionary Justice, and Islamic Jihad for the Liberation of Palestine, kidnapped foreigners on the streets of Beirut. The conditions set for their release were rarely specific, and the refusal of the U.S. and other Western governments to "deal with terrorists" left them languishing in unknown prisons for years, almost forgotten by the outside world.

The changing Middle East situation and Lebanon's slow return to normalcy in the '90s began to move the hostage release process forward. Release negotiations were pursued by UN General-Secretary Javier Pérez de Cuéllar (who retired at the end of 1991). The UN team worked on two levels: Pérez de Cuéllar ran a high-profile diplomatic campaign by repeatedly visiting Iran, Syria, and Israel; while his long-time associ-

ate Giandomenico Picco conducted behind-the-scenes talks with Shia operatives in the Biqa' Valley located in the eastern part of Lebanon. By August their efforts began to bear fruit when British journalist John McCarthy was released. In late October Jesse Turner was released; 4 weeks later Thomas Sutherland and British church envoy Terry Waite were freed. By November 30 Picco had received a schedule for the release of Joseph Cicippio, Alan Steen, and Terry Anderson. Cicippio was turned over to the U.S. ambassador for Syria on December 2, Steen was freed on December 3, and the last American held by the Revolutionary Justice Organization, Terry Anderson, was released on December 4. At the end of 1991 two German relief workers, Heinrich Strübig and Thomas Kemptner, remained in captivity pending the release of two Arab brothers being held in a German jail for hijacking and abduction. Picco continued to negotiate to bring the hostage crisis to a close.

THE ECONOMY

Since the mid-1970s the Lebanese economy has been going steadily downhill. The Civil War and resulting instability caused most banks and financial institutions to move out of Beirut to more secure locations, notably Jordan, Bahrain, and Kuwait. Aside from the cost in human lives, Israeli raids and the 1982 invasion severely damaged the economy. The cost of the invasion in terms of damages was estimated at $1.9 billion. Remittances from Lebanese emigrants abroad dropped. The Lebanese pound, valued at 4.74 to the U.S. dollar in 1982, reached 600 to $1.00 in 1987.

Yet by a strange irony of fate, some elements of the economy continued to display robust health. Gold reserves held by the central bank reached $4.5 billion in 1988, the country had no foreign debt, and investment of funds abroad or in dollar accounts helped to shield many middle-class Lebanese from economic disaster.

A proposal by the prime minister prior to the abortive presidential elections that gold reserves be sold to finance public spending and shore up the currency aroused a storm of protest. Opportunists to the end, the Lebanese adjusted to the latest Battle of Beirut in 1989 with more aplomb and inventiveness than they had shown during the 15 previous years of civil war. A newspaper advertisement announced, "Civilian fortifications, 24-hour delivery service. Sandbags and barrels, full or empty." With the Syrian-Christian artillery exchanges concentrated at night,

Establishment of Mount Lebanon as a sanctuary for religious communities 9th–11th centuries A.D.	Shihab and Ma'an emirs are granted autonomy under overall Ottoman control 1700–1840	The first Civil War, between Maronites and Druze, ending in foreign military intervention 1860–1864	French mandate 1920–1946	Internal crisis and the first U.S. military intervention 1958	Civil War, ended (temporarily) by an Arab League-sponsored cease-fire and peace-keeping force of Syrian troops 1975–1976	

1980s–199

Israeli invasion and occupation of Beirut; massacre of Palestinians in refugee camps by Christian militiamen	Syrian troops re-occupy Beirut, restore order, but are unable to reconcile warring factions; foreigners are seized in a new outbreak of hos-tage taking; the economy nears collapse as the currency is devalued and banks halt trading	Leaders form a government of "National Unity"; the withdrawal of Israeli forces from Lebanon is completed; nearly all foreign hostages are released

most residents fled the city then, returning after the muezzin's first call for morning prayers had in effect silenced the guns, to shop, to stock up on fuel smuggled ashore from small tankers, or to sample the luxury goods that in some mysterious way had appeared on supermarket shelves.

But except for the fortunate ones, the general population began to feel the economic impact of years of civil war for the first time in 1986 and 1987. A Lebanese filmmaker summed up the situation with devastating accuracy: "We are getting divided into the very poor and the very rich, and the middle class is getting squeezed out. The poor, you can see them everywhere now, for the first time."[13]

The long, drawn-out civil conflict badly affected Lebanese agriculture, the mainstay of the economy. Both the coastal strip and the Biqa' Valley are extremely fertile, and in normal times produce crop surpluses for export. Lebanese fruit, particularly apples (the most important cash crop) and grapes, is in great demand throughout the Arab world. But these crops are no longer exported in quantity. Israeli destruction of crops, the flight of most of the farm labor force, and the blockade by Israeli troops of truck traffic from rural areas into Beirut had a devastating effect on production.

Lebanon produces no oil of its own, but before the Civil War and the Israeli invasion, the country derived important revenues from transit fees for oil shipments through pipelines across its territory. The periodic closing of these pipelines and damage to the country's two refineries sharply reduced revenues. The well-developed manufacturing industry, particularly textiles, was equally hard hit.

But the Lebanese, over the years, have shown an extraordinary resilience in recovering from economic disaster. Even before the central government had completed its disarming of militias there were hopeful signs. The port of Beirut opened early in 1991 after a 2-year shutdown, and the first formal budget since 1985 was approved and went into effect. Projecting a $667 million deficit, the government agreed to end subsidies on bread, flour, and gasoline to comply with requirements of the World Bank for resumption of foreign aid, and the U.S. Bechtel Corporation was given a $69 million contract to plan the rebuilding of the country's infrastructure, almost ruined after years of war.

NOTES

1. Abdo Baaklini, *Legislative and Political Development: Lebanon 1842–1972* (Durham: Duke University Press, 1976), pp. 32–34.

2. David C. Gordon, *The Republic of Lebanon: Nation in Jeopardy* (Boulder: Westview Press, 1983), p. 4.

3. Samir Khlaf, *Lebanon's Predicament* (New York: Columbia University Press, 1987), p. 69.

4. Gordon, *op. cit.*, p. 19.

5. *Ibid.*, p. 25. See also Baaklini, *op. cit.*, pp. 200–202, for a description of the coexistence process as used by Sabri Hamadeh, for many years head of the assembly.

6. Whether the Civil War ever really ended is open to question. A cartoon in a U.S. newspaper in August 1982 shows a hooded skeleton on a TV screen captioned "Lebanon" saying, "And now we return to our regularly scheduled civil war." Gordon, *op. cit*, p. 113.

7. Shia religious leader Imam Musa al-Sadr's political organization was named Harakat al-Mahrumin ("Movement of the Disinherited") when it was founded in 1969–1970. See Marius Deeb, *The Lebanese Civil War* (New York: Praeger, 1980), pp. 69–70.

8. Gordon, *op. cit.*, p. 110.

9. *Ibid.*, p. 125

10. Charles Issawi, "Economic Development and Political Liberalism in Lebanon," in Leonard Binder, ed., *Politics in Lebanon* (New York: John Wiley, 1966), pp. 80–81.

11. The Taif Accord, signed under Arab League auspices in Taif, Saudi Arabia, changes the power-sharing arrangement in the Lebanese government from a 6:5 Christian-Muslim ratio to one of equal representation in the government. The powers of the president are also reduced.

12. *Middle East Economic Digest* (October 10, 1990).

13. Quoted in *The Christian Science Monitor* (March 3, 1987).

DEVELOPMENT

The 1990–1991 budget projected spending at $1 billion and revenues of $330 million, mostly from customs fees and duties from the newly reopened ports of Beirut and Tripoli. The resumption of oil refining at the Tripoli refinery will generate 15,000 barrels per day for export; the crude oil comes via pipeline from Syria.

FREEDOM

The Taif Accord and amendments to the Lebanese Constitution establish a 50-50 division between Christians and Muslims in an enlarged 108-member Chamber of Deputies. Three seats are reserved for Shia Muslims and 2 each for the Sunni Muslim, Druze, and Alawi communities.

HEALTH/WELFARE

The disbanding of militias has created a severe employment problem since the militiamen (some of whom earned as much as $40,000 a year from rackets in addition to their militia salaries) have no skills and are virtually unemployable. The government hopes to integrate a small number into the army or police once they are "rehabilitated."

ACHIEVEMENTS

One of the few successful projects in the rebuilding of Lebanon is the UNICEF-sponsored reconstruction program in the south. It began in 1981 with small projects in various villages, such as the provision of a potable water supply, school construction, and health clinics. The funding of just under $2 million comes from other Arab countries.

Libya (Socialist People's Libyan Arab Jamahiriya)

GEOGRAPHY

Area in Square Kilometers (Miles): 1,758,610 (679,536) (larger than Alaska)
Capital (Population): Tripoli (990,700)
Climate: arid

PEOPLE

Population
Total: 4,280,000
Annual Growth Rate: 3.0%
Rural/Urban Population Ratio: 31/69
Ethnic Makeup of Population: 97% Berber and Arab; 3% southern European and southern Asian

Health
Life Expectancy at Birth: 64 years (male); 69 years (female)
Infant Mortality Rate (Ratio): 77/1,000
Average Caloric Intake: 147% of FAO minimum
Physicians Available (Ratio): 1/823

Religion(s)
97% Sunni Muslim; 3% others

Education
Adult Literacy Rate: 60%

COMMUNICATION
Telephones: 102,000
Newspapers: 1 daily in Tripoli

TRANSPORTATION
Highways—Kilometers (Miles): 25,675 (16,021)
Railroads—Kilometers (Miles): none
Usable Airfields: 115

TOWARD GREATER SELF-SUFFICIENCY

The Great Man-Made River (GMR) is a network of pipelines and reservoirs designed to bring subsurface water from the Sahara Desert northward to provide irrigation for expanded coastal farming and potable water for cities. This project is Colonel Muammar al-Qadhafi's showpiece in a campaign to make arid Libya self-sufficient in food production by the end of the century.

GOVERNMENT
Type: direct popular democracy
Independence Date: December 24, 1951
Head of State: Colonel Muammar al-Qadhafi (no official title; de facto chief of state)*; legislation through local people's congresses and elected General People's Congress (GPC)
Political Parties: none
Suffrage: universal adult

MILITARY
Number of Armed Forces: 85,000
Military Expenditures (% of Central Government Expenditures): n/a
Current Hostilities: none

ECONOMY
Currency ($ U.S. Equivalent): 0.27 Libyan dinar = $1
Per Capita Income/GNP: $5,500/$20 billion
Inflation Rate: n/a
Total Foreign Debt: n/a
Natural Resources: petroleum; natural gas
Agriculture: wheat; barley; olives; dates; citrus fruits; peanuts; livestock
Industry: crude petroleum; food processing; textiles; handcrafts

FOREIGN TRADE
Exports: $6.7 billion
Imports: $5.1 billion

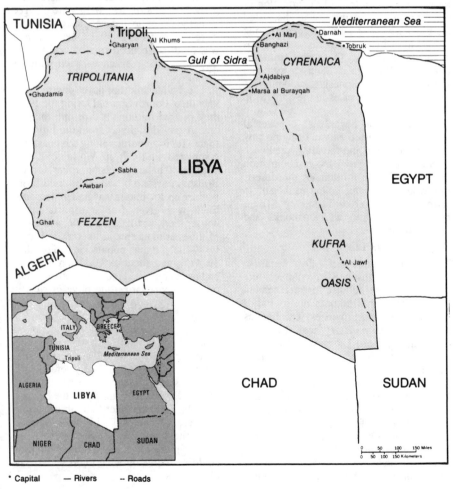

* Capital   — Rivers   -- Roads

*Note: Other commonly used spellings of Colonel Qadhafi's name include Qaddafi, Gaddafi, and Khadafy.

LIBYA

The Socialist People's Libyan Arab Jamahiriya (Republic), commonly known as Libya, encompasses 679,536 square miles, the fourth largest of the Arab countries. Since it became a republic in 1969, it has played a role in regional and international affairs more appropriate to the size of its territory than of its population.

Libya consists of three geographical regions: Tripolitania, Cyrenaica, and the Fezzan. Most of the population live in Tripolitania, the northwestern part of the country where Tripoli, the capital and major port, is located. Cyrenaica, in the east along the Egyptian border, has a narrow coastline backed by a high plateau (2,400-feet elevation) called the Jabal al-Akhdar ("Green Mountain"). It contains Libya's other principal city, Benghazi. The two regions are separated by the Sirte, an extension of the Sahara Desert that reaches almost to the Mediterranean Sea. Most of Libya's oil fields are in the Sirte.

The Fezzan occupies the central part of the country. It is entirely desert except for a string of widely scattered oases. Its borders are with Chad, Algeria, Niger, and Sudan. The boundary with Chad has been in dispute since Libyan troops occupied the 120-mile-long Aouzou Strip in northern Chad in 1973, claiming rights inherited from the French colonial period.

HISTORY

Until modern times Libya did not have a separate identity, either national or territorial. It formed a part of some other territorial unit and in most cases was controlled by outsiders. However, control was usually limited to the coastal areas. The Berbers of the interior were little affected by the passing of conquerors and the rise and fall of civilizations.

Libya's culture and social structure have been influenced more by the Islamic Arabs than by any other invaders. The Arabs brought Islam to Libya in the early seventh century. Arab groups settled in the region and intermarried with the Berber population to such an extent that the Libyans became one of the most thoroughly Arabized peoples in the Islamic world.

Coastal Libya, around Tripoli, was an outlying province of the Ottoman Empire for several centuries. Like its neighbors Tunis and Algiers, Tripoli had a fleet of corsairs who made life dangerous for European merchant ships in the Mediterranean. When the United States became a Mediterranean trading nation, the corsairs of Tripoli included American ships among their targets. The *USS Philadel-phia* was sent to Tripoli to "teach the corsairs a lesson" in 1804, but it got stuck on a sandbar and was captured. Navy Lieutenant Stephen Decatur led a commando raid into Tripoli harbor and blew up the ship, inspiring the words to what became the official U.S. Marine hymn: "From the halls of Montezuma to the shores of Tripoli. . . ."

The Sanusiya Movement

At various stages in Islam's long history, new groups or movements have appeared, committed to purifying or reforming Islamic society and taking it back to its original form of a simple community of believers led by just rulers. Several of these movements, such as the Wahhabis of Saudi Arabia, were important in the founding of modern Islamic states. The movement called the *Sanusiya* was formed in the nineteenth century. In later years it became an important factor in the formation of modern Libya.

The founder, the Grand Sanusi, was a religious teacher from Algeria. He left Algeria after the French conquest and settled in northern Cyrenaica. The Grand Sanusi's teachings attracted many followers. He also attracted the attention of the Ottoman authorities, who distrusted his advocacy of a strong united Islamic world in which Ottomans and Arabs would be partners. To escape from the Ottomans, the Grand Sanusi's son and successor moved Sanusiya headquarters to Kufra, a remote oasis in the Sahara, in 1895.

The Sanusiya began as a peaceful movement interested only in bringing new converts to Islam and founding a network of *zawiyas* ("lodges") for contemplation and monastic life throughout the desert. But when European countries began to seize territories in North and West Africa, the Sanusi became warrior-monks and fought the invaders.

Italy Conquers Libya

The Italian conquest of Libya began in 1911. The Italians needed colonies, not only for prestige but also for resettlement of poor and landless peasants in Italy's crowded southern provinces. The Italians expected an easy victory against a weak Ottoman garrison. Libya would become the "Fourth Shore" of a new Roman Empire from shore to shore along the Mediterranean. But the Italians found Libya a tougher land to subdue than they had expected. Italian forces were pinned to Tripoli and a few other points on the coast by the Ottoman garrison and the fierce Sanusi warrior-monks.

The Italians were given a second chance after World War I. The Ottoman Empire had been defeated, and Libya was ripe for plucking. The new Italian government of swaggering dictator Benito Mussolini sent an army to occupy Tripolitania. When the Italians moved on Cyrenaica, the Grand Sanusi crossed the Egyptian border into exile under British protection. The Italians found Cyrenaica much more difficult to control than Tripolitania. It is ideal guerrilla country, from the caves of Jebel al-Akhdar to the stony plains and dry hidden *wadis* (river beds) of the south. It took 9 years (1923–1932) for Italy to overcome all of Libya, despite its vast superiority in troops and weapons. Sanusi guerrilla bands harried the Italians, cutting supply lines, ambushing patrols, and attacking convoys. Their leader, Shaykh Omar Mukhtar, became Libya's first national hero.

The Italians finally overcame the Sanusi by the use of methods that do not surprise us today but seemed unbelievably brutal at the time. Cyrenaica was made into a huge concentration camp with a barbed-wire fence along the Egyptian border. Nomadic peoples were herded into these camps, guarded by soldiers to prevent them from aiding the Sanusi. Sanusi prisoners were pushed out of airplanes, wells were plugged to deny water to the people, and flocks were slaughtered. In 1931 Omar Mukhtar was captured, court-martialed, and hanged in public. The resistance ended with his death.

The Italians did not have long to cultivate their Fourth Shore. During the 1930s they poured millions of lire into the colony. A paved highway from the Egyptian to the Tunisian border along the coast was completed in 1937; in World War II it became a handy invasion route for the British. A system of state-subsidized farms was set up for immigrant Italian peasants. Each was given free transportation, a house, seed, fertilizers, a mule, and a pair of shoes as inducements to come to Libya. By 1940 the Italian population had reached 110,000, and about 495,000 acres of land had been converted into productive farms, orchards, vineyards, and olive groves.[1]

Independent Libya

Libya was a major battleground during World War II as British, German, and Italian armies rolled back and forth across the desert. The British finally defeated the Germans and occupied northern Libya, while a French army occupied the Fezzan. The United States later built an important air base, Wheelus Field, near Tripoli. Thus the three major Allied powers all had an interest in Libya's future. But they could not agree on what to do with occupied Libya.

(UN photo/Rice)

After the 1969 Revolution, Libya strove to develop many aspects of the country. These local chiefs are meeting to plan community development.

Italy wanted Libya back. France wished to keep the Fezzan as a buffer for its African colonies, while the United Kingdom preferred self-government for Cyrenaica, under the Grand Sanusi, who had become staunchly pro-British during his exile in Egypt. The Soviet Union favored a Soviet trusteeship over Libya, which would provide the Soviet Union with a convenient outlet in the Mediterranean. The United States waffled, but finally settled on independence, which would at least keep the Soviet tentacles from enveloping Libya.

Due to lack of agreement, the Libyan "problem" was referred to the United Nations General Assembly. Popular demonstrations of support for independence in Libya impressed a number of the newer UN members, and in 1951 the General Assembly approved a resolution for an independent Libyan state, a kingdom under the Grand Sanusi, Idris.

THE KINGDOM OF LIBYA

Libya has been governed under two political systems since independence: a constitutional monarchy (1951–1969), and a Socialist republic (1969–), which has no constitution because all power "belongs" to the people. Monarchy and republic have had almost equal time in power. But Libya's spectacular economic growth and aggressive foreign policy under the republic need to be understood in relation to the solid, if unspectacular, accomplishments of the regime that preceded it.

Libya at independence was an artificial union of the three provinces. The Libyan people had little sense of national identity or unity. Loyalty was to one's family, clan,

village, and, in a general sense, to the higher authority represented by a tribal confederation. The only other loyalty linking Libyans was the Islamic religion. The tides of war and conquest that had washed over them for centuries had had little effect on their strong, traditional attachment to Islam.[2]

Political differences also divided the three provinces. Tripolitanians talked openly of abolishing the monarchy. Cyrenaica was the home and power base of King Idris; the king's principal supporters were the Sanusiya and certain important traditional families. The distances and poor communications between the provinces contributed to the impression that they should be separate countries. Leaders could not even agree on a choice between Tripoli and Benghazi for the capital. The king distrusted both cities as being corrupt and overly influenced by foreigners. He had his administrative capital at Baida, in the Jebel al-Akhdar.

The greatest problem facing Libya at independence was economic. Per capita income in 1951 was about $30 per year; in 1960 it was about $100 per year. Approximately 5 percent of the land was marginally usable for agriculture, and only 1 percent could be cultivated on a permanent basis. Most economists considered Libya to be a hopeless case, almost totally dependent on foreign aid for survival. It is interesting to note that the Italians were seemingly able to force more out of the soil, but one must remember that the Italian government poured a great deal of money into the country to develop the plantations, and credit must be given to the extremely hard-working Italian peasant farmer.

Despite its meager resources and lack of political experience, Libya was valuable to the United States and the United Kingdom in the 1950s and 1960s because of its strategic location. The United States negotiated a long-term lease on Wheelus Field in 1954, as a vital link in the chain of U.S. bases built around the southern perimeter of the Soviet Union due to the Cold War. In return, U.S. aid of $42 million sweetened the pot, and Wheelus became the single largest employer of Libyan labor. The British had two air bases and maintained a garrison in Tobruk.

Political development in the kingdom was minimal. King Idris knew little about parliamentary democracy, and he distrusted political parties. The 1951 Constitution provided for an elected legislature, but a dispute between the king and the Tripolitanian National Congress, one of several Tripolitanian parties, led to the outlawing of all political parties. Elections were held every 4 years, but only property-owning adult males could vote (women were granted the vote in 1963). The same legislators were reelected regularly. In the absence of political activity, the king was the glue that held Libya together.

THE 1969 REVOLUTION

At dawn on September 1, 1969, a group of young army officers abruptly carried out a military coup in Libya. King Idris, who had gone to Turkey for medical treatment, was deposed, and a "Libyan Arab Republic" was proclaimed by the unknown officers. These officers, whose names were not known to the outside world until weeks after the coup, were led by Captain

Muammar Muhammad al-Qadhafi. He went on Benghazi radio to announce to a startled Libyan population: "People of Libya . . . your armed forces have undertaken the overthrow of the reactionary and corrupt regime. . . . From now on Libya is a free, sovereign republic, ascending with God's help to exalted heights."[3]

Qadhafi's new regime made a sharp change in policy from that of its predecessor. Wheelus Field and the British bases were evacuated and returned to Libyan control. Libya took an active part in Arab affairs and supported Arab unity, to the extent of working to undermine other Arab leaders whom Qadhafi considered undemocratic or unfriendly to his regime.[4] However, his efforts to unite Libya with other Arab states have not been successful. A 1984 agreement for a federal union with Morocco, which provided for separate sovereignty but a federated assembly and unified foreign policies, was abrogated unilaterally by Morocco's King Hassan II after Qadhafi accused the king of "Arab treason" for meeting with Israeli leader Shimon Peres. Undeterred, Qadhafi tried again in 1987 with neighboring Algeria, receiving a medal from Algerian President Chadli Bendjedid but no other encouragement.

REGIONAL POLICY

Although distrustful of the mercurial Libyan leader, other North African heads of state have continued to work with him on the basis that it is safer to have Qadhafi inside the circle than isolated outside. Tunisia restored diplomatic relations in 1987, and Qadhafi agreed to compensate the Tunisian government for lost wages of Tunisian workers expelled from Libya during the 1985 economic recession. Qadhafi also reversed an earlier position by agreeing to accept binding international arbitration by the International Court of Justice in a dispute with Tunisia over ownership of oil rights in the Gulf of Gabes. Libya also joined other North African states in the new Arab Maghrib Union in 1989.

The oft-expressed U.S. accusation that Libya is a major sponsor of international terrorism was given new life in 1991, when U.S. and British officials accused two Libyans of involvement in the 1988 bombing of Pan American Airways Flight #103 over Lockerbie, Scotland. Although it refused to extradite its own nationals, Libya agreed to submit the case to the World Court in order to determine its legal obligations.

QADHAFI'S SOCIAL REVOLUTION

Qadhafi's desert upbringing and Islamic education gave him a strong, puritanical moral code. In addition to closing foreign

(Gamma-Liaison/Christian Vioujard)

Muammar al-Qadhafi led a group of army officers in the military coup of 1969 that deposed King Idris. In later years Qadhafi gained worldwide notoriety for his seeming sanction of terrorism.

bases and expropriating Italian and Jewish properties, he moved forcefully against symbols of foreign influence. The Italian cathedral in Tripoli became a mosque, street signs were converted to Arabic, nightclubs were closed, and production and sale of alcohol were prohibited.

But Qadhafi's revolution went far beyond changing names. In a three-volume work entitled *The Green Book,* he described his vision of the appropriate political system for Libya. Political parties would not be allowed, nor would constitutions, legislatures, even an organized court system. All of these institutions, according to Qadhafi, eventually become corrupt and unrepresentative. Instead, people's committees would run the government, business, industry, and even the universities. Libyan embassies abroad were renamed people's bureaus and were run by junior officers. (The takeover of the London bureau in 1984 led to counterdemonstrations by Libyan students and the killing of a British police officer by gunfire from inside the bureau. The Libyan bureau in Washington, D.C. was closed by the U.S. Federal Bureau of Investigation and the staff deported on charges of espionage and terrorism against Libyans in the United States.) The country was renamed the Socialist People's Libyan Arab Jamahiriya and titles of government officials were eliminated. Qadhafi became "Leader

of the Revolution," and each government department was headed by the secretary of a particular people's committee.

Qadhafi then developed a so-called Third International Theory, based on the belief that neither capitalism nor communism could solve the world's problems. What was needed, he said, was a middle way that would harness the driving forces of human history—religion and nationalism—to interact with each other to revitalize humankind. Islam would be the source of that middle way, because "it provides for the realization of justice and equity, it does not allow the rich to exploit the poor."[5]

THE ECONOMY

Modern Libya's economy is based almost entirely on oil exports. Concessions were granted in 1955 to various foreign companies to explore for oil, and the first oil strikes were made in 1957. Within a decade Libya had become the world's fourth-largest crude-oil exporter. The industry continued to expand in the 1960s, as pipelines were built from the oil fields to new export terminals on the Mediterranean coast. The lightness and low-sulfur content of Libyan crude oil make it highly desirable to industrialized countries, and, with the exception of the United States, differences in political viewpoint have had little effect on Libyan oil sales abroad.

After the 1969 Revolution Libya became a leader in the drive by oil-producing countries to gain control over their petroleum industries. The process began in 1971, when the new Libyan government took over the interests of British Petroleum (BP) in Libya. The Libyan method of nationalization was to proceed against individual companies rather than to take on the "oil giants" all at once. It took more than a decade before the last company, Exxon, capitulated. However, the companies' $2 billion in assets were left in limbo in 1986, when the Reagan administration imposed a ban on all trade with Libya to protest Libya's involvement in international terrorism. President George Bush extended the ban for an additional year in 1990, although he expressed satisfaction with reduced Libyan support for terroristic activities, one example being the expulsion from Tripoli of the Palestine Liberation Front, a radical opponent of Yassir Arafat's Palestine Liberation Organization.

Construction of new refineries and pipelines in recent years along with new oil and gas discoveries have enabled Libya to build a strong industrial sector emphasizing petrochemicals. The industrial complex at Marsa Brega, near Tripoli, is now a major producer of urea and related fertilizer products, with production sufficient for domestic needs and a surplus for export. Libya is also self-sufficient in cement, with five plants in operation, and in steel.

Until recently industrial-development successes based on oil revenues enabled Libyans to enjoy an ever-improving standard of living, and funding priorities were shifted from industry to agricultural development in the budget. But a combination of factors—mismanagement, lack of a cadre of skilled Libyan workers, absenteeism, low motivation of the work force, and a significant drop in revenues (from $22 billion in 1980 to $7 billion in 1988)—cast doubts on the effectiveness of Qadhafi's *Green Book* socialistic economic policies.

In 1988 the leader began closing the book. Controls on both imports and exports were eliminated and profit sharing for employees of small businesses encouraged as production incentives. In 1990 the General People's Congress (GPC), prodded strongly by Qadhafi, approved a major shake-up in the government. Eleven new secretaries (equivalent to Cabinet ministers) were appointed to spur economic development, and new Secretariats (Ministries) were formed to promote cooperation with Libya's neighbors. The oil industry, criticized for its inefficiency, was placed under a new Secretariat for Petroleum Affairs, superseding the National Oil Company, which had previously managed production.

Libya is also developing its considerable uranium resources. A 1985 agreement with the Soviet Union provided the components for an 880-megawatt nuclear power station in the Sirte region. Libya has enough uranium to meet its foreseeable domestic peacetime needs, although exploitation of reported large-scale uranium resources in the Aouzou Strip (assuming its award to Libya) would add significantly to the country's nuclear-power facilities.

The fledgling Libyan arms industry generated much international concern in 1989, with reports that a chemical plant built by West German technicians was producing mustard gas and other chemical weapons. The main evidence cited was a large stockpile of thiodiglycol, used in the manufacture of pharmaceuticals but also the basic chemical element in mustard gas.

New oil discoveries and higher prices for its low-sulfur crude helped stabilize the Libyan economy in the early 1990s. But in the long run, the key to orderly economic development lay in expanded agricultural production. Qadhafi declared 1990 the "Year of Agriculture," noting that self-sufficiency had been achieved in poultry, vegetables, and cereals. The Libyan leader's centerpiece for this plan is the Great Man-Made River. Construction began in 1984, and the first phase was completed in 1991. It consists of a network of underground pipes to bring water from subsurface sources at Tarir and Tazerbo, deep in the Sahara, northward to the Mediterranean coastal belt, which contains most of Libya's arable land. When completed, the project will irrigate 396,000 acres of new land and supply cities such as Benghazi with adequate potable water. Despite some serious questions about the GMR's long-term feasibility, its impact on water resources, and Libya's ability to manage the technical details once the foreign companies doing the work have left, the government in 1992 initiated Phase Two of the project, which will expand the pipe network and build storage reservoirs in Tripolitania.

AN UNCERTAIN FUTURE

The revolutionary regime's major success was a redistribution of wealth to bring the benefits of oil revenues to all Libyans. Annual per capita income rose to $2,168 in 1970 and reached a peak of $10,900 in 1980 before dropping to $5,500 in 1990. Even so, the quantum leap of wealth in 3 decades brought undreamed-of benefits to Libyans, including permanent homes for the seminomadic Qadadfas of the Sirte, kin of Qadhafi. An extensive social-welfare system, partially financed from workers' contributions, provided free medical care, pensions, low-cost housing and education, changing not only the lives but also the outlook and values of a generation of Libyans.

But rule by the people also means rule by the strong, as Qadhafi himself stated in *The Green Book*. Over the years most of the leader's old associates became alienated from him, either from disagreements about foreign policy or opposition to the "people's socialism" of *The Green Book*. In the 1980s Qadhafi began to send hit squads abroad to silence the opposition. A number of opposition leaders and dissident students were hunted down and killed in a shadowy war of Libyan against Libyan.

Until recently opposition to Qadhafi was confined almost entirely to exiles abroad, centered in former associates living in Cairo, Egypt, who had broken with the Libyan leader for reasons either personal or related to economic mismanagement. But the economic downturn and dissatisfaction with the leader's wildly unsuccessful foreign-policy ventures increased popular discontent at home. In 1983 Qadhafi introduced two domestic policies that generated widespread resentment: he called for the drafting of women into the armed services, and he recommended that all children be educated at home until age 10. The 200 basic people's congresses, set up in 1977 to recommend policy to the national General People's Congress (which in theory is responsible for national policy), objected strongly to both proposals. Qadhafi then created 2,000 more people's congresses, presumably to dilute the opposition, but withdrew the proposals. In effect, said one observer, *The Green Book* theory had begun to work, and Qadhafi didn't like it.

Qadhafi's principal support base rests on the armed forces and the Revolutionary Committees, formed of youths whose responsibility is to guard against infractions of *The Green Book* rules. "Brother Colonel" also relies upon a small group of collaborators from the early days of the Revolution, and his own relatives and members of the Qadadfa form part of the inner power structure. This structure is highly informal, and it may explain why Qadhafi is able to disappear from public view from time to time, as he did after the 1986 U.S. air raid on Tripoli, and emerge having lost none of his popularity and charismatic appeal.

The Libyan leader is well protected, but discontent within the military has led to two attempts by army units to overthrow him. The most serious attempt took place in 1984, when soldiers sympathetic to the newly formed opposition National Front for the Salvation of Libya, based in Cairo, invaded his Tripoli barracks but were repelled in a bloody gun battle. Even the U.S. air attack on the same barracks in 1986 failed to separate Qadhafi from his military support base.

INTERNAL CHANGES

Qadhafi has a talent for the unexpected that has made him an effective survivor. In 1988 he ordered the release of all political prisoners and personally drove a bulldozer through the main gate of Tripoli prison to inaugurate "Freedom Day." Exiled opponents of the regime were invited to return under a promise of amnesty, and a number did so. In June the GPC approved a Charter of Human Rights as an addendum to *The Green Book*. The new charter outlaws the death penalty, bans mistreatment of prisoners, and guarantees every accused person the right to a fair trial. It also permits formation of labor unions, confirms the right to education and suitable employment for all Libyan citizens, and places Libya on record as prohibiting production of nuclear and chemical weapons.

| Establishment of the Regency of Tripoli 1711 | Tripoli becomes an Ottoman province directly governed, with the Sanusiyah controlling the interior 1835 | The first Italian invasion 1911 | Libya becomes an Italian colony, Italy's "Fourth Shore" 1932 | An independent kingdom is set up by the UN under King Idris 1951 | The Revolution overthrows Idris; the Libyan Arab Republic is established 1969 | Qadhafi decrees a cultural and social revolution with government by people's committees 1973–1976 |

1980s–1990

| A campaign to eliminate Qadhafi's exiled opponents abroad; the United States imposes economic sanctions in response to suspected Libya-terrorist ties | U.S. planes attack targets in Tripoli and Benghazi; Libyan troops are driven from Chad, including the Aouzou Strip | Libya's relations with its neighbors improve |

THE WAR WITH CHAD

Libyan forces occupied the Aouzou Strip in northern Chad in 1973, claiming it as an integral part of the Libyan state. Occupation gave Libya access also to the reportedly rich uranium resources of the region. In subsequent years Qadhafi played upon political rivalries in Chad to extend the occupation into a de facto one of annexation of most of its poverty-stricken neighbor. But in late 1986 and early 1987 Chadian leaders patched up their differences and turned on the Libyans. In a series of spectacular raids on entrenched Libyan forces, the highly mobile Chadians, traveling mostly in Toyota trucks, routed the Libyans and drove them out of northern Chad. Chadian forces then moved into the Aouzou Strip and even attacked nearby air bases inside Libya. The defeats, with casualties of some 3,000 Libyans and loss of huge quantities of Soviet-supplied military equipment, exposed the weaknesses of the overequipped, undertrained, and poorly motivated Libyan Army. In 1988 Qadhafi declared that the Libyan occupation had been a mistake. In 1989 he signed a cease-fire with Chadian leader Hissène Habré and agreed to submit the dispute over ownership of Aouzou to international arbitration. However, Habré was overthrown by another Chadian leader in December 1990; the new ruler was reportedly pro-Libyan, suggesting that Qadhafi might have his piece of uranium-rich Chadian territory after all.

Perhaps the major change in Libya's foreign policy in recent years has involved relations with its neighbors. The country took an active part in formation of the Arab Maghrib Union, and Qadhafi pledged in 1990 that Moroccan workers would be brought in to carry out the second phase of the GMR. The Libyan leader's persistent efforts to unite with other Arab countries in full integration resulted in 1990 in yet another merger agreement, this one with Sudan. The agreement between leaders specified that full integration of the countries would be completed within 4 years; on its side, Libya agreed to supply all Sudanese oil needs.

Following the Arab Maghrib Union pact, Libya opened its borders with Tunisia to free trade and passage of travelers in both directions. In 1991 Qadhafi declared that Libya's border with Egypt was open to unrestricted trade, driving a tractor to demolish a border post and make his point.

Like a number of other revolutions in the developing world of Asia, Africa, and the Middle East, the Libyan Revolution is far from finished. It is entirely possible that as the revolutionary process continues, another junior officer may emerge from the ranks to seize power and proclaim yet another revolution. But it is highly unlikely that any new Libyan leader will have the color and charisma of Qadhafi or that he will possess comparable skills of oratory based on misinformation about global affairs. The world according to Qadhafi is a place where Israelis manage American foreign policy, the United States aims at encirclement of the Soviet Union through Libya, and the Arab na-

tions must undertake a massive population expansion in order to out-produce the industrialized nations. To Libyans less well informed than their leader, these views make perfectly good sense, but their number is steadily decreasing as Libya becomes more and more caught up in the rest of the world.

NOTES

1. " . . . irrigation, colonization and hard work have wrought marvels. Everywhere you see plantations forced out of the sandy, wretched soil. . . ." A. H. Broderick, *North Africa* (London: Oxford University Press, 1943), p. 27.

2. Religious leaders issued a *fatwa* ("binding legal decision") stating that a vote against independence would be a vote against religion. Omar el Fathaly et al., *Political Development and Bureaucracy in Libya* (Lexington: Lexington Books, 1977).

3. See the *Middle East Journal*, vol. 24, no. 2 (Spring 1970), Documents Section.

4. John Wright, *Libya: A Modern History* (Baltimore: Johns Hopkins University Press, 1982), pp. 124–126. Qadhafi's idol was former Egyptian President Nasser, a leader in the movement for unity and freedom among the Arabs. While he was at school in Sebha, the Fezzan, he listened to Radio Cairo's Voice of the Arabs and was later expelled from school as a militant organizer of demonstrations.

5. *The Times* (London, June 6, 1973).

DEVELOPMENT

Discovery of the new offshore Bourri oil field, with reserves of 2 billion barrels, and the inauguration of the Tobruk refinery in 1989 will boost oil production and revenues. Libya has been self-sufficient in energy since the 1960s.

FREEDOM

Libya has no written constitution, and political parties are outlawed. The main instrument of government is the General People's Congress. The Cabinet is responsible to the Congress. Popular congresses were set up in 1977 to administer regions and municipalities. Popular committees manage all industries and educational institutions.

HEALTH/WELFARE

The republic has vastly expanded education, health, and social services. By 1982 1 million students were enrolled in schools at all levels. There are now 2 universities. Although still dependent on foreign teachers and doctors, Libya has more than 2,000 students in medical and teacher training.

ACHIEVEMENTS

The revolutionary regime committed itself from the start to improve living conditions through broad use of oil revenues. By the mid-1980s 745,000 housing units were completed and all towns and villages, even in remote oases, were linked to major cities by paved roads.

Morocco (Kingdom of Morocco)

GEOGRAPHY

Area in Square Kilometers (Miles): 446,300 (172,272) (larger than California)
Capital (Population): Rabat (901,500 in metropolitan area)
Climate: Mediterranean and desert

PEOPLE

Population
Total: 26,249,000
Annual Growth Rate: 2.5%
Rural/Urban Population Ratio: 53/47
Ethnic Makeup of Population: 99% Arab-Berber; 1% non-Moroccan and Jewish

Health
Life Expectancy at Birth: 61 years (male); 63 years (female)
Infant Mortality Rate (Ratio): 79/1,000
Average Caloric Intake: 115% of FAO minimum
Physicians Available (Ratio): 1/4,725

Religion(s)
99% Sunni Muslim; 1% Christian and Jewish

Education
Adult Literacy Rate: 67%

COMMUNICATION
Telephones: 265,670
Newspapers: 12 dailies; 18 weeklies

TRANSPORTATION
Highways—Kilometers (Miles): 58,000 (35,960)
Railroads—Kilometers (Miles): 1,891 (1,179)
Usable Airfields: 72

GOVERNMENT
Type: constitutional monarchy
Independence Date: March 2, 1956
Head of State: King Hassan II
Political Parties: the National Assembly of Independents, Popular Movement, Independent Democrats, Constitutional Union Party, and Socialist Union of Popular Forces make up a ruling coalition; opposition Istiqlal, National Union of Popular Forces
Suffrage: universal over 20

MILITARY
Number of Armed Forces: 195,500
Military Expenditures (% of Central Government Expenditures): 15%
Current Hostilities: none

ECONOMY
Currency ($ U.S. Equivalent): 7.8 dirhams = $1
Per Capita Income/GNP: $880/$18.7 billion
Inflation Rate: 8.7%
Total Foreign Debt: $20.9 billion
Natural Resources: phosphates; iron; manganese; lead; cobalt; silver; copper; oil shale; fish
Agriculture: wheat; barley; livestock; wine; vegetables; olives; fishing
Industry: phosphate mining; mineral processing; food processing; textiles; construction

FOREIGN TRADE
Exports: $3.3 billion
Imports: $5.5 billion

* Capital   — Rivers   -- Roads

MOROCCO

The Kingdom of Morocco is the western-most country in North Africa. Morocco's population is the second largest (after Egypt) of the Arab states. Moroccan territory includes at present the Western Sahara, a former Spanish colony annexed in 1976 after the withdrawal of the Spanish administration. The annexation was opposed by a Saharan nationalism movement, the Polisario Front. If Morocco acquires permanent control over the Western Sahara, the country's land area will be increased by 102,000 square miles, a territory the size of Colorado.

Two other territories physically within Morocco remain outside Moroccan control. They are the cities of Ceuta and Melilla, both located on rocky peninsulas that jut out into the Mediterranean Sea. They have been held by Spain since the fifteenth century. (Spain also owns several small islands off the coast in Moroccan territorial waters.)

The economic advantages to Morocco of the free-port status of Ceuta and Melilla, plus the fact that they employ a large expatriate Moroccan labor force, have thus far outweighed the desire among Moroccan leaders to press hard for their return. Morocco's King Hassan II speaks periodically of the need for their retrocession, and in 1986 a new Spanish law effectively excluding Muslim residents of both cities from many of the benefits of Spanish citizenship, even if they have lived there all their lives, spawned conflict between them and Spanish police and generated a pro-Moroccan nationalist movement. In 1988 the question of ownership became moot when the Spanish Parliament passed a law formally incorporating Ceuta and Melilla into Spain as Spanish cities with locally elected legislatures. As a sweetener for the action, Spain loaned Morocco $1.1 billion at low interest rates and supported Morocco's successful request to the European Community for preferential treatment for its citrus and fish exports to EC countries.

SPLENDID ISOLATION

Morocco is a rugged land, dominated by several massive mountain ranges. The Rif Range, averaging 7,000 feet in elevation, runs parallel to the Mediterranean, isolating the northern region from the rest of the country. The Atlas Mountains dominate the rest of interior Morocco. The Middle Atlas begins south of the Rif, separated by the Taza Gap (the traditional gateway for invaders from the east), and extends from northeast to southwest to join the High Atlas, a snowcapped range containing North Africa's highest peak. A third range, the Anti-Atlas, walls off the desert from the rest of Morocco. These ranges and the general inaccessibility of the country isolated Morocco throughout most of its history, not only from outside invaders but internally as well, because of the geographical separation of peoples.

Moroccan geography also explains the country's dual population structure. About 35 percent of the population are Berbers, descendants of the original North Africans. The Berbers were, until recently, grouped into tribes, often taking the name of a common ancestor, such as the Ait ("Sons of") 'Atta of southern Morocco.[1] Invading Arabs converted them to Islam in the eighth century but made few changes in Berber life. Unlike the Berbers, the majority of the Arabs who settled in Morocco were, and are, town dwellers. To a much greater degree than the Arabs, Berbers were conditioned by traditional family structure and values; "a web of kinship bound the rural individual to his tribal territory, to his immediate family, and to his more distant kin."[2]

The fact that the Arabs were invaders caused the majority of the Berbers to withdraw into mountain areas. They accepted Islam but held stubbornly to their independence. Much of Morocco's past history consists of efforts by various rulers, both Berber and Arab, to control Berber territory. The result was a kind of balance-of-power political system. The rulers had their power bases in the cities, while the rural groups operated as independent units. Moroccan rulers made periodic military expeditions, called *mahallas*, into Berber territory to collect tribute and if possible to secure full obedience from the Berbers. When the ruler was strong, the Berbers paid up and submitted; when he was weak, they ignored him. At times Berber leaders might invade "government territory," capturing cities and replacing one ruler by another more to their liking. When they were not fighting with urban rulers, different Berber groups fought among themselves, so the system did little for Moroccan national unity.

HISTORY

Morocco has a rich cultural history, with many of its ancient monuments more or less intact. It has had a ruling monarchy for 12 centuries, in some form or other. The ancestors of the current monarch, King Hassan II, came to power in the seventeenth century. One reason for their long rule is the fact that they were descended from the Prophet Muhammad. Thus, Moroccans have a real sense of Islamic traditions and history through their ruler.

The first identifiable Moroccan "state" was established by a descendant of Muhammad named Idris, in the late eighth century. Idris had taken refuge in the far west of the Islamic world to escape civil war in the east. Because of his piety, learning, and his descent from Muhammad, he was accepted by a number of Berber groups as their spiritual and political leader. His son and successor, Idris II, founded the first Moroccan capital, Fez. Father and son established the principle whereby descent from the Prophet was an important qualification for political power as well as social status in Morocco.

The Idrisids ruled over only a small portion of the current Moroccan territory, and after the death of Idris II their "nation" lapsed into decentralized family rule. In any case, the Berbers had no real idea of nationhood; each separate Berber group thought of itself as a nation. But in the eleventh and twelfth centuries two Berber confederations developed that brought imperial grandeur to Morocco. They were the Almoravids and the Almohads. Under their rule, North Africa developed a political structure separate from that of the Eastern Islamic world, one strongly influenced by Berber values.

The Almoravids began as camel-riding nomads from the Western Sahara who were inspired by a religious teacher to carry out a reform movement to revive the true faith of Islam. (Almoravid comes from the Arabic *al-Murabitun*, "men of the ribat," rather like the crusading religious orders of Christianity in the Middle Ages.) Fired by religious zeal, the Almoravids conquered all of Morocco and parts of western Algeria.

A second "imperial" dynasty, the Almohads, succeeded the Almoravids but improved on their performance. They were the first, and probably the last, to unite all of North Africa and Islamic Spain under one government. Almohad monuments, such as the Qutubiya tower, the best-known landmark of Marrakesh, and the Tower of Hassan in Rabat, still stand as reminders of their power and the high level of their architectural achievements.

The same fragmentation, conflicts, and Berber/Arab rivalries that had undermined their predecessors brought down the Almohads in the late thirteenth century. From then on, dynasty succeeded dynasty in power. An interesting point about this cyclical pattern is that despite the lack of political unity, a distinctive Moroccan style and culture developed. Each dynasty contributed something to this culture, in architecture, crafts, literature, and music. The interchange between

Morocco and Islamic Spain was constant and fruitful. Poets, musicians, artisans, architects, and others traveled regularly between Spanish and Moroccan cities. One can visit the city of Fez today and be instantly transported back into the Hispano-Moorish way of life of the Middle Ages.

Mulay Ismail

In the late seventeenth century the Alawis, the dynasty currently ruling Morocco, came to power. The Alawis were originally from Arabia and were descended from the Prophet Muhammad. They used their prestige from being descended from Muhammad to win the support of both Arabs and Berbers. The real founder of the dynasty was Mulay Ismail (1672–1727), one of the longest-reigning and most powerful monarchs in Morocco's history. Mulay Ismail unified the Moroccan nation. The great majority of the Berber groups accepted him as their sovereign. The sultan built watchtowers and posted permanent garrisons in Berber territories to make sure they continued to do so. He brought public security to Morocco also, and it was said that in his time a Jew or an unveiled woman could travel safely anywhere in the land, which was not the case in most parts of North Africa, the Middle East, and Europe.

Mulay Ismail was a contemporary of Louis XIV, and the reports of his envoys to the French court at Versailles convinced him that he should build a capital like it. He chose Meknes, not far from Fez. The work was half finished when he died of old age. The slaves and prisoners working on this "Moroccan Versailles" threw down their shovels and ran away. The enormous unfinished walls and arched Bab al-Mansur ("Gate of the Victorious") still stand today as reminders of Mulay Ismail's dream.

Mulay Ismail had many wives and left behind 500 sons but no instructions as to which one should succeed him. After years of conflict one of his grandsons overcame the other claimants and took the throne as Muhammad II. He is important for giving European merchants a monopoly on trade from Moroccan ports (in wool, wax, hides, carpets, and leather) and for being the first non-European monarch to recognize the United States as an independent nation, in 1787.[3]

The French Protectorate

In the nineteenth and early twentieth centuries Morocco became increasingly vulnerable to outside pressures. The French, who were established in neighboring Algeria and Tunisia, wanted to complete their conquests. The nineteenth-century

(Hamilton Wright/Government of Morocco)

Morocco has a rich history. The Karawiyyin Mosque at Fez was founded in the ninth century A.D. and is the largest in North Africa. It is also the seat of one of Africa's oldest universities.

sultans were less and less able to control the mountain Berbers and were forced to make constant expeditions into the "land of dissidence," at great expense to the treasury. They began borrowing money from European bankers, not only to pay their bills but also to finance arms purchases and the development of ports, railroads, and industries to create a modern economy and prove to the European powers that Morocco could manage its own affairs. Nothing worked; by 1900 Morocco was so far in debt that the French took over the management of its finances. (One sultan, Abd al-Aziz, had bought one of everything he was told about by European salesmen, including a gold-plated toy train that carried food from the kitchen to the dining room of his palace.) Meanwhile, the European powers plotted the country's downfall.

In 1904 France, the United Kingdom, Spain, and Germany signed secret agreements partitioning the country. The French would be given the largest part of the coun-

try, while Spain would receive the northern third as a protectorate plus some territory in the Western Sahara. In return, the French and Spanish agreed to respect the United Kingdom's claim to Egypt and Germany's claim to East African territory.

The ax fell on Morocco in 1912. French workers building the new port of Casablanca were killed by Berbers. Mobs attacked foreigners in Fez, and the sultan's troops could not control them. French troops marched to Fez from Algeria to restore order. The sultan, Mulay Hafidh (Hafiz), was forced to sign the Treaty of Fez, establishing a French protectorate over southern Morocco. The sultan believed he had betrayed his country and died shortly thereafter, supposedly of a broken heart. Spain then occupied the northern third of the country, and Tangier, the traditional residence of foreign consuls, became an international city ruled by several European powers.

The French protectorate over Morocco covered barely 45 years (1912–1956). But in that brief period the French introduced significant changes into Moroccan life. For the first time in its history, southern Morocco was brought entirely under central government control, although the "pacification" of the Berbers was not complete until 1934. French troops also intervened in the Spanish Zone to help put down a rebellion in the Rif led by Abd al-Krim, a *Qadi* ("religious judge") and leader of the powerful Ait Waryaghar tribe.[4]

The organization of the protectorate was largely the work of the first French resident-general, Marshal Louis Lyautey. Lyautey had great respect for Morocco's past and its proud, dignified people. His goal was to develop the country and modernize the sultan's government while preserving Moroccan traditions and culture. He preferred the Berbers to the Arabs and set up a separate administration under Berber-speaking French officers for Berber areas.[5]

Lyautey's successors were less respectful of Moroccan traditions. The sultan, supposedly an independent ruler, became a figurehead. French *colons* (settlers) flocked to Morocco to buy land at rock-bottom prices and develop vineyards, citrus groves, and orchards. Modern cities sprang up around the perimeters of Rabat, Fez, Marrakesh, and other cities. In rural areas, particularly the Atlas, the French worked with powerful local chiefs *(qaids)*. Certain unscrupulous qaids used the arrangement to become enormously wealthy. One qaid, al-Glawi, as he was called, strutted about like a rooster in his territory and often said that he was the real sultan of Morocco.[6]

Morocco's Independence Struggle

The movement for independence in Morocco developed slowly. The only symbol of national unity was the sultan, Muhammad ibn Yusuf. But he seemed ineffectual to most young Moroccans, particularly those educated in French schools, who began to question the right of France to rule a people against their will.

The hopes of these young Moroccans got a boost during World War II. The Western allies, the United Kingdom and the United States, had gone on record in favor of the right of subject peoples to self-determination after the war. When President Franklin Roosevelt and Prime Minister Winston Churchill came to Casablanca for an important wartime conference, the sultan was convinced to meet them privately and get a commitment for Morocco's independence. The leaders promised their support.

However, Roosevelt died before the end of the war and Churchill was defeated for reelection. The French were not under any pressure after the war to end the protectorate. When a group of Moroccan nationalists formed the Istiqlal ("Independence") Party and demanded the end of French rule, most of them were arrested. A few leaders escaped to the Spanish Zone or to Tangier, where they could operate freely. For several years Istiqlal headquarters was the home of the principal of the American School at Tangier, an ardent supporter of Moroccan nationalism.

With the Istiqlal dispersed, the sultan represented the last hope for national unity and resistance. Until then he had gone along with the French, but in the early 1950s he began to oppose them openly. The French began to look for a way to remove him from office and install a more cooperative ruler.

In 1953 the Glawi and his fellow qaids decided, along with the French, that the time was right to depose the sultan. The qaids demanded that he abdicate; they said his presence was contributing to Moroccan instability. When he refused, he was bundled into a French plane and sent into exile. An elderly uncle was named to replace him.

The sultan's departure had the opposite effect from what was intended. In exile he became a symbol for Moroccan resistance to the protectorate. Violence broke out, French settlers were murdered, and a Moroccan Army of Liberation began battling French troops in rural regions. Although the French could probably have contained the rebellion in Morocco, they were under great pressure in neighboring Algeria and Tunisia, where resistance movements were also under way. In 1955, somewhat abruptly, the French capitulated. Sultan Muhammad ibn Yusuf returned to his palace in Rabat in triumph, and the elderly uncle retired to potter about in his garden in Tangier.

INDEPENDENCE

Morocco became independent on March 2, 1956. (The Spanish protectorate ended in April and Tangier came under Moroccan control in October, although it kept its free-port status and special banking and currency privileges for several more years.) It began its existence as a sovereign state with a number of assets—a popular ruler, an established government, and a well-developed system of roads, schools, hospitals, and industries inherited from the protectorate. Against these assets were the liabilities of age-old Arab/Berber and inter-Berber conflicts, little experience with political parties or democratic institutions, and an economy dominated by Europeans.

The sultan's goal was to establish a constitutional monarchy. His first action was to give himself a new title, King Muhammad V, symbolizing the end of the old autocratic rule of his predecessors. He also pardoned the Glawi, who crawled into his presence to kiss his feet and crawled out backwards as proof of penitence. (He died soon thereafter.) However, the power of the qaids and pashas ended; "they were compromised by their association with the French, and returned to the land to make way for nationalist cadres, many . . . not from the regions they were assigned to administer."[7]

Muhammad V did not live long enough to reach his goal. He died unexpectedly in 1961 and was succeeded by his eldest son, Crown Prince Hassan. Hassan II has ruled Morocco since then, and while he fulfilled his father's promise immediately with a Constitution, in most other ways he has set his own stamp on Morocco.

The Constitution provided for an elected Legislature and a multiparty political system. In addition to the Istiqlal, a number of other parties were organized, including one representing the monarchy. But the results of the French failure to develop a satisfactory party system soon became apparent. Berber/Arab friction, urban/rural distrust, city rivalries, and inter-Berber hostility all resurfaced. Elections failed to produce a clear majority for any party, not even the king's own party.

In 1965 riots broke out in Casablanca. The immediate cause was labor unrest, but the real cause lay in the lack of effective leadership by the parties. The king declared a state of emergency, dismissed the Legislature, and assumed full powers under the Constitution.

For the next dozen years Hassan II ruled as an absolute monarch. He continued to insist that his goal was a parliamentary system, a "government of national union." But he depended on a small group of cronies, members of prominent merchant families, the large Alawi family, or powerful Berber leaders as a more reliable group than the fractious political parties. The dominance of "the king's men" led to growing dissatisfaction and a feeling that the king had sold out to special interests. The opposition spread to the army, previously considered Hassan's most loyal supporter. Army officers, most of them Berbers, objected to government corruption and the king's flamboyant lifestyle, his numerous palaces, and his free association with foreigners. (The king, who has a law degree from a French university, is very much at ease in Euro-

(Hamilton Wright/Government of Morocco)

Tangier, Morocco was once a free city and port. It now is Morocco's northern metropolis just across the Strait of Gibraltar from Spain.

pean cultures as well as in his own Islamic Moroccan culture.) The king became identified as the cause of the nation's problems. In 1971, and again in 1972, the military attempted to overthrow him. In both cases the king narrowly escaped with his life, suggesting to most Moroccans that his *baraka* ("charisma") was stronger than that of his opposition. The attempts, however, prompted Hassan II to revive the parliamentary system. The new Constitution in 1972 defined Morocco "as democratic and social constitutional monarchy in which Islam is the established religion."[8] However, the king holds broad constitutional powers. Royal power is based on the leadership of the Alawi family, the king's spiritual role as "Commander of the Faithful," and his control of patronage. When Hassan puts on an army uniform, or rides to the mosque on Fridays in the traditional white *jellaba* under an umbrella symbolizing royalty, or meets with his Cabinet dressed in a business suit, he symbolizes these three roles of leadership.

THE WESTERN SAHARA

The Western Sahara, which Morocco annexed after Spain ended its rule over the colony in 1976, is primarily a regional rather than an internal Moroccan problem, although it has adversely affected Morocco's economy due to the heavy cost

of occupation. However, the annexation had important results for Moroccan political development. The "Green March," organized by the king, of 350,000 unarmed Moroccans into Spanish territory in 1975 to dramatize Morocco's claim, was supported by all segments of the population and the opposition parties. In 1977 opposition leaders agreed to serve under the king in a "government of national union." The first elections in 12 years were held for a new legislature, and several new parties, including Socialist and Marxist ones, took part.

The 1984 elections continued the national unity process. A majority of seats in the 306-member Legislature were won by the monarchist Constitutional Union Party. But in December 1989 the king ordered a 2-year postponement of the scheduled 1990 elections. He said that more time was needed for the UN-sponsored peace plan for the Western Sahara and for economic stabilization.

FOREIGN POLICY

Broad national support for Hassan's annexation of the Western Sahara has enabled the king to resist pressures from other African states to negotiate a settlement with the Polisario (the Saharian Nationalist Movement). Hassan signed an abortive federal union with Libya in 1984, and although he abrogated it unilaterally,

Libya kept its part of the unification bargain by terminating its aid to the Polisario.

Diplomatic relations were restored with Algeria, and the border was opened to free movement in both directions. In 1989 Morocco ratified a 1972 agreement formally demarcating its southern border with Algeria and joined with its neighbors in the Arab Maghrib Union.

In 1991 Hassan accepted the UN plan for a ceasefire in the Western Sahara, scheduled a referendum, and announced an amnesty for all Sahrawi (people of Western Sahara) exiles as well as Polisario members.

THE ECONOMY

Morocco has too much of certain resources and too little of other critical ones. It has two-thirds of the world's known reserves of phosphate rock and is the top exporter of phosphates. The major thrust in industrial development is in phosphate-related industries, in large phosphoric-acid and fertilizer plants.

The country also has important undeveloped iron-ore deposits and a small but significant production of rare metals such as mercury, antimony, nickel, and lead. The major obstacle to development is the lack of oil. There are shale-oil deposits estimated at 200 billion tons at Timadhit and Tarfaya in the far south, but extraction

| The foundations of Moroccan nation are established by Idris I and II, with the capital at Fez A.D. 788–790 | The Almoravid and Almohad dynasties, Morocco's "imperial period" 1062–1147 | The current ruling dynasty, the Alawi, establishes its authority under Mulay Ismail 1672 | Morocco is occupied and placed under French and Spanish protectorates 1912 | Independence under King Muhammad V 1956 | The accession of King Hassan II 1961 | Unsuccessful attempts by army officers to overthrow Hassan 1971, 1972 | The Green March into the Western Sahara dramatizes Morocco's claim to the area 1975 |

1980s–1990

| Bread riots to protest price increases in basic commodities; agreement with Libya for a federal union; the king unilaterally abrogates the 1984 treaty of union with Libya | Completion of the sixth section of the Sand Wall around Western Sahara; an exchange of prisoners with Algeria; Morocco joins the Arab Maghrib Union | Morocco accepts a UN plan for a ceasefire in the Western Sahara and amnesties Sahrawi exiles and Polisario members |

using available methods is considered economically unfeasible. A small gas field near Essaouira is the only hydrocarbons discovery made to date.

Collapse of the global phosphates market in the mid-1980s was an important factor in Morocco's developing debt crisis. However, phosphate exports rose sharply in 1988–1989 as world prices stabilized. Exploitation of new reserves and expansion of production in the huge Bou Craa mines of the Western Sahara should enable Morocco to improve upon its position as a leading world exporter of phosphates.

By 1983 total foreign indebtedness had reached $13 billion. An economic recovery plan was set up with the help of the World Bank in that year. By 1986 the trade deficit had been cut 27 percent. Exports of phosphoric acid rose from 280,908 tons in 1989 to 974,992 tons in 1990, after India, Morocco's largest customer, resumed purchases. The country's overall economic stability prompted the Club of Paris to reschedule $32 billion in Moroccan commercial debts as Morocco became the first low-income nation to benefit from the Club's extended debt-repayment terms.

Agriculture, which employs half the labor force and accounts for 15 to 20 percent of gross domestic product (GDP), generated its first surplus in many years in 1988.

OUTLOOK

The austerity program and economic reforms imposed on Morocco by the World Bank as prerequisites for additional loans have helped the country recover signifi-

cantly from the dark days of the "bread riots" of 1984. Food is again cheap and plentiful. The GDP has increased and inflation has been held down. But serious social pressures remain. Half the population is under age 20, and there are by far too many workers entering the job market each year (250,000 per year) for the jobs available.

Yet the country continues to be politically stable. Apart from the improved economy, a major factor is the broad popularity of the king. "North, South, East, West—the King is numero uno," observed a busboy in a posh Casablanca restaurant. Admittedly, the ruler's popularity is enhanced by his tight grip on internal affairs, through an efficient security service and a patronage system that keeps the "2,000 families" who have dominated economic life for centuries tied to the palace. Hassan has also defused any threat from Islamic fundamentalists by cultivating his image as Commander of the Faithful and descendant of the Prophet Muhammad. The king's success in drawing together the other North African nations in an Arab Maghrib Union and generating Arab League intervention in Lebanon also won him plaudits at home and abroad, encouraging diplomats to characterize him as the "Great Survivor."

NOTES

1. See David M. Hart, *Dadda 'Atta and His Forty Grandsons* (Cambridge: Menas Press, 1981), pp. 8–11. Dadda 'Atta was a historical figure, a minor saint or marabout.

2. Harold D. Nelson, ed., *Morocco, A Country Study* (Washington: American University, Foreign Area Studies, 1978), p. 112.

3. The oldest property owned by the U.S. government abroad is the American Consulate in Tangier; a consul was assigned there in 1791. *Ibid.*, p. 40.

4. See David Woolman, *Rebels in the Rif: Abd 'al Krim and the Rif Rebellion* (Stanford: Stanford University Press, 1968). On the Ait Waryaghar, see David M. Hart, *The Ait Waryaghar of the Moroccan Rif: An Ethnography and a History* (Tucson: University of Arizona Press, 1976). Abd 'al Krim had annihilated a Spanish army and set up a Republic of the Rif (1921–1926).

5. For a detailed description of protectorate tribal administration, see Robin Bidwell, *Morocco Under Colonial Rule* (London: Frank Cass, 1973).

6. He once said: "Morocco is a cow, the Qaids milk her while France holds the horns." Nelson, *op. cit.*, p. 53.

7. Mark Tessler, "Morocco: Institutional Pluralism and Monarchical Dominance," in W. I. Zartman, ed., *Political Elites in North Africa* (New York: Longman, 1982), p. 44.

8. Nelson, *op. cit.*, p. 205.

DEVELOPMENT

The 1988–1992 5-year-plan forecasts a 4% annual growth rate, based on a 15% increase in phosphate exports and reduced fuel imports. In 1989 Hassan moved to speed up development projects with an edict that investment proposals not approved within 2 months would start up automatically without having to go through the ponderous bureaucracy.

FREEDOM

Human rights improved significantly in 1990–1991, following negative reports from Amnesty International. Hassan II appointed a Human Rights Council to "wash clean the country's face." New laws reduced by half the time allowed for prisoner detention without trial, and the king amnestied more than 2,000 prisoners on the 30th anniversary of his accession.

HEALTH/WELFARE

A 1991 law increased the minimum wage after a nationwide strike was called to demand a "national pact" of government, private employers, and unions to deal with the economy.

ACHIEVEMENTS

A 10-year campaign by government and private groups to control runaway population growth showed dramatic results in 1991, despite illiteracy and a lagging economy. The average number of children per woman of childbearing age dropped from 7 in 1980 to 4.5 in 1990, with contraceptive use among men and women increasing 40 percent.

Oman (Sultanate of Oman)

GEOGRAPHY

Area in Square Kilometers (Miles):
212,460 (82,009) (about the size of
New Mexico)
Capital (Population): Muscat (85,000)
Climate: coast, hot and humid;
interior, hot and dry

PEOPLE

Population
Total: 1,305,000
Annual Growth Rate: 3.1%
Rural/Urban Population Ratio: 90/10
Ethnic Makeup of Population: almost
entirely Arab; small Baluchi,
Zanzibari, and Indian groups

Health
Life Expectancy at Birth: 63 years
(male); 67 years (female)
Infant Mortality Rate (Ratio):
36/1,000
Average Caloric Intake: n/a
Physicians Available (Ratio): 1/1,071

Religion(s)
75% Ibadhi Muslim; remainder Sunni
Muslim, Shia Muslim, some Hindu

Education
Adult Literacy Rate: 20%

COMMUNICATION
Telephones: 23,000
Newspapers: 3 dailies; 2 weeklies

"ATLANTIS OF THE SANDS"

The ancient fortress city of Ubar, situated in a region of Oman so remote
that it is known as Rub'al Khali, or "Empty Quarter," was recently
found through satellite-imaging techniques. The technology told scientists where to look by showing them where water tables would be large
enough to support a city. The ruins of Ubar were described in the Koran
as the "city of towers" and in Arabian fables as the center of the
frankincense trade for 30 centuries. Trade, commerce, and religious
ritual may have been active in Ubar as far back as 3,000 to 4,000 B.C.
The discovery may help us to understand the history of an area from
which Islam, Christianity, and Judaism evolved.

TRANSPORTATION
Highways—Kilometers (Miles):
24,700 (15,314)
Railroads—Kilometers (Miles): none
Usable Airfields: 114

GOVERNMENT
Type: absolute monarchy
Independence Date: 1951
Head of State: Sultan and Prime
Minister Qabus ibn Said
Political Parties: none
Suffrage: none

MILITARY
Number of Armed Forces: 25,500
*Military Expenditures (% of Central
Government Expenditures):* 42%
Current Hostilities: none

ECONOMY
Currency ($ U.S. Equivalent): 0.38
Omani rial = $1
Per Capita Income/GNP: $5,220/$7.5
billion
Inflation Rate: n/a
Total Foreign Debt: $2.97 billion
Natural Resources: oil; copper;
asbestos; some marble; limestone;
gypsum
Agriculture: dates; alfalfa; wheat;
bananas; coconuts; limes; vegetables;
fish
Industry: crude petroleum; fisheries;
copper mine and smelter;
construction; cement

FOREIGN TRADE
Exports: $3.9 billion
Imports: $2.2 billion

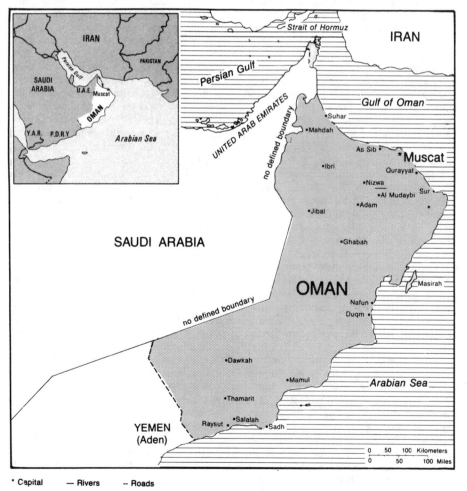

* Capital   — Rivers   -- Roads

OMAN

The Sultanate of Oman was, at least until 1970, one of the least-known countries in the world. Yet it is a very old country with a long history of contact with the outside world. Merchants from Oman had a near monopoly on the trade in frankincense and myrrh. Oman-built, shallow-draught, broad-beamed ships called *dhows* criss-crossed the Indian Ocean, trading with India and the Far East.

In the twentieth century Oman has become important to the outside world for two reasons. First, it has been producing oil since the 1960s; and second, it has a strategic location on the Strait of Hormuz, the passageway for supertankers carrying Middle Eastern oil to the industrialized nations. Eighty percent of Japan's oil needs passes through Hormuz, and 60 percent of Western Europe's. A Swiss journalist called the Omanis "sentinels of the Gulf" because they watch over this vital traffic.

GEOGRAPHY

Oman is the second-largest country in the Arabian Peninsula. However, the population is small and large areas are uninhabited or sparsely populated. The geographic diversity—rugged mountains, vast gravelly plains, and deserts—limits large-scale settlement. Prior to the discovery of oil, Oman's geography was an obstacle to agricultural development. The bulk of the population lives in the coastal area around Muscat, the capital, and the Batinah coast on the Persian Gulf opposite Iran. Here an ingenious system of underground irrigation channels (*falaj*) makes intensive agriculture feasible. Another important area of development is the southwestern coast of Dhofar Province, source of the legendary frankincense tree, still an important Omani export.

Behind Oman's coast is a spine of rugged mountains, the Jabal al-Akhdar ("Green Mountain"), with peaks over 10,000 feet. The mountains form several disconnected chains, interspersed with deep, narrow valleys where village houses hang like eagles' nests from the mountain tops above terraced gardens and palm groves.

Most of Oman's oil wells are located in the interior of the country. The interior is a broad, hilly plain dotted with oasis villages, each one a fortress with thick walls to keep out desert raiders. The stony plain eventually becomes the Rub al-Khali ("Empty Quarter"), the great uninhabited desert of southeastern Arabia.

Omani territory includes the Musandam Peninsula, at the northeastern tip of Arabia projecting into the Strait of Hormuz. The peninsula is separated from the rest of Oman by the Union of Arab Emirates (U.A.E.). Oman's borders are still undefined, due to a historical dispute over ownership of the oasis of Buraimi, which is now controlled by the U.A.E. but has been claimed at various times by Saudi Arabia, Oman, and the former British protectorate of Abu Dhabi (one of the U.A.E. member states).

HISTORY

As was the case elsewhere in Arabia, the early social structure of Oman consisted of a number of tribal groups. Many of them were and still are nomadic (Bedouin), while others became settled farmers and herders centuries ago. The groups spent much of their time feuding with one another. Occasionally, several would join in an alliance against others, but none of them recognized any higher authority than their leaders.

In the seventh century A.D. the Omanis were converted to Islam. However, they developed their own form of Islam, called *Ibadism,* meaning "Community of the Just," a branch of Shia Islam. The Ibadi peoples elect their own leader, called an Imam. The Ibadi Imams do not have to be descendants of the prophet Muhammad, as do the Imams in the main body of Shia Muslims. The Ibadi community believes that anyone, regardless of background, can be elected Imam, as long as the individual is pious, just, and capable. If no one is available who meets those requirements, the office may remain vacant.

Ibadi Imams ruled interior Oman with the support of family shaykhs until the eighteenth century. But well before then, coastal Oman was being opened up to foreign powers. The Portuguese captured Muscat in the 1500s for use as a stopping place for their ships on the trade route to India. (An Omani served as navigator to Portuguese admiral Vasco da Gama in his voyage across the Indian Ocean to India.) They built two great forts guarding the entrance to Muscat harbor, forts that still stand, giving the town its picturesque appearance. The Portuguese were finally driven out in 1650. Since that time Oman has not been ruled directly by any foreign power.

The current ruling dynasty in Oman is the Al Bu Said Dynasty. It has been in power since 1749, when a chief named Ahmad ibn Said defeated an Iranian invasion and established his authority over most of Oman. As Middle Eastern rulers go, the Al Bu Saids have been in power for a very long time. But for most of the period, Oman actually had two rulers, a sultan ruling in Muscat and an Imam ruling in the interior at the same time.

The most successful Omani sultan before the twentieth century was Said ibn Sultan (1804–1856). He added Dhofar Province and Zanzibar, on the East African coast, to Omani territory. Sultan Said had good relations with the United Kingdom. He signed a treaty with the British which stated, "the friendship between our two states shall remain unshook to the end of time." The sultan also signed a friendship treaty with the United States in 1833, and in 1836, to the surprise of the New York Port authorities, an Omani ship docked in New York harbor. Its captain said that the sultan had sent him to get to know the Americans whom he had heard so much about and to arrange trade contacts. Friendship between the United States and Oman operates on a different basis today. Now it is the Omanis who allow the Americans the use of the British-built Masirah Island base and share responsibility for patrolling the Strait of Hormuz, the strategic entrance point for the strife-ridden Persian Gulf. But this friendship has its roots in Sultan Said's mission.

After Said's death, ethnic, tribal, and religious differences reasserted themselves and Oman lost its importance in regional affairs. Its territory was again restricted to its small corner of southeastern Arabia. The opening of the Suez Canal in 1869 diverted shipping to new Red Sea routes, and ships no longer called at Muscat harbor. Piracy and the slave trade, both of which had provided revenues for the sultan, were prohibited by international law. For the rest of the nineteenth century and most of the twentieth century Oman sank back into isolation, forgotten by the world. Only the United Kingdom paid the Omanis any attention, giving the sultan a small monthly subsidy in the event that Oman might be of some future use to it.

In the early twentieth century the Imams of inner Oman and the sultans ruling in Muscat came to a complete parting of the ways. In 1920 a treaty between the two leaders provided that the sultan would not interfere in the internal affairs of inner Oman. Relations were reasonably smooth until 1951, when the United Kingdom recognized the independence of the Sultanate of Muscat-Oman, as it was then called, and withdrew its advisers. Subsequently, the Imam declared inner Oman as a separate state from the sultanate. A number of Arab states supported the Imam on the grounds that the sultan was a British puppet. Conflict between the Imam and the sultan dragged on until 1960, when the sultan finally reestablished his authority.

Oman's ruler for nearly 4 decades in the twentieth century was Sultan Said ibn Taimur (1932–1970). The most unusual aspect of his reign was the way in which he stopped the clock of modernization. Oil was discovered in 1964 in inland Oman, and within a few years wealth from oil royalties began pouring in. But the sultan was afraid the new wealth would corrupt his people. He refused to spend money except for the purchase of arms and a few personal luxuries such as an automobile, which he liked to drive on the only paved road in Salalah, his southern capital in Dhofar Province. He would not allow the building of schools, houses, roads, or hospitals for his people. Before 1970 there were only 16 schools in all of Oman. The sole hospital was the American mission in Muscat, established in the 1800s by Baptist missionaries, and all 10 of Oman's qualified doctors were practicing abroad because the sultan did not trust modern medicine. The few roads were rough caravan tracks; many areas of the country, for example the Musandam Peninsula, were inaccessible.

The sultan required the city gates of Muscat to be closed and locked 3 hours after sunset. No one could enter or leave the city. Flashlights were prohibited, since they were a modern invention; so were sunglasses and European shoes. Anyone found on the streets at night without a lighted kerosene lantern was liable to imprisonment. In the entire country there were about 1,000 automobiles; to import an automobile, one had to have the sultan's personal permission. On the darker side, slavery was still a common practice. Women were almost never seen in public and were veiled from head to foot if they so much as walked to a neighbor's house to visit. Prisoners could be locked up in the old Portuguese fort at Muscat on the slightest pretext and left to rot.

THE COUP d'ETAT OF 1970

As the 1960s came to an end there was more and more unrest in Oman. The opposition centered around Qabus ibn Said, the sultan's son. Qabus had been educated in England, but when he came home his father shut him up in a house in Salalah, a town far from Muscat, and refused to give him any responsibilities. He was afraid of his son's "Western ideas."

On July 23, 1970, supporters of Crown Prince Qabus overthrew the sultan, and Qabus succeeded him. Sultan Qabus brought Oman into the twentieth century in a hurry. The old policy of isolation was reversed. In 1981, worried about a possible spread of the Iran-Iraq War, Oman joined the Gulf Cooperation Council and allowed

(UN photo/A221)

Boys studying the Koran at a village in Oman. When Qabus ibn Said came to power in 1970, replacing his father, he targeted education, health care, and transportation as prime development areas.

the U.S. military to use the facilities on Masirah Island in return for $200 million in aid.

Qabus also ended a long-running rebellion in Dhofar that he had inherited from his father. The rebellion had developed originally from the social and economic neglect of the province by the Taimur government. The Dhofar rebels were supported and armed by the People's Democratic Republic of Yemen (P.D.R.Y.), Oman's neighbor. Relations between the two countries remained poor even after the sultan had crushed the rebellion in 1975, with the help of troops from the United Kingdom and Iran. However, common Arab interests and prospects for economic complementarity seem to have brought about a rapprochement. In 1988 the P.D.R.Y. leader, Ali Haydar al-Attas, made an official visit to Oman and signed an agreement to demarcate the border and cooperate in economic development.

OMANI SOCIETY

Today Omanis typically live in two worlds. They may wear both a *kanjar*, the traditional curved dagger, and a digital watch; travel by Land Rover or Mercedes; dress in *dishdasha* and skullcap yet do business by telephone in English; and spend holidays abroad. The pace of modernization is dizzying. Yesterday Muscat had a small dirt airstrip; today a huge industrial park with shops, factories, and high-rise apartments covers the old runway. Broad, paved highways curve along the coast and branch inland to the Imam's old fortress towns and oasis villages, where only camel tracks existed before 1970.

Sultan Qabus set education, health care, and transportation as his top priorities. The results have been astonishing. Within 2 decades there were 490 schools, with 7,700 teachers and 150,000 students, one-third of them girls, and plans were well under way for the country's first university. Such is the thirst for education that children often walk many miles to attend the nearest school in their district. In a land where most of the people are illiterate, one symbol of the new Oman is the schoolchild trudging along a dusty road carrying a book bag.

The sultan also set out to blanket his country with roads and health clinics. By the mid-1980s all but a few remote Musandam villages were served by graded

| The Portuguese seize Muscat and build massive fortresses to guard the harbor 1587–1588 | The Al Bu Said Dynasty is established; extends Omani territory 1749 | The British establish a de facto protectorate; the slave trade is supposedly ended late 1800s | Independence 1951 | Sultan Said ibn Taimur is deposed by his son, Prince Qabus 1970 | With British and Iranian help, Sultan Qabus ends the Dhofar rebellion 1975 | 1980s–199 |

An agreement with the United States allows the American military the use of Masirah air base

Sultan Qabus sets up a Consultative Assembly as an advisory body, as the first step toward democratization

The sultan focuses on expanding Oman's industrial base

roads. Medical services used to be provided by the local traditional doctors, but now the health team comes to the villages fully equipped in a Land Rover.

THE ECONOMY

Oman has been exporting oil since 1967, and oil revenues provide 96 percent of its income. There are two main oil fields, one near Muscat, the other in Dhofar. Several new Dhofar wells started production in 1985. New oil discoveries plus increased output brought production up to 700,000 barrels per day in 1990; reserves are now estimated at 4 billion barrels.

Prior to oil development Oman and the Yemen Arab Republic (Y.A.R.) were the only two Arabian Peninsula countries where agriculture was extensively practiced. More than 60 percent of the labor force are engaged in agriculture, although that sector provides less than 3 percent of gross domestic product. Farming is limited by lack of arable land, undependable rainfall, inefficient methods, and lack of manpower as more and more rural people move to the cities. To encourage Omanis to "stay on the farm," Sultan Qabus proclaimed 1988 the Year of Agriculture.

The country's varied geography and range of climate allow cultivation of many different crops. These include dates and limes, grown on the Batinah coast, bananas and papayas from Dhofar (which receives extensive rainfall from Indian Ocean monsoon winds), and market garden vegetables grown in interior oases. Some 82,000 acres of total arable land is under cultivation.

Oman also produces natural gas. The new Sohar gas-liquefaction plant, activated in 1988, helped to increase production by 17.5 percent. New gas fields brought into production in 1990 in central Oman will add significantly to exports. Oman also produces and exports copper ore. The copper mines, which were first worked by the Sumerians 5,000 years ago, were reopened in 1982. At current extraction rates, the copper reserves are estimated to be sufficient only for another decade.

The fishing industry employs 10 percent of the working population, but obsolete equipment and lack of canning and freezing plants have severely limited the catch in the past. Another problem is the unwillingness of Omani fishermen to move into commercial production; most of them catch just enough fish for their own use. The Oman Fish Company was formed in 1987 to develop fishery resources, financing the purchase by fishermen of aluminum boats powered by outboard motors to replace the seaworthy but slow traditional wooden dhows. The company has also set up processing and cold-storage plants inland for preparation and marketing of the catch. A marine-science and fisheries research center, opened in 1987, provides research and training facilities for the industry as well as an experimental turtle-breeding pool for the study and preservation of endangered Indian Ocean species.

PROSPECTS

The Omani tradition of independence that predates the current sultanate and the national pride generated by economic success and Sultan Qabus's strong leadership augur well for Oman's future. On the 20th anniversary of his accession Qabus formed a new *Majlis al-Shura* (Consultative Council) to encourage greater citizen participation in the nation's development. Another decree set up a regional assembly with representatives from each of Oman's *wilayas* (provinces); it meets annually to confer with the sultan and Majlis al-Shura and to provide input on development plans.

DEVELOPMENT

The 5-year-plan for 1991–1995 has as its major goal the broadening of the industrial base, with industrial parks at three sites. Some 70 light industries, including a joint-venture paint factory with Jøtun, a Norwegian concern, are in operation at Rusail, outside of Muscat.

FREEDOM

Sultan Qabus set up a Consultative Assembly in 1981 in response to suggestions that he was unaware of public opinion. Ten of its 55 members represent government; the remainder, appointed by Qabus, represent private industry and the various Omani regions. A Council of Ministers advises the ruler on legislation and foreign policy, but in practice his power is absolute.

HEALTH/WELFARE

With native Omani labor in short supply—most jobs are held by expatriates—the 5-year-plan allocates $104 million to train 100,000 nationals and to create 160,000 jobs.

ACHIEVEMENTS

Higher oil prices and subsequent increased revenues resulting from Iraq's invasion of Kuwait generated the first budget surplus in a decade in 1990, as gross domestic product rose by 7.4 percent. A major road-building program will complete more than 2,500 miles of paved roads in the sultanate.

Qatar (State of Qatar)

GEOGRAPHY

Area in Square Kilometers (Miles): 11,000 (4,427) (about the size of Connecticut)
Capital (Population): Doha (250,000)
Climate: hot and dry

PEOPLE

Population

Total: 498,000
Annual Growth Rate: 3.7%
Rural/Urban Population Ratio: 13/87
Ethnic Makeup of Population: 40% Arab; 18% Pakistani; 18% Indian; 10% Iranian; 14% others

Health

Life Expectancy at Birth: 68 years (male); 72 years (female)
Infant Mortality Rate (Ratio): 29/1,000
Average Caloric Intake: n/a
Physicians Available (Ratio): 1/679

Religion(s)

95% Muslim; 5% others

Education

Adult Literacy Rate: 60%

COMMUNICATION

Telephones: 129,290
Newspapers: 4 dailies; 2 weeklies

THE VANISHING QATARI LIFESTYLE

A century ago an English traveler described Qatar as "miles and miles of low barren hills, with hardly a single tree." Black Bedouin tents pitched in a palm grove were the only signs of human life. Today one is more likely to pass a white marquee set up beside a paved highway, under it a city family from Doha, seeking to find its nomad roots—although a shiny BMW or Toyota parked nearby guarantees a quick return to urban life.

TRANSPORTATION

Highways—Kilometers (Miles): 840 (522)
Railroads—Kilometers (Miles): none
Usable Airfields: 4

GOVERNMENT

Type: traditional monarchy
Independence Date: September 3, 1971
Head of State: Emir and Prime Minister Khalifa bin Hamad al-Thani
Political Parties: none
Suffrage: none

MILITARY

Number of Armed Forces: 7,000
Military Expenditures (% of Central Government Expenditures): 25%
Current Hostilities: none

ECONOMY

Currency ($ U.S. Equivalent): 3.63 riyals = $1
Per Capita Income/GNP: $15,500/$5.4 billion
Inflation Rate: −9%
Total Foreign Debt: n/a
Natural Resources: petroleum; natural gas; fish
Agriculture: farming on small scale
Industry: oil production and refining; natural gas development; fishing; cement; petrochemicals; steel; fertilizer

FOREIGN TRADE

Exports: $2.6 billion
Imports: $1.1 billion

* Capital — Rivers -- Roads

QATAR

Qatar is a shaykhdom on the eastern (Gulf) coast of Arabia, a peninsula 4,427 square miles in area. It is the second-smallest Middle Eastern state, after Bahrain, but due to oil wealth it has an extremely high per capita annual income. Before 1949, when oil exports began, there were about 20,000 Qataris, all descendants of peoples who had migrated to the coast centuries ago in search of a dependable water supply. Since then rapid economic growth has attracted expatriate workers and immigrants from other Arab countries and distant Muslim states such as Pakistan. As a result, native Qataris are outnumbered four to one by immigrants and expatriates, which makes for some tension.

HISTORY

Although the peninsula has been inhabited since 4000 B.C., little is known of its history before the nineteenth century. At one time it was ruled by the al-Khalifa family, current rulers of Bahrain. It became part of the Ottoman Empire formally in 1872, but the Turkish garrison was evacuated during World War I. The Ottomans earlier had recognized Shaykh Qassim al-Thani, head of the important al-Thani family, as emir of Qatar, and the British followed suit when they established a protectorate after the war.

The British treaty with the al-Thanis was similar to ones made with other shaykhs in Arabia and the Persian Gulf in order to keep other European powers out of the area and to protect their trade and communications links with India. In 1916 the British recognized Shaykh Abdullah al-Thani, grandfather of the current ruler, as ruler of Qatar and promised to protect the territory from outside attack either by the Ottomans or overland by hostile Arabian groups. In return, Shaykh al-Thani agreed not to enter into any relationship with any other foreign government and to accept British political advisers.

Qatar remained a tranquil British protectorate until the 1950s, when oil exports began. Since then the country has developed rapidly, but not to the extent of the dizzying change visible in other oil-producing Arab states.

INDEPENDENCE

Qatar became independent in 1971, and the ruler, Shaykh Ahmad al-Thani, took the title of emir. Disagreements within the ruling family led the emir's cousin, Shaykh Khalifa, to seize power in 1972. Shaykh Khalifa made himself prime minister as well as ruler and initiated a major pro-gram of social and economic development, which his cousin had opposed.

Shaykh Khalifa limited the privileges of the ruling family. There were more than 2,000 al-Thanis, and most of them had been paid several thousand dollars a month whether or not they worked. Khalifa reduced their allowances and also appointed some nonmembers of the royal family to the Council of Ministers, the state's chief executive body. He subsequently issued a decree establishing a Consultative Council of 30 elected members to advise the Council of Ministers on legislation and to debate the national budget. In 1989 the emir made a number of major changes in the Cabinet, appointing technicians and specialists in various fields to revitalize national development. The ruler also turned over day-to-day operations of government to Crown Prince Hamad, his designated successor.

FOREIGN RELATIONS

Because of its small size, great wealth, and proximity to regional conflicts, Qatar is vulnerable to outside intervention. The government especially fears that the example of the Iranian Shia Revolution may bring unrest to its own Shia Muslim population. After the discovery of a Shia plot to overthrow the government of neighboring Bahrain in 1981, Qatari authorities rounded up and deported several hundred Shia Qataris of Iranian origin. But thus far the government has avoided singling out the Shia community for heavy-handed repression, preferring to concentrate its efforts on economic and social progress. On the tenth anniversary of independence, the emir said in a speech that "economic strength is the strongest guarantee that safeguards the independence of nations, their sovereignty, rights and dignity." [1]

Vulnerability to possible outside attack led Qatar to sign a bilateral defense agreement with Saudi Arabia in 1982. It had previously joined the Gulf Cooperation Council and has been active in developing arrangements to eliminate import tariffs and travel restrictions among GCC members and in setting up a mutual defense system. An earlier British effort to form a federation of Qatar, Bahrain, and the United Arab Emirates in 1968–1969 did not work out, but the very real possibility of Iranian-sponsored subversion accelerated the pace of cooperation. In 1987 the Qatari ruler issued a decree allowing citizens of the other GCC states to own real estate in Qatar.

The country abandoned its usual low profile in regional affairs after the 1990 Iraqi invasion of Kuwait. The emir endorsed Arab League and GCC resolutions condemning the invasion and invited foreign troops to use Qatari bases to repel aggression if necessary. (Some 24 U.S. aircraft were based in Qatar during the subsequent Gulf War.) The majority of Palestinians resident in the emirate were expelled in October 1990 after the Palestine Liberation Organization publicly supported Iraq in its invasion.

THE ECONOMY

Qatar's economy is based almost entirely on oil production and export. Reserves are estimated at 2.5 billion barrels. At the current rates of extraction of 390,000 barrels per day, these reserves should be used up early in the next century. Aside from prudent investment of oil revenues, the state has undertaken a major development of its large natural-gas reserves. The offshore North Field gas project began operating in 1991, with production scheduled to rise to 800 million cubic feet per day in 1992. It is expected to more than make up for the shortfall in current revenues caused by dwindling oil production.

Development of diversified industries to reduce Qatar's dependence on oil exports has been a top priority for the government since independence. Umm Said, the port of Doha, is the main industrial center. Whereas not long ago it was mud flats, by 1983 Umm Said had a steel mill, fertilizer plants, gas-liquefaction plants for animal feedstock, and a 50,000 barrels-per-day oil refinery. Fertilizer plants produced 1.5 million tons of urea and ammonia in 1988, while global price increases of 100 percent brought large increases in revenues.

Although industrial growth in Qatar depends upon factors not subject to local control, notably oil prices, agriculture depends entirely on subsurface water for irrigation. Water demand has risen 10 percent annually since 1980, seriously depleting the underground aquifer. The country's water supply comes mostly from huge desalination plants, which are already outmoded due to population growth. In 1988 a project was begun to cultivate food crops on sand, using solar energy and seawater. Due to this project and other innovative agricultural techniques, Qatar has been able to produce enough food to meet domestic needs and to export vegetables to other Gulf states. Qatar's largest dairy, the al-Rakkiya, accommodates 1,200 dairy cattle on what were formerly desert sands.

SOCIETAL CHANGES

Qatar was originally settled by nomadic peoples, and their influence is still strong. Traditional Bedouin values, such as honesty, hospitality, pride, and courage when

The United Kingdom recognizes Shaykh Abdullah al-Thani as emir
1916

The start of oil production
1949

An abortive federation with Bahrain and the Trucial States (U.A.E.), followed by independence
1971

The ruler is deposed by Crown Prince Shaykh Khalifa
1972

1980s–1990s

Qatar joins the Gulf Cooperation Council; the country's first university is enlarged to accommodate 6,000 students

New laws are approved restricting activities of non-Qataris in trade and industry; the first national census is taken

Qatar condemns the Iraqi invasion of Kuwait and expels resident Palestinians

faced with adversity, have carried over into modern times.

Most Qataris belong to the strict puritanical Wahhabi sect of Islam, which is also dominant in Saudi Arabia. They are conservative and cautious. But perhaps because of the large number of immigrants and the presence of a large number of non-Muslim foreign workers, Qataris are less conservative than are their Saudi neighbors. For example, movies are shown in Qatar but not in Saudi Arabia.

Unlike other Islamic lands, where women have had to fight every step of the way to gain social and civil rights comparable to those of men, in Qatar the position of women has changed smoothly, almost imperceptibly. The first school for girls opened in 1956, and by 1982–1983 the ratio of boys to girls in primary schools was about the same. However, there were more girls than boys in secondary school and at the University of Qatar. Women are entering many new fields in addition to the traditional ones of nursing and teaching. They work as doctors, journalists, radio and television announcers, and set designers.

The movement of women into the work place often creates family tensions in other societies, but Qataris seem able to take it in stride. One woman, a designer in her mid-twenties who is married with one child, told an interviewer, "There are Qataris who allow their wives more freedom than an Englishman would give to his wife. But we hold to our traditions. What I want is for us to change, but wisely. Trouble arises when people try to be mod-

ern too fast. Change should take place within the framework of our habits and traditions."[2] A woman doctor said, "I don't want my daughter to wear the *batula* [the black beak-shaped face-mask veil traditionally worn by women in the Gulf]. It has no importance now. Times are different. When I was young everybody wore it. Now girls go to school and university and the batula doesn't suit them."[3]

THE FUTURE

What will Qatar be like when the oil stops flowing? Twenty years ago Doha consisted of two rows of mud-brick houses along a ditch; today it is a thriving seaport of 250,000 people, with traffic jams and supermarkets. Qatar, like other oil-producing countries, is affected by global reductions in demand, lower prices, and the inevitable slowdown in development projects. The Gulf War, although it brought with it higher oil prices and increased revenues, stalled the industrial-diversification process. A large number of key projects were delayed, including the North Field gas pipeline and the Doha aluminum smelter.

Qatar's small size and the close links between the ruling family and the people give the country more the appearance of a family-run corporation than of a nation-state. The monarchy is absolute, but it is also paternalistic. Upward mobility and success are common experiences, and for many they occur at a relatively young age; a number of government and industrial leaders are in their thirties.

Mohammed, the head of the electricity department of the Ministry of Power and-Water, is a typical example of the Qatari of today. His father was a mechanic, and he knows nothing of his grandfather's people. Yet Mohammed operates comfortably in two worlds, the Western world of high-powered technology and the world of the traditional close-knit Qatari family. He is the model of the Western technocrat, wearing tailored European suits, his hair short and neatly trimmed. "Yet under this exterior lurks a mind more Arab than Western in its working, never moving on one level only, never accepting anything at face value."[4] These qualities and this distinctive cast of mind seem likely to carry Qatar comfortably into the not-too-distant future when its last oil well out in the desert runs dry.

NOTES

1. Qatar News Agency (November 23, 1981).
2. Helga Graham, *Arabian Time Machine: Self Portrait of an Oil State* (London: Heinemann, 1978), p. 207.
3. *Ibid.*, p. 183.
4. *Ibid.*, p. 108.

DEVELOPMENT

Qatar has never drawn up formal development plans. In past years the government has plowed annual surpluses into housing, hospitals, schools, and other services. The goal is complete self-sufficiency by the year 2000.

FREEDOM

In theory, Qatar is a constitutional monarchy, but in practice, absolute power is vested in the ruler. A majority of members of the Council of Ministers (Cabinet) are al-Thanis. But increasingly, high government positions are being filled by technically competent Qataris trained and educated in the West.

HEALTH/WELFARE

By 1989 Qatar's national health system was able to supply 20 doctors, 3 dentists, and 51 nurses per 10,000 population, the highest ratio of any Arab state. Some 6,000 families were provided with public housing in 1983, and a noncontributory pension fund was set up for all public employees.

ACHIEVEMENTS

A pilot project to plant mangroves along the Qatari shoreline, undertaken with Japanese technical help, is expected to bring a major increase in the shrimp harvest, since mangrove roots provide an ideal shrimp breeding ground.

Saudi Arabia (Kingdom of Saudi Arabia)

GEOGRAPHY

Area in Square Kilometers (Miles):
2,331,000 (899,770) (about ¼ the
size of the continental United States)
Capital (Population): Riyadh
(1,380,000)
Climate: arid, with great extremes of
temperature

PEOPLE

Population

Total: 16,758,000
Annual Growth Rate: 4.1%
Rural/Urban Population Ratio: 24/76
Ethnic Makeup of Population: 90%
Arab; 10% Afro-Asian

Health

Life Expectancy at Birth: 62 years
(male); 66 years (female)
Infant Mortality Rate (Ratio):
67/1,000
Average Caloric Intake: 116% of FAO
minimum
Physicians Available (Ratio): 1/973

Religion(s)

100% Muslim

Education

Adult Literacy Rate: 50%

COMMUNICATION

Telephones: 1,624,000
Newspapers: 8 dailies in Arabic; 3
dailies in English

TRANSPORTATION

Highways—Kilometers (Miles):
92,802 (57,537)

Railroads—Kilometers (Miles): 1,036
(642)
Usable Airfields: 176

GOVERNMENT

Type: hereditary monarchy in al-Saud
family
Independence Date: September 23,
1932 (unification)
Head of State: King and Prime
Minister Fahd ibn Abdul Aziz al-Saud
Political Parties: none; prohibited
Suffrage: none

MILITARY

Number of Armed Forces: 67,500
*Military Expenditures (% of Central
Government Expenditures):* 36%
Current Hostilities: none

ECONOMY

Currency ($ U.S. Equivalent): 3.74
Saudi rials = $1
Per Capita Income/GNP: $6,020/$70
billion
Inflation Rate: −4%
Total Foreign Debt: n/a
Natural Resources: hydrocarbons;
iron ore; gold; copper
Agriculture: dates; grain; livestock
Industry: petroleum production;
petrochemicals; cement; fertilizer;
light industry

FOREIGN TRADE

Exports: $26.2 billion
Imports: $21.5 billion

CHANGING THE FACE OF MECCA

Mecca, located in a dusty valley 45 miles inland from the Red Sea, is not only the Kingdom of Saudi Arabia's spiritual capital but also contains the holiest shrines of Islam. It was Muhammad's birthplace and the scene of his conversion, early ministry, and ultimate triumph. The annual Hajj (Great Pilgrimage) to Mecca draws Muslim pilgrims from the four corners of the world. In 1989 the Saudi government began a huge building project to meet the needs of the growing number of pilgrims. It includes a shopping mall, luxury hotels, and other amenities, located across from the Great Mosque and the Ka'ba, the black-draped cube-shaped building in its inner courtyard that is the focus and center of the pilgrimage.

* Capital　— Rivers　-- Roads

SAUDI ARABIA

The Kingdom of Saudi Arabia is the giant of the Arabian Peninsula, with an area of nearly 900,000 square miles. It is also a giant in the world economy, because of its oil. To many people in the United States and elsewhere, the name Saudi Arabia is a synonym for oil wealth. Indeed, its huge oil reserves, large financial surpluses from oil production, and its ability to use oil as a political weapon (as in the 1973 embargo) enable the country to play an important part in regional and international affairs.

In relation to its size, Saudi Arabia has a small population (16,758,000), with three-quarters of the people living in urban areas. Urban growth has been very rapid, since only 1 percent of the land can be used for agriculture and all employment opportunities are in the cities or the oil-producing regions. Due to its small population, the country has traditionally relied upon foreign labor, both skilled and unskilled, in its development. The economic recession of the 1980s and more recently the Gulf War have sharply reduced the number of foreign workers. The labor force was 4,081,000 in 1990.

The country contains three geographical regions: the Hejaz, along the Red Sea; the Nejd, a vast interior plateau that comprises the bulk of Saudi territory; and the Eastern Province. The kingdom's largest oases, al-Hasa Safwa, are located in this third region, along with the major oil fields and industrial centers. The Empty Quarter (al-Rub' al-Khali), an uninhabited desert where rain may not fall for a decade or more, occupies the entire southeastern quadrant of the country.

THE WAHHABI MOVEMENT

In the eighteenth century most of the area included in present-day Saudi Arabia was the home of nomads, as it had been for centuries. These peoples had no central government and owed allegiance to no one except their chiefs. They spent much of their time raiding one another's territories in the struggle for survival. Inland Arabia was a great blank area on the map, a vast, empty desert.

The only part of present-day Saudi Arabia under any government control in the eighteenth century was the Hejaz, which includes the Islamic Holy Cities of Mecca and Medina. It was a province of the Ottoman Turkish Empire, the major power in the Middle East at that time.

Saudi Arabia became a nation, in the modern sense of the word, in 1932. But the origins of the Saudi nation go back to the eighteenth century. One of the tribes that roamed the desert beyond Ottoman control was the tribe of Saud. Its leader, Muhammad ibn Saud, wanted to gain an advantage over his rivals in the constant search for water and good grazing land for animals. He approached a famous religious scholar named Abd al-Wahhab, who lived in an oasis near the current Saudi capital, Riyadh (then a mud-walled village). Abd al-Wahhab promised Allah's blessing to ibn Saud in his contests with his rivals. In return, the Saudi leader agreed to protect al-Wahhab from threats to his life by opponents of the strict doctrines he taught and preached, and he swore an oath of obedience to these doctrines. The partnership between these two men gave rise to a crusading religious movement called Wahhabism.

Wahhabism is basically a strict and puritanical form of Sunni Islam. The Wahhabi code of law, behavior, and conduct is modeled on that of the original Islamic community established in Mecca and Medina by the Prophet Muhammad. Although there has been some relaxation of the code due to the country's modernization, it remains the law of Saudi Arabia today. As a result, Saudi society is not only more conservative and puritanical than many other Islamic societies but is also governed much more strictly. A Ministry of Public Morals Enforcement, for example, has the responsibility to ensure that women (including foreigners) are dressed and veiled in accordance with Islamic modesty, and its squads patrol the streets to guarantee compliance. More recently the Committee to Promote Virtue and Prevent Vice, a private organization of young Muslims who wear short beards and robes, has taken to enforcing the rules more vigorously. Their leader, the Shaykh Bin Baz (noted for his public statements that the world is flat) is also the head of the Saudi *ulema* (religious leaders), giving the organization the needed aura of Islamic respectability.

Wahhabi strictures were tested in November 1990 when a group of women from prominent families defied the ban on driving and drove their cars on public streets in Riyadh. Fearing a religious backlash, the Interior minister issued a decree formalizing the ban. Said one woman, "It's 1990, we're on the brink of World War III and Saudi Arabia has just formally banned driving by women. It's crazy. It's sad. It's ridiculous."[1]

Due to the Wahhabi-Saud partnership, religious leaders in the country (many of whom are descendants of Abd al-Wahhab) have a great deal of influence in the government. They may delay or even annul government actions that they believe are contrary to Islamic principles. Thus, they have successfully prevented the opening of movie theaters in the kingdom.

HISTORY

The puritanical zeal of the Wahhabis led them to declare a "holy war" against the Ottoman Turks, who were then in control of Mecca and Medina, in order to restore these Holy Cities to the Arabs. In the early 1800s Wahhabis captured the cities. Soon the Wahhabis threatened to undermine Ottoman authority elsewhere. Wahhabi raiders seized Najaf and Karbala in Iraq, centers of Shia pilgrimage, and desecrated Shia shrines. In Mecca they removed the headstones from the graves of members of the Prophet's family, because in their belief all Muslims are supposed to be buried unmarked.

The Ottoman sultan did not have sufficient forces at hand to deal with the Wahhabi threat, so he called upon his vassal, Mohammad Ali, the khedive (viceroy) of Egypt. Muhammad Ali organized an army equipped with European weapons and trained by European advisers. In a series of hard-fought campaigns, the Egyptian Army defeated the Wahhabis and drove them back into the desert.

Inland Arabia reverted to its old ways of conflict. The only difference between the Saudis and their rivals was the bond of Wahhabism. It did not help them in their conflicts, and in the 1890s the Saudis' major rivals, the Rashidis, seized Riyadh. The Saudi chief escaped across the desert to Kuwait, a town on the Persian Gulf that was under British protection. He took along his 11-year-old son, Abd al-Aziz ibn Saud.

IBN SAUD

Abd al-Aziz ibn Saud, or Ibn Saud as he is usually known in history, was, like George Washington, the father of his country, in both a political and a literal sense.[2] He grew up in exile in Kuwait, where he brooded and schemed about how to regain the lands of the Saudis. When he reached age 21, in 1902, he decided on a bold stroke to reach his goal. Crossing the desert with a small band of followers, he scaled the walls of Riyadh at night and seized the fortress by surprise at daybreak. This daring exploit won him the support of the people of Riyadh, who drove the Rashidis out of the town.

Over the next 3 decades Ibn Saud steadily expanded his territory. He said his goal was "to recover all the lands of our forefathers."[3] In World War I he became an ally of the British, fighting the Ottoman Turks in Arabia. In return, the British provided arms for his followers and gave him a monthly allowance. The British continued to back Ibn Saud after the war, and in 1924 he entered Mecca in triumph.

(Aramco photo)

The Great Mosque at Mecca, in Saudi Arabia, is the holiest of shrines to Muslims. Historically, Mecca was the site at which Islam was founded in the seventh century A.D. by the Prophet Muhammad. Pilgrims today flock to the Great Mosque to fulfill their Muslim duties as set down by the Five Pillars of Islam.

His major rival, Sharif Husayn, who had been appointed by the Ottoman government as the "Protector of the Holy Places," fled into exile. (Sharif Husayn was the great-grandfather of King Hussein I of Jordan.)

Ibn Saud's second goal, after recovering his ancestral lands, was to build a modern nation under a central government. He used as his motto the Koranic verse, "God changes not what is in a people until they change what is in themselves" (*Sura XIII, II*). The first step was to gain recognition of Saudi Arabia as an independent state. The United Kingdom recognized the country in 1927, and other countries soon followed suit. In 1932 the country took its current name of Saudi Arabia, a union of the three provinces of Hejaz, Nejd, and al-Hasa.

INDEPENDENCE

Ibn Saud's second step in his "grand design" for the new country was to establish order under a central government. To do this, he began to build settlements and to encourage the nomads to settle down, live in permanent homes, and learn how to grow their own food rather than relying on the desert. Those who settled on the land

were given seeds and tools, were enrolled in a sort of national guard, and were paid regular allowances. These former Bedouin warriors became in time the core of the Saudi armed forces.

Ibn Saud also established the country's basic political system. The basis for the system was the Wahhabi interpretation of Islamic law. Ibn Saud insisted that "the laws of the state shall always be in accordance with the Book of Allah and the Sunna (Conduct) of His Messenger and the ways of the Companions."[4] He saw no need for a written constitution, and as yet Saudi Arabia has none. Ibn Saud decreed that the country would be governed as an absolute monarchy, with rulers always chosen from the Saud family. He was unfamiliar with political parties and distrusted them in principle; political organizations were therefore prohibited in the kingdom. Yet Ibn Saud was himself democratic, humble in manner, and spartan in his living habits. He remained all his life a man of the people and held every day a public assembly (*majlis*) in Riyadh at which any citizen had the right to ask favors or present petitions. (The custom of holding a daily majlis has been observed by Saudi rulers ever since.) More often

than not, petitioners would address Ibn Saud not as Your Majesty but simply as Abd al-Aziz (his given name), a dramatic example of Saudi democracy in action.

Ibn Saud died in 1953. He had witnessed the beginning of rapid social and economic change in his country due to oil revenues. Yet his successors have presided over a transformation beyond the imaginations of the warriors who scaled the walls of Riyadh half a century earlier. Almost the only building left in Riyadh from that period is the Masmak Fort, headquarters of the Rashidi leader, still standing in the midst of tall modern buildings as a reminder to young Saudis of the epic age in their nation's history.

Ibn Saud was succeeded by his eldest surviving son, Crown Prince Saud. A number of royal princes felt that the second son, Faisal, should have become the new king because of his greater experience in foreign affairs and economic management. Saud's only experience was as governor of Nejd.

The new king was like his father in a number of ways, although he was large and corpulent and lacked Ibn Saud's forceful personality. He was more comfortable in a desert tent than in running a bureaucracy or meeting foreign dignitaries. Also, like his father, he had no idea of the value of money. Ibn Saud would carry a sackful of riyals (the Saudi currency) to the daily majlis and give them away to petitioners. His son, Saud, not only doled out money to petitioners but also gave millions to other members of the royal family. One of his greatest extravagances was a palace surrounded by a bright pink wall.[5]

By 1958 the country was almost bankrupt. The royal family was understandably nervous about a possible coup supported by other Arab states, such as Egypt and Syria, which were openly critical of Saudi Arabia because of its lack of political institutions. The senior princes issued an ultimatum to Saud: first he would put Faisal in charge of straightening out the kingdom's finances, and when that had been done he would abdicate. The financial overhaul was completed in 1964, and with the kingdom again on a sound footing, Saud abdicated in favor of Faisal.

This incident offers a good example of how the Saudi monarchy operates in crisis situations. Decisions are made collectively, and although the king is an absolute monarch to his subjects, he serves as "head of the family" and in reality must consult with the senior princes on all matters of policy. Decisions are also made in secret in order to give the impression of family unity to the outside world. The reasons for a decision must always be guessed at; the Saudis never explain them. It is a system very different from the open, freewheeling one of Western democracies, yet it has given Saudi Arabia stability and leadership on occasions when crises threatened the kingdom.

FAISAL AND HIS SUCCESSORS

The reign of King Faisal (1964–1975) is second in importance only to that of Ibn Saud in terms of state-building. One author wrote of King Faisal during his reign, "He is leading the country with gentle insistence from medievalism into the jet age."[6] Faisal's gentle insistence showed itself in many different ways. Encouraged by his wife, Queen Iffat, he introduced education for girls into the kingdom. Before Faisal, the kingdom had had no systematic development plans. In introducing the first 5-year development plan, the king said that "our religion requires us to progress and to bear the burden of the highest tradition and best manners."[7]

In foreign affairs, Faisal ended the Yemen Civil War on an honorable basis for both sides, took an active part in the Islamic world in keeping with his role as Protector of the Holy Places, and in 1970 founded the Organization of the Islamic Conference, which has given the Islamic nations of the world a voice in international affairs. Faisal laid down the basic strategy that his successors have followed, namely, avoidance of direct conflict, mediation of disputes behind the scenes, and use of oil wealth as a political weapon when necessary. The king never understood the American commitment to Israel, any more than his father had. (Ibn Saud had met U.S. President Franklin D. Roosevelt in Egypt during World War II. Roosevelt, already motivated by American Jewish leaders to help in the establishment of a Jewish homeland in Palestine, sought to convince Ibn Saud, as head of the only independent Arab state at that time, to moderate Arab opposition to the project.) But Faisal's distrust of communism was equally strong. This distrust led him to continue the ambivalent yet close Saudi alliance with the United States that has continued up to the present.

Faisal was assassinated in 1975 by a deranged nephew while he was holding the daily majlis. The assassination was another test of the system of rule by consensus in the royal family, and the system held firm. Khalid, Faisal's eldest half-brother and junior by 6 years, succeeded him without incident and ruled until 1982. King Khalid, who was already in poor health, delegated most of his powers to his half-brother Fahd. He died

suddenly in 1982, and Crown Prince Fahd, the current ruler, succeeded him.

THE MECCA MOSQUE SIEGE

One of the most shocking events in Saudi history since the founding of the kingdom was the seizure of the Great Mosque in Mecca, Islam's holiest shrine, by a group of fundamentalist Sunni Muslims in November 1979. The leader of the group declared that one of its members was the *Mahdi* (in Sunni Islam, the "Awaited One") who had come to announce the Day of Judgment. The group occupied the mosque for 2 weeks. The siege was finally overcome by army and national-guard units, but with considerable loss of life on both sides. No one knows exactly what the group's purpose was, nor did it lead to any general expressions of dissatisfaction with the regime. But the incident reflects the very real fear of the Saudi rulers of a coup attempted by the ultrareligious right, perhaps a reawakening of the Wahhabi spirit of long ago.

Although the Saudi government remains staunchly conservative, it has before it the example of Iran, where a similar Islamic fundamentalist movement overthrew a well-established monarchy. Furthermore, the Shia Muslim population of the country is concentrated in al-Hasa Province, where the oil fields are located. The government's immediate fear after the Great Mosque seizure was of an outside plot inspired by Iran. When this plot did not materialize, the Saudis feared Shia involvement. Outside of increased security measures, the principal result of the incident has been a large increase in funding for the Shia community.

THE ECONOMY

Oil was discovered in Saudi Arabia in 1938, but exports did not begin until after World War II. The oil fields are located in the eastern provinces and in the Neutral Zone. New discoveries in 1989 and 1990 increased proven oil reserves to 257.5 billion barrels, the largest in the world. Natural-gas deposits are 3.5 billion cubic meters, sufficient to serve the newly developed national gas grid. The oil industry was controlled by Aramco (Arabian-American Oil Company), a consortium of four U.S. oil companies. In 1980, it came under Saudi government control, but Aramco continued to manage marketing and distribution services. The last American president of Aramco retired in 1989 and was succeeded by a Saudi.

King Faisal's reorganization of finances and development plans in the 1960s set the kingdom on an upward course of rapid development. The economy took off after 1973, when the Saudis, along with other

Arab oil-producing states, reduced production and imposed an export embargo on Western countries as a gesture of support to Egypt in its war with Israel. After 1973 the price per barrel of Saudi oil continued to increase, to a peak of $34.00 per barrel in 1981. (Prior to the embargo it was $3.00 per barrel; in 1979 it was $13.30 per barrel.) The outbreak of the Iran-Iraq War in 1980 caused a huge drop in world production. The Saudis took up the slack.

The huge revenues from oil made possible economic development on a scale undreamed of by Ibn Saud and his Bedouin warriors. The old fishing ports of Yanbu, on the Red Sea, and Jubail, on the Persian Gulf, were transformed into new industrial cities, with oil refineries, cement and petrochemical plants, steel mills, and dozens of related industries. Riyadh experienced a building boom; Cadillacs bumped into camels on the streets and the shops filled up with imported luxury goods. Every native Saudi, it seemed, profited from the boom through free education and health care, low-interest housing loans, and guaranteed jobs.

The boom also attracted a large foreign labor force, drawn by the high wages. Most came from poor countries such as Yemen, Pakistan, South Korea, and the Philippines. The remittances sent home by these workers became a vital source of income to their countries.

The global oil slump of the 1980s hit Saudi Arabia particularly hard. Revenues plummeted and many development projects were postponed or cancelled. Oil production dropped to a low of 4.5 million barrels per day (in 1988), rising to 8.9 million b/d in 1992, above its OPEC quota.

THE FUTURE

Historically, Saudi Arabia's size, distance from major Middle Eastern urban centers, and oil wealth have insulated the country from the winds of political change. Domestic and foreign policy alike evolve from within the ruling family. Officials who undertake independent policy actions are quickly brought into line, an example being the freewheeling former Oil Minister Shaykh Zamani. The ruling family is also closely aligned with the ulema; Saudi rulers since Ibn Saud's time have held the title "Guardians of the Holy Mosques" (of Mecca and Medina), giving them a preeminent position in the Islamic world. Except for the army, the ulema form the only organized group in the kingdom outside of the royal family, and they help to legitimize the government, although at a price.

Wahhabis seize Mecca and Medina 1800	Ibn Saud captures Riyadh in a daring commando raid 1902	Ibn Saud is recognized by the British as the king of Saudi Arabia 1927	Oil exports get under way under management of Aramco 1946	King Saud, the eldest son and successor of Ibn Saud, is deposed in favor of his brother Faisal 1963	Faisal is assassinated; succession passes by agreement to Khalid 1975	The Great Mosque in Mecca is seized by a fundamentalist Muslim group 1979	

1980s–19█

King Khalid dies; succession passes to Crown Prince Fahd; Saudi jets shoot down an Iranian jet for violation of Saudi air space	The first formal budget since 1985 is approved; expenditures reflect reduced revenues	A bloody clash between Iranian pilgrims in Mecca and Saudi security forces leads to sacking of the Saudi Embassy in Teheran; Saudi Arabia hosts foreign troops and shares command in the Gulf War

In recent years pressures to broaden the political system have increased. In general, the demand for change pits Western-educated liberals against hardline religious leaders. But unexpectedly in June 1991 the ulema submitted a list of eleven "demands" to the rulers, the most important being more equal distribution of wealth and the formation of a *majlis al-Shura* (Consultative Council). With the need for such a council widely recognized, it appeared that the religious leaders wished to associate themselves with an inevitable move toward a more participatory system rather than to back themselves into a corner opposing it. In March 1992 the king approved a 60-member Consultative Council to act as an advisory body with powers to initiate legislation and to review foreign policy. A bill of rights is to be prepared that would put limits on the powers of the religious police and confirm the right to private property.

FOREIGN POLICY

The Iraqi invasion and occupation of Kuwait caused a major shift in Saudi policy, away from mediation in regional conflicts and bankrolling of popular causes (such as the Palestinian) to one of direct confrontation. For the first time in its history the Saudi nation felt threatened directly by the actions of an aggressive neighbor. Diplomatic relations were broken with Iraq and subsequently with Jordan and Yemen, due to their support for the Iraqi occupation. Yemeni workers were rounded up and expelled, and harsh restrictions were imposed on Yemeni busi-ness owners in the kingdom. Establishment of the UN-U.S.–led coalition against Iraq led to the stationing of foreign non-Muslim troops on its soil, also a historic first. Aside from concern over their own vulnerability, Saudi leaders were motivated strongly by an interest in restoring a fellow partriarchal ruling family, the al-Sabahs, to power in Kuwait.

A by-product of the Gulf War and alignment with the United States was stepped-up Saudi purchases of U.S. arms. The country became the major world purchaser of American weaponry—$14.5 billion in 1990 alone. Saudi Arabia also contributed $11.5 billion in cash to cover U.S. war costs.

The country's often difficult relationship with Iran underwent another change in 1991. The fall of the Iranian monarchy and establishment of the Islamic Republic had initially been welcomed by Saudi rulers because of the new regime's fidelity to Islamic principles. But in 1987 Iranian pilgrims attending the pilgrimage to Mecca undertook anti-Saudi demonstrations that led to a violent confrontation with police, resulting in more than 400 casualties. The two countries broke diplomatic relations, and in 1988 Saudi Arabia established a quota system for pilgrims on the basis of 1 pilgrim per 1,000 population. The quota system was described as necessary to reduce congestion on the annual pilgrimages, but in fact it would limit Iran to 50,000 pilgrims and limit Iranian-inspired political activism. Iran boycotted the pilgrimage in 1988 and 1989 as a result. But the country's neutral stance during the Gulf War helped heal the breach. Diplomatic relations were restored in 1991. As a Saudi official observed, "If the Iranians open their hand to us, we will open our heart to them."[8]

NOTES

1. James Lemoyne, in *The New York Times* (November 23, 1990).

2. He had 24 sons by 16 different women during his life (1880–1953). See William Quandt, *Saudi Arabia in the 1980's* (Washington: Brookings Institution, 1981), Appendix E, for a genealogy.

3. George Rentz, "The Saudi Monarchy," in Willard A. Beling, ed., *King Faisal and the Modernization of Saudi Arabia* (Boulder: Westview Press, 1980), pp. 26–27.

4. *Ibid.*, p. 29.

5. The wall was torn down by his successor, King Faisal. Justin Coe, in *The Christian Science Monitor* (February 13, 1985).

6. Gordon Gaskill, "Saudi Arabia's Modern Monarch," *Reader's Digest* (January 1967), p. 118.

7. Ministry of Information, Kingdom of Saudi Arabia, *Faisal Speaks* (n.d.), p. 88.

8. Peter Ford, in *The Christian Science Monitor* (June 6, 1991).

DEVELOPMENT

Sharply reduced oil revenues forced the government to borrow funds internally in 1988, for the first time in 25 years. An income tax on expatriate workers was introduced early in the year but was withdrawn after foreign companies threatened to remove all of their nationals.

FREEDOM

Although the country is an absolute monarchy, local administration exists under municipal, district, and tribal councils.

HEALTH/WELFARE

Education holds a high priority in the kingdom. In the 1960s and 1970s thousands of Saudis were sent abroad for technical training, most to the United States. A domestic university system was developed rapidly with the help of foreign specialists. Saudi students are not politicized and student unrest is absent.

ACHIEVEMENTS

Large-scale financing of agricultural projects and subsidies to growers have enabled Saudi Arabia to become self-sufficient in wheat, barley, poultry, eggs, and milk, with a surplus for export. Some 35% of Saudi Arabia's non-oil exports come from food products.

Sudan (Democratic Republic of Sudan)

GEOGRAPHY

Area in Square Kilometers (Miles):
2,504,530 (967,500) (about ¼ the size
of the continental United States)
Capital (Population): Khartoum
(476,200)
Climate: dry in the north to tropical
in the south

PEOPLE

Population

Total: 25,164,000
Annual Growth Rate: 2.7%
Rural/Urban Population Ratio: 78/22
Ethnic Makeup of Population: 52%
black; 39% Arab; 6% Beja; 3%
others

Health

Life Expectancy at Birth: 49 years
(male); 52 years (female)
Infant Mortality Rate (Ratio):
104/1,000
Average Caloric Intake: 99% of FAO
minimum
Physicians Available (Ratio): 1/11,600

Religion(s)

70% Sunni Muslim in north; 20%
indigenous beliefs; 5% Christian; 5%
others

Education

Adult Literacy Rate: 30%

COMMUNICATION

Telephones: 68,500
Newspapers: 2 dailies in English, 2 in
Arabic; party newspapers

TRANSPORTATION

Highways—Kilometers (Miles):
20,000 (12,428)
Railroads—Kilometers (Miles): 5,516

LAND OF BROWNS AND BLACKS

Sudan is really two nations, a Muslim Arab north ("Brown") and a
Christian or animistic south ("Black"), peopled by various sub-Saharan
groups. One of these is the Dinka, incredibly tall, spear-carrying cattle
herders. A young Dinka, 7-foot, 6-inch Manute Bol, was the star center
on the University of Bridgeport, Connecticut, basketball team during
the 1984–1985 season, although he had never played the game before
coming to the United States.

The southerners fought a 17-year war with the north to gain regional
autonomy, and President Nimeiri's imposition of Islamic law over them
in 1983 led to renewed rebellion. In 1985 the new government abolished
Islamic law courts, but it has yet to come to terms with the southerners
on regional autonomy.

(3,428)
Usable Airfields: 78

GOVERNMENT

Type: republic; currently under
military rule
Independence Date: January 1, 1956
Head of State: Lieutenant General
Omar Hassan al-Bashir, chair of the
Revolutionary Council
Political Parties: suspended since
July 1989
Suffrage: universal adult

MILITARY

Number of Armed Forces: 74,500
*Military Expenditures (% of Central
Government Expenditures):* n/a
Current Hostilities: none

ECONOMY

Currency ($ U.S. Equivalent): 11.4
Sudanese pounds = $1
Per Capita Income/GNP: $480/$8.5
billion
Inflation Rate: 70%
Total Foreign Debt: $12.97 billion
Natural Resources: oil; iron ore;
copper; chrome; other industrial
metals
Agriculture: cotton; peanuts; sesame;
gum arabic; sorghum; wheat
Industry: textiles; cement; cotton
ginning; edible oils; distilling;
pharmaceuticals

FOREIGN TRADE

Exports: $520 million
Imports: $1.4 billion

SUDAN

Sudan is the largest nation in Africa, with a land area of 967,500 square miles. The bulk of the population is concentrated in the province of Khartoum (also the name of the capital) and in the central region, which includes the Blue Nile and the White Nile, the country's principal rivers.

The name of the country underscores its distinctive social structure. Centuries ago Arab geographers named it Bilad al-Sudan, "Land of the Blacks." The northern half, including Khartoum, is Arabic in language, culture, and traditions, and Islamic in religion. The southern half is sub-Saharan African, made up of a number of black African peoples, the Shilluk, Dinka, Nuer, Azande, and many others. Some of them are Christian due to the efforts of European mission schools established during the British occupation. Others believe in traditional religions. The two halves of Sudan have little or nothing in common. The country's basic political problem is how to achieve unity between these two different societies that were brought together under British rule to form an artificial nation.

HISTORY

The ancient history of Sudan, at least the northern region, was always linked with that of Egypt. The pharaohs and later conquerors of Egypt—Persians, Greeks, Romans, and eventually the Arabs, Turks, and British—periodically attempted to extend their power farther south. The connection with Egypt became very close when the Egyptians were converted to Islam by invading armies from Arabia in the seventh century A.D. As the invaders spread southward, they converted the northern Sudanese people to Islam, developing in time an Islamic Arab society in northern Sudan. Southern Sudan remained comparatively untouched because it was separated by geographical barriers, mountain ranges and the great impassable swamps of the Nile.

The two regions were forcibly brought together by conquering Egyptian armies in the nineteenth century. The conquest became possible after the exploration of sub-Saharan Africa by European explorers. After the explorers and armies came slave traders and then European fortune hunters, interested in developing the gold, ivory, diamonds, timber, and other resources of sub-Saharan Africa.

The soldiers and slave traders were the most brutal of all these invaders, particularly in southern Sudan. In fact, many of the slave traders were Muslim Sudanese from the north. The Civil War between the Islamic north and the Christian/animist south, which began in 1955 and is still going on, had its roots in the nineteenth-century experiences of the southerners, as "memories of plunder, slave raiding and suffering" at the hands of slavers and their military allies were passed down from generation to generation.[1]

ORIGINS OF THE SUDANESE STATE

The first effort to establish a nation in Sudan began in the 1880s, when the country was ruled by the British as part of their protectorate over Egypt. The British were hated as foreign, non-Muslim rulers. The Egyptians, who made up the bulk of the security forces assigned to Sudan, were hated for their arrogance and mistreatment of the Sudanese.

In 1881 a religious leader in northern Sudan announced that he was the Mahdi, the "Awaited One," who, according to Sunni Islamic belief, would appear on earth, sent by God to rid the Sudan of its foreign rulers. The Mahdi called for a *jihad* (holy war or struggle) against the British and the Egyptians.

Sudanese by the thousands flocked to join the Mahdi. His warriors, fired by revolutionary zeal, defeated several British-led Egyptian armies. In 1885 they captured Khartoum, and soon thereafter the Mahdi's rule extended over the whole of present-day Sudan. For this reason, the Mahdi is remembered, at least in northern Sudan, as Abu al-Istiqlal, "Father of Independence."[2]

The Mahdi's rule did not last long; he died in 1886. His chief lieutenant and successor, the Khalifa Abdallahi, continued in power until 1898, when a British force armed with guns mowed down his spear-carrying, club-wielding army. Sudan was ruled jointly by the United Kingdom and Egypt from then until 1955. Since the British already ruled Egypt as a protectorate, for all practical purposes joint rule meant British rule.

Under the British, Sudan was divided into a number of provinces, and British university graduates staffed the country's first civil service.[3] But the British followed two policies that have created problems for Sudan since it became independent. One was "indirect rule" in the north. Rather than developing a group of trained Sudanese administrators who could take over when they left, the British governed indirectly through local chiefs and religious leaders. The second policy was to separate southern from northern Sudan through "Closed Door" laws which prohibited northerners from working in, or even visiting, the south.

INDEPENDENCE

Sudan became independent on New Year's Day, 1956, as a republic headed by a civilian government. The country is still officially a republic, but in its few decades of existence it has had six different governments—only one of which was voted into office. The first civilian government lasted until 1958, when a military group seized power "to save the country from the chaotic regime of the politicians."[4] But the military regime soon became as "chaotic" as its predecessors. In 1964 it handed over power to another civilian group. The second civilian group was no more successful than the first had been, as the politicians continued to feud, and intermittent conflict between government forces and rebels in the southern region turned into all-out civil war.

In 1969 the Sudanese Army carried out another military coup, headed by Colonel Ja'far (Gaafar) Nimeiri. Successive Sudanese governments since independence, including Nimeiri's, have faced the same basic problems: the unification of north and south, an economy hampered by inadequate transportation and few resources, and the building of a workable political system. Nimeiri's record in dealing with these difficult problems is one explanation for his longevity in power. A written Constitution was approved in 1973. Although political parties were outlawed, an umbrella political organization, the Sudan Socialist Union, provided an alternative to the fractious political jockeying that divided the nation before Nimeiri.[5]

Nimeiri's firm control through the military and his effectiveness in carrying out political reforms were soon reflected at the ballot box. He was elected president in 1971 for a 6-year term and was reelected in 1977. Yet broad popular support did not generate political stability. There were a number of attempts to overthrow him, the most serious in 1971 and 1976, when he was actually captured and held for a time by rebels.

One reason for his survival may be his resourcefulness. After the 1976 coup attempt, for example, instead of having his opponents executed, he invited them and other opposition leaders to form a government of national unity. One of Nimeiri's major opponents, Sadiq al-Mahdi, great grandson of the Mahdi and himself an important religious leader, accepted the offer and returned from exile.

Nimeiri's major achievement was to end temporarily the Civil War between north and south. An agreement was signed in 1972 in Addis Ababa, Ethiopia, mediated by Ethiopian authorities, between his government and the southern Anya Anya resistance movement. The agreement provided for regional autonomy for the south's three provinces, greater representation of southerners in the National People's Assembly, and integration of Anya Anya units into the armed forces without restrictions.

THE COUP OF 1985

Nimeiri was reelected in 1983 for a third presidential term. Most of his political opponents had apparently been reconciled with him, and the army and state security forces were firmly under his control. It seemed that Sudan's most durable leader would round out another full term in office without too much difficulty. But storm clouds were brewing on the horizon. Nimeiri had survived for 16 years in power largely through his ability to keep opponents divided and off balance by his unpredictable moves. From 1983 on, however, his policies seemed designed to unite rather than divide them.

The first step in Nimeiri's undoing was his decision to impose Islamic law (Sharia) over the entire country. The impact fell heaviest on the non-Muslim southern region. In a 1983 interview Nimeiri explained his reasons for the action. His goal from the start of his regime, he said, was "to raise government by the book [i.e., the Koran] from the level of the individual to that of government." If the Sudanese, with their numerous ethnic and cultural differences and the country's vast size, were governed properly by God's Book, they would provide an example of peace and security to neighboring countries.[6]

In Nimeiri's view, the application of Islamic restrictions on alcohol, tobacco, and other prohibited forms of behavior was appropriate to Sudanese Muslims and non-Muslims alike, since "Islam was revealed to serve man and all its legislation has the goal of regulating family, social, and individual life and raising the level of the individual."[7]

The new draconian measures were widely resented, but particularly in the south, where home-brewed beer and cigarettes were popular palliatives for a harsh existence. When Nimeiri continued his "Islamic purification" process with a reorganization of Sudanese administration into several large regions in order to streamline the cumbersome bureaucracy inherited from the British, the southerners reacted strongly. Consolidation of three autonomous provinces into one directly under central-government control was seen by them as a violation of the commitment made to regional autonomy that had ended

the Civil War. An organized guerrilla army, the Sudan Peoples Liberation Army (SPLA), resumed civil war under the expert leadership of U.S.–trained Colonel John Garang. The rebels' new strategy was not only to oppose government troops but also to strike at development projects essential to the economy. Foreign workers in the newly developed oil fields in southwestern Sudan were kidnapped or killed, and as a result Chevron Oil Company halted all work on the project.

A crackdown on Islamic fundamentalist groups, particularly the Muslim Brotherhood, added to Nimeiri's growing list of opponents. Members of the Brotherhood had been active in implementing Islamic law as the law of the land, but Nimeiri felt they had gone too far. By late 1984 it appeared that the president had angered or alienated everybody in the country, all for different reasons.

In the end it was the failure of his economic policies rather than anything else that brought about the fall of the leader. The International Monetary Fund imposed strict austerity requirements on Sudan in 1984 as a prerequisite to a $90 million standby loan to enable the country to pay its mounting food and fuel bills. The food bills were aggravated by famine, fuel bills by the necessity to import almost all fuel requirements. The IMF insisted on drastic budget cuts, devaluation of currency, and an end to subsidies on basic commodities. If Nimeiri had been able to carry out these reforms, he would have stood a chance of restoring the country to solvency and his own rule to respec-

tability. Protests turned to riots, mainly over the end of price subsidies and a consequent 33 percent increase in the prices of such necessities as bread, sugar, and cooking oil. Other protests erupted over the application of Islamic law, especially the ban on alcohol, which brought thousands of Sudanese into the streets shouting "We want beer! We want beer!"

Nimeiri's departure for the United States to seek further economic help triggered a general strike in 1985. A genuine national movement arose, uniting students and professionals with the urban poor, all demanding that Nimeiri resign. Fearing anarchy or an uprising by young army officers, the senior military leaders moved quickly, took over the government, and ordered Nimeiri deposed. Crowds in Khartoum shouted, "Nimeiri the butcher is finished; the country belongs to the people." "He's nothing, let him sell lemons," cried one demonstrator, and others tore Nimeiri's picture from devalued banknotes.[8]

The new military government, headed by General Abd al-Rahman Swareddahab, a highly respected senior officer, promised to hold elections within a year to restore civilian rule and to revive political parties. That promise was kept, and in 1986 elections were held for a new People's Assembly. Two revived pre-Nimeiri parties, the Umma and the Democratic Unionist Party (DUP), won the majority of seats, with the fundamentalist National Islamic Front emerging as a strong third party. Sadiq al-Mahdi, head of the Umma, automatically became prime minister; his

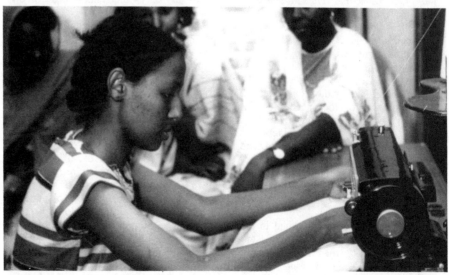

(UN photo/Louise Gubb)

The attainment of political stability is important to Sudanese development, but it will be the economy that makes for lasting peace. Unfortunately, the economy of Sudan is dependent on a narrow agricultural base, and job training is extremely important. This woman in a sewing class in Khartoum represents the need for creating a productive pool of workers.

principal rival, DUP leader Ahmed Ali al-Mirghani, was chosen as president. The new prime minister chose a coalition Cabinet to begin the arduous process of restoring the democratic process to Sudan after 15 years of Nimeiri.

But the euphoria over the departure of "Nimeiri the Butcher" soon gave way to the realization that the problems that had daunted him remained unresolved. They included heavy foreign indebtedness, a weak economy, inefficient agricultural production, an inadequate transportation system, party and personal rivalries, and extreme distrust between north and south in the divided Sudanese nation.

INTERNAL PROBLEMS

The al-Mahdi government had no more success than its predecessors in resolving Sudan's endemic political disunity. Efforts to limit the application of Islamic law throughout the country were blocked by the National Islamic Front in 1988, and as a result the Civil War intensified. SPLA success in capturing the principal towns in the south led the DUP to sign a separate agreement with the rebels for a ceasefire. The People's Assembly rejected the agreement, and the DUP then withdrew from the government.

Faced with the imminent collapse of civilian authority, the armed forces again seized power, in Sudan's fourth military coup since independence. The army moved after food shortages and soaring inflation, fed by war costs of $1 million a day, led to riots in Khartoum and other cities. A Revolutionary Council headed by Lieutenant General Omar Hassan al-Bashir suspended the Constitution and arrested government leaders.

The country's latest military regime has made little progress toward resolving chronic economic problems or finding a solution to the Civil War. Insistence on the application of Islamic law to the entire nation continues to block peace negotiations with the SPLA. In 1991 a new federal structure of nine "states" replaced the former regional/provincial structure, and early in 1992 Bashir formed a 300-member Legislative Assembly which would be granted full governing powers by the military regime at some unspecified future date.

Although a stalemate continued in the war, the government's position was enhanced in late 1991 when the SPLA split into rival factions, one backing Colonel John Garang and the other, the "Nasir faction," led by his chief Lieutenant Commander Rick Machar. Machar accused Garang of a dictatorial reign of terror within the organization. The break led to

internal conflict in November, organized along tribal lines as Nuer troops of the Nasir faction invaded Dinka tribal territory (the Dinkas are Garang's main supporters). The fighting left more than 5,000 dead, and some 100,000 Dinkas fled their homeland as refugees.

The regime's commitment to Islamic fundamentalism and determination to apply Islamic law in Sudan won outside support from Iran in particular. Bashir made a state visit to that country in 1990, and upon his return Sudan was declared officially an Islamic nation. As a consequence, Iran provided both light and heavy battle weapons for the government forces in the Civil War. Iran also agreed to cover all Sudan's oil needs for 1991 and 1992. (The end of the Civil War in Lebanon led Lebanese-based terrorist groups to relocate to Sudan as a more hospitable environment.) Sudan sided with Iraq during the Kuwait invasion and the ensuing Gulf War. As a result, all U.S. humanitarian aid to Sudan was stopped.

THE ECONOMY

Although the attainment of political stability is important to Sudanese development, in the long run it depends on the economy—creating jobs, educating youth, building a future for the country's population that will keep pace with population growth. Unfortunately, the Sudanese economy is still a weak reed to lean on. The economy is largely dependent on agriculture. The most important crop is cotton, and cotton exports are affected by world demand and the resulting price fluctuations. Until recently the only other export crop of importance was gum arabic.

Because Sudan has great agricultural potential due to its rivers, alluvial soils, and vast areas of unused arable land, Nimeiri had set out in the 1970s to develop the country into what experts told him could be the "breadbasket" of the Middle East. Enough food could be grown through the expansion of agriculture, he was told, to meet all domestic needs, raise the country's low standard of living, and cover the food needs of all the Arab countries, most of which are not self-sufficient and must import food. To reach this ambitious goal, cotton plantations were converted to production of grain crops. The huge Kenana sugar-refinery complex was started with joint foreign and Sudanese management, the long-established Gezira cotton scheme was expanded, and work began on the Jonglei Canal, intended to drain a vast marshy area called the Sudd (swamp) in the south, in order to bring hundreds of thousands of acres of marshlands under cultivation.

But the breadbasket was never filled. It was as if the Sudanese government had had a good idea but had implemented it from the wrong end. Mismanagement and lack of skilled labor delayed some projects, while others languished because the roads and communications systems needed to implement them did not exist. The most critical need was for domestic sources of oil. Oil was discovered in the southwest in the early 1980s by Chevron Oil Company. Early projections were for production of 50,000 barrels per day by 1986. But the work came to a halt in 1984 due to the resumption of the Civil War. The country has continued to import its oil, much of it from Iraq due to favorable terms. Shortly after the Iraqi invasion of Kuwait, which Sudan (not surprisingly) supported, Bashir signed an agreement with Libyan leader Muammar al-Qadhafi to integrate Sudan and Libya within 4 years. In return, Libya agreed to meet all Sudan's oil needs during that period.

But the foreign aid that Sudan so desperately needs has yet to be provided. In 1989 and 1990 negotiations with the International Monetary Fund broke down when the military government refused to accept IMF recommendations for a 50 percent currency devaluation, tariff increases on imports, higher interest rates to curb inflation, and price controls on basic commodities, as prerequisites for further financing.

A major problem with oil development, apart from the Civil War, stems from lack of transport facilities. The nearest refinery is at Port Sudan, 840 miles from the oil fields on the Red Sea. Rather than build a new on-site refinery, the Nimeiri government decided to construct a $1 billion pipeline from the fields to the refinery. The southern Sudanese objected to the proposed pipeline, on the grounds that it would take away oil revenues that were rightfully theirs. The pipeline project, along with Nimeiri's imposition of Islamic law on them, were the main causes for the renewal of the Civil War.

FAMINE: AN EVER-PRESENT REALITY

The Sudanese economy outside the cities was a barter one in which little money changed hands. Until Nimeiri imposed steep price increases on bread, soap, and cooking oil, average people were little affected by budget deficits and staggering fuel bills.

But from 1973 their lives were affected increasingly by circumstances beyond their control, as a cycle of drought spread from the sub-Saharan Sahel region across Africa to affect Sudan and its near neigh-

| An Egyptian province under Muhammad Ali 1820 | Mahdi rebellion against the British and Egyptians 1881 | The British recapture Khartoum; establishment of joint Anglo-Egyptian control 1899 | Sudan becomes an independent republic 1956 | Civil War 1956–1971 | Nimeiri seizes power, ends the Civil War 1969, 1971 | 1980–1990s |

| Riots and strikes in response to austerity measures; Nimeiri is overthrown by army leaders in a bloodless coup | Millions of people dying of starvation; relief agencies are ordered to leave the country as rebels interfere with food deliveries | Civil War resumes in the south between government forces and the SPLA; thousands die in Nuer/Dinka conflict |

bors. The drought became critical in 1983, and millions of refugees from Ethiopia and Chad, the countries most affected, moved into temporary camps in Sudan. Then it was Sudan's turn to suffer. Desperate families fled from their villages as wells dried up, cattle died, and crops wilted. By 1985 an estimated 9 million persons, half of them native Sudanese, were dying of starvation. Emergency food supplies from many countries poured into Sudan, but due to inadequate transportation, port delays, and diversion of shipments by incompetent or dishonest officials, much of this relief could not be delivered to those who most needed it. Bags of grain already unloaded lay on the docks, waiting for trucks that did not come because they were immobilized somewhere else, stuck in the sand or mired in the mud of one of Sudan's few passable roads. Equally distressing things were happening along Sudan's one railroad, from Khartoum to Kosti and on to the heart of the drought-stricken region at Nyala. While refugees starved in Darfur Province, heavy rains to the east washed out track sections. Out of one shipment of 6,000 tons, half vanished before arrival at Nyala. "Use your imagination," a UN distribution official told a reporter, indicating corruption or theft, or both.[9] Meanwhile, at the far end of this thin lifeline, children grew weaker daily from malnutrition as their parents waited for the promised rations. Hassan Atiya, Sudanese deputy commissioner for refugees, estimated the death rate for children at

2,000 per day in the worst famine of this century.

Sudan's political instability compounded the hunger problem. SPLA control of the south had forced the government to suspend the April 1986 elections there, so the region was unrepresented in the National Assembly. The rebels refused to allow delivery of relief supplies on government planes and shot one down to make their point.

Although the drought cycle finally ended in 1987 with the resumption of normal spring rains, the ongoing Civil War continued to interfere with food production and deliveries. Both sides used food as a weapon to manipulate relief agencies rather than help in getting food to the needy. As a result, about 260,000 Sudanese died of starvation in that year.

Intermittent interference with food-relief shipments continues to threaten hundreds of thousands of refugees from the south with malnutrition or all-out famine. Operation Lifeline, a UN relief program begun in 1989, had some success in providing emergency supplies, due largely to SPLA cooperation. But in Feburary 1992 the regime cancelled all shipments to southern Sudan as it prepared for its first dry-season offensive against the fragmented rebels.

NOTES

1. Dunstan Wai, *The African-Arab Conflict in the Sudan* (New York: Africana Publishing Co., 1981), p. 32.

2. Southerners are not so favorable; in the south the Mahdi's government was as cruel as the Egyptian. *Ibid.*, p. 31.

3. Peter M. Holt, in *The History of the Sudan,* 3rd edition (London: Weidenfeld and Nicolson, 1979), p. 123, quotes the British governor as saying that they were recruited on the basis of "good health, high character and fair abilities."

4. *Ibid.*, p. 171.

5. The SSU is defined as "a grand alliance of workers, farmers, intellectuals, business people and soldiers." Harold D. Nelson, ed., *Sudan, A Country Study* (Washington: American University, Foreign Area Studies, 1982), p. 199.

6. Quoted in Tareq Y. Ismael and Jacqueline S. Ismael, *Government and Politics in Islam* (New York: St. Martin's Press, 1985), Appendix, pp. 148–149.

7. *Ibid.*, p. 150.

8. *The Christian Science Monitor* (April 16, 1985).

9. David K. Willis, in *The Christian Science Monitor* (July 11, 1985).

DEVELOPMENT

The Civil War and related problems have brought development programs to a standstill. The IMF declared Sudan ineligible for further aid in 1986. A freeze on wages and prices is expected to reduce inflation from 70% to 50% and may produce a small budget surplus.

FREEDOM

Until 1989 government was vested in a Supreme Council with a Cabinet responsible to a People's Assembly. This structure has been preserved by the military leaders, but political parties, press freedom, and trade unions are currently suspended.

HEALTH/WELFARE

Despite war losses, Sudan's population continues to grow at a rate of 2.7% annually. However, the loss of some 500,000 skilled professionals—doctors, teachers, engineers, agricultural experts—who have migrated to other Arab countries has hurt economic development.

ACHIEVEMENTS

Sudan has substantial gold reserves. The gold mine at Gebeit near Port Sudan went into production in 1987 and now exports $15 million in gold nuggets per year.

Syria (Syrian Arab Republic)

GEOGRAPHY

Area in Square Kilometers (Miles): 185,170 (71,500) (about the size of North Dakota)
Capital (Population): Damascus (1,361,000)
Climate: predominantly dry, but considerable variation between the interior and coastal regions

PEOPLE

Population

Total: 13,300,000
Annual Growth Rate: 3.3%
Rural/Urban Population Ratio: 34/66
Ethnic Makeup of Population: 90% Arab; 10% Kurd, Armenian, Circassian, and Turk

Health

Life Expectancy at Birth: 64 years (male); 68 years (female)
Infant Mortality Rate (Ratio): 44/1,000
Average Caloric Intake: 120% of FAO minimum
Physicians Available (Ratio): 1/1,347

Religion(s)

74% Sunni Muslim; 12% Alawite; 6% Druze and other Muslim sects; 8% Christian

---

ANCIENT CIVILIZATIONS

In Syria, as in other areas of the Middle East, the visitor is surrounded by the ruined monuments of many long-vanished civilizations. Some are not only visible but still in use. The Roman waterwheels of Hama, for example, turn creakingly, bringing water up from the Orontes River for thirsty citizens as they have for centuries. One comes upon others suddenly. Palmyra (Tadmor), "Bride of the Desert," appears abruptly at the edge of the ferocious Syrian desert like a mirage of Roman civilization, with its broken columns and arches. Still others must be dug up laboriously from mounds. At Tell Mardikh, due north of Hama, archaeologists have uncovered the ruins of Ebla, a powerful state of 4,000 years ago with a written language and an elaborate royal court. Ebla was a meeting place for ancient civilizations, just as modern Syria is a bridge between Mediterranean and West Asian cultures.

Education

Adult Literacy Rate: 40%

COMMUNICATION

Telephones: 507,989
Newspapers: 3 dailies in Damascus; others in other major cities

TRANSPORTATION

Highways—Kilometers (Miles): 30,452 (18,880)
Railroads—Kilometers (Miles): 1,878 (1,164)

Usable Airfields: 94

GOVERNMENT

Type: republic
Independence Date: April 17, 1946
Head of State: President Hafez al-Assad
Political Parties: Ba'th (Arab Socialist Resurrection Party), dominant; various minor parties, several forming a Progressive National Front as token opposition in the People's Assembly
Suffrage: universal at 18

MILITARY

Number of Armed Forces: 346,000
Military Expenditures (% of Central Government Expenditures): 40%
Current Hostilities: Syria has had troops in Lebanon as a peacekeeping force since 1975

ECONOMY

Currency ($ U.S. Equivalent): 21 Syrian pounds = $1
Per Capita Income/GNP: $1,680/$17 billion
Inflation Rate: 17%
Total Foreign Debt: $5.2 billion
Natural Resources: crude oil; phosphates; chrome; iron; manganese ores; asphalt; rock salt; marble; gypsum
Agriculture: cotton; wheat; barley; sugar beets; tobacco; sheep and goat raising
Industry: petroleum; mining; manufacturing; textiles; food processing; construction

FOREIGN TRADE

Exports: $3.0 billion
Imports: $2.1 billion

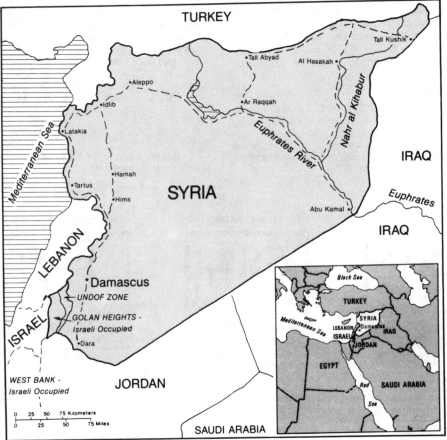

124

SYRIA

The modern Syrian state is a pale shadow of Syria as it existed centuries ago. Ancient Syria was a powerful kingdom stretching from the Euphrates River to the Mediterranean Sea in the time of Christ. It included the modern countries of Israel, Jordan, Lebanon, Iraq, and southern Turkey. During the first 2 centuries of Islam the *caliphs* ("successors" of Muhammad) ruled a vast empire from their capital at Damascus. Damascus (today the capital of the republic) and Aleppo, Syria's other major city, both claim, with reason, to be the oldest continuously inhabited city in the world. Arab geographers viewed Syria as a large geographical unit, *Bilad ash-Sham*.

Modern Syria is a nation of artificial boundaries. Its borders were determined by agreement between France and the United Kingdom after World War I. The country's current boundaries are with Turkey, Iraq, Jordan, Israel, and Lebanon. The only one of these boundaries in dispute is the Golan Heights, which was seized and annexed unilaterally by Israel in the 1970s. The border with Turkey is defined by a single-track railroad, perhaps the only case in the world of a railroad put to that use. Syria's other borders are artificial lines established by outside powers for convenience.

Syria is artificial in another sense: its political system was established by outside powers. Since becoming independent in 1946, the Syrians have struggled to find a political system that works for them. The large number of coups and frequent changes in government are evidence of this struggle. The most stable government in Syria's independent history is the current one, which has been in power since 1970.

Syrian political instability stems from the division of the population into separate ethnic and religious groups. The Syrians are an amalgamation of many different ethnoreligious groups that have settled the region over the centuries. The majority of the population are Sunni Muslim Arabs. The Alawis form the largest minority group. Although the Alawis are nominally Shia Muslims, the Sunni Muslims distrust them, not primarily because of religion but because of their secret rituals and because as a minority they are very clannish. A second large minority is the Druze, who are distrusted by both Sunni Muslims and Alawis because their religion, an offshoot of Islam, has Christian and Jewish elements and secret rituals. There are a number of Christian denominations, the most important being the Armenians, and a community of Jews with ancient origins. Syria also has a number of groups that are distinguished from the rest of the population by language or origin, the largest group being the Kurds (who are Sunni Muslims).

Although Syrian cities are slowly becoming more homogeneous in population, the different communities still constitute a majority in certain areas. Thus, the Alawis make up 60 percent of the population of the northern coast, the Druze (about 6 percent of the total population) are dominant in the Jabal Druze area in southwestern Syria, and the Kurds live predominantly in the mountains north of Aleppo.

HISTORY

Syria's greatest period was probably that of the Umayyad caliphs (A.D. 661–750), rulers of a vast Islamic empire. The first Umayyad caliph, Muawiya, is considered one of the political geniuses of Islam. He described his political philosophy to a visitor as follows:

> I apply not my lash where my tongue suffices, nor my sword where my whip is enough. If there be one hair binding me to my fellow men I let it not break. If they pull I loosen; If they loosen I pull.[1]

During this period of Umayyad rule Damascus became a great center of learning and culture. But later Umayyad caliphs were no more successful than their modern Syrian counterparts in developing effective government. They ruled by fear, repression, and heavy taxation. They also made new non-Arab converts to Islam pay a special tax from which Arab Muslims were exempted. They were finally overthrown by non-Arab Muslim invaders from Iraq. From that time until Syria became an independent republic, its destinies were determined by outsiders.

Syria was ruled by the Ottoman Turks for 4 centuries as a part of their empire. It was divided into provinces, each province being governed by a pasha whose job it was to collect taxes and keep order (with the help of an Ottoman garrison). In mountain areas such as Lebanon, then part of Syria, the Ottomans delegated authority to the heads of powerful families or leaders of religious communities. The Ottomans recognized each of these communities as a *millet*, a Turkish word meaning "nation." The religious head of each millet represented the millet in dealings with Ottoman officials. The Ottomans in turn allowed each millet leader to manage the community's internal affairs. The result was that Syrian society became a series of sealed compartments. The millet system has disappeared, but its effects have lingered on to the present, making national unity difficult.

The French Mandate

In the nineteenth century, as Ottoman rule weakened and conflict developed among Muslim, Christian, and Druze communities in Syria, the French began to intervene directly in Syria to help the Maronite Christians. French Jesuits founded schools for Christian children, and in 1860 French troops landed in Lebanon to protect the Christian Maronites from massacres by the Druze. French forces were withdrawn after the Ottoman government agreed to establish a separate Maronite region in the Lebanese mountains. This arrangement brought about the development of Lebanon as a nation separate from Syria. The Christians in Syria were less fortunate. About 6,000 of them were slaughtered in Damascus before Ottoman troops restored order.[2]

In the years immediately preceding World War I numbers of young Syrian Christians and some Muslims were exposed through mission schools to ideas of nationalism and human rights. A movement for Arab independence from Turkish rule gradually developed, centered in Damascus and Beirut. After the start of World War I the British, with French backing, convinced Arab leaders to revolt against the Ottoman government. The Arab army recruited for the revolt was led by the Emir Faisal, second son of the Sharif Husayn of Mecca, leader of the powerful Arab Hashimite family and the Arab official appointed by the Ottomans as "Protector of the Holy Shrines of Islam." Faisal's forces, along with a British army, drove the Ottomans out of Syria, and in 1918 the emir entered Damascus as a conquering hero. In 1920 he was proclaimed king of Syria.

Faisal's kingdom did not last long. The British had promised the Arabs independence in a state of their own in return for their revolt. However, they had also made secret agreements with France to divide the Arab regions of the defeated Ottoman Empire into French and British protectorates. The French would have Syria and Lebanon; the British would have Palestine and Iraq. The French now moved to collect their pound of flesh. They sent an ultimatum to Faisal to accept French rule. When he refused, a French army marched to Damascus, bombarded the city, and forced him into exile. (Faisal was brought back by the British and later installed as king of Iraq under a British protectorate.)

What one author calls the "false dawn" of Arab independence was followed by the establishment of direct French control over Syria.[3] The Syrians reacted angrily to what they considered betrayal by their former allies. Resistance to French rule continued throughout the mandate period (1920–1946), and the legacy of bitterness over their betrayal affects Syrian attitudes toward outside powers, particularly Western powers, to this day.[4]

The French did some positive things for Syria. They built schools, roads, and hospitals, developed a productive cotton industry, established order and peaceful relations among the various communities. But the Syrians remained strongly attached to the goals of Arab unity and Arab independence, first in Syria, then in a future Arab nation.[5]

INDEPENDENT SYRIA

Syria became independent in 1946. The French had promised the Syrians independence during World War II but delayed their departure after the war, hoping to keep their privileged trade position and military bases. Eventually, pressure from the United States, the Soviet Union, and the United Kingdom forced the French to leave both Syria and Lebanon.

The new republic began under adverse circumstances. Syrian leaders had little experience in government; the French had not given them much responsibility and had encouraged personal rivalries in their divide-and-rule policy. The Druze and Alawi communities feared they would be under the thumb of the Sunni majority. In addition to these problems, the establishment in 1948 of the State of Israel next door in Palestine caused great instability in Syria. The failure of Syrian armies to defeat the Israelis was blamed on weak and incompetent leaders.

For 2 decades after independence Syria had the reputation of being the most unstable country in the Middle East. There were four military coups between 1949 and 1954 and several more between 1961 and 1966. There was also a brief union with Egypt (1958–1961), which ended in an army revolt. One reason for Syria's chronic instability is that political parties, at least until the 1960s, were simply groups formed around leading personalities. At independence the country had many such parties. Other parties were formed on the basis of ideology, such as the Syrian Communist Party. In 1963 one party, the Ba'th, acquired control of all political activities. Since then, Syria has been a single-party state.

THE BA'TH

The Ba'th Party (the Arabic word *ba'th* means "resurrection") began in the 1940s as a political party dedicated to Arab unity.

It was founded by two Damascus school teachers, both French educated: Michel Aflaq, a Greek Orthodox Christian, and Salah Bitar, a Sunni Muslim. In 1953 the Ba'th merged with another political party, the Arab Socialist Party. Since then, the formal name of the Ba'th has been the Arab Socialist Resurrection Party.

The Ba'th was the first Syrian political party to establish a mass popular base and to draw members from all social classes. Its program called for freedom, Arab unity, and socialism. The movement for Arab unity led to the establishment of the branches of the party in other Arab countries, notably Iraq and Lebanon. The party appealed particularly to young officers in the armed forces, and it attracted strong support from the Alawi community because it called for social justice and the equality of all Syrians.

The Ba'th was instrumental in 1958 in arranging a merger between Syria and Egypt in the United Arab Republic (U.A.R.). The Ba'thists had hoped to undercut their chief rivals, the Syrian Communist Party, by the merger. But they soon decided they had made a mistake. The Egyptians did not treat the Syrians as equals but as junior partners in the firm. Syrian officers seized control and expelled the Egyptian advisers. It was the end of the U.A.R.

For the next 9 years power shifted back and forth among military and civilian factions of the Ba'th Party. The process had little effect on the average Syrian, who liked to talk about politics but was wary, with good reason, of any involvement. Gradually the military faction got the upper hand, and in 1970 Lieutenant General Hafez al-Assad, the Defense minister of one of the country's innumerable previous governments, seized power in a bloodless coup.[6]

THE ASSAD REGIME

Hafez al-Assad has been head of Syria longer than any of his predecessors since independence. He was elected president for a 7-year term in 1971 and reelected in 1978, in 1985, and in 1991. Although Assad was slowed down by a heart attack in 1983, he remains the dominant figure in Syrian politics, and his ability to neutralize potential rivals or deal ruthlessly with opposition movements has enabled him to remain in power despite belonging to a minority group.

Syria can be called a presidential republic, in the sense that the head of state has extensive powers, which are confirmed in the Constitution approved in 1973. He decides and executes policies, appoints all government officials, and commands the

armed forces. He is also head of the Ba'th Party. Under the Constitution, he has unlimited emergency powers "in case of grave danger threatening national unity or the security . . . of the national territory . . . " (Article 113), which only the president can determine.

Another important difference between Assad and most of his predecessors is that he has made some effort to broaden the governing process and thereby make his regime more popular. Several small Socialist parties whose programs are acceptable to the Ba'th have been allowed to function as token opposition, and national elections were held for a People's Assembly in 1986 and again in 1990. The Ba'th won 60 percent of seats in the Assembly in 1986, but in 1990 the party's margin was less in an enlarged 250-member Legislature. The difference was because candidates were allowed to run as independents. They won 84 seats to 132 for the Ba'th and 32 for the opposition parties, now grouped into a Progressive National Front. However, the extent of the Assembly's power is the approval of laws issued by the Ba'th Central Committee and concurrent approval of the national budget.

ROLE IN LEBANON

Assad's position was strengthened domestically in the 1970s due to his success (or perceived success) in certain foreign-policy actions. The Syrian Army fought well against Israel in the October 1973 War, and Syria subsequently received both military and financial aid from the Soviet Union as well as its Arab brothers. The invitation by the Arab League for Syria to intervene in Lebanon, beginning with the 1975–1976 Lebanese Civil War, was widely popular among Syrians. They never fully accepted the French action of separating Lebanon from Syria during the mandate period, and they continue to maintain a proprietary attitude toward Lebanon.

Assad's determination to avoid conflict with Israel has led him in past years to keep a tight rein on Syrian-based Palestine Liberation Organization operations. The al-Saiqa Palestinian Brigade is integrated into the Syrian Army, for example. However, Assad's agreement to join a Middle East conference with other Arab states and Israel in 1991 resulted in the release of all PLO activists held in detention in Syria.

When the Lebanese Civil War broke out, Assad pledged that he would control the Palestinians in Lebanon and sent about 2,000 al-Saiqa guerrillas to Beirut in early 1976. The peacekeeping force approved by the Arab League for Lebanon included 30,000 regular Syrian troops. For all practical purposes, this force maintained a balance of power among Lebanese factions until the Israeli invasion of June 1982. It then withdrew to the eastern Biqa' Valley, avoiding conflict with Israeli forces and providing sanctuary to Palestinian guerrillas escaping from Beirut.

From this vantage point, Syria made a number of attempts to broker a peace agreement among the various Lebanese factions. However, all of them failed, owing in large measure to the intractable hostility separating Muslim from Christian communities and intercommunal rivalries among the militias. In 1987, faced with a near-total breakdown in public security, Assad ordered 7,000 elite Syrian commandos into West Beirut. Syrian forces maintained an uneasy peace in the Lebanese capital until 1989, when they were challenged directly by the Christian militia of General Michel Aoun. (Earlier, Aoun had declared himself president after the Lebanese Chamber of Deputies had refused to endorse Syria's candidate for the position.) Syrian forces surrounded the Christian enclave and early in 1990 mounted a massive assault, backed by heavy artillery, that finally broke the Christian resistance. Aoun took refuge in the French Embassy. The Syrians acted in response to a request from the legitimate Lebanese government of President Elias Hrawi to assist the Lebanese Army in establishing government authority over the Christian population. Inasmuch as this had been Assad's primary objective in sending Syrian forces into Lebanon, it seemed he had achieved his goal.

INTERNAL OPPOSITION

Since 1979 opposition to the Assad regime has increased steadily. One of the causes is the dominance of the Alawi minority. Although many non-Alawis hold high government positions, the Alawis are the majority in the officer corps, the police, and the intelligence services (the latter two were headed at one time by Assad's brothers). One brother, Rifaat Assad, and his rivals engaged in armed confrontation during the president's illness in a struggle over the succession in 1984. After Assad recovered, he sent Rifaat out of the country for several months. Rifaat was eventually reinstated and made one of three vice presidents.

The main opposition to the regime comes from the Muslim Brotherhood, an underground Sunni organization that operates throughout the Arab world. Its goal is a unified, democratic Arab/Islamic state under just leaders. The Brotherhood opposes Assad for what it calls his autocratic leadership and repression of political opposition and for allowing corruption in government. The Brotherhood was implicated in a wave of assassinations of prominent Alawis, which had claimed 300 victims by 1981. Its main stronghold was the ancient city of Hama, famed for its Roman waterwheels. In 1982 Assad's regular army moved against Hama after an ambush of government officials there. The city was almost obliterated by tanks and artillery fire, with an estimated 120,000 casualties. Large areas were bulldozed as a warning to other potentially disloyal elements in the population.[7]

Memories of Hama, along with an unwritten "mutual cooperation pact" between the regime and the country's large merchant class, have kept potential opposition under control in recent years. It is a control admittedly reinforced by the presence of some 15 intelligence and paramilitary agencies, the *mukhabarat,* which keeps close tabs on the population. But despite the narrow support base provided by his status as member of a minority group, Assad has given Syria the stability that his predecessors did not provide. His most recent election victory, in December 1991, was marked by huge rallies honoring "our savior, hero of the people."

The urban populations resent government by people from the provinces. The Alawis are resented by Sunni Muslims because of their high visibility and privileges; it is whispered that they are not true Muslims.[8] Urban rivalries have always been strong in Syria; the rivalry of Damascus and Aleppo goes back centuries. In the final analysis, the regime's survival depends upon its ability to establish a process of succession going beyond Assad, preserving the single-party state in a more representative fashion to provide the just institutions demanded by its opponents.

Such institutions as a free press, representative political parties, appellate courts, and a Parliament responsible for legislation exist in Syria only in principle. Some observers have compared Assad's Syria to Franco's Spain, also a pluralistic society ruled by a dictator. In the latter case, the monarchy seemed an appropriate instrument of succession. But with Assad's brother no longer a part of the Syrian power structure, the only family continuity in sight for the Syrian president is his son Basil, a captain in the *mukhabarat* and clearly lacking the experience and statecraft of his father.

Only in recent years has Assad begun to deal with abuses of power. In 1987 several Cabinet ministers resigned after they had been accused of corruption by the People's Assembly. A newly formed economic security court handed down stiff sentences for misuse of funds and other crimes to a number of government officials and businesspeople.

In December 1991 Assad was reelected for a fourth 7-year term, by a 99.8-percent majority. Continuing his announced liberalization process, some 2,800 political prisoners were released after the election referendum. Most were Muslim Brotherhood members arrested in the 1980s. Assad also abolished the office of vice president, held by a triumvirate which included his brother Rifaat.

THE ECONOMY

At independence Syria was primarily an agricultural country, although it had a large merchant class and a free-enterprise system with considerable small-scale industrial development. When it came to power, the Ba'th party was committed to state control of the economy. Agriculture was collectivized, land expropriated from large landowners and converted into state-managed farms. Most industries were nationalized in the 1960s. The free-enterprise system all but disappeared.

Cotton was Syria's principal export crop and money earner until the mid-1970s. But with the development of oil fields, petroleum became the main export. Syria produced enough oil for its own needs until 1980. However, the changing global oil market, political differences with its Western customers, and the reluctance of foreign oil companies to invest in oil exploration due to the country's strict nationalization policies hampered economic development. Discovery of a new oil field at Thayyim, south of Deir ez-Zor, in 1984 and a major natural-gas find near ancient Palmyra, in the Syrian Desert, vastly improved the economy. By 1991 oil production was 480,000 barrels per day. New discoveries in the Palmyra and Deir ez-Zor areas should boost output to 500,000 b/d.

Expansion of cultivable areas for wheat and barley plus favorable weather have brought a significant improvement in agricultural production. The cereals harvest tripled in 1990 to reach 900,000 tons and nearly tripled again in 1991. The Assad regime has moved steadily away from state control of economic development; a 1991 law encourages private investment by allowing industries to import needed machinery duty-free and gives a 7-year tax exemption to companies developing projects of benefit to national development.

Ever since the Ba'th came to power, two problems have hampered Syrian development. One is economic. The Ba'th

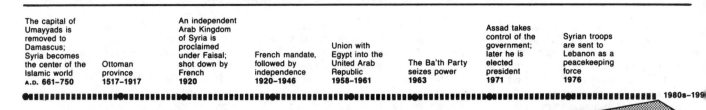

| The capital of Umayyads is removed to Damascus; Syria becomes the center of the Islamic world A.D. 661–750 | Ottoman province 1517–1917 | An independent Arab Kingdom of Syria is proclaimed under Faisal; shot down by French 1920 | French mandate, followed by independence 1920–1946 | Union with Egypt into the United Arab Republic 1958–1961 | The Ba'th Party seizes power 1963 | Assad takes control of the government; later he is elected president 1971 | Syrian troops are sent to Lebanon as a peacekeeping force 1976 | 1980s–199 |

emphasis on state socialism has forced the normally freewheeling private-enterprise system underground, gasping for air under layers of state control and bureaucratic corruption. It was not until 1988 that some hope emerged for the revival of the system, as the Assad government revealed its growing disenchantment with Ba'thist social practice.

Strengthening private enterprise should be a great asset for the Syrian economy. But Syria's often difficult relations with its Arab neighbors remain as obstacles to national development. As an example, disagreements with neighboring Iraq from time to time have shut off Iraqi crude-oil shipments through Syrian pipelines to refineries on the Mediterranean. For years Syria earned more from transit fees than it did from its own oil production. In 1985 Kuwaiti opposition to Syria's policies in Lebanon led the Kuwait National Assembly to cancel $334 million pledged to Syria as a frontline Arab state in the struggle with Israel. The political stability achieved under Assad had just begun to affect the economy when the 1973 Arab-Israeli War caused extensive damage to Syrian factories and refineries.

Syria's role as a major sponsor of international terrorism also adversely affects economic stability. In 1986 the United Kingdom, Germany, and other European states broke diplomatic relations and adopted strict economic sanctions against the Assad regime after the British uncovered a Syrian-financed plot to blow up an Israeli airliner in the London airport. In 1987 the Syrians began "polishing up

their image" and thus reduced their international political isolation. Germany restored diplomatic relations, and the United States returned its ambassador to Damascus. An agreement with Turkey established joint border patrols to halt smuggling and ensure that Kurdish guerrillas fighting the Turkish central government would no longer have the right to sanctuary in Syrian territory. Syria continued its alliance with Iran—the only Arab state to do so—and was given a million tons of free oil as its part of the bargain.

Resolution of the long ordeal of the U.S. hostages in Lebanon was due in large measure to Syrian-Iranian cooperation. This in turn became possible after Syria's ouster of Lebanese Maronite Christian leader General Michel Aoun and establishment of the authority of the Syrian-backed Muslim government over most of the country.

NOTES

1. The statement is found in many chronicles of the Umayyads. See Richard Nyrop, ed., *Syria, A Country Study* (Washington: American University, Foreign Area Studies, 1978), p. 13.

2. Philip Khoury, *Urban Notables and Arab Nationalism: The Politics of Damascus 1860–1920* (Cambridge: Cambridge University Press, 1983), pp. 8–9.

3. Umar F. Abd-Allah, *The Islamic Struggle in Syria* (Berkeley: Mizan Press, 1983), p. 39.

4. A. H. Hourani, *Syria and Lebanon, A Political Essay* (London: Oxford University Press, 1954), p. 54, notes that "His (Faisal's) government had more solid foundations in popular consent than any perhaps since Umayyad times."

Assad suffers an apparent heart attack and is hospitalized for several months; Assad approves amnesty for members of the Muslim Brotherhood, formerly the main opposition to his rule

Syria's association with international terrorism leads the United Kingdom to break relations and European powers to impose economic sanctions; Syrian troops return to Beirut but are only partly successful in restoring order

Assad's efforts to gain the release of hostages in Lebanon leads the United States and other countries to resume aid and diplomatic relations

5. "Syrians had long seen themselves as Arabs . . . who considered the Arab world as rightly a single entity." John F. Devlin, *Syria: Modern State in an Ancient Land* (Boulder: Westview Press, 1983), p. 44.

6. He was barred from attending a Cabinet meeting, and then surrounded the meeting site with army units, dismissed the government and formed his own. *Ibid.*, p. 56.

7. Thomas L. Friedman, in *From Beirut to Jerusalem*, coined the phrase "Hama rules" to describe Assad's domestic political methods. "Hama rules" are no rules at all.

8. Abd-Allah, *op. cit.*, pp. 42–48, describes them as believing in a Trinity, worshipping natural objects, giving less than absolute obedience to the Koran as the word of God, and following a religious teacher who claimed to be a Prophet and messenger 200 years after Muhammad.

DEVELOPMENT

Significant expansion of oil production and favorable harvests have greatly enhanced Syria's economic prospects in the 1990s. The growth rate in 1990 was 6 percent, with a budget surplus recorded for the first time in 30 years.

FREEDOM

The 1973 Constitution defines Syria as a socialist popular democracy with a preplanned socialist economy. In practice, the Ba'th Party dominates the government, with extensive powers reserved to the president. A popularly elected People's Assembly is responsible for approval of laws emanating from the Ba'th or directly from the Cabinet.

HEALTH/WELFARE

Education and health services in Syria show uneven growth. In the 1980s there were more than 2 million students in primary and secondary schools and 113,000 in the country's 5 universities. In contrast, large-scale emigration from rural to urban areas led to major shortages in housing and health facilities.

ACHIEVEMENTS

Syria's most ambitious development is the Euphrates Dam, begun in 1968 by Soviet technicians and put into operation in 1974. By 1979 it was providing 70% of all electricity needs. However, disputes with Turkey and Iraq over sharing of Euphrates water have hampered the dam's effectiveness.

Tunisia (Republic of Tunisia)

GEOGRAPHY

Area in Square Kilometers (Miles):
164,149 (63,378) (about the size of
Missouri)
Capital (Population): Tunis
(1,000,000)
Climate: hot, dry summers; mild,
rainy winters

PEOPLE

Population
Total: 8,094,000
Annual Growth Rate: 2.1%
Rural/Urban Population Ratio: 46/54
Ethnic Makeup of Population: 98%
Arab; 1% European; 1% others

Health
Life Expectancy at Birth: 66 years
(male); 67 years (female)
Infant Mortality Rate (Ratio):
46/1,000
Average Caloric Intake: 116% of FAO
minimum
Physicians Available (Ratio): 1/2,198

Religion(s)
98% Muslim; 1% Christian; less than
1% Jewish

Education
Adult Literacy Rate: 46%

COMMUNICATION

Telephones: 218,810
Newspapers: 2 Arabic dailies; 4
French dailies

PEACE AT LAST

In 1985, after 2,000 years, the mayors of Rome and Carthage (now a
Tunis suburb) signed a treaty symbolically ending the state of war
between their ancestor city-states. The treaty was a reminder of the great
days of Roman Africa with its capital at Carthage. The Bardo Museum
in Tunis houses the world's finest collection of Roman African mosaics
in the world. Students came here to work under mosaic masters from
Alexandria (Egypt) in the first century A.D. They soon developed their
own distinct impressionistic style, incorporating native themes, showing
rural hunting and harvesting scenes, fishing expeditions with boat
models of the period, and family picnics. One of the largest mosaics,
showing the triumph of Neptune, covers 1,465 square feet.

TRANSPORTATION

Highways—Kilometers (Miles): 18,952
(11,750)
Railroads—Kilometers (Miles): 2,241
(1,389)
Usable Airfields: 29

GOVERNMENT

Type: republic
Independence Date: March 20, 1956
Head of State: Zine el-Abidine Ben
Ali
Political Parties: Constitutional
Democratic Party (ruling); Tunisian
Communist Party; Social Democratic
Movement; others
Suffrage: universal over 21

MILITARY

Number of Armed Forces: 38,000
*Military Expenditures (% of Central
Government Expenditures):* 5.7%
Current Hostilities: none

ECONOMY

Currency ($ U.S. Equivalent): 0.87
Tunisian dinar = $1
Per Capita Income/GNP: $1,260/$9.6
billion
Inflation Rate: 3.5%
Total Foreign Debt: $6.9 billion
Natural Resources: oil; phosphates;
iron ore; lead; zinc
Agriculture: wheat; barley; olives;
citrus fruits; grapes; vegetables; fish
Industry: mining (phosphates);
petroleum; olive oil; textiles; food
processing; construction

FOREIGN TRADE

Exports: $2.9 billion
Imports: $4.7 billion

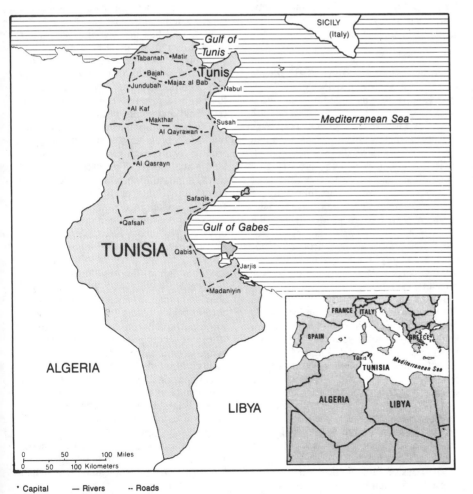

* Capital — Rivers -- Roads

TUNISIA

Tunisia, the smallest of the four North African countries, is less than one-tenth the size of Libya, its neighbor to the east. However, its population is nearly twice the size of Libya's, although it is increasing at a slower rate.

Tunisia's long coastline has exposed it over the centuries to a succession of invaders from the sea. The southern third of the country is part of the Sahara Desert, and the central third consists of high, arid plains. Only the northern region has sufficient rainfall for agriculture; this region contains Tunisia's only permanent river, the Medjerda.

The country is predominantly urban. There is almost no nomadic population, and there are no high mountains to provide refuge for independent mountain peoples opposed to central government. The Tunis region and the Sahel, a coastal plain important in olive production, are the most densely populated areas. Tunis, the capital, is not only the dominant city but also the hub of all government, economic, and political activity.

HISTORY

Tunisia has an ancient history that is urban rather than territorial. Phoenician merchants from what is today Lebanon founded a number of trading posts several thousand years ago. The most important one was Carthage, founded by tradition in 814 B.C. It grew wealthy through trade and developed a maritime empire. Its great rival was Rome; after several wars the Romans defeated the Carthaginians and destroyed Carthage. Later the Romans rebuilt the city and it became great once again, the capital of the Roman province of Africa. Rome's African province was one of the most prosperous in the empire. The wheat and other commodities shipped to Rome from North African farms were vitally needed to feed the Roman population. When the ships from Carthage were late due to storms or lost at sea, or seized by pirates, as sometimes happened, the Romans suffered hardship. Tunisia today has yet to reach the level of prosperity it had under Roman rule.

The collapse of the Roman Empire in the fifth century A.D. affected Roman Africa as well. Cities were abandoned; the irrigation system that had made the farms prosperous fell into ruin. (A number of these Roman cities, such as Dougga, Utica, and Carthage itself, which is now a suburb of Tunis, have been preserved as historical monuments of this period.)

Arab armies from the east brought Islam to North Africa in the late seventh century. After some resistance, the population accepted the new religion, and from that time on the area was ruled as the Arab-Islamic province of *Ifriqiya*. The Anglicized form of this Arabic word, "Africa," was eventually applied to the entire continent.

The Arab governors did not want to have anything to do with Carthage, since they associated it with Christian Roman rule. They built a new capital on the site of a village in the outskirts of Carthage, named Tunis. The fact that Tunis has been the capital and major city in the country for 14 centuries has contributed to the sense of unity and nationhood that most Tunisians have.[1]

The original Tunisian population consisted of Berbers, a people of unknown origin. During the centuries of Islamic rule many Arabs settled in the country. Other waves of immigration brought Muslims from Spain, Greeks, Italians, Maltese, and many other nationalities. Tunisia also had until recently a large community of Jews, most of whom emigrated to the State of Israel when it was founded in 1948. The blending of ethnic groups and nationalities over the years created a relatively homogeneous and tolerant society, with few of the conflicts that marked other societies in the Islamic world.

The Beylical State

From the late 1500s to the 1880s Tunisia was a self-governing province of the Ottoman Empire. It was called a regency because its governors ruled as "regents" on behalf of the Ottoman sultan. Tunis was already a well-established, cosmopolitan city when it became the regency capital. Its rulers, called *beys,* were supported by an Ottoman garrison and a corsair fleet of fast ships that served as auxiliaries to the regular Ottoman navy. The corsairs, many of them Christian renegades, ruled the Mediterranean Sea for 4 centuries, raiding the coasts of nearby European countries, and preyed on merchant vessels, seizing cargoes and holding crews for ransom.[2]

In the nineteenth century European powers, particularly France and England, began to interfere directly in the Ottoman Empire and to seize some of its outlying provinces. France and England had a "gentleman's agreement" about Ottoman territories in Africa—the French were given a free hand in North Africa and the British in Egypt. In 1830 the French seized Algiers, capital of the Algiers Regency, and began to intervene in neighboring Tunisia in order to protect their Algerian investment.

The beys of Tunis worked very hard to forestall a French occupation. In order to do this, they had to satisfy the European powers that they were developing modern political institutions and rights for their people. Ahmad Bey (1837–1855) abolished slavery and piracy, organized a modern army (trained by French officers), and established a national system of tax collection. Muhammad al-Sadiq Bey (1859–1882) approved in 1861 the first written Constitution in the Islamic world. This Constitution had a declaration of rights and provided for a hereditary (but not an absolute) monarchy under the beys. The Constitution worked better in theory than in practice. Provincial landowners and local chiefs opposed it because it undermined their authority. The peasants, whom it was supposedly designed to protect, opposed it because it brought them heavy new taxes, collected by government troops sent from Tunis. In 1864 a popular rebellion broke out against the bey, and he was forced to suspend the Constitution.

The French Protectorate

In 1881 a French army invaded and occupied all of Tunisia, almost without firing a shot. The French said they had intervened because the bey's government could not meet its debts to French bankers and capitalists, who had been lending money for years to keep the country afloat. There was concern also about the European population. Europeans from many countries had been pouring into Tunisia, ever since the bey had given foreigners the right to own land and set up businesses.

The bey's government continued under the French protectorate, but it was supplemented by a French administration which held actual power. The French collected taxes, imposed French law, and developed roads, railroads, ports, hospitals, and schools. French landowners bought large areas and converted them into vineyards, olive groves, and wheat farms. For the first time in 2,000 years Tunisia exported wheat, corn, and olive oil to the lands on the other side of the Mediterranean.

Because Tunisia was small, manageable, and urban, its society, particularly in certain regions, was influenced strongly by French culture. An elite developed whose members preferred the French language to their native Arabic and who sent their children to French high schools and to colleges or universities in France. The Tunisian Nationalist Movement was developed largely from members of this group, who had matured enough to feel that a friendly association of the two countries as equals would be of mutual benefit. The movement began in the 1920s.[3] The French allowed a certain amount of political freedom, and the nationalists took the

(UN photo/B. Graham)

In the 1970s Tunisia experienced a steady and rapid increase in income. Tourism sparked hotel development, such as the one pictured above (left), and exports of phosphates, petroleum, and olive oil fueled substantial economic growth. As demand for these products has since decreased, Tunisia's economic future has become uncertain.

name Destour (in Arabic, *Dustur*), meaning "Constitution."

In the 1930s a new generation of Tunisians began to talk seriously of independence. Most of them had been educated in France. The youths of the new generation became convinced that nationalism, "in order to be effective against the French, had to break loose from its traditional power base in the urban elite and mobilize mass support."[4] In 1934 a group of young nationalists quit the Destour and formed a new party, the Neo-Destour. The goal of the Neo-Destour Party was independence from France. From the beginning, its principal leader was Habib Bourguiba.

HABIB BOURGUIBA

Bourguiba, born in 1903, once boasted that he had "invented" Tunisia. In a sense, he was right. The Neo-Destour Party, under his leadership, became the country's first mass political party. It drew its membership from shopkeepers, craftspeople, blue-collar workers, and peasants, along with French-educated lawyers and doctors. The party became the vanguard of the nation, mobilizing the population in a campaign of strikes, demonstrations, and violence in order to gain independence. It was a long struggle. Bourguiba spent many years in prison. But eventually the Neo-Destour tactics succeeded. On March 20, 1956, the French ended the protectorate and Tunisia became an independent republic led by Habib Bourguiba.

One of the problems facing Tunisia today is that its political organization has changed very little since independence. A Constitution was approved in 1959 that established a "presidential republic"—that is, a republic in which the elected president has very great power. Habib Bourguiba was elected president in 1957.

Bourguiba was also the head of the Neo-Destour Party, the country's only le-

gal political party. The Constitution provides for a National Assembly, which is responsible for enacting laws. But to be elected to the Assembly, a candidate had to be a member of the Destour Party. Bourguiba's philosophy and programs for national development in his country were often called Bourguibism. It was tailored to the particular historical experience of the Tunisian people. Since ancient Carthage, Tunisian life has been characterized by the presence of some strong central government able to impose order and bring relative stability to the people. The predominance of cities and villages over nomadism reinforced this sense of order. The experience of Carthage, and even more so that of Rome, set the pattern. "The Beys continued the pattern of strong order while the French developed a strongly bourgeois, trade-oriented society, adding humanitarian and some authoritarian values contained in French political philosophy."[5] Bourguiba always considered himself the tutor of the Tunisian people, guiding them toward moral, economic, and political maturity.

In 1961 Bourguiba introduced a new program for Tunisian development that he termed "Destourian Socialism." It combined Bourguibism with government planning for economic and social development. The name of the Neo-Destour Party was changed to Destour Socialist Party (PSD) to indicate its new direction. Destourian Socialism worked for the general good, but it was not Marxist; Bourguiba stressed national unanimity rather than class struggle and opposed communism as the "ideology of a godless state." Bourguiba took the view that Destourian Socialism was directly related to Islam. He said once that the original members of the Islamic community (in Muhammad's time in Mecca) "were socialists . . . and worked for the common good."[6]

For many years after independence Tunisia appeared to be a model among new nations, because of its stability, order, and economic progress. Particularly notable were Bourguiba's reforms in social and political life. Islamic law was replaced by a Western legal system with various levels of courts. Women were encouraged to attend school and enter occupations previously closed to them and were given equal rights with men in matters of divorce and inheritance.

Bourguiba strongly criticized those aspects of Islam that seemed to him to be obstacles to national development. He was against women veiling, polygyny, and ownership of lands by religious leaders, which kept the lands out of production. He even encouraged people not to fast during Ramadan, because their hunger made them less effective in their work.

There were few challenges to Bourguiba's leadership. His method of alternately dismissing and reinstating party leaders who disagreed with him effectively maintained Destourian unity. But in later years Bourguiba's periodic health problems, the growth of Islamic fundamentalism, and the disenchantment of Tunisian youth with the single-party system raised doubts about Tunisia's future under the PSD.

The system was provided with a certain continuity by the election of Bourguiba as president-for-life in 1974, when a constitutional amendment was approved specifying that at the time of his death, or in the event of his disability, the prime minister would succeed him and hold office pending a general election. One author observed: "Nobody is big enough to replace Bourguiba. He created a national liberation movement, fashioned the country and its institutions."[7] Yet he failed to recognize or deal with changing political and social realities in his later years.

The new generation now coming of age in Tunisia is deeply alienated from the old. Young Tunisians (half the population are under age 15) increasingly protest their inability to find jobs, their exclusion from the decision-making process, the unfair distribution of wealth, and the lack of political organizations. It seems as if there are two Tunisias: the old Tunisia of genteel politicians and freedom fighters; and the new one of alienated youth, angry peasants, and frustrated intellectuals. Somehow the two have gotten out of touch with each other.

The division between these groups has been magnified by the growth of Islamic fundamentalism, which in Bourguiba's view was equated with rejection of the secular, modern Islamic society that he created. The Islamic Tendency Movement (MTI) emerged in the 1980s as the major fundamentalist group. The MTI applied for recognition as a political party after Bourguiba agreed to allow political activity outside of the Destour Party and had licensed two opposition parties. But the application was rejected.

THE END OF AN ERA

Riots over an increase in the price of bread in 1984 signaled a turning point for the regime. For the first time in the republic's history an organized Islamic opposition challenged Bourguiba, on the grounds that he had deformed Islam to create a secular society. Former Bourguiba associates urged a broadening of the political process and formed political movements to challenge the Destour monopoly on power. Although they were frequently jailed and their movements proscribed or declared illegal, they continued to press for political reform.

However, Bourguiba turned a deaf ear to all proposals for political change. Having survived several heart attacks and other illnesses to regain reasonably good health, he seemed to feel that he was indestructible. In 1986 and 1987 he not only assumed direct control over party and nation but also turned against most of his long-term friends and colleagues. These included senior officials, his son Habib, Jr., his wife Wassila, whom he divorced and accused of urging changes in the succession amendment, and members of her family. The two legal opposition parties were forced out of local and national elections by arrests of leaders and a shutdown of opposition newspapers. The Tunisian trade-union confederation (UGTT) was disbanded, and the government launched a massive purge of fundamentalists.

The purge was directed by General Zine el-Abidine Ben Ali, the minister of the Interior, regarded by Bourguiba as one of the few people he could trust. There were mass arrests of Islamic militants, most of them belonging to the outlawed Islamic Tendency Movement. In 1987 a trial of MTI activists ended with seven death sentences and long prison terms for others, including the leader of the movement, Rachid Ghannouchi. But Bourguiba intervened, demanding a new trial and the death sentence for Ghannouchi.

Increasingly, it seemed to responsible leaders that Bourguiba was becoming senile as well as paranoid. "The government lacks all sense of vision," said a long-time observer. "The strategy is to get through the day, to play palace parlor games." A student leader was more cynical: "There is no logic to his [Bourguiba's] decisions; sometimes he does the opposite of what he did the day before."[8]

A decision that would prove crucial to the needed change in leadership was taken by Bourguiba in September 1987, when he named Ben Ali as prime minister. Six weeks later Ben Ali carried out a bloodless coup, removing the aging president under the 1974 constitutional provision that allows the prime minister to take over in the event of a president's "manifest incapacity" to govern. Seven prominent Tunisian doctors signed such a statement. "Perhaps I should have given up sooner," said the former president-for-life in a moment of sad lucidity as he was gently taken away to temporary house arrest.[9] Recognizing Bourguiba's "historic role" in the building of the Tunisian state, the Ben Ali government in 1990 allowed him to receive visitors and to move freely about his hometown of Monastir.

NEW DIRECTIONS

President Ben Ali (elected to a full 5-year term in April 1989) has initiated a series of bold reforms designed to wean the country away from the one-party system. Political prisoners were released under a general amnesty; they included MTI leader Ghannouchi and Habib Achour, former head of the UGTT. Prodded by Ben Ali, the Destour-dominated National Assembly passed laws ensuring press freedom and the right of political parties to form as long as their platforms are not based exclusively on language, race, or religion. The Assembly also abolished the constitutional provision establishing the position of president-for-life, which had been created expressly for Bourguiba. Henceforth Tunisian presidents will be limited to three consecutive terms in office.

Ben Ali also undertook the major job of restructuring and revitalizing the Destour Party. In 1988 it was renamed the Constitutional Democratic Assembly (RCD). Ben Ali told delegates to the first RCD Congress that no single party could represent all Tunisians. There can be no democracy without pluralism, fair elections, and freedom of expression, he said.

Elections in 1988 underscored Tunisia's fixation on the single-party system. RCD candidates won all 141 seats in the Chamber of Deputies, taking 80 percent of the popular vote. Two new opposition parties, the Progressive Socialist Party (PSP) and the Progressive Socialist Rally, participated but failed to win more than 5 percent of the popular vote, the minimum needed for representation in the Chamber. MTI candidates, although required to run as independents because of the ban on "Islamic" parties under the revised election law, dominated urban voting, taking 30 percent of the popular vote in the cities. However, the winner-take-all system of electing candidates shut them out as well.

Local and municipal elections in 1990 confirmed the RCD stranglehold on Tunisian political life; its performance was the exact opposite of that of the National Liberation Front in neighboring Algeria, which found itself seriously threatened by Islamic fundamentalist power. RCD candidates won control of 253 out of 254 municipal councils. The elections, however, did little to advance the cause of multiparty democracy to which Ben Ali had declared himself committed. All six opposition parties boycotted the elections. Opposition leaders said that the election process was meaningless because the RCD and the Tunisian state were indivisible and the media were prohibited from supporting or encouraging a pluralist political system.

THE ECONOMY

The challenge to Ben Ali lies not only in broadening political participation but also in improving the economy. After a period of impressive growth in the 1960s and 1970s, the growth rate began dropping steadily, largely due to decreased demand and lowered prices for the country's three main exports (phosphates, petroleum, and olive oil). Tunisia is the world's fourth-ranking producer of phosphates, and the most important industries are those related to production of superphosphates and fertilizers.

Tunisia's oil reserves are estimated at 1.65 billion barrels. The main producing fields are at El Borma and offshore in the Gulf of Gabes. New discoveries near Sfax, off Cap Bon, and at Ezzaouia have

| Wars between Rome and Carthage, ending in the destruction of Carthage and its rebuilding as a Roman city 264–146 B.C. | The establishment of Islam in Ifriqiya, with its new capital at Tunis A.D. 800–900 | The Hafsid dynasty develops Tunisia as a highly centralized urban state 1200–1400 | Ottoman Turks establish Tunis state to control Mediterranean sea lanes 1500–1800 | French protectorate 1881–1956 | Tunisia gains independence, led by Habib Bourguiba 1956 | An abortive merger with Libya 1974 | 1980s–1990s |

| Bourguiba assumes direct control of the government, even purging family members and longtime associates; the government cracks down on Islamic fundamentalists | Bourguiba is removed from office in a "palace coup" on grounds of mental incapacity; he is succeeded by Ben Ali | Ben Ali is elected to a full 5-year term as president; Tunisia's economic picture brightens |

led to increases in production after a long period of stagnation. Production in 1990 was 4.3 million barrels, a 30-percent increase.

Problems also affect the phosphate industry. The quality of the rock mined is poor in comparison with that of other phosphate producers, such as Morocco. The Tunisian industry experienced hard times in the late 1980s with the drop in global phosphate prices; one-fourth of its 12,000-member-work force was laid off in 1987. However, improved production methods and higher world demand led to a 29-percent increase in exports in 1990.

Tunisia's associate-member status in the European Community has brought the country some economic benefits. Despite competition from EC members Spain and Portugal, production and exports of olive oil to Europe were 165,000 tons, the highest in 15 years.

The economic stabilization program begun in 1986 as a consequence of International Monetary Fund insistence on reforms as a prerequisite for further loans began to show results in 1988, aided by good harvests and increased remittances from Tunisians working abroad. By 1990 the growth rate was up to 6.5 percent. A 10-percent minimum daily wage increase for workers (to $11) and a "pact for social peace" reached in 1990 between the government and the UGTT, which would set wage increases of 7 to 12 percent annually over a 3-year period, helped ease the financial blow to families from price increases on basic commodities set for Tunisia by IMF guidelines. Subsidies for these commodities represented a heavy drain on the budget.

Despite a fairly heavy foreign debt burden, Tunisia in the early 1990s continued to be a favored country for foreign aid, receiving more loans from the World Bank than any other Arab or African country, due to its relative political stability and high level of education. The country's goal of becoming a "Mediterranean Singapore," well-run and able to absorb large amounts of foreign capital, seemed within reach.

THE FUTURE

The major unknown in the Tunisian political equation concerns the future role of Islam. President Ben Ali's goal has been to restore Islam to a place in national politics appropriate to a secular state, without relinquishing any of the social gains achieved by his predecessor. In 1987 he reopened the Zitouna University, the ancient center of Islamic studies in Tunis, and increased funding for mosque construction and maintenance. But political parties whose platform and goals are considered exclusively Islamic still have not been legalized. Al-Nahda (Rebirth), a more radical Islamic fundamentalist movement than MTI, emerged in the 1990s to present a more dangerous challenge to the regime. An attack on RCD headquarters in Tunis in 1991 led to a crackdown on the movement; some 300 militants were arrested, and three of its leaders subsequently were hanged. Following the fundamentalists' election victory in neighboring Algeria, Ben Ali appointed new hardline ministers of Defense and Interior to forestall possible repercussions in Tu-

nisia that might endanger Tunisia's long-established secular Islamic identity.

NOTES

1. Harold D. Nelson, ed., *Tunisia: A Country Study* (Washington: American University, Foreign Area Studies, 1979), p. 68.
2. Attacks on American shipping by Tunisian corsairs led the U.S. to sign a treaty with the bey in 1799, guaranteeing an annual tribute in return for protection. *Ibid.*, p. 27.
3. The nationalists were nearly all graduates of Sadiki College, a "high school" with a European curriculum that included courses in European politics. They also went on to complete their education in France. *Ibid.*, p. 39.
4. *Ibid.*, p. 42.
5. What Nelson means, in this case, by "authoritarianism" is that the French brought to Tunisia the elaborate bureaucracy of metropolitan France, with levels of administration from the center down to local towns and villages. *Ibid.*, p. 194.
6. *Ibid.*, p. 196.
7. Jim Rupert, in *The Christian Science Monitor* (November 23, 1984).
8. Louise Lief, in *The Christian Science Monitor* (April 10, 1987).
9. *The Economist* (November 14, 1987), p. 50.

DEVELOPMENT

Along with political liberalism, the Ben Ali government has begun to dismantle state socialism. A package of economic reforms was introduced in 1989. It includes devaluation of the dinar to help local producers compete in foreign markets, turning most state-run enterprises over to the private sector, eliminating most price controls, and providing favorable incentives for foreign investors.

FREEDOM

Freedom of press and expression are now guaranteed by law, and no one may be persecuted for holding ideas contrary to those of others or for membership in any organization, except for those that advocate violent change or the reestablishment of Islamic law codes and restrictions, especially those that affect women. Since 1987, 10,000 political prisoners have been amnestied.

HEALTH/WELFARE

Since independence Tunisia has been a leader among Arab states in social change, especially in women's rights. The 1956 Code of Personal Status outlawed polygyny, set minimum ages for marriage (17 years for females), gave women divorce and inheritance rights equal with men, and guaranteed equal pay for equal work.

ACHIEVEMENTS

Tunisia's strict adherence to IMF requirements for loans has helped to stabilize the economy. In 1991 the IMF lowered its funding ceiling for developments, from $273 million to $104 million, in recognition of the country's internal economic stability and its success in lowering its foreign debt.

Turkey (Republic of Turkey)

GEOGRAPHY

Area in Square Kilometers (Miles): 766,640 (296,000) (about 2 times the size of California)
Capital (Population): Ankara (3,306,000)
Climate: moderate coastal areas; harsher temperatures inland

PEOPLE

Population
Total: 56,549,000
Annual Growth Rate: 2.0%
Rural/Urban Population Ratio: 40/60
Ethnic Makeup of Population: 80% Turkish; 15% Kurdish (Kurds not recognized as separate ethnic group); 5% others

Health
Life Expectancy at Birth: 64 years (male); 69 years (female)
Infant Mortality Rate (Ratio): 80/1,000
Average Caloric Intake: 122% of FAO minimum
Physicians Available (Ratio): 1/360

Religion(s)
98% Muslim (mostly Sunni); 2% others (mostly Christian and Jewish)

Education
Adult Literacy Rate: 70%

COMMUNICATION
Telephones: 2,800,000
Newspapers: 54 dailies

TRANSPORTATION
Highways—Kilometers (Miles): 58,851 (36,487)
Railroads—Kilometers (Miles): 8,430 (5,226)
Usable Airfields: 107

GOVERNMENT
Type: republican parliamentary democracy
Independence Date: October 29, 1923
Head of State: President Turgut Ozal; Prime Minister Mesut Yilmaz
Political Parties: True Path/Socialist Democratic Populist (SHP), dominant; Motherland Party (ANAD), main opposition; Welfare Party (Islamic fundamentalist); other minor parties
Suffrage: universal over 21

MILITARY
Number of Armed Forces: 647,400
Military Expenditures (% of Central Government Expenditures): 11.6%
Current Hostilities: none

SHADOW PLAY

One of the most popular forms of entertainment in Turkey is the *Karagoz*, or "shadow play." It dates back to the sixteenth century. There are two main characters: Karagoz, who represents common sense and irony, and his friend Hacivad, who represents formal superficial knowledge. The most popular legend about the origins of the form is that the two characters were workers repairing a mosque. Their conversation was so humorous that all work ceased, making the sultan so angry that he had them hanged. He then suffered terrible remorse, and to console him a courtier built a screen and manipulated puppets behind it to represent the two dead men. There are many versions of Karagoz, all requiring great voice skill and knowledge of poetry and music. For a time Karagoz was also used as political satire.

ECONOMY
Currency ($ U.S. Equivalent): 3,369 Turkish lira = $1
Per Capita Income/GNP: $1,783/$68 billion
Inflation Rate: 68%
Total Foreign Debt: $41 billion
Natural Resources: coal; chromite; copper; boron
Agriculture: cotton; tobacco; cereals; sugar beets; fruits; nuts; livestock products
Industry: textiles; food processing; mining; iron and steel; cement; petroleum; leather goods

FOREIGN TRADE
Exports: $11.6 billion
Imports: $15.8 billion

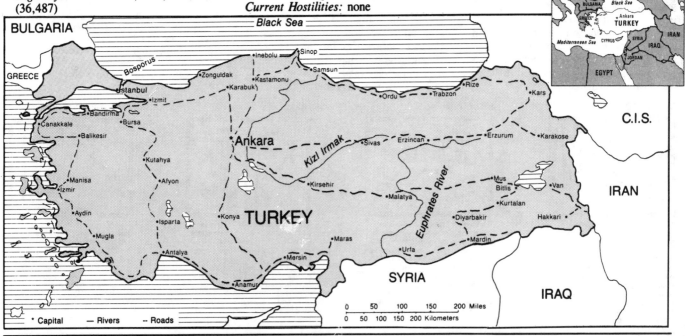

TURKEY

Except for a small area in extreme southeastern Europe called Thrace, the Republic of Turkey consists of the large peninsula of Asia Minor (Anatolia), which forms a land bridge between Europe and Asia. Asiatic Turkey is separated from European Turkey by the Bosporus, a narrow strait connecting the Black Sea with the Aegean Sea and the Mediterranean Sea via the Sea of Marmara. Throughout history the Bosporus and the Dardanelles, at the Mediterranean end, have been important strategic waterways, fought over by many nations.

Except for the Syrian border, Asiatic Turkey's borders are defined by natural limits, with seas on three sides and rugged mountains on the fourth. European Turkey's frontiers with Greece and Bulgaria are artificial and fluctuated considerably in the nineteenth and twentieth centuries before the Republic of Turkey was established.

Modern Turkey occupies a much smaller area than did its predecessor, the Ottoman Empire. The Ottoman Turks were the dominant power in the Middle East for more than 5 centuries. After the defeat of the empire in World War I, Turkey's new leader, Mustafa Kemal Ataturk, turned away from the imperial past, limiting the new republic to territory with a predominantly Turkish population. Since then Turkey has not attempted to dominate its neighbors and has concentrated mainly on internal development and peaceful relations. The exception is Cyprus, where Turkish forces have intervened to protect the Turkish minority against the Greek majority of the population.

Asia Minor has an ancient history of settlement. Most of the peninsula is a plateau ringed by mountains. The mountains are close to the coast, and over the centuries, due to volcanic action, the coastline became cracked, with deep indentations and islands just offshore. The inland plateau has an area of arid steppe with dried-up salt lakes at the center, but most of it is rolling land, well suited to agriculture. Consequently, at an early period people settled in small, self-contained villages and began to cultivate the land. Over the centuries nomadic peoples migrated into Asia Minor, but the geographical pattern there did not encourage them to remain nomadic.

In terms of national unity, the modern Turkish state has not had the thorny problem of ethnic conflicts, with two exceptions. One is the Armenians, an ancient Christian people who ruled over a large part of what is now eastern Turkey many

centuries ago. The great majority were forced to leave their homeland during World War I, because the Turkish government at that time suspected them of aiding the invading Russian armies. Hundreds of thousands of Armenians died or were killed during this series of forced emigrations. Although the republican government has consistently disclaimed responsibility for all wartime actions of its Ottoman predecessor, including the massacres of Armenians, in the 1970s and 1980s Armenian terrorist groups carried out a number of attacks on Turkish diplomats abroad, in an effort to force the Turkish government to admit at least a measure of guilt. The violence refocused international attention on the Armenian "question." The U.S. Congress on several occasions, most recently in February 1990, narrowly defeated a proposed resolution to designate April 24 as a "national day of remembrance for the Armenian genocide of 1915–1923"; although it was a purely symbolic gesture, it was viewed by the Turks as a gratuitous insult to a loyal ally.

The other exception to Turkish homogeneity is that of the Kurds, who make up 15 to 20 percent (estimates vary widely) of the population. The Kurds are an ancient people of unknown origin who have lived for 2 or more millennia in the mountainous areas where modern Turkey, Iran, Iraq, and Syria meet. Turkey's Kurds, who number somewhere between 8 and 12 million, form the largest component of this "people without a nation or sovereignty over a particular territory." Their clannish social structure and fierce spirit of independence have led to periodic Kurdish uprisings against the governments that rule them. In Turkey, the Ataturk regime crushed Kurdish rebellions in the 1920s, and from then on Kurds were

(UN photo/Rice)

Turkey has been populated with a myriad of peoples, dating back to the seventeenth century B.C.; Hittites, Greeks, Romans, Christians, Muslims, and Kurds have inhabited the area. This ancient Turkish artifact is mute evidence of one of these many bygone civilizations.

referred to officially as "Mountain Turks." The Kurdish language, which is distinct from Turkish, was prohibited in schools and for use in public documents. Turkey's Kurds are concentrated in the southeast, where they live in compact villages and work as herders or small farmers.

Outside Turkey's borders, the only significant population of ethnic Turks is in Bulgaria. They have lived there since the period of Ottoman rule in Eastern Europe and until recently at peace with their Christian neighbors. However, in the late 1980s the Bulgarian government instituted a policy of forced assimilation of its Turkish minority that led some 310,000 to take refuge in Turkey. The Turkish government protested the new policy, and it was reversed after the overthrow of the Bulgarian Communist regime. By 1991 about 90,000 Turks had returned to Bulgaria. In October 1991 the predominantly Turkish Movement for Rights and Freedom Party won 10 percent of seats in the 240-member Bulgarian Legislature, in that country's first free parliamentary election in 40 years.

HISTORY: A PARADE OF PEOPLES

The earliest political unit to develop in the peninsula was the Empire of the Hittites (1600–1200 B.C.), inventors of the two-wheeled chariot and one of the great powers of the ancient Near East. Various peoples succeeded the Hittites. One, the Lydians, invented money as a means of exchange in the time of the Lydian King Croesus. The modern expression "rich as Croesus" comes from this king's habit of panning gold from a nearby river, which he pressed into coins to pay for his kingdom's purchases. According to legend, another early Anatolian king, Midas, had the gift of turning anything he touched into gold, hence the expression "the Midas touch."

The Greeks settled Asia Minor still later, followed by the Romans. When Christianity developed as a religion, many cities on the peninsula became important centers of Christian faith, such as Ephesus, Antioch, and Nicaea. A Roman citizen from Tarsus, named Saul, became the greatest missionary of the new Christian Church as the Apostle Paul.

Following the collapse of the Roman Empire in the fifth century A.D., Asia Minor became the largest part of the East Roman or Byzantine Empire, named for its capital, Byzantium. The city was later renamed Constantinople, in honor of the Roman Emperor Constantine, after the emperor had become Christian. For a thousand years this empire was a center and fortress of Christianity against hostile neighbors and later the forces of Islam.

The Ottoman Centuries[1]

Various nomadic peoples from Central Asia began migrating into Islamic lands from the ninth century onward. Among them were the ancestors of the Turks of today. They settled mostly along the borders between Christian and Islamic powers in Asia Minor and northwest Iran. Although divided into families and clans and often in conflict, the Turks had a rare sense of unity as a nation. They were also early converts to Islam. Its simple faith and requirements appealed to them more than did Christian ritual, and they readily joined in Islam's battles as Ghazis, "warriors for the faith." Asia Minor, having been wrested from the Greeks by the Turks, also gave the Turks a strong sense of identification with that particular place. To them it was Anadolu (Anatolia), "land of the setting sun," a "sacred homeland" giving the Turks a strong sense of national identity and unity.

The Ottomans were one of many Turkish clans in Anatolia. They took their name from Osman, a clan leader elected because of certain qualifications considered ideal for a Ghazi chieftain—wisdom, prudence, courage, skill in battle, and justice, along with a strong belief in Islam.[2] Osman's clan members identified with their leader to such an extent that they called themselves Osmanlis, "sons of Osman," rather than Turks, a term they equated with boorish, unwashed peasants.

Although the Ottomans started out with a small territory, they were fortunate in that Osman and his successors were extremely able rulers. Osman's son, Orkhan, captured the important Greek city of Bursa across the Sea of Marmara from Constantinople. It became the first Ottoman capital. Later Ottoman rulers took the title of sultan to signify their temporal authority over expanding territories. Within a century after Osman's death they had crossed the straits into Europe and surrounded the Byzantine capital. On May 29, 1453, Mehmed II, the seventh Ottoman sultan, captured Constantinople, completing the transformation of a frontier principality of unknown Ghazis into a world empire.

Ottoman power continued to expand after the death of Mehmed II. By the 1600s it included most of Eastern Europe, North Africa, and the Middle East. This large territory was headed by the sultan, who was also the caliph of Islam, ensuring him the spiritual authority over Muslims that supplemented his temporal authority. The Ottomans developed a strong army and fleet that were more than a match for European Christian powers for several centuries. The core of the army was the Janissaries, an elite body of soldiers recruited from Christian villages, forced to convert to Islam and given special privileges as the sultan's personal guard. Janissary garrisons were assigned to important cities in the empire, and in certain cities, notably the North African provinces, they ran the government, ignoring the sultan's appointed governors.

Another factor that made the Ottoman system work was the religious organization of non-Muslim minority groups as self-governing units called *millets*, a Turkish word meaning "nation." Each millet was headed by its own religious leader, who was responsible to the sultan for the leadership and good behavior of his people. The three principal millets in Turkey were the Armenian and Greek Orthodox Christian communities and the Jews. Although Christians and Jews were not considered equal to freeborn Muslims, they were under the sultan's protection. Usually their lives were not interfered with, and Greek and Jewish merchants in particular rendered important services to the Ottoman government as intermediaries in trade with European countries.

The Sick Man of Europe

In the eighteenth and nineteenth centuries the Ottoman Empire gradually weakened, while European Christian powers grew stronger. European countries improved their military equipment and tactics and began to defeat the Ottomans regularly. The sultans were forced to sign treaties and lost territories, causing great humiliation, since they had never treated Christian rulers as equals before. To make matters worse, the European powers helped the Greeks and other Balkan peoples to win their independence from the Ottomans.

The European powers also took advantage of the millet system to intervene directly in the Ottoman Empire's internal affairs. French troops invaded Lebanon in 1860 to restore order after civil war broke out there between the Christian and the Druze communities. The European powers claimed the right to protect the Christian minorities from mistreatment by the Muslim majority, saying that the sultan's troops could not provide for their safety.

One or two sultans in the nineteenth century tried to make reforms in the Ottoman system. They suppressed the Janissaries, who by then had become an unruly mob, and organized a modern army equipped with European weapons, uniforms, and advisers. One sultan issued a charter stating that all of his subjects would have equal rights "regardless of religion, race or language, in matters such as taxation, education, property rights and encouragement of good citizenship."[3] In 1876 Sultan Abdul-Hamid II, prodded by the British, issued a Constitution providing for a Grand National Assembly, representing all classes, races, and creeds within the empire, and limiting the ruler's absolute powers "to the counsel and will of the nation, on the model of the British system of government."[4]

Unfortunately, the forces of reaction, represented by the religious leaders, the sultan's courtiers, and the sultan himself, were stronger than the forces for reform. Abdul-Hamid had no real intention of giving up the absolute powers that Ottoman sultans had always had. The first Grand National Assembly met in 1877, and when the members ventured to criticize the sultan's ministers, he dissolved it.

The European powers became convinced that the Ottomans were incapable of reform. European rulers compared the healthy state of their economies and the growth of representative government in their countries to the grinding poverty and lack of rights for Ottoman subjects, as a healthy person looks at an ill one in a hospital bed. The European rulers referred to the sultan as "the Sick Man of Europe" and plotted his death.[5]

However, the Sick Man's death was easier to talk about than to carry out. The main reason was that the European rulers distrusted one another almost as much as they disliked the sultan. If one European ruler seemed to be getting too much territory, trade privileges, or control over the sultan's policies, the others would band together to block that ruler.

World War I:
Exit Empire, Enter Republic

During World War I the Ottoman Empire was allied with Germany against the United Kingdom, France, and Russia. Ottoman armies fought bravely against heavy odds but were eventually defeated. A peace treaty signed in 1920 divided up the empire into British and French protectorates, except for a small part of Anatolia which was left to the sultan. The most devastating blow of all was the occupation by the Greeks of western Anatolia, under the provisions of a secret agreement that brought Greece into the war. It seemed to the Turks that their former subjects had become their rulers.

At this point in the Turkish nation's fortunes, however, a new "gray wolf" appeared to lead them in a very different direction. His name was Mustafa Kemal.

(UN photo/S. Jackson)

Historically, Turkey has been occupied by many different peoples. This recent picture is of rural women washing clothes in a Roman bath in Isikli, western Turkey, that dates back to the fifth century A.D.

During the war Mustafa Kemal was one of the few successful Ottoman military commanders, organizing brilliant tactical retreats and defeating the British in 1915 when they attempted to capture the Dardanelles.

Mustafa Kemal took advantage of Turkish anger over the occupation of Anatolia by foreign armies, particularly the Greeks, to launch a movement for independence. It would be a movement not only to recover the sacred Anatolian homeland but also for independence from the sultan.

The Turkish independence movement began in the interior, far from Constantinople. Mustafa Kemal and his associates chose Ankara, a village on a plateau, as their new capital. They issued a so-called National Pact stating that the "New Turkey" would be an independent republic. Its territory would be limited to areas where Turks were the majority of the population. The nationalists resolutely turned their backs on Turkey's imperial past.

The Turkish War of Independence lasted until 1922. It was fought mainly against the Greeks. The nationalists were able to convince other occupation forces to withdraw from Anatolia by proving that they controlled the territory and represented the real interests of the Turkish people. The Greeks were defeated in a series of fierce battles, and in 1922 France and the United Kingdom signed a treaty recognizing Turkey as a sovereign state headed by Mustafa Kemal.

THE TURKISH REPUBLIC

The Turkish republic has passed through several stages of political development since it was founded. The first stage, dominated by Mustafa Kemal, established its basic form. "Turkey for the Turks" meant that the republic would be predominantly Turkish in population; this was accomplished by rough surgery with the expulsion of the Armenians and most of the Greeks. Mustafa Kemal also rejected imperialism and interference in the internal affairs of other nations. He once said, "Turkey has a firm policy of ensuring [its] independence within set national boundaries."[6] Peace with Turkey's neighbors and the abandonment of imperialism enabled Mustafa Kemal to concentrate on internal changes. By design, these changes would be far-reaching in order to break what he viewed as the dead hand of Islam on Turkish life. Turkey would become a secular democratic state on the European model. A Constitution was approved in 1924, the sultanate and the caliphate were both abolished, and the last Ottoman sultan went into exile. Religious courts were also abolished, and new European law codes were introduced to replace Islamic law. An elected Grand National Assembly was given the responsibility for legislation, with executive power held by the president of the republic.

The most striking changes were made in social life, most bearing the personal stamp of Mustafa Kemal. The traditional Turkish costume and polygyny were outlawed. Women were encouraged to work, allowed to vote (in 1930), and given equal rights with men in divorce and inheritance. Turks were required to have surnames; Mustafa Kemal took the name Ataturk, meaning "Father of the Turks."

Mustafa Kemal Ataturk died on November 10, 1938. His hold on his country had been so strong, his influence so pervasive, that a whole nation broke down and wept when the news came. The anniversary of his death is still observed by a moment of silence.

Ismet Inonu, Ataturk's right-hand man, succeeded Ataturk and served as president until 1950. Ataturk had distrusted political parties; his brief experiment with a two-party system was abruptly cancelled when members of the officially sponsored "loyal opposition" criticized the Father of the Turks for his free life-style. The only political party he allowed was the Republican People's Party (RPP). It was not dedicated to its own survival or to repression, as are political parties in many single-party states. The RPP based its program on six principles, the most important, in terms of politics, being *devrimcilik* ("revolutionism" or "reformism"). It meant that the party was committed to work for a multiparty system and free elections. One author noted, "The Turkish single party system was never based on the doctrine of a single party. It was always embarrassed and almost ashamed of the monopoly [over power]. The Turkish single party had a bad conscience."[7]

Agitation for political reforms began during World War II. When Turkey applied for admission to the United Nations, a number of National Assembly deputies pointed out that the UN Charter specified certain rights that the government was not providing. Reacting to popular demands and pressure from Turkey's allies, Inonu announced that political parties could be established. The first new party in the republic's history was the Democratic Party, organized in 1946. In 1950 the party won 408 seats in the National Assembly to 69 for the Republican People's Party. The Democrats had campaigned vigorously in rural areas winning massive support from farmers and peasants. Having presided over the transition from a one-party system with a bad conscience to a two-party one, President Inonu stepped down to become head of the opposition.

CIVILIAN POLITICS, MILITARY RULE

Modern Turkey has struggled for decades to develop a workable multiparty political system. An interesting point about this struggle is that the armed forces have seized power three times, and three times they have returned the nation to civilian rule. This fact makes Turkey very different from other Middle Eastern nations, whose army leaders, once they have seized power, are unwilling to give it up. Ataturk deliberately kept the Turkish armed forces out of domestic politics. He believed that the military had only two responsibilities: to defend the nation in case of invasion and to serve as "the guardian of the reforming ideals of his regime."[8] Since Ataturk's death, military leaders have seized power only when they have been convinced that the civilian government had betrayed the ideals of the founder of the republic.

The first military coup took place in the 1960s after a decade of rule by the Democrats. Army leaders charged them with corruption, economic mismanagement, and repression of the opposition. After a public trial, the three top civilian leaders were executed. Thus far they have been the only high-ranking Turkish politicians to receive the death sentence. (After the 1980 coup a number of civilian leaders were arrested, but the most serious sentence imposed was a ban on political activity for the next 10 years for certain party chiefs.)

The military leaders reinstated civilian rule in 1961. The Democratic Party was declared illegal, but other parties were allowed to compete in national elections. The new Justice Party, successor to the Democrats, won the elections but did not win a clear majority. As a result, the Turkish government could not function effectively. More and more Turks, especially university students and trade-union leaders, turned to violence as they became disillusioned with the multiparty system. As the violence increased, the military again intervened, but stopped short of taking complete control.

In 1980 the armed forces intervened for the third time, citing three reasons: failure of the government to deal with political violence, the economic crisis, and the revival of Islamic fundamentalism, which they viewed as a total surrender of the secular principles established by Ataturk. (A political party, the National Salvation Party, openly advocated a return to Islamic law and organized huge rallies in several Turkish cities in 1979–1981.) The National Assembly was dissolved, the Constitution was suspended, and martial law was imposed throughout the country. The generals said they would restore parliamentary rule, but not before terrorism had been eliminated.

Thus far Turkey's generals have kept the major part of their promise. A systematic campaign to eliminate political violence has been largely successful. A new Constitution was approved in 1982. It moves Turkey closer to a presidential republic, with wide powers reserved for the president. General Kenan Evren, leader of the 1980 coup and head of the ruling National Security Council (NSC) of 5 generals, was elected president for a 7-year term.

The only real surprise in Turkey's reconstructed political system resulted from the revival of political parties. (All former political parties had been banned after the 1980 coup.) Elections were allowed for a new Assembly in 1983. Three new parties were allowed to participate, two of them favored by the country's military leaders. The third, the Motherland Party, ran an American-style political campaign, using the media to present its candidates to the country, and won handily. Its leader, Turgut Ozal, became the first prime minister in this newest phase of Turkey's long, slow progress toward effective multiparty democracy.

Whether civilian rule will succeed in Turkey in its third attempt remains to be seen. Ozal, an economist by profession, served as minister of finance under the military government in 1980–1982. In that capacity, he developed a strict austerity program that stabilized the economy. But the prime ministership was another matter, especially with five generals looking over his shoulder. The Motherland Party's popularity declined somewhat in 1986–1987. But the decline owed more to a broadening of the political process than to voter disenchantment. Two new parties, True Path, a liberal left-wing group, and the right-wing Free Democrats, won seats in the Assembly.

The nation took a significant step forward—although some analysts called it sideways—toward full restoration of the democratic process on September 6, 1987. Voters narrowly approved the restoration of political rights to a hundred politicians who were banned from party activity for 10 years after the 1980 coup. The vote was 50.23 percent "yes" to 49.77 percent "no" in a nationwide referendum, a difference of fewer than 100,000 votes. The results surprised many observers, particularly the most prominent political exiles, former Prime Ministers Suleyman Demirel of the Justice Party and Bulent Ecevit, leader of the banned Republican People's Party. They had expected a heavy vote in their favor. Ozal's argument that the nation should not return to the "bad old days" before the 1980 coup, when the personal vendetta between these two leaders had polarized politics and paralyzed the economy, with several dozen murders a day, clearly carried weight with the electorate.[9]

Thus encouraged, Ozal scheduled new elections for November 1, 1987, a year ahead of schedule. But in October the constitutional court ruled that a December 1986 electoral law was invalid, because it had eliminated the primary system, thereby undermining the multiparty system. The elections were held on November 29 under new electoral guidelines. Ozal's Motherland Party (ANAP) won handily, taking 292 of 450 seats in the National Assembly. The Social Democrat Populist Party (SHP), a newcomer to Turkey's political wars, was second with 99 seats, while Demirel's True Path Party was a distant third with 59. Ecevit's party failed to collect the necessary 10 percent of the popular vote and was excluded from participation.

However, the Ozal government's failure to produce quick results with its economic reforms, along with factional infighting in the Motherland Party, continued to eat away at its popular support. In November 1988 a proposed constitutional amendment allowing the government to advance the dates of local elections and thus build on its parliamentary majority was defeated by the voters in a nationwide referendum. Ozal himself was wounded in an assassination attempt while addressing a party convention. Ironically, the would-be assassin was a member of the Gray Wolves, an outlawed right-wing terrorist group responsible for much of the violence of the 1970s.

ANAP's large parliamentary majority enabled Ozal to have himself elected president to succeed General Evren in 1989, at the end of the latter's term in office. Although the Turkish presidency is largely a ceremonial office, Ozal continued to run the nation as if it were not, with less successful results than those he had attained during his prime ministership. As a result, popular support for his party continued to erode. In the October 1991 elections for a new National Assembly, candidates of the opposition True Path Party won 180 seats to 113 for ANAP, taking 27.2 percent of the popular vote to 24 percent for the majority party. The

Social Democratic Populist Party (SHP) garnered 20 percent of the vote and the Islamic fundamentalist Welfare Party (RP) 16 percent, underscoring the balanced nature of the Turkish political spectrum.

Since no party held a majority in the Assembly, the interim Cabinet of Prime Minister Mesut Yilmaz remained in office until November, when True Path formed a coalition government with other former opposition parties to hold 266 seats in the Legislature. ANAP now became the opposition. However, True Path leader Suleyman Demirel failed to win the necessary two-thirds majority in the Assembly for a constitutional amendment to remove Ozal from office, on charges of exceeding presidential powers in running the government. As had been the case throughout his political career, the president's personal popularity continued to outweigh that of his party.

REGIONAL CONFLICT

Turkey remained neutral during the Iran-Iraq War, although the country sided with Iraq to the extent of protecting Iraqi oil shipments through the pipeline across its territory and extended Iraq $2 billion in export credits. When Iraqi forces invaded Kuwait, Ozal ranged his country firmly on the side of the United Nations coalition. The pipeline was shut down, and Iraqi and Kuwaiti assets of $200 million in Turkish banks were frozen. Turkish troop strength along the Iraqi border was increased to 100,000, and the Grand National Assembly approved sending Turkish units to join coalition forces and the stationing of foreign troops on Turkish soil. The measure was strengthened in 1991 to set up a multinational "rapid strike force" to ensure the security of the Kurdish population of northern Iraq.

THE KURDISH PROBLEM INTENSIFIES

Until recently the almost total exclusion of the Kurdish population from national life, even in nomenclature, aroused little resistance. However, the breakdown of law and order throughout the country in the 1970s led to a revival of Kurdish nationalism. The Workers' Party of Kurdistan (PKK), founded in 1978 as a Marxist-Leninist party, took part in the general violence but went farther than other left-wing groups (or for that matter the Kurdish mainstream) in demanding a separate Kurdish state. The PKK was outlawed after the 1980 military takeover; several of its leaders were executed and 1,500 members arrested and jailed. The torture and mistreatment of Kurdish prisoners has been strongly criticized by human-rights groups and is one of the main reasons why

Turkey's application for membership in the European Community thus far has been unsuccessful.

The PKK shifted to guerrilla operations in 1984. Since then more than 2,000 persons have been killed, including a large number of Kurdish civilians along with Turkish border guards and guerrilla fighters. After a series of PKK raids on remote villages, intended to draw counter-raids by Turkish forces and thus enlist the support of the villagers, had increased Turkish casualties, the entire southeastern region was placed under martial law.

With the outbreak of the Gulf War, Turkey's Kurdish problem intensified. The PKK set up bases in northern Iraq to supplement its main base in northern Lebanon, where the guerrillas came under Syrian protection. Guerrillas infiltrating into Turkish territory with Kurdish refugees fleeing Iraqi Army attacks assaulted Turkish police and border posts. As Turkish casualties increased, the army and air force launched reprisal raids into Iraqi territory in attempts to destroy the PKK bases. One reason for Turkey's willingness to accept the UN–U.S. rapid strike force based on its soil was to keep up pressure on the PKK and thus discourage Kurdish separatism.

The Ozal government has also belatedly recognized that the "Kurdish problem" is as much economic as it is political. The giant Ataturk Dam on the Euphrates, which became operational in 1990, is the showpiece of a $21 billion development program for southeastern Turkey. The government also relaxed the ban on use of the Kurdish language in schools and on government documents, implicitly recognizing Kurdish separate cultural rights within the Turkish nation. Reflecting the changing Middle East political equation that resulted from the Gulf War and Kurdish aspirations, the newly formed Kurdish People's Labor Party won 22 seats in the National Assembly in the 1991 elections. The party is committed to Kurdish economic and social development and rights similar to those enjoyed by the Turkish majority.

THE ECONOMY

Turkey has a relatively diversified economy, with a productive agriculture and considerable mineral resources. Cotton is the major export crop, but the country is the world's largest producer of sultana raisins and hazelnuts. Other important crops are tobacco, wheat, sunflower-oil seeds, sesame and linseed oils, and cotton-oil seeds. Opium was once an important crop, but due to illegal exportation, poppy growing was banned by the govern-

The founding of Constantinople as Roman Christian capital, on the site of ancient Byzantium A.D. 330	The capture of Constantinople by Sultan Mehmed II; the city becomes the capital of the Islamic Ottoman Empire 1453	The Ottoman Empire expands deep into Europe; the high-water mark is the siege of Vienna 1683	The defeat of Ottomans and division of territories into foreign protectorates 1918–1920	Turkey becomes a republic 1925	The two-party system is established; the opposition Democrat Party comes to power 1946–1950	The first military coup overthrows the Menderes government 1960

1980s–19...

Civilian rule returns with election of new Grand National Assembly under the 1981 Constitution	Kurdish guerrillas launch attacks on villages and police posts in eastern provinces; the government imposes emergency rule; Ozal's Motherland Party wins a huge majority of National Assembly seats	Turkey strongly supports coalition efforts in the Gulf War; the Kurdish problem intensifies; the economy improves

ment in 1972. The ban was lifted in 1974 after poppy farmers were unable to adapt their lands to other crops; production and sale are now government controlled.

Mineral resources include bauxite, chrome, copper, and iron ore, and there are large deposits of lignite. Turkey is one of the world's largest producers of chromite (chromium ore). Another important mineral resource is meerschaum, used for pipes and cigarette holders. Turkey supplies 80 percent of the world market for emery, and there are rich deposits of tungsten, perlite, boron, and cinnabar, all important rare metals.

The major economic weakness is in the lack of petroleum. There is one producing oil field, with reserves estimated at 10 billion barrels. There are four refineries. Revenues from the Iraqi pipeline were cut off by the Gulf War, but Saudi Arabia met Turkey's needs. About 45 percent of Turkey's oil must be imported.

The country does have a fairly large skilled labor force, and Turkish contractors have been able to negotiate contracts for development projects in oil-producing countries, such as Libya, with partial payment for services in oil shipments at reduced rates. The large Turkish expatriate labor force, much of it in Germany, provided an important source of revenue through worker remittances, although the European recession of the late 1980s dried up much of this revenue.

Despite foreign debts of $41 billion, a 68-percent inflation rate, and poor agricultural harvests in 1988 and 1989 due to drought, the Turkish economy recovered in 1990 to become one of the region's strongest, with a 9-percent growth rate. This was due largely to government policies of encouraging bilateral trade, investment guarantees to foreign firms, and elimination of import duties on 4,000 items. Turnover of state-run industries to private investors, while incomplete, has helped stimulate the economy. Despite major obstacles such as its poor human-rights record, the difference in purchasing power and salaries from those of EC countries, and political differences with Greece, Turkish leaders remain optimistic about membership in the European Community. "I think we'll catch the EC train, maybe the last cars, but we will catch it," observed a veteran newspaper editor.[10]

NOTES

1. Cf. Lord Kinross, *The Ottoman Centuries: The Rise and Fall of the Turkish Empire* (New York: William Morrow, 1977).
2. *Ibid.*, p. 25.
3. *Ibid.*, p. 501.
4. *Ibid.*, p. 511.

5. British Prime Minister William Gladstone said in 1880 that the Ottoman government was "a bottomless pit of fraud and falsehood." *Ibid.*, p. 538.
6. V. A. Danilov, "Kemalism and World Peace," in A. Kazancigil and E. Ozbudun, eds., *Ataturk, Founder of a Modern State* (Hamden: Archon Books, 1981), p. 110.
7. Maurice Duverger, *Political Parties* (New York: John Wiley, 1959), p. 277.
8. C. H. Dodd, *Democracy and Development in Turkey* (North Humberside: Eothen Press, 1979), p. 135.
9. *The Economist* (August 22, 1987) noted that ballots would be colored orange (for "yes") and blue (for "no") to simplify the process for rural voters, who make up half of the electorate and are mostly illiterate.
10. Hasan Cemal, editor of *Cumhuriyet*, quoted in Clyde Haberman, "On Iraq's Other Front," *New York Times Magazine* (November 18, 1990), p. 75.

DEVELOPMENT

Lack of oil and heavy defense expenditures have made effective economic development difficult. The 1990–1994 5-year-plan sets targets of an 8.3% annual growth rate and a 12% reduction in inflation. GNP went up 9 percent in 1990 and inflation was reduced to 63 percent despite price increases and a deficit of $985 million.

FREEDOM

Turkey has alternated between democratic government and authoritarian repression since independence. The 1980 military coup resulted in a new penal code with restrictions on press and speech freedoms and certain political activities. These have been restored. Leaders of the former political parties suppressed after the coup are now permitted to resume political activity.

HEALTH/WELFARE

The early priority placed on education in the republic has resulted in a large pool of skilled Turkish labor that has been important in providing a labor force for oil-producing developing states such as Libya.

ACHIEVEMENTS

The first stage of the giant Ataturk Dam on the Euphrates River became operational in 1990, with output of 9 million cubic meters of water for power generation. This will rise to 29 million cubic meters when the dam is fully operational. It is the centerpiece in a $21 billion development project for the impoverished, densely populated southeast.

United Arab Emirates

GEOGRAPHY

Area in Square Kilometers (Miles):
82,880 (30,000) (about the size of Maine)
Capital (Population): Abu Dhabi (670,000)
Climate: hot, dry desert; cooler in eastern mountains

PEOPLE

Population

Total: 2,250,000 (80,000 native)
Annual Growth Rate: 6.5%
Rural/Urban Population Ratio: 22/78
Ethnic Makeup of Population: 19% indigenous Arab; 23% other Arab; 50% south Asian; 8% East Asian and Westerner

Health

Life Expectancy at Birth: 69 years (male); 73 years (female)
Infant Mortality Rate (Ratio): 24/1,000
Average Caloric Intake: n/a
Physicians Available (Ratio): 1/659

Religion(s)

94% Muslim; 6% Hindu, Christian, and others

Education

Adult Literacy Rate: 68%

COMMUNICATION

Telephones: 367,333
Newspapers: 2 notable dailies; 1 weekly

TRANSPORTATION

Highways—Kilometers (Miles): 2,200 (1,364)
Railroads—Kilometers (Miles): none
Usable Airfields: 33

GOVERNMENT

Type: federation of emirates
Independence Date: December 2, 1971
Head of State: Shaykh Zayed bin Sultan al-Nuhayyan, ruler of Abu Dhabi and president of the ruling Council; Shaykh Maktoum al-Rashid, Ruler of Dubai, vice president and prime minister; rulers of the other 5 emirates also sit on the Council
Political Parties: none
Suffrage: none

MILITARY

Number of Armed Forces: 44,000

Military Expenditures (% of Central Government Expenditures): 44%
Current Hostilities: none

ECONOMY

Currency ($ U.S. Equivalent): 3.67 dirhams = $1
Per Capita Income/GNP: $18,430/$34.8 billion
Inflation Rate: n/a
Total Foreign Debt: n/a
Natural Resources: oil; natural gas; cement aggregate
Agriculture: vegetables; dates; limes; alfalfa; tobacco
Industry: petroleum; light manufacturing

FOREIGN TRADE

Exports: $15.0 billion
Imports: $9.6 billion

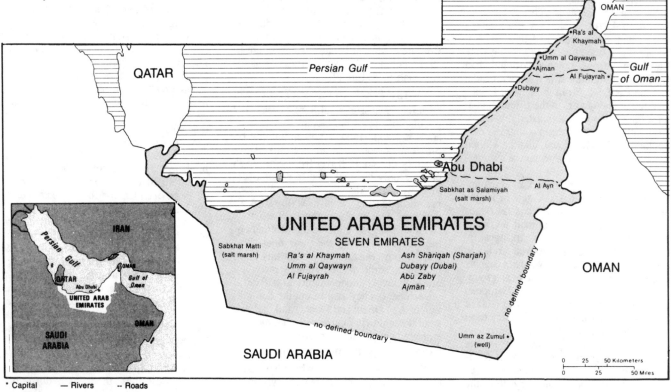

THE UNITED ARAB EMIRATES

The United Arab Emirates (U.A.E.) is a federation of seven independent states with a central governing Council located on the northeast coast of the Arabian Peninsula. The seven states—called *emirates,* from the title of their rulers—are Abu Dhabi, Ajman, Dubai, Fujairah, Ras al-Khaimah, Sharjah, and Umm al-Qaiwain. They came under British protection in the 1800s and were given their independence from the United Kingdom by treaty in 1971. At that time they joined in the federal union. From its modest beginnings, the U.A.E. has come to play an important role in Middle East Arab affairs because of its oil wealth.

Abu Dhabi, the largest emirate, contains 87 percent of the U.A.E. in area. Its capital, also called Abu Dhabi, is the largest city in the federation. Dubai, the second-largest emirate, has the federation's only natural harbor, which has been enlarged to handle supertankers. Abu Dhabi, Dubai, and Sharjah produce oil, and Sharjah also has important natural-gas reserves and cement. Fujairah port is a major entrepôt for shipping, handling both throughput container and direct traffic. The other emirates have little in the way of resources and have yet to find oil in commercial quantities.

HISTORY

The early inhabitants of the area were fishermen and nomads. They were converted to Islam in the seventh century A.D., but little is known of their history before the sixteenth century. At that time European nations, notably Portugal, had taken an active interest in trade with India and the Far East. From the time of Prince Henry the Navigator, in the fifteenth century, the Portuguese dominated this trade. Gradually, other European countries, particularly Holland, France, and the United Kingdom, challenged Portuguese supremacy.

As more and more European ships appeared in Arabian coastal waters or fought one another over trade, the coastal Arabs felt threatened with loss of their territory. Meanwhile, the Wahhabis, militant Islamic missionaries, spread over Arabia in the eighteenth century. Wahhabi agents incited the most powerful coastal group, the Qawasim, to interfere with European shipping. European ships were seized along with their cargoes, and their crews were held for ransom. To the European countries this was piracy, but to the Qawasim it was defense of Islamic territory against the infidels. Ras al-Khaimah was their chief port, but very soon the whole coast of the modern U.A.E. became known as the Pirate Coast.

Piracy lasted until 1820, when the British, who now controlled India and thus dominated the eastern trade, convinced the principal chiefs of the coast to sign a treaty that ended pirate activities. A British naval squadron was stationed in Ras al-Khaimah to enforce the treaty. In 1853 the arrangement was changed into a "Perpetual Maritime Truce." Because it specified a *truce* between the British and the chiefs, the region became known as the Trucial Coast and the territory of each chief was a trucial state. A British garrison was provided for each ruler, and a British political agent was assigned to take charge of foreign affairs. The United Kingdom paid the rulers annual subsidies; in most cases, it was all the money they could acquire. There were originally five Trucial States (also called *emirates*); Sharjah and Ras al-Khaimah were reorganized as separate emirates in 1966.

The arrangement between the United Kingdom and the Trucial States continued to work smoothly for more than a century, through both world wars. Then, in the 1960s, the British decided for economic and political reasons to give up most of their overseas colonies, including those in the Arabian Peninsula, which were technically protectorates rather than colonies. In 1968 they proposed to the Trucial Coast emirs that they join in a federation with Bahrain and Qatar, neighboring oil-producing protectorates. But Bahrain and Qatar, being larger and richer, decided to go it alone. Thus, the United Arab Emirates, when it became independent in 1971, included only six emirates. Ras al-Khaimah joined in 1972.

PROBLEMS OF INTEGRATION

Differences in size, wealth, resources, and population have hampered the U.A.E. since it was formed. Another integration problem is poor communications. Until recently one could travel from emirate to emirate only by boat, and telephone service was nonexistent. These limitations are disappearing rapidly as the U.A.E. develops. One problem that still exists is rivalry among the emirs and resentment of the rich emirates by the poor ones. The small, poor emirates have been unwilling to give up some of their rights (since they are technically independent) to a federal government. They also resent the domination of Abu Dhabi and Dubai, and feel that wealth is unfairly distributed, that the rich emirates get the lion's share.

BUILDING A FEDERAL UNION

Unlike the United States, which has had 2 centuries to develop its federal system of government, the U.A.E. has had only 2 decades. The system was defined in the 1971 Constitution. The government consists of a ruling Council of the 7 emirs, plus a Council of Ministers (Cabinet) and a 40-member Federal National Legislature, whose members are appointed from the 7 emirates on a proportional basis according to size and population. The federal capital is in Abu Dhabi, and the president of the Council, Shaykh Zayed, is also ruler of Abu Dhabi. This fact has caused friction, particularly between Abu Dhabi and Dubai. Dubai and Ras al-Khaimah refused for a time to integrate their military units into the U.A.E. armed forces.

The 1979 Revolution in Iran, which seemed to threaten the U.A.E.'s security, accelerated the move toward centralization of authority over defense forces, abolition of borders, and merging of revenues. Iran's threat to close the Strait of Hormuz was particularly worrisome, since the U.A.E. economy depends on oil exports. In 1981 the U.A.E. joined with other Persian Gulf states in the Gulf Cooperation Council to establish common defense and economic cooperation policies. Abu Dhabi and Dubai also pledged to contribute 50 percent of their revenues toward the federal budget.

The governments of the emirates themselves are best described as patriarchal. Each emir is head of his own large "family" as well as head of the emirate. The ruling emirs gained their power a long time ago from various sources—foreign trade, pearl fishing, or ownership of lands—and in recent years they have profited from oil royalties to confirm their positions as heads of state.

Disagreements within the ruling families have sometimes led to violence or "palace coups," there being no rule or law of primogeniture. The ruler of Umm al-Qaiwain came to power when his father was murdered in 1929. Shaykh Zayed deposed his brother, Shaykh Shakbut, in 1966, when the latter refused to approve a British-sponsored development plan for the protectorate. In 1987 Shaykh Abd al-Aziz, elder brother of the ruler of Shajah, attempted to overthrow his brother on the grounds that economic development was being mishandled. The U.A.E. Supreme Council mediated a settlement, and Abd al-Aziz retired to Abu Dhabi. However, he continued to demand authority over Sharjah's economic policies in his capacity as minister for National Development. In 1990 the ruler dismissed him by simply abolishing the position.

Ajman and Umm al-Qaiwain are coastal ports with agricultural hinterlands; one author describes them as "dormitory

Peace treaties between the United Kingdom and Arab shaykhs establishing the Trucial States **1853, 1866**	Establishment of the Trucial Council under British advisers, the forerunner of federation **1952**	Independence **1971**	The U.A.E. becomes the first Arab oil producer to ban exports to the U.S. after the Yom Kippur War **1973**	Balanced federal Assembly and Cabinet are established **1979**

1980s–1990s

The first free-trade zone is established, in Dubai port; an emergency fuel stockpile is set up to avoid shortages

A bilateral defense treaty with Saudi Arabia is signed

Diplomatic relations are established with the Soviet Union and China

towns for the Sharjah-Dubai conurbation, laid out in featureless blocks of flats as depressing as any in the industrial suburbs of the West." Ras al-Khaimah has continually disappointed hopeful oil seekers; its only natural resource is aggregate, which is used in making cement. Fujairah, the seventh emirate, is physically separated by Omani territory from the rest of the U.A.E. Its principal assets are its cement plant and its deep-water port. The port handled 2.3 million tons of cargo in 1990, a 56-percent increase over 1989.

These differences have not only made the development of a unified, balanced economy difficult to achieve, but they have also interfered with progress toward full federation. The emirs of the smaller states remain reluctant to surrender their power over police protection, tax collection, ministerial appointments, and other reserved powers to federal jurisdiction.

AN OIL-DRIVEN ECONOMY

In the past the people of the Trucial Coast made a meager living from breeding racing camels, some farming, and pearl fishing. Pearls were the main cash crop. But twentieth-century competition from Japanese cultured pearls ruined the Arabian pearl-fishing industry.

In 1958 Shaykh Zayed, then in his teens, led a party of geologists into the remote desert near the oasis of al-Ain, following up the first oil-exploration agreement signed by Abu Dhabi with foreign oil companies. Oil exports began in 1962, and from then on the fortunes of the Gulf Arabs improved dramatically. Production

was 14,200 barrels per day in 1962. In 1982 it was 1.1 million b/d, indicating how far the country's oil-driven economy had moved in 2 decades. Estimated oil reserves of 100 billion barrels and natural-gas reserves of 3.5 billion cubic feet are expected to last a century even at the increased output resulting from the Gulf War, which found the U.A.E. in the frontline of combat. Production in 1990 was 1.7 million barrels per day, which was cut back in 1991 to 1.5 million b/d to comply with Organization of Petroleum Exporting Countries (OPEC) quotas. Abu Dhabi is the largest producer, with Dubai second and Sharjah a distant third.

Its wealth has given the U.A.E. the luxury of being able to move away from overdependence on oil. A large industrial zone opened in Abu Dhabi in 1982 with a refinery and fertilizer and other plants. Dubai took an early lead in non-oil development, setting up aluminum and petrochemical plants as well as the world's largest dry dock. In the 1980s the extension of the Iran-Iraq War to the Gulf, with attacks on tankers by both sides and danger from floating mines, brought about a boom in the ship-repair business.

An indirect source of economic wealth for the emirates ended abruptly in 1992, when 12 tons of confiscated ivory seized from poachers was burned in Dubai as a gesture of support for a UN ban on ivory trading. Until then the emirate had been a major transit point for illegal ivory shipments.

The economic boom and the U.A.E.'s small population have made dependence

on expatriate labor inevitable; by 1987 foreign nationals accounted for 75 percent of the labor force. (Today that figure is 80 percent.)

The fall-off in oil revenues during the mid-1980s was more than compensated for by the Gulf War and cut-off of Iraqi production. A 50-percent rise in revenues through expanded production and higher prices will permit completion of a number of industrial projects in the poorer non-oil-producing emirates, which had been delayed due to the slump in oil prices worldwide.

In the long run, the challenge facing U.A.E. remains one of adapting a traditional society to the world of high technology. Barely 20 years ago the Gulf Arabs traveled by camels, lived in tents or palm-frond huts, and struggled to survive in a harsh environment. Now they drive Mercedes or Land Rovers, live in air-conditioned homes, vacation in Paris, Rome, and London. Sinbad the Sailor, the legendary traveler, would be amazed if he returned to his old harbor, the creek at Dubai. He would hardly know what to think of the sprawling industrial world going up on the old Trucial Coast; many of his fellow Arabs have the same difficulty adjusting to their changing world.

DEVELOPMENT

Oil wealth has enabled the U.A.E. to transform a meager agriculture to near self-sufficiency in less than 2 decades. The total area under cultivation doubled between 1973 and 1979. Large-scale dairy and poultry farms are now in operation. The aluminum smelter at Dubai exceeded rated capacity in 1988, with 180,000 tons produced. It also operates its own desalination plant.

FREEDOM

The U.A.E. has a federal system with a ruling Council of rulers, each of whom is responsible for local administration, tax collection, and police protection. Overall responsibility for government and foreign affairs rests with the Council.

HEALTH/WELFARE

Education has expanded rapidly since independence. With 49% of the population under age 15, a massive school-construction program got under way in 1988.

ACHIEVEMENTS

The U.A.E.'s system of government works because of the small number of *citizens* (as opposed to residents), the daily *majlis* (the public assembly where grievances are dealt with on the spot), and the prestige of individual rulers who serve on the ruling Council.

Yemen (Republic of Yemen)

GEOGRAPHY

Area in Square Kilometers (Miles):
South Yemen: 287,849 (110,000);
North Yemen: 195,000 (75,290); total
482,849 (185,290) (about twice the
size of Oregon)
Capital (Population): San'a (political
capital) (432,000); Aden (economic
capital) (327,000)
Climate: hot, with minimal rainfall
except in moutain zones

PEOPLE

Population
Total: 12,000,000
Annual Growth Rate: 3.6%
Rural/Urban Population Ratio: 72/28
(changing rapidly)
Ethnic Makeup of Population: almost
all ethnic Arab

Health
Life Expectancy at Birth: 47 years
(male); 49 years (female)
Infant Mortality Rate (Ratio):
132/1,000
Average Caloric Intake: 76% of FAO
minimum
Physicians Available (Ratio): 1/5,621

Religion(s)
99%–100% Sunni Muslim (South
Yemen); Sunni and Shia Muslim
(North Yemen)

Education
Adult Literacy Rate: 26% (South
Yemen); 14% (North Yemen)

COMMUNICATION
Telephones: 70,000
Newspapers: n/a

TRANSPORTATION
Highways—Kilometers (Miles):
39,200 (24,304)
Railroads—Kilometers (Miles): none
Usable Airfields: 15

GOVERNMENT
Type: republic, formed by merger of
former Yemen Arab Republic and
People's Democratic Republic of
Yemen
Independence Date: formally united
May 22, 1990 (date of merger)
Head of State: (Colonel) Ali Abdullah
Saleh, president, Presidential Council
with 2 members from each Yemen;
Prime Minister Haydar Abu Bakr al-
Attas; the Constitution calls for a
301-member Legislature
Political Parties: 23 registered in
1990 for November 1992 scheduled
elections
Suffrage: universal adult (over 18)

MILITARY
Number of Armed Forces: 64,000
(combined defense forces)
*Military Expenditures (% of Central
Government Expenditures):* 35%
Current Hostilities: none

ECONOMY
Currency ($ U.S. Equivalent): 12
Yemeni rials = $1
Per Capita Income/GNP: $390/$1
billion (South); $640/$4.5 billion
(North)
Inflation Rate: 16%–20%
Total Foreign Debt: $7 billion
Natural Resources: oil; natural gas;
gold; rock salt; small deposits of coal
and copper
Agriculture: cotton; fruits and
vegetables; cereals; *qat* (a bush
whose leaves produce a mild
narcotic); livestock and poultry;
coffee
Industry: oil refining; food
processing; textiles; fisheries and fish
processing

FOREIGN TRADE
Exports: n/a
Imports: n/a

A WORLD OF CONTRASTS

San'a, Yemen's political capital, has been inhabited for more than 2,000 years. Its *suq* (market) is a microcosm of medieval and modern Yemen in confusing juxtaposition. Vendors still hawk spices, henna, and *kohl,* and men bargain for *jambiyas.* But alongside these items are the goods of the modern world—cameras, digital watches, plastic sandals. The skyline of medieval San'a rises above, its multicolored "skyscraper" buildings and slender minarets now disfigured by television aerials. Suq and city alike are threatened by traffic pollution. In 1985 San'a was designated an international historical landmark by UNESCO. A billion-dollar campaign is underway to restore the market, rehabilitate medieval merchants' homes, and develop a handcrafts center.

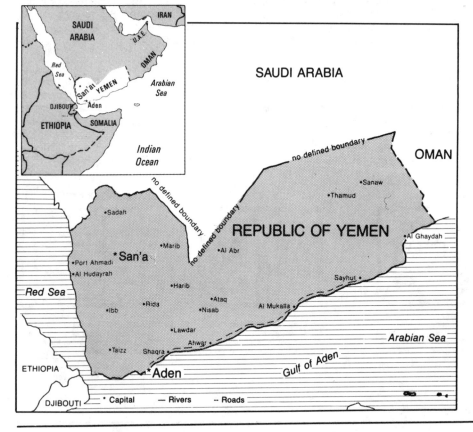

YEMEN

The Republic of Yemen occupies the extreme southwest corner of the Arabian Penninsula. It consists of three distinct regions, which until 1990 had been separated geographically for centuries and divided politically into two states, the Yemen Arab Republic (North Yemen, or Y.A.R.) and the People's Democratic Republic of Yemen (South Yemen, or P.D.R.Y.). Until the twentieth century the entire area was known simply as Yemen, and with the merger of the two states it has resumed its former geographic identity. The former Yemen Arab Repbulic's territory consists of two distinct regions: a hot, humid coastal strip, the Tihama, along the Red Sea; and an interior region of mountains and high plains that shade off gradually into the bleak, waterless south Arabian desert.

The Yemeni interior is very different not only from the Tihama but also from other parts of the Arabian Peninsula. It consists of highlands and rugged mountains ranging up to 12,000 feet. At the higher elevations the mountain ridges are separated by deep, narrow valleys, usually with swift-flowing streams at the bottom. The ample rainfall allows extensive use of terracing for agriculture. The main crops are coffee, cereals, vegetables, and qat, a shrub whose leaves are chewed as a mildly intoxicating narcotic.

This part of Yemen has been for centuries the home of warlike but sedentary peoples who have always formed a stable, stratified society living in villages or small cities. These groups have been the principal support for the Shia Zaidi Imams, whose rule was the political nucleus of Yemen from the ninth century A.D. to the establishment of the republic in 1962. The Yemeni political capital, San'a, is located in these northern highlands.

The former People's Democratic Republic of Yemen, almost twice the size of its neighbor but less favored geographically, consists of the port and hinterland of Aden (today the economic capital); the Hadhramaut, a broad valley edged by desert and extending eastward along the Arabian Sea coast; the Perim and Kamaran islands, at the south end of the Red Sea; and Socotra Island, off the Arabian coast adjacent to the Dhofar Province of Oman.

Until the recent discoveries of oil, South Yemen was believed to have no natural resources. It has very little rainfall, and a hot, humid climate. The dominant physical feature is the Wadi Hadhramaut. It is one of the few regions of the country with enough water for

irrigation. Except for Aden, the area has little rainfall; in some sections rain may fall only once in every 10 years. Less than 2 percent of the land is cultivable.

ANCIENT CIVILIZATIONS

In ancient times the whole of Yemen was known to the Greeks, Romans, and other peoples as Arabia Felix ("Happy Arabia"), a remote land that they believed to be fabulously wealthy. They knew it as the source of frankincense, myrrh, and other spices as well as other exotic products brought to Mediterranean and Middle Eastern markets by Arab merchants from the East. In Yemen itself, several powerful kingdoms grew up from profits earned in this Eastern trade. One kingdom in particular, the Sabaeans, also had a productive agriculture based on irrigation. The water for irrigation came from the great Marib Dam, built around 500 B.C. Marib was a marvel of engineering, built across a deep river valley. The Sabaean economy supported a population estimated at 300,000 in a region that today supports only a few thousand herders.

The Sabaeans were followed by the Himyarites. Himyarite rulers were converted to Christianity by wandering monks in the second century A.D. The Himyarites had contacts with Christian Ethiopia across the Red Sea and for a time were vassals of Ethiopian kings. An Ethiopian army invaded South Arabia but was defeated by the Himyarites in A.D. 570, the "Year of the Elephant" in Arab tradition, so called because the Ethiopian invaders were mounted on elephants. (The year was also notable for the birth of Muhammad, founder of Islam.)

Sabaeans and Himyarites ruled long ago, but they are important to Yemenis as symbols of their long and rich historical past. The Imams of Yemen, who ruled until 1962, used a red dye to sign their official documents in token of their relationship to Himyarite kings. (The word *Himyar* comes from the same root as *hamra*, "red.")

The domestication of the camel and development of an underground irrigation system of channels (*falaj*) made this civilization possible. Ships and camel caravans brought the frankincense, myrrh, and musk from Socotra, and silks and spices from India and the Far East to northern cities in Egypt, Persia, and Mesopotamia. Aden was an important port for this trade, due to its natural harbor and its location at the south end of the Red Sea. The trade brought large profits to merchants based in Aden. The region's agriculture was well developed due to the falaj and to water provided by the great Marib Dam.

THE COMING OF ISLAM

Yemenis were among the first converts to Islam. The separation of the Yemenis into mutually hostile Sunni and Shia Muslims took place relatively early in Islamic history. Those living in the Tihama, which was easily accessible to missionaries and warriors expanding the borders of the new Islamic state, became Sunnis, obedient to the caliphs (the elected "successors" of Muhammad). The Yemeni mountaineers were more difficult to reach; and when they were converted to the new religion, it was through the teachings of a follower of the Shi'at Ali, "Party of Ali," those who felt that Muhammad's son-in-law Ali and his descendants should have been chosen as the rightful leaders of the Islamic community. Yemenis in Aden and the Hadhramaut, as well as those in the Tihama, became Sunni, creating the basis for an intra-Yemeni conflict which still exists today.

THE ZAIDI IMAMATE

In the late ninth century A.D. a feud between certain nominally Muslim groups in inland Yemen led to the invitation to a religious scholar living in Mecca to come and mediate in their dispute. Use of an outside mediator was common in Arabia at that time. This scholar brought with him a number of families of Ali's descendants, who sought to escape persecution from the Sunnis. He himself was a disciple of Zaid, Ali's great-grandson. He settled the feud, and in return for his services he was accepted by both sides of the conflict as their religious leader, or Imam. His followers received lands and were given a protected status, so that in time they became a sort of theocratic aristocracy. This was the beginning of the Zaidi Imamate, a theocratic state that lasted for a thousand years (until 1962) in Yemen.

Although the first Zaidi Imam had come to Yemen as a mediator, he had some personal qualities that enabled him to control the unruly mountain people and bend them to his will. He was a shrewd judge of Yemeni character, using his knowledge and his prestige as a member of the family of Ali to give personal favors and his power of *baraka* (special powers from God) to one group, or withholding these gifts from another. He also had great physical strength and was reputed to possess magical powers (presumably part of his baraka). It was said of him that he could grind corn with his fingers and pull a camel apart barehanded. He wrote 49 books on Islamic jurisprudence and theology, some of which are still being studied by modern Yemeni scholars. He could also bring good (or bad) fortune to a subject merely by a touch or a glance from his piercing black eyes.[1]

In a reversal of the ancient process whereby south Arabian merchants carried goods to far-flung cities of the north, from the late 1400s on, the towns of the bleak Arabian coast attracted the interest of European seafaring powers as waystations or potential bases for control of their expanding trade with the East Indies, India, and China. Aden was a potentially important base, and expeditions by Portuguese and other Europeans tried without success to capture it at the time. In 1839 a British expedition finally succeeded. They found a town of "800 miserable souls, huddled in huts of reed matting, surrounded by guns that would not fire," or so the American traveler Joseph Osgood described the scene.

Under British rule, Aden became an important naval base and refueling port for ships passing through the Suez Canal and down the Red Sea en route to India. For many British families bound for India, Aden was the last land, with the last friendly faces, that they would see before arriving many days later in the strange wonderland of India. The route through the Suez Canal and down the Red Sea past Aden was the lifeline of the British Empire. In order to protect Aden from possible attack by hostile peoples in the interior, the British signed a series of

treaties with their chiefs, called shaykhs or sometimes sultans. These treaties laid the basis for the South Arabian Protectorates. British political agents advised the rulers on policy matters and gave them annual subsidies to keep them happy. One particular agent, Harold Ingrams, was so successful in eliminating feuds and rivalries that "Ingrams's Peace" became a symbol of the right way to deal with proud, independent local leaders.

The Zaidi Imams continued to rule inland Yemen until the nineteenth century, when the Ottoman Turks, who controlled the Tihama, sent an army to conquer all of Yemen (except for Aden, which remained under British protection.) The Turks installed an Ottoman governor in San'a and made Yemen a province (*vilayet*) of the empire. But this action did not sit well with the mountain peoples. A Yemeni official told a British visitor: "We have fought the Turks, the tribes . . . and we are always fighting each other. We Yemenis submit to no one permanently. We love freedom and we will fight for it."[2]

The Turkish occupation sparked a revolt. Turkish forces were unable to defeat the mountain peoples, and in 1911 they signed a treaty that recognized the Imam Yahya as ruler in the highlands. In return, the Imam recognized Turkish rule in the Tihama. At the end of World War I the Turks left Yemen for good. The British,

who now controlled most of the Middle East, signed a treaty with Imam Yahya, recognizing his rule in all Yemen. (The northern boundary was fixed by treaty with Saudi Arabia in 1934; the eastern boundary with Saudi Arabia Yemen has yet to be defined.)

The two Yemens followed divergent paths in the twentieth century, accounting in large measure for the difficulties that they have faced in incorporating into a single state. North Yemen remained largely uninvolved in the political turmoil that engulfed the Middle East after World War II. Imam Yahya ruled his feudal country as an absolute monarch, with a handful of advisers, mostly tribal leaders, religious scholars, and members of his family. John Peterson notes that the Imamate "was completely dependent on the abilities of a single individual who was expected to be a competent combination of religious scholar, administrator, negotiator, and military commander."[3] Yahya was all of these, and his forceful personality and ruthless methods of dealing with potential opposition (with just a touch of magic) ensured his control over the population.

Yahya's method of government was simplicity itself. He held a daily public meeting (*jama'a*) seated under an umbrella outside his palace, receiving petitions from anyone who wished to present them and signing approval or disapproval

(UN photo/Kay Muldoon)

Yemen has long been an important trade center. As time passed, warring tribes and alternate trade routes greatly diminished the economic strength of the country. Agriculture is an important element in its economy, but technology has not yet caught up with this industry, as this picture illustrates.

in Himyarite red ink. He personally supervised tax collections and kept the national treasury in a box under his bed. The Imam distrusted the Ottomans, against whom he had fought for Yemeni independence, and refused to accept their coinage. He also rejected British pounds sterling because they represented a potential foreign influence.

Yahya was determined to keep foreign influences out of Yemen and to resist change in any form. Although Yemen was poor by the industrial world's standards, it was self-sufficient, free, and fully recognized as an independent state. Yahya hoped to keep it that way. He even refused foreign aid because he felt it would lead to foreign occupation. But he was unable to stop the clock entirely and to keep all foreign ideas or influences out of Yemen.

Certain actions that seemed to be to his advantage worked against him. One was the organization of a standing army. In order to equip and train an army that would be stronger than tribal armies, Yahya had to purchase arms from abroad and to hire foreign advisers to train his troops. Promising young officers were also sent for training in Egypt, and on their return they formed the nucleus of opposition to the Imam.

In 1948 Imam Yahya was murdered in an attempted coup. He had alienated not only army officers who resented his repressive rule, but also leaders from outside the ruling family who were angered by the privileges given to the Imam's sons and relatives. But the coup was disorganized, the conspirators unsure of their goals. Crown Prince Ahmad, the Imam's eldest son and heir, was as tough and resourceful as his 80-year-old father had been.[4] He gathered support from leaders of other clans and nipped the rebellion in the bud.

Imam Ahmad (1948–1962) ruled as despotically as his father had ruled. But the walls of Yemeni isolation inevitably began to crack. Foreign experts came to design and help build the roads, factories, hospitals, and schools the Imam felt were needed. Unlike Yahya, Ahmad was willing to modernize a little. Several hundred young Yemenis were sent abroad for study. Those who had left the country during Imam Yahya's reign returned. Many Yemenis emigrated to Aden to work for the British and formed the nucleus of a "Free Yemen" movement.

In 1955 the Imam foiled an attempted coup. Other attempts, in 1958 and 1961, were also unsuccessful. The old Imam finally died in 1962 of emphysema, leaving his son, Crown Prince Muhammad al-Badr, to succeed him.

THE MARCH TO INDEPENDENCE

The British wanted to hold on to Aden as long as possible because of its naval base and refinery. It seemed to them that the best way to protect British interests was to set up a union of Aden and the South Arabian Protectorates. This was done in 1963, with independence promised for 1968. However, the British plan proved unworkable. In Aden, a strong anti-British nationalist movement developed in the trade unions among the dock workers and refinery employees. This movement organized a political party, the People's Socialist Party, strongly influenced by the socialist, anti-Western, Arab-nationalist programs of President Gamal Abdel Nasser in Egypt.

The party had two branches, the moderate Front for the Liberation of Occupied South Yemen (FLOSY) and the leftist Marxist National Liberation Front (NLF). About all they had in common was their opposition to the British and the South Arabian sultans, whom they called "lackeys of imperialism." FLOSY and the NLF joined forces in 1965–1967 to force the British to leave Aden. British troops were murdered; bombs damaged the refinery. By 1967 the British had had enough. British forces were evacuated, and the United Kingdom signed a treaty granting independence in South Yemen under a coalition government made up of members of both FLOSY and the NLF.

THE 1962 REVOLUTION

Muhammad al-Badr held office for a week. Then he was overthrown by a military coup. Yemen's new military leaders formed a Revolution Command Council and announced that the Imam was dead. Henceforth, they said, Yemen would be a republic. It would give up its self-imposed isolation and would become part of the Arab world. But the Revolution proved to be more difficult to carry out than the military officers had expected. The Imam was not dead, as it turned out, but had escaped to the mountains. The mountain peoples rallied to his support, helping him to launch a counterrevolution. About 85,000 Egyptian troops arrived in Yemen to help the republican army. The coup leaders had been trained in Egypt, and the Egyptian government had not only financed the Revolution but also had encouraged it against the "reactionary" Imam.

For the next 8 years Yemen was a battleground for civil war. The Egyptians bombed villages and even used poison gas against civilians in trying to defeat the Imam's forces. But they were unable to crush the people hidden in the wild mountains of the interior. Saudi Arabia also

backed the Imam with arms and kept the border open. The Saudi rulers did not particularly like the Imam, but he seemed preferable to an Egyptian-backed republican regime next door.

After Egypt's defeat by Israel in the 1967 Six-Day War, the Egyptian position in Yemen became untenable, and Egyptian troops were withdrawn. It appeared that the royalists would have a clear field. But they were even more disunited than the republicans. A royalist force surrounded San'a in 1968 but failed to capture the city. The Saudis then decided that the Imam had no future. They worked out a reconciliation of royalists and republicans which would reunite the country. The only restriction was that neither the Imam nor any of his relatives would be allowed to return to Yemen.

Thus, as of 1970, two "republics" had come into existence side by side in Yemen. The Yemen Arab Republic was more of a tribal state than a republic in the modern political sense of the term. Prior to 1978 its first three presidents either went into exile or were murdered, victims of rivalry within the army. Colonel Ali Abdullah Saleh, a career army officer, seized power in that year and was subsequently chosen as the republic's first elected president. He was reelected in 1983 and again in 1988 for consecutive 5-year terms. (With unification, he became the first head of state of all Yemen in 1990.)

During his tenure Saleh provided internal stability and allowed some broadening of the political process in North Yemen. A General People's Congress was established in 1982. A Consultative Council, elected by popular vote, was established in 1988 to provide some citizen input into legislation. Saleh displayed great skill in balancing tribal and army factions and used foreign aid to develop economic projects such as dams for irrigation to benefit highland and Tihama Yemenis alike.

SOUTH YEMEN: A MARXIST STATE

With the British departure the South Arabian Federation collapsed. Aden and the Hadhramaut were united under Aden political leadership in 1970 as the People's Democratic Republic of Yemen. It began its life under adverse circumstances. Britain ended its subsidy for the Aden refinery, and the withdrawal of British forces cut off the revenues generated by the military payroll.

But the main problem was political. A power struggle developed between FLOSY and the NLF. The former favored moderate policies, good relations with other Arab states, and continued ties with

| Collapse of Marib Dam, destroying flourishing Himyarite civilization A.D. 500 | Establishment of Zaidi Imamate in highland Yemen 890 | Yemen is occupied by the Ottoman Turks; eventually becomes an Ottoman province 1517, 1872 | Capture of Aden by a British naval expedition 1839 |

the United Kingdom. The NLF were leftist Marxists. By 1970 the Marxists had won. FLOSY leaders were killed or went into exile. The new government set its objectives as state ownership of lands, state management of all business and industry, a single political organization with all other political parties prohibited, and support for antigovernment revolutionary movements in other Arab states, particularly Oman and Saudi Arabia.

During its 2 decades of existence the P.D.R.Y. modeled its governing structure on that of the Soviet Union, with a Presidium, Council of Ministers, a Supreme People's Legislative Council and provincial and district councils, in descending order of importance. The ruling (and only legal) political party took the name Yemen Socialist Party in 1978 to emphasize its Yemeni makeup.

Although the P.D.R.Y. government's ruthless suppression of opposition enabled it to establish political stability, rivalries and vendettas among party leaders led to much instability within the ruling party. The first president, Qahtan al-Sha'bi, was overthrown by pro-Soviet radicals within the party. His successor, Salim Rubayyi Ali, was executed after he had tried and failed to oust his rivals on the party Central Committee. Abd al-Fattah Ismail, the country's third president, resigned in 1980 and went into exile due to a dispute over economic policies. Ali Nasir Muhammad, the fourth president, seemed to have consolidated power and to have won broad party support, until in 1986 he also tried to purge the Central Committee of potential opponents. The peoples of the interior, who formed Muhammad's original support base, stayed out of the fighting. After 10 days of bloody battles with heavy casualties, the president's forces were defeated and he fled first to Ethiopia and later to the Y.A.R., where he was granted asylum. The new president, Haydar Abu Bakr al' Attas, who had been his predecessor's prime minister, pledged greater cooperation with his Arab neighbors and unity with the Y.A.R.

UNIFICATION

Despite their natural urge to unite in a single Yemeni nation, the two Yemens were more often at odds with each other than united in pursuing common goals.

(UN photo/Kay Muldoon)

Agriculture has suffered in Yemen due to the lack of irrigation. This farmer must resort to the traditional way of using his camels to draw water.

This was due in part to the age-old highland-lowland, Sunni-Shia conflict which cut across Yemeni society. But it was also due to their very different systems of government. There were border clashes in 1972, 1975, and 1978–1979, when the P.D.R.Y. was accused of plotting the overthrow of its neighbor. (A P.D.R.Y. envoy brought a bomb hidden in a suitcase to a meeting with the Y.A.R. president, and the latter was killed when the bomb exploded.)

Improved economic circumstances and internal political stability in both Yemens revived interest in unity in the 1980s, especially after oil and natural-gas discoveries in border areas promised advantages to both governments through joint exploitation. In May 1988 President Saleh and P.D.R.Y. Prime Minister al-Attas signed the May Unity Pact, which ended travel restrictions and set up a Supreme Yemeni Council of national leaders to prepare a constitution for the proposed unitary state.

From then on the unity process snowballed. The P.D.R.Y. regime in 1989 freed supporters of former President Ali Nasir Muhammad, who had been convicted of treason in absentia; the supporters had been jailed after his overthrow. Breaking with precedent, the Yemen Socialist Party agreed to allow other political parties to form, and the first all-Yemeni party, the Yemeni Unionist Party, was organized by a group of educated Northerners and Southerners. Early in 1990 the banks, postal services, ports administration, and customs of the two republics were merged, followed by the merger under joint command of their armed forces.

Formal unification took place on May 22, 1990, with approval by both governments and ratification of instruments by their legislative bodies. Ali Abdullah Saleh was unanimously chosen as the republic's first president, with a 4-member Presidential Council formed to oversee the transition. The draft constitution of the new republic established a 39-member Council of Ministers headed by P.D.R.Y. Prime Minister al-Attas, with ministries divided equally between North and South. The third arm of government, a 301-member legislature, would be elected in a general election, scheduled for November 1992.

The penultimate step in forming the new Yemeni republic came in May 1991, as voters approved the formal Constitution in a national referendum. (The voting process was flawed—several parties, notably the Yemen Reform Group and League of the Sons of Yemen, charged that children had been registered, many people had voted twice, there had been no outside supervision of the referendum such as by the Arab League, and a majority of eligible voters were unregistered.)

THE ECONOMY

Both Yemens until very recently were among the poorest and least developed countries in the Middle East. This description is somewhat misleading in the North Yemen's case, since the highland regions have traditionally supported a sizable population, due to fertile soil, dependable and adequate rainfall, and effective use of limited arable land through terracing and other sound techniques. South Yemen's only resources

South Arabian Protectorates established by British 1882–1914	Yemen is recognized as an independent nation under Imam Yahya 1934	A revolution overthrows Imam al-Badr; a military group proclaims a republic in North Yemen 1962	Civil war between supporters of Badr and Egyptian-backed republicans 1962–1969	Protectorates merge with Aden Crown Colony; Wivil war 1962–1969	British forces withdraw from Aden; the National Liberation Front proclaims South Yemen an independent republic 1967

1980s–1990s

Major oil and natural-gas discoveries	Oil exports begin after several false starts and production problems	The two Yemens unite on May 22, 1990

were its fisheries and, during the British period, the bunkering and refining facilities of Aden and its refinery. About 70 percent of the P.D.R.Y.'s budget came from foreign aid, most of its supplied by the former Soviet Union and other Eastern Bloc countries. Government control of the economy and nationalization of the few foreign firms doing business in Aden discouraged foreign investment. The reduction in Soviet aid from $400 million in 1988 to $50 million in 1989 was one of the economic factors that encouraged unification from the South Yemeni side.

The Yemen Arab Republic's economy was altered drastically in the 1980s. One development was the emigration of more than a million Yemenis to work in Saudi Arabia and other Arab oil-producing states. Remittances from expatriate workers generated a cash economy in the country, resulting in inflation, huge increase in imports of consumer goods, and depreciation of the currency.

Agriculture has suffered more than Yemen's fledgling industry with the change in economic patterns. Lack of irrigation and a shortage of credit facilities adversely affect agricultural development. Coffee was formerly the main export crop, but with the shift to a consumer economy, farmers converted much coffee-growing land to production of qat, the use of which is addictive in Yemeni society and therefore yields larger profits than coffee. One promising development is the rebuilding,

with foreign aid, of the Marib Dam to restore the lands of the Sabaeans to their former productivity.

The new republic's economic future is promising for a number of reasons. The major one is its oil prospects. The U.S. Hunt Oil Company struck oil in the Marib area in the late 1980s. Reserves are estimated at 1 billion barrels. Other discoveries followed, and by 1990 production had reached 250,000 barrels per day, with refining and export from the new Marib refinery built near the fields. In 1987 the Soviet national oil company Technoexport struck oil at three sites in the Shabwa area northeast of Aden. Reserves are estimated at 3.3 billion barrels, with an additional 5 billion barrels in the neutral zone formerly shared by the two Yemens and now integral Yemeni territory. A large natural-gas field was discovered in 1988 near the Asad al-Kamil oil field; its reserves are estimated at 5.5 trillion cubic feet.

Had the Iraqi invasion of Kuwait not taken place, the Yemeni republic could also have counted on continued significant revenues from the remittances of its expatriate workers. The great majority of its expatriate labor force was employed in Saudi Arabia. However, Yemen's support for Iraq and its rejection of the UN resolutions authorizing sanctions against Iraq and expulsion of Iraqi forces from Kuwait led to a Saudi crackdown on Yemeni workers. A number of them were arrested and jailed and hundreds more deported as

security risks; the customary exemption of visas for Yemenis was revoked, and they were required to have a Saudi sponsor to open a small business or even simply to work. About 1 million expatriate workers had returned to Yemen by 1991, creating severe housing shortages in cities such as Hodeida, whose population jumped from 154,000 to half a million. With few sources of income available to the returnees, they represented an unemployment burden as well as a fiscal liability; their remittances had been 20 percent of the gross domestic product in previous years.

NOTES

1. Robin Bidwell, *The Two Yemens* (Boulder: Westview Press, 1983), p. 10.

2. Quoted in Robert Stookey, *Yemen: The Politics of the Yemen Arab Republic* (Boulder: Westview Press, 1978), p. 168.

3. John Peterson, "Nation-building and Political Development in the Two Yemens," in B. R. Pridham, ed., *Contemporary Yemen: Politics and Historical Background* (New York: St. Martin's Press, 1985), p. 86.

4. Yemenis believed that he slept with a rope around his neck to terrify visitors, that he could turn twigs into snakes, and that he once outwrestled the devil. Bidwell, *op. cit.*, p. 121.

DEVELOPMENT

The new republic has inherited oil and natural-gas resources, developed in its predecessor states in the 1980s by U.S. and Soviet oil companies. Reserves are estimated at 3.3 billion barrels of oil and 430 billion cubic centimeters of gas. Despite favorable long-term prospects, foreign debts are over $7 billion.

FREEDOM

A Constitution was approved in 1991 making Yemen a parliamentary republic. Elections are scheduled for November 1992 for the country's first all-Yemeni Parliament. Some 23 political parties are presenting candidates, including the Marxist Yemen Socialist Party, formerly dominant in South Yemen but now a minority party.

HEALTH/WELFARE

A UN program set up in 1990 will aid small farmers and fishermen with credits for equipment, seeds, fertilizers, boat modernization, etc., financed through the Cooperative Agricultural Credit Bank. The program also targets rural women, who have traditional responsibility for rearing livestock, especially sheep.

ACHIEVEMENTS

The new Aden free-trade zone opened in 1991. With some 50 industrial plants based there, it will be a boon to national development and foreign trade.

Articles from the World Press

Topic Guide to Articles

TOPIC AREA	TREATED AS AN ISSUE IN:	TOPIC AREA	TREATED AS AN ISSUE IN:
Leadership	3. A New Arab Order 4. The End of Arab Nationalism 13. Iraq, the Pariah State 17. Kuwait: The Morning After 18. Surface Appearances Matter 19. Turkey: Star of Islam	**Recession**	7. Arab Economies After the Gulf War
		Refugees	14. Profile: The Kurds 15. Unpromised Lands
Mathematics	10. The Arab World: Where Geometry and Algebra Intersect	**Religion**	2. Past Glories Shape Destinies 8. The Koran and Islamic Life 12. Riddle of Riyadh 15. Unpromised Lands
Middle Eastern Relations	3. A New Arab Order 4. The End of Arab Nationalism 19. Turkey: Star of Islam	**Roots**	1. How the Modern Middle East Map Came to Be Drawn 2. Past Glories Shape Destinies 8. The Koran and Islamic Life 9. Land of a Thousand and One Courtesies 14. Profile: The Kurds
Nationalism	3. A New Arab Order 4. The End of Arab Nationalism 21. Yemen: Unification		
Natural Resources	7. Arab Economies After the Gulf War 16. Another Obstacle to Peace 17. Kuwait: The Morning After	**Science**	10. The Arab World: Where Geometry and Algebra Intersect
Pan-Arab Movement	3. A New Arab Order 4. The End of Arab Nationalism	**Social Reform**	5. Human Rights and Elusive Democracy 6. Breaking Through the Wall 11. Women, Islam and the State 12. Riddle of Riyadh 17. Kuwait: The Morning After
Political Reform	5. Human Rights and Elusive Democracy 6. Breaking Through the Wall 19. Turkey: Star of Islam		
Politics	1. How the Modern Middle East Map Came to Be Drawn 2. Past Glories Shape Destinies 3. A New Arab Order 6. Breaking Through the Wall 12. Riddle of Riyadh 13. Iraq, the Pariah State 21. Yemen: Unification	**Standard of Living**	3. A New Arab Order 4. The End of Arab Nationalism 7. Arab Economies After the Gulf War 13. Iraq, the Pariah State
		Women's Rights	11. Women, Islam and the State 12. Riddle of Riyadh

Article 1   *Smithsonian,* May 1991

How the modern Middle East map came to be drawn

When the Ottoman Empire collapsed in 1918, the British created new borders (and rulers) to keep the peace and protect their interests

David Fromkin

Lawyer-historian David Fromkin is the author of a prizewinning book entitled A Peace to End All Peace.

The dictator of Iraq claimed—falsely—that until 1914 Kuwait had been administered from Iraq, that historically Kuwait was a part of Iraq, that the separation of Kuwait from Iraq was an arbitrary decision of Great Britain's after World War I. The year was 1961; the Iraqi dictator was Abdul-Karim Qasim; and the dispatch of British troops averted a threatened invasion.

Iraq, claiming that it had never recognized the British-drawn frontier with Kuwait, demanded full access to the Persian Gulf; and when Kuwait failed to agree, Iraqi tanks and infantry attacked Kuwait. The year was 1973; the Iraqi dictator was Ahmad Hasan al-Bakr; when other Arab states came to Kuwait's support, a deal was struck, Kuwait made a payment of money to Iraq, and the troops withdrew.

August 2, 1990. At 2 A.M. Iraqi forces swept across the Kuwaiti frontier. Iraq's dictator, Saddam Hussein, declared that the frontier between Iraq and Kuwait was invalid, a creation of the British after World War I, and that Kuwait really belonged to Iraq.

It was, of course, true, as one Iraqi dictator after another claimed, that the exact Iraq-Kuwait frontier was a line drawn on an empty map by a British civil servant in the early 1920s. But Kuwait began to emerge as an independent entity in the early 1700s—two centuries before Britain invented Iraq. Moreover, most

other frontiers between states of the Middle East were also creations of the British (or the French). The map of the Arab Middle East was drawn by the victorious Allies when they took over these lands from the Ottoman Empire after World War I. By proposing to nullify that map, Saddam Hussein at a minimum was trying to turn the clock back by almost a century.

A hundred years ago, when Ottoman governors in Basra were futilely attempting to assert authority over the autonomous sheikdom of Kuwait, most of the Arabic-speaking Middle East was at least nominally part of the Ottoman Empire. It had been so for hundreds of years and would remain so until the end of World War I.

The Ottomans, a dynasty, not a nationality, were originally a band of Turkish warriors who first galloped onto the stage of history in the 13th century. By the early 20th century the Ottoman Empire, which once had stretched to the gates of Vienna, was shrinking rapidly, though it still ruled perhaps 20 million to 25 million people in the Middle East and elsewhere, comprising perhaps a dozen or more different nationalities. It was a ramshackle Muslim empire, held together by the glue of Islam, and the lot of its non-Muslim population (perhaps 5 million) was often unhappy and sometimes tragic.

In the year 1900, if you traveled from the United States to the Middle East, you might have landed in Egypt, part of the Ottoman Empire in name but in fact governed by British "advisers." The Egyptian Army was commanded by an English general, and the real ruler of the country

was the British Agent and Consul-General—a position to which the crusty Horatio Herbert Kitchener was appointed in 1911.

The center of your social life in all likelihood would have been the British enclave in Cairo, which possessed (wrote one of Lord Kitchener's aides) "all the narrowness and provincialism of an English garrison town." The social schedule of British officials and their families revolved around the balls given at each of the leading hotels in turn, six nights out of seven, and before dark, around the Turf Club and the Sporting Club on the island of El Gezira. Throughout Egypt, Turkish officials, Turkish police and a Turkish army were conspicuous by their absence. Outside British confines you found yourself not in a Turkish-speaking country but in an Arabic-speaking one. Following the advice of the *Baedeker,* you'd likely engage a dragoman—a translator and guide—of whom there were about 90 in Cairo ("all more or less intelligent and able, but scarcely a half of the number are trustworthy").

On leaving Egypt, if you turned north through the Holy Land and the Levant toward Anatolia, you finally would have encountered the reality of Ottoman government, however corrupt and inefficient, though many cities—Jerusalem (mostly Jewish), Damascus (mostly Arab) and Smyrna, now Izmir (mostly Greek)—were not at all Turkish in character or population.

Heading south by steamer down the Red Sea and around the enormous Arabian Peninsula was a very different matter. Nominally Ottoman, Arabia was in large part a vast, ungoverned desert wilderness through which roamed bedouin tribes knowing no law but their own. In those days Abdul Aziz ibn Saud, the youthful scion of deposed lords of most of the peninsula, was living in exile, dreaming of a return to reclaim his rights and establish his dominion. In the port towns on the Persian Gulf, ruling sheiks paid lip service to Ottoman rule but in fact their sheikdoms were protectorates of Great Britain. Not long after you passed Kuwait you reached Basra, in what is now Iraq, up a river formed by the union of the great Tigris and Euphrates.

A muddy, unhealthy port of heterogeneous population, Basra was then the capital of a province, largely Shiite Arab, ruled by an Ottoman governor. Well north of it, celebrated for archaeological sites like Babylon and Nippur, which drew tourists, lay Baghdad, then a heavily Jewish city (along with Jerusalem, one of the two great Jewish cities of Asia). Baghdad was the administrative center of an Ottoman province that was in large part Sunni Arab. Farther north still was a third Ottoman province, with a large population of Kurds. Taken together, the three roughly equaled the present area of Iraq.

Ottoman rule in some parts of the Middle East clearly was more imaginary than real. And even in those portions of the empire that Turkish governors did govern, the population was often too diverse to be governed effectively by a single regime. Yet the hold of the Turkish sultan on the empire's peoples lingered on. Indeed, had World War I not intervened, the Ottoman Empire might well have lasted many decades more.

In its origins, the war that would change the map of the Middle East had nothing to do with that region. How the Ottoman Empire came to be involved in the war at all—and lost it—and how the triumphant Allies

found themselves in a position to redesign the Middle Eastern lands the Turks had ruled, is one of the most fascinating stories of the 20th century, rich in consequences that we are still struggling with today.

The story begins with one man, a tiny, vain, strutting man addicted to dramatic gestures and uniforms. He was Enver Pasha, and he mistook himself for a sort of Napoleon. Of modest origins, Enver, as a junior officer in the Ottoman Army, joined the Young Turks, a secret society that was plotting against the Ottoman regime. In 1913, Enver led a Young Turk raiding party that overthrew the government and killed the Minister of War. In 1914, at the age of 31, he became the Ottoman Minister of War himself, married the niece of the sultan and moved into a palace.

As a new political figure Enver scored a major, instant success. The Young Turks for years had urgently sought a European ally that would promise to protect the Ottoman Empire against other European powers. Britain, France and Russia had each been approached and had refused; but on August 1, 1914, just as Germany was about to invade Belgium to begin World War I, Enver wangled a secret treaty with the kaiser pledging to protect the Ottoman domains.

Unaware of Enver's coup, and with war added to the equation, Britain and France began wooing Turkey too, while the Turks played off one side against the other. By autumn the German Army's plan to knock France out of the war in six weeks had failed. Needing help, Germany urged the Ottoman Empire to join the war by attacking Russia.

Though Enver's colleagues in the Turkish government were opposed to war, Enver had a different idea. To him the time seemed ripe: in the first month of the war German armies overwhelmingly turned back a Russian attack on East Prussia, and a collapse of the czar's armies appeared imminent. Seeing a chance to share

in the spoils of a likely German victory over Russia, Enver entered into a private conspiracy with the German admiral commanding the powerful warship *Goeben* and its companion vessel, the *Breslau*, which had taken refuge in Turkish waters at the outset of hostilities.

During the last week of October, Enver secretly arranged for the *Goeben* and the *Breslau* to escape into the Black Sea and steam toward Russia. Flying the Ottoman flag, the Germans then opened fire on the Russian coast. Thinking themselves attacked by Turks, the Russians declared war. Russia's allies, Britain and France, thus found themselves at war with the Ottoman Empire too. By needlessly plunging the empire into war, Enver had put everything in the Middle East up for grabs. In that sense, he was the father of the modern Middle East. Had Enver never existed, the Turkish flag might even yet be flying—if only in some confederal way—over Beirut and Damascus, Baghdad and Jerusalem.

Great Britain had propped up the Ottoman Empire for generations as a buffer against Russian expansionism. Now, with Russia as Britain's shaky ally, once the war had been won and the Ottomans overthrown, the Allies would be able to reshape the entire Middle East. It would be one of those magic moments in history when fresh starts beckon and dreams become realities.

"What is to prevent the Jews having Palestine and restoring a real Judaea?" asked H. G. Wells, the British novelist, essayist and prophet of a rational future for mankind. The Greeks, the French and the Italians also had claims to Middle East territory. And naturally, in Cairo, Lord Kitchener's aides soon began to contemplate a future plan for an Arab world to be ruled by Egypt, which in turn would continue to be controlled by themselves.

At the time, the Allies already had their hands full with war against Germany on the Western Front. They resolved not to be distracted by the Middle East until later. The issues and ambitions there were too divisive. Hardly had the Ottoman Empire entered the war, however, when Enver stirred the pot again. He took personal command of the Ottoman Third Army on the Caucasus frontier and, in the dead of winter, launched a foolhardy attack against fortified positions on high ground. His offensive was hopeless, since it was both amateurishly planned and executed, but the czar's generals panicked anyway. The Russian government begged Lord Kitchener (now serving in London as Secretary of State for War) to stage a more or less instant diversionary action. The result was the Allied attack on the Dardanelles, the strait that eventually leads to Constantinople (now Istanbul).

Enver soon lost about 86,000 of his 100,000 men; the few, bloodied survivors straggled back through icy mountain passes. A German observer noted that Enver's army had "suffered a disaster which for rapidity and completeness is without parallel in military history." But nobody in the Russian government or high command bothered to tell the British that mounting a Dardanelles naval attack was no longer necessary. So on the morning of February 19, 1915, British ships fired the opening shots in what became a tragic campaign.

Initially, the British Navy seemed poised to take Constantinople, and Russia panicked again. What if the British, having occupied Constantinople, were to hold onto it? The 50 percent of Russia's export trade flowing through the strait would then do so only with British permission. Czar Nicholas II demanded immediate assurance that Constantinople would be Russia's in the postwar world. Fearing Russia might withdraw from the war, Britain and France agreed. In return, Russia offered to support British and French claims in other parts of the Middle East.

With that in mind, on April 8,

1915, the British Prime Minister appointed a committee to define Britain's postwar goals in the Middle East. It was a committee dominated by Lord Kitchener through his personal representative, 36-year-old Sir Mark Sykes, one of many remarkable characters, including Winston Churchill and T. E. Lawrence, to be involved in the remaking (and remapping) of the Middle East.

A restless soul who had moved from school to school as a child, Sykes left college without graduating, and thereafter never liked to stay long in one spot. A Tory Member of Parliament, before the war he had traveled widely in Asiatic Turkey, publishing accounts of his journeys. Sykes' views tended to be passionate but changeable, and his talent for clever exaggeration sometimes carried over into his politics.

As a traditional Tory he had regarded the sultan's domains as a useful buffer protecting Britain's road to India against Britain's imperial rivals, the czar chief among them. Only 15 months earlier, Sykes was warning the House of Commons that "the disappearance of the Ottoman Empire must be the first step towards the disappearance of our own." Yet between 1915 and 1919, he busily planned the dismantling of the Ottoman Empire.

The Allied attack on the Dardanelles ended with Gallipoli, a disaster told and retold in books and films. Neither that defeat, nor the darkest days of 1916-17, when it looked for a while as though the Allies might lose the war, stopped British planning about how to cut up the Turkish Middle East. Steadily but secretly Sykes worked on. As the fight to overthrow the Ottoman Empire grew more intense, the elements he had to take into account grew more complex.

It was clear that the British needed to maintain control over the Suez Canal, and all the rest of the route to their prized colonial possession, India. They needed to keep the Russians and Germans and Italians and French

in check. Especially the French, who had claims on Syria. But with millions of men committed to trench warfare in Europe, they could not drain off forces for the Middle East. Instead, units of the British Indian Army along with other Commonwealth forces attacked in the east in what are now Iraq and Iran, occupying Basra, Baghdad and eventually Mosul. Meanwhile, Allied liaison officers, including notably T. E. Lawrence, began encouraging the smallish group of Arabian tribesmen following Emir (later King) Hussein of the Hejaz, who had rebelled against the Turks, to fight a guerrilla campaign against Turkish forces.

Throughout 1917, in and near the Hejaz area of Arabia (see map), the Arabs attacked the railway line that supported Turkish troops in Medina. The "Arab Revolt" had little military effect on the outcome of the war, yet the fighting brought to the fore, as British clients and potential Arab leaders, not only Hussein of the Hejaz, but two of his sons, Faisal and Abdullah. Both were deadly rivals of Ibn Saud, who by then had become a rising power in Arabia and a client of the British too.

British officials in Cairo deluded themselves and others into believing that the whole of the Arabic-speaking half of the Ottoman Empire might rise up and come over to the Allied side. When the time came, the Arab world did not follow the lead of Hussein, Abdullah and Faisal. But Arab aspirations and British gratitude began to loom large in British, and Arab, plans for the future. Sykes now felt he had to take Arab ambitions into account in his future planning, though he neglected those of Ibn Saud (father of today's Saudi king), who also deserved well of Britain.

By 1917 Sykes was also convinced that it was vital for the British war effort to win Jewish support against Germany, and that pledging support for Zionism could win it. That year his efforts and those of others resulted in the publication of a statement by Arthur James Balfour, the British

Foreign Secretary, expressing Britain's support for the establishment of a Jewish national home in Palestine.

The year 1917 proved to be a turning point. In the wake of its revolution Russia pulled out of the war, but the entrance by the United States on the Allied side insured the Allies a victory—if they could hold on long enough for U.S. troops to arrive in force. In the Middle East, as British India consolidated its hold on areas that are now part of Iraq, Gen. Edmund Allenby's Egyptian-based British army began fighting its way north from Suez to Damascus. Lawrence and a force of Arab raiders captured the Red Sea port of Aqaba (near the point where Israel and Jordan now meet). Then, still other Arabs, with Faisal in command, moved north to harass the Turkish flank.

By October 1918, Allenby had taken Syria and Lebanon, and was poised to invade what is now Turkey. But there was no need to do so, because on October 31 the Ottoman Empire surrendered.

As the Peace Conference convened in Paris, in February 1919, Sykes, who had been rethinking Britain's design for the Middle East, suddenly fell ill and died. At first there was nobody to take his place as the British government's overall Middle East planner. Prime Minister David Lloyd George took personal charge in many Middle East matters. But more and more, as the months went by, Winston Churchill had begun to play a major role, gradually superseding the others.

Accordingly, early that year the ambitious 45-year-old politician was asked by the Prime Minister to serve as both War Minister and Air Minister. ("Of course," Lloyd George wrote Churchill, "there will be but one salary!") Maintaining the peace in the captured—and now occupied—Arab Middle East was among Churchill's new responsibilities.

Cheerful, controversial and belligerent, Churchill was not yet the revered figure who would so inspire his countrymen and the world in 1940. Haunted by the specter of a brilliant father, he had won fame and high office early, but was widely distrusted, in part for having switched political parties. Churchill's foresighted administration of the Admiralty in the summer of 1914 won universal praise, but then the botched Dardanelles campaign, perhaps unfairly, was blamed on him. As a Conservative newspaper put it, "we have watched his brilliant and erratic course in the confident expectation that sooner or later he would make a mess of anything he undertook." In making Churchill minister of both War and Air in 1919, Lloyd George was giving his protégé a try at a political comeback.

By the end of the war, everyone was so used to the bickering among the Allies about who was going to get what in the postwar Middle East that the alternative—nobody taking anything—simply didn't enter into the equation. Churchill was perhaps the only statesman to consider that possibility. He foresaw that many problems would arise from trying to impose a new political design on so troubled a region, and thought it unwise to make the attempt. Churchill argued, in fact, for simply retaining a reformed version of the Ottoman Empire. Nobody took him seriously.

After the war, a British army of a million men, the only cohesive military force in the region, briefly occupied the Middle East. Even as his real work began, however, Churchill was confronted with demands that the army, exhausted from years of war, be demobilized. He understood what meeting those demands meant. Relying on that army, Prime Minister Lloyd George had decided to keep the whole Arab Middle East under British influence; in the words he once used about Palestine: "We shall be there by conquest and shall remain." Now Churchill repeatedly warned that once British troops were withdrawn, Britain would not be able to impose its terms.

Lloyd George had predicted that it would take about a week to agree on the terms of peace to be imposed on the defeated Ottoman Empire. Instead it took nearly two years. By then, in Churchill's words, the British army of occupation had long since "melted away," with the dire consequences he predicted.

In Egypt, demonstrations, strikes and riots broke out. In Arabia, Ibn Saud, though himself a British client, defeated and threatened to destroy Britain's protégé Hussein. In Turkey, the defeated Enver had long since fled the country to find refuge in Berlin. From there he journeyed to Russia, assumed leadership of Bukhara (in what is now the Uzbek Republic of the USSR) in its struggle for independence from Moscow, and was killed in battle against the Red Army of the Soviet Union in 1922. Turkish nationalists under the great Ottoman general Mustafa Kemal (later known as Kemal Ataturk) rebelled against the Allied-imposed treaty and later proclaimed the national state that is modern Turkey.

In Palestine, Arabs rioted against Jews. In what is now Saddam Hussein's Iraq, armed revolts by the tribes, sparked in the first instance by the imposition of taxes, caused thousands of casualties. "How much longer," the outraged London *Times* asked, "are valuable lives to be sacrificed in the vain endeavour to impose upon the Arab population an elaborate and expensive administration which they never asked for and do not want?"

By the end of 1920, Lloyd George's Middle East policy was under attack from all sides. Churchill, who had warned all along that peacetime Britain, in the grip of an economic collapse, had neither the money, the troops, nor the will to coerce the Middle East, was proved right—and placed even more directly in charge. On New Year's Day 1921 he was appointed Colonial Secretary, and soon began to expand his powers, consolidating within his new department responsibility for all Britain's domains in Arabic-speaking Asia.

He assembled his staff by combing the government for its ablest and most experienced officials. The one offbeat appointment was T. E. Lawrence. A young American journalist and promoter named Lowell Thomas, roaming the Middle East in search of a story, had found Lawrence dressed in Arab robes, and proceeded to make him world-famous as "Lawrence of Arabia." A complex personality, Lawrence was chronically insubordinate, but Churchill admired all the wonderful stories he'd heard of Lawrence's wartime exploits.

Seeking to forge a working consensus among his staff in London and his men in the field, Churchill invited them all to a conference that opened in Cairo on March 12, 1921. During the ten-day session held in the Semiramis Hotel, about 40 experts were in attendance. "Everybody Middle East is here," wrote Lawrence.

Egypt was not on the agenda. Its fate was being settled separately by its new British proconsul, Lord Allenby. In 1922 he established it as an independent kingdom, still largely subject to British control under terms of a unilateral proclamation that neither Egypt's politicians nor its new king, Fuad, accepted.

All Britain's other wartime conquests—the lands now called Israel, the West Bank, Jordan and Iraq—were very much on the agenda, while the fate of Syria and Lebanon, which Britain had also conquered, was on everybody's mind. In the immediate aftermath of the war, it was control of Syria that had caused the most problems, as Lloyd George tried to keep it for Britain by placing it under the rule of Lawrence's comrade-in-arms, Prince Faisal, son of Hussein. After Syria declared its independence, the French fought back. Occupying all of Syria-Lebanon, they drove Faisal into exile. The French also devised a new frontier for Lebanon that invited eventual disaster, as

would become evident in the 1970s and '80s. They refused to see that the Muslim population was deeply hostile to their rule.

Churchill, meanwhile, was confronted by constant Arab disturbances in Palestine. West of the Jordan River, where the Jewish population lived, Arabs fought against Jewish immigration, claiming—wrongly, as the future was to show—that the country was too barren to support more than its existing 600,000 inhabitants. Churchill rejected that view, and dealt with the Arab objections to a Jewish homeland by keeping—though redefining—

Britain's commitment to Zionism. As he saw it, there was to be a Jewish homeland in Palestine, but other homelands could exist there as well.

The 75 percent of Palestine east of the Jordan River (Transjordan, as it was called, until it became Jordan in 1950) was lawless. Lacking the troops to police it and wanting to avert additional causes of strife, Churchill decided to forbid Jews from settling there, temporarily at least.

Fittingly while still War and Air Minister, Churchill had devised a strategy for controlling the Middle East with a minimum number of Brit-

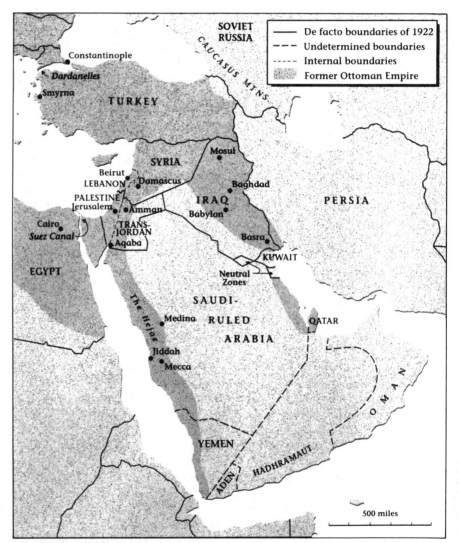

Map shows the Middle East redrawn by the British as of 1922. Iraq has just been created out of three more or less incompatible Ottoman provinces. Part of Palestine has become Transjordan (today's Jordan), which is still ruled by one of Abdullah's descendants.

ish troops by using an economical combination of airpower and armored cars. But it would take time for the necessary units to be put in place. Meanwhile tribal fighting had to be contained somehow. As the Cairo conference met, news arrived that Abdullah, Faisal's brother, claiming to need "a change of air for his health," had left Arabia with a retinue of bedouin warriors and entered Transjordan. The British feared that Abdullah would attack French Syria and so give the French an excuse to invade Transjordan, as a first step toward taking over all Palestine.

As a temporary expedient Churchill appointed Abdullah as governor of a Transjordan to be administratively detached from the rest of Palestine. He charged him with keeping order by his prestige and with his own bedouin followers—at least until Britain's aircraft and armored cars were in place. This provisional solution has lasted for seven decades and so have the borders of Transjordan, now ruled over by Abdullah's grandson, Hussein, the Hashemite King of Jordan.

The appointment of Abdullah seemed to accomplish several objectives at once. It went partway toward paying what Lawrence and others told Churchill was Britain's wartime debt to the family of King Hussein, though Hussein himself was beyond help. Too stubborn to accept British advice, he was losing the battle for Arabia to his blood rival, Ibn Saud. Meanwhile Prince Faisal, Britain's preferred Arab ruler, remained in idle exile.

Other chief items on the Cairo agenda were the Ottoman territories running from the Persian Gulf to Turkey along the border of Persia, which make up present-day Iraq. Including what were suspected—but not proved—to be vast oil reserves, at a time when the value of oil was beginning to be understood, these territories had been the scene of the bloodiest postwar Arab uprisings against British rule. They caused so many difficulties of every sort that Churchill flirted with the idea of abandoning them entirely, but Lloyd George would have none of it. If the British left, the Prime Minister warned, in a year or two they might find that they had "handed over to the French and Americans some of the richest oil fields in the world."

As a matter of convenience, the British administered this troubled region as a unit, though it was composed of the three separate Ottoman provinces—Mosul, Baghdad and Basra, with their incompatible Kurdish, Assyrian Christian, Jewish, Sunni Muslim, and Shiite populations. In making it into a country, Churchill and his colleagues found it convenient to continue treating it as a single unit. (One British planner was warned by an American missionary, "You are flying in the face of four millenniums of history . . .") The country was called Iraq—"the well-rooted country"—in order to give it a name that was Arabic. Faisal was placed on the throne by the British, and like his brother Abdullah in Transjordan, he was supposed to keep Iraq quiet until the British were ready to police it with aircraft and armored cars.

One of the leftover problems in 1921 was just how to protect Transjordan's new governor, Abdullah, and Iraq's new king, Faisal, against the fierce warriors of Ibn Saud. In August 1922 Ibn Saud's camel-cavalry forces invading Transjordan were stopped outside Amman by British airplanes and armored cars. Earlier that year, the British forced Ibn Saud to accept a settlement aimed at protecting Iraq. With this in mind, the British drew a frontier line that awarded Iraq a substantial amount of territory claimed by Ibn Saud for Arabia: all the land (in what is now Iraq) west of the Euphrates River, all the way to the Syrian frontier. To compensate Ibn Saud's kingdom (later known as Saudi Arabia) the British transferred to it rights to two-thirds of the territory of Kuwait, which had been essentially independent for about two centuries. These were valuable grazing lands, in which oil might exist too.

It is this frontier line between Iraq, Kuwait and Arabia, drawn by a British civil servant in 1922 to protect Iraq at the expense of Kuwait, that Iraq's Saddam Hussein denounced as invalid when he invaded.

In 1922, Churchill succeeded in mapping out the Arab Middle East along lines suitable to the needs of the British civilian and military administrations. T. E. Lawrence would later brag that he, Churchill and a few others had designed the modern Middle East over dinner. Seventy years later, in the tense deliberations and confrontations of half the world over the same area, the question is whether the peoples of the Middle East are willing or able to continue living with that design.

Article 2

INSIGHT / MARCH 4, 1991

Past Glories Shape Destinies of Arabs

SUMMARY: Westerners confused by the actions of some Arab leaders would do well to study history, for in the Middle East the past pervades the present. Indeed much of the unrest there stems from discontent, if not anger, lingering from centuries of Ottoman domination, followed by colonialism by Western powers. Visions of ancient days of Arab triumphs have moved modern leaders to action as well — sometimes to their detriment.

Where is there victory in defeat, honor in death, brotherhood in oppression and unity in war? No sphinx's riddle this: It is the Arab world, where reality threatens, dreams are the stuff of everyday life and it "might have been" is the creed that thrills a million souls.

For many in the West, the war with Iraq is the first glimpse into Araby. It is a strange sight. Holy men in Baghdad and Riyadh each declaring jihad against the other. Newspapers in Amman, Jordan, celebrating an Iraqi victory at Khafji, known to most others as a 36-hour rout. Intrigue, blood and God — these are the currencies of the Middle East.

The past pervades the present. The lightning defeat of 1967, when the West Bank, Sinai and the old city of Jerusalem were lost in less than one week, still fires the flames of vengeance in Arab armies.

The British-French-Israeli attempt to regain Suez 35 years ago is the prototype of Western conspiracies in the modern Middle East.

But if the leaders of the modern Arab world exist to right the wrongs of the 20th century, so too they strive to relive the glories of centuries past. The triumphs of Nebuchadrezzar II, who conquered Jerusalem in 597 B.C., and of Saladin, who united Egypt, Syria and Palestine in 1174, have inspired generations of Arab despots. Saddam Hussein is only the most recent.

Glorious battles, crushing defeats, occupation, liberation, 1967 and 597 B.C., all are as real as yesterday. "If you go back to the early Middle Ages, the seventh, eighth, up to the 11th century, you find a world around the Mediterranean where the Arabs led," says Raphael Patai, an Arabist and student of Middle Eastern cultures. "They were ahead of Europe in practically every respect, in philosophy, medicine, astronomy. It is an undeniable fact."

Preoccupation with ancient glories is perhaps no surprise, given that Arab history since has been one of relative decline. The Middle East was freed of centuries of Ottoman domination only to be gobbled up by the British and French empires. Even the final liberation of the Middle East, many Arabs feel, was laced with Western contempt: kings crowned, capitals named, institutions built. "Look at our borders," cries one Arab intellectual. "Straight lines. They didn't even bother to make them crooked."

"After 400 years of Ottoman occupation and then being carved up by Britain and

France and the United Nations, we are at the bottom of a cycle," says Rami Khouri, a prominent Jordanian publisher and journalist. "If the Arab world had been allowed to develop on its own, we would not be seeing the troubles we have today."

If the Arab world had developed on its own, it is likely the borders drawn so haphazardly by the British and the French would not be there. Perhaps there would be no untenable states, no Jordans and Syrias with few resources, no Persian Gulf emirates, little more than tribes with flags and armies; perhaps there would be an Iraq with a port on the sea and no Kuwait.

Many lay responsibility for the current misfortunes of the Arabs at Western feet. "We are a very beleaguered people," says Kemal Abu Jaber, director of the Jordan Center for Middle East Studies and a former Cabinet minister. "We feel isolated, hounded, vilified, demonized, abused by the West in general and the Zionist organization in particular."

The West, popular opinion has it, is out to crush the Arabs and Islam. Jordan's King Hussein recently proclaimed that the United States is waging "a war against all Arabs and Muslims." Saddam Hussein plays the same tune, but over the years there is nary an Arab leader who has not touched on the American, or the Zionist, or the American-Zionist plot to destroy the Arab world and Islam.

The most dastardly evidence of the plan to subjugate Islam — the seedling of the new Crusades — is the state of Israel. Out of British Palestine, the United Nations created a Jewish state. It was imposed on the Arabs, the catechism goes, to atone for the crimes of the Germans, to expiate the guilt of the Americans. And then the Americans compounded their sin by supporting that state politically and financially. "The mother of Middle East problems is the Arab-Israeli conflict," says Abu Jaber.

In the name of Palestine there have been three wars, and a fourth now in progress — remember, Saddam says he invaded Kuwait to liberate Jerusalem. For most of this century millions in the Arab world have put their faith in the claims of tin pot dictators, petty tyrants, field marshals, kings and presidents-for-life who have promised to liberate Palestine and regain Arab dignity.

So too, in the name of that quest, successive leaders have denied their people basic human rights and political liberties, all the more reason to blame the Jewish state for the woes of the Arab people. But once this problem is swept aside, successive leaders have claimed, Arabia will flourish as of yore.

Instead, however, the Arab world's battle against Israel has brought disaster upon disaster, including what is termed the "second Holocaust" — the Six-Day War. It was the worst of humiliations, Arabs explain; it is the loss that Arab armies exist to avenge and the barometer by which all other battles are judged in the Middle East.

Because the Egyptian armies succeeded in crossing Israel's Bar Lev Line in the October War of 1973, and despite the fact that the Israeli army pushed back as far into Egypt, the war was labeled a victory. An inaccurate missile falls by happenstance into a residential neighborhood in Tel Aviv, scaring two elderly Jews to death, and it is a triumph. In the same way, "the fact that Saddam can take 30 days of U.S. bombing and not collapse is a victory," says an allied partisan in the Gulf. "Expectations are so low, our standard is 1967."

One reason the Arab world rates itself so low is because — a popular theory goes — the world is allied against it. "The fact is that the Muslims used to feel themselves on top and now they feel behind," says Daniel Pipes, director of the Foreign Policy Research Institute in Philadelphia.

"They are deeply troubled by this and see conspiracies as one way to explain the current reality." Thus, the West stole Islamic power by some secret means, a favorite theory of Iran's late Ayatollah Ruhollah Khomeini. Or the West set up the Middle East so it would never be stable, never a challenge to occidental hegemony.

Conspiracy theories are not confined to rationalizing the decline of Arab power. Indeed, they are a favorite tool of Arab leaders to explain their own inadequacies to a curious and ill-used public. Egyptian

President Gamal Abdel Nasser suggested to King Hussein that they "reveal" the reason for their defeat at the hands of the Israelis in the Six-Day War: British and American aircraft helping the Jewish state. Saddam Hussein has insisted that "treacherous Zionism is behind every unjust conspiracy or aggression against Iraq and the Arabs."

Pride plays no small part in the desperate need for explain-all conspiracies. The loss of face and honor in the Six-Day War scarred the Arab world. Losing to a greater opponent is an honorable defeat; to lose to Jews is something else again. "The Arabs have looked down on the Jews for many centuries. As long as they were subservient and behaved as the Arabs wanted, they were tolerated," says Patai. "But to face the fact that these subservient people suddenly have changed and are strong enough to defeat us, this is a very bitter pill to swallow." Thus Nasser brushed off the whole 1967 episode with a typical, "We have not been defeated, we have been betrayed."

The very idea that preservation of face and honor could be of such paramount importance is alien to most Westerners, gone with pantaloons and the duel. Witness, however, the frantic attempts to find a way for Saddam to withdraw from Kuwait and "save face," the promises from the king of Saudi Arabia and the president of Egypt that should Saddam retire to Baghdad, he would not be dishonored.

The same view dictated that Saddam go to war rather than receive a letter from George Bush that his foreign minister deemed "rude." The idea that Saddam was forced to fight rather than lose face permeates the Middle East. "My guess is that the West and in particular the United States

calculated the crisis from Aug. 2 in such a way as to preclude any meaningful dialogue," says Abu Jaber. "It was calculated to bring Iraq to a position where it had no choice but to surrender or be pulverized."

"I heard President Bush say on two or three occasions that the man [Saddam] is a liar. Would he ever refer to President Francois Mitterrand or John Major this way?" asks Abu Jaber. "Even now, should the United States see fit to talk to the Iraqis in a proper way," there could be a solution.

Of course, plenty of Arabs will not dance to Saddam's tune, do not believe he is out to liberate anyone, believe he is a liar and a thief, and dismiss his self-portrait as Arab savior. "The Arabs don't trust their governments," says the Gulf resident. "People are so desperate they are willing to put themselves in the hands of any tyrant. But they don't believe him."

Little wonder, as truth has become a rare commodity in Arab politics: Leaders lie to each other and to their people. At the start of the 1967 Arab-Israeli war, Nasser called up King Hussein, the Jordanian himself has recounted, and told him that most of Israel's air force was destroyed; Egyptian troops were engaged in battle on the Sinai Peninsula and had entered Israel through the Negev Desert. On the strength of that information — whether he believed it or not — the king entered the war with Israel and lost the West Bank. In truth, what Nasser said was nothing more than fantasy.

It may seem curious that when Saddam called up King Hussein in that first week of August and assured him of an intent to withdraw from Kuwait, a vision of promises past did not rise before the king. But perhaps it did. A savvy veteran of Arab politics, the king has learned that sometimes it is politic to believe a lie.

Nasser's appeals to King Hussein led to Jordan's entry into the 1967 war.

Psst, Saddam Has a Story He Wants You to Hear

Heard about the deliberate allied bombing of residential areas in Iraq? Tension between the Arab and Western soldiers in the allied coalition in the Persian Gulf? Hundreds of allied "air targets" shot down? Israeli jets in Turkey? Thousands of dead Iraqi children? Seen the film showing American GIs begging for mercy from their Iraqi captors (it was shown Jan. 19 in Mauritania)? The infamous baby milk factory, shattered to smithereens?

What about the five Pakistanis and 72 Americans dead at each other's hands? Drinking and carousing at Muslim holy places? Pentagon-procured Egyptian prostitutes? The Saudi royal family quavering in exile in Morocco? Egyptians and Syrians mutinying? Hundreds of churches and synagogues built in Saudi Arabia? Egypt's Hosni Mubarak almost overthrown? Israeli jets in Iraqi markings attacking Turkey, Syria and Egypt?

All Iraqi disinformation.

To Westerners, most of this stuff looks like garbage. In the Middle East and the Third World it is being eaten up like so much caviar. The Algerian, Bangladeshi, Iranian, Indian, Jordanian, Nigerian, Pakistani and Zambian media — not known for their muckraking abilities — have picked up and made up fabulous tales of death and debauchery. Even the Soviets (from whom the Iraqis learned their disinformation techniques) have uncritically parroted Iraqi News Agency releases.

"The Moroccan press has been carrying stories that American and Moroccan troops have been fighting and killing each other," says William Rugh, an expert on the Arab press at the U.S. Information Agency. "But they may not be dishonest — they may honestly believe that the Americans are defiling the holy places in Saudi Arabia and shooting Moroccan troops. [They're] maybe not as fastidious about sources as we would like, but it's not necessarily deliberate lying."

The key to such successful disinformation, explains Todd Leventhal, a USIA disinformation specialist, is not the grain of truth that some believe gives a story credibility.

"It's one of those cliches that there's a grain of truth but it has no basis in fact," he says. "Take for example the [assertion of] Israeli involvement — there's no Israeli involvement in the multinational coalition whatsoever. There's not the single slightest grain of truth in that. But what there is is a strong predisposition to believe in the target audience. And that's what counts."

The curious may wonder why Iraq is bothering to preach to the converted. The answer is that Saddam Hussein is aiming over the heads of the less pliable leadership to the hearts of the masses. Jordan is a prime example: King Hussein is a middle-of-the-road kind of guy, yet he steadily followed the lead of his violently pro-Iraqi subjects and finally fell headlong into the Iraqi camp. If Saddam comes out of this war alive he will not lack friends among the Arab people.

But the West is not immune to Iraqi disinformation either. Scenes of civilian casualties in Iraq are getting more and more play both in Europe and in the United States, contrasted, as they are, with the protestations of the U.S. military that the allies are only aiming for strategic targets. It is difficult, U.S. officials argue, to show pictures of unhurt civilians and call it proof positive of allied good intentions.

U.S. experts suspect that some footage supplied by Iraqi television — heartrending scenes of injured children and overflowing hospitals — may have come from other conflicts. There is eight years' worth of Iran-Iraq war film to choose from. And independent reporting is hard to come by. Western journalists leaving Iraq report that eager Information Ministry officials drove them hundreds of miles to find civilian casualties.

Such stories are unlikely to bring the American people out in Jordan-style protests. But if credible or even somewhat credible reports continue to flow from Baghdad about civilian deaths, there is a danger of erosion of support for the war in the West.

"Over the longer haul it gives us a political climate that's very difficult to operate in," says George Carver, a former adviser on Vietnamese affairs to the CIA.

"In the Vietnam War, the Vietnamese were unable to defeat the French in battle, but they waged the first Indochina war in such a fashion as to make the continuation of the struggle a politically unsalable commodity in Paris," says Carver. "And they waged the second Indochina war with the intent to ultimately make its continuation politically unsalable in Washington." Their success is a lesson that cannot have been lost on Saddam.

Certainly, the Arab people have often been fed little more by their leaders. No war been entered without fervent assurances from the powers that be that it would be won, and fast. None has been won. Leaders have regularly trumpeted their affection for fellow Arab leaders. It has not escaped much of the Arab world that unity is not forthcoming.

"What you have in the Arab heart and mind is the existence of a myth and reality at the same time," says Abu Jaber. "The myth is that there is an Arab nation which everyone declares that he sees on the official level. And the reality is that this is not the fact and every nation is acting out of its own narrow interests."

The constant clash of government gospel and naked truth have created an alternate reality in the Arab world, where little is as it seems. There are few states where the press is free, even fewer where the state does not hover threateningly over journalists. "We buy the paper for the sports section," says the Gulf resident. "When we want the truth, we listen to the BBC."

Not everyone cares for what the British Broadcasting Corp. has to offer, however. Refugees fleeing Iraq in the first days of the Gulf war told a reporter of the widespread civilian deaths, the indiscriminate bombing by the allies. An Egyptian pulled the reporter aside and confided that "in truth," the bombing was impressively well placed on strategic targets.

There is, however, one inescapable reality. After 50-odd years of Arab independence, the Middle East is a patchwork of dictatorship and autocracy, of disastrous socialist experiments and serendipitous oil wealth. It is a place where in comparison to the history that every Arab knows from the youngest age, there is no glory and no influence; there are no great Arab armies, and in place of the Saladins are Saddams.

"There is a huge gap between hope and reality, and that is why much of the Arab world is turning toward Islam," says Khouri. "People in the Middle East turned to religion in the early Eighties as a means of challenging and protesting the existing political order."

The fly in the Islamic ointment is that religion is also the preferred means for the leadership of the Arab world to maintain

Swimming in Blood and Other Flowery Phrases

"Is it not time to prevent confused persistence on this deviant path to which you were led by satanic propensities before you make the people in the Arabian Peninsula . . . bear the consequences of this horrible propensity for evil hysteria after Bush and his little agents infused your hearts with evil pretexts?"

— Saddam Hussein to King Fahd ibn Abdul Aziz of Saudi Arabia, Jan. 14

In Saddam Hussein's lexicon, George Bush is: Criminal Bush, Oppressor Bush, Satan, Criminal Tyrant, Loathsome Criminal, Evil Butcher, America's Satan, Criminal Failure, the Grand Satan, Satan of the Era. Saudi Arabia's King Fahd is the Midget Agent, Traitor Fahd, Agent Fahd, Enemy of God, Ally of the Forces of Evil and Shame, an ignorant ingrate, infidel, blasphemer and, worst of all, Jewish.

Rhetoric is art to the Arabic speaker — proverbs, rhyme, seductive imagery and, most of all, exaggeration are commonplace. Language is poetry, writing is art. English it ain't.

"When Saddam says Americans will swim in their own blood, if you take away the flowery rhetoric and the problems with translation, it is the equivalent in tone and meaning as when George Bush says, 'We're going to kick his ass,' " says Rami Khouri, a Jordanian journalist and publisher.

What with all the effort put into formulating language, it is hardly surprising that words have come to take the place of action. Take the decades of protestations about the liquidation of the state of Israel, about the strength of the Arab armies, about the brotherhood of Arab nations; oft-averred, never realized.

Witness, too, the hundreds of conferences, parleys, emergency meetings of the dozens of formal groupings in the Arab world: the Gulf Cooperation Council, the Arab League, the Arab Cooperation Council, to name just a few. All have convened time and again, all have accomplished close to nothing. "They convene a conference, there is much talk, they even pass a resolution. And then they go home," says Raphael

Patai, an Arabist and longtime student of the language.

This habit has not been lost on outsiders or local observers. Indeed, many an Arab leader has exhorted his people to get off their duffs and act. King Abdullah of Jordan, grandfather of the present-day Jordanian monarch, concluded after a lifetime of experience with wishful thinking that "Arabs must give up daydreaming and apply themselves to realities."

Egypt's Hosni Mubarak has learned that lesson. A self-described technocrat, he has tossed traditions out the window, does not talk too much, eschews flowery language and generally does what he says he will.

Ironically, so does Saddam Hussein. He and his followers are much given to bombast, especially when it comes to Israel (Hated Daughter of the United States) and its people (Criminal Zionist Spiders, Arrogant Zionists, Filthy Zionists). But give him this: What Saddam threatens, he does. Or at least he tries.

just that order. Saddam Hussein, new champion of Allah, is one in a long line of such prophets. That he liquidated much of his country's religious leadership seems not

to mar his image as a true believer among many of his followers.

And that those followers are in the very countries where Islam has been a force for

democratization — Jordan, Algeria, Yemen — may not bode well for the future of the Arab world.

— *Danielle Pletka*

Article 3

The Economist, September 28, 1991

A new Arab order

Or just the settling of scores?

A FEW days before Iraq invaded Kuwait, the man who was then its foreign minister, Tariq Aziz, sent a letter to the boss of the Arab League. Among other things, it said this:

Iraq considers that the Arabs, over and above national boundaries, are one nation, that what belongs to them should belong to all and benefit all and that what hurts one of them hurts all . . . Despite its division into states, the Arab world nevertheless remains one country, every inch of which must be considered in accordance with a nationalistic vision and, more particularly, in accordance with the demands of a common Arab security. We must avoid falling into a narrow and selfish point of view when considering the interests and rights of this or that country.

This letter deserves a special place in the annals of modern Arab history. With hindsight it is easy to see its attempt to belittle the idea of national sovereignty for what it was: a pretext for Iraq to swallow up a neighbour. At the time the sentiments expressed by Mr Aziz were not the least bit remarkable. Until the invasion of Kuwait, it was almost obligatory for Arab leaders to decorate their pronouncements with lofty invocations of the pan-Arab idea.

The deepest change the Gulf war wrought in the Arab world may turn out to have been the smashing of this idea once and for all. Ever since the emergence of the modern system of Middle Eastern states at the end of the first world war, Arabs have felt themselves pushed and pulled between two forms of nationalism. One, *wataniyya*, means loyalty to a particular country. The other, *qawmiyya*, means loyalty towards a larger sense of Arab nationhood, a loyalty that is supposed to transcend the borders imposed on the Arabs by western imperialism. Since the Gulf war *qawmiyya* has fallen out of favour. Arab regimes no longer feel the need to disguise actions they take for their own national interests as actions that serve the wider Arab cause.

This change is neatly illustrated by what has happened to the Arab League, the organisation which since 1945 has been the joint mouthpiece of all the Arab governments. The Arab League has not held a big summit since Iraq invaded Kuwait. Its last such gathering took place in Baghdad in May 1990, three months before the invasion. That meeting resounded to the traditional slogans of pan-Arabism. Saddam Hussein, who had recently started brandishing his chemical missiles at Israel, was the hero of the moment. Fears of a Zionist attack on Iraq, masterminded by "imperialism", were conjured up from nowhere. Egypt's President Hosni Mubarak was a lonely voice speaking out against the anti-western din.

After the invasion of Kuwait, everything changed. President Mubarak convened an emergency meeting of the League in Cairo. The League demanded an Iraqi withdrawal (breaking, in a token of things to come, a time-honoured *qawmiyya* rule that its decisions should be unanimous). Later Egypt arranged to return the organisation's headquarters from Tunis to Cairo, from where it had been withdrawn a decade earlier as a protest against Egypt's peace with Israel. Egypt spent a decade in exile from the League for having dared to go its own way in relations with Israel. Today the Egyptians are back in charge. Their own former foreign minister, Esmat Abdel-Meguid, is now the League's secretary-general.

After Baathism

The curious thing is that although the Egyptians have regained control of the Arab League, they are not hurrying to restore its influence. Instead, they are systematically stopping it from tackling issues of substance. As a body with a constitution that reflects the pan-Arab idea, and of which all Arab governments are members, the League has become an inconvenience. For the moment, the regimes that took the Kuwaiti side in the recent war—Egypt, Syria, Saudi Arabia and the Gulf sheikhdoms—are chiefly interested in consolidating their individual gains. Healing wounds and repairing Arab unity are not yet on the agenda.

Is an Arab world composed of self-assertive nation states going to be healthier than one spellbound by the idea of pan-Arabism? It may, at least, become more honest. In one sense pan-Arabism has been dead since the 1960s. Except for Libya's Moammar Qaddafi, no Arab leader since Nasser has striven seriously for the political unification of the Middle East. That is hardly surprising. Having gained control, often violently, of the "artificial" nations manufactured by colonialism, each regime

acquired a vested interest in preserving the system of states it felt obliged to disparage. To the extent that pan-Arabism lived on through the 1970s and 1980s, it was as an ideology to be waffled about rather than as a programme to be acted upon.

It was an ideology, however, which continued to have some practical consequences, most of them baleful. One was to magnify the conflict between the Arabs and their non-Arab enemies. In many countries, *qawmiyya* was used as a way to buttress the domestic standing of unelected regimes. Stirring talk about the grandeur of the larger Arab identity helped governments draw attention to external threats, such as imperialism and Zionism, and away from tribal and ethnic conflicts closer to home. It is no accident that the two countries which have taken pan-Arabism furthest are the Baathist regimes of Iraq and Syria. Both are despotisms wracked by sectarian splits—between Sunnis, Shias, Kurds and Alawites.

Baathists say they believe (remember Mr Aziz's letter) in the withering away of individual Arab states and the putting of pan-Arab interests above selfish ones. It is not surprising, after Mr Hussein's invasion of Kuwait, that this doctrine no longer delights his neighbours. Caring about a wider Arabhood is one thing; being trampled on in Arabhood's name by a bully is another. To defeat Mr Hussein the Gulf Arabs and their allies broke many of their own unwritten rules. One was accepting military help from the United States, Israel's friend. Their refusal to falter even after Mr Hussein fired his missiles at Israel was even more remarkable. Attacking Israel is the noblest action of the good pan-Arabist.

Some American officials interpret this falling apart of the pan-Arab creed as part of the new opportunity in the Middle East—analagous, in a way, to the collapse of communism in Europe. Having broken so many taboos in the course of the war, might not the Arabs now be readier to break another, by ending their policy of perpetual enmity to Israel? Perhaps. In the bad old days of *qawmiyya*, it took a self-confident Egypt to step out of the Arab consensus and reach an accommodation with Israel. Now the confidence of the countries that sided against Iraq has soared, and the "Arab consensus" no longer exists. This, it is true, has made a lot of governments receptive to previously unimaginable ideas. But the post-war re-ordering also has a darker side.

Pan-Arabism was a stultifying, anti-western dogma which helped to trap the Arabs in the past. What, though, if the backlash against *qawmiyya* is taken too far? Then the end of pan-Arabism might create a Middle East whose separate governments felt free to pursue their own narrow interests with a wilful contempt for the concerns of their neighbours. That would go against a trend in other parts of the world, where in the interests of prosperity countries are co-operating more with their neighbours and even pooling aspects of sovereignty. An Arab world whose separate governments adopted too narrow an interpretation of their self-interest could stir up dangerous resentments.

None for all

In a small way, it is starting to happen already. From Washington or London, the recent war can look like an uplifting episode. Kuwait was liberated; the world learnt that Americans and Arabs, Christians and Muslims, could fight shoulder-to-shoulder against a common enemy. From Riyadh or Baghdad it all seems different. Arabs associate the Gulf war with betrayal. Half the Arabs felt betrayed by Iraq's invasion of Kuwait, the other half by Iraq's eviction from Kuwait. The instinct of people who feel betrayed is revenge, not reconciliation. Some of the changes that have taken place since the war—changes in which outsiders are pleased to detect a new maturity in Arab politics—may amount to little more than the settling of scores.

Take the case of Saudi Arabia, probably the war's main beneficiary. The destruction of Iraq's military power, coming so soon after Iraq had destroyed Iran's, has probably removed for many years the danger of Saudi Arabia coming under attack by a foreign power. But, more than that, the war demonstrated for the first time that the kingdom possesses a usable defence guarantee from the United States. Since the war, President Bush has reiterated that the Gulf remains a "vital national interest" for America. A year ago the Saudi royal family had to agonise over whether to accept military help from the United States. Now it has emerged from the war bathed in self-confidence.

This is a considerable change. Saudi Arabia was once a byword for timidity in foreign affairs. Before the war, the kingdom used its oil wealth fairly indiscriminately as a way to buy off potential threats. It lavished Danegeld on Mr Arafat's PLO, helped Yemen, its poor but populous neighbour to south, and was a long-standing supporter of Jordan. The Saudis regarded Jordan's King Hussein (whose family's origins are in the Hejaz, in Saudi territory) as a kindred spirit, a trustworthy ally with pro-western instincts.

No longer. The Saudis feel betrayed by their former allies and are determined to mete out punishment. The PLO and Jordan have been crossed off the aid roster. Tens of thousands of Palestinians, Jordanians and Yemenis have been thrown out of their jobs in Saudi Arabia, and out of Saudi Arabia itself. Kuwaitis feel similarly vengeful. They have slashed the number of jobs for non-Kuwaiti citizens in the emirate. Before the war, fewer than one in three of the people living in Kuwait were formally Kuwaiti citizens. Now the government plans to reduce the number of foreign nationals to less than half the population. More than half of the nearly 400,000 Palestinians who lived in Kuwait before the war have fled or been pushed out.

The animus the Saudis and Kuwaitis feel towards Mr Arafat and King Hussein is easy to understand. During the war Palestinians, Jordanians and Yemenis came to be seen as pro-Iraqi fifth columnists. Maybe a few really were. But western governments are trying to persuade the Saudis that the revenge being exacted on them is both disproportionate and counter-productive. The

Americans, too, felt let down by King Hussein during the war, and showed their anger by cutting off the aid Jordan had been receiving from the United States. Later, though, the Americans accepted that, for all his weaknesses, King Hussein had a contribution to make to Arab-Israeli peacemaking. If he fell from power, Jordan could fall into the hands of militant Islamists, or Palestinians committed to endless war with Israel.

America and Britain want Saudi Arabia to forgive the king his wartime transgressions, as they have. But it is easier to be magnanimous from far away. To date, the Saudis have been unreceptive. They say that their grievance against King Hussein goes too deep to be casually revoked. Some top Saudis continue to believe that the king was party to an Iraqi conspiracy to dismember their own country. For evidence, they point to the king's revival, before the war, of his Hashemite family's old title as the *sharifs* of Mecca, inside Saudi Arabia. This hurt, because the Saudi royals take their own job as the custodians of Mecca intensely seriously. The allegation that King Hussein was part of an Iraqi plot against Saudi Arabia is almost certainly nonsense. But forgiveness is not nigh.

Enter the Damascus Eight

The climate of revenge has not been kind to regional institutions in the Middle East. The Arab League is neutered, the Arab Co-operation Council (whose members were Egypt, Jordan, Iraq and Yemen) has disappeared. Into the vacuum has stepped an informal alliance consisting of the eight Arab countries that took the anti-Iraqi side in the war. Six are the members of the Gulf Co-operation Council (Saudi Arabia, Kuwait and the other Gulf sheikhdoms). The others are Syria and Egypt. This alliance of victors has come to be known as the Damascus Eight, after a declaration their leaders issued from the Syrian capital in March, shortly after the end of the war.

At the time, the Damascus Declaration was taken to herald the birth of a new alignment of forces in the Arab world. The Americans viewed it with favour. Marrying the military muscle of populous Syria and Egypt to the money of the underpopulated Gulf sheikhdoms looked like a logical way to organise the Middle East. A defence agreement between the military two and the moneyed six would help keep the Arabian peninsula's oil safe from future predators. It might also provide a mechanism by which to redistribute some of the wealth of the Arab world. Better still, it would lock the previously hostile Syrians into a closer relationship with Egypt and Saudi Arabia, America's most intimate Arab allies.

The trouble with self-confidence

The logic of the Damascus Declaration, although it looks elegant enough on paper, has been hard to put into practice. Syria and Egypt may want to portray themselves as the defenders of the Gulf Arabs. They certainly expect to be rewarded for doing so. But this expectation bumps awkwardly against the new self-confidence of Saudi Arabia. During the war it was useful for the Saudis to exaggerate the part played by the Syrian and Egyptian expeditionary forces. That helped to undermine Mr Hussein's claim that the battle for Kuwait was a war between Islam and the West. But everybody knows that the real military job was done by the United States, and the Saudis no longer feel the need to pretend otherwise. They are confident that their American partnership, plus a plan to double the size of their own armed forces, add up to a perfectly adequate security arrangement for the Gulf.

From a strictly military point of view, the Saudis are probably right. Indeed, some GCC countries feel that turning the Damascus Eight into a defence organisation could add to, rather than diminish, the region's insecurity. The Omanis calculate that the continued presence of Syrian and Egyptian forces in the Gulf will damage relations with Iran, the unpredictable giant just across the water. The Gulf monarchies are particularly unhappy about the idea of large numbers of Syrian officers staying on, lest they infect the local soldiery with their wild republican notions. Egyptian soldiers pose less of a worry, except that Egypt may have exaggerated ideas about the economic compensation it deserves for keeping its troops in the peninsula.

Without pressure from the Americans, the idea of a defence pact might have collapsed completely. Kuwait, in particular, would like to depend for its defence on forces from Britain and America. But the United States, eager to avoid an open-ended defence commitment in the Gulf, continues to push for some sort of inter-Arab defence arrangement. Last July the Damascus Eight held a meeting in Kuwait in an attempt to reach a compromise. It adjourned without agreement. In the end, the Gulf Arabs will probably let a token force of Egyptians and Syrians be stationed on the territory of individual GCC members who invite them. Kuwait will have its own bilateral defence arrangement with America. This muddle is a far cry from the "regional security structure" President Bush listed as one of his main post-war goals.

As so often in the Middle East, the argument about the defence of the Gulf is, at least in part, really an argument about something else. It is about how to put the political and economic relationship between the richer and poorer parts of the Arab world on a surer footing.

When Mr Hussein invaded Kuwait, he exposed an unpalatable truth about the Middle East. In the northern tier of the Arab world—Syria, Iraq, Egypt and Jordan—most people heartily dislike their oil-rich cousins from the Arabian peninsula. On balance, Arab public opinion during the Gulf probably sympathised more with Mr Hussein than with his Kuwaiti victims. At times, Kuwait had dished out large sums in aid to fellow Arabs (4% of its GDP in 1982), yet had earned a widespread reputation for being haughty and selfish. During the war, Mr Hussein exploited the envy northern Arabs felt towards the Gulf. Iraq itself has oil reserves second in size only to Saudi Arabia's, but this did not stop Mr Hussein from convincing millions of Arabs outside the Gulf that he was a Muslim Robin Hood who had stolen Kuwait only in order to give out its riches to the Arab poor.

The charge of miserliness infuriates GCC governments. Some have a history of making generous transfers to their neighbours. In addition, for more than 20 years, they have opened their doors to migrant workers from all over the Arab world, enabling them to remit salaries home and so benefit from the Gulf's oil bonanza. Since the war, the GCC maintains, it has continued to show exemplary generosity. For taking an anti-Iraqi line during the war Syria has already received about $2 billion from the Gulf (money it promptly spent on weapons) and Egypt has had debts cancelled. There will probably be more help to come, if the GCC goes ahead with a plan for a special $10 billion development fund.

Winners and losers

This is something, but not nearly enough to wash away the mountain of resentment that has come to divide rich Arabs from poor. Indeed, the mountain will probably grow taller in the war's aftermath. The war was expensive, and the oil price is flat, which means that there will be less wealth to spread around. Meanwhile Yemenis, Jordanians and Palestinians are locked out of the victors' Middle East. Their leaders are not welcome inside the Damascus Eight, their workers are no longer welcome in the Gulf. The newly assertive Saudis are in no mood to pay large sums to Syria and Egypt for contributing a token force to the Gulf's defence. Saudi Arabia intends to give out less money in government-to-government grants, more in grants for particular projects that happen to meet with its approval.

In the post-war Arab order the Saudis will be throwing their weight around more and their money about less. They have every right to do this, and their confidence fits in well with the decline of *qawmiyya* as a force in the region's politics. No need to mourn pan-Arabism: it helped launch dictators into foolish wars. But what a pity it would be if the price of its passing came to be an Arab world ever more divided against itself.

Article 4   THE NEW REPUBLIC **AUGUST 12, 1991**

A personal and political odyssey.

THE END OF ARAB NATIONALISM

Fouad Ajami

FOUAD AJAMI teaches at the School of Advanced International Studies of the Johns Hopkins University.

It is now a little more than half a century ago that George Antonius (an Alexandria-born Greek Orthodox writer of Palestinian background) published his manifesto, *The Arab Awakening.* All the grand themes of Arab nationalism were foreshadowed in Antonius's work: the "secularism" of the Arab nationalist movement, the primacy of the Pan-Arab movement over "smaller" loyalties, the fragmentation of that movement at the hands of the colonial powers, and the presumed centrality of the Palestinian question to the entire Arab world. Antonius wrote with an Anglo-American audience in mind. That too continues to devil the proponent of Arab nationalism: the narrative nationalist history with its gaze fixed on the outside world, petitioning, alternating between a search for foreign patrons and an equally frenzied search for foreign scapegoats and demons.

Today, the children of Antonius are adrift. On the first anniversary of Saddam Hussein's invasion of Kuwait, the edifice they built is in ruins. In Saddam, the "Arab awakening" hatched a monster. With his cruel bid for an imperium in Iraq's image, the Arabs were to witness what the Arab national movement had wrought.

The defects of the Arab nationalist narrative should have been all too easy to see. The kind of world men and women bumped into when they stepped out of the abstract texts of Arab nationalism—the world of daily experience—was nowhere to be found in the works of the Arab nationalist historiography. Some years ago, when I began to grope my way out of this historiography, I read an influential book of that genre, *Arabic Thought in the Liberal Age* by Albert Hourani. But in truth there had been no liberal age in Arab politics. "Reason is helpless before the fist," the great Russian writer Alexander Herzen had written about Russian liberalism and its fragility. And Reason had proved helpless in the Arab world. The ground under the feet of liberalism cracked over and over again.

I.

I was born in the hinterland of Lebanon in 1945. My people broke out of my remote birthplace into the city of Beirut in the late 1940s. But that world stuck to our fingers. My great-grandfather had come from Tabriz in Iran to a remote hamlet in south Lebanon, sometime in the mid-1850s. The years covered the trail that my great-grandfather had traveled. The Persian connection was severed, but was given away in the name by which he became known in his new home: Dahir Ajami, Dahir the Persian. No pamphleteers or authors who celebrated the "Arab awakening" ventured near my stern, impoverished ancestral village on the Lebanese-Israeli border.

To my early work on modern Arab politics I must have brought the truth bequeathed me by the small Shiite world I had been born into. The Shiites were the stepchildren of the Arab world. In its principal cities they were strangers, a people of the countryside. To its (Sunni) orthodox, they were sectarians. Modern Arab nationalism never quite accommodated them. My elders inhabited a world of private concerns: the land my grandfather owned, the price of tobacco paid out by the tobacco monopoly, the money to be made in Liberia and Sierra Leone by my uncles and aunts.

I, on the other hand, came into my own in the public world of Beirut. I was the beneficiary of the struggle of the preceding generation—the passage to Beirut, the money made in faraway places. I grew up in the atmosphere of Muslim West Beirut. Across the line—a cable car ride away, in Christian East Beirut—there was an entirely different sensibility: the Maronite mountain with its ethos of independence, and its sense of being set apart from the Muslim world around it. The Maronites had a strong sense of themselves; they had their formidable clergy, their own schools, traffic with Europe, special ties to France. They possessed a special history—the flight of their ancestors from the (oppressed) plains of Syria in the seventh century to the freedom of Mount Lebanon. Their history was not mine.

I was formed by an amorphous Arab nationalist sensibility. There was the shadow of the Egyptian Gamal Abdel Nasser that lay over the Muslims of Lebanon. There was the drama of the struggle over Palestine—between Arab and Jew, and the pull of the Palestinian cause. The Egyptian leader who came to dominate our world in West Beirut—really in Muslim Lebanon as a whole—had made the cause of Palestine his rallying cry. The towns and villages of Mandatory Palestine were a veritable extension of my ancestral land in south Lebanon. For my elders a fight had taken place between *Arab Filastin* (the Arab of Palestine) and *al Yahud* (the Jews). The Palestinians had lost. That tale was told as men and women spoke of calamities and weather, of the yield of particular harvests.

My family bore the Palestinians no particular animus. Nor did they think that their ordeal was of great concern to us. (The animus would come much later, in the 1970s, when the Palestinians would overrun my mother's beloved town of Khiam and gun down many of her large clan.) My mother had her small world and the stark sensibility of her peasant world. *Al Dahr Ghaddar,* fate was vengeful; it played with the lives of men, and fate had dealt the Palestinians what it had. For my generation the struggle that had played itself out in Palestine was transformed and made political and grand, part of our burden. We knew precious little of what had actually happened during the fight between Arab and Jew. We could not claim that history. (That awaited the new Zionist histories. There were no reliable accounts, no archives or honest diaries.) We knew that the "traitors" were punished—that King Abdullah of Jordan was murdered, that King Farouk of Egypt was packed off to exile. We thought that the "new men" would annul the weakness and the shame of the past. The "traditional" world was declared dead and buried. Such were the threads out of which the politics of my generation were made.

It was out of this material—the promise of Arab nationalism and Nasserism, and then the undoing of that era—that I wrote my first book, from afar, in the United States. Several years later, in the mid-1980s, I embarked on a different enterprise. The Shiite world I knew in Lebanon—the small villages and towns passed over by history and large events, the Shiite slums on the outskirts of Beirut—had risen in rebellion. The Iranian revolution had spilled into Lebanon. It had given a timid population a sense of their own worth. The Shiite tradition of quietism and political withdrawal was being remade. I had struggled to go beyond the world of my kinsmen. Now I had set out on an intellectual return of my own. That was the gift of America to me. I was willing to look into that Shiite past.

I found an instrument: the life of the Iranian-born mullah, Imam Musa al Sadr. I decided to write a biography of him. Sadr had come into the small world of the Shiites of Lebanon in 1959; he "disappeared" in Libya, in 1978, while on a visit to its leader Muammar al Qaddafi. I had seen Musa al Sadr only once in my boyhood. He had come to visit my school in West Beirut in 1963. A Persian-born Shiite cleric was anathema to me at the time, to my claim to "Arabism," my place in the city, my very "modernity." But the tall, striking-looking cleric who was born in Qom to a religious family of high calling had gone on to fame and power. He survived the hostility of young, nervous assimilies like myself. An intensely political man, he had transformed the Shiites of Lebanon. He gave his followers some of his daring. Years before Ayatollah Khomeini emerged as the "armed Imam," the handsome young cleric fashioned out of the symbols of Shiism a new politics of commitment and activism.

A drawn-out battle for West Beirut and for the Shiite ancestral lands in south Lebanon ensued between the Shiites and remnants of the Palestine Liberation Organization. In the mid-1970s the Palestinians had overrun much of the ancestral land of the Shiites. They had established a turf of their own. It was an uneven fight: the Palestinians had the resources extended to them by the Arab state; they had behind them the weight of Arab nationalism and the primacy it gave the issue of Palestine. But the Israeli invasion of 1982 had transformed the political landscape in Beirut and in south Lebanon. It shattered the Palestinian sanctuary and thus served as the midwife of a Shiite bid for power. Emboldened, the Shiites now struck at the Palestinians.

The "war of the camps" between the Palestinians and the Shiites raged in the spring of 1985. My book about Musa al Sadr was released in 1986. The lines were drawn. The book was a work of biography, but only in part. Through the life of Musa al Sadr, I had written of the grievances of the people he had led in Lebanon. On their way out of self-contempt the Shiites had clashed with the Palestinians and with West Beirut's traditional Sunni elites. A city once pampered and precious had fallen to the rabble. The reign of the Palestinian gunmen and the leftist parties that had diminished the world of West Beirut and its notables had been passed off as the reign of "progressive" men. The coming of age of a Shiite underclass was depicted as a dawn of a new age of barbarism. To challenge this was to run afoul of classes and men who had taken their ascendancy over West Beirut as a birthright. That, too, now lay between me and the upholders of the Arab nationalist orthodoxy.

I had marked myself in yet another way. A few years earlier, in 1980, I had gone to Israel and was to visit the country many times in the intervening years. I had an academic pretext: I did Middle Eastern work and it made sense for me to go. But a stronger motivation took me there. I was intensely curious about the Israelis and their world. The land of Israel lay just across the border from my ancestral village in south Lebanon. At night, a searchlight from the Israeli town of Metullah could be seen from the high ridge on which my village lay. The searchlight was a subject of childhood fascination. The searchlight was from the land of the Jews, my grandfather said. The oral history transmitted to me by my grandfather—we possessed no written records, no diaries—was of places now on the other side of a great barrier: Safa, Acre, Tiberias. They were places of my grandfather's memory. About these places, and about Metullah, I retained within me an unrelenting sense of curiosity.

My first crossing to Israel in 1980 was by land from Jordan, over the Allenby Bridge. It would have been too brave, too forthright to fly into Israel. I covered up my first passage by pretending that I had come to the West Bank. Northern Israel had been a stone's throw from my ancestral village and the neighboring villages of my kinsmen. Smugglers would slip there and come back with tales of Israel. In the open, barren country, by the border, that land of the Jews could be seen and the chatter of its people heard across the barbed wire. Over the years, though, it had become a forbidden land. Venturing there (even with an American passport) still had the feel of something illicit about it.

I knew a good many of the country's academics and journalists. I had met them in America, and they were eager to tutor me about their country. Gradually the country opened to me. I didn't know Hebrew; there was only so much of Israeli life that was accessible to me. But the culture of its universities, the intensity of its intellectual debates would soon strip me of the nervousness with which I had initially approached the place. The Palestinian story was not mine. I could thus see Israel on its own terms. I was free to take in the world that the Zionist project had brought forth. Above all, I think I had wanted to understand and interpret Arab society without the great alibi that Israel had become for every Arab failing under the sun. In a curious way, my exposure to Israel was essential to my coming to terms with Arab political life and its material.

II.

There was something odd as the 1980s drew to a close: the dominant historiography written by the Arab nationalists and their "foreign friends" was emptied of any truth. Reality stared it in the face. The carnage and the waste had wreaked havoc on the Arab world. From West Beirut and from the American University of Beirut, which was home to an active Palestinian contingent of academics and publicists, the literati and the scribes had taken to the road—to Paris and London, to Washington, D.C. It was getting harder to conceal and to apologize. But the dominant historiography knew no other way. It could not bear to look outside itself. It had its text, its masters, its beneficiaries. The exiles who fled the terrors of Beirut walked into liberal, open societies. Away from the hell, they fell back on the old truths.

You would have thought that the great troubles—the carnage in Beirut and in the Syrian city of Hama, the bankruptcy of the Palestinian movement, the defection of the Egyptian state from the anti-Israeli assignment given it by Arab nationalists—would have shaken the confidence of the Pan-Arabists. But they pushed on. Vanity—and a good deal of their politics is vanity and wounded pride—was too deep. An Arab historian with American citizenship was lifted out of Beirut in the summer of 1982 by the U.S. Embassy; he arrived on America's shores to rail against American imperialism and to offer up the old pieties. Christian Arabs who in private expressed deep fears of the "Muslim tide" stepped out into the public domain to speak of the "progressive" role of the Islamic movement, to praise its "anti-imperialist character." The failings of that world could not be acknowledged or named. They were written off as the sins of the Orientalists and the failings of American policy. The rage against America was the other side of the dependence and of the failure. It was hard for the Arab nationalists to acknowledge the simple facts of postcolonial life: that men beget the history they deserve, that Arab life is what the Arabs have made of it.

Then, in the summer of 1990, there arrived Arab nationalism's moment of truth: Saddam's storming of Kuwait. There were deadly ideas and delusions in the Arab world. The Iraqi despot plucked them at will, turned them into weapons of his own. He did not emerge out of a void. The culture's sins of omission and commission had converged to make him into the predator he became. He was a son, and a favored son at that. Secularism, Arab unity, the promise of a new center of Arab power, the atavistic spirit of the folk, and the prerogatives of the dominant Sunni stratum—all these were Saddam's to manipulate. The Iraqi despot offered himself to the imagination of the thwarted: a strongman who could hold off the challenge of the "fire-worshiping Persians" to the east and who, in time, would stand up to the "Zionist entity" by the Mediterranean. In a culture of words, he seemed like a man of his deeds. His admirers—Arabs and some foreign enthusiasts as well—dwelled on his record as a "nation builder": the emancipation of women, the urbanization of the country, the drop in infant mortality. On the banks of the Tigris, the admirers said, a powerful Arab state was being built, an alternative to the feeble Egyptian state that had slipped into the American orbit.

That Saddam was a murderer at home was of little concern to the Arab intelligentsia who saw him as an answer for the ills and weaknesses of his world. By the time he swept into Kuwait, Saddam Hussein had behind him two decades of cruel deeds. But the cruelty of the man never troubled the pamphleteers and ideologues. The end—some dream of national power—justified the means.

It should have taken no great literacy in strategic

matters to guess that Saddam's bid for mastery over the Gulf would end in defeat and ruin, that its outcome would be a replay of the Six-Day War of 1967, that the Arabs who took a ride with the Iraqi dictator were in for another great betrayal. A society that lived through that ordeal of 1967 should have been immune to another pied piper: the Egyptian rockets that didn't fire, the air force that was destroyed on the ground, the promised rendezvous in Tel Aviv that had turned into a monumental Arab defeat, the barefoot Egyptian soldiers lost in the Sinai desert. And above all the Maximum Leader at the time, Gamal Abdel Nasser, offering that incredible explanation of the defeat: Israel had attacked from the west when he had expected the attack to come from the east and the north. But a quarter century later, in a culture susceptible to legend and to the promise of the strongman, there was another peddler of delusions. The false gifts of the dictators: for these gifts there were ample takers.

It would be tempting to see the "Guns of August 1990" as a great rupture in Arab politics. Instead of the old evasions, there would be an honest reckoning with things as they really are. Men would give political matters their right names. In the fantasy of a world chastened by the ordeal it has just gone through, the written word would descend into the lives of men. It would name things with some clarity and precision. It would acknowledge the bankruptcy of Arab nationalism. The Arab exiles would tell the truth as to why they left the old world behind; their writings would incorporate the fact of their exile and its meaning.

In the fantasy Arabs would leave behind the scapegoating and the search for alibis that have marked so much of what they have written and said over the last three to four decades. The verdict of the struggle between Israeli and Palestinian would be accepted. No love need be extended the Jewish state—just live and let live. The Arab political mind would simply wander away from Israel. The dominant Arab historiography—closed, sure of itself, bearing the dead weight that demagogues and scribes have burdened it with—would pass from the scene. That terrifying power of *Takhwin* (the power to declare other men traitors) that the enforcers have allocated to themselves would be broken. The hooded men who knock at the door at dawn, in Nablus and Ramallah, would no longer be "children of the stones" meting out justice, but cruel players in the Night of the Long Knives.

It will not be easy. On pain of extinction, cultures often stubbornly refuse to look into themselves. They retreat into the nooks and crannies of their received history, offer up the standard evasions, fall back on the consolations they know. The war in the Gulf was a battle between a local despot and a foreign savior. In the scheme of such things, it was quick and decisive. Men did not really have to change to be rescued; the rescue came from afar. This leaves open all sorts of possible

escapes. Those who fell for Kuwait's conqueror could claim that they were misunderstood, that they were only patriots responding to the coming to the Arab world of yet another Western army. Or they could plead distress and "mitigating circumstances": we were oppressed, we had only wanted to be heard, there was no place for us in the "new world order" the foreigner came to uphold. In other words, Saddam could be thwarted (almost) but the sensibility and the moral outlook from which he fed could survive.

Still, there are some hopeful signs of a break with that long trail of delusions. "The dream of the intifada has become a nightmare," a Palestinian activist, Adnan Damiri, recently wrote in *Al-Fajr*, the PLO-sponsored daily paper on the West Bank. Poems had been written in praise of "the stone" and the children of the stones. The stone building a bright new world and disposing of the old weaknesses. The dark side of the intifada—the revolution devouring its own children, the reign of terror and virtue against "collaborators" that has taken a toll of some 400 lives—was brushed aside. Palestinian society has been here before. The Arab Rebellion of 1936-39 was consumed by its own fury. Then, too, an initial euphoria gave way to indiscriminate terror and recriminations and the hunt for collaborators. After the stones were thrown the world stood still: worse yet for the Palestinians, their condition—their economic and educational standards—had deteriorated over the course of the intifada. The work of the "founding fathers" of the Palestinian movement—the exiled leadership of the PLO in Tunis, the intellectuals who front for the PLO—has led to ruin. Out of the exhibitionism and the bravado and the delusions of their leaders the Palestinians had come out empty-handed.

Arab society had indulged the Palestinians for some four decades. Cynicism toward the cause of the Palestinians and its standard-bearers there was aplenty. But at the end of the day there came the indulgence. This was the logic of the tribal feud between Arab and Jew. Clearly this now belongs to the past. The daring with which the Lebanese (and the Syrians behind them) went about dismantling what remains of the Palestinian sanctuary in Lebanon is as good an indication as any of the new state of things in the Arab world. No one came to the rescue of the Palestinians. The Egyptian intellectual class (traditionally a pillar of support for the Palestinians) was virtually silent. No Kuwaitis or Saudis threatened to cut off funds and aid from those storming Palestinian positions. The lands of the Gulf and the Peninsula had wearied of the affairs of the Palestinians, and of the slogans and pamphlets of Arab nationalism. To the world of the "desert men" has come a new sense of confidence in the path they have chosen, a great sense of vindication that they have been spared the turmoil and the ruin of the "city Arabs" to their north. The deference to those who had produced and quoted the texts of Arab nationalism and spun its symbols has vanished from the lands of the Gulf.

III.

I went to Kuwait three months after its liberation, a country betrayed by the very deities it had sought to propitiate. Kuwaitis had paid homage to Arab nationalism; they had made much of the cause of the Palestinians. To see the country again for the first time after its calamity was to come face to face with the bitterness of that betrayal. The old headquarters of the PLO—what was once the center of a state within a state—is gutted. The graffiti on the walls damn Yasir Arafat and Saddam Hussein as "traitors." The building that housed the Palestinian Federation of Women is boarded up. The Hawali district, the Palestinian quarter in Kuwait City, seems like a marked place. Among Kuwaitis of every stripe, the bonds with the Palestinians have been shattered. In place of the old Pan-Arabism there is an attachment to American power and to an American presence. American missionaries had once built a hospital in Kuwait City. The building is run down and decayed. There had been plans to bulldoze it. "This will stay now," a Kuwaiti friend guiding me through the city said. "It might yet be restored."

There remain the last citadels of Arab nationalism—exile communities of intellectuals in France and the United States, and to a lesser extent in Britain. Like fortresses at the end of the road that are yet to receive the dispatches that all is lost and the battle is over, these fortresses fight on. The old, tattered flags are unfurled. All the orthodoxies of the "Arab awakening" are still upheld. The children of Nablus are celebrated by the exiles, those of Basra left to the tender mercies of the monster at the helm of the Iraqi state. From distant lands the Arab world can be all that the exiles wish it to be. From these distant shores you could flail at the Americans and the French and the British and the Zionists. A story could be told of a world that was whole and pretty and "progressive," and was then done in by cruel powers. All that the Arabs did to themselves is edited out of the narrative.

But the story that matters unfolds down river, as it were: in the Arab lands themselves. And there even those who yesterday partook of the old legends—spread them, paid homage to them—are beginning to acknowledge the great disorder the old ways had wrought. My favorite example is Souad Al Sabah, a member of the ruling family of Kuwait. A few years earlier she had been something of a cheerleader for Saddam Hussein during the Iran-Iraq war. She had written a well-known poem, which at the time turned no heads, in praise of the "Iraqi sword." Back then the "Iraqi sword" was hacking away at Persians and Kurds and others who fell beyond the lines of the clan and folk. After Saddam's barbarism against her birthplace, she wrote a poignant new poem, "Who Killed Kuwait?" It is a long poem; I'll offer only a sample (a rough translation) of it:

Who killed Kuwait?
The Killer did not descend from the sky
or emerge from a world of dreams
Didn't we all take part in the chorus of the Regime?

Didn't we all applaud the master of the Regime?
Didn't we all make pretty the mistakes of the rulers
with the sweetest of words, with the most deceitful of words
Didn't we all march like sheep in the caravan of the rulers?

He who killed Kuwait is our own flesh and blood
He is the embodiment of all our ways.
We made him in accord with our own measurements.
No one can say "no."
We all participated in the crime
We all took part in the making of the devil
We all applauded the tyrants and tyranny
We can't complain about our idols.
Was not the making of idols our profession?

In the Arab world "after the storm," these new words of Souad al Sabah would stick and be taken to heart. Were Arabs to turn a corner and still meet the past again, the terrible ordeal of Kuwait and its lessons would have been for naught. When the moral calamity of writing a poem in praise of the "Iraqi sword" is fully assimilated we shall have a better Arab world. In that world the dissident would cease to be a demon. "You go not till I set you up a glass, where you may see the inmost part of you," Hamlet says to his mother. From Baghdad there came out, in the summer of 1990, the most peculiar bearer of a glass. He did not quite know what he was doing, but he held up a glass to the Arabs all the same. It would be no fault of the bearer of the glass if the Arabs refused to look and to see. ●

Article 5

Middle East Report • January-February 1992

Rally in Jordan protesting US policy towards Iraq.

Human Rights and Elusive Democracy

Ahmed Abdalla

Ahmed Abdalla is the author of The Student Movement and National Politics in Egypt *(London: Al-Saqi, 1985), and editor of* The Army and Democracy in Egypt *[in Arabic] (Cairo, 1990) and* Egyptian History: Between the Scientific Approach and Party Politics *[in Arabic] (Cairo, 1988).*

The practice of human rights cannot wait until all political systems have become democratic. Human rights, in their vast range, can be protected under non-democratic regimes and violated under democratic ones. Still, human rights and democracy, though not interchangeable, can form the most humane relationship of all.

In the global trend towards neo-liberalism, the Middle East is no exception. The situation is not stagnant. Something is happening here, too. But it is a matter of measure. It is not the swift change we have seen in Eastern Europe; it is in the same direction but not in the same proportion. The simple observation of the trend is no reason for complacency. The actual scores attained in the broad realm of democratic change remain subject to assessment, and a difficult one at that.

Four avenues help to trace what has taken place. First, a study of the dialectics of form and content can gauge the substance and significance of formal adoption of such items of democracy as constitutions, elections, parliaments, parties and a free press. Their introduction, restoration or reformation may mean little change in structures, despite the glossy paper on which they are advertised. Ignored constitutions, rigged elections, silent parliaments, harassed parties and an information-starved press offer little ground for speaking seriously of democracy. Restrictions on the establishment of political parties, especially for existing movements and de facto parties, deprive democracy of one key ingredient. An example is the Egyptian authorities' adamant refusal to legitimize parties for the Islamist, Nasirist and communist movements, which are the most active in the country's political life.[1] The attitude of the Tunisian authorities towards their Islamist movement, al-Nahda, is similar.[2] But what is more significant about the neo-liberal experiments of Middle Eastern countries is the fact that a transfer of power is not contemplated. Algeria, the only country in the region where events have forced such a possibility, is under some outside pressure not to let this happen.[3]

Secondly, a study of the dialectics of past and present, by examining the inertia of daily practices of despotism, tells how little a measure of democracy most countries in the Middle East have attained. Such a study suggests the prospects of sustainable democracy in this part of the world. Present attempts at democratizing regimes are hampered by anti-democratic ideas and deeds in daily life, at different levels of politics and society.

Thirdly, a study of the dialectics of elites and masses can outline a code of conduct between the two, on the basis of accountability and responsibility. The broadening of democratic processes should benefit both rulers and ruled. In neo-liberal regimes of the Middle East, the elites are benefiting disproportionately. The opposition elite is less harassed than before, and has better opportunity for self-expression. Certain circles are allowed to be very critical of governments: opposition parties within their headquarters, the opposition press within its limited circulation, university professors within their auditoriums. But there has been no such allowance at the level of street politics. The more popular instruments for expression—e.g., television and workers' and students' movements—are more tightly controlled. At police stations or government departments, ordinary citizens may not detect any difference.

Fourthly, a study of the dialectics of the whole and the part indicates that implantation of fragmented items of democracy does not necessarily provide a democratic whole. It could mean merely a change in technique, from wholesale to piecemeal authoritarianism. Regimes can be more selective in imprisoning political opponents, minimizing adverse reactions and fostering democratic pretensions. This is what actually happens in the Middle East.

It may be idealistic to seek in the Middle East, over a short period of time, a democracy that is substantive, devoid of despotism, popular, and complete. Foundations for this are not sufficient.[4] The Egyptian journalist Ahmed Baha-eddin has often reminded his readers that what exists is "pluralism" rather than "democracy"; is the first leading to the second?

How appropriate is it to use the term "democracy" to describe these neo-liberal regimes of the Middle East? It should be at least qualified as "elusive" democracy. Democracy itself is a relative proposition. The French prime minister, Michel Rocard, said in 1989 that the aim of his government was to establish "the democracy of daily life"—exactly 200 years after the French Revolution.

These elusive democracies furnish the paradoxical example of holding more elections but providing less selection to choose from. In Egypt and Tunisia, for example, the heads of state changed the constitution to allow them unlimited terms in office. The quasi-monopolistic position of their ruling parties is untouched.

These regimes provide another paradoxical example of wider representation coupled with narrower participation. While the number of political parties represented in parliament and political life has generally increased, people's participation in elections and politics has generally decreased. Under these regimes flagrant violations of human rights may be more subtle. The few who are imprisoned now endure the torture assigned to both them and their colleagues outside. Perhaps this amounts to an application of the Egyptian proverb: Hit hard the ones in chains; the free ones will be deterred. In many cases, physical torture has given way to forms of punishment that have long-run consequences, such as dismissal or transfer from work, affecting income.

The apparent democracy of Middle Eastern regimes is inherently fragile, endangered from within and from without. Its weak foundations at home are worsened by the pressures of economic crisis. It is also threatened at the borders—by regional conflicts over Palestine, the Persian Gulf, the Sahara, southern Sudan and the rest. Some regimes, like Morocco and Jordan, have tried to broaden the national consensus by coupling support for external conflicts to a measure of political liberalization. Others pull the curtain on democracy by invoking the old slogan: No voice should be louder than the voice of the battle.

A clear setback has taken place in Sudan, and earlier pronouncements on pluralism in Syria and Iraq have come to an abrupt end. Before being invaded, Kuwait hesitated to expand political participation beyond the royal family, and the rest of the Gulf remained dormant. The principle of non-interference in the affairs of neighboring countries was used to isolate the relatively more democratic countries. The poorer countries raised the slogan of democracy while the rich ones did not need to add it to their wealth. Understandably, the needy turned a blind eye to human rights violations by the wealthy whose assistance they sought. Such was the case of Egypt vis-à-vis the Iraqi regime, as Baghdad was bombing its Kurdish population with chemical weapons and harassing Egyptians working in Iraq. Democracy has no regional power to advocate and defend it. None has had the luxury to do so.

The second Gulf war, which broke out while the victims and costs of the first had hardly been counted, effectively arrested the slow progress of democratization in the region. Autocratic handling of the situation became the order of the day. The irony is clear in the case of a country like Egypt, which was caught by these events while its parliament was under dissolution and its cabinet busy negotiating the repayment of debts. President Mubarak formulated all policy and took all decisions. The scope for opposing official policy was narrowed to two weekly opposition journals; all daily press, weekly magazines, radio and television supported official policy.[5]

Human rights were affected in two ways. Besides people killed, injured, pillaged, raped and displaced, tens of thousands of foreign workers, especially Asians, escaped Kuwait and other countries, leaving their property behind and having to wait for weeks in border areas under appalling conditions until they found transport home. Most Europeans and Americans, those not taken hostage by the Iraqi authorities, had easier access home.[6]

Secondly, human rights became an issue in the propaganda war between adversaries. Baghdad was not only denounced for its violations of human rights during the war but for its long-standing record on this count. Egyptians remembered Iraq's earlier victims, and everybody remembered the Kurds. The Iraqis, in their turn, reminded their adversaries of the Palestinians under Israeli siege, and of the Lebanese under Israeli and Syrian siege.

This war proved useful in one way. By exposing the scope of destruction to which despotic rule can lead, the limits of democracy of the alleged democrats and the fragility of regimes with oil as the sole property, it is challenging peoples of the region to find for themselves more valid regimes. The solid establishment of democracy and the preservation of human rights are clearly becoming the core of debate aimed at facing the challenge.

Human rights work might thus face good prospects, but so far it has been a precarious task, if not a nasty ordeal, which begins with controversy over the very meaning of human rights.[7] On a practical note, the conditions of elusive democracy and regional instability require human rights workers to make themselves less elusive and more stable. To prove their impartiality, human rights workers have tended to present themselves as apolitical. This reflects a pragmatic sense of service to the cause, and a reluctance to divert energy into areas of political controversy.

Such thinking is misguided. Human rights workers, many of whom are past and present activists of various political movements, need no façade or camouflage to present their case and defend their cause—neither the apolitical mask nor the legalist and judicial blanket with which they often cover themselves. The human rights movement is a political movement par excellence, and it should courageously present itself as such. It should advertise itself as the largest reservoir of consensus politics, where all political movements are represented and their activists are capable of surpassing their differences to uphold a common cause.

To argue their cause, human rights activists require a measure of political education commensurate to the requirements of the political context within which they act. They require training in the skills of political debate. The use of legal instruments should be seen as one of the political tools with which to hammer at human rights issues. Human rights organizations should be seen as broad-based "democratic fronts" rather than solely as offices of legal or humanitarian assistance (though this type of assistance should remain one of their primary tasks, to which they recruit the support of other

movements, political and non-political). As political movements, human rights organizations must aim to be masters of objectivity and efficiency in speech and action.

With the scale of national violations and regional war tragedies in the Middle East, the defense of rights is a large enterprise, requiring resources and capabilities. One task is to devise how the human rights movement in the Middle East can claim its share of oil wealth. The finances of the movement cannot continue relying on small, unsteady, individual donations. The Arab Organization for Human Rights should be envious of the Arab Thought Forum in Amman, which gets donations from banks and companies to hold intellectual encounters. Alternative finances could include local and national taxes for human rights work and collective dues paid by all political organizations which benefit from the work of human rights organizations. Donations and payments should not translate into oversight. Human rights organizations should reserve the right to criticize the violations of members and donors, as well as the violations of victims who become perpetrators.[8] Financing ought to be similar to that at the UN, where members are obligated to pay dues even though they might disagree with the resolutions.

Finally, the enterprise of human

rights is multifaceted. Human rights work entails a great deal of research, education, legal defense, humanitarian relief and political campaigning. It encompasses local, national, regional and international dimensions. The juxtaposition of these dimensions—mass apathy at the local level, power struggles at the national level, territorial claims at the regional level and claims of dominance at the international level—is what makes human rights work a complex matter in the Arab world, despite the apparent simplicity of the task.

Footnotes

1 See "Forces Disallowed Legitimacy," in *Arab Strategic Report 1988* (Cairo: Center for Political and Strategic Studies at Al-Ahram [CPSSA], 1989), pp. 510-542.

2 See "State and Groupings of Political Islam," in *Arab Strategic Report 1987* (Cairo: CPSSA, 1988), pp. 236-252.

3 The worry over an Islamist takeover in Algeria expressed by Western ambassadors there is recounted in Hussein Ahmed Amin, "A Western Working Lunch and an Arab Working Dinner," *Al-Ahali*, December 9, 1990.

4 Charles Issawi's classic essay on social foundations of democracy in the Middle East is in Walter Laquer, ed., *The Middle East in Transition* (London: Routledge and Kegan Paul, 1958).

5 On the limits of freedom of expression in Egypt, see the report of the Egyptian Organization for Human Rights (EOHR), June 27, 1990.

6 See EOHR's appeal for equality in treatment of victims, September 15, 1990.

7 See, for example, Amani Kandil, "Human Rights: The Cause of the Future," *Ai-Ahram*, August 7, 1987; Mohamed El Sayed Said, "Human Rights in the Third World: The Question of Priorities," *Journal of Arab Affairs*, (Spring 1990), pp. 61-83; Ahmed Abdalla, "On Human Rights," *Al-'Arab*, September 15, 1987.

8 I wrote about human rights violations by opposition forces in Egypt for the first conference of EOHR, Cairo, December 1988. The EOHR criticized Islamists for resorting to violence and sectarian confrontation in its September 1990 bulletin.

Breaking through the Wall of Fear in the Arab World

"Ironically, the most significant impact of the Persian Gulf war may have been. . .that the 'wall of fear' separating citizens from autocratic rulers has been broken through. If this is true, United States President George Bush and his colleagues in the anti-Iraq coalition may have unleashed whirlwinds of change that will engender profound instability in the Arab world. While the great powers applaud participation and exalt democracy, they loathe instability; yet the achievement of greater participation and democratization without accompanying instability is difficult to imagine."

Augustus Richard Norton

Augustus Richard Norton *is a professor of political science at the United States Military Academy. He is, with Muhammad Muslih, the coauthor of* Rising Tides in the Middle East *(New York: Foreign Policy Association, 1992); and, with Jerrold Green, the coauthor of* Rulers under Siege: Middle East Politics in the 1990s *(New York: Harcourt Brace Jovanovich, forthcoming). The views expressed in this article are those of the author and should not be construed to represent the policy or position of the United States government or any of its constituent institutions.*

D emocracy's appeal is growing in nearly every corner of the world. Yet there is a tendency to presume that Arab societies are insulated from the global trend toward democratization. The very idea of democracy in Arab countries strikes some as laughable; certainly there is no widespread tradition of democracy in the Arab world. But putting aside the prejudice that underpins some of the commentary, part of the unwillingness to believe in the possibility of democracy in the Arab world is simple ignorance of recent political developments in the Arab states.

In 1984 one of America's leading political scientists wrote that "with a few exceptions, the limits of democratic development in the world may well have been reached."[1] Since then democracy has blossomed in Europe, Latin America, and Africa. The democratic changes in these regions should chasten any rush to pronounce on prospects in Arab lands, especially when one considers the historical novelty of the democratic ideal in Eastern Europe, not to mention the Soviet Union, where democracy's roots are neither thick nor deep.

This is not to argue that all the Arab states will metamorphose into democracies overnight, or even that some will. As in Europe, a few autocratic regimes will cling to power while others will experiment with opening up government, permitting free or semi-free elections and sharing or pretending to share power.

As elsewhere, the global revolution in communications has had a striking impact in the Middle East. Governments can no longer hide behind a cloak of secrecy. Through reliable alternative news sources such as the British Broadcasting Corporation (BBC), Radio Monte Carlo, and sometimes the Cable News Network (CNN), the man and the woman in the street have access to information about their government and the rest of the world. Coupled with education—literacy rates among Arab adults have steadily risen—the communications revolution gives people an unprecedented ability to judge their governments.

Opinions are now being publicly expressed in the Arab world. People are complaining about widespread corruption in government, insisting that leaders address their needs, and demanding a voice in decision making. But the opinions of Arab populations are not monolithic. They embrace diverse ideological perspectives, especially among Islamist groups in countries where a freer political life has encouraged competition rather than solidarity.

No conversion to Jeffersonian democracy is under way in the Arab world, but the pressure to open up political systems is increasingly obvious. For their part, many Arab politicians are pragmatic. In advocating increased political participation they are acknowledging the need to vent some of the public's dissatisfaction and relieve the pressure in their countries.

Faced with restive and increasingly assertive populations, some governments continue to choose repression over concession, but others experiment with democratization. Egypt is the most advanced fledgling democracy in the Arab world. President Hosni Mubarak has pursued a mixed strategy of co-optation, sharing the blame as well as the benefits, and reasonably free elections engineered to ensure victory for the ruling National Democratic party (NDP). Both the secular Wafd party and the fundamentalist Muslim Brotherhood boycotted the November 1990 parliamentary elections to protest anticipated vote-rigging and electoral procedures skewed to favor the ruling party. The NDP won an overwhelming but empty victory; not even the appearance of an effective parliamentary opposition was preserved (notwithstanding the six seats won by the left-wing Tagama party). Still, compared to the autocracy of former President Anwar el-Sadat and the intolerance of Gamal Abdel Nasser's presidency, Egypt is freer than it has ever been.

Jordan, Algeria, Tunisia, and Yemen are also moving in fits and starts down the path of democratization. The badly battered Lebanese democracy may be regaining its vitality, and incipient political liberalization has even been noted in Libya. Kuwait is an open question. The opposition there has demanded the reconvening of the freely elected parliament and the reestablishment of the 1962 constitution, both of which were suspended in 1986 by Kuwait's emir, Sheik Jaber al-Ahmad al-Sabah. Before Iraq's August 1990 invasion, the Kuwaiti regime had responded to opposition demands by holding out the possibility of citizen participation in a pliant political structure of its own making; thus in June 1990, the regime created an Advisory National Council rather than reconvene parliament.

As with earlier ventures into pseudo-participation by Nasser and Iran's Mohammed Riza Shah Pahlavi, the effect was simply to call attention to the absence of free political structures. After his return to liberated Kuwait, the emir attempted to dampen enthusiasm for the opposition and increase support for his family's rule by bribing virtually all Kuwaitis: he simply forgave all outstanding commercial loans and mortgages. The emir's many critics were quick to note the ease with which he dipped into the treasury to pay for the scheme. Whether he did more than provide them with ammunition against the regime will only become clear in October 1992, when the long-demanded parliamentary elections are scheduled to be held.

DWINDLING LEGITIMACY

Arab governments are widely viewed with disdain by their own citizens. While Americans routinely refer to "our government," an Arab rarely thinks in these terms. Instead, it is a matter of "us" and "them."

Insecure and marginally legitimate rulers regard any attempt to organize citizens outside the government's authority as a dangerous challenge. They view with the utmost suspicion any labor unions, professional organizations, civic clubs, interest groups, and other non-governmental organizations making up civil society that are outside the direct control of the government.

In some settings, among the Palestinians, in Lebanon and Egypt, and in parts of Arab North Africa, civil society is vibrant and varied. In Algeria liberalization has promoted a flourishing civil society with more than 12,000 professional and cultural groups. But in most of the Arab world civil society is weak and fragmented, signifying the absence of freedom. In Iraq the government has aggressively destroyed any vestige of civil society that it cannot dominate, making it hard to imagine any peaceful transfer of power to a group outside the Baathist regime.

The Arab-Israeli conflict has often been exploited to justify the creation of garrison states in which freedom and prosperity are sacrificed in the interest of national security. Can a regime that lacks electoral approval and that roots its legitimacy in the confrontation with Israel, the "unity" of the Arab nation, and a commitment to justice for the Palestinians survive a resolution of the Arab-Israeli conflict?

This is a particularly relevant question for Syrian President Hafez al-Assad, whose dilemma became transparent in October 1991 at the Madrid Middle East peace conference, which was cosponsored by the United States and the Soviet Union. The Syrian regime bases its legitimacy on its role as the militant standard-bearer of Arabism and self-appointed protector of Palestine. (Symptomatically, when the Syrians received $2 billion from Saudi Arabia for their participation in the anti-Iraq alliance during the Persian Gulf war, they spent most of the money on missiles, despite critical domestic economic problems.)

Even as the Palestinian delegates in Madrid enthusiastically pursued negotiations with Israel, seizing what may be a last opportunity, the Syrians were reluctant to proceed. This was not merely tactical, but reflected their acknowledgment that steps toward normalizing relations with Israel necessarily undermine the regime's formula for legitimacy. Yet the Syrians could not afford to be left at the starting gate, especially given the world dominance held by the United States and the disastrous economic conditions in Syria that make further Saudi largesse essential. If the peace process moves forward, as now seems likely, the regime must try to refashion its claims to legitimacy.

THE ALGERIAN BELLWETHER

One of the most important and promising political experiments under way in the Arab world is in Algeria, where the National Liberation Front (FLN) has ruled since the country's independence from France in 1962.

After bloody rioting in October 1988, when discontent stemming from unemployment and a general economic crisis erupted in Algeria's major cities, the constitution was revised to permit the creation of political parties in the formerly one-party republic. Nearly two dozen political parties were spawned, and municipal and provincial parliamentary elections were held in June 1990. Several of the largest new opposition parties boycotted the elections, saying national elections should be held first. The boycott benefited the fundamentalist Islamic Salvation Front (FIS), which campaigned on the platform "Islam is the solution." The party won control of 32 of 48 provincial assemblies and more than half the 1,541 municipal councils. Even President Chadli Bendjedid's hometown voted for the FIS.

The FIS victory was stunning. The FLN remained in control of the national government, but its grip was tenuous. Bendjedid, who along with the powerful army leadership is apparently convinced that the political system must be opened up to survive, announced parliamentary elections for early 1991, then postponed them until June.

The old order will not go quietly. The present holders of power and privilege are attempting to manipulate the laws to preserve their power, and they may succeed. The Algerian parliament, still an FLN preserve, passed an election law on April 1 that proved gerrymandering is a universal craft. Capitalizing on the FLN's strength in rural districts, the new law created electoral districts that gave disproportionate weight to FLN strongholds. In the most egregious cases, pro-FLN voters in rural areas cast ballots that were effectively weighted to equal 10 FIS votes in the city. In addition, runoff procedures were modified so that only the top vote-winners could compete. This prevented voters from choosing a third party that might mark the middle ground between the FLN and the FIS.

The two leading figures in the FIS have split on some issues: Sheik Ali Abbasi al-Madani has espoused coexistence with other political parties while Ali Belhadj, a firebrand, has been outspoken in his skepticism about pluralism. Both men, however, blasted the new election law and urged their supporters to protest it. Demonstrations in late May prompted a declaration of martial law and the appointment of a new prime minister, Sid Ahmed Ghozali, who met with Madani in early June and promised "free and clean elections" by year's end.

Tension persisted. The army jailed hundreds of FIS members, and by the end of June both Madani and Bel-

hadj had been arrested for plotting against the government. The two leaders remain in custody, though most of their followers have been released. The elections, which had already been postponed once, were eventually rescheduled for December 26. As many as 64 parties will compete in the December elections, if they are held. At least half a dozen of these will pose serious competition for the FIS.

Following the uproar in May and June, the Algerian parliament had a chance to amend the election law but instead made it tougher. For instance, despite a request by Ghozali, procedures for absentee balloting that permit a man to vote for his wife were retained. The prime minister referred the matter to the Constitutional Council, the body empowered to overturn unconstitutional legislation. In early November the Constitutional Council invalidated the section of the electoral law authorizing absentee balloting; it said the right to vote is necessarily the right to cast a ballot secretly and personally.

Algeria has become a bellwether for the possibility of a genuine political opening in the Arab world, and the results of the proposed elections are likely to inspire imitation elsewhere. Whether the imitation will assume the form of a design for controlling dissent or a step toward pluralism remains to be seen.

SAUDI ARABIA: A REGRESSIVE CASE

While Algeria may be moving forward toward pluralism, albeit hesitantly, in other Arab states autocratic rulers are retrenching, tightening social controls after glimpses of a freer political life during the Gulf crisis. The most obvious example is Saudi Arabia.

In what is certainly the most socially conservative Arab state, middle-class professionals have long pressured the regime to allow popular participation in decision making. Since 1962 there have been periodic promises to establish a *majlis al-shura*, or consultative council; typically, the promise is dusted off during a moment of popular discontent, and then promptly put back on the shelf for a few more years. The latest such occurrence took place in November 1990, in the midst of the Gulf crisis and on the heels of promises by Kuwait's ruling family to restore parliamentary life in the emirate. However, one year later, in November 1991, Saudi Arabia's King Fahd announced that the council would finally be established, along with a written body of laws. Thus, nearly 30 years after it was first announced, the council may come into existence. But rather than being a precursor to parliamentary representation, as some Saudi liberals hope, the *majlis al-shura* will be a conservative body more likely to stifle than to instill change.

As the protector of the two holiest cities of Islam,

King Fahd is especially sensitive to any charge that he is jeopardizing the sanctity or purity of Mecca and Medina. Although the learned men, or *ulema*, of the puritanical Wahhabi sect do not rule in Saudi Arabia, they are keenly concerned with the state of public morals and deeply influence the regime and the monarch; a challenge to the regime's Islamic probity is a challenge to its core legitimacy.* Hence King Fahd had to heed conservative grumbling over his agreement to permit the United States–led, predominantly non-Muslim military alliance against Iraq to deploy in the kingdom during the Gulf crisis.

When presented with an opportunity to emphasize his credentials as upholder of the faith during the Gulf crisis, the king seized it. On November 6, 1990, some four dozen Saudi women in Riyadh audaciously dismissed their drivers and drove their own cars, thus violating the informal but well-understood ban on women driving cars. Saudi liberals—who later petitioned the king to create a parliament and an independent judiciary, to reduce the power religion has on society and to review the status of women—were initially heartened by the demonstration.

The regime, however, reacted harshly, ostracizing the participants, firing several from their teaching positions, and exploiting the incident to stress the regime's Wahhabist credentials. A leading Wahhabi deliberative body lent support to the king with a *fatwa*, or authoritative religious opinion, that found that "women should not be allowed to drive motor vehicles as the *sharia* [religious law] instructs that things that degrade or harm the dignity of women must be prevented."[2]

Last June, in a move that was widely interpreted as an attempt by the *ulema* to collect for their wartime sufferance of Western troops in the kingdom while countering the entreaties of Saudi liberals, the *ulema* presented a memorandum urging King Fahd to undertake a series of conservative reforms. These included the creation of an *ulema*-dominated parliament, stricter application of Islamic law in the country, and consistent punishments for corruption. Although the conservative reforms have not been implemented, there is little doubt that political life in Saudi Arabia will continue to be the exclusive preserve of the regime, not its citizens.

THE ISLAMIST MOVEMENTS

In recent years, Islamist movements in the Arab world have proliferated dramatically. Enjoying broad popular appeal that crosses economic classes and employing a populist theme—"The answer is Islam"— these movements have been remarkably successful in winning votes where there are contested elections. In 1989 Islamists captured 34 of 80 seats in the Jordanian parliament and managed to construct a working majority through an alliance with leftist representatives. As noted earlier, the FIS has changed the complexion of Algerian politics, and the venerable Muslim Brotherhood in Egypt has competed successfully in two national elections since 1984. In Kuwait the Islamic Constitutional Movement is poised to play a leading role.

Several points need to be made about these movements. First, their vitality stems from the general impoverishment of civil society. Where civil society has been suppressed, Islamist groups have often prospered; in effect, they have had the field to themselves. Religious institutions are a part of the cultural landscape of the Arab world, and the fundamental Islamic institution, the mosque, is a natural meeting place that is often reasonably free from government control. As civil society is enlivened, it is only natural that the influence of the Islamist groups will be challenged.

Second, the Islamist groups are a symptom of the broad social and economic changes that have swept the region. Many of the people attracted to these groups have college educations but cannot find decent jobs, or have heard politicians' promises but have borne the brunt of government inefficiency. It is no accident that many of the Islamist groups have cemented their group solidarity by providing services that government either has not provided or has provided incompetently. Thus in many settings, such as Egypt and Lebanon, Islamist groups act as quasi-governmental social welfare and medical agencies, filling a vacuum left by government.

Third, in countries where the government has attempted to halt the rise of Islamist groups, there has been a marked solidarity among the various organizations. Where government has treaded more lightly, or at least more selectively, there has been fissuring and competition. Examples of the latter include Algeria and Egypt, where Islamists willing to play by the government's rules have abandoned those unwilling to do so.

Fourth, when Islamist groups move from opposition to positions of public responsibility, they submit themselves to a more prosaic standard of evaluation. For instance, in the Algerian municipalities where they assumed authority, FIS officials often failed to deliver on their promises, and lost some support accordingly. It is one thing to castigate government for its incompetence and corruption, and another to collect the garbage efficiently.

Moreover, playing the game of politics has left the Islamists vulnerable to political exploitation, notably in Jordan. On New Year's Day 1991, Jordan's King Hussein oversaw the appointment of five members of the Muslim Brotherhood and two other Islamists to Cabinet posts, including the portfolios of education, social development, and religious affairs and education. The monarch's motive was to put a lid on the public temper, which was at a boil because of the Gulf crisis and its damaging economic effect on Jordan. Less than six months later, the Islamists had served their purpose, and the king dismissed the government, appointing as prime minister Tahir Masri, a moderate thought to be more congenial to the unfolding Middle East peace process. On June 9, a National Charter that endorsed a multi-party political system, freedom of the press, and equal rights for women was promulgated.

Fifth, although the Islamist groups see themselves as part of the world community of Muslims (the *umma*), they are willing to voice their demands within states. Some observers believe this is some sort of trick, but the evidence points in another direction—namely, to the Islamists' realistic acceptance of the existence of the state. Obviously, some Islamists reject pluralism and democracy, but many others do not.

Sixth, as during the Gulf crisis, when popular opinion in much of the Arab world often ran strongly against the United States–led alliance, Islamist leaders are forced into the difficult role of balancer between their benefactors (particularly Saudi Arabia) and their followers. In general they have displayed a noteworthy capacity for pragmatism.

As many of the preceding points illustrate, the Islamist movements are basically social reform movements. Yet they retain a keen interest in Jerusalem, the third-holiest city of Islam, and in the fate of Palestine as a part of the *dar-al-Islam* (roughly, the land of Islam). Of course, the Islamists do not have a corner on the market in dogmatic obstinacy—one need only look at Israel's secular Likud party to see that. The unfolding Middle East peace process will show how the Islamists respond to the necessity of a larger compromise.

THE 1991 WATERSHED

Commentary about the Gulf war has often noted that the events represented a watershed. In an age of instant news, when history plays out before our eyes, it is understandable that some are impatient to declare that the Middle East is back to business as usual since the Gulf war did not bring instant sweeping reform. But the history of the region teaches that watersheds become apparent over the long run. It is likely that the events of 1990 and 1991 represent a particularly rich watershed, one simultaneously marking important international changes and catalyzing inchoate political trends in the region, especially at the level of state-society relations.

Ironically, the most significant impact of the Persian Gulf war may have been, as one Arab scholar noted recently, that the "wall of fear" separating citizens from autocratic rulers has been broken through. If this is true, United States President George Bush and his colleagues in the anti-Iraq coalition may have unleashed whirlwinds of change that will engender profound instability in the Arab world. While the great powers applaud participation and exalt democracy, they loathe instability; yet the achievement of greater participation and democratization without accompanying instability is difficult to imagine. And there is of course no necessary connection between popular (often populist) political voices and Western-style government; the contrary is often the case.

If Arab governments are exhibiting a new tolerance for contested elections, this is no guarantee that the election results will not be manipulated or that the polling will be fully fair. The international community must be willing to supervise elections in the Middle East. Relatively free elections have been conducted under international supervision in Namibia, Nicaragua, and Haiti. International supervision does not render an election result coup-proof, but it does inhibit tampering with the results. Certainly Kuwait and Lebanon would be obvious candidates in the Arab world. In the first instance, international supervision would reduce the regime's temptation to ignore or reverse the results. In the second, supervision would be a means of facilitating the relegitimation of the Lebanese parliament, which last stood for election in 1972, as well as of putting some distance between Lebanon and its overly intrusive neighbors, Israel and Syria.

Liberalization will sometimes exacerbate tensions rather than moderate them. But whatever their transitional excesses, democratizing governments must eventually balance arms budgets against social programs and address the demands of those to whom they are accountable. Aggressive wars are not easily launched in political systems in which leaders must win support for their policies through consultation and consensus-building. Dictators, by contrast, are not subject to these constraints.

One as yet unmeasurable result of the Gulf crisis is that many Arab intellectuals and policymakers now argue that malaise in the Arab world is a product of the lack of freedom there. This may well prove to be the war's most significant revelation. In the short run, loosening the grip of authoritarian regimes will be a messy process, and incrementally minded Western officials will resist encouraging an overly rapid liberalization of Arab politics. But statesmen with a longer view will appreciate that promoting liberalization is the key to pre-empting the emergence of absolute rulers like Iraqi President Saddam Hussein. And no matter what statesmen decide, the train of political liberalization seems to have left the station.

[1]Samuel P. Huntington, "Will More Countries Become Democratic?" *Political Science Quarterly*, vol. 99, no. 2 (Summer 1984), p. 218.

[2]See Eleanor Abdella Doumato, "Women and the Stability of Saudi Arabia," *Middle East Report*, July–August 1991, pp. 34–37.

Article 7   Middle East Report • May-June 1991

Arab Economies after the Gulf War
Power, Poverty, and Petrodollars

President Bush and King Fahd confer through a translator during Bush's November 1990 visit to Saudi Arabia.   David Valdez/White House

Yahya Sadowski

Yahya Sadowski, an editor of this magazine, is an analyst at the Brookings Institution in Washington, DC.

On February 6, 1991, Secretary of State James Baker admitted before the House Foreign Affairs Committee that economic factors, particularly widespread Arab resentment that oil wealth was not more equitably distributed, had played a role in the dynamics leading to the Gulf war and would remain one of the primary "sources of conflict" in the region. To ease these tensions, he proposed the creation of an economic organization through which oil-rich states could fund the reconstruction and development of their poorer neighbors.[1] The following day, Baker advocated the creation of a multinational "Middle East Development Bank" to attain these objectives.[2]

Baker's proposals were among several ambitious plans for economic reconstruction following the victory of Operation Desert Storm. After a March 5 meeting in Damascus of the Arab coalition that had arrayed against Iraq, Egyptian delegates emerged with their own plan for the oil-rich Gulf states to contribute $15 billion annually to their poorer neighbors. Arab nationalists, long the harshest critics of income inequal-

ity in the region, floated still other proposals.[3]

All these proposals presumed that the treasures of Arab oil-exporting states were brimming with dollars. After all, uncertainty over the future of the Gulf had driven crude oil prices from about $15 per barrel at the beginning of July 1990 up to $40 per barrel by September. Because Iraqi and Kuwaiti oil was held off the market, Saudi Arabia and other OPEC members were able to increase production dramatically without undercutting prices. *Business Week* surmised that expanded pumping and higher prices could earn Saudi Arabia as much as $45 billion in 1990 ($20 billion more than in 1989), and perhaps $65 billion in 1991.[4] Surely this would be enough to repair the immediate Gulf war damage and still fund a more prosperous and equitable regional economy.

This ebullience in Washington and in some Arab capitals was misplaced. Even before the US began to bomb Iraq on January 16, 1991, the bills being presented to the Gulf states were outstripping their revenues. There was no "windfall" of petroleum profits waiting to be redistributed. For anyone who "follows the money," it is evident that the Middle East as a whole will be much poorer in the 1990s than in the 1980s.

What Price Victory?

Those in Washington and elsewhere who hope that the Gulf war will midwife a "new economic order" in the Middle East pin much of their hopes on contributions from Saudi Arabia—historically the largest oil exporter with the largest petroleum reserves, highest cash income earnings and most pivotal political position of any Gulf state.

Saudi Arabia emerged from the fighting relatively unscathed. A handful of Scud missiles hit Riyadh; Iraqi artillery set fire to the refinery at Khafji; and oil spills threatened desalinization plants. Yet the Saudis are finding their economic assets drained by the Gulf war. The day Iraq invaded Kuwait, business confidence in Gulf investments plummeted. The crisis dashed Saudi hopes that foreign concerns would invest $5-6 billion in new petrochemical works at Jubayl.[5] The government had to cancel a dozen major projects as $10 billion of anticipated investment dried up.[6] The Saudi stock market crashed. Saudi citizens began converting their savings accounts into dollars in preparation for fleeing the region, triggering a run on most banks. Eleven percent of all bank deposits were withdrawn, and the government had to pump $4.4 billion into the financial system to keep it from crashing.[7]

The Saudis initially had to house and feed 200,000 Kuwaitis who fled to the kingdom.[8] They also paid the airfare to send home hundreds of thousands of Asian "guest workers" who had fled Kuwait, and footed the bill for thousands of Saudi citizens who fled Eastern Province towns like Khafji. The cost of these emergency measures may have totalled as much as $3-4 billion.[9]

To prepare the kingdom for war, by the end of 1990 Riyadh had spent at least $13 billion on new arms purchases. It also expects to be offered an additional $17 billion American arms package (though this may be scaled back under Congressional pressure).[10] The kingdom stepped up troop training and is contemplating doubling the size of the armed forces, both of which will add to the bills.[11]

In a September meeting with James Baker, King Fahd agreed to cover the full "in country" costs of US troops dispatched to the kingdom, including fuel, water, transportation, and rented or rapidly constructed housing. The US Treasury did not keep tabs on these expenditures, but American officials estimated they ran upwards of $500 million a month through the end of 1990.[12] When war broke out in January, the king pledged an additional $13.5 billion to cover allied military costs through March.[13]

At his meeting with Baker, King Fahd also agreed to contribute $3-4 billion to a special US Treasury fund to help countries like Turkey and Jordan bear the consequences of supporting the UN Security Council embargo against Iraq.[14] Riyadh gave $1.5 billion in loans and grants to Egypt and, together with Kuwait, wrote off $6.6 billion of Cairo's debts. The Saudis also made a subvention of at least $1 billion to Syria.[15]

Not all of these costs had an immediate impact on the Saudi budget. Riyadh has taken its time to meet its cash pledges to support the American military and to aid states hurt by the embargo of Iraq, although it began making in-kind contributions (including $180 million a month in jet and diesel fuel) immediately. Some of the Egyptian debt never would have been repaid in any case. Still, using even the most conservative estimates, the cash cost of coping with the Gulf crisis drained $27.9 billion from the Saudi treasury by the end of 1990. By August 1991, Saudi Arabia will have spent some $64 billion on the war and associated costs, and some well-placed Saudis estimate the sum may actually reach as high as $80 billion.[16]

The Oil Windfall

In actuality, the windfall from oil exports proved much smaller than the projected $45-95 billion.[17] When Iraq invaded Kuwait, Saudi Arabia was producing oil at a rate of 5.6 million barrels per day (bpd). As soon as the UN imposed its embargo on Iraqi and Kuwaiti exports, the Saudis—at American urging—began to expand their own production to cover the shortfall. But it was not until November that Saudi production reached 8.7 million bpd, and Riyadh spent $4.7 billion taking old oil facilities out of mothballs or constructing new ones.[18] Even then, all that production was not exported. The Saudis themselves consume 800,000 bpd and they supplied at least 300,000 bpd free to allied troops.[19] (Once combat began in January 1991, Riyadh had to *import* jet and diesel fuel to keep up with allied military consumption.) The actual volume of Saudi exports stayed well below the levels assumed by many Western economists.

More importantly, the profit which the Saudis earned on each barrel exported was much lower than commonly assumed. Although prices in the international oil exchanges peaked at $40 per barrel in early October, they steadily retreated from then on, staying below $30 from December onwards. The day after US fighter jets began bombing Iraq, prices collapsed by $10 and have hovered around $20 per barrel ever since.[20]

International oil price quotations give an exaggerated sense of Saudi profits in any case. A significant share of Saudi oil is sold on long-term contracts, which may not reflect short-term jumps in international prices. The prices quoted by international exchanges are usually for high-quality "sweet" oils, while most Saudi exports consist of less valuable "sour" crudes. In September, when the price for sweet oil on the New York Mercantile Exchange hit $40 per barrel, the bulk of Saudi exports were earning only $28, which includes $1-3 per barrel in production and delivery costs.[21]

Most petroleum industry analysts agree that the actual Saudi receipts from oil sales in 1990 totalled $40-41 billion.[22] This represents $14-16 billion more than the kingdom had expected to earn from oil sales before the Gulf crisis erupted. The expenses Riyadh incurred as a result of the crisis exceeded the value of this windfall by at least $10 billion.

Saudi planners knew that they were running a large deficit in 1990, but hoped they might make this up in 1991. If they could earn $20 per barrel and export 8 million bpd, by

December 1991 they would earn $58.4 billion dollars—enough to cover a $31 billion operating budget and most of the crisis-related expenses.[23]

Will oil prices remain high enough for Riyadh to earn $20 per barrel? Saudi production expansion guaranteed there was no drop in world oil supply (or even in strategic stockpiles) during 1990. Recession and mild weather in the industrialized countries actually reduced oil demand in the first quarter of 1991 by 0.5 percent.[24] Iraq and Kuwait will need oil revenues to rebuild their societies as soon as possible.[25]

World oil supplies could well exceed demand for the foreseeable future. There is not much chance that OPEC can get its members to reduce production enough to avoid this glut. Saudi Arabia proclaims to want a price of $21 per barrel, but does not appear ready to accept a significant decrease in its new market share.[26] Prices could well drop below $15 a barrel.[27]

If oil prices do fall back to pre-crisis levels, the Saudis will have to cover war-related expenses out of assets. These are not negligible: during the oil booms of the 1970s the kingdom laid away billions of dollars in sundry funds and accounts. But for much of the last decade, Riyadh had been tapping accounts to fund current expenses and budget deficits. The 1990 Saudi budget had projected $38 billion in outlays but only $28 billion in oil revenues; $6.7 billion of the difference was to be financed by tapping the reserve funds controlled by the Saudi Arabian Monetary Agency (SAMA) and by issuing bonds.[28]

No outsider knows for sure just how large SAMA's assets are. Optimists claim that it had $50-70 billion in solid assets in June 1990—enough to cover the costs of the Gulf crisis. But pessimists (including Zaki Yamani) suggest that these figures include non-performing loans to Iraq and Egypt, leaving the real value of SAMA funds closer to $25 billion. If this is true, SAMA's liquid assets could potentially be wiped out by the confrontation with Iraq.[29]

Saudi Arabia is not about to become a "poor" country, but the costs of the Gulf war will exceed all of its petrodollar windfall and most of its liquid assets, compelling Riyadh to borrow abroad. In early February 1991, when Iraq dumped oil from Kuwaiti terminals into the Gulf to imperil Saudi Arabia's desalinization plants, Riyadh reacted cautiously: the kingdom lacked the money to contemplate any massive effort to clean up the spill. On February 13, the *Washington Post* noted that the Saudis were preparing to make major sales of their holdings in US government securities, and later that month Riyadh borrowed $3.5 billion as a loan syndicated by J.P. Morgan Co.[30]

The war's economic burden will weigh less heavily on Saudi Arabia than on most of the other oil-rich Gulf states. The emir of Kuwait, like King Fahd, has been making handsome contributions to allied war coffers. He also has had to pay $500 million a month to sustain the Kuwaiti refugee population.[31] Estimates of the cost of rebuilding Kuwait now generally start at $60 billion.[32] Kuwait has earned no oil export revenues since August 2, and Iraqi troops dynamited 60-85 percent of its wells before they withdrew. It may take 5-10 years to restore the emirate's oil production to pre-war levels.[33] The

costs of rebuilding the country will have to be paid largely by liquidating part of Kuwait's $90 billion portfolio of foreign assets and taking out sizable loans secured against the rest.[34]

Iraq has been economically demolished by the war. On August 2, Baghdad was already shouldering a $23 billion fiscal deficit and $80 billion in foreign debts.[35] Once the UN embargo was imposed, it began to lose $1.25 billion a month in oil revenues.[36] Allied air strikes rapidly erased much of its economic infrastructure: bridges, power plants, factories and refineries. Now that the war is over, Baghdad may find commercial bankers unwilling to roll over old credits, much less extend new ones. Foreign firms, which built many of Iraq's industries, may be reluctant to resume work in a country where their employees have been held as "guests by force." As for Iraq's foreign assets, confiscated shortly after the invasion of Kuwait, the allies plan to hold them as part of the reparations owed to the victims of Saddam's invasion.

Some of the smaller states of the southern Gulf—Qatar and the United Arab Emirates—have been hit less hard by the war.[37] But even before the conflict, their oil revenues were not large enough to make a major contribution to the economic development of the region. The US proposal to orchestrate the economic reconstruction of the region through a Middle East Development Bank, then, suffers from a major flaw: no state in the region really has the assets necessary to fund such an institution.

Regional Consequences

The diversion of oil profits into the Gulf war and reconstruction (and away from development projects) is going to have a major impact on the economies of the Middle East for years to come. It is too soon to make hard predictions, but certain broad effects are already apparent.

Within the Gulf states themselves, the war has dealt a body blow to the one economic sector—apart from oil—which had shown potential: finance. In March 1990 Offshore Banking Units (OBUs) in Bahrain held $73.3 billion in deposits and seemed to be on the verge of recovering from the problems which had afflicted them in the 1980s.[38] When Iraq invaded Kuwait, thousands of their depositors withdrew $13.7 billion in assets (21 percent) and sent them abroad. Local commercial banks lost 15 percent of their deposits.[39] A similar run consumed 11 percent of Saudi bank deposits (see above), and in the UAE withdrawals rose to 25 percent of liabilities. Kuwaiti banks ceased operations entirely. Iraq looted KD 365 million in securities and $800 million in gold which had been deposited with the central bank of Kuwait.[40]

Rapid government intervention prevented any of these banks from going bankrupt, but this cannot brighten the prospects for the region's financial system. The rapid rise of military spending by Gulf governments makes it clear there will be no "excess funds." Indeed, local regimes began to pare back their normal menu of investment projects, leaving an even smaller scope for banking operations. Japanese and Western financiers are reluctant to deal with Gulf banks, arguing that political uncertainties and shrunken assets make them unreliable partners. No one expects a collapse of Gulf financial institutions, but bankers themselves foresee a period of retrenchment in which larger and more solvent firms will swallow their competitors—and the survivors adopt more conservative and modest lending policies.[41]

The Gulf banks had been one of the major channels through which petrodollars had percolated from the Gulf into the rest of the Arab world. Aid from the oil-rich countries to their poorer neighbors had been declining throughout the 1980s. As the Gulf states divert their revenues to meeting war and reconstruction costs, aid will probably become even less available. Aid to states which appeared sympathetic to Iraq was suspended almost immediately. Saudi Arabia and Kuwait completely halted their contributions to the Palestine Liberation Organization, which had been running over $100 million per year.[42] Jordan, too, quickly lost the $300 million in aid it had been receiving annually from Iraq and Kuwait, and now Riyadh also has cut its support, suspending concessionary oil shipments to Amman (worth $1 million per day and representing half of Jordan's consumption). It also suspended economic aid to Amman, which had totalled $200 million annually and supplied 15 percent of the state budget.[43]

Restricting aid to the Palestinians and Jordan freed up monies which the Saudis could then reallocate to countries which supported the kingdom in the Gulf conflict—chiefly Egypt, Syria, and Morocco. A similar change, benefitting Saudi allies while punishing "unfriendly" states, was evident in the most important single mechanism for redistributing petrodollars: labor migration. Before the crisis, all of the oil-rich Gulf states had employed large numbers of expatriate—largely Arab—workers who provided professional services (teachers, doctors, lawyers, engineers) or performed manual labor (construction, agriculture) which local citizens either could not or would not. Remittances formed a major source of hard currency for their home countries. The invasion of Kuwait massively disrupted this system. Half of the Palestinians and most of the Jordanians who were working in Kuwait fled the country after August 2, and those who remained could not get money out. The Palestinians of the West Bank lost access to $100 million a year. In Jordan, half of the $800 million Amman derived from remittances each year came from workers in Kuwait.[44]

These disruptions were compounded when Qatar and other Gulf states began to restrict the entry of Palestinian workers, widely suspected of pro-Iraqi sympathies. In September, Saudi Arabia punished Yemen for its neutral policy on the war by requiring Yemeni workers in the kingdom to find Saudi sponsors or face expulsion. By November 700,000 had already returned to Yemen and another 30,000 were leaving Saudi Arabia every day. This put an end to $1-2 billion a year in remittances, a loss of 20 percent of the country's foreign currency receipts. (Saudi, Iraqi and Kuwaiti economic aid to Yemen also ended.)[45]

The interruption of workers' remittances also hit Egypt hard. At the beginning of 1990, some 150,000 Egyptians had been working in Kuwait and another million in Iraq. After Iraq invaded Kuwait, over 400,000 Egyptians fled these countries, costing Egypt an estimated $1.1 billion in annual hard currency revenues.[46] Saudi Arabia supplied Cairo with aid to assist in relocating refugees and issued some 684,000 work visas to Egyptians by early 1991.[47]

The substitution of Egyptian workers for Jordanians, Palestinians and Yemenis in Saudi Arabia and Kuwait will reinforce the same pattern evident in the reallocation of aid from those two states. Egypt and Syria may enjoy some relief from the economic constraints which had plagued them in the 1980s. Jordan, Yemen and Sudan, which the Saudis felt had shown too much sympathy for Baghdad, will find their economic problems enormously aggravated.

This does not bode well for any "new economic order" in the Middle East. The Gulf war has made the region as a whole much poorer than it was in 1989, and the inequalities between the "have and have-not" states are likely to become even more pronounced. The growth of poverty and income disparities will translate into popular resentment and sooner or later will fuel political conflict. Instead of a "new order," the future probably holds a return to "the Arab cold war."[48]

Footnotes

1 *New York Times* (NYT), February 7, 1991.

2 *Washington Post* (WP), February 8, 1991.

3 *Financial Times* (FT), March 8, 1991; *al-Majalla*, October 15, 1990, pp. 16-17; and *al-Ahram al-Iqtisadi*, February 11, 1991, pp. 12-13.

4 *Business Week*, September 17, 1990, p. 30. Other sources predicted Saudi revenues for 1991 might run as high as $93 billion; see *Middle East Economic Digest* (MEED), October 19, 1990, pp. 4-5.

5 *FT*, August 21, 1990.

6 *WP*, August 21, 1990.

7 *MEED*, September 21, 1990, pp. 26-27 and October 19, 1990, p. 36.

8 *FT*, December 12, 1990.

9 *WP*, August 21, 1990; and *MEED*, August 31, 1990, pp. 18-19.

10 *FT*, December 12, 1990.

11 *FT*, December 12, 1990; and *MEED*, October 19, 1990, pp. 4-5.

12 *WP*, September 7, 1990; and *NYT*, September 7, 1990.

13 *NYT*, February 11, 1991; and *MEED*, February 8, 1991, p. 8.

14 *Wall Street Journal* (WSJ), November 6, 1990; and *NYT*, February 11, 1991.

15 *NYT*, December 6, 1990; and *FT*, October 30, 1990.

16 *WP*, April 3, 1991.

17 For an example of such optimism, see *NYT*, September 7, 1990.

18 *MEED*, December 14, 1990, p. 19.

19 *FT*, December 20, 1990.

20 *WP*, January 18, 1991.

21 *WP*, January 4, 1991.

22 *FT*, January 2, 1991.

23 These crisis-related expenses would include not only the $10-20 billion deficit left over from 1990, but the $13.5 billion the Saudis committed to support American military operations

for the first three months of 1991, and the $17 billion in American arms purchases still pending.

24 *FT*, February 6, 1991.

25 *MEED*, November 2, 1990, p. 15.

26 *MEED*, February 1, 1991, p. 5; and *NYT*, February 11, 1991.

27 *NYT*, October 19, 1990; *WSJ*, December 10, 1990. It is plausible that OPEC prices may begin recovering by the year 2000; see *Economist*, August 4, 1990, p. 51-52.

28 *MEED*, January 12, 1990, p. 31 and October 19, 1990, pp. 4-5.

29 *Euromoney*, September 1990, pp. 70-76.

30 *WP*, February 13, 1991.

31 *FT*, December 12, 1990.

32 *WSJ*, February 27, 1991; and *NYT*, February 27, 1991.

33 *NYT*, March 6, 1991.

34 *Business Week*, January 21, 1991, pp. 44-45; and *MEED*, February 8, 1991, p. 6.

35 *MEED*, January 12, 1990. p. 26; and *WP*, November 9, 1990.

36 *FT*, August 7, 1990; and *NYT*, February 6, 1991.

37 *The Middle East*, January 1991, pp. 25-26.

38 The key problems had been a) too many banks offering similar services operating in a tiny market, b) a heavy reliance on loans to developing countries which had performed poorly, and c) problems collecting debts within Gulf countries because of impediments raised by Islamic law.

39 *The Middle East*, January 1991, p. 33.

40 *FT*, October 4, 1990; and *al-Majalla*, January 23-29, 1991, pp. 46-48.

41 For a slightly more upbeat assessment—which suggests that local commercial banks will survive while the OBUs take a beating—see *MEED*, February 8, 1991, pp. 11-12.

42 *FT*, December 28, 1990.

43 *NYT*, September 21, 1990; *FT*, October 1, 1990; and *NYT*, October 21, 1990.

44 *al-Quds*, September 26, 1990, cited in FBIS September 27, 1990, p. 27; and *al-Ra'y*, September 20, 1990, cited in FBIS, September 20, 1990, pp. 33-36.

45 *NYT*, October 22 and October 26, 1990; and *MEED* November 30, 1990, pp. 4-5.

46 *FT*, August 23, 1990; *al-Majalla*, September 12-18, 1990, pp. 40-43; and *MEED*, January 25, 1991, p. 18.

47 *NYT*, February 5, 1991.

48 Malcolm Kerr coined this term to describe the feud between Arab nationalists and pro-Western monarchists which plagued the region during the 1960s; see his *The Arab Cold War: Gamal Abd al-Nasir and His Rivals, 1958-1970* (New York: Oxford University Press, 1971).

Article 8

THE WORLD & I
FEBRUARY 1991

THE KORAN AND ISLAMIC LIFE

Mustansir Mir

Mustansir Mir is assistant professor of Islamic studies in the Department of Near Eastern Studies at the University of Michigan in Ann Arbor. His most recent book is Verbal Idioms of the Koran *(Ann Arbor: Center for Near Eastern and North African Studies, 1989).*

A small town of three thousand in the province of the Punjab in Pakistan has a tradition that is strictly maintained: every member of the population, male and female, young and old, must be a *hafiz,* that is, one who has committed the entire Koran to memory. It might seem remarkable that a child of ten, or even younger, should be able to reproduce a book the size of the New Testament from memory, but this is not at all unusual in the Muslim world. *Huffaz* (pl. of hafiz) are found in every Muslim country, in some countries thousands of them. In many cases they are non-Arab, and so do not know the language of the Koran, although they have learned to read the Koranic script. Together, these huffaz form a human chain that serves, among other things, to preserve and transmit the sacred scriptures of Islam from one generation to another.

The Koran is made up of the revelations received by the Prophet of Islam, Muhammad. Born in Arabia in 570 C.E., Muhammad had his first revelatory experience at the age of forty (610). Thereafter the revelations came in small and large portions until his death (632), and were given the arrangement in which we possess them, according to some authorities by Muhammad himself, according to others by Muhammad's Companions not too long after his death. The Koran has 114 chapters of varying length: the longest chapter has 286 verses, while the shortest chapters have only 3. The chapters are arranged roughly according to the principle of diminishing length.

CONTENT, STRUCTURE, AND LANGUAGE

The Koranic material deals with doctrine, law, ethics, and history. The essentials of the doctrine are: an uncompromising belief in the oneness of God (even the Christian trinitarian interpretation of deity is rejected); belief in prophets who receive, through the agency of angels, revelation (which sometimes takes the form of a scripture) from God and convey it to mankind; and belief in the Day of Judgment. Concise statements of the doctrine are to be found in the four-verse long 112 chapter, and in 2:255[*], 1:285; 4:136; 31:34; and 59:23.

The law covers both worship and conduct. On the one hand the Koran enjoins the believers to offer ritual prayer regularly, give to the poor, fast the month of Ramadan (ninth in the lunar calendar), and, means permitting, perform a pilgrimage to Mecca at least once in their lifetime. On the other hand, it gives them instructions, sometimes brief but sometimes detailed, in several fields of law: social (marriage and divorce), civil (inheritance, bequest, usury), criminal (theft, homicide, fornication, false accusation of unchasti-

---

[*] 2 is the number of the Koranic chapter, 255 the number of the verse in that chapter.

It might seem remarkable that a child of ten, or even younger, should be able to reproduce a book the size of the New Testament from memory, but this is not at all unusual in the Muslim world.

y), procedural (number and qualifications of witnesses), and international war between Muslims and non-Muslims, civil war). Most of the legal material is found in the Medinan chapters of the Koran. Verses 167 through 283 of chapter 2 make up the most extended treatment of legal matters in the Koran. Other significant discussions of the law are to be found in chapters 4, 5, 24, 33, and 49.

Philosophically, Koranic ethics is based on the notion of universal human brotherhood: all human beings are the progeny of Adam and Eve, and all have been created by God (4:1). As such, not only non-Muslims but enemies, too, have certain rights. In its actual formulation, Koranic ethics deals mostly with matters that would arise in a Muslim society, and is practical in character, stressing (as in 2:83, 177; 4:8) the importance of obeying one's parents, being considerate to one's relatives and neighbors, and taking care of orphans and the needy.

Koranic history is, principally, religious history, which is presented to highlight a moral, substantiate a claim, and encourage the believers or warn the unbelievers. Many of the major figures in this history are biblical—Adam, Noah, Abraham, Moses, and Jesus. As a rule, no attempt is made to present detailed accounts of their lives or work. Chapters 11, 21, and 23 deal with many prophets, chapter 20 largely with Moses, chapter 12 specifically with Joseph. A number of ancient Arabian prophets are also mentioned.

To an ordinary reader the structure of the Koran will appear unusual, even puzzling. The Koran seems to move from one subject to another without warning—this is especially true of longer chapters—and one wonders whether it can be called a coherent work at all. A number of modern Muslim scholars, unlike traditional ones (who do not seem to have been bothered by the problem), have seen in the Koranic presentation significant patterns.

These scholars have argued that the living context of the book links up the seemingly disparate themes and motifs of the Koran. At the same time that it presented a doctrine, the Koran replied to the objections of opponents, gave guidelines for the organization of community life, told stories and parables to elucidate its content, urged the faithful to make financial contributions to the cause of the religion, explained the ritual, rebuked the weak of faith, cited past history in support of its message, and so on. Once the living context of the individual chapters is identified and fully understood, so goes the argument, the disparateness vanishes, giving way to a deep underlying unity. Here it would be pertinent to speak briefly about the peculiar nature of classical Arabic, the language of the Koran.

In a sense the language of the Koran is simple; the vocabulary employed is quite small. But a certain feature of the language is likely to cause difficulties. Unlike modern languages, in which the burden of communication falls on the speaker or the writer, classical, and particularly pre-Islamic, Arabic requires the listener or reader to participate in the act of communication. Thus, for example, a speaker could omit transitional words and phrases, relying on the listener to supply them. The disjointedness of the Koran that a modern reader would be quick to notice is to a considerable extent due to the suppression of such words and phrases, and is an index of the structural changes that have occurred in the language.

The Koran, from the Muslim view, is from God not only with respect to the meanings it conveys but also to the words in which those meanings are presented. This implies that the language of the Koran is invested, on the one hand, with a matchless aesthetic quality and, on the other, with a sacred quality so that a translation of the Koran may not be called Koran. While the dogma of the "inimitability" of the Koran has been variously interpreted, it is a fact that Koranic language has served as a model of excellence for the speakers and writers of Arabic through the ages.

For purposes of study and reference, the Koranic chapters are often divided into Meccan and Medinan. During the first twelve years of his ministry (610–622), Muhammed was in his native city, Mecca, where he preached to an increasingly hostile oligarchy, the tribe of Quraysh; the revelations received in Mecca are called Meccan. Forced to leave Mecca, with only a few hundred converts, Muhammad went to the city of Medina, where he established a state, organized the Muslims into a well-knit community, and, after a series of battles, brought nearly all of Arabia, including Mecca, under his control; the revelations received in Medina (622–632) are called Medinan. The Meccan-Medinan division is not simply a geographical division, it is significant in a more substantive sense: In Mecca, where the Muslims were a persecuted minority, the revelations dealt almost exclusively with religious and moral subjects; in Medina, where the Muslims enjoyed a position of authority, the revelations dealt with a host of social and practical matters. The division is significant from the viewpoint of Koranic style also. The Meccan chapters are much more poetic, whereas the Medinan chapters are more matter-of-fact.

THE KORAN AND THE BIBLE

The Koran is strikingly similar to, and strikingly dissimilar from, the Bible. Both emphasize the importance of the monotheistic doctrine, of the agency of prophethood for making the will of God known to man, and of the need for man to live in a state of constant moral alertness. But the Koran is a much shorter book than the Bible, and does not have the variety of material found in the Bible. It is planned differently, too. For one thing, it is not organized on the chronological principle, as most of the Bible is; themes take precedence over chronology. For another, it does not contain the detailed histories of the Bible, but is selective. Still further, the Koran's preoccupation with Judgment Day is much more intense than that of the Bible, especially the Old Testament—the Koran being closer in this respect to the New Testament. Finally, a conspicuous difference has to do with the verbal focus on God. Unlike the Bible, the Koran contains, sometimes almost in every other verse, a reference to this or that attribute of God, such as his mercy, justice, wisdom, majesty, omnipotence, omniscience, and omnipresence. These references are meant, among other things, to induce in man the state of moral alertness the Koran requires of him.

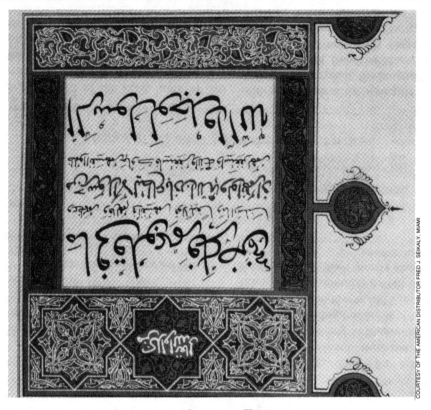

■ **Ornamentation of a seventeenth-century Koran.**

THE KORAN AND MUSLIM SOCIETY

The importance of the Koran in Muslim society is manifold.

Fundamental text. As the fundamental text of Islam, the Koran lays down the Islamic creed and expounds the rights and obligations of the believers. It constitutes the highest authority one can cite in support of a view or opinion. Needless to say, because its authority is uncontested, some may attempt to manipulate its interpretation for their own ends. As a safeguard, scholars have adopted a set of interpretive rules.

Religious, social, and artistic uses. The Koran is at the heart of Muslim liturgy. Since, as noted above, the Koran in translation may not be called the Koran, liturgical recitation of the Koran must be in the original language. In the five daily prayers, therefore, it is recited in Arabic. In Ramadan, the month of fasting, special congregational prayers are held in mosques at night in which huffaz recite the Koran from beginning to end. The art of Koran-recitation is called *tajwid*, and

tajwid competitions, which are held at local, regional, national, and international levels, are widely attended. In many countries, Koran-recitation forms part of the ceremony blessing a new house, launching a business, or commemorating a deceased person. The Koran is also recited to avert evil or as a token of gratitude for success in a venture. Many Koran-reciters have made recordings of the Koran that are best-sellers, and commuters use the cassette-recorders in their cars to listen to their favorite Koran-reciter. Besides Koran-recitation, Koranic calligraphy is an esteemed art. The absolute Koranic prohibition of idolatry resulted in a distrust of representational art, but, in compensation as it were, the art of callig-

raphy was developed and perfected. Walls, domes, and arches of mosques are frequently decorated with Koranic verses. And even in this age of typesetting, the Arabic Koran is often written in hand by expert calligraphers and then printed on presses.

Role in Islamic intellectual history. Not only is the Koran the central religious text of Islam, it was responsible for transforming, almost overnight, a nonliterate culture into a literate one. The art of writing in Arabia owes its systematic development to the need for transmitting the Koranic text in written form. The need to solve the problems of grammar and language in the Koran led to the formulation of grammar (*nahw*). The need

The art of Koran-recitation is called tajwid, *and tajwid competitions, which are held at local, regional, national, and international levels, are widely attended.*

o solve the issue of divine omnipotence and human freedom, an important issue in the Koran, laid the foundations of Muslim theology (*kalam*), part of which later developed into Muslim philosophy. The need to understand the laws and injunctions of the Koran gave rise to the science of jurisprudence (*fiqh*).

The importance of studying nature as a repository of God's signs engendered among Muslims of earlier centuries a spirit of investigation and an empirical outlook that made possible Muslim achievements in several scientific fields. Today, in the hands of thoughtful Muslims, the Koran yields principles and guidelines for a critical reassessment of Islamic tradition and history.

General educational value. The majority of the world Muslim population is non-Arab. And yet a Muslim, no matter what his native language, is normally expected to be able to read the Koran in Arabic. Muslim children usually learn to read the Koranic script at an early age. In a country like Pakistan, learning the Koran's Arabic script helps the child in learning the derived script of his native language, for example Urdu. But even when this is not the case, as in Indonesia, learning the Koranic script is a matter of religious importance. Furthermore, learning Koran-recitation facilitates, and is often accompanied (formally or informally, in Arabic or in any other language) by the learning of basic Koranic terms, concepts, and doctrines.

ECUMENISM, JIHAD, AND DISSENT

How does the Koran view other faiths? Two things are quite clear. First, there were messengers sent before Muhammad: "There has not been a community which has not seen the advent of a warner [i.e. prophet]." reads 16:36. This means that, in principle at least, divine guidance was or has been available to the followers of religions other than Islam. In a sense, then, humanity is linked through the dispensers of that guidance—prophets. Second, two pre-Islamic

religions, for all the criticism they are subjected to, enjoy a special status in the Koran: Judaism and Christianity. If humanity is linked in a general way through the institution of prophecy, the religions of Islam, Judaism, and Christianity are linked in a special way through that model religious personality, Abraham. What ecumenist possibilities does this two-fold linkage hold?

One may respond to this question by saying that while in principle Islam would be ecumenically disposed toward any religion, it is with Judaism and Christianity that it can best come to ecumenical terms in a substantive sense; Judaism and Christianity, too, one might say, would feel greater kinship with Islam than with most other religions. But in the pluralistic world of today, and especially in a pluralistic society like the United States, ecumenism calls, on the one hand, for more detailed statements on Islam's relations with Judaism and Christianity, and, on the other, for fresh answers to questions pertaining to Islam's relations with other religions. Such answers, yet to be provided, can result only from interreligious dialogue, in which, it must be noted, Muslim participation has been relatively recent. The one crucial Koranic verse whose interpretation is likely to determine or condition the Muslim position on the issue is 2:62: "Indeed those people who have believed [i.e. Muslims], those who became Jews, the Christians, the Sabeans—all those who believe in God and the Last Day and perform good deeds, shall have their reward with their God, and shall have no fear and experience no grief." While it would be wrong to interpret this verse in such a way as to abolish the differences that exist between Islam and the other religions, it would be equally mistaken to interpret it in such a

way as to preclude the possibility, from the Islamic viewpoint, of any ecumenical effort. At this point we may note a certain modern development.

The Koran, like the Bible, contains statements that could be used for and against an ecumenical approach, and much would therefore depend on what perspective is placed on them. Compare the following two "sword verses," one each from the Koran and the New Testament: "Do not think that I have come to bring peace on earth; I have not come to bring peace but a sword" (Matt. 10:34); "then kill the idolaters wherever you find them, besiege them, and lie in wait for them in every place" (9:5). Ecumenism is, in its origin, a Christian phenomenon. But Matt. 10:34, interpreted strictly, would hardly make for a credible Christian ecumenical stance. As for Koran 9:5, traditional Muslim scholars use it to posit a world that is sharply divided between the world of Muslims ("Abode of Islam," or "Abode of Peace") and the world of non-Muslims ("Abode of Unbelief," and hence "Abode of War"), the only relationship between these two abodes being that of hostility.

But a number of renowned modern scholars of Islam, scholars who cannot be accused of selling their Islam cheap, have taken issue with this interpretation. A case in point is Abu Zahrah of Egypt, one of whose many fine works deals with the subject of Islam and international relations. His essential thesis is that, in international relations, Islam takes peace rather than war as its starting-point, and that in settling a conflict war is the last rather than the first resort. It is in light of this thesis that he interprets the history of early Islamic conquests. Even more important than the position taken by Abu Zahrah is the interpretative method

The Koran, like the Bible, contains statements that could be used for and against an ecumenical approach, and much would therefore depend on what perspective is placed on them.

he uses to arrive at that position: He contextualizes the Koranic verses, and the context he uses is not only the immediate context of the passage or section in which a particular verse occurs but also the entire thought-context of the Koran.

This combination of textual and philosophical perspectives is not only theoretically defensible but it also maintains, at least in respect to the issue under discus-

sion, the integrity of the Koranic content. It accords their proper place to both pro-peace and prowar statements in the Koran, within the thought-framework of the Koran. Such an interpretation would seem to provide a Koranic basis for resolving, wherever possible and to the extent possible, international conflicts by peaceful means. Today all Muslim countries are members of the United Nations, and

there is nothing in the Koran that prohibits Muslims from abiding by the agreed upon charter of a body like the United Nations.

It must, however, be kept in mind that an ecumenical endeavor is by definition joint and concerted, and the follower of one religion should therefore desist from prescribing ecumenical terms for the followers of another religion. The actu

■ Page from an eighteenth-century ornamental Koran belonging to Sultan Mohammed III of Morroco.

Today all Muslim countries are members of the United Nations, and there is nothing in the Koran that prohibits Muslims from abiding by the agreed-upon charter of a body like the United Nations.

al character of an ecumenical understanding, moreover, will be determined by the particular configuration of the religious and non-religious factors at a given time. What is of the utmost importance is that one be clear as to what ecumenism really involves. First, ecumenism should be a practical rather than a theoretical objective. Respect for, rather than abolition of, differences should be the aim. Second, ecumenism is not an all-or-nothing proposition. Partial agreement and limited cooperation is not to be frowned at if total agreement and full cooperation is not possible. Third, the search for ecumenism should involve genuine representatives of the communities in question rather than those who are merely vocal or vociferous.

In medieval times, the Christian propaganda machinery saw fit to present Islam as the primitive creed of sword-brandishing hordes from Arabia. To their credit, Western scholars themselves have done much to rectify the distorted image. But certain conceptual hobgoblins remain, especially on the popular level, and one of them is *jihad*. The word means literally "struggle," and is used for any effort made to promote or protect the religion of Islam. When this effort takes the particular form of armed action, it is called *qital*. Every country or society, Muslim or non-Muslim, regards qital as a legitimate means of self-defense, and it would be childish to wish otherwise. But neither the specific term *qital* nor the more inclusive term *jihad* is presented anywhere in the Islamic sources as an approved, or even permissible, way of making converts. The Koranic teaching on the subject is succinctly stated in 2:256, which says: "There is no compulsion in religion," and in 76:3, which says that it is entirely up to a human being to choose his religious faith and destiny.

What does the Koran say on the issue of dissent and liberty? The Koran does not address the issue as such. There are, however, several indications of the Koranic position. The above-quoted dictum, "There is no compulsion in religion," basically means that no one can be compelled to accept Islam. But there is no reason why the principle underlying the state-ment, namely, that an individual has the right to choose and profess what he will, should be restricted to formal acceptance or rejection of a creed. Umar, the second caliph of Islam (seventh century), once rebuked one of his governors, and also the son of the governor, for mistreatment of an ordinary citizen: "Since when," he said angrily, "did you start enslaving men who were born free?" It is, however, not simply a question of citing one or two apposite verses to establish that the Koran upholds individual freedom; it is also a question of the overall spirit and outlook of that scripture, and a careful study of the Koran cannot fail to show that the Koran, insofar as we can judge its intent, does put a high premium on individual liberty. The Koran's repeated urging of man to use reason in choosing his destiny and follow a reasonable course of conduct is predicated on the two-fold premise that man has the freedom to choose, and that that freedom must be guarded.

LIBERTY AND DISSENT IN THE SALMAN RUSHDIE CASE

This, in simple terms, is the Koranic position on liberty and dissent. What does this position imply in reference to free publication and censorship? Does it hold up in practice? The question acquires some urgency in view of the recent flare-up over Salman Rushdie's novel, *The Satanic Verses*.

In the first place, it should be noted that the general Muslim reaction—that of outrage—to the publication of the novel, cannot be used to impugn the Koranic position stated above; the two are really quite different phenomena. In the second place, the nature of that reaction was almost completely misunderstood in the West. The difference of perspective was quite fundamental. While the West saw the issue in ethnocentrically interpreted legal terms of liberty and censorship, the Muslim world saw it in broader humanistic terms of fair play and foul play. Consider the very different Muslim attitude to two other works. Dante's *Divine Comedy* presents Muhammad and other revered personalities of Islam in gulfs of hell. The work is, in its basic intent, literary, and that is how it was perceived in the Muslim world. It was not censored, and has been available in bookstores and libraries in Muslim countries. The nineteenth-century British scholar Sir William Muir's biography of the Prophet of Islam contains material that is inflammatory from an Islamic viewpoint and also shows evident bias on the author's part. Again, however, in its basic intent it is a scholarly work, and that is how it was perceived by Muslims; it, too, is available in Muslim countries.

If Rushdie's book was treated differently, it obviously was taken to be neither as a literary nor as a scholarly work, but one of malicious satire and wanton sacrilege. The insensitive attitude and conveniently selective approach of Western media that gloatingly promoted the work puzzled and infuriated a community that already felt violated. Compounding the problem, of course, was the fact that Rushdie bears a Muslim name, which brings up the issue of cultural treason as opposed to political treason. Also called in question were the motives of the writer, who had received a huge advance payment. It must be added that the exaggerated importance given to the book by certain acts committed and certain statements made in the Muslim world only aggravated a phenomenon that, had the soberer advice of some Muslim circles been heeded, would have eventually played itself out.

ACCESSIBILITY OF THE KORAN

The Koran is not a rare book. It is easily available, and despite the usually inadequate, not to say bad, translations it is available in, its essential message can easily be derived by an intelligent layman. One who is seriously interested in finding out the Koranic position on some of the issues discussed herein, or, better still, in acquiring a serious overall understanding of a book that about a billion Muslims regard as their scripture, would do well to spend some time perusing the book on his own. This might be more rewarding than reading several books or articles on sundry Koranic subjects.

REFERENCES

Bell, Richard. *Introduction to the Qur'an.* rev. and enl. by W. Montgomery Watt. Edinburgh: Edinburgh University Press, 1970.

Irving, Thomas Ballantine; Khurshid, Ahmad, and Muhammad Manazir, Ahsan. *The Qur'an: Basic Teachings.* Leicester, England: Islamic Foundation, 1979.

Rahman, Fazlur. *Major Themes of the Qur'an.* Minnesota and Chicago: Bibliotheca Islamica, 1980.

Stanton, H.U. Weitbrecht. *The Teaching of the Qur'an.* New York: Bible and Tannen, 1969 (first published 1919).

APPENDIX

Several translations of the Koran are in common use. Of the following, all but No. 2 are available in paperback.

(1) *The Meaning of the Glorious Koran,* by Mohammed Marmaduke Pickthall, a British convert to Islam (Mentor, n.d.; first published 1930). Adheres to traditional interpretations and is quite literal.

(2) *The Holy Qur'an: Text, Translation, and Commentary,* new rev. n.d. (Brentwood, Maryland: Amana Corporation, 1985). Copious notes. The original edition (1934) should preferably be used.

(3) *The Koran Interpreted,* by A.J. Arberry, 2 vols. (New York: MacMillan, 1956). Tries to recapture the poetic beauty of the Koran, with sometimes awkward results. May be used in conjunction with Pickthall.

(4) *The Message of the Koran,* by Muhammad Asad, an Austrian convert to Islam (Gibraltar, 1980). Is an interpretive rendering, using parenthetic additions for clarity and continuity with extensive notes.

(5) *The Koran,* by N.J. Dawood, 4th rev. ed. (New York: Penguin, 1974). Idiomatic and highly readable, but rather careless, at times inaccurate. The traditional order of the Koranic chapters is altered, perhaps needlessly.

> *While the West saw the issue in ethnocentrically interpreted legal terms of liberty and censorship, the Muslim world saw it in broader humanistic terms of fair play and foul play.*

Article 9   *The UNESCO Courier,* February 1990

Land of a thousand and one courtesies

YANN RICHARD

An Islamic tradition handed down by the Persian poets tells how Abraham, not wishing to eat alone, once sought to share his meal with an old man he met in the desert. When the time came to pray, he realized that his guest was a Zoroastrian and wanted to send him away. But an angel restrained Abraham, saying, "God has fed this man for a hundred years, how could you refuse him a meal?"

Strangers are invariably surprised by the ceremonial that unfolds before them on a visit to an Iranian household. Whatever the time of day or night, whatever the reason for the visit or the social status of the visitor, a drink will be offered first of all. To enter someone's house is like coming to the end of a journey through the dust of the desert and slaking one's thirst in a garden.

Usually the tea is prepared in the Russian manner, left to brew for a long time in a teapot standing on a samovar and served with added water in small glasses. Sugar is not added to the tea but placed on the tongue. Sweetmeats are always provided to accompany the golden liquid. Each town has its own speciality, such as tamarisk jellies, sugared almonds flavoured with the essence of Egyptian willow, assorted baklavas (nut and honey pastries) from Yazd, all kinds of biscuits, some flavoured with jasmine, others stuffed with walnuts, pistachios or almonds...

YANN RICHARD, of France, is a researcher at the French National Centre for Scientific Research (CNRS). He lived for several years in Iran, where he worked with the French Institute of Iranology, Tehran. He has published several studies on Iranian culture, and is co-author (with B. Hourcade) of *Téhéran au-dessous du volcan* ("Tehran under the Volcano", Autrement publishers, Paris, 1987) and editor of a collection of articles on Iran and the West published by the Maison des Sciences de l'Homme, Paris, in 1989.

In summer, to alleviate the torrid heat of the road, cool syrups made from melon or watermelon juice are served on arrival. The accomplished hostess can blend the colours and flavours of different fruits in the most unexpected ways.

Don't think that you can drop in on someone and then quietly slip away as soon as your business is concluded. In face of the sometimes excessively polite formulas used by the master of the house when he insists that you stay to eat (in the case of an unexpected visit it is good manners not to accept too quickly), you must decide for yourself what common courtesy requires. Even if there is little to talk about, a visit should not last less than an hour, otherwise your friends will be offended by the implication that they have failed to entertain you properly.

Conversation follows a ritual course, beginning with mutual inquiries about matters of health. At first bad news is avoided, and it is only broached after a decent interval in order to spare people's feelings. Depending on the closeness of the friendship between them, people either discuss general topics or more personal matters. What is so-and-so up to these days? When the conversation flags, such basic questions as "How are you getting on?" are used to get it started again. It would be a mistake to lose patience with these conventions, which simply exist to fill gaps in the conversation and to create a companionable atmosphere.

When your thirst has been quenched you will be brought dishes of dried fruit, cakes, fresh fruit.... It has been decided that you will stay and any pretext will be used to keep you. You can't leave without tasting our fruit! How can you refuse, faced with such a tempting array of grapes, figs, peaches and cucumbers?

Pause between mouthfuls and you will notice that the room where you are being entertained does not seem to be in regular use. It is certainly not the place where the family watches television or reads the papers. Even poor families have a place where guests can be entertained, although in modern apartments space is limited. Wealthier families used to Western-style comfort keep a guest-room furnished with armchairs and a sofa, while in more modest rural homes cushions are arranged around the central carpet. Guests who have travelled far sleep in the same room, for which carefully folded sheets, blankets and a mattress are always at hand and will be laid on the carpet for the night.

The urbanization of the last thirty years, the wear and tear of city life, cramped apartments... all these factors make it increasingly difficult to offer hospitality. Moreover, travelling has become commonplace and the arrival of a relative from the airport after a flight lasting an hour or two bears little resemblance to that of the exhausted dust-caked traveller of not so very long ago, who had suffered extremes of heat and cold and had not slept for several nights. Such hardships are only a memory today, when proliferating hotels and restaurants cater for the growing number of people who wish to travel anonymously, without imposing on the hospitality of a relative or friend and incidentally sparing themselves the duty to reciprocate.

Most large family get-togethers, which are less common today than they used to be, tend to take place during the major festivals of the religious or civic calendar. On these occasions succulent dishes are laid out on cloths spread over the carpet, and twenty or thirty people gather to eat. But in contrast to the welcome ceremonies described above, people talk as little as possible during these meals, and eat hurriedly, which is a pity since people would often be happy to take a second helping and savour the meal at their leisure.

Enormous quantities of food are prepared for these family reunions, and if supplies were to run out, the master of the house would give the shameful impression that he is ungenerous. When you have finished, don't forget to say that you are full. Extra guests commonly turn up at the last minute, when someone brings along an unexpected visitor, a relative or a friend. There are never any seating problems as everyone squeezes up around the cloth, and if the meal is served on a table it is often in the form of a buffet since there are rarely enough chairs to go round.

Once the meal is over, more tea is served and the ceremony quickly comes to an end. The master of the house will beg you to excuse the frugality of his hospitality and the poor quality of his food, but of course you will protest by insisting that your hosts have done everything they could, that is to say a great deal, and that you are very grateful to them.

Although the master and mistress of the house always stay in the background, try to satisfy your every need and give you the place of honour, do not think that a guest's role is simply to relax. First of all you must humbly accept the honours bestowed on you, respond to the polite remarks addressed to you, and help yourself to the dishes offered to you even if you don't want them. All these signs of good manners will show the host that his attempts at hospitality have not been in vain. The guest loses his independence and becomes, as a Persian saying ironically puts it, "the master's donkey"!

The guest's paramount duty, however, is to return the courtesy. At New Year *(Now Rouz)* a return visit is practically taken for granted, as anyone who has received guests has been placed under an obligation to them. It may seem surprising that people you have just entertained in your home insist on receiving you the following day, but to refuse would be embarrassing as it would put them at a disadvantage and leave them in your debt. The uninitiated who accept the lavish hospitality of Iranians often forget this duty to reciprocate and earn themselves a black mark socially. One way to make up for not being able to return the invitation is to bring a present.

But compensation for generosity may come much later. Someone from the provinces living in Tehran or another big city will feel particularly honoured to receive people from his village, even if they stay for several days. Such a visit is a tribute to his social success and raises his standing in the neighbourhood. Guests of this kind are therefore a blessing, because although they may cost their host something in food and effort, their visit enhances his prestige.

One benefit of hospitality, and not the least, is that it puts paid to disagreement and conflict. While "bread and salt" are being shared there is no question of perpetuating grievances or of picking quarrels. A tacit truce by both parties, host and guest, creates a feeling of solidarity that nothing can destroy. The same principle, when institutionalized, guarantees the traditional right

of asylum in places held to be sacred: mosques, the homes of great ulemas (religious leaders), the stables or kitchens of the shah or, more recently, embassies and consulates.

When the time has come to take your leave, the host will see you out. This is another way of placing you under an obligation. Among the formalities of leave-taking, you will often hear the same words you heard when you arrived. No irony is intended: this is not a polite way of showing you the door but a way of assuring you in all sincerity that the visit has been beneficial for the household and that you will always be just as welcome in the future.

Article 10

The UNESCO Courier
November 1989

THE ARAB WORLD Where geometry and algebra intersect

Historian of science Roshdi Rashed on the Arab contribution to the history of mathematics

How would you describe the beginnings of Arab mathematics?

Arab research into mathematics seems to have begun early in the ninth century when, in Baghdad, the movement to translate the great Greek authors into Arabic was at its height. For instance, Al-Hajjaj ibn Matar made two translations of Euclid's *Elements* and Ptolemy's *Almagest,* and Hilal ibn Hilal al-Himsi translated the first four volumes of Apollonius of Perga's *Conics.* Several works by Archimedes, Pappus and Diophantus, among others, were also translated in the same century.

This major undertaking was noteworthy for two very important features, in that the translations were made by leading mathematicians and were inspired by the most advanced research of the time. For example, volumes V to VII of Apollonius' *Conics* were translated by the great mathematician Thabit ibn Qurrah, who died in the year 901. Moreover, all the indications are that Qusta ibn Luqa was prompted to translate the *Arithmetica* of Diophantus around 870 on account of studies already being carried out on indeterminate analysis.[1]

Many other examples could be cited to demonstrate the close links between such translations and the innovative research already being done at this high point in the dissemination of Hellenistic mathematics in Arabic.

Al-Khwarizmi is the best known of the Arab mathematicians. What was his contribution to mathematical thinking?

It was at this time, in the ninth century, at the Baghdad Academy, or "House of Wisdom" as it was known, that al-Khwarizmi wrote a

Detail from a treatise on equations by Sharif al-Din al-Tusi (late 12th-early 13th century). The manuscript dates from 1297.

work that represented a new departure in terms of both content and style. This was the *Kitab al-jabr wa'l muqabalah* ("The Book of Integration and Equation"),[2] from which algebra emerged for the first time as a separate and independent mathematical discipline. This was a crucial development, and was recognized as such by al-Khwarizmi's contemporaries, as much for its new mathematical style as for the nature of its subject-matter and above all for the rich promise it held out for further advances.

In terms of style, it was both algorithmic, in that the author set out a series of computational procedures, and demonstrative. A new mathematics had to be devised that was general enough to be capable of handling different types of formulation while existing independently of those formulations. In al-Khwarizmi's work, an algebraic expression could refer to a number or to an irrational quantity or to a geometrical magnitude. This new mathematics and its combination of the demonstrative and applied approaches was a striking innovation for the thinkers of the time.

The novelty of the conception and style of al-Khwarizmi's algebra, which did not hark back to any previously known tradition, cannot be over-emphasized. The new algebra already afforded a glimpse of the enormous potential for applying one mathematical discipline to another that lay ahead from the ninth century onwards. In other words, while algebra, by virtue of its widespread scope and the new concepts it introduced, made such applications possible, their number and variety were thereafter constantly to change the face of mathematics.

Al-Khwarizmi's successors increasingly applied arithmetic to algebra and vice versa, arithmetic and algebra to trigonometry, algebra to the Euclidian theory of numbers, and algebra to geometry and vice versa. All these applications paved the way for new disciplines or at least for new chapters in the history of mathematics.

Could you give us a significant example of the encounter between arithmetic and algebra?

One example that springs to mind is the contribution which Arab mathematics made to classical number theory.

By the end of the ninth century, the most important Greek texts on arithmetic, such as Euclid's own volumes on the subject, the *Introductio arithmeticae* of Nicomachus of Gerasa, and the *Arithmetica* of Diophantus of Alexandria, had all been translated. Further chapters in the theory of numbers were opened in the wake of these translations and could in a sense be said to have been a reply to them. For example, two significant steps were taken in respect of the theory of amicable numbers. The first of these led, in the context of Euclidian arithmetic, to a new set of findings, while, as a result of the application of algebra to the theory of numbers, the second step culminated some centuries later in the creation of a field of number theory that owed nothing to the Greeks. We can look into these two aspects more closely.

Although Euclid put forward a theory of perfect numbers at the end of Volume IX of his *Elements*, neither he nor Nicomachus of Gerasa had developed the theory of amicable numbers.[3] Thabit ibn Qurrah, who translated the work of Nicomachus and revised a translation of the *Elements*, decided to work on this theory. He came up with and demonstrated, in pure Euclidian style, a remarkable formula for amicable numbers which now bears his name.

If we disregard the mystique which had surrounded amicable numbers and look only at the mathematics, it has to be acknowledged that, up to the end of the seventeenth century at least, the history of amicable numbers merely consisted of a passing reference to Ibn Qurrah's formula and its transmission by later mathematicians. These included such Arabic-speaking mathematicians as al-Antaki, al-Bagdadi, ibn al-Banna, al-Umawi and al-Kashi, whose differing origins in both time and place clearly show the widespread dissemination of Ibn Qurrah's formula, which crops up again in the work of Pierre de Fermat in 1636 and in that of René Descartes in 1638.

The second step is noteworthy for the fact that the celebrated physicist and mathematician Kamal al-Din al-Farisi, who died in 1320, wrote a paper in which he deliberately set out to demonstrate Ibn Qurrah's formula, but by a different path. Al-Farisi based his new demonstration on a systematic knowledge of the divisors of a whole number and of the operations that can be applied to them. However, this demonstration involved a reorganization which gave rise not only to a change in the perspective of Euclidian arithmetic, but to the promotion of new topics in number theory. It accordingly became possible to speak of a non-Hellenistic area in number theory.

In order to make it possible to engage in this new study of divisors, al-Farisi had to establish explicitly certain facts that had only been latent in Euclid's *Elements*. He also had to make use of the advances in algebra since al-Karaji's time in the tenth and eleventh centuries, and especially

ROSHDI RASHED, of France, is director of research at the National Centre for Scientific Research (CNRS). He is the author of many studies on the history of Arab mathematics. Several of his articles were published in *Entre arithmétique et algèbre, Recherches sur l'histoire des mathématiques arabes* (Les Belles Lettres publishers, Paris, 1984).

of combinatory methods. Hence, al-Farisi's approach was by no means confined to demonstrating Ibn Qurrah's formula, but enabled him to embark on a new study involving the first two arithmetical functions: the sum of the divisors of a whole number and the number of those divisors.

This style, which applied algebra and combinatory analysis to Euclidian arithmetic, was still prevalent in Europe in the seventeenth century, at least until 1640. The analysis of al-Farisi's conclusions and of the methods he used thus goes to show that, by as early as the thirteenth century, it had been possible to produce a set of propositions, findings and techniques that had hitherto been ascribed to the mathematicians of the seventeenth century.

What about the new relationship that was established between algebra and geometry?

We have already seen that the mathematical landscape was no longer the same from the ninth century onwards; it was transformed and its frontiers were rolled back. Greek arithmetic and geometry became increasingly widespread. In addition, non-Hellenistic areas were developed within the corpus of Hellenistic mathematics itself. The relationship between the old disciplines was no longer the same, and a host of other groupings were formed. This changing pattern is crucial to an understanding of the history of mathematics generally, for the new relationship between algebra and geometry gave rise to techniques of enormous potential.

The mathematicians of the tenth century embarked on a two-way exercise in conversion which had never previously been envisaged—the translation of geometrical problems into the language of algebra, and vice versa. They translated into algebraic terms solid problems that could not be constructed with ruler and compass, such as the trisection of the angle, the two means, and the regular heptagon. Moreover, algebraists and also geometers such as Abu al-Jud b. al-Leith, when faced with the difficulty of using radicals to solve a cubic equation, were able to turn to the language of geometry and apply the intersecting curves technique to the study of this type of equation.

The first attempts to provide a basis for these conversions were made by al-Khayyam (c. 1048-1131). In his bid to go beyond the specific cases represented by a particular form of cubic equation, al-Khayyam developed a theory of algebraic equations of a degree less than or equal to three which at the same time provided a new model for the formulation of equations. He then studied cubic equations using conic sections in order to reach positive real solutions for them. In order to construct his theory, al-Khayyam had to visualize the new relationship between algebra and geometry in clearer terms before being able to formulate it. From then onwards, the theory of equations appeared, albeit still tentatively, to bridge the gap between algebra and geometry.

In his celebrated treatise *Algebra,* al-Khayyam produced two remarkable findings which historians have wrongly attributed to Descartes. These are the generalized solution of all third-degree equations by means of two intersecting curves, and the possibility of performing a geometric calculation by defining a unit length, which was a fundamental concept.

Some fifty years after al-Khayyam, his successor Sharaf al-Din al-Tusi made a further step forward. In an attempt to demonstrate the existence of the point of intersection of two curves, he arrived at the problems of finding and separating the roots of the equation and of dealing with the conditions under which they existed. In order to find a solution he defined the notion of maximum values for an algebraic expression and tried to find concepts and methods for determining such "maxima".

This not only led al-Tusi to the development of concepts and methods, such as derivatives, that were only to be named as such at a later date, but also compelled him to change his approach. He discovered the need to use local procedures, whereas his predecessors had only considered the overall properties of the objects being studied. All these findings and the theory embracing them are obviously important and have often been attributed to mathematicians who only came several centuries later.

These are the main features of the dialectic between algebra and geometry. To complete the picture, however, two impediments which slowed down the progress of the new mathematics should be mentioned. These were a reluctance to use negative numbers as such, at a time when they had not yet been defined, and the shortcomings of symbolic notation. Both issues were to preoccupy later mathematicians.

In political historiography distinctions are made between Antiquity, the Middle Ages, the Renaissance and modern times. Do you think that this breakdown is relevant in an account of the history of mathematics, and especially of the Arab contribution?

It is true that "medieval" mathematics has been contrasted with "modern" mathematics. The first

Right, part of a Latin translation of al-Khwarizmi's treatise on algebra in a manuscript dating from 1145. Far right, a commentary on Euclid's **Elements of Geometry** *by Nasir al-Din al-Tusi (1201-1274). (15th-century Persian manuscript)*

historical corpus, covering Latin, Byzantine and Arab mathematics, and Indian and Chinese mathematics as well, could be distinguished from another body of work which came into being with the Renaissance. I don't feel that this dichotomy is relevant in either historical or epistemological terms. Arab mathematics clearly represents a continuation and outgrowth of Hellenistic mathematics, which was its breeding-ground. This is also true of the mathematics which grew up in the Latin world from the twelfth century onwards. Finally, the work accomplished in both Arabic and Latin (or Italian) between the ninth century and the early seventeenth century cannot be split into separate periods.

On the contrary, all the indications are that the type of mathematics involved was the same. This is borne out by the fact that we can now compare the work on algebra and numerical computation produced by al-Samaw'al in the twelfth century with that of Simon Stevin in the sixteenth century; al-Farisi's findings in number theory with those of Descartes; the methods used by al-Tusi for the numerical resolution of equations with that of François Viète in the sixteenth century or al-Tusi's search for *maxima* with that of Fermat; al-Khazin's work on integral Diophantine analysis in the tenth century with that of Bachet de Meziriac in the seventeenth cen-

1. The last five books of Diophantus' *Arithmetica* are principally devoted to the solution of indeterminate equations, i.e. those with more than one variable and a large number of solutions. *Editor*
2. The word *algebra* is derived from the title of this work which was translated into Latin many times in the Middle Ages and had a strong influence on medieval Western science. The word *algorithm*, which designates any method of computation (such as the decimal system) involving a series of steps, is derived from the Latinized form of al-Khwarizmi's name. *Editor*
3. A number is *perfect* if it is equal to the sum of its own divisors (for example $6 = 3 + 2 + 1$; $28 = 14 + 7 + 4 + 2 + 1$). Two integers form a pair of amicable numbers if the sum of the proper divisors of one is equal to the other. This is true of the numbers 220 and 284, which were for a long time the only known pair of amicable numbers.

tury, and so on. If we were to disregard the work of al-Khwarizmi, Abu Kamil, al-Karaji and others, how could we understand the work of Leonardo of Pisa and the other Italian mathematicians in the twelfth and thirteenth centuries, or the mathematics of the seventeenth century?

True, the later seventeenth century was marked by the emergence of new methods and new areas of mathematical interest in Europe. However, that break did not necessarily occur all of a sudden, nor did it take place at the same time in every discipline. Moreover, the dividing lines seldom coincide with the works of different authors, but often cut right across them. In number theory, for example, the innovation did not lie in Descartes' and Fermat's use of algebraic methods, as has been claimed, since they simply rediscovered al-Farisi's findings. The break can actually be identified within Fermat's own work around 1640, with his invention of the "infinite descent" method and his study of certain quadratic forms.

It was really from the mid-seventeenth century onwards that the tangled threads come together and the main breaks in continuity are identifiable. The contribution made by the Arab mathematicians thus fitted into a coherent pattern which grew up between the ninth century and the first half of the seventeenth century.

Article 11

Middle East Report • November-December 1991

WOMEN, ISLAM AND THE STATE

Deniz Kandiyoti

Deniz Kandiyoti, a senior lecturer in the Social Sciences Division of Richmond College, London, is the editor of Women, Islam and the State *(Temple University Press, 1991).*

Most commentary on gender and politics in the Middle East assigns a central place to Islam, but there is little agreement about the analytic weight it carries in accounting for the subordination of women or the role it plays in relation to women's rights.[1] Using the Quran, the *hadith* and the lives of prominent women in the early period of Muslim history as sources, conservatives confirmed that existing gender asymmetries are divinely ordained, while feminists discerned possibilities for a more progressive politics of gender based on the egalitarian ideals of early Islam. These exegetical exercises mainly showed that, for both feminists and anti-feminists,

Islamic doctrine continued to provide the only legitimate discourse within which to debate women's rights.

Contemporary analysts have renounced these treatments as essentialist, ahistorical and lacking in class perspectives.[2] These newer studies focused on the processes of socioeconomic transformation accompanying the region's incorporation into the world economy; the concerns of Middle East scholars started mirroring those of Third World "women and development" specialists.[3] The influence of feminist theory also made itself increasingly felt. Debates about the subordination of women now occurred in a more complex theoretical field, in which the analytic primacy of Islam was temporarily eclipsed.

The rise of Islamist movements has stimulated new interest in the relationship between religion and politics in the region, and the role of the state in expressing and implementing this relationship. The most immediate and visible targets in "Islamization" programs were the dress, mobility and general status of women, putting the question of Islam and women's rights back on the agenda with a renewed urgency. For Moroccan sociologist Fatima Mernissi, Muslim fundamentalism is an assertion of identity in the face of rapid social changes threatening existing authority relations (especially between genders), and a response to the boundary problems created by the intrusions of colonialism, new technology, consumerism and economic dependency.[4] I have argued elsewhere that socioeconomic transformation has aggravated social inequalities, dislocating local communities and producing massive migratory movements and the influx of women into the labor force. All of this has dealt a severe blow to the material and normative underpinnings of patriarchy, increasing the attractions of compensatory, conservative ideologies.[5]

While such arguments may account for part of the popular appeal of Islamist ideologies, they cannot explain the differential incorporation of these ideologies into actual state policies. Significant variations in the condition of women in Muslim societies derive from, among other things, the different political projects of modern nation-states. The ways in which women are represented in political discourse, the degree of formal emancipation they have achieved, their forms of participation in economic life and the nature of the social movements through which they express their demands are closely linked to state-building processes. Studies on women in Muslim societies have not always acknowledged the extent to which aspects of state practice define and mediate the place of Islam itself.

Relationships between Islam, the state and the politics of gender comprise at least three distinct components: 1) links between Islam and cultural nationalism; 2) processes of state consolidation and the modes of control states establish over local kin-based, religious and ethnic communities; and 3) international pressures that influence priorities and policies.

Cultural Nationalism & Women's Rights

All Muslim societies have had to grapple with the problems of establishing modern nation states and forging new notions of citizenship. Diverse processes of nation-building have produced a spectrum of distinct, shifting and actively contested syntheses between cultural nationalism and Islam. Women's rights were debated and legislated in the search for new ideologies to legitimize emerging forms of state power.

Turkey stands out with its early experience of secularism, as the multi-ethnic Ottoman empire dissolved in favor of an Anatolia-based nation state. Kemal Ataturk not only dismantled the central institutions of Ottoman Islam by abolishing the Caliphate, but took additional measures to heighten Turkey's "Turkish" national consciousness at the expense of a wider identification with the Muslim *umma*. The nationalist alliance that brought Kemal to power included men of religion who resisted any changes in the position of women, but collaboration between the Ottoman Islamic establishment and Allied occupation forces after World War I had undermined their legitimacy. The abrogation of the *shari'a*, the adoption of a secular Civil Code in 1926 and the enfranchisement of women in 1934 became part of a broader struggle to liquidate the institutions of the Ottoman state and establish a republican notion of citizenship. Despite the growth of Islamist political platforms in recent years, the Turkish state has not, to date, acted to reverse the legislative reforms of the early republican era.

In Iran, Reza Shah openly claimed to derive inspiration from Mustafa Kemal's reforms. His ban on veiling in 1936 was certainly more drastic than Kemal's pedagogic and indirect approach. However, at the point of modern state-building Iran was a much more fragmented polity than the Ottoman empire. Reza Shah's regime, furthermore, was not the heir of a war of national liberation but a military-based monarchy, with a much shallower basis for legitimacy. While Reza Shah consolidated his rule by eliminating alternative sources of power, the Shi'a clergy was able to resist co-optation into the institutions of the Pahlavi state. Unlike the Ottoman clerical establishment, the clergy in Iran remained strong enough both economically and in its mass-based networks to reenter the political arena after the 1960s.[6]

State-building projects in the Arab world have ranged from experiments with "Arab socialism" to continuing monarchic rule. Despite reforms permitting educational, juridical and state institutions greater autonomy from religious authorities, *shari'a*-inspired legislation in family and personal status codes persists even where secular laws have been adopted in every other sphere. Equal citizenship rights of women guaranteed by national constitutions are circumscribed by personal laws granting men special privileges in the areas of marriage, divorce, custody, maintenance and inheritance. Does this conservatism in the areas of women and the family derive from the centrality of Islam to Arab cultural nationalism, and represent an attempt to preserve Arab cultural identity in the face of Western imperialism as many Arab commentators maintain?[7] Al-Khalil takes issue with the notion that Arab nationalism, at least in its Ba'thist version, could ever embody a secular project. He argues that the demarcation of Arab national identity was made possible through arguments about the primacy of the Arabs within Islam, and that a particular version of Islam, Sunnism, was made co-terminus with national identity.[8] The fact that Sunnism and Shi'ism can be mobilized as the respective markers of Arab and Iranian national identities was made amply evident and was fully exploited during the Iran-Iraq war.

The tensions and juxtapositions between Islam and national identity are clearest in the South Asian subcontinent. Pakistan emerged from partition as a state that claimed its separate identity and sovereignty on the grounds of religion; Islam was constitutive of nationhood in itself. Although Pakistan originated as a homeland for the Muslims of India rather than as an Islamic state, Islam was increasingly evoked as the legitimizing ideology of Pakistani unity. The "Islamization" package introduced by General Zia ul-Haq gave legal sanction to crude forms of sexual discrimination, which Pakistani women's organizations loudly protested.

This emphasis on control of women as a means of establishing Islamic credentials must be set in the historical context of pre-partition India. Ayesha Jalal argues that conservative entrenchment on issues pertaining to women and family life lay at the heart of Muslim cultural resistance to both Hinduism and British colonialism.[9] The Bengalis, on the other hand, favored a linguistic and cultural nationalism in order to wrest their independence from their Pakistani co-religionists; Bangladesh emerged from the conflict of 1971 as a secular People's Republic. State secularism subsequently eroded under successive regimes until finally General Ershad declared Bangladesh an Islamic state in 1988. The Islamization policies of Bangladesh, though, have remained more tentative than those of Pakistan, continuing to express the contradictions of its nationalist history, of its varied internal constituencies and of the conflicting agendas of various foreign aid donors.[10]

In India, the question of Muslim women's rights easily turns into a confrontation of minority (Muslim) and majority (Hindu) interests. As a result, any progressive attempts to redefine or expand these rights is thwarted by the logic of communal politics.[11]

State Consolidation & Family Legislation

The fact that women represent the "inner sanctum" of diverse national collectivities and the focal point of kinship-based solidarities, as opposed to a more abstract and problematic allegiance to the state, has presented a dilemma for the "modernizing" states of the Muslim world. Modern states have had to confront and to some extent eradicate the local particularisms in order to create new forms of civic consciousness and to liberate all available forces of development, including the labor potential of their female citizens. Depending on the nature of their political projects, states have variously challenged, accommodated or abdicated to local/communal patriarchal interests, with important consequences for family legislation and more general policies affecting women.

Muslim modernists at the turn of the century put family reform high on their agendas. They denounced sex segrega-

tion, arranged marriages, repudiation and polygamy and argued that the subjugation of women hinders national progress. Such views remained in the realm of polemic in societies with small urban populations, weak industrial bases and vast rural or tribal hinterlands. The limited outreach of pre-modern states left many aspects of their citizens' lives untouched; regulation of marriage and family life remained under local kin control. Attempts at greater state penetration of society under Muhammad Ali in 19th century Egypt and in the late Ottoman empire remained limited compared to the dramatic expansion of state power in this century.

The attempts of post-independence states to absorb and transform kin-based communities in order to expand their control had an important bearing on policies relating to women and the family. Mounira Charrad argues that variations in the balance of power between the national state and locally based communities in Tunisia, Morocco and Algeria during accession to independence account for significant differences in family legislation.[12] In Iraq, the Ba'th had an interest both in recruiting women into the labor force in the context of a continuing labor shortage, and in wresting women's allegiance away from loyalties to kin, family or ethnic group and shifting that allegiance to the state-party. Women were recruited into state-controlled agencies and put through public education as well as vocational training and political indoctrination. The 1978 Personal Status law, although limited in its objectives, aimed at reducing the control of extended families over women. In Lebanon, governments formally relinquished matters of family and personal status to the religious authorities of existing communities. This was part of the strategy of Lebanon's ruling elite to maintain the balance of sectarian power in the state.[13] The People's Democratic Republic of Yemen, by contrast, introduced the 1974 family law which, despite numerous concessions to Islamic laws and local customs, aimed to free women from traditional forms of kin control and create possibilities for their emergence as economic and political actors in the service of national development.[14]

Other considerations that have a bearing on state policies relating to women include the extent to which states are pressed to mobilize their internal resources.[15] Oil states, which were until recently able to recruit foreign migrant labor, were clearly less reliant on female labor than, say, Turkey or Egypt, though recent developments in the Gulf may force a partial redefinition of the existing sexual divisions of labor. Conversely, states whose foreign earnings are highly contingent on remittances from male international migrants may increasingly rely on female labor in their domestic economies. This is particularly true in countries that have shifted their industrial priorities from import-substitution to export-led strategies of development which stimulate the recruitment of low-paid female labor.

The interventionist measures of post-independence states, either through family legislation or education, employment and population control policies, were primarily geared to national development. Their record with respect to the emancipation of women is quite mixed. Typically authoritarian and *dirigiste* regimes did not encourage the creation of democratic civil societies in which women's gender interests could be autonomously represented. Women's attempts at independent organizations were considered divisive and actively discouraged. This was the case during the single-party regime in Turkey, under the Pahlavis in Iran, and under Nasir in Egypt who, immediately after granting women suffrage in 1956, outlawed all feminist organizations.[16] Instead, state-sponsored women's organizations were set up which were generally the docile auxiliaries of the ruling state-party. Nonetheless, in regimes as diverse as those of Ataturk, Reza Shah and Nasir, an emphasis on national consolidation and unity and the creation of a modern, centralized bureaucracy were congruent with the mobilization of women to aid the expansion of new cadres and the creation of a uniform citizenry.

Some regimes have recently reversed what appeared to be the steady expansion of women's rights in the early stages of national consolidation. Others are expecting legitimacy crises, the political outcomes of which may also encroach on women's rights. The expansion of women's citizenship rights coincided with the secularist thrust of nationalist state-building projects. The political and distributive failures of such projects in Pakistan and India, for example, have aggravated conflicts expressed in religious, ethnic and regional terms. States have themselves used and exploited sectional rivalries in their patronage networks and distributive systems, exposing any initial universalist pretensions as shallow and fragile. Radical Islamist discourse typically identifies these failures not as merely political ones but as "moral" failures, requiring a complete overhaul of the world views underpinning them. As religious and ethnic identities become increasingly politicized, they tend to sacrifice women's hard-won civil rights on the altar of a politics of identity that prioritizes control of women. Governments struggling to shore up their legitimacy may choose tactically to relinquish control of women to their immediate communities and families, thus depriving female citizens of full legal protection.[17]

In those cases where the state itself sponsors religious fundamentalism, as in Iran, Pakistan or Saudi Arabia, the exercise of patriarchal authority extends to the clergy, the police or even other unrelated men, who take it upon themselves to monitor the dress and conduct of women.[18] One of the deepest ironies behind this emphasis on the control of women is the fact that the ties of economic and political dependence in which most states are enmeshed restricts their autonomy quite severely in almost every other sphere. This brings us to a consideration of the international context in which state policies are formulated and implemented.

The International Context

At the regional level, the cleavages between oil-rich and resource-poor countries had an important effect on the flow of migration, aid and political influence in the Muslim world. Migrants went from poorer countries such as Egypt, Yemen, Bangladesh, Turkey and Pakistan to the oil countries of the Gulf, while a reverse flow of cash and political influence strengthened the cultural and political prominence of local Islamist tendencies. This prompted diverse accommodations with Islam in aid-dependent countries. Internal Islamist constituencies either received a measure of acceptance and favor from ruling parties or governments, or created pressures pushing governments to declare their own commitment to religious orthodoxy as a means of upstaging more radical Islamist platforms.

Meanwhile, international monitoring of local economies reached unprecedented levels with the adoption of structural adjustment packages and stabilization measures imposed by the International Monetary Fund and diverse development projects sponsored by Western donor agencies. The shift from tight state control over the economy to private sector and foreign investment initiatives, and the adoption of export-led development strategies, had significant gender effects, notably a significant increase of the female labor force in the low-paid, casual and non-unionized sectors of the economy.

Since the International Women's Year in 1975 and the United Nations Decade for Women (1975-1985), the women-and-development lobby has exerted pressure on national governments to recognize the role of women in combating poverty, illiteracy and high birth rates and to eliminate all forms of legal discrimination based on sex. Since 1973, the Percy Amendment to the US Foreign Assistance Act has required that bilateral aid should promote projects integrating women into development efforts. Monitoring bureaucracies were set up within the US Agency for International Development, the World Bank and the foreign aid departments of the main European donor nations. Although these initiatives are still marginal to mainstream development funding, they indicate the success of international women's movements in placing gender issues on policy agendas. The "official" feminist rhetoric of modernizing, post-independence states has now been appropriated by supra-national monitoring bodies, but with contradictory consequences at the local level.

Bangladesh, an impoverished country with a high level of dependence on foreign aid, offers interesting perspectives on the interaction between local politics and international influences. The declaration of the United Nations Decade for Women in 1975 coincided with the military coup that brought Zia ul-Rahman to power. Zia accumulated considerable political capital by championing the causes of the women and development lobby. However, he also needed the support of rightwing constituencies, including the army, to counter the opposition of the Awami League.

Oil-rich countries like Saudi Arabia, meanwhile, joined the ranks of major aid donors and increased their influence considerably. Zia embarked on an Islamization program which culminated in General Ershad's declaration of Bangladesh as an Islamic state in 1988. Both Zia's and later Ershad's strategies strove to balance the conflicting gender ideologies implicit in different aid packages: the development projects encouraged women's participation in the labor force and public life, while aid from wealthier Muslim countries strengthened religious education and the pro-religious parties advocating stricter controls over women. The government, which supports US-funded attempts at population control, also funds Islamic organizations condemning them.[19]

Parallels may be found in other countries, where we see local machinery channeling development funds into projects designed to empower women against a background of increasingly conservative ideologies, and sometimes policies, concerning their appropriate roles. Donor governments and funding agencies aim to harness women directly to their vision of a more effective, though not necessarily more equitable, international economic order. The very manner in which the recipients of aid are integrated into this order encourages the rise of unstable and repressive regimes.

The development policies favored by such regimes have by and large led to more visible disparities in wealth, fueling widespread popular resentment and discontent, often in the absence of adequate democratic channels of expression. Islamist tendencies and movements enter this equation in ways specific to each context, which does not invite easy generalizations. A conclusion that does seem permissible is that when they do become a factor, tighter control over women and restrictions of their rights constitute the lowest common denominator of their policies.

Footnotes

1 A debate indicative of these disagreements may be found in Mai Ghoussoub, "Feminism—or the Eternal Masculine—in the Arab World," *New Left Review* 161 (January-February 1987), pp. 3-13; Rema Hammami and Martina Rieker, "Feminist Orientalism and Orientalist Marxism," *New Left Review* 170 (July-August 1988), pp. 93-106.

2 Nikki R. Keddie, "Problems in the Study of Middle Eastern Women," *International Journal of Middle East Studies* 10 (1979), pp. 225-40; Judith E. Tucker, "Problems in the Historiography of Women in the Middle East: The Case of Nineteenth Century Egypt," *International Journal of Middle East Studies* 15 (1983), pp. 321-36.

3 See the themes in: "Women and Work in the Middle East," *MERIP Reports* #95 (March-April 1981); "Women and Labor Migration," *MERIP Reports* #124 (June 1984); "Women and Politics," *MERIP Reports* #138 (January-February 1986).

4 Fatima Mernissi, "Muslim Women and Fundamentalism," *MERIP Reports* #153 (July-August 1988), pp. 8-11.

5 Deniz Kandiyoti, "Islam and Patriarchy: A Comparative Perspective," in Nikki Keddie and Beth Baron, eds., *Shifting Boundaries: Women and Gender in Middle Eastern History* (New Haven: Yale University Press, forthcoming 1992).

6 Afsaneh Najmabadi, "The Hazards of Modernity and Morality: Women, State and Ideology in Contemporary Iran," in Deniz Kandiyoti, ed., *Women, Islam and the State* (London: Macmillan, and Philadelphia: Temple University Press, 1991).

7 Nadia Hijab, *Womanpower* (Cambridge: Cambridge University Press, 1988); Nawal el Saadawi, "The Political Challenges Facing Arab Women at the End of the 20th Century," in Nahid Toubia, ed., *Women in the Muslim World* (London: Zed Books, 1988); Leila Ahmed, "Early Feminist Movements in Turkey and Egypt," in Farida Hussain, ed., *Muslim Women* (London: Croom Helm, 1984); Fatima Mernissi, *Beyond the Veil* (London: Al-Saqi Books, 1985).

8 Samir Al Khalil, *The Republic of Fear* (London: Hutchinson, 1989).

9 Ayesha Jalal, "The Convenience of Subservience: Women and the State of Pakistan," in *Women, Islam and the State.*

10 Naila Kabeer, "The Quest for National Identity: Women, Islam and the State of Bangladesh," in *Women, Islam and the State.*

11 Amrita Chhachhi, "Forced Identities: The State, Communalism, Fundamentalism and Women in India," in *Women, Islam and the State.*

12 Mounira Charrad, "State and Gender in the Maghrib," in *Middle East Report* #163 (March-April 1990), pp. 19-24.

13 Suad Joseph, "Elite Strategies for State Building: Women, Family, Religion and the State in Iraq and Lebanon," in *Women, Islam and the State.*

14 Maxine Molyneux, "The Law, the State and Socialist Policies with Regard to Women: The Case of PDRY 1967-1990," in *Women, Islam and the State.*

15 I am grateful to Suad Joseph for calling my attention to this consideration in her comments on an earlier paper.

16 For an extensive discussion of women's movements in Egypt see: Margot Badran, "Competing Agenda: Feminists, Islam and the State in 19th and 20th Century Egypt," in *Women, Islam and the State.*

17 This was the case in India, where Muslim women's access to secular law in matters of divorce was blocked by the Muslim Women's Act of 1986. Another significant but little noticed, and subsequently denied, development was the Iraqi government's legal exemption for Iraqi men announced in March 1990 entitling them to kill female members of their family if they suspect them of adultery.

18 Amrita Chhachhi, *op.cit.* See also Eleanor Abdella Doumato, "Women and the Stability of Saudi Arabia," in *Middle East Report* #171 (July-August 1991), pp. 34-37.

19 Naila Kabeer, *op.cit.*

Article 12

The Wall Street Journal, November 1989

Riddle of Riyadh: Islamic Law Thrives Amid Modernity

Women Learn Car Mechanics But Not How to Drive; They Still Defend System

Geraldine Brooks

Staff Reporter of The Wall Street Journal

AL KHUBAR, Saudi Arabia—Desert tradition demands that any traveler who turns up at a Bedouin's tent must be offered shelter for at least three nights. But in modern-day Saudi Arabia, a woman arriving with a reservation at a five-star hotel seems unwelcome for even one night.

At the gleaming Gulf Meridien hotel, a Western reporter with a reservation finds herself directed to the police station rather than to her room. An apologetic desk clerk explains that it is illegal for an unaccompanied woman to stay in a Saudi hotel without a certificate from the police establishing that she isn't a prostitute. "In the morning the police check the registrations," he explains, "and in the past we've had staff jailed and deported for allowing a woman to check in."

Six-lane freeways have replaced camel trails, and 24-hour Safeway supermarkets have superseded dusty *souqs*. But more remarkable than what has changed is what hasn't. The glittering city-centers still feature Friday-afternoon beheadings that are open to the public. And inside the walls of modern villas, family life holds tenaciously to the old ways. Islam rules here.

Temporarily Brooks Brothers

It is a mistake to assume Westernization inevitably accompanies industrialization, says Don Kerr, a Saudi Arabia expert at the London Institute for Strategic Studies. For a brief time, he says, the thousands of young Saudis who go to universities in the West pick up Western tastes and a Western vocabulary. "But while they may have temporarily swapped the *thobe* [traditional robe] for a little number from Brooks Brothers, the change was no more significant

than that—a surface covering," he says. "When it came to things that are really important, they operate on the same basis they have always done."

The Koran and the tribe remain the important things. The Koran is both holy book and constitution in Saudi Arabia, and from it the state derives the right to chop off the hands of thieves and to order shopkeepers to close for prayers. Tribal tradition, meanwhile, props up one of the world's most absolute of monarchies and rigidly restricts social life.

Until about a year ago, Saudis of both sexes used to lace up their skates and glide around the sheet of high-density white plastic that substitutes for ice in Jeddah's scorching climate. "We used to get a thousand skaters over a weekend," recalls Gerry Willis, the rink's British manager. But then the sheik who owns the rink decided that the Madonna music, the flashing lights and the male-female mixing was "all a bit too free" says Mr. Willis, Now both sexes can still skate, but only during segregated hours.

Rules of the Road

Women still aren't permitted to drive in Saudi Arabia, and riding alone in a taxi is frowned upon. But traveling in groups also poses problems. Earlier this month, a Filipino driver in Riyadh picked up three American women, who didn't all want to cram into the back seat. One sat in the front passenger seat and, as a result, the driver says, he was hauled to jail and beaten by the religious police—the Committee for the Propagation of Virtue and the Prevention of Vice—for sitting alongside a woman who wasn't his wife.

In the case of the visiting reporter, a bearded young lieutenant at the police station eventually provided the neces-

sary paper work for a hotel stay. But that was only after the Saudi businessman whose company the reporter planned to visit presented himself for a late-night interrogation. "Once, in Riyadh, they stopped me from checking in with my wife," the businessman confided. He had to have documents faxed to the hotel proving the two were married before he was allowed to take his wife to his room.

Most Saudis seem to put up with such excesses as part of the cost for a stable and secure life.

"The Islamic religion is also our law," explains Lolwah al-Ammari, a Saudi businesswoman educated at Whittier College in California. "If you understand Islam, you can find a reason for every act." To Mrs. al-Ammari, restrictions on women's travel are "protection for you, not chains around you." She adds, "You are supposed to travel with a male to protect you, because in old times travel took days, months maybe. So the whole idea is love and protection."

Mrs. al-Ammari covers her hair and wears a long cloak when she goes out, but doesn't wear the black cloth that most women still drape over their faces. "I can't breathe well and I can't see well" through it, she says. Yet she doesn't consider it a major obstacle to women's advancement. "Women have gone to university wearing the veil," she says. "It is only a piece of cloth. "It's not covering my mind."

To help keep traditions, censorship is rigorous. An American executive living in Jeddah was recently astonished to open a letter from the Hyatt hotel chain, only to find the swimsuited model on the brochure inside had earned the censor's attention. "Somebody had opened the envelope, colored in her legs from the crotch down, and then resealed it. It was meticulously done," the businessman says.

Foreign publications also are individually previewed. Copies of this newspaper circulated here got the felt-pen treatment last month when an advertisement for ergonomically designed airline furniture featured Leonardo da Vinci's famed nude drawing of "Man."

References to Jews often are censored as well. The television series "War and Remembrance," which dealt with World War II, including the Holocaust, appeared in the Saudi video version with all reference to Jews blanked out. "You could see the characters mouthing the word 'Jew' but no sound was coming out," recalls one viewer.

Saudis are zealous about keeping the desert kingdom free of any religious symbols that aren't Islamic. Christian churches, even private religious services, are banned. A few years back, employees of the national airline were surprised by an abrupt redesign of the carrier's logo, making a slight alteration in the shape of the letter "a" in the word Saudia. The airline repainted its fleet of planes, remade neon signs and changed the appliques on employees' uniforms.

A staffer, baffled by so much expense for a minor change, got the following explanation: The space between the first two letters of the old Saudia logo had formed a cross-shape. The cross, as a symbol of Christianity, may not be displayed in Saudi Arabia. A spokesman for Saudia, however, labels this account as "airline folklore" and says religious considerations didn't play a part in the redesign, which aimed to make the logo conform "more to the style of Arabic calligraphy."

With or without a cross, the airline is unmistakably Islamic. Each flight begins with a recorded recitation of Mohammed's prayer for travelers played over the public address system, and each plane is equipped with a ceiling-mounted Mecca compass, so that traveling Moslems can be sure which direction to turn to in prayer. Alcoholic drinks aren't served by the airline and aren't allowed to be carried by passengers.

On the ground in Saudi Arabia, Islam dominates the landscape. Billboards proclaiming "Allahu Akbar"—God is Great—share roadside space with advertisements for tea bags and air freshener. Mosques rise alongside gas stations, at airports, in hotel foyers and on every city block. Even travel routes are determined by religion, with giant highway signs labeled "Moslems" and "Non-Moslems," directing unbelievers on to routes that won't allow them to pass through, or even glimpse, the sacred cities of Mecca and Medina. To stress that Islam comes first, King Fahd has ordered that his preferred title is "Custodian of the Two Holy Mosques," rather than "His Majesty."

But while Islam may prescribe life here, "there are plenty of safety valves," says a Western diplomat in Riyadh. "A Saudi can travel if he finds it too restrictive." For a Saudi woman, it isn't quite so easy. She must have the permission of a male relative to leave the country.

Women, nonetheless, often are the staunchest defenders of the system, pointing to the gains they have made in education and, increasingly, in Saudi Arabia's segregated work force.

As a young girl, Basilah al-Homoud got most of her education in Syria. Her father moved the whole family there because her older sister wanted to be a dentist and at that time in Saudi Arabia dentistry and other advanced studies weren't open to women.

But times have changed. Now Mrs. al-Homoud is completing her master's degree in business administration at a university in Jeddah. She is also the director of Dar al-Fikr, a school for girls in the city. Along with pure academic subjects, the school stresses know-how in practical matters such as computers, cooking and motor mechanics. But Mrs. al-Hamoud isn't aiming to turn out a generation of auto engineers. "If [a student's] driver says the car's broken down, I want her to know if he's telling the truth," Mrs. al-Homoud explains.

A staunch traditionalist, Mrs. al-Homoud says, "When my father told me I had been proposed to, he said 'Do you want to see him, do you want to sit with him?' I said, 'If you sit with him, it is enough for me.' "

But lest outsiders think nothing changes in Saudi Arabia, Mrs. al-Ammari, who is a member of a 10-woman consortium running a computer-training business, tells a story: Just a generation ago, her mother was kidnapped and sold to a man who became her husband. At the age of eight, it was her second wedding. She had already been married once by family arrangement.

Article 13   CURRENT HISTORY • January 1992

Iraq, the Pariah State

"Iraq succumbed to hubris in 1990: Saddam Hussein hoped to make his country rich beyond belief and infinitely more powerful by incorporating Kuwait. Then he promised that the war for Kuwait would be 'the mother of all battles,' but it turned out to be 'the mother of all defeats.' . . . [O]ne of the most highly developed countries in the Middle East has been crippled and left with limited sovereignty and a limited regional and international role."

AHMED HASHIM

AHMED HASHIM, *a Washington-based consultant on the Middle East who specializes on Iraq, is the author of "The Strategic Culture of the Garrison State: Iraqi Views on Deterrence, Compellance, and War-Fighting vis-à-vis Israel, 1988–1991," in David Wurmser, ed.,* Regional Security in the Middle East: Arab and Israeli Concepts of Deterrence and Defense *(Washington, D.C.: United States Institute of Peace, 1992).*

Iraq's invasion of Kuwait on August 2, 1990, and its subsequent ejection from the emirate were watershed events in Iraq's modern history. The invasion precipitated the world's first post–cold war crisis and united almost the entire international community against Iraq. In the United Nations (UN) Security Council, the Western powers (Britain, France, and the United States) led the opposition to Iraq on the diplomatic front and helped push through a series of Security Council resolutions condemning the invasion and imposing trade sanctions.*

Activity was not limited to the diplomatic front. Fearing an Iraqi attack, Saudi Arabia requested United States military aid, which began to arrive on August 7. This set the stage for a massive deployment of United States forces to the region, soon joined by smaller contingents from Britain, France, Egypt, Syria, and many other countries to form a formidable anti-Iraq international coalition. On November 29 the UN Security Council authorized this coalition to use "all necessary means"—including force—to eject Iraq from Kuwait on or after January 15, 1991.

---

*The main Security Council resolutions on the Persian Gulf crisis are excerpted in *Current History*, February, 1991, pp. 79, 90.

As the crisis continued, the coalition's goals were increasingly defined by the United States. These included the defense of Saudi Arabia; Iraq's immediate, complete, and unconditional withdrawal from Kuwait; and the restoration of security and stability to the Persian Gulf. Attempts by France, Iran, the Soviet Union, and others to reach a negotiated settlement stalled because of United States insistence on an unconditional Iraqi withdrawal, and because Iraq insisted that Kuwait was Iraqi territory and that the Kuwait crisis should be linked to the resolution of other problems in the Middle East.

January 15 came and went without Iraq's withdrawal; on January 17, the coalition began a massive aerial attack against targets in Iraq and Kuwait. Six weeks of this punishing air campaign were followed by a lightning ground assault on February 24 that routed Iraqi forces at a surprisingly low cost to the coalition. On February 27, 100 hours after the attack had begun, United States President George Bush halted the ground offensive. Kuwait had been liberated, and a large swath of southern Iraq was held by the coalition. Baghdad accepted the coalition's cease-fire terms on March 3, which included an immediate release of prisoners of war; 2 days later Iraq's leader annulled the annexation of Kuwait.

One month later, on April 6, Baghdad accepted the terms for a permanent cease-fire in accordance with Security Council Resolution 687, which stipulated continuing an arms embargo for the indefinite future; UN-supervised destruction of all chemical and biological weapons, long-range ballistic missiles, and nuclear infrastructure; Iraqi compensation to Kuwait and other countries for damages incurred during the war; an unequal demilitarized zone along the border with Kuwait extending 6 miles into Iraq and 3 miles inside

Kuwait to be patrolled by UN observers; and UN demarcation of the border between the two countries. Iraqi compliance with these demands would result in the gradual lifting of sanctions. Iraq reacted with predictable outrage to Resolution 687, saying it was a vindictive and unwarranted derogation of Iraqi sovereignty. However, it had no option but to accept the terms.

OPPOSITION AND REBELLION

The end of the war also found Baghdad challenged by an array of Iraqi opposition groups based outside the country and spanning the political spectrum from Islamic fundamentalists, Kurdish autonomists, and nationalists to dissident Baathists, leftists, and liberals. Opposition to the regime was longstanding, but Iraq was a well-policed and "self-policing" society, where the public had internalized the "correct" patterns of behavior. Iraqis had tolerated an authoritarian regime in return for socioeconomic policies that were the most progressive in the Arab world: under Hussein's reign, the Iraqi people had become the best-educated and healthiest Arabs in the Gulf region.

But the Gulf crisis dramatically changed the opposition's fortunes soon after its start. The allied coalition's mobilization against Saddam raised hopes among the opposition that it would no longer be ignored by the international community; dissident groups redoubled their efforts to establish a common anti-Saddam platform and began to court members of the coalition. In December 1990 almost all the members of the Iraqi opposition convened a conference in Damascus and established a steering group, the Joint Action Committee, that condemned Saddam's "dictatorship" and called for his removal and free elections.

Although the opposition had hoped a popular revolt would remove Saddam from power, it was not prepared for the insurrections that erupted at war's end among the Shiites in southern Iraq and the Kurds in the north. The revolt in the south began after disgruntled infantry streamed back into Basra with harrowing tales of defeat at the hands of a superior foe and mismanagement of the war by their own government. The soldiers, allied with Muslim fundamentalists, launched attacks against government installations and Baath party buildings. Baath party cadre and security officials—most of whom were Shiites—who did not flee or go into hiding were hunted down and murdered.

Within days the revolt had spread to major cities, including the Shiite holy centers of Karbala, An Najaf, Diwaniyah, Hilla, and Mahmudiya. The rebellion profited immensely from the coalition's military presence in southern Iraq, since it inhibited the Iraqi army from using the full range of its remaining firepower; moreover, the coalition said it would not allow Iraq to use fixed-wing aircraft or chemical weapons against the insurgents.

Iran, despite disclaimers to the contrary, played an important role in the rebellion, infiltrating into southern Iraq ideologically committed and well-trained paramilitary units—the At-Tawibin and Badr divisions made up of fundamentalist exiles and Iraqi prisoners of war from the Iran-Iraq war who had joined the Iranians. Iran also infiltrated members of its own Pasdaran, or Revolutionary Guards. (At the end of the revolt it was reported that Iraq had captured 6,000 Pasdaran infiltrators.) These units from Iran were generally better armed, better motivated, and better organized than the initiators of the rebellion.

The Iraqi government fought back with its best-trained and most loyal units, the Republican Guards, who made liberal use of their superior firepower and helicopter gunships. Savage street fighting took place in the holy cities, where the rebels fought to the death. The military exacted a terrible revenge against the rebels and those suspected of aiding them, and many civilians caught in the cross fire fled into Iran, coalition-held territory, or the inaccessible marshy region of southern Iraq.

Iraq regained control of Basra on March 12, and Karbala fell to government forces on March 15. The next day Baghdad claimed the rebellion was over, and accused "rancorous traitors" and foreign governments of instigating it. The government's announcement was premature, however, because between March 20 and 29 the capital itself witnessed minor disturbances in the largely Shiite quarters, but these were quickly contained by security forces.[1]

Why did the Shiite insurrection fail? First, it was not a general insurrection. The revolt was initially an explosion of pent-up rage characterized by looting and destruction and offering no ideological vision. But when it achieved a semblance of organization and success as a result of leadership provided by the units from Iran, it developed an ideology that proved disastrous: carried away by their euphoria, the rebels raised the green banner of Islam, displayed portraits of deceased Iranian leader the Ayatollah Ruhollah Khomeini, and called for Islamic rule in Iraq. This dismayed opposition groups outside Iraq, including Shiite fundamentalists, who denied that they intended to bring about Islamic rule.

Most important was the reaction of Sunni Arabs and the Shiite middle class. For this secular-minded segment of the population, the thought of a fundamentalist regime coming to power with Iran's aid was horrifying. Furthermore, the atrocities against government officials were seen as harbingers of the bloodbath to come if the rebels prevailed. And members of the coalition, who had made clear their desire to see Saddam overthrown, were thoroughly disconcerted by a rebellion that might result in the fragmentation of Iraq or install a pro-Iranian fundamentalist regime. Their very neutrality during the revolt enabled the Iraqi military to move about freely and crush it.

THE KURDISH REVOLT

The Kurdish revolt erupted in both rural and urban areas when Kurdish civilians, including professionals and intellectuals as well as tens of thousands of Fursan members (Kurdish irregulars), joined the Iraqi Kurdistan Front (IKF), which was made up of smaller Kurdish groups, and the rival Kurdish Democratic party and the Patriotic Union of Kurdistan. Massoud Barzani, the head of the Kurdish Democratic party, and Jalal Talabani, the leader of the Patriotic Union of Kurdistan, acted quickly to take control of the rebellion and engaged their veteran guerrilla units in attacks against government forces. Within days and for the first time in their history, the guerrillas took several major urban centers, including the oil center of Kirkuk. By mid-March the IKF had declared that 75 percent of Kurdistan was in rebel hands. The group rapidly moved to restore essential services and civil administration in the "liberated" areas.

After crushing the revolt in the south, Baghdad moved its forces north and launched an offensive to retake all urban centers by April 1. Lacking experience in urban warfare and hoping to spare the urban population, the guerrillas fled into the mountains, but they found that they could not conduct war in rural areas because they had been depopulated and turned into free-fire zones.

The reason for the Kurdish collapse is clear: the guerrillas were not as combat ready as the Iraqi forces. Talabani noted that "we did not realize that the Republican Guards were still in such good shape."

Neither the IKF nor the international community expected what happened as the revolt collapsed: hundreds of thousands of civilians began an exodus from northern Iraq that, at its height, encompassed more than 50 percent of the Kurdish population. Thousands of people died because of cold weather or lack of food as they escaped to the safety of Iran or Turkey. The exodus may have been prompted by fear of reprisals by government forces, including the possibility that chemical weapons might be used, as they had been in 1988. The refugee problem received enormous international media coverage, prompting a massive humanitarian effort to provide the refugees with food, medicine, and shelter. On April 5 the UN Security Council adopted Resolution 688, which approved the establishment of "safe havens" in Iraq north of the thirty-sixth parallel that would be protected by coalition military forces; Kurdish civilians were encouraged to return to these protected zones.

Despite their commitment to overthrow Saddam, the defeated Kurds had no choice but to negotiate. Baghdad balked at many of the Kurds' demands: it adamantly refused to cede Kirkuk, arguing that the city did not have a Kurdish majority; it also had no intention of losing control over a substantial part of the country's oil. The Kurds believed that the government was not negotiating in good faith, and they were not impressed by the political reform program proposed by the government in March.

Negotiations dragged on throughout the summer and autumn. The Kurds were reluctant to sign an agreement, and there were reports of a growing rift between Barzani and Talabani. Barzani distrusted international guarantees and wished to conclude an agreement with Baghdad, while Talabani supported the mainstream opposition's belief that Kurdish autonomy and democracy in Iraq would develop if Saddam were overthrown.

SANCTIONS AND ECONOMIC DEVASTATION

The damage Iraq suffered in its war with Iran between 1980 and 1988 pales in comparison with what it has suffered as a result of sanctions, the allied air campaign, and the insurrections.[2] The trade sanctions that the UN approved on August 6, 1990, seriously affected food stocks; before the war Iraq imported 75 percent of its wheat, 100 percent of its soybean meal, and 90 percent of its maize, sugar, and vegetable oil. Economic sanctions also had a severe impact on local industry, which relied heavily on foreign suppliers for spare parts, raw materials, machinery, and expertise. By the fall of 1991, the private sector suffered from shortages of materials and goods; according to the head of the Iraqi industrial association, 16,000 private ventures were either working at reduced capacity or on the verge of halting operations.

The international community believed that in the short term sanctions would not persuade Iraq to leave Kuwait; the Iraqi government would try to attenuate the effects by careful stockpiling and rationing of available food stocks, reducing the population's already high caloric intake, and by circumventing the sanctions through limited trade with its neighbors. But it was thought that long-term enforcement of the embargo would cause economic dislocation and would paralyze Iraq as the country ran out of food, spare parts, and raw materials after mid-1991. However, the issue of whether sanctions would have forced Iraq out of Kuwait became moot when the coalition decided to use force instead.

The coalition's massive air bombardment of Iraq was aimed not only at the Iraqi military, its supply dumps, and its communications lines, but also at a wide array of economic and industrial targets. The bombing would amplify the economic impact of sanctions, incite the

Iraqi people to oppose Saddam, degrade Iraq's ability to sustain itself as an industrial and military power, and create leverage over postwar Iraq, which would not be able to repair extensive damage without outside help.

Iraq suffered particularly extensive damage in three critical areas: the national electric power grid, telecommunications, and the oil industry. Coalition air forces damaged 17 of Iraq's 20 electric power plants; 11 were totally destroyed. At the height of the summer of 1991, when electricity demand was at its peak, Iraqi power-generating capacity was 40 percent of the prewar level of 9,500 megawatts. The damage to the electric power grid forced closures or the slowing down of operations in the public-health sector, refrigeration plants, and sewage treatment units; the last resulted in raw sewage flowing through streets and into rivers. The incidence of diarrheal diseases increased dramatically.

Telephone exchanges and radio and television stations as well as the country's extensive road and bridge network were targeted and suffered extensive damage: half of Iraq's telephone lines were destroyed as were scores of bridges, including many of those spanning the Tigris and Euphrates rivers. The damage to much of what had been a modern infrastructure hindered the ability of government and relief agencies to deliver foodstuffs to rural regions, where shortages were more acute.

The oil industry has been absolutely critical to Iraq's economic development over the years, providing the country with as much as 95 percent of its foreign-exchange earnings. Coalition forces dropped 1,200 tons of high explosives on 28 major oil installations. The immediate goal was to curtail Iraq's refining capacity and thus its ability to deliver fuel to the armed forces. Facilities in the south suffered the greatest damage because of their proximity to important military targets (Republican Guard concentrations and supply dumps), while the facilities around Kirkuk suffered less during the war and incurred minor damage during the Kurdish insurgency.

The Iraqis have repaired some of the facilities. By the autumn of 1991 Iraq was able to produce 450,000 barrels of oil a day for domestic consumption and 50,000 barrels a day for export to Jordan. Total production capacity, however, was estimated at 1.5 million barrels a day; 1 million of this could be exported by pipelines through Turkey if sanctions are lifted. The Iraqi Ministry of Oil has said that by the end of 1992 Iran could achieve its prewar production level of 3.2 million barrels a day if it receives desperately needed chemical additives, spare parts, and help to repair damage to the oil industry.

A UN mission that visited Iraq in mid-March issued a report saying the war had "wrought near-apocalyptic results" on a highly urbanized and mechanized society.

The report drew the world's attention to the combined effects of sanctions and war damage on the population, noting rapidly dwindling stocks of food and medicine and declining health and sanitary conditions. Iraq repeatedly requested that it be allowed to sell oil to satisfy basic needs, but in its first formal review of sanctions in June the Security Council concluded that lifting the sanctions was not justified since Iraq had not fully complied with the provisions of Resolution 687.

Another UN report on Iraq's economic and social crisis in mid-July urgently requested that Iraq be permitted to import $7-billion worth of food, medicine, and spare parts. The Security Council "relented" and on August 15 passed Resolution 706, allowing Iraq to sell $1.6-billion worth of oil over a six-month period. Proceeds from the sale will go into an escrow account to be divided into three unequal amounts: almost $1 billion will be used to buy food and medicine, while the rest is to be divided between reparations and paying UN peacekeeping expenses.

The task of reconstruction is enormous; Iraqi officials claim that the Kuwait affair cost them $200 billion. This is in addition to $200 billion spent on the Iran-Iraq war. Long-term reconstruction will depend on foreign-exchange revenues, trade, foreign technical expertise, and the willingness of the Iraqi private sector to take a more vigorous role in the economy. Iraqis know that they cannot engage in long-term reconstruction if the sanctions remain in place. Even if the sanctions are lifted the country will face formidable obstacles; indebtedness makes the country a terrible credit risk, and reparations payments will siphon off as much as 30 percent of Iraq's income for the indefinite future.

A FORMIDABLE MILITARY

Initial figures of Iraqi losses during the war led to the hasty conclusion that Iraq's remaining army consisted largely of poorly equipped, low-grade infantry divisions. By summer's end this was found to be inaccurate; the war had destroyed between 45 and 50 percent of a huge inventory, but Iraq retained 2,400 tanks; 4,400 armored personnel carriers and infantry fighting vehicles; between 1,000 and 2,000 artillery pieces, mortars, and howitzers; and 250 multiple rocket launchers.

The air force suffered the most devastating losses: of a prewar total of 700 warplanes, Iraq had no more than 300 left. Iran had allowed 115 Iraqi warplanes, including many of Iraq's top-of-the-line Soviet- and French-built fighters and about 30 Iraqi Airways civilian jets, to flee the country and land in Iran during the course of the war. Most of Iraq's helicopter fleet survived intact, as was evident during the insurrections.

The army has been restructured; instead of a ramshackle 1-million-man force, the Iraqis now have between 350,000 and 400,000 troops, of which the Republican Guards constitute a substantial and growing element. Most of the other units are special forces and regular army armored and mechanized divisions shorn of the low-grade infantry divisions that performed dismally in both the Iran-Iraq war and the Persian Gulf war. Throughout last spring and summer the army received substantial pay and benefit increases in order to restore its morale. The army is a now a leaner, more professional force that would be more formidable if Iraq were allowed to rearm.

Iraq's comprehensive military industries program was severely damaged by the war. By 1987 Iraq was self-sufficient in ammunition and many basic weapons, and it had established a burgeoning semicovert nonconventional weapons program. Many of the installations that produced weapons were destroyed by the coalition bombing, but in midsummer 1991, UN inspection teams and other sources reported that Iraq had accumulated extensive stockpiles of chemical weapons and ballistic missiles. It also had an extensive and sophisticated uranium enrichment program that would have eventually given Iraq a steady supply of enriched uranium—the key ingredient in a fission bomb. The UN teams were impressed by the breadth, scope, and progress of Iraq's "Manhattan Project" and by the skill of Iraqi engineers and scientists.

SADDAM'S GRIP ON POWER

The portrait of Saddam as an omnipotent ruler was shattered by his defeat in the war and by the intensity of the insurrections. Profound bitterness was expressed by many who felt that Saddam had badly miscalculated or blundered into a trap laid for him by the coalition. Yet he is the symbol of Iraq's achievements; he brought Iraq into an era of military strength and scientific progress. The message is clear: only under Saddam can Iraq regain its former strength. But he cannot rule alone, and has moved to strengthen his control over the state apparatus.

The powerful position of Hussein's followers from his hometown of Tikrit has been enhanced. The innermost circle of power is made up of Tikritis who are Saddam's close relatives. These half-brothers, sons, cousins, and sons-in-law occupy the top positions in the Special Bureau and the security/intelligence services; the latter is under the control of Sabawi Ibrahim, one of Saddam's half-brothers: Ali Hassan al-Majid, a paternal cousin of Saddam's who is noted for his "flair" in pacifying unruly regions, was appointed interior minister in March 1991. Tikritis and other Sunni Arabs have reinforced their positions in the officer corps, which has been purged of politically suspect officers and those who failed in their duties during the war. Hussein Kamel Hassan, Saddam's

cousin and son-in-law, is minister of defense,** while the new chief of staff, General Iyad Fatih al-Rawi—a former head of the Republican Guards—is a Sunni Arab.

Loyalty to Saddam is cemented by family ties and by other factors, such as collective fear of and reliance on Saddam, who has adroitly handled his family over the years and who has not hesitated to punish and reward. They also fear that if Saddam is overthrown their lives could be jeopardized. A third source of loyalty is economic; Tikritis have prospered despite the regime's strong anticorruption ethic. When the government introduced its privatization measures in 1987, Tikritis bought state enterprises at low prices and then sold them at considerable profit to middle-class businessmen.

CONTROL OF THE CENTER

Saddam also manages to remain in power through his control of and support in the "center." This refers not only to the geographic center of support in the Sunni Arab heartland and Baghdad, but also to a socioeconomic and cultural center made up of those with the nation's highest standards of living.

The center held during the rebellions for several reasons. First, there was hostility toward the goals of the rebellions in the north and the south: the Kurds are seen as putative separatists who should not be allowed to control the oil-rich northern province of At-Tamim. And the Shiite rebellion held the possibility of an Islamic fundamentalist regime.

Second, the center held because of loyalty among the part of the population that has confidence in the Baath party's commitment to secularism, economic development, and the promotion of a distinct and nonsectarian Iraqi nationalism, or because of what can be called the "legitimacy of the worst alternative"—the belief that if Saddam is overthrown the situation will not improve but, rather, deteriorate dramatically. Third, fear of the pervasive presence of the security and military apparatus may have inspired caution.

The center has its grievances and problems, including declining standards of living: annual inflation is 2,000 percent, and wages and salaries have not risen in real terms for the last three years. Job security in the stagnant economy is nonexistent, and unemployment has reached 20 percent; poverty has increased, and the middle class has seen its savings wiped out. Many have been forced to pawn their valuables or take second jobs. The poor increasingly rely on the state for basic needs, but the rationed products distributed by the government provide only 55 percent of the calories needed daily,

---

**Hassan was replaced as defense minister by Majid on November 6.

according to Minister of Commerce Mohammed Mahdi Salih.

Saddam realized that restoring law and order was not enough. To maintain the people's loyalty the regime had to implement political reforms and reconstruct the country quickly; this was the theme of Saddam's speech on March 16, his first after the war ended. That same month Saddam appointed Saadun Hamadi, a Shiite and veteran Baathist, as prime minister; he headed a Cabinet of technocrats charged with reconstruction, political and economic reforms, and bringing an end to Iraq's international isolation.

In his speech, Saddam declared that the leadership's commitment to building a "democratic society based on a constitution, law, institutions, and [party] pluralism. . .is an irrevocable and final decision." Hamadi expressed the belief that Iraq would move slowly from the revolutionary phase of politics, under which Iraq has existed since 1968, to constitutional politics characterized by the supremacy of law. Sweeping political reforms were to include the implementation of a constitution that had been drafted in 1990, a free press, eventual abolition of the supralegal Revolutionary Court (charged with trying crimes against the state) and the ruling Revolutionary Command Council, and the establishment of a multiparty system.

The regime may find it difficult to shed its authoritarianism and may fear that if it goes too far too quickly it may lose control like the Communist regimes in Eastern Europe did in 1989. The new multiparty law approved by the Revolutionary Command Council on September 3 is indicative of both the regime's definition of competitive party politics and its fears. The law dropped an earlier provision banning any party whose ideology was inimical to Baathism; it insisted, however, that all parties "should value and be proud of of Iraq's heritage, glorious history and achievements attained by national struggle; particularly by the great revolutions of. . .1958 and. . .1968" that overthrew the monarchy and brought the Baath party to power.

Under the new multiparty law, parties may not be founded on the basis of apostasy, racism, regionalism, or anti-Arabism; an initial ban on religious parties was lifted but Communist, sectarian, and separatist groups are proscribed. Only the Baath party may engage in political activity in the armed forces and security services, a condition betraying both the fear that hostile forces might proselytize in these institutions as a means of overthrowing the Baath party and the regime's determination to ensure that the ruling party's domination of political life remains unchallenged. In September Saddam made clear that Western-style democracy is not welcome in Iraq and that Iraqis who support the importation of it to Iraq would not be allowed to hold any leading positions.

The surprise removal of Hamadi from office on September 14 at the Iraqi Baath party's tenth congress raised questions about the future of political reforms. Hamadi was perceived as committed to implementation of the reforms, and he may have expressed his views too forcefully for some at the congress. The Beirut newspaper *Al-Hayat* claims that Hamadi fell victim to the party's old guard, which feared for the party's position. But the situation may have been more complicated than that. Hamadi may have run afoul of the leadership for not having achieved solid progress in the task of reconstruction; Saddam had vowed in March that ministers would be given four to six months to prove themselves. The new prime minister, Muhammad Hamza al-Zubaydi, is a political lightweight who is not expected to be too independent-minded.

THE PARIAH STATE

Iraq's relations with the outside world remain stymied despite persistent Iraqi efforts to break the isolation. Iraqis point out that they are not surprised by the stance taken by the United States and Britain during the crisis and after the war, but France's active participation in the coalition was an unpleasant surprise given the special relationship the two countries had developed over two decades.

From an Iraqi perspective the West went to war not because of fundamental concern over Kuwait but because it could not countenance the emergence of a militarily strong and politically influential Iraq; under Saddam, Iraq was breaking the shackles of military, political, and technological dependence. This threatened the West's domination of the region as well as posing a danger to its creation, "the Zionist entity," that is, Israel. But not long after the end of the war Iraq expressed an interest in restoring political and economic relations with the Western powers that were its main trading partners before the crisis.

The West has not been forthcoming, and Iraq's relations with this powerful group of countries are dictated by the latter's continued insistence that Saddam must be removed from power. A coup by the army or the party did not materialize at the war's end, and despite calls for the Iraqi people to overthrow Saddam, Washington was not interested in helping the rebels during the insurrections, fearing, as has been noted, that Iraq might become fragmented or fall under Iranian domination. "We don't want to involve ourselves in the internal conflict in Iraq," was White House Press Secretary Marlin Fitzwater's comment in late March.

In order to remove Saddam, the United States and its closest allies have maintained unremitting pressure in the form of sanctions and the humiliating derogation of Iraqi national sovereignty mandated by Security Council Resolution 687. The aim is to persuade Iraqis that neither their lives nor the status of their country will be normalized until Saddam leaves office.

Iraq succumbed to hubris in 1990: Saddam Hussein hoped to make his country rich beyond belief and infinitely more powerful by incorporating Kuwait. Then he promised that the war for Kuwait would be "the mother of all battles," but it turned out to be "the mother of all defeats." The Iraqi leader himself has reportedly compared the damage from the war with that wrought on the country by the Mongol hordes of Hülegu in 1258. The comparison is not inapt: one of the most highly developed countries in the Middle East has been crippled and left with limited sovereignty and a limited regional and international role.

[1]For the Iraqi opposition and Shiite revolt, see Antoine Jalkh, "L'opposition irakienne dans tous les états," *Arabies* (Paris), no. 51 (March 1991); Phebe Marr, "Iraq's Future: Plus Ça Change. . .Or Something Better?" (mimeo., Center for Arab Studies, 1991); Pierre Martin, "Les chiites d'Irak de retour sur la scène politique," *Monde Arabe Maghreb Machrek* (Paris), no. 132 (April–June 1991); Peter Galbraith, "Civil War in Iraq," Staff Report to the Committee on Foreign Relations, US Senate, May 1991 (Washington, D.C.: United States Government Printing Office, 1991); and The Economist Intelligence Unit, *Iraq Country Report* (London), nos. 1, 2, and 3 (1991).

[2]The analysis of economic devastation is based on Martti Ahtisaari, "Report of the United Nations Mission to Assess Humanitarian Needs," March 27, 1991; and Sadruddin Aga Khan, "Report to the [UN] Secretary-General on Humanitarian Needs in Iraq," July 15, 1991.

Article 14   *MECRA*, Spring/Summer 1991

PROFILE: The Kurds of Kurdistan

Dr. Jamal A. Shurdom

Dr. Shurdom is an expert in international affairs, national security, and strategic studies. He is a consultant and the executive director of MECRA, and is the editor in chief of the internationally distributed periodical: The Middle East Research/Analysis. A Fulbright Scholar, he was a professor at the University of Jordan, Political Science Department (1980–86), and currently is an adjunct professor at Rollins College, Florida. He is the author of a series of articles in Arabic and English in major newspapers, magazines, and periodicals on topics related to the Middle East, East-West relations, and national security. He has several books in the process of being published, notably, The U.S. Foreign Policy Strategy in the Arab World Since the 19th Century. To contact Dr. Shurdom, call or write to: Mr. Wallace J. Sadowski, Jr., Director Public Relations, MECRA, P.O. Box 2511, Saint Leo, Florida 33574. Tel. 407–767–8338.

GEOGRAPHY

Kurdistan occupied an area estimated to be 74,000 square miles. Located on a plateau and mountain region in southwest Asia, it lies astride the Zagros mountains (in Iran), extends to the eastern part of the Taurus mountains (Turkey) and reaches south across the Mesopotamian plain. It is located along the upper reaches of the Tigris and Euphrates rivers. Kurds are concentrated chiefly in these regions: parts of eastern Turkey; northeastern Iraq; northwestern Iran; northeastern Syria; and Soviet Armenia. There is an obvious transportation problem in the area: most available transportation is provided by animals (mules, oxen, donkeys, ponies, etc.).

POPULATION

The Kurds "are people of mysterious origin. They have been famed throughout history for hardiness and longevity and for their chivalrous nature. The Kurds are an ethnic group bonded by a common language. They live in the mountainous areas of Anatolia, Iraq, Iran, Turkey, Syria, and Soviet Armenia" in the area called Kurdistan. According to estimates, the Kurds number between 19 to 20 million. Approximately 4.5 million reside in eastern Turkey, 4 million in Iraq, 4.5 million in Iran, and the rest are scattered in the Russian Caucasus and in Kazakastan, on the eastern side of the Caspian Sea. New estimates show that there are about half million Kurds in Azerbaijan and

Armenia Syria (half million) and the rest of the world. In Turkey, Kurds "dwell near the frontiers around Lake Van, as well as near Diyarbakir and Erzurum. In Iraq, they live within the Kirkuk, Sulaimaniyah and Mosul regions. In Iran, Kurds live in Azerbaijan and Khurasn, and a number of Kurds also live in Fars. Ethnically, the Kurds are closely related to the Iranians. Traditionally, they were pastoral nomadic herdsmen. Some are now seminomadic, and engage in some agriculture."

The creation of national boundaries after World War I prevented the Kurds from continuing their life style, and put some constraints on their "seasonal migration." Most are now urbanized. Since the 7th century A.D., Kurds have been devout Muslims of the Sunnite branch. Kurdish dialects belong to the northwestern branch of the Iranian language. Today, Kurdistan (or Kordestan) consists geographically only of a province in Northwest Iran, bounded on the west by Iraq. The capital of this province is Sanadaj.

HISTORY

Historically, the Kurdistan region has constantly been under foreign domination. The Kurdish people have struggled against foreign rule from time immemorial. Historians say that "Kurdistan is commonly identified with ancient Corduene, which was inhabited by the Carduchi (mentioned in Xenophon)." In the 7th century A.D. the Arabs conquered Kurdistan, at which time the Kurds were converted to the Islamic religion. In the 11th century, the region fell under the domination of the Seljuk Turks. From the 13th to 15th century it was ruled by the Mongols, and afterward, until 1920, by the Ottoman Empire. The Kurdish people "were oppressed throughout their political history." They have striven for centuries, attempting to achieve an independent political identity.

At the end of World War I the Kurds were encouraged by the Turkish defeat and by American President Wilson's Fourteen Point plea for national self-determination, to revive their claim for Kurdish independence at the Paris Peace Conference of 1919. In 1920, an agreement for a Kurdish autonomous state was reached in the Treaty of Sevres, as a result of the "liquidation of the Ottoman Empire," but it was never implemented. However, because of Turkey's military revival under Kemal Ataturk, the Treaty of Lausanne (1923), which superseded Sevres, ignored Kurdistan aspirations. In 1925 and 1930 the Kurds revolted against the Turks, but these attempts failed, the Kurds were forcibly quelled, and remaining manifestations of Kurdish nationalism suppressed. Today, those Kurds who live in Turkey are not allowed to identify themselves as Kurds or to claim ethnic identity as Kurds. One expert

described Turkish treatment by saying that "the tongues of Kurds are cut out if they are caught speaking their native language instead of Turkish." The Turkish government is pursuing a melting pot policy, in which Kurds will be melted into Turks.

In Iran the Kurds have suffered religious persecution as Sunni Muslims. They rebelled against the Iranians during the 1920s and, at the end of World War II, a Soviet-backed Kurdish "republic" existed briefly. The persecution of Kurds by Iranians seems to have continued, especially after the Iranian revolution of 1979. As in Turkey, the Kurds are not permitted to exercise their heritage. The intention is to integrate them into Iranian culture. The Kurdish desire for an independent Kurdish state is simply rejected because of the Iranian views of national security.

In Iraq, the Kurds challenged the Iraqi government over the Ba'ath Party's failure to fulfill a promise "to achieve autonomous status for Kurdistan during the 1960's and 1970's." This led to bloody confrontations between Iraqi troops and Kurdish forces led by General Mustafa al-Barzani. In 1970, the Iraqis promised the Kurds self-rule, with the city of Irbil as the capital of the Kurdish state. The Kurdish rebel leaders rejected the Iraqi proposal, arguing that the Iraqi president "would retain all real authority, and demanding that Kirkuk, an important oil center, be included in the proposed Kurdish state." In 1974 an attempt by the Iraqi government to implement limited autonomy in Kurdistan, and the Kurdish refusal, led to the outbreak of bloody fighting, which continued until the end of the year. During the Iraqi-Iranian War the Kurds unsuccessfully attempted to secede from Iraq, but the Iraqi army managed to defeat these rebellions and forcibly return the Kurds to Iraqi control.

After the Gulf War, and the defeat of the Iraqi army by the United States and the Allied forces, the Kurds, exploiting the golden opportunity presented by the apparent weakness of the defeated Iraqi army, and encouraged by the United States, unsuccessfully launched a large-scale military operation in the north of Iraq (the Kurdish region). The White House (U.S.) aides stated that "the Administration under an order signed last fall covertly has aided Iraq's oppositions." The Kurdish guerrillas hoped to achieve their independence with the military support of American and Allied forces. However, because of lack of support by U.S. and Allied forces, once again a Kurdish rebellion was forcibly suppressed by Iraqi forces.

On March 31, 1991 Saddam Hussein's army "pushed forward a lightning offensive against rebellious Kurds, capturing their headquarters, Duhuk, 25 miles from Turkish borders." Instead, as a result of the revolt, hundreds of thousands of Kurdish refugees have fled their homes in Iraq to neighboring Turkey and Iran. The U.S., Iran, and Turkey have provided humanitarian assistance, but offered no military support for the rebellion. Turkey's firm supportive role in the most recent Gulf war cost it about $7 billion, left it with more than 250,000 Kurdish refugees on its border and threatens to increase political instability. On April 15, the State Department cited reports that an estimated 400 to 1000 refugees are dying from disease each day along the Turkish border.

However, on May 2, Jalal Talabani, a Kurdish leader and member of the Patriotic Union of Kurdistan said Saddam Hussein's government agreed to "abolish the ruling Revolutionary Command Council, with a freely elected parliament supplanting other governing bodies." Talking to Western reporters, he also said that he secured an amnesty for Kurdish and Shiite prisoners captured during the uprising after the Gulf war (Shiite Muslim Iraqi rebels rose up against Hussein at the end of the war in southern Iraq). Furthermore, on May 12, in Baghdad, after meeting Saddam Hussein, the most respected Kurdish leader Massoud Barzani, head of the Kurdish Party, said that the Kurdish guerrillas were nearing an agreement with Saddam Hussein on Kurdish autonomy in northern Iraq. Barzanai said, "We are approaching an agreement with steady and studied steps." Then on May 13, the U.N. took administrative control of the main Kurdish refugee camp in the border town of Zakho. On May 22, 1991, the Iraqi Army agreed to a pull-out plan from the key Kurdish city of Dohuk and that allied forces would move in to protect Kurdish refugees returning to northern Iraq. And, on June 4, 1991, the Iraqi government said that they were hopeful for a Kurdish autonomy pact, but Baghdad insists on control of the oil center in the Kirkuk area. However, an Iraqi official said, "We expect signing a (pact) in the next 10 days."

In the final analysis, "the Kurds, like the Palestinians, remain refugees in their own historical homeland." It seems obvious that Iraq, Iran, Turkey, Syria, and the Soviet Union have a single strategy: the Kurdish struggle for independence and the idea of a sovereign, independent, Kurdish state. Such a state is a direct threat, in their view, to their nation's security; therefore, they are opposed to the emergence of a Kurdish state in any circumstances. Any Iraqi-Kurdish agreement on Kurdish autonomy is seen as a potential perplexing political problem for the Turks and the Iranians. This opposition seems to discourage the U.S., and its Gulf War Allies, from siding militarily with the Kurdish rebels. Pressure from our ally, Turkey, is especially heavy not to support an independent Kurdish state.

Historically, however, although the Kurds have never achieved political unity, they, "as individuals and in small groups, have had a lasting impact on developments in Southeast Asia." Remember, the famous Muslim hero, Salah el-Din al-Ayyubie, who gained fame during the Crusades, is the Muslim hero who liberated the holy city of Jerusalem in 1187, and is perhaps the most famous of all Kurds. The Kurds' political struggle will most likely be continued by one form of rebellion or another. It will certainly face complex obstacles on the bumpy road to political freedom. The common strategy of all neighboring states, to prevent the creation of an independent Kurdish state, makes it almost impossible for the Kurdish people to achieve independence.

The Kurds, as a result, will continue to suffer and will be sacrificed to the interests of other nations for a long time to come, unless a political miracle occurs to cause the interests and the strategy of its neighbors to diverge.

Article 15

THE NEW REPUBLIC JUNE 3, 1991

The statelessness of Kurds and Palestinians.

UNPROMISED LANDS

By Martin Peretz

Among the national minorities in the Middle East that have been kept from political self-expression, the Kurds are not alone. But they are the largest such minority. Neither Arabs nor Semites, they are an ancient, distinct people who can honestly trace their history back to the time of Cyrus the Great. They speak an Indo-European language all their own. Twenty-odd million of them, roughly as many as ethnic Persians, live in the contiguous territory of what was once called Kurdistan. The Kurds, unlike the tribes of Lebanon or some of the nationalities trapped in the Soviet Union, do not claim independence to the exclusion of other indigenous groups. They have a homogeneous country and a history of their own. Few people deserve the sobriquet "nation" more richly than these people, who have run their own daily affairs on their own lands for millennia.

Twice in this century the Kurds were given auguries of self-determination, and twice were betrayed. The Treaty of Sèvres, which in 1920 allocated the vast territories of the defeated Ottoman Empire, envisaged an autonomous Kurdish state leading to independence. But it was never ratified by the Turks, and the decisive ally, Britain, whose troops had occupied all of Mesopotamia since 1918, became increasingly committed to its new satrapy of Iraq. At the behest of Britain, the League of Nations awarded Iraq the Kurdish area of Mosul and, more to the point, the oil riches around it. With that act, the future of Kurdish prosperity was handed to their future oppressors.

After the Second World War, a Kurdish republic was proclaimed by rebels in the part of Iran then occupied by the Soviet Union. The republic lasted a year. After the Red Army's retreat in 1946, and with the collusion of Britain and the United States, Tehran crushed the Kurds. Although there have been various risings in Kurdistan in the intervening forty-five years, they all seemed forlorn. The Kurds' fate echoed again and again their initial betrayal after the First World War. They had had no friends then to argue for them in Western capitals. They have few such friends now.

Nowhere has the Kurdish agony been more excruciating and unremitting than in Iraq. There, ever since the British in 1921 handed over political power to a feeble Sunni chieftain from the Arabian desert (the French had just ousted him, after one year, as ruler of Damascus), the Kurds have been the targets of relentless, routine persecution. In 1969 sixty-seven Kurdish women and children were burned alive in a cave into which they had escaped to seek refuge from shelling. Two years later some 40,000 Kurds were expelled from the country. During 1974 and 1975 the regime napalmed Kurdish villages and dispossessed many thousands of civilians. Samir al-Khalil's scrupulous book, *Republic of Fear*, testifies to summary executions, assassinations, and public hangings.

This bloody history somehow eluded President Bush and Secretary of State Baker. They were thus dumbfounded by Baghdad's recent brutalities. The hatreds mystified them, and did not truly outrage them. The crimes did not cross formal borders, after all; nor did they correlate with the traditional idea of a civil war, where brother fights against brother. But they were crimes nonetheless; and crimes that would have been particularly noxious to a new world order with any genuine claims to moral or historical seriousness.

In the aftermath of Desert Storm, we pushed the Shiites' suffering out of our minds. But the Kurds did not go so gently. They fled by the hundreds of thousands, their dead and dying paraded for weeks on end in prime time. So, despite his efforts to evade responsibility, George Bush was finally forced to acknowledge that the United States had to do something for them. What he did not acknowledge—because he did not grasp it—was what it was precisely that we owed them.

Humanitarian aid is not enough. The Kurds of Iraq

are not survivors of an earthquake. They are the permanently endangered victims of a government that won't integrate them into the body politic as long as they are Kurds and can't integrate them precisely because they are Kurds. That is to say, their plight is hopeless because they are not Arabs. And Iraq is an Arab state: a Sunni Arab state, at that. As Hannah Arendt pointed out once after self-determination replaced empire in Eastern Europe, in many cultures only nationals can truly "be citizens, only people of the same national origin could enjoy the full protection of legal institutions." Nowhere is this truer than in the Middle East.

This is a notion difficult for Americans to grasp. Ours, after all, is ostensibly a nationality of nationalities: our ideal and imperfect practice is a citizenship devoid of ethnic or cultural determinism. Or at least it has been until recently when everything from public contracts to the composition of juries, from the character of election districts to academic appointments, is constrained by these considerations. But the Arendtian proposition is axiomatic in those regions where modern liberalism has yet to permeate, where men are either kin or enemies. It is true today among peoples in the Soviet empire and in Yugoslavia, in Romania and Czechoslovakia, in India and Indonesia, in Ireland and South Africa. The Middle East is hardly a more open and inclusive place than these.

Arendt argued further—and in a vein still more alien to American sensibilities—what she thought leaders of the great nations "knew only too well, that minorities within nation-states must sooner or later be either assimilated or liquidated." It is an unbearable thought, but borne out across the globe. In the Arab world there is the added irony that the dominant "state people" are often themselves minorities, numerically weaker and sometimes culturally less coherent than the groups they rule. Assimilating the majorities is neither enticing to them nor, history tells them, feasible. Total liquidation ordinarily being impossible, mass murders are common measures of temporary pacification. That's why the Arab wars are forever.

There are many examples of this, but take Syria. There the "state people" and especially its ruling elites are drawn not simply from the schismatic Alawite Muslim sect (12 percent of the population) but more narrowly from the Matawira tribe and, even more narrowly, from the Numailatiyya clan. Indeed, those who hail from Qardaha, Hafez Assad's birthplace, are the most favored among the tiny cohort that rises to the top. These Alawites are joined by a myth of common unity, as distinct from the Sunnis, the Druze, and the remnant Christian sects. Other Syrians are just that: "other." In states where one group routinely wields the whip over another—even where they may both be Arab—citizenship is an abstraction connoting neither loyalty nor rights. Aside from those in the ruling group, there are no citizens, merely stateless people.

There are two major stateless peoples in Iraq, its Kurds and its Shiites, and several smaller sects and ethnicities. The regime itself is run by an ideological kleptocracy drawn, as in Syria, from a "state people," which is a fragment of a fragment of the populace. This group brutalizes because nothing but brutality would sustain its power. Indeed, the Iraqi ruling group is far more ferocious than the Alawites in Syria. The Alawites, a heretic creed made up mostly of rural believers, brutalize because of their own fear. The Sunni elites in Iraq, however, brutalize with the swagger that comes from the knowledge that, although they make up only one-fifth of their country, they are of the dominant branch of Islam. But even in Baghdad itself the Sunnis are a small minority, which is why, had the coalition forces gone on to the capital, they would have been welcomed as liberators.

There is no mystery here. As the Shiite historian Abas Kelidar has written, almost no one "accepts the state of Iraq in its present form . . . it remains an artificial political entity . . . nationalism as advocated by the Iraqi political elite could appeal to only one community." The identity cards of the Shiites named them as Iranians, regardless of where they had been born. Thus, it was easy to expel them, and expelled they were. In the late 1970s, 200,000 of them were put across the border with nary a peep from anyone in the West.

Saddam Hussein preferred to liquidate his Kurdish problem by inducing them to flee. Let them, he thought, vex his old enemy Turgut Ozal of Turkey, already burdened by more than 9 million Kurds who do not think of themselves as Turks. Saddam has now been forced to pretend that he welcomes his Kurds back and that he will grant them some measure of self-rule. He has even produced from the Talabani family of longtime and certified Kurdish quislings some mountaineers quick to cut a deal with Baghdad. But Saddam's refusal to accept U.N.-supervised safe havens betrays his enduring motives. And the Kurds' seasoned instincts tell them that they are being brought to the slaughter. Most of them, of course, are not going home. They are going to hastily constructed refugee camps where they will linger until the protecting coalition forces leave. Then the safety of the Kurds will depend for the long haul on U.N. forces—hardened troops from places such as Finland and Fiji—like those who kept the peace so well in Lebanon.

This is not, then, the end of a problem but its beginning. When the short haul is over, the worst is likely to happen again. Modest estimates put the Kurdish civilian death toll at 250,000 in the decade before the current atrocities. It is in the very logic of Iraq's pan-Arab ambitions that the Kurds shall be such objects once more, the more so in that Baghdad's more grandiose plans have, for the moment at least, been frustrated.

Pushing the Kurds into "safe havens" in an unchanged Iraq is no way out. The coaxing of the Kurds back into Iraq is really bullying them back into the areas of danger. It is an example of what Arendt described in *The Origins of Totalitarianism*: "Nonrecognition of statelessness always means repatriation, i.e., deportation to a country of origin, which either refuses to recognize the prospective repatriate as a citizen or, on the contrary, urgently wants him back for punishment." The sin of the Kurds was not some particular acts or thoughts but, as with other stateless peoples, "what they unchangeably were."

Without national rights, in short, the Kurds are without human rights. The Bush administration won't for a moment acknowledge this awful truth. It is true nonetheless, because the political culture of Iraq makes it a case *in extremis* of a state that is not an instrument of law but an instrument of the "state people," this minority of the Sunni minority. There is an important distinction between human rights and national rights that is illumined by the Iraqi case. Many peoples in the world crave political expressions of their national rights. But, failing to achieve these, they are not everywhere without human rights, which are the elementary freedoms—to physical safety, to work, to opinions—said to be inalienable and independent of citizenship and nationality. The Basques have these in Spain without national rights, as do Irish nationalists in the United Kingdom, and, if I dare say so, the Palestinian Arabs in Israel. But in Iraq the most elementary freedoms depend on both citizenship and nationality. When the administration let stand the structure of Iraqi power it let stand the utter rightslessness of the Kurds.

The complicity of the administration in the forfeiting of the human rights of the Kurds is a direct consequence of its calamitous and callous endgame in the war against Iraq. It is a remarkable spectacle. Within hours the United States abdicated the power it had won in the Gulf, leaving behind incalculable anguish in Kurdistan and in southern Iraq: demolished homes, razed villages, disintegrated social structures, and, of course, the irreplaceable dead. To have won a war against a monstrous regime and nonetheless to have permitted it the mass murder of civilians is a debacle that will sully American policy for years to come. The tragedy, moreover, is not yet finished. The Baath is still on good behavior, and will be as long as American soldiers remain in place. The food, the blankets, the medical inoculations provided by coalition personnel have only temporarily impeded Baghdad's objectives.

But what is more remarkable is the rationale for this abandonment of the national cause and human rights of the Kurds. Neither the president nor the secretary of state has conceded what is obvious to serious observers: the United States turned its back on the Kurds of the north and the Shiites of the

south, before we even knew quite what was actually occurring there, out of deference to Saudi anxieties and sensibilities. Saudi Arabia is the ally that the Bush administration values most highly. (Neither Bush nor Baker has ever felt that special tie that has bonded Americans to Israel through thick and thin.) And if the Saudis feared a non-Arab state in Kurdistan and a non-Sunni state in the Shiite areas of Iraq, we'd do everything to prevent these from coming to pass. So the administration, in an extraordinary military achievement, had won a unique opportunity for the liberation of the Kurds, but chose instead to betray them in order to take up another cause—a cause tangential to the events of the Gulf war and far from the region where the United States wields the most leverage. The cause was the plight of a people whose claims to nationhood are less profound than the Kurds', and whose lonely role in the Gulf war was vociferously to support our enemy. I mean, of course, the Palestinian Arabs, James Baker's perennial obsession.

To compare the claims to nationhood of the Kurds and the Palestinian Arabs makes for some interesting ironies in the politics of the Middle East. The passion for a distinctive Palestinian state among the Arabs, unlike that among Kurds for a Kurdish state, is derived less from that people's intrinsic history than from their intimate encounter with the Jews. It is no longer politically correct to say that without Zionism there is no Palestinian people, but it contains a good deal of truth. Until 1948, as Professor Aziz Haidar of Bir Zeit University on the West Bank put it, the Palestinians "did not constitute a group that had any sort of crystallized ethnic identity—cultural, religious, or based on community, life-style, or language. Instead, they were a part of the Middle Eastern Arab population. Actually, the differences between the Palestinians and the bordering peoples of the region were less obvious than the differences within the Palestinian population itself." A more apologetic scholar, Muhammad Y. Muslih, concedes the same: until the 1920s "there is no Arabic name for Palestinian nationalism." And even after there was a nationalist nomenclature, the particular idea remained in constant struggle with more generalized pan-Arab aspirations. The establishment of the Jewish state in Palestine after the war was, of course, made possible by the fact that a large amount of land in Palestine was already owned by Jewish national institutions. Much of it had been sold by Arab notables. One can understand poor Arab peasants doing that for cash. It is slightly harder to comprehend why members of the Arab Executive and the Arab Higher Committee—many of them ostensibly militant nationalists, some of whom had actually organized riots against the Jews—sold land to the Zionists. Lists of such sellers go on for many pages in the scholarly studies dealing with this matter. One thing you cannot say about the Kurds is that they sold or abandoned their patrimony.

This does not mean, of course, that the Palestinians

do not deserve some form of autonomy, along the lines of the Camp David accords. They do. Some species of subsovereignty, like the paradigm proposed for the Kurds by Brian Uruquart, former undersecretary general of the United Nations, would allow the Palestinians self-rule and reassure the Israelis on security issues. My comparison between the two stateless peoples is intended simply to raise the question of why an ancient historic people like the Kurds can be effortlessly sidetracked, while the Palestinians, with a newer and more ambiguous identity, press on everybody's agenda.

Even those sympathetic to the plight of the Kurds, such as Harvard professor Stanley Hoffmann, rarely go so far as to support their right to an independent state. But they do not flinch at such options for the Palestinians. At a recent Harvard meeting, Professor Hoffmann preferred to offer the Kurds succor under international "Minority Treaties," the kind through which the League of Nations was so effective in protecting the Jews, Slavs, and Gypsies from their tormentors. Why such meager measures for the Kurds and such urgency for the Palestinians? "Because the Palestinians won't settle for less." It does not make for a particularly convincing moral—or prudential—argument.

The administration was certain the epilogue to the Gulf war would be a prologue to Arab-Israeli peace. So certain, in fact, that it blinded itself to the actual epilogue taking place in the north of Iraq. We were told that Saudi Arabia and Kuwait had shown new flexibility and new openness toward Israel. Baker would produce these valued allies at the beginning of the process. And they would produce not only conciliatory Syrians but also Palestinians who were more than mere marionettes of the PLO in Tunis. Reassured about a changing climate in the Arab world, Israel would then be expected to be forthcoming toward the Palestinians. But, as an old Arab proverb has it, "The words of the night are erased by the day." Baker has been able to deliver almost nothing of what he had promised from the salient Arabs. Instead of Saudi Arabia taking the lead in the accommodation of the Arab world to Israel, it has chosen to hide behind the robes of the Gulf Cooperation Council, and to do this only after frantic pleas from America.

In retrospect, one wonders why any of us believed that the Saudis would come out from the shadows to sit with the Jews. Saudi Arabia is not central, the secretary now opines, because it is not a front-line state. Well, in every war it was a front-line state, and more than symbolically. It always sent troops and, more important, it always sent money. So having rescued the Saudi monarchy from the clutches of Saddam, the administration still has precious little leverage over it. It prefers to use its leverage over Israel: the financial power to make the Soviet migration a success or a failure. Even a hard-line government like Shamir's cannot be altogether indifferent to these realities.

It is a curious logic that abdicates power in the Gulf and asserts it in Israeli-Palestinian affairs. The United States fought linkage all along in the Gulf, and yet now linkage is the cornerstone of its postwar policy. We defeated Saddam only to keep him in play. We thwarted Saddamism only to give a new lease on life to its deadly and cherished illusions. And one of those illusions is that the Palestinian Arabs deserve so much more, and deserve it so much more urgently, than the people whose future we accidentally brightened, only to condemn to sudden and certain eclipse.

Article 16

U.S.NEWS & WORLD REPORT, DECEMBER 16, 1991

Another obstacle to peace

The land and water of the West Bank are difficult to divide

In the 25 years since Israel occupied the West Bank during the Six-Day War, Israeli politicians and settlers have laid claim to the biblical lands of Judea and Samaria on the basis of religion, history and national security. But with direct negotiations between Israel and the Palestinians finally underway, a new argument against any territorial compromise is increasingly being heard in Israel: Not only would giving up land compound the problems of defending Israel, it also would imperil the nation's fragile water supply.

Diplomats and political scientists usually consider nationalism, religion and security to be the core of the Israeli-Palestinian conflict. The West Bank commands the strategic high ground that rises 3,000 feet above potential invasion routes into the narrow coastal plain that is home to two thirds of Israel's population and most of its industry. But resource experts and geographers argue that immutable geological facts are just as important in explaining the conflict. Disputes over the region's water—such as Syria's attempt to divert the Jordan River's headwaters in the 1960s—have flared into violence many times before.

A dreary place. The West Bank, 2,000 square miles of rocky slopes and deserts—about the size of Delaware—is, biblical authority notwithstanding, at first glance a godforsaken place. W. H. Bartlett, a 19th-century English traveler, recorded his impressions of "this dreary

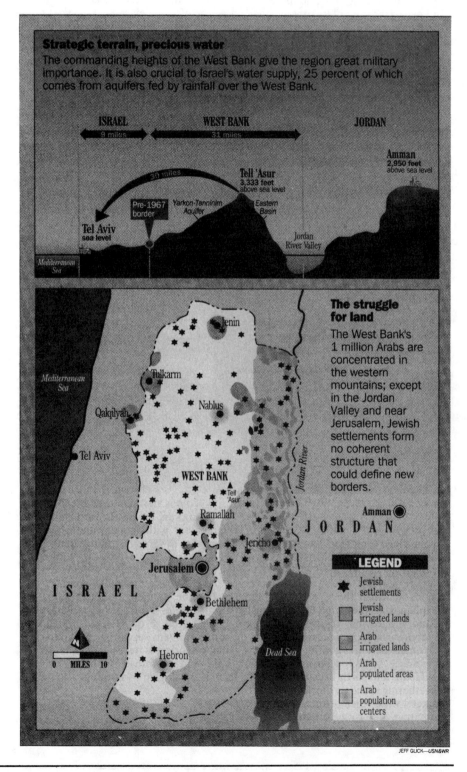

Strategic terrain, precious water
The commanding heights of the West Bank give the region great military importance. It is also crucial to Israel's water supply, 25 percent of which comes from aquifers fed by rainfall over the West Bank.

ISRAEL — 9 miles — WEST BANK — 31 miles — JORDAN

Amman 2,950 feet above sea level

Tell 'Asur 3,333 feet above sea level

30 miles

Pre-1967 border

Yarkon-Tanninim Aquifer

Eastern Basin

Jordan River Valley

Tel Aviv sea level

Mediterranean Sea

The struggle for land
The West Bank's 1 million Arabs are concentrated in the western mountains; except in the Jordan Valley and near Jerusalem, Jewish settlements form no coherent structure that could define new borders.

Jenin
Mediterranean Sea
Tulkarm
Nablus
Qalqilyah
Tel Aviv
WEST BANK
Tell 'Asur
Ramallah
Jericho
Jerusalem
JORDAN
Amman
ISRAEL
Bethlehem
Hebron
Dead Sea
Jordan River
0 MILES 10

LEGEND
★ Jewish settlements
Jewish irrigated lands
Arab irrigated lands
Arab populated areas
Arab population centers

JEFF GLICK—USN&WR

region" en route from Jericho to Jerusalem: "Though excessively wild, there is not the least compensation in grandeur of scenery." The area's only natural resources are 500,000 acres of cultivable land — an Iowa county's worth — and 20 to 30 inches of rain that falls each year on the mountain highlands, feeding three underground aquifers.

But two of these aquifers supply Israel with some 25 percent of its growing water needs. If some diabolical agent had set out to arrange the West Bank's resources and topography in order to foil any peaceful resolution, he could hardly have done a better job. These mountain highlands, located in the western half of the West Bank, are also home to nearly all of the West Bank's 1 million Arab residents. Any territorial compromise that adjusts borders to give Israel the hydrologically and militarily significant terrain would also give it the bulk of the Arab population of the West Bank.

The high profile given the activities of Jewish settlers has made it seem that the conflict is over land. In truth, there is little land to fight about. Arab farmers cultivate nearly all the valleys and terraced steep hillsides in the rainy mountain regions; under the 19th-century Ottoman law that Israel applies to the occupied territories, only uncultivated stony fields and wastelands can be claimed as state property — and thus provided to Jewish settlers. Usable land in the largely unoccupied, arid eastern half is limited by water. Only a little more than 10,000 acres of West Bank land are under cultivation by Israeli settlers; nearly 1 million acres are farmed in Israel.

"I'm always struck at how small the areas are relative to their political importance," says John Hayward, a water expert at the World Bank. "It's not the land—it's the water the land can supply." The major West Bank aquifer, the Yarkon-Tanninim, flows in a layer of limestone from the western slopes of the Judean and Samarian hills westward across the Green Line, the pre-1967 Israeli-Jordanian border.

Wells within Israel proper were tapping this water long before the Six-Day War.

But as population and water demand on both sides of the Green Line have grown, control of the western slopes has attained a new and vital importance for Israel. It is the rain falling on the West Bank that recharges the aquifer; any new wells drilled between the recharge area and the Israeli taps could cut off the supply and, by lowering the water tables in the part of the aquifer that extends to the west of the Green Line, allow saline water from greater depths to seep in, permanently ruining what is left.

Israel currently pumps 320 million cubic meters of water (Mm^3) a year from the Yarkon-Tanninim; the West Bank Arabs are allowed to pump 20 Mm^3. (A million cubic meters a year, by way of comparison, would supply 2,500 American households.) A second West Bank aquifer that feeds springs to the north supplies Israel with 140 Mm^3 and the West Bank Arabs with 20 Mm^3. Most of the total of 120 Mm^3 of water allotted to the million Palestinians comes from a third aquifer that flows to the east. The 70,000 Israeli settlers in the West Bank receive 40 to 50 Mm^3.

"Israeli reliance on West Bank water will be a major obstacle to Israeli withdrawal," a recent study by the U.S. Consulate in Jerusalem concluded. Israeli restrictions prevent Palestinians from drilling new wells, mainly to protect the aquifers that Israel taps from across the Green Line. Israeli drilling of new, deep wells in the West Bank, mainly to supply irrigation water for Jewish agricultural settlements in the arid Jordan Valley, has at the same time lowered water tables and dried up some Palestinian springs and shallow wells. Palestinians say that more than two thirds of the farmers in the Jordan Valley village of al-Ouja, for example, were forced to abandon their land when their 150-year-old spring went dry.

The conflict can only intensify. A scathing critique by Israel's comptroller earlier this year warned that Israel is already overpumping the underground water supplies of the West Bank. Given the growing demand for water within Israel, as well as a projected increase in the Palestinian population and in per capita water use as the standard of living grows, Israeli water authorities plan to allow no increase in the amount of water made available to Palestinians for agricultural use, approximately 80 Mm^3 per year.

Bedroom suburbs. The pattern of settlement in the West Bank is another manifestation of geography's power to thwart any territorial compromise. Arab towns and villages grew up where the rains fall, in the western reaches that abut the Green Line. The Jewish settlements, built on uncultivable land wedged between these Arab towns and fields, form no coherent economic or social structure; they are largely bedroom suburbs of Jerusalem and Tel Aviv. Nor are they much help in defining a new border.

The major exception is a string of Jordan Valley settlements, created under the previous Labor Party government to establish a defensible border zone that would be retained in a deal that returned the heavily Arab areas to Jordanian sovereignty. These isolated outposts were to delay an enemy attack while Israel mobilized, but in the age of modern armored warfare, it's an open question how effective they would be. Their economic viability, meanwhile, is increasingly in doubt, dependent as they are on heavily subsidized irrigation water.

The Jewish presence in the West Bank remains quite small; most settlements have only a few hundred residents. (The largest, with populations in the thousands — and the ones that *could* conceivably form a border structure — are mostly around Jerusalem and in the Etzion Bloc, an area halfway between Jerusalem and Hebron that Jews owned before 1948.) Washington calls the settlements "an obstacle to peace," but the unyielding land of the West Bank may prove to be a much greater impediment.

BY STEPHEN BUDIANSKY WITH DAVID MAKOVSKY IN JERUSALEM AND KHALED ABU TOAMEH IN THE WEST BANK

Article 17

CURRENT HISTORY • January 1992

> "The Iraqi invasion and occupation was a horrible and costly experience for virtually everyone touched by it. Yet it was not unrelievedly bad. For the first time in more than a generation, Kuwaitis were called on to risk their lives and property, and they achieved substantial results."

Kuwait: The Morning After

MARY ANN TÉTREAULT

MARY ANN TÉTREAULT *is a professor of political science and geography at Old Dominion University and the author of* Revolution in the World Petroleum Market (*Westport, Conn.: Quorum Books, 1985) and "Autonomy, Necessity, and the Small State: Ruling Kuwait in the Twentieth Century," in* International Organization (*Autumn 1991). In the spring of 1990 she was a Fulbright fellow in Kuwait, where she conducted interviews with members of the political opposition and the government.*

The expulsion of Iraqi forces from Kuwait last February and March by a United States–led coalition ended a seven-month national nightmare.* But the country Kuwaitis woke up to was filled with ironies. The best of their old lives—the stark beauty of the desert, the new seafront development where families had walked and played on cool evenings, the oil industry that generated the wealth on which their comfort rested—had been devastated, not only by the accidents of war but by deliberate Iraqi sabotage. The worst of their old lives—the insecurity that besets, in the words of Kuwaiti historian Hassan Ali al-Ebraheem, a "small state living in a bad neighborhood," and Kuwait's fumbling and increasingly autocratic regime—was restored to them seemingly intact.

The crisis divided the Kuwaitis into "insiders," those who endured the Iraqi invasion and occupation, and "outsiders," those who fled the country and then watched from safe havens. Perhaps because most members of the government were outsiders, insider experiences have been devalued and repressed. Unlike the progress on reconstruction of Kuwait's physical infrastructure, repair of the political community has barely begun, and it is doubtful that it will meet with the same success.

---

*The author wishes to thank Connie Moray and Denise Wilman, and Karen Elliot House of *The Wall Street Journal* for their assistance on this article.

The August 2, 1990, Iraqi invasion and the subsequent occupation of Kuwait destroyed the myth of Arab brotherhood, and with it many lives and billions of dollars in property in Kuwait. Even though many Iraqi soldiers were reported to have been capriciously cruel rather than systematically vicious, the population was terrorized by arrests, torture, kidnapping, rape, and murder. Kuwaitis caught with weapons, leaflets, or other tokens of resistance were killed, sometimes in front of their families, who had been brought out to watch.

The invasion was about holding, looting, and terrorizing Kuwait—not its integration into Iraq. According to an official associated with Kuwait's reconstruction program, "The Iraqis stole everything that could be loaded onto a five-ton truck and carried it away. . . . automobiles, typewriters, telephones, computers, televisions, domestic appliances, furniture, and every other possible sort of movable possession." Stores, offices, private homes, and even hospitals were looted.

In the months before the invasion, Kuwait was producing about 2 million barrels a day of crude oil and refining 750,000 barrels daily—most of it for export—in its own high-tech refineries. Smashing the Kuwaiti oil industry was one of Iraqi President Saddam Hussein's primary goals. His army had more than five months to accomplish this, from the invasion to the beginning on January 17 of the Persian Gulf war to evict Iraqi forces. During their occupation, soldiers preset explosive charges at oil wells, pumping and storage facilities, and refineries, and mined the surrounding areas.

Detonation of these charges damaged 749 of Kuwait's 1,330 active oil and gas wells. About 650 of the damaged wells caught fire. Despite a slow start in putting out blazes and repairing equipment, limited oil production resumed at two onshore fields in June, while the Ahmadi refinery, the least damaged of Kuwait's three interlinked refining complexes, was restarted in August. By September about

30 firefighting teams from 11 countries were at work. The last fire was extinguished in early November, many months sooner than most experts had thought possible.

THE KUWAITI RESISTANCE

Before the invasion, the most frequently heard criticism of Kuwaitis was that they were lazy and incompetent, dependent on the government and foreigners to do everything for them. But their ordeal under occupation revealed how much of this behavior had been socially constructed. After the invasion, Kuwaiti insiders rapidly established resistance groups whose activities went far beyond the paramilitary operations that Iraqi troops almost completely suppressed in three months. The groups organized mass demonstrations and held clandestine political meetings at mosques and *diwaniyyahs*.[1] Because the Iraqis were not concerned with providing for the population, the most important resistance activities related to keeping people alive: the acquisition and distribution of food and other necessities, garbage removal, the provision of medical care, and the dissemination of information.[2] Resistance workers were in danger of immediate execution if they were caught at any of these tasks.

Insiders lived very differently from the way most Kuwaitis had before the invasion. In the resistance, Kuwaitis from the middle and upper classes worked side by side with those of lower social status and with Palestinians and other foreigners. Age barriers, religious differences, and the separation by gender common in the societies of the Arabian peninsula were forgotten by those helping a population under siege; everyday life was democratized.

After the war insiders were vocal in their criticism of the Kuwaiti government; they had withstood all that Saddam could do to them, and no longer feared their own government. They pointed out official ineptitude in responding to Iraq's demands before the invasion: the poor strategy and performance of those in top positions, including the ministers of defense and the interior and the acting chief of staff, all three of whom were members of the ruling Sabah family; and the discounting of assessments by lower ranking officers of the military danger to Kuwait from Iraq. They decried the tight control of the news media that had left many ignorant of the scope of the threat facing them until it was too late either to flee or to defend themselves. The regime, however, simply ignored these criticisms.

DEMOLISHING THE RESISTANCE

Despite disenchantment with the government, both insiders and outsiders remained loyal to the ruling family, which for them symbolized their unity as a people and their 250-year history as a political community. No Kuwaiti quisling could be found to front for Iraq during the occupation. After liberation the return of Kuwait's emir, Sheik Jaber al-Ahmed al-Sabah, was eagerly anticipated throughout the country.

However, the emir, who put off his return to liberated Kuwait for 15 days, chose not to mark his resumption of authority by reinstating Kuwait's social contract. In what seemed a clear reneging on promises he had made at an October 1990 meeting of Kuwaiti exiles in Jiddah, Saudi Arabia, the emir did not rescind his July 1986 suspension of the civil liberties provisions of the Kuwaiti constitution, nor did he recall the parliament, which he had closed at the same time. Instead, martial law was imposed, as the government-in-exile had announced it would be.

Martial law was defended as necessary for the disarming of unruly teenagers, former collaborators, and a feared fifth column of Iraqis masquerading as Kuwaitis. It was probably also aimed at resistance organizations like the Movement of the Second of August, whose members had vowed to remain armed until the government was purged of those they considered responsible for the debacle. Martial law failed to protect Kuwaiti opponents of the regime. Two of these, Hamad al-Jouan and Hussein al-Bani, were shot under suspicious circumstances; Jouan was seriously wounded and Bani was killed.

Domestic and foreign pressures for some movement toward democratization intensified in response to the shootings and to repeated disruptions of opposition political meetings. On June 2 the emir announced that parliamentary elections would be held in October 1992. However, a separate proclamation banned political meetings, and press censorship continued. In the meantime, the emir said that a national council, whose members had been chosen by extraconstitutional means the preceding summer, would meet to advise him and prepare for the coming elections. Although opposition leaders opposed the convening of the national council, the promise of elections and hints that women and naturalized Kuwaitis might be enfranchised in time to vote defused the domestic unrest. The crowds attending opposition rallies soon dwindled to a few hundred people.

RULE AS USUAL?

Kuwait's first postwar Cabinet was named in April 1991. It was widely condemned as unrepresentative and incompetent by critics from across the political spectrum. It included no one from the opposition or who had remained inside Kuwait during the occupation. The emir showed his contempt for insider concerns by retaining the interior and defense ministers in the Cabinet, though they were shuffled to less prominent positions. Khalid Sultan, a businessman and leader of an Islamist (Muslim fundamentalist) group, said the Cabinet "is politically unacceptable and management-wise it lacks what it takes to rebuild a broken country, from the prime minister down." The former minister of planning in the Cabinet-in-exile, Suleiman Mutawa, found the ruler's choices incomprehensible: "Nobody wants the al-Sabah[s] out, so what are they worried about? What prevents them from bringing in good managers?"

These questions penetrate to the heart of the domestic malaise that has afflicted Kuwait for nearly a decade. Good managers could become rivals of the ruling family and challenge what before the invasion had been the Sabah family's increasingly exclusive hold on Kuwait's government, economy, and society. This explains why, despite the proven competence of resistance organizations, the government denied insiders a formal role in reconstruction, even during the first few weeks after liberation, when food and fuel shortages threatened while truckloads of supplies rotted because outsiders were unable to distribute them.

But squeezing out potential rivals of the ruling family is only one mechanism in the regime's arsenal of social controls. University of Michigan political scientist Jill Crystal points to two others: the purchase of citizen support through the provision of material benefits, especially to those who are the most compliant, and pitting social groups against one another, especially citizens against foreign workers but also citizens against citizens.[3]

The regime's role as paternalistic dispenser of benefits dates to the creation of Kuwait's welfare state in the 1950s. Every social group in the country felt the regime's largesse, even wealthy merchants, the traditional antagonists of the ruling family. For them, the most important benefits included profits from the sale of land to the government at vastly inflated prices, and the requirement in the 1960 Law of Commercial Companies that all companies operating in Kuwait be at least 51 percent Kuwaiti-owned. For the masses and the elite in Kuwait, government benefits included free housing, utilities, education, and health care, and subsidized food staples and petroleum products.

After the Iraqi invasion the living expenses of outsiders were paid by the government, and each outsider received a lump-sum payment of $1,720. After liberation insiders received their salaries, even though most had refused to work as part of the resistance-organized noncompliance with the occupation; expatriate employees, most of whom had remained in their positions, did not receive back pay because, the government said, they had worked for the occupiers. Both Kuwaitis and non-Kuwaitis have been assured that the money they had in Kuwaiti banks at the time of the invasion will be returned, and all Kuwaiti foreign liabilities, private and public, have also been guaranteed by the government. Estimates of the cost of the salaries and support payments range from $3 billion to $4 billion, a substantial sum for a country in Kuwait's present financial position but still manageable.

If the claims of foreigners living in Kuwait are set aside, these measures seem reasonable. But other proposed benefits are excessive and unfair—even perverse—in their likely effects. In a surprise move, the emir announced in April that the debts of Kuwaiti insiders held by Kuwaiti banks—primarily mortgages and consumer loans amounting to some $5 billion—would be forgiven by the state. This was a boon to those with large debts but small comfort to citizens who had already repaid their mortgages or had no personal debt. Even as reparations this plan is flawed because it does not distinguish between those who suffered large losses and those who lost relatively little under the occupation. A similarly constructed bailout of Kuwaiti commercial banks and businesses, which would cost about $17.5 billion, may be adopted as well.

FOREIGNERS AS SCAPEGOATS

The exclusion of foreign workers living in Kuwait from salary supports and the proposed bailouts are examples of the third major method used by the regime to strengthen its hand against civil society. Public criticism after liberation pushed the government to try even harder to build support for itself and to reunite the country; one way it did this was to make foreigners scapegoats.

At the second conference of the government-in-exile, held in January 1991 in Jiddah, government spokesmen "harp[ed] on the theme that Kuwaiti society had been infiltrated by agents provocateurs, and that the loyalties of Palestinians resident in Kuwait were suspect and needed to be determined."[4] After liberation, the government rounded up foreigners. Because the foreigners and bedouns (people without citizenship papers, many of them desert nomads) who had made up the majority of Kuwait's police force had been deprived of their jobs, the roundup depended on the services of untrained and often thuggish young Kuwaitis.

Non-Kuwaiti Arabs, Asians, and bedouns were beaten, kidnapped, murdered, or forced to leave the country. Some were arrested and tried as collaborators. Police were implicated in most cases of brutality against foreigners, but private citizens were also reported to have been involved. On April 4, Salim Mukhtar, a prominent Palestinian, was shot under circumstances similar to those surrounding the shooting of Hamad al-Jouan; at least one report attributed the killings to "royal death squads."[5] United States Army officers investigating human rights abuses reported that direct evidence had been found linking some cases to the ruling family, including the son of the crown prince.

There was little outcry by Kuwaitis against these human rights violations. Insiders especially had a great deal of pent-up anger and a desire to pay back in kind the brutal treatment that the Iraqis and collaborators had inflicted on them and their families.

In the last days of the occupation thousands of Kuwaitis, including children, were trucked to Iraq. (As of late September, some 300 Kuwaiti children were still unaccounted for, while more than 1,500 Kuwaiti adults and 400 adults of other nationalities who had been living in Kuwait continued to be held in Iraq.)

But Kuwait's treatment of foreign nationals and the kangaroo-court aspects of the postwar trials of accused collaborators provoked an international outcry. Amnesty International, which only a few months earlier had condemned the treatment of Kuwaitis by their Iraqi occupiers, now condemned Kuwaiti actions. In response to pressures from human rights organizations and the United States, in late June 1991 the Kuwaiti government announced that all those who had been given the death penalty for collaboration would have their sentences commuted. Eventually the Red Cross was permitted to visit detainees and to observe expulsions from the country. However, as late as October reports that detainees were being beaten continued to surface in the press.

RINGMASTERS AND SIDESHOWS

Most of the postwar reconstruction of Kuwait has concentrated on rebuilding the physical plant and infrastructure, while little attention has been given to political reconstruction and almost none to the Kuwaiti people's emotional and moral rehabilitation. In one sense this reflects Kuwait's status as a sideshow in the process preoccupying most world leaders participating in "the crisis in the Gulf"—that is, the decay of the cold war international order and the new distribution of world power. Kuwait's liberation was an exercise in great-power military logistics and public relations, with powers and pretenders to power vying for prestige. The coalition that liberated Kuwait had made no prior plans regarding the country's postwar internal or external security, leaving its disoriented leaders responsible for everything from mine clearing to the development and implementation of a new defense strategy.

The interest of the Persian Gulf war's ringmasters in rebuilding Kuwait seems sadly limited, centering mainly on how much Kuwait can pay for past and future services. Pledges and payments to Kuwait's liberators started even before hostilities commenced. Kuwait's government-in-exile pledged $5 billion to the United States in support of the military buildup in the region after the

invasion; for the war itself, Kuwait pledged an additional $13.5 billion to the United States and $6 billion to other countries of the coalition. Kuwait's foreign aid agency, the Kuwait Fund for Arab Economic Development, wrote off all outstanding loans to coalition members Egypt and Syria, and in December granted them $175 million in new loans. Kuwait also agreed to support other activities in Egypt, offering as much as $650 million in additional funds.

The fight over who would be awarded the reconstruction contracts was even more crass. It was widely believed after liberation that a deal had been negotiated that would allocate fixed percentages of the value of contracts to prominent coalition members, chiefly the United States. The most severe criticism on the allocation of contracts came from the Arab governments, particularly Egypt's. Egypt did not receive any contracts in the spring of 1991 and was also angered at the treatment of Egyptian guest workers in Kuwait. Egyptians, like those from other countries that had sided with Iraq during the crisis, lost their jobs in large numbers, were harassed, deported, denied salaries, and even killed. In May, Egypt unilaterally decided to pull all its troops out of Kuwait, confirming the deterioration in relations between the two countries and derailing plans for a postwar security arrangement for Kuwait based on an Egyptian and Syrian troop presence. In a belated attempt to repair the relationship, the Kuwaiti government agreed to honor the labor contracts of all Egyptian workers, permitting more than 80,000 of them to return to Kuwait and buying out the contracts of the others under the terms awarded to retirees. It is also reported to have awarded some contracts to Egyptian companies.

Because more money will probably be used to replace looted property than to rebuild (except in the oil industry), estimates of reconstruction costs for Kuwait have been revised downward, from more than $100 billion to a more moderate $30 billion. For the ringmasters this is a great disappointment. For Kuwait it is still a substantial sum of money, most of which will leave the country, since virtually everything must be replaced or rebuilt using materials, equipment, and even workers from abroad.

DEFINING KUWAIT'S IDENTITY

The number and status of foreign workers to be allowed into Kuwait is a bellwether issue. For several years the government has wanted to cut back the number of foreign residents. At the last official census, conducted in 1985, 60 percent of Kuwait's population was non-Kuwaiti. There were many announcements last March and April that the foreign population would be reduced as a security measure to ensure that Kuwaitis would never again be a minority in their own country;

the wholesale deportation of Palestinians and other foreign workers was justified on that basis.

Yet even here the regime is torn between its own and the national interest. It makes pronouncements on reducing the number of foreign workers but encourages Kuwaitis to return to their pre-invasion habits and a lifestyle based on the widespread use of domestic servants. The Kuwaiti private sector, interested in low costs and labor productivity, has also made its preference for foreign workers clear. Midway through the autumn of 1991, the government had not yet set official limits on guest workers, nor was there any mechanism to allocate them to the jobs where they were most needed.

Kuwaitis are asking their government for more than servants and laborers. In July members of the national council—almost two-thirds of whom are from non-elite backgrounds—advised the emir to give each Kuwaiti family $69,000, half of which would be an outright gift and the remainder a long-term, interest-free loan. This would require almost $10 billion and, more problematic for Kuwait's long-term prospects, would reinforce the welfare syndrome that before the invasion had kept Kuwaitis dependent on the government and scorned by their neighbors.

The Iraqi invasion and occupation was a horrible and costly experience for virtually everyone touched by it. Yet it was not unrelievedly bad. For the first time in more than a generation, Kuwaitis were called on to risk their lives and property, and they achieved substantial results. Insiders put their efforts into resisting their occupiers; many outsiders devoted themselves to keeping their country's plight before the world community, to fighting for liberation, and, after returning to Kuwait, to rebuilding their society.

The government also rose to the occasion in many ways. It showed its best side in the fall of 1990, when the prospects of an early end to the crisis dimmed with each passing day. The emir's speech at the October 1990 meeting in Jiddah inspired Kuwaitis from across the political spectrum to steel themselves against the terrors of occupation and war. It was not until liberation was almost at hand that the regime reverted to its autocratic and manipulative ways, foreshadowing the ugly and contentious period under martial law that lasted from February 28 to June 26.

The setting of an October 1992 date for parliamentary elections provides time for Kuwait's government and people to reflect on the kind of country they want and to mobilize the resources they will need to create it. The unique Reserve Fund for Future Generations—which, although supposed to remain untouched until 2010, financed the government-in-exile, Kuwait's share of the liberation costs, and reconstruction—could be further plundered by the regime to finance giveaways to buy popular support, at least for a while.

But the regime could choose differently. It could lead the country to constitutional government, requiring not only power sharing among elites but burden sharing across the entire population. Opposition leaders could fight among themselves, vying for power, prestige, and the substantial economic rewards the regime offers the acquiescent. Or they could continue what they began under domestic repression and subsequent occupation—building bridges between the various social groups that the regime worked so hard to divide. For political as well as moral reasons, they must overcome their religious prejudices and include Kuwait's large Shiite Muslim minority as full participants in any expanded political life.

These choices must be made in an extremely insecure environment. Kuwait's neighbors have opposed its democratization since the 1930s; one of them, Iraq, remains enough of a threat to allow the regime to justify domestic repression for the sake of national security. The ringmasters who benefited from the Persian Gulf war and who buy Kuwaiti oil must pay some of the bills for rebuilding the country and must cooperate in a security regime that permits Kuwait to solve domestic problems in its own way.

Before the war Kuwait shared many of the attractive characteristics of the ancient Greek city-states, especially the quality of what political philosopher Hannah Arendt would describe as its "public space"; the *diwaniyyahs* allowed widespread and enthusiastic participation in politics. The country also shared some of the unattractive characteristics of those ancient communities: discrimination against foreigners, second-class status for women, and disdain for hard work and expertise. Kuwaitis are having second thoughts about at least some of these in light of what they have learned about themselves and the world in the past year and a half. It is important that these lessons be remembered and built on.

The future shape of Kuwaiti society will depend on a strong commitment to democratization and human rights in Kuwait by the United Nations and the countries of the coalition that liberated it. This must be coupled with their acceptance of shared responsibility in the creation of security arrangements that permit the countries of the Gulf region not only to survive but to flourish. And the outlines of that future Kuwait will also depend on the outcome of the current struggle between insiders and outsiders to define Kuwait.

---

[1]*Diwaniyyahs* are informal gatherings, generally of adult men, held regularly at the homes of prominent members of the community for purposes of discussion. The *diwaniyyah* is the most important public forum in Kuwaiti society.

[2]The organization and activities of the resistance are detailed in Shafeeq Ghabra, "The Iraqi Occupation of Kuwait: An Eyewitness Account," *Journal of Palestine Studies* (London), vol. 20, no. 2 (Winter 1991), and in press accounts.

[3]See Jill Crystal, *Oil, Politics, and the Gulf: Rulers and Merchants in Kuwait and Qatar* (Cambridge: Cambridge University Press, 1990).

[4]The Economist Intelligence Unit, *Iraq Country Report*, No. 1 (1991), p. 7.

[5]The Economist Intelligence Unit, *Iraq Country Report*, No. 2 (1991), p. 12.

The Wall Street Journal, April 23, 1991

Article 18

Surface Appearances Matter Very Deeply To a Sultan of Clean

Oman's Qaboos bin Said Likes His Realm to Be Spotless; Even the Fish Don't Smell

Tony Horwitz

Staff Reporter of The Wall Street Journal

MUSCAT, Oman—Maqbool Sultan is late for a board meeting, but he still attends to certain crucial details.

Climbing into his BMW, the Chamber of Commerce president straps a dagger to the belt of his crisp white robe and rewraps his mauve headscarf. Then, speeding down a spotless highway, he brakes at the sight of a dingy office building. "Needs paint," he says with a frown. Stopping for gasoline, Mr. Sultan instinctively checks the hood—not for oil, but for dust. "Our government," he says, gazing at a nearby carwash, "is very fussy about appearances."

So fussy, in fact, that Omanis can be fined for driving a dirty car or leaving a building unpainted. Office workers can be docked for not wearing traditional garb—a robe and sashlike turban, with daggers de rigueur for official meetings.

Air conditioners must be concealed with wooden lattices, construction sites and laundry lines must be shielded from view. Muscat even provides drawings for a wooden laundry screen that homeowners can build themselves.

Sanitized to Perfection

Such a passion for the pristine wouldn't seem shocking in Scandinavia. But in a region of the world renowned for dust, discord and dubious plumbing, this small Arab nation is a blinding oasis of order.

"It's hard to believe you're in the Middle East," says Dieter Christensen, a Columbia University ethnomusicologist doing research in Oman. "People even obey traffic rules. It's eerie."

It's also, at times, a bit *too* antiseptic. Touring the narrow alleys of Muscat's well-swept souk, Mr. Christensen stops to have a silver ring repaired. Without

asking, the craftsman finishes the job by scouring decades of grime from the jewelry. "I think it had more character before," the professor says with a sigh.

Life in Muscat, a capital city of 300,000, wasn't always so unsullied. A 19th century Englishman described the trading port as "ill-built, crowded, not over-clean." In the 1960s, Muscat remained a walled backwater with only six miles of paved roads and a sultan so medieval that he forbade Western "corruptions" such as riding bicycles and wearing sunglasses.

Then, in 1970, the sultan's son, Qaboos bin Said, seized power in a bloodless coup and set about modernizing his kingdom—and prettifying it. Now, all new structures—even bus shelters—must incorporate Islamic architectural features, such as domes and arches. Homes can only be painted in traditional, pastel colors.

To ensure that his edicts are obeyed,

Sultan Qaboos (pronounced like the last car of a train) sometimes tours his realm surreptitiously, usually at night, checking roadside decorations—urns of flowers and replicas of oversized incense burners and coffee pots—and ordering eyesores demolished. "Ugliness of any kind distresses him," says Ralph Daly, a Scotsman who advises the palace on conservation and the environment.

The British-educated sultan, always sartorially resplendent, sometimes in gold-braided cape and tasseled, rainbow-colored turban, was unavailable for comment. But Mr. Daly and other acquaintances describe him as a cultured, carefully groomed ruler with a taste for choral music and a love of horses, seashells and flowers.

Unlike other Arab leaders, who dot the landscape with military monuments and portraits of themselves, the 50-year-old Omani sultan prefers floodlit waterfalls cascading down the seaside cliffs, and sculptures of desert antelope feeding on Muscat's volcanic rock. Muscat appears to have more roadside benches than Yellowstone. And litterbugs, of course, are harshly punished: a $50 fine on first offense, imprisonment on second.

Sultan Qaboos, says Mr. Daly, "is that rare Arab leader who looks at a landscape as something more than good or bad grazing land." Though arid, Muscat is lush with foliage—watered with treated effluent. Appropriately, the World Federation of Rose Societies recently named a newly bred flower after the sultan.

The sultan is fortunate in possessing oil wells, and also in attracting likeminded officials to carry out his campaign for clean. Muscat's top health official, Said Amor, pledges to make Oman "the Singapore of the Middle East."

The bespectacled inspector knows of what he speaks; he honeymooned in the Asian nation in 1977 and has been trying to impose severe Singaporese standards on Muscat ever since. Making his rounds in a fuel-injection Volvo, the health official stops at Muscat's sprawling fish market, where turbaned anglers once slapped tuna and squid down on a pebbly beach, and sold their catch open-air.

Now, thanks to Mr. Amor, the fish repose in a tidy pavilion, shielded from the sun and drenched with tap water to keep from spoiling. The floor is hosed and swept, and disinfected at day's end with pine-oil. Khaki-clad inspectors patrol the market, making sure that fishermen don't revert to old habits.

"We still have some problems with odor," Mr. Amor says, shaking his head as a fisherman tosses a spoiled sardine from boat to beach. Mr. Amor's newest scheme: encouraging fishermen to lay their catch on beds of broken ice.

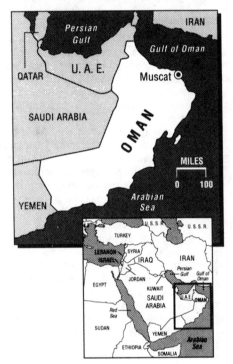

"Much prettier," he explains. "More hygienic."

These finer touches seem lost, however, on many fishermen, who continue to slog barefoot through piles of gutted fish, and who have a colorful—and doubtless unhygienic—habit of stashing their earnings beneath their turbans, to keep the bills dry.

Otherwise, Muscat has been completely sanitized. The traveler in search of Cairo's gritty bustle, or the color and mayhem of Marrakesh, will find this Arab city wanting. What bustle exists in Muscat's bazaar is largely devoted to

sweeping (twice a day, by an army of street cleaners). The Portuguese fortresses that flank Muscat's half-moon harbor are so well-preserved and finely lighted as to seem more fairy-tale than real. And the only unwashed surface in sight is the face of the cliff where 19th-century sailors scrawled the names of visiting ships.

"I'm surprised the Omanis haven't whitewashed that, too," says a diplomat at a harbor-side embassy. "They hate graffiti."

If Muscat's shimmer disappoints tourists, few Omanis seem to care. Until the late 1980s, Oman allowed no tourists at all, fearful of the garish commercialism tourism so often breeds. "We don't want Oman to become like Disneyland," explains Mr. Amor.

There seems little danger of that. Nor did the Gulf war, and an influx of U.S. forces into Muscat, muss Oman's hair too much. The sultanate played a crucial role in allowing the U.S. to preposition equipment and use its airstrips. Omani forces also joined Desert Storm. But the country weathered the conflict well out of missile range.

Now, with the war over and with Muscat's beautification virtually complete, officials can turn their attention to Oman's vast, untidy interior.

In the mountain town of Nakhl, an hour's drive west of Muscat, the cramped streets are thick with trash, the cars dusty, the mudwalled homes unpainted. But even here, the government is making inroads. "Don't Litter—Keep Your Town Clean!" says a poster beside a schoolyard, where students play soccer with soda cans. On the unpaved road winding from town, there are green trash barrels, public toilets, and experimental date-palm saplings enclosed with protective wire mesh.

"We are getting more like Muscat every day," says Mohamed Jaffer, an elementary school principal. Mr. Jaffer even confesses, rather sheepishly, that he recently enclosed the air conditioner at his home with the required wooden latticework. But then, Nakhl's 20,000 people still are some way from becoming city slickers.

"Muscat has hundreds of people picking up trash," Mr. Jaffer says. "Here, we still depend on goats."

Article 19

THE ECONOMIST DECEMBER 14TH 1991

TURKEY

Star of Islam

M OST people think the end of the cold war has made Turkey matter even less than they thought it mattered before. The Turks were mildly useful in the containment and defeat of communism, but that has been achieved; the Turks can now return to the periphery where they belong. This is culturally arrogant and geopolitically blind.

Consider the most likely outlook for the world of the next 15 or 20 years, and the problems this sort of world is likely to cause for the democracies of Europe and America; ask what Turkey can do to help with these problems, and what the consequences might be if Turkey cannot, or will not, help; and realise that Turkey is no longer in the least peripheral. It sits at the centre of the possible next cold war.

The outlook for the next bit of history, in bare bones, is as follows. The Russian danger has gone away, until and unless Russia reassembles the economic strength, and the will, to make another bid for the control of Europe. There will be economic friction, and bad temper, between the winners of the cold war, America, Europe and Japan, but bad temper seems unlikely to degenerate into anything desperately worse between now and 2010.

Eastern Asia astonishingly contains both the last remnants of defeated Marxism and the world's most efficient examples of victorious capitalism, but no great crisis between them is in prospect: eastern Asia's ideological wars were won and lost a generation ago. Only a nuclear North Korea might make that untrue. Southern Asia may have to live through an attempt by India to become the local superpower, but the new world order (and India's own internal disorder) can probably contain that. Latin America and Africa, after communism and apartheid, at last have a chance to concentrate on their enormous private business.

That leaves only one large stretch of the world notably liable to produce turmoil and mayhem on a large scale in the coming 15-20 years: the appro-

Look eastward, Europe, and see why you need a successsful Turkey, says Brian Beedham

	Population, 1990 est, millions	Population growth, %*	Real GNP growth, %*
Algeria	25.0	2.7	0.7
Bahrain	0.5	3.9	2.6▲
Egypt	53.2	2.7	1.6
Iran	54.6	3.2	–3.6▲
Iraq	19.0	4.1	n.a.
Jordan	4.0	3.3	1.9
Kuwait	2.1	4.6	1.9▲
Lebanon	2.7	nil	n.a.
Libya	4.5	6.8	n.a.
Mauritania	2.0	2.7	3.5
Morocco	25.1	2.6	4.4
Oman	1.5	4.0‡	3.6
Qatar	0.4	3.9	n.a.
Saudi Arabia	14.9	5.6	2.9
Sudan	25.2	2.9	n.a.
Syria	12.1	3.4	2.6▲
Tunisia	8.2	2.2	2.2
Turkey	56.5†	2.2	5.3
UAE	1.6	3.5	–2.6
Yemen	11.3	2.2	n.a.
Azerbaijan	7.1	1.5	n.a.
Kazakhstan	16.7	1.1	n.a.
Kirgizia	4.4	1.8	n.a.
Tajikistan	5.1	2.6	n.a.
Turkmenia	3.6	7.5	n.a.
Uzbekistan	20.3	2.5	n.a.

*Annual average, 1985-89 †actual ‡1986-89 ▲1985-88
Sources: World Bank; Economist Intelligence Unit; United Nations; Turkish national statistics

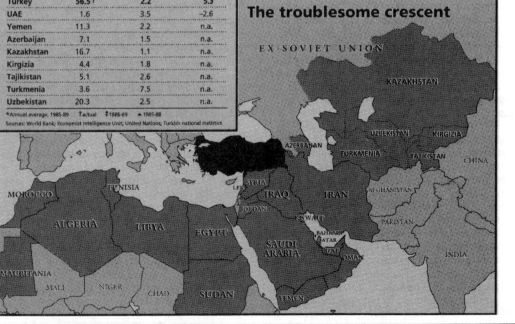

The troublesome crescent

priately crescent-shaped piece of territory that starts in the steppes of Kazakhstan and curves south and west through the Gulf and Suez to the north coast of Africa. This western part of Islam is a potential zone of turbulence for a depressing variety of reasons.

Except in a handful of oil-owning states, its chances of keeping its peoples materially happy are not good: not the worst in the world, but not all that far off. It has too many inhabitants, too little fertile land, barely the rudiments of an industrial economy. Of the 19 countries south of the old Soviet border that constitute the main part of the crescent, at least 13 or 14 had populations growing faster than their economies in the second half of the 1980s. In short, they got poorer. The economic gloom is unlikely to be removed by the intelligent innovations of competitive politics. With one admirable exception—not counting non-Muslim Israel—the area does not yet have a single working democracy.

Worse, it does have an ideology. Now that Marxism has been lowered into its grave, Islam is the 20th century's last surviving example of an idea that claims universal relevance.

The problem is not the Muslim religion itself, or the Muslim conviction (shared by plenty of non-Muslims) that religion ought to shape the believer's daily life. The problem is that in the late 20th century the Islamic body of ideas operates in remarkably difficult circumstances, very much as another body of ideas called Christianity did at the time when Christianity was as young as Islam is now, 600-odd years ago. Many of its followers are simple and emotional people. Many of the politicians who rule over them are unscrupulously willing to use Islam as a banner, and a weapon, against the outside world. Not all Muslims are ideologues; probably most are not. Enough are to make Islam an uncomfortable neighbour.

This economically unhappy, politically prickly stretch of the world sits next door to a Europe that has a chance, for the first time in its life, to be democratic all the way from the Atlantic to the Urals. Europe and Islam have had a difficult time with each other over the past 1,300 years. The fear and hatred are still there. Listen to the tirades of Muslim fundamentalists against the satanic West; see how the politics of France and Germany are twisted by right-wing hysteria about Muslim immigrants.

This will produce ructions. There will almost certainly be upheavals in the next couple of decades in several of the Islamic crescent's two dozen countries, caused by economic misery, bad government and a religion-driven feeling that things ought to be better. There may be more attempts by some of the region's poorer countries to grab the wealth of the few rich ones, like Iraq's grab at Kuwait last year. The authoritarian style of local politics will quite possibly produce another Saddam Hussein or two. The pressure of growing numbers of very poor people will send new waves of immigrants towards Europe, which on present evidence will make Europe slam its doors, which will understandably set Europe's Muslim neighbours looking for ways to re-open those doors. It will not be an easy period.

The beckoning finger

Enter the centrality of Turkey. Into this worrying part of the world points a long rectangle of a country that offers, by and large, an admirable exception to the region's general unsatisfactoriness.

Turkey is a working democracy. The democracy has been embarrassingly interruptible (three course-corrections by the army between 1960 and 1980), and it is still weak in the civil-rights department; but the election on October 20th showed that multi-party choice is vigorously back in operation, and the chances of another military intervention are small, and diminishing. Turkey also has a fairly promising economy. Its national income is growing cheeringly faster than its population, and since 1980 the Turks have abandoned their old fascination with economic self-sufficiency and the merits of state-run industry. They now have a bad case of inflation, and too many dead-loss state companies they have not yet had the courage to get rid of. But, if they keep their heart in it, the Turks can go into the 21st century successfully pluralist in both politics and economics.

It matters as much to the West as to the Turks themselves that they should do so. During the cold war it used to be said that Turkey's value to the West was purely military. It was not true then, and it is not true now. The Turks could do little during the cold war to help hold off the Russians on the vital central front, in Germany. The point of Turkey's membership of NATO was political: it interposed a warning finger between the Soviet Union and the Middle East. In the new shape of things Turkey still has the finger's role; but now the finger says "Come this way", not "Keep out".

True, it is useful that the United States is strengthening the force of bomber aircraft it keeps in south-eastern Turkey, to discourage present and future Saddam Husseins. It is a pity that the brigade of allied soldiers posted in the south-east to protect the Iraqi Kurds has now been withdrawn (because it got entangled in the Turks' quarrel with their own Kurds); but an allied force could be rapidly re-assembled if the politicians decided one was needed again. It is handy to have military clout close to where the clout might have to be delivered. Yet this is not what Turkey can chiefly do to help.

The temptation to opt out

Turkey's chief value is to be an example to the region around it—a living demonstration of the proposition that a Muslim country can become a prosperous democracy, a full member of the modern world. Various explanations have been offered for the rest of western Islam's failure to achieve this. Some people put it down to the humiliation of having had to live for 500 years next to Europe's technological superiority, after the earlier blaze of Arab and Ottoman glory. Others say the reason is that Muslims cannot draw the necessary dividing line between the spiritual and the secular, between the formulation of rules for man's dealings with God and his dealings with other men. Whatever the explanation, Turkey seems to prove it wrong.

The Turks show no sign of feeling inferior to anybody. They are still a manifestly Muslim people; the public evidence of religious belief is more obvious now than a generation ago, in an unassertive, Church-of-England sort of way. And yet, since Kemal Ataturk sent the last Ottoman sultan packing 70 years ago, Turkey has done all the basic things needed for the creation of a modern society: first the necessary separation of church and state; then the introduction of multi-party elections in 1946; and now, since 1980, the opening up of its economy to the outside world. It has been a slow business, with many halts and hesitations, but it has gone ahead.

If Turkish Muslims can do it, why not Arab Muslims and ex-Soviet ones too? This is Turkey's invitation to its semi-circle of Muslim neighbours. The trouble is that the effectiveness of the invitation depends on a continuation of the Turkish good example. There are a couple of reasons for wondering whether the Turks will stay the course in the 1990s.

One is the disappointment of the late 1980s, and the consequences it produced in the confused election on October 20th 1991. The spectacular real economic growth of the mid-1980s has started to hiccup: down to 1.6% in 1989, back up to 9.2% last year, sharply down again this year. The government has failed to get to grips with the budget deficit, so inflation has risen inexorably, to a year-on-year 66% in October.

Moreover, the man who seemed to embody the decisiveness of the mid-1980s has lost his glamour. Turgut Ozal, prime minister from 1983 to 1989 and president since then, still sees more clearly than most other Turks where his country needs to go, but he is a rotten politician. He has let too many of his relatives get rich in unaccountable ways. He has also, since 1989, failed to treat the presidency as the Olympian post the constitution says it should be.

The result is that the Motherland Party, which he created, got only 24% of the votes in October. The other four chief contenders got 27%, 21%, 17% and 11%. That is a mark of voter indecision. And the sort of government the election made inevitable could produce policy indecision too. Four of those five parties—the exception is the Islamic-nationalist far right, the 17% bunch—agree that Turkey should be a free-market democracy, as much like the free democracies of Europe and North America as possible. But they quibble about the details. Worse, they are divided by angry personal antagonisms. The bitterest (but far from the only one) is that between President Ozal and Suleyman Demirel, his new 27%-of-the-votes prime minister. The election result does not look like a prescription for clear-cut, decisive government.

At the same time the break-up of the Soviet Union has brought in a new factor. Most of the people who live in the six Muslim republics of the ex-Soviet south are related to the Turks, and speak a Turkic language. The population of the six, as it happens, almost exactly equals Turkey's population of 56m. This could be a good thing or a bad thing. The good possibility is that Turkey will help to lead these places too towards a free-market, democratic future; the catchment-area for Turkey's good example may have suddenly expanded northeastwards. The danger is that, for some Turks, the reappearance of this Turkish family to the east opens up an alternative to the west-looking policy of the past 70 years. The family, instead of being pulled by Turkey into new ways, may pull Turkey back into old ones.

It would be an exaggeration to call the danger urgent. Talk in Turkey of pan-Turanism, a Turkic commonwealth, is still confined to the wilder shores of right-wing romanticism. But it is worth remembering that for 70 years—the lifetime of modern, post-Ottoman Turkey—the Turks, like the post-1945 Germans, have had a one-option foreign policy. The iron curtain separated Turkey, as it separated Germany, from the cousins to the east. There was nowhere to look but westward. Now the iron curtain has gone; the family can meet again; a counter-current of blood and emotion is at work. It will be as big a pity for Europe and America as for Turkey itself if 1991's combination of disappointment at home and new horizons abroad diverts Turkey from the course it set itself 70 years ago.

Article 20

DISCOVER • DECEMBER • 1991

Land of Bronze

High in the mountains of Turkey, Aslihan Yener may have found the 5,000-year-old secret behind the Bronze Age.

THOMAS BASS

Thomas Bass is the author of Camping with the Prince and Other Tales of Science in Africa.

in was a big deal in the Bronze Age. And the ancient Assyrians were the biggest dealers of the day. They supplied the tin that, added to copper, made the bronze that led to the proliferation of the tools and weapons that were the high-tech hallmarks of the age.

At least that's what most archeologists thought until recently, because this is the impression the Assyrians left for history, and no one else had left anything to contradict them. The Assyrian claim to fame, written 4,000 years ago in cuneiform on slabs of clay, was unearthed among a large stash of trading tablets discovered in southern Turkey in the 1940s and 1950s. These bills of lading documented the boom years of Bronze Age trade at the eastern end of the Mediterranean, when the newly civilized world was first plunging into the global marketplace.

In these tablets the Assyrians, who lived in what is now northern Iraq, characterized their trading partners to the north—the Anatolians—as "stupid." They took great delight in describing how they made 100 percent profits by swapping rare goods obtained from other countries for the Anatolians' silver and gold. One of their most lucrative imports was tin, they claimed, because it was absent from the mountains in Anatolia.

Copper was readily available from mines throughout the Near East, but tin was much scarcer. If the Assyrians were to be believed—and archeologists had no reason to doubt them—the nearest source of tin was 1,000 miles away, in the mines of the Hindu Kush Mountains of Afghanistan. Controlling that tin supposedly put the Assyrians, who were shrewd middlemen and shipping agents, in a powerful position.

"It was an intensely entrepreneurial time," says archeologist Aslihan Yener of the Smithsonian Institution. "Even kings were dabbling in the market." For 2,500 years tin—and its bronze product—would remain the metal on which civilization was built. "All weapons, all agricultural tools, everything from the pins in your hair to the plow in your fields was made of bronze," says Yener. Given the competitive spirit of the day, Yener implies, it would not be so surprising if the Assyrians were inclined to, well, lie.

For the past several years Yener has been amassing the evidence proving the Assyrians did just that, and in the process she is rewriting Bronze Age history. This soft-spoken, unassuming woman hardly looks the part, but she is the Indiana Jones of Near Eastern archeology. While hanging off mountaintops and spelunking into treacherous mine shafts, she has unearthed one remarkable find after another. Her finds are giving archeologists new respect for the sophistication of ancient economies, as well as recasting Anatolia as a major power player in the metals market.

In 1989 Yener discovered what she claims is a Bronze Age tin mine in the Taurus Mountains of southern Turkey, on the Mediterranean coast. "We found a mine smack in the middle of the Near East, where believers of the Assyrian trading tablets said it couldn't be," she says. "But it was in front of our noses all along!" Along with the mine, Yener discovered the archeological remains of what seems to be a great mining city devoted to processing Near Eastern tin—a veritable Pittsburgh of the Bronze Age.

All this has made Kutlu Aslihan Yener something of a hero in present-day Anatolia, or Turkey, where she was born in 1946 into an illustrious family of palace physicians and provincial governors (it also included a few Young Turks who got into trouble trying to overthrow the sultan). Her businessman father moved the family to New Rochelle, New York, when Yener was six months old.

Yener did not set out to be an archeologist. When she entered Adelphi University in 1964, she enrolled as a chemistry major. "It was the age of Sputnik," Yener recalls. "There was a lot of emphasis on science, and I was interested in the fundamental blocks that make up the world. But then along came the later sixties, and I got the travel bug."

The bug took her back to Turkey. She transferred to Robert College—now Bosporus University—in Istanbul and switched her specialization to art history, which allowed her to visit the Roman ruins scattered along Turkey's Mediterranean coast. "The ruins are quite spectacular, but it wasn't the artifacts above ground that fascinated me. It was the traces of the earlier cultures buried underground," she says. "What I wanted to understand were the systems and contexts that produced the pre-Roman art in Turkey."

Her pursuit of these systems took her back to New York to complete her doctorate in archeology at Columbia. Calling on her background in chemistry, Yener's original project was "to apply atomic bomb techniques to archeology. I wanted to open a new window into the ancient world by analyzing the lead isotopes in mines and metals throughout the Near East."

Mines from different regions, and the metallic objects produced from them, have distinct ratios of lead isotopes mixed in with other metals. These isotopic fingerprints can be measured in nanograms down at the atomic level. If an object and a mine have the same ratio, this is strong evidence that one came from the other.

What Yener wanted to do was to use these atomic tracers to map the global economy of the Bronze Age metals trade. She had thought for a long time that her colleagues put too much faith in items like the Assyrian accounts. This was like writing the history of modern world trade from a single source, that source being the vouchers from a trucking company in Brooklyn. "In the past, it was the verbal Assyrians versus the mute Anatolians," she says. "But by tracing the exchange in metals independently of any written accounts, we could finally allow the Anatolians to speak up for themselves. Lead isotopes are the twentieth century's trading tablets."

Before setting up a full-fledged archeological Interpol for matching the lead fingerprints of mines and artifacts throughout the Near East, Yener thought she should start with a smaller test case—the Taurus Mountains of Turkey. For centuries, traders and invaders have stormed in and out of Asia Minor through these mountains, and they looked like a promising region for finding ancient mines. In 1983 Yener began looking for trace elements of lead in silver, which had provided both the money and standard unit of weight for Bronze Age bankers.

It took Yener a while to convince her colleagues from the Turkish Geological Research and Survey Directorate that she had the mettle for scrambling into five-tiered mines that stretched for miles under the snow-covered peaks. "I was always the last person up the slopes," she remembers. "It was a challenge to me, but I *had* to know what was up there. I was driven by sheer curiosity.

"My colleagues were all men, and the Turkish workers on the project had no way of addressing me, because they had never dealt with a young woman who was director of an expedition. But the day came when I finally won their respect. We had climbed up to examine a mine at eighty-five hundred feet, when I fainted from exhaustion and lack of oxygen." Not, perhaps, a performance to inspire confidence. "But on coming around, I found the team geologist shaking my hand. He was congratulating me for attaining heights that no archeologist in Turkey had ever scaled before."

On these peaks Yener discovered a maze of ancient mine shafts and other Bronze Age treasures. "We were flabbergasted," she says. "In one six-square-mile area, where I thought there might be thirty or forty mines, we found eight hundred and fifty." Apart from the mines, Yener found hillsides honeycombed with settlements and mountain strongholds,

many of them with their slag heaps and stone mining tools still in place. These ancient industrial parks straddled mountaintops that today are visited only by the occasional nomad running his sheep to summer pasture.

Yener took lead-isotope signatures from silver in the mines and compared them with the signatures of various Bronze Age artifacts, including silver bracelets, earrings, goblets, and bowls that had once filled the treasure halls of Troy, on Anatolia's north coast. Her isotopic fingerprints of the Taurus silver mines matched those of the Trojan hoard. They also matched the lead net sinkers salvaged from the world's oldest recovered shipwreck, a Bronze Age sailing vessel found off the Turkish coast. Historians, perusing ancient records, had long suspected that the "Silver Mountains of the Akkadians," a misty Bronze Age legend, were really the Taurus Mountains of Turkey; now Yener's tracers added modern confirmation.

Yener barely had time to savor this news before she made her next discovery: tin. "We found trace elements of tin in an old, mined-out vein that still held a small amount of stannite, a naturally occurring form of bronze." To Yener, this was clear evidence that, contrary to textbook archeology, Bronze Age tin came from close to home. "But my critics, who still believed what the Assyrians had written, kept telling me this wasn't good enough. They wanted tin oxide, the only natural source of tin ore, and they wanted it from a mine." So for five years Yener and her colleagues in the Turkish geological survey combed the mountains and panned through 80 tons of soil washed down by mountain streams. They found nothing. But that was to be expected, Yener decided; if the ancient Turks were mining tin, they would have removed it all thousands of years earlier.

Yener's big break came in the sum-

"THE MINE LOOKS LIKE A SERIES OF RABBIT TUNNELS. BUT I'M AMAZED AT THE ENGINEERING ABILITY OF THESE MINERS OF FORTY-FIVE HUNDRED YEARS AGO."

mer of 1987, in Istanbul, when she got a phone call from a friend who works for the geological survey. He said that as he spoke he was holding a test tube full of what looked like purple grains of sand with a glassy surface. This was cassiterite, or tin ore, that he had panned out of a stream while searching for gold in the Taurus foothills.

Yener ditched her plans to spend the summer digging through old Taurus slag heaps and drove 15 hours straight to the mountains. "I got very excited when I saw it," she says of her first glimpse of Turkish tin. "It was burgundy colored, rather than the more familiar black, which is one of the reasons everyone had overlooked it all these years."

After hiking into a remote valley 24 miles north of her old silver mine, Yener found Bronze Age pottery and mining tools littering the hillsides. At a site called Kestel she also found a mine full of bats and sheep dung, and in its perilous limestone galleries, some of them no more than two feet wide, were veins in the rock that bore traces of that beautiful burgundy ore.

"I've gotten so used to it that it's like a home now," says Yener of the mine. She and her research team have spent the past four summers re-excavating it. "The mine looks like a series of rabbit tunnels going off in different directions. It's horribly damp and mucky as you crunch through the animal bones de-

posited over the years. But I'm amazed at the engineering ability of these miners of forty-five hundred years ago."

While she was convinced she had found the missing tin of antiquity, the old supporters of the Assyrian traders were still dubious. Yener's mine had been worked so thoroughly that its tin content was a measly 3 percent. "Again there was a hue and cry that this couldn't possibly have been a significant source of tin. We needed an untapped deposit or another piece of major evidence to prove that this had once been a working tin mine."

An untapped deposit in a mountain of miners was unlikely, but a mining village or foundry would have helped Yener's case immensely. "After all our work, we still couldn't find the processing site and mining village," she says. "Where were the miners living? It was a great mystery. Then one week before the end of the 1989 season, my students went to look at some stones on a hill opposite the mine. They came back with bags of pottery. It was the ugliest, crummiest looking stuff I had ever seen—real mountainware. But it was Bronze Age pottery, nonetheless, so I went over to survey the hilltop and found an incredible cache of hammerstone tools, fifty thousand of them scattered over an area just over half a mile in diameter."

In the summer of 1990, as soon as the snow was off the ground, Yener returned to excavate what turned out to be a semisubterranean city that was larger than Bronze Age Troy and may have had a population of about 10,000. The city is on a hill called Goltepe. "Workshops and houses had been cut into the bedrock, and the city was fortified, which meant it was either a year-round settlement or highly important."

The digging also unearthed a lot more pottery. "Some of it was covered with a glassy sheen that I recognized as metallic slag," Yener says. "Naysayers—the last holdouts for the Assyrian traders—suggested these were baking dishes or lanterns. But I knew, after all the years I had been studying them, that these were crucibles for processing tin."

Yener carried some of her newly excavated potsherds to the X-ray fluorescent unit at the Smithsonian. Different trace elements reflect different wavelengths of X-rays. The Smithsonian lab produced a computer-generated graph of the different elements coating the pots. "When the tin peaks came shooting up on the graph, we started dancing up and down and hugging each other," Yener says. "The crucibles were lined with thirty percent tin; parts of them registered ninety-nine percent pure tin."

Charcoal found near the crucibles has since been radiocarbon dated to 4,500 years ago, placing the pots exactly at the

MAP BY WALTER STUART

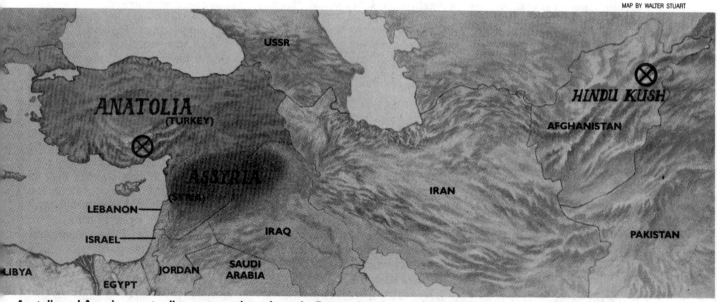

Anatolia and Assyria were trading partners throughout the Bronze Age, from 4000 to 1000 B.C.

time when Bronze Age technology was starting to take off. Apparently, the tin ore was pulverized with stone pestles and then mixed with arsenic to lower its melting temperature. It was then placed in these crucibles and covered with charcoal. By blowing on the coals through reeds—a process shown in Egyptian pictographs—the metal workers got their fires hot enough to smelt tin.

Yener's pots have not entirely silenced the doubters. But even the hardened skeptics now admit there's a strong case for a source of Bronze Age tin much closer to the Mediterranean centers than distant Hindu Kush. And the discovery points to a much more complex economy than archeologists had allowed for. With competing sources of tin, some local and some foreign, there must have been price competition, trade wars, and all sorts of maneuvering to dominate the market. "Tin was like oil today," Yener says. "It was the most important component in your high-tech culture. Knowing that there were competing sources complicates the picture, but I like complications like these."

Now that Yener has discovered the elusive tin of antiquity, she intends to study the people who used it. "My next lifetime will be devoted to understanding the folk culture of the miners." She also wants to find out how the Bronze Age discovered bronze in the first place. Who, 5,000 years ago, came up with the bright idea of mixing together two metals to make an alloy stronger than its individual parts? "When it comes to the invention of Bronze Age metallurgy," says Yener, with a glint in her eye, "we have a big gap in our knowledge. And boy, do I go for the gaps!"

Article 21

Middle East Report • May-June 1991

Yemen: Unification and the Gulf War

Sheila Carapico

On May 22, 1990, the People's Democratic Republic of Yemen (the PDRY, or South Yemen) and the Yemen Arab Republic (the YAR, or North Yemen) joined to become the Republic of Yemen. "A Tale of Two Families" reflects the malaise in North Yemen on the eve of unification; the situation in the south, since the 1986 street battles in Aden, was even worse.[1]

Unity offered beneficial economies of scale in oil, power, administrative apparatus and tourism. It made political sense, too, reflecting the view of most Yemenis that the division into separate countries was artificial and imposed.

Formal unification heralded unprecedented pluralism and political opening. Televised debates in parliament, dominated by the former ruling parties of the YAR and the PDRY, the General People's Congress and the Yemeni Socialist Party, exposed bureaucratic corruption. Some three dozen new parties, of Nasirist, Ba'thi, liberal and religious orientations, began publishing newspapers and organizing for May 1992 elections. Sana' University students demonstrated to replace national security police with student workers as campus guards. Military checkpoints virtually disappeared from Sana', Aden, and the highway between them. In June and July of 1990, the mood was like that in Prague.

The sudden suspension of Saudi, Kuwaiti and Iraqi aid, the embargo of Iraqi oil shipments, the collapse of tourism and the decline in regional commerce cost Yemen nearly $2 billion in 1990, although a sudden infusion of migrants' remittances cushioned the blow. While ministries struggled to pay faculty and health workers' salaries previously financed from the Gulf, investment plans were scaled back, the *riyal*'s value dropped, prices rose sharply, and a half-million returnees camped outside Sana'.

Yemen's refusal to join the coalition caused the deepest rift in Washington-Sana' relations since June 1967, but it also captured US attention. US Secretary of State James Baker visited Sana' but failed to persuade the government to join the US-Saudi axis. President 'Ali 'Abdallah Salih repeated Yemen's condemnation of Iraq's invasion but observed that intervention by a massive multinational force was liable to "destabilize the entire region."

American dependents, Peace Corps, USAID, USIA, their European counterparts, and business people gradually evacuated Yemen. Once the war began, the remaining 20 US diplomats and marines moved into the embassy, and oil industry employees stayed off the streets. Yemeni media now carried Baghdad's war coverage, along with denunciations of Voice of America and the BBC. After some demonstrations, and then a calm, someone threw grenades at the Sana' International School, there were small explosions at several embassies, and the heavily fortified US compound came under machine-gun fire from a passing car.

For all its popularity, Yemeni unification is anathema to Saudi Arabia. Although the YAR's more conservative social, economic and political system appeared to dominate the new union, a unified Yemen of 13 or 14 million people posed a potential military threat, the Saudis felt, and its relative freedom of press, assembly and participation, including women's participation, could set a dangerous example. Riyadh tersely congratulated the new republic, but covertly subsidized an opposition "reform" party of conservative tribes and fundamentalists.

Washington has traditionally dealt with North Yemen through Riyadh.[2] Sana' got a modest $30 million or so annually in US development assistance, but the PDRY was on the State Department's list of "terrorist states." Economic plans of the unified state called for freer trade and investment, and Soviet influence seemed on the wane. When 'Ali 'Abdallah Salih became the first Yemeni president to visit Washington in January 1990, two months after being designated to lead the future unified state, the Bush administration approved $50 million in trade credits. YAR ambassador Muhsin al-'Aini stayed on in Washington, while the PDRY's 'Abdallah al-Ashtal remained as the new country's UN delegate.

It was against the backdrop of this most important event in its recent history that Yemen responded to the Iraqi invasion of Kuwait. Initially opinion was divided, but the balance shifted after Saddam Hussein, in his first major speech of the crisis, declared that Iraq had been inspired by the Yemeni example to pursue Arab unity by erasing colonial boundaries, and Saudi commentators lambasted Sana' for refusing to commit troops to the kingdom's defense. The Saudi request for US troops to confront Iraq prompted extraordinary protest demonstrations, and the consensus at many qat chews shifted decisively against Saudi Arabia. At the same time, pro-Saudi elements formed a Committee for the Defense of the Rights of Kuwait.

Mindful of both the public mood and longer term interest in maintaining ties with the West and the Gulf, the government declared and held to a policy of neutrality. The Salih regime condemned the invasion, hostage-taking and annexation, but did not support sanctions or use-of-force resolutions. UN representative al-Ashtal became the Security Council's most prominent, consistent advocate for diplomacy.

The al-Sauds took this neutrality as an affront. They cut aid in August. Next, they summarily revoked special residence and working privileges for over a million of the Yemenis in the kingdom, life-long residents as well as short-term sojourners, forcing the majority to sell what they could at distressed prices and head south.

News of the US bombing of a Baghdad shelter full of civilians and of the ground assault politicized Sana' as never before. While the Arab League's minority anti-war faction met at the Hadda Ramada, Tahrir Square overflowed with tens of thousands of enraged students and expelled migrants.

In the confluence of these events—a new nationalism, sudden lifting of political constraints, a war jeopardizing national and individual well-being, and a leading role at the UN—Yemenis and their government feel they have found a political voice. Popular slogans against the war and the Gulf monarchies have helped legitimize a regime which, in turn, tried to play a mediating role in the Arab League and the Security Council. Saudi and US "punishment" has so far only heightened a sense of nationalist self-righteousness. This will deepen if Yemen and other poor Arab states that declined to back the war are forced to pay.

Footnotes

1 For one account, see Fred Halliday, "Moscow's Crisis Management: The Case of South Yemen," *Middle East Report*, #151 (March-April 1988).

2 After the fall of the shah, the US rushed $100 million in arms to Sana' when Saudi Arabia requested weapons to protect the YAR from the PDRY. See *New York Times*, February 12 and 13, 1979; *New York Times*, February 13, 1979; and *Washington Post*, December 4, 1986, for articles describing the *quid pro quo* for Saudi involvement in Iran-Contra dealings. The context for these events is discussed by Nadav Safran, *Saudi Arabia: The Ceaseless Quest for Security* (Cambridge: Belknap, 1985), especially pages 282-294 and 387-397; and Anthony Cordesman, *The Gulf and the Search for Strategic Stability: Saudi Arabia, the Military Balance in the Gulf and Trends in the Arab-Israeli Military Balance* (Boulder: Westview, 1986). The case for Saudi hegemony is made in Saeed Badeeb, *The Saudi-Egyptian Conflict over Yemen 1962-70* (Boulder: Westview, 1986).

Credits

Sources for Statistical Reports

U.S. State Department, *Background Notes* (1988–1991).

The World Factbook (1992).

World Statistics in Brief (1991).

World Almanac (1992).

The Statesman's Yearbook (1990–1991).

Demographic Yearbook (1991).

Statistical Yearbook (1992).

World Bank, World Development Report (1991).

Ayers Directory of Publications (1991).

Glossary of Terms and Abbreviations

Abd—Slave, servant of God (as in Gamal Abdel Nasser: Abd al-Nasir).

AFESD (Arab Fund for Economic and Social Development)—Established in 1973 to make low-interest loans within the Arab states. Membership: all of the Arab states except Egypt (suspended in 1979) plus the PLO. Headquarters: Kuwait City, Kuwait.

Alawi (Nusayri)—A Shia Muslim minority group in Syria, currently in power under President Assad.

Arab Monetary Fund—Established in 1977 to work for Arab economic integration, provide loans to meet balance of payments deficits, and promote inter-Arab trade. Membership: all of the Arab states except Egypt (suspended 1979), plus Somalia, Mauritania, and the PLO. Headquarters: Abu Dhabi, United Arab Emirates.

Asabiyya—Tribal or group solidarity, a concept developed by the fourteenth-century Islamic philosopher Ibn Khaldun to explain Muslim, particularly North African, social behavior.

Ayatollah—"Sign of God," the title of highest rank among the Shia religious leaders in Iran.

Ba'th (Arab Socialist Resurrection Party)—A Socialist political party that has two main branches, ruling in Syria and Iraq respectively, plus members in other Arab countries.

Caliph (in Arabic, *Khalifa*)—Agent, representative, or deputy; in Sunni Islam, the line of successors to Muhammad.

Colon—Settler, colonist (French), a term used for the French population in North Africa during the colonial period (1830–1962).

Council of Arab Economic Unity—Established in 1964 to promote an Arab Common Market, coordinate Arab development plans and formation of joint Arab companies and unions, and form an Arab customs union. Membership: Iraq, Jordan, Kuwait, Libya, Mauritania, Somalia, Sudan, Syria, United Arab Emirates, Yemen, and the PLO. Headquarters: Amman, Jordan.

Dar al-Islam—"House of Islam," territory ruled under Islam. Conversely, Dar al-Harb, "House of War," denotes territory not under Islamic rule.

Dhimmis (in Arabic, *ahl al-dhimma*, "the protected peoples")—Subject peoples such as Christians and Jews living under Islamic rule but protected in return for payment of a head tax and inferior status.

Druze (or Druse)—An offshoot of Islam that has developed its own rituals and practices and a close-knit community structure; Druze populations are found today in Lebanon, Jordan, Syria, and Israel.

Emir (or Amir)—A title of rank, denoting either a patriarchal ruler, provincial governor, or military commander. Today it is used exclusively for rulers of certain Arabian Peninsula states.

Fatwa—A legal opinion or interpretation delivered by a Muslim religious scholar-jurist.

Fida'i (plural Fida'iyun, also Fedayeen, cf. Mujahideen)—Literally, "fighter for the faith"; a warrior who fights for the faith against the enemies of Islam.

FLN (National Liberation Front)—The resistance movement against the French in Algeria that succeeded in establishing Algerian independence.

GCC (Gulf Cooperation Council)—Established in 1981 as a mutual-defense organization by the Arab Gulf states. Membership: Bahrain, Kuwait, Oman, Qatar, Saudi Arabia, and United Arab Emirates. Headquarters: Riyadh, Saudi Arabia.

Hadith—"Traditions" of the Prophet Muhammad, the compilation of sayings and decisions attributed to him that serve as a model and guide to conduct for Muslims.

Hajj—Pilgrimage to Mecca, one of the Five Pillars of Islam; also used as a title for one who has made the pilgrimage.

Hijrah (Hegira)—The Prophet Muhammad's emigration from Mecca to Medina in A.D. 622 to escape persecution; the start of the Islamic calendar.

Histadrut—The largest Israeli labor confederation.

Ibadi—A militant early Islamic group that split with the majority (Sunni) over the question of the succession to Muhammad. Their descendants form the majority of the population in Oman and the Yemen Arab Republic.

IBRD (International Bank for Reconstruction and Development)—Established in 1945 to make loans at conventional interest rates to countries for development projects. Headquarters: Washington, D.C. Affiliated organizations are the International Development Assistance Organization (IDA), the International Finance Corporation (IFC), and the International Monetary Fund (IMF).

Ihram—The seamless white robe worn by all Muslims making the hajj.

Ijma—Consensus, the agreement of the majority of members of a particular Islamic community for collective action on important matters, such as a peace treaty.

Ijtihad—Independent reasoning and interpretation of matters of Islamic law. When made authoritatively, as by an ayatollah, such interpretations have the force of law.

Ikhwan—Brothers, as in a religious confraternity. When capitalized (i.e., Ikhwan al-Muslimin), refers to the Muslim Brotherhood, a secret but widespread Sunni organization opposed to Muslim secular governments.

Imam—Religious leader, prayer-leader of a congregation. When capitalized, refers to the descendants of Ali who are regarded by Shia Muslims as the rightful successors to Muhammad.

Intifadah—Uprising, that is, of the Palestinians against Israeli occupation.

Islam—Submission, i.e., to the will of God, as revealed in the Koran. The religion of Muslims.

Ismailis—Members of a branch of Shia Islam who accept a line of only five Imams descended from Muhammad through Ali. Their spiritual leader is the Aga Khan.

Ithna 'ashariyyah—"Twelvers," the main body of members of Shia Islam who accept a line of 12 Imams, ending with the Hidden Imam or Mahdi.

Jahiliyya—The "time of ignorance" of the Arabs before Islam. Sometimes used by Islamic fundamentalists today to describe secular Muslim societies, which they regard as sinful.

Jama'a—The Friday communal prayer, held in a mosque (*jami'*). By extension, the public assembly held by Muslim rulers for their subjects in traditional Islamic states such as Saudi Arabia.

Jamahiriyya—Popular democracy (as in Libya).

Jihad—The struggle of Muslims collectively or individually to do right and defend the community; commonly, "holy war."

Jizya—A poll-tax or tithe imposed on non-Muslim peoples living in the territories of Islam.

Khan—A title of rank in eastern Islam (Turkey, Iran, etc.) for military or clan leaders.

Kharijites—An early Muslim group who opposed the succession in Muhammad's family but also opposed the election of the first four caliphs as undemocratic. They assassinated Ali after he had negotiated a truce with his opponents upon becoming caliph; in their view, he had bartered away his right to the office.

Khedive—Viceroy, the title of rulers of Egypt in the nineteenth and twentieth centuries who ruled as regents of the Ottoman sultan.

Kibbutz—A collective settlement in Israel.

Koran (in Arabic, Qur'an)—"Recitation," the book of God's revelations to Muhammad via the Angel Gabriel that form the basis for Islam.

League of Arab States (Arab League)—Established in 1945 as a regional organization for newly independent Arab countries. Membership: all the Arab states except Egypt (suspended in 1979) plus the PLO.

Maghrib—"West," the hour of the sunset prayer; in Arabic, a geographical term for North Africa.

Mahdi—"The Awaited One" in both Sunni and Shia Islam, the Messiah, who will appear on earth to reunite the divided Islamic community and announce the Day of Judgment. In Shia Islam he is the Twelfth and Last Imam (al-Mahdi al-Muntazir) who disappeared 12 centuries ago but is believed to be in a state of occultation (suspended between heaven and earth).

Majlis—Assembly, Parliament, Legislature.

Mandates, System of—An arrangement set up under the League of Nations after World War I for German colonies and territories of the Ottoman Empire inhabited by non-Turkish populations. The purpose was to train these populations for eventual self-government under a temporary occupation by a foreign power, which was either the United Kingdom or France.

Marabout—Particularly in North Africa, a local saint or holy man respected for his intercessory powers with God on behalf of a community.

Mawlid (Mouloud)—Birthday, usually used only for the birthday of the Prophet Muhammad, a major holiday in the Islamic world.

Millet—"Nation," a non-Muslim population group in the Ottoman Empire recognized as a legitimate religious community and allowed self-government in internal affairs under its own religious leaders, who were responsible to the sultan for its behavior.

Muezzin—A prayer-caller, the person who announces the five daily obligatory prayers from the minaret of a mosque.

Mufti—A legal scholar empowered to issue fatwas. Usually one mufti is designated as the Grand Mufti of a particular Islamic state or territory.

Mujahideen (*see* Fida'i)—A common term for resistance fighters in Afghanistan and opposition militants in Iran.

Mujtahid—An independent legal interpreter whose judicial opinions reflect one of the four schools of Islamic law.

Muslim (*see* Islam)—One who submits (to the Will of God).

OAPEC (Organization of Arab Petroleum Exporting Countries)—Established in 1968 to coordinate oil policies—but not setting prices—and to develop oil-related inter-Arab projects, such as an Arab tanker fleet and dry-dock facilities. Membership: all Arab oil-producing states. Headquarters: Kuwait.

OIC (Organization of the Islamic Conference)—Established in 1971 to promote solidarity among Islamic countries, provide humanitarian aid to Muslim communities throughout the world, and provide funds for Islamic education through construction of mosques, theological institutions of Islamic learning, etc. Membership: all states with an Islamic majority or significant minority. Headquarters: Jiddah, Saudi Arabia.

OPEC (Organization of Petroleum Exporting Countries)—Established in 1960 to set prices and coordinate global oil policies of members. A majority of its 13 member states are in the Middle East. Headquarters: Vienna, Austria.

PLO (Palestine Liberation Organization)—Established in 1964 to develop political and military strategies for the creation of a sovereign Arab state in Palestine and its liberation from Israeli control. Overall PLO authority is vested in the Palestine National Council (PNC). Fatah (acronym for the Palestine National Liberation Movement, a guerrilla military group) joined the PLO in 1968, when a charter for Palestinian Arab national independence was issued. The PNC (in theory) supervises the Palestine Liberation Army, a body of 16,000 troops dispersed since 1982 in various Arab states. The PLO holds observer status at the United Nations. Funding comes from annual contributions from the Arab states, mainly Saudi Arabia, plus a 3- to 6-percent tax levied on the incomes of all Palestinians. Headquarters (temporary): Tunis, Tunisia.

Polisario—A national resistance movement in the Western Sahara that opposes annexation by Morocco and is fighting to establish an independent Saharan Arab state, the Sahrawi Arab Democratic Republic (SADR).

PSD (Parti Socialiste Destourien)—The dominant political party in Tunisia since independence and until recently the only legal party.

Qadi (Cadi, Kadi)—An Islamic judge.

Qaid (Caid, Kaid)—Particularly in North Africa, a native Muslim official appointed to administer a region or territory by the French during the protectorate period.

Qasba (Casbah, Kasba)—A fortified section of an Islamic city; citadel.

Qibla—The section of wall in an Islamic mosque that faces in the direction of Mecca, marked by a recess or niche (*mihrab*).

Qizilbash—("Red heads" in Turkish, from their red battle-caps) An eastern Islamic group who helped found the sixteenth-century Safavid monarchy in Iran.

Quraysh—The group of clans who made up Muhammad's community in Mecca.

Salat—The five obligatory daily Islamic prayers, the second of the Five Pillars of Islam.

Shahada—The confession of faith by Muslims, the first of the Five Pillars of Islam.

Shari'a—"The Way," the corpus of the sacred laws of Islam as revealed to Muhammad in the Koran.

Sharif—"Holy," a term applied to members of Muhammad's immediate family and descendants through his daughter Fatima and son-in-law Ali.

Shaykh (Sheikh, Sheik)—A patriarchal leader of an Islamic community, usually elected for life; also used for certain religious leaders and community elders as a title of honor.

Shia (commonly, but incorrectly, called Shiite)—Originally meant "Party," i.e., of Ali, those Muslims who supported him as Muhammad's rightful and designated successor. Today, broadly, a member of the principal Islamic minority.

Sufi—An Islamic mystic.

Sunna—Custom or procedure, the code of acceptable behavior for Muslims based on the Koran and hadith. Not to be confused with Sunni, the name for the majority group in Islam.

Suq (Souk)—A public weekly market in Islamic rural areas, always held in the same village on the same day of the week, so that the village may have the word incorpo-

rated into its name. Also refers to a section of an Islamic city devoted to the wares and work of potters, cloth merchants, wood workers, spice sellers, etc.

Taqiyya—Dissimulation, concealment of one's religious identity or beliefs (as by Shia under Sunni control) in the face of overwhelming power or repression.

Tariqas—The religious brotherhoods or orders of Sunni Islam.

U.A.R. (United Arab Republic)—The name given to the abortive union of Egypt and Syria (1958–1961).

Ulema—The corporate body of Islamic religious leaders, scholars, and jurists.

Umma—The worldwide community of Muslims.

UNHCR (United Nations High Commissioner for Refugees)—Established in 1951 to provide international protection and material assistance to refugees worldwide. UNHCR has several refugee projects in the Middle East.

UNIFIL (UN Interim Force in Lebanon)—Formed in 1978 to ensure Israeli withdrawal from southern Lebanon. After the 1982 Israeli invasion UNIFIL was given the added responsibility for protection and humanitarian aid to the people of the area. Headquarters: Naqoura, Lebanon.

UN Peacekeeping Forces—Various military observer missions formed to supervise disengagement or truce agreements between the Arab states and Israel. They include UNDOF (UN Disengagement Observer Force). Formed in 1974 as a result of the October 1973 Arab-Israeli War and continued by successive resolutions. Headquarters: Damascus, Syria.

UNRWA (United Nations Relief and Works Agency for Palestine Refugees)—Established in 1950 to provide food, housing, and health and education services for Palestinian refugees who fled their homes after the establishment of the State of Israel in Palestine. Headquarters: Vienna, Austria. UNRWA maintains refugee camps in Lebanon, Syria, Jordan, the occupied West Bank and the Gaza Strip. UNRWA has also assumed responsibility for emergency relief for refugees in Lebanon displaced by the Israeli invasion and by the Lebanese Civil War.

Wilayat al-Faqih—Supreme guardianship of the law, according to Iran's 1980 Constitution.

Bibliography

GENERAL WORKS

Patrick Bannerman, *Islam in Perspective: A Guide to Islamic Society* (London: Routledge, 1988).

Berch Berberoglu, ed., *Power and Stability in the Middle East* (London: Zed Books, 1989).

Leonard Binder, *Islamic Liberalism: A Critique of Developmental Ideologies* (Chicago: University of Chicago Press, 1988).

H. Hrair Dekmejian, *Islam in Revolution* (Syracuse: Syracuse University Press, 1985).
> Detailed analysis of Islamic fundamentalism with case studies of fundamentalist politics in several Middle Eastern countries.

Dilip Hiro, *Holy Wars: The Rise of Islamic Fundamentalism* (New York: Routledge, 1989).

Jacques Jomier, *How to Understand Islam*, Translated by John Bowden (New York: Crossroad, 1989). First published in France in 1988 as *Pour Connaitre Islam*, by Editions du Cerf.

David Lamb, *The Arabs: Journeys Beyond the Mirage* (New York: Random House, 1987).
> A good general introduction by the former *Los Angeles Times* correspondent.

Ira M. Lapidus, *A History of Islamic Societies* (Cambridge: Cambridge University Press, 1988).

Trevor Mostyn, *Coming of Age in the Middle East* (London: Kegan Paul International, 1987).

Emmanual Sivan, *Radical Islam: Medieval Theology and Modern Politics* (New Haven: Yale University Press, 1985).
> An insightful monograph dealing with the ideas of Islam as they affect modern politics.

Rafiq Zakaria, *The Struggle Within Islam* (London: Penguin Books, 1989).

Samir Zubaida, *Islam, the People and the State: Essays on Political Ideas and Movements in the Middle East* (New York: Routledge, 1989).

NATIONAL HISTORIES

Algeria
Mahfoud Bennune, *The Making of Contemporary Algeria* (Cambridge, England: Cambridge University Press, 1988).

John P. Entelis, *Algeria: The Revolution Institutionalized* (Boulder: Westview Press, 1986).

Assassi Lassassi, *Non-Alignment and Algerian Foreign Policy* (Hanta, England: Aldershot, 1989).

Bahrain
Michael Jenner, *Bahrain: Gulf Heritage in Transition* (London: Longman, 1984).

Fuad I. Khuri, *Tribe and State in Bahrain* (Chicago: University of Chicago Press, 1981).

Mahdi A. al-Tajir, *Bahrain 1920–1945: Britain, The Shaykh and the Administration* (London: Croom Helm, 1987).

Egypt
Hamid Ansari, *Egypt: The Stalled Society* (Binghamton: State University of New York Press, 1986).

Raymond A. Hinnebusch, Jr., *Egyptian Politics Under Sadat* (Cambridge: Cambridge University Press, 1985).

Monte Palmer, *The Egyptian Bureaucracy,* with Ali Leila (Syracuse: Syracuse University Press, 1988).

Robert Springborg, *Mubarak's Egypt: Fragmentation of the Political Order* (Boulder: Westview Press, 1989).

John Waterbury, *The Egypt of Nasser and Sadat: Political Economies of Two Regimes* (Princeton: Princeton University Press, 1983).

Iran
Hooshang Amirahmadi & M. Parvin, eds., *Post-Revolutionary Iran* (Boulder: Westview Press, 1988).

S. A. Arjomand, *The Turban for the Crown: The Islamic Revolution in Iran* (New York: Oxford University Press, 1988).

James A. Bill, *The Eagle and the Lion: The Tragedy of American-Iranian Relations* (New Haven: Yale University Press, 1988).

Frances Bostock & Geoffrey Jones, *Planning and Power in Iran: Ebtehaj's Economic Development Under the Shah* (London: Frank Cass, 1989).

Roy Mottahedeh, *The Mantle of the Prophet: Religion and Politics in Iran* (New York: Simon & Schuster, 1985).

R. K. Ramazani, ed., *Iran's Revolution: The Search for Consensus* (Bloomington: Indiana University Press, 1990, in conjunction with the Middle East Institute).

William Shawcross, *The Shah's Last Ride* (New York: Simon & Schuster, 1988).

Amir Taheri, *Nest of Spies: America's Journey to Disaster in Iran* (New York: Pantheon Books, 1988).

Iraq
F. W. Axelgard, *A New Iraq? The Gulf War and Implications for Foreign Policy* (New York: Praeger, 1988. The Washington Papers, No. 133).

Arthur H. Blair, *At War in the Gulf: A Chronology* (College Station, Texas A&M University Press, 1992).

Samir Khalil, *Republic of Fear: The Politics of Modern Iraq* (Berkeley: University of California Press, 1989).

Phoebe Marr, *A History of Modern Iraq* (London: Longman, 1983).

Reeva S. Simon, *Iraq Between the Two World Wars* (New York: Columbia University Press, 1986).

Israel
Ze'ev Chafets, *Hard Hats and Holy Men: Inside the New Israel* (New York: Quill/William Morrow, 1987).

Yehoshafat Harkabi, *Israel's Fateful Hour* (New York: Harper & Row, revised edition, 1989).

Conor Cruse O'Brien, *The Siege: The Saga of Israel and Zionism* (New York: Simon & Schuster, 1986).

Shlomo Swirski, *Israel, the Oriental Majority* (London: Zed Books, 1989).

Milton Viorst, *Sands of Sorrow: Israel's Journey From Independence* (New York: Harper & Row, 1987).

Palestinian Conflict
Thomas L. Friedman, *From Beirut to Jerusalem* (New York: Farrar Straus & Giroux, 1989). By the former chief Middle East correspondent of the *New York Times*.

Zachary Lechman & Joel Beinin, eds., *Intifada: The Palestinian Uprising Against Israeli Occupation* (Boston: South End Press, 1989). A MERIP publication.

Muhammad Y. Muslih, *The Origins of Palestinian Nationalism* (New York: Columbia University Press, 1988). Published in cooperation with the Institute of Palestine Studies.

Don Peretz, *Intifada: The Palestinian Uprising* (Boulder: Westview Press, 1990).

Jordan

Peter Gubser, *Jordan: Crossroads of Middle Eastern Events* (Boulder: Westview Press, 1983).

Paul Jureidini and R. D. McLaurin, *Jordan: The Impact of Social Change on the Tribes* (New York: Praeger, 1984, The Washington Papers, No. 108).

James Lunt, *Hussein of Jordan* (New York: William Morrow, 1989). A biography.

Robert B. Satloff, *Troubles on the West Bank: Challenges to the Domestic Stability of Jordan* (New York: Praeger, 1986. The Washington Papers, No. 123).

Mary Wilson, *King Abdullah, Britain and the Making of Jordan* (New York: Oxford University Press, 1987).

Kuwait

A. M. Abu-Hakima, *The Modern History of Kuwait, 1750–1965* (London: Luzac, 1983).

Jill Crystal, *Kuwait: The Transformation of an Old State* (Boulder, Westview, 1992).

Stephen Gardiner and Ian Cook, *Kuwait: Making of a City* (London: Longman, 1983).

Jacqueline Ismael, *Kuwait: Problems of Modernization* (Syracuse: Syracuse University Press, 1981).

Lebanon

Helena Cobban, *The Making of Modern Lebanon* (Boulder: Westview Press, 1985).

Thomas L. Friedman, *From Beirut to Jerusalem* (New York: Farrar, Straus & Giroux, 1989).

David C. Gordon, *Lebanon: Nation in Jeopardy* (Boulder: Westview Press, 1983).

Samir Khalaf, *Lebanon's Predicament* (New York: Columbia University Press, 1987).

Kamal S. Salibi, *A House of Many Mansions: The History of Lebanon Reconsidered* (Berkeley: University of California Press, 1988).

Libya

David Blundy and Andrew Lycett, *Qaddafi and the Libyan Revolution* (Boston: Little, Brown, 1987).

John Davis, *Libyan Politics: The Zuwaya and Their Government* (Berkeley: University of California Press, 1987).

Lillian Craig Harris, *Libya: Qadhafi's Revolution and the Modern State* (Boulder: Westview Press, 1986).

Mohammed El-Khawar, *Qadhafi: His Ideology in Theory and Practice* (Brattleboro: Amana Books, 1986).

Ronald B. St. John, *Qadhafi's World Design: Libyan Foreign Policy 1969–1987* (Atlantic Highlands: Saqi Books, 1987).

Martin Sicker, *The Making of a Pariah State: The Adventurist Politics of Mu'ammar Qadhafi* (New York: Praeger, 1987).

M. G. El-Warfally, *Imagery and Ideology in U.S. Policy Toward Libya* (Pittsburgh: University of Pittsburgh Press, 1988).

Morocco

M. E. Combs-Schilling, *Sacred Performances: Islam, Sexuality and Sacrifice in Moroccan Society* (New York: Columbia University Press, 1989).

John P. Entelis, *Culture and Counterculture in Moroccan Politics* (Boulder: Westview Press, 1988).

Lawrence Rosen, *Bargaining for Reality* (Chicago: University of Chicago Press, 1984).

Oman

Calvin H. Allen, Jr., *Oman: The Modernization of the Sultanate* (Boulder: Westview Press, 1987).

Patricia Russo, *Oman and Muscat, an Early Modern History* (New York: St. Martin's Press, 1986).

John C. Wilkinson, *The Imamate Tradition of Oman* (Cambridge: Cambridge University Press, 1987).

Qatar

Zuhair A. Nafi, *Economic and Social Development in Qatar* (Dover: F. Pinter, 1983).

Abeer abu Saud, *Qatari Women Past and Present* (London: Longman's, 1984).

Saudi Arabia

Mordechai Abir, *Saudi Arabia in the Oil Era* (Boulder: Westview Press, 1988).

Anthony Cordesman, *Western Strategic Interests in Saudi Arabia* (London: Croom Helm, 1987).

Sumner S. Huyette, *Political Adaptation in Saudi Arabia: A Study of the Council of Ministers* (Boulder: Westview Press, 1985).

Sandra Mackey, *The Saudis* (Boston: Houghton Mifflin, 1987).

Sudan

Tony Barnett and Abbas Abdel Karim, *Sudan: State, Capital and Transformation* (London: Croom Helm, 1988).

Robert O. Collins, *Shadows on the Grass: Britain in the Southern Sudan 1918–1956* (New Haven: Yale University Press, 1983).

Dennis Tully, *Culture and Context in Sudan* (Albany: State University of New York Press, 1988).

John O. Voll and Sarah Potts Voll, *The Sudan: Unity and Diversity in a Multicultural State* (Boulder: Westview Press, 1985).

Peter Woodward, *Condominium and Sudanese Nationalism* (New York: Harper & Row, 1979).

Syria

Raymond A. Hinnebusch, *Peasant and Bureaucracy in Ba'thist Syria* (Boulder: Westview Press, 1989).

Derek Hopwood, *Syria 1945–1986: Politics and Society* (London: Allen & Unwin, 1988).

Philip S. Khoury, *Syria and the French Mandate* (Princeton: Princeton University Press, 1987).

Moshe Ma'oz, *Asad, the Sphinx of Damascus: A Political Biography* (New York: Weidenfield & Nicholson, 1988).

Patrick Seale, *Asad of Syria: The Struggle for the Middle East* (Berkeley: University of California Press, 1989).

Valerie Yorke, *Domestic Politics and Regional Security: Jordan, Syria and Israel* (Aldershot, England: International Institute of Strategic Studies, 1988).

Tunisia

Lisa Anderson, *The State and Social Transformation in Tunisia and Libya, 1830–1980* (Princeton: Princeton University Press, 1986).

Kenneth J. Perkins, *Tunisia: Crossroads of the Islamic and Mediterranean Worlds* (Boulder: Westview Press, 1986).

Norma Salem, *Habib Bourguiba, Islam and the Creation of Tunisia* (London: Croom Helm, 1984).

Turkey

George S. Harris, *Turkey: Coping with Crisis* (Boulder: Westview Press, 1985).

Dankwart A. Rustow, *Turkey: America's Forgotten Ally* (New York: Council on Foreign Relations, 1987).

Irvin C. Schick and Ertoghrul A. Tonak, *Turkey in Transition* (New York: Oxford University Press, 1987).

William Spencer, *The Land and People of Turkey* (New York: J. B. Lippincott, 1990).

Frank Tachau, *Turkey: The Politics of Authority, Democracy and Development* (New York: Praeger, 1984).

United Arab Emirates

Frauke Heard-Bey, *From Trucial States to United Arab Emirates* (London: Longman, 1982).

Aida S. Kanafani, *Aesthetics and Ritual in The United Arab Emirates* (Beirut: American University of Beirut, 1983).

Malcolm C. Peck, *The UAE: A Venture in Unity* (Boulder: Westview Press, 1986).

Yemen

Paul Dresch, *Tribes, Government and History in Yemen* (New York: Oxford University Press, 1989).

Helen Lackner, *P.D.R. Yemen, Outpost of Socialist Development in Arabia* (London: Ithaca Press, 1985).

Richard F. Nyrop, ed., *The Yemens, Country Studies* (Washington: American University, Foreign Area Studies, 1986).

B. R. Pridham, ed., *Contemporary Yemen: Politics and Historical Background* (New York: St. Martin's Press, 1985).

REGIONAL AND ETHNIC STUDIES

Nejla Abu-Izzeddin, *The Druzes: A New History of their History, Faith and Society* (Leiden: E. J. Brill, 1984).

Lois Beck, *The Qashqa'i of Iran* (New Haven: Yale University Press, 1986).

Robert Brenton Betts, *The Druze* (New Haven: Yale University Press, 1988).

Gene R. Garthwaite, *Khans and Shahs: A Documentary Analysis of the Bakhtiyari in Iran* (Cambridge: Cambridge University Press, 1983).

Magali Morsy, *North Africa 1800–1900* (London: Longman, 1984).

Emile A. Nakhleh, *The Gulf Cooperation Council: Problems and Prospects* (New York: Praeger, 1986).

Ian Richard Netton, ed., *Arabia and the Gulf: From Traditional Societies to Modern States* (New York: Barnes & Noble, 1986).

LITERATURE IN TRANSLATION

Roger Allen, ed., *In the Eye of the Beholder: Tales of Egyptian Life from the Writings of Yusuf Idris* (Minneapolis: Bibliotheca Islamica, 1978).

Kamal Boullata, ed., *Women of the Fertile Crescent: An Anthology of Modern Poetry* (Washington: Three Continents Press, 1978).

Leo Hamalian and John D. Yohannan, eds., *New Writing from the Middle East* (New York: Mentor Books/New American Library, 1978).

Herbert S. Joseph, ed., *Modern Israeli Drama, an Anthology* (Rutherford: Fairleigh Dickinson Press, 1983).

Djanet Lachmet, *Lallia (Le Cowboy)* (New York: Carcanet Books, 1986). Transl. by Judith Still.

H. T. Norris, *The Berbers in Arabic Literature* (London: Longman, 1982).

Nicolas Saudray, *The House of the Prophets* (New York: Doubleday, 1985).

Dan V. Segre, *Memoirs of a Fortunate Jew* (Bethesda: Adler & Adler, 1987).

Charles G. Tuety, *Classical Arabic Poetry* (London: Kegan Paul International, 1985).

Abdullah al-Udari, *Modern Poetry of the Arab World* (New York: Penguin Books, 1987).

Barbara K. Walker, with Filiz Erol and Mine Erol, *To Set Them Free: The Early Years of Mustafa Kemal Ataturk* (Grantham: Tompson and Rutter, 1981).

CURRENT EVENTS

To keep up to date on rapidly changing events in the contemporary Middle East and North Africa, the following are especially useful:

Africa Report
Bimonthly, with an "African Update" chronology for all regions.

Africa Research Bulletin (Exeter, England)
Monthly summaries of political, economic, and social developments in all of Africa, with coverage of North-Northeast Africa.

Current History, A World Affairs Journal
One issue per year is usually devoted to the Middle Eastern region.

MEED (Middle East Economic Digest) (London, England)
Weekly summary of economic and some political developments in the Middle East-North African region generally and in individual countries. Provides special issues from time to time on such topics as "Japan in the Middle East," "The Transportation Industry," and "Kuwait: A Profile."

PERIODICALS

The Christian Science Monitor
One Norway Street, Boston, MA 02115

The Economist
25 St. James's Street, London, England

Le Monde (Weekly edition, in English)
7 Rue des Italiens, Paris, France
A summary of the previous week's news, with separate sections on various geographical regions. The Middle East and North Africa are treated separately.

The Middle East and North Africa
Europa Publications, 18 Bedford Square, London, England
A reference work, published annually and updated, with country surveys, regional articles, and documents.

The Middle East Journal
1761 N Street, NW, Washington, DC 20036
This quarterly periodical, established in 1947, is the oldest one specializing in Middle East affairs, with authoritative articles, book reviews, documents, and a quarterly chronology.

Middle Eastern Studies
Gainsborough House, Gainsborough Road, London, England
Quarterly historical magazine.

New Outlook
9 Gordon Street, Tel Aviv, Israel
Bimonthly news magazine, with articles, chronology and documents. Reflects generally Israeli leftist peace-with-the-Arabs views of the movement Peace Now with which it is affiliated.